Preface

This volume contains the proceedings of EKAW 2000 (12th International Conference on Knowledge Engineering and Knowledge Management), held in Juan-les-Pins, on 2–6 October. Previously, EKAW was the European Knowledge Acquisition Workshop. In 1997, it had evolved towards the European Workshop on Knowledge Acquisition, Modeling and Management. Since 2000, EKAW has become an open conference, focusing on knowledge engineering and knowledge management. It aims at gathering researchers working in any area concerning methods, techniques and tools for the construction and the exploitation of knowledge-intensive systems and for knowledge management. EKAW 2000 attracted numerous submissions of papers, from all over the world.

Research in knowledge engineering tries to offer some answers to the following questions:

- How to build knowledge-intensive systems, such as expert systems, knowledge-based systems, or knowledge management systems? In the past years, strong advances in knowledge engineering consisted of methodologies and tools for supporting knowledge acquisition from human experts and for supporting knowledge-level modeling of knowledge-based systems. In the last years, there was a strong emphasis on ontologies and problem-solving methods, with the aim of enhancing knowledge reusability. Knowledge engineering can also benefit from machine learning techniques that can be helpful for automatic building of a knowledge base (for example, automatic knowledge acquisition from textual sources of information).
- How to evaluate knowledge-intensive systems, with both qualitative and quantitative measures, according to various criteria (user-centered criteria, quantitative criteria, etc.)?
- How to make knowledge-intensive systems evolve? Cooperation with the stakeholders involved and machine learning are examples of approaches helpful for evolution and refinement of a knowledge base.

We have noticed the following current trends in knowledge engineering:

- There is a growing importance for knowledge management as a privileged application of knowledge engineering methodologies and techniques. Knowledge management aims at capturing and representing individual or collective knowledge in organizations or communities, in order to enhance knowledge access, sharing and reuse. Therefore knowledge management is a privileged potential application of knowledge engineering. But other communities (such as Computer Supported Cooperative Work (CSCW)) have been involved in knowledge management for years – even before the knowledge engineering community. The need for a multidisciplinary approach and other techniques stemming from these other communities is recognized more and more. Such

communities emphasize the cooperative and organizational approaches for knowledge management.
- The exploitation of texts and documents either as sources from which a knowledge base can be built, or as way of materializing organizational memory led to a growing significance of knowledge acquisition from texts or text mining. This is possible thanks to the recent advances in natural language processing techniques, and thanks to cooperation between knowledge engineering and linguistics communities.
- There is a growing influence of the Web, both as a fabulous source of knowledge and as a fabulous means of knowledge diffusion. It enables a convergence with the research of other communities (e.g. database community, information retrieval community, and text mining), which try to contribute to the semantic Web. The Web also raises new problems that are challenging to the knowledge engineering community.
- Ontology engineering continues to play an essential role in research on knowledge engineering, as confirmed by the papers published in these proceedings. They aim at answering the following questions: What methodology should be used for building an ontology? In particular, how can it exploit knowledge acquisition from texts with the support of natural language processing tools? How can ontologies be specified and exchanged (in particular, through the Web)? Since standards are important, how can we compare the languages proposed by the knowledge engineering community for modeling and formalizing knowledge with respect to the existing recommendations of W3C for the semantic Web, such as resource description framework (RDF) and RDF Schema? How can we reuse existing ontologies? What influence does reuse have on ontology life cycle? How can we integrate several ontologies, possibly cooperatively?
- Cross-fertilization between knowledge engineering and other disciplines such as software engineering, linguistics, CSCW, and machine learning, is not new but continues to be promising.

These are the main trends of research in knowledge engineering, as they appear in the papers accepted at EKAW 2000. These papers are gathered into the following topics:

- Knowledge modeling languages and tools,
- Ontologies,
- Knowledge acquisition from texts,
- Machine learning,
- Knowledge management and e-commerce,
- Validation, evaluation, certification,
- Problem-solving methods,
- Knowledge representation and
- Methodologies.

The main lesson about these current trends in knowledge engineering is the confirmation of the need to remain open to other communities, to new technologies or to new kinds of applications.

Rose Dieng Olivier Corby (Eds.)

Knowledge Engineering and Knowledge Management

Methods, Models, and Tools

12th International Conference, EKAW 2000
Juan-les-Pins, France, October 2-6, 2000
Proceedings

Springer

Volume Editors

Rose Dieng
Olivier Corby
INRIA
2004 route des Lucioles, BP 93
06902 Sophia Antipolis Cedex, France
E-mail: {Rose.Dieng, Olivier.Corby}@inria.fr

Cataloging-in-Publication Data applied for

Die Deutsche Bibliothek - CIP-Einheitsaufnahme

Knowledge engineering and knowledge management : methods, models, and tools ; 12th international conference ; proceedings / EKAW 2000, Juan-les-Pins, France, October 2 - 6, 2000. Rose Dieng ; Olivier Corby (ed.). - Berlin ; Heidelberg ; New York ; Barcelona ; Hong Kong ; London ; Milan ; Paris ; Singapore ; Tokyo : Springer, 2000
(Lecture notes in computer science ; Vol. 1937 : Lecture notes in artificial intelligence)
ISBN 3-540-41119-4

CR Subject Classification (1998): I.2

ISBN 3-540-41119-4 Springer-Verlag Berlin Heidelberg New York

Springer-Verlag Berlin Heidelberg New York
a member of BertelsmannSpringer Science+Business Media GmbH

Printed in Germany

Typesetting: Camera-ready by author, data conversion by PTP-Berlin, Stefan Sossna
Printed on acid-free paper SPIN: 10781250 06/3142 5 4 3 2 1 0

Acknowledgements

We deeply thank the members of the program committee and the additional reviewers that gave their time to make thorough and constructive reviews of the papers. We also thank Monique Simonetti very much for her remarkable organization. We are grateful to the Conseil Régional Provence Alpes Côte d'Azur for its financial support, to INRIA for its significant organizational support and to the other sponsors of EKAW 2000 (AAAI, AFIA, GRACQ, IIIA, MLNET and Club CRIN Ingénierie du Traitement de l'Information).

August 2000

Rose Dieng
Olivier Corby

Conference Chairs

Rose Dieng	INRIA Sophia Antipolis
Olivier Corby	INRIA Sophia Antipolis

Program Committee

Stuart Aitken	University of Glasgow (UK)
Hans Akkermans	Free University Amsterdam (The Netherlands)
Nathalie Aussenac-Gilles	IRIT–CNRS Toulouse (France)
Richard Benjamins	University of Amsterdam (The Netherlands)
Brigitte Biébow	Université Paris-Nord (France)
Jeff Bradshaw	Boeing (USA)
Frances Brazier	Free University of Amsterdam (The Netherlands)
Joost Breuker	University of Amsterdam (The Netherlands)
Paul Compton	University of New South Wales (Austria)
John Domingue	Open University (UK)
Dieter Fensel	Free University of Amsterdam (The Netherlands)
Jean-Gabriel Ganascia	LIP6-University Paris VI (France)
Yolanda Gil	ISI, University of Southern California (USA)
Asunción Gómez Pérez	Universidad Politecnica de Madrid (Spain)
Nicola Guarino	National Research Council (Italy)
Udo Hahn	University of Freiburg (Germany)
Knut Hinkelmann	Insiders (Germany)
Rob Kremer	University of Calgary (Canada)
Franck Maurer	University of Calgary (Canada)
Riichiro Mizoguchi	Osaka University (Japan)
Martin Molina	Technical University of Madrid (Spain)
Hiroshi Motoda	Osaka University (Japan)
Enrico Motta	Open University (UK)
Mark Musen	Stanford University (USA)
Kieron O'Hara	University of Nottingham (UK)
Enric Plaza I Cervera	Spanish Scientific Research Council, CSIC (Spain)
Ulrich Reimer	Swiss Life (Switzerland)
Chantal Reynaud	University of Nanterre & University of Paris-Sud (France)
François Rousselot	LIIA-ENSAIS, University of Strasbourg (France)
Marie-Christine Rousset	University of Paris-Sud (France)
Franz Schmalhofer	DFKI, Kaiserslautern (Germany)
Guus Schreiber	University of Amsterdam (The Netherlands)
Nigel Shadbolt	University of Southampton (UK)
Derek Sleeman	University of Aberdeen (UK)
Rudi Studer	University of Karlsruhe (Germany)
Jan Treur	Free University Amsterdam (The Netherlands)
Mike Uschold	Boeing (USA)
Andre Valente	FasTV (USA)

Frank Van Harmelen	Free University of Amsterdam (The Netherlands)
Gertjan Van Heijst	Kenniscentrum CIBIT (The Netherlands)
Thomas Wetter	University of Heidelberg (Germany)

Steering Committee

Nathalie Aussenac-Gilles	IRIT–CNRS Toulouse (France)
Richard Benjamins	University of Amsterdam (The Netherlands)
Joost Breuker	University of Amsterdam (The Netherlands)
B. Chandrasekaran	Ohio State University (USA)
Dieter Fensel	Free University of Amsterdam (The Netherlands)
Brian Gaines	University of Calgary (Canada)
Riichiro Mizoguchi	Osaka University (Japan)
Enrico Motta	Open University (UK)
Mark Musen	Stanford University (USA)
Nigel Shadbolt	University of Southampton (UK)
Rudi Studer	University of Karlsruhe (Germany)
Frank Van Harmelen	Free University Amsterdam (The Netherlands)

Additional Referees

Jean-Paul Barthès
Ghassan Beydoun
Jim Blythe
Didier Bourigault
Monica Crubézy
Mehdi Dastani
John Debenham
Jérome Euzenat
Yolanda Gil
Adil Hameed
Ian Horrocks
Zhisheng Huang
Catholijn Jonker
Gilles Kassel
Jihie Kim
Nada Matta
Tim Menzies
Amedeo Napoli
Claire Nedellec
Borys Omelayenko
Frank Puppe
Hans-Peter Schnurr
Carla Simone
Gerd Stumme
York Sure
Jennifer Tennison
Leon Van der Torre
Yannick Toussaint
Niek J.E. Wijngaards
Manuel Zacklad

Organizing Committee

Olivier Corby	INRIA, Sophia Antipolis
Rose Dieng	INRIA, Sophia Antipolis
Monique Simonetti	INRIA, Sophia Antipolis

Sponsoring Institutions

INRIA, Conseil Régional Provence Alpes Côte d'Azur, AAAI, AFIA, Club CRIN Ingénierie du Traitement de l'Information, GRACQ, IIIA, MLNET

Table of Contents

Knowledge Modelling Languages and Tools

Ontologies

Knowledge Acquisition from Texts

Machine Learning

Knowledge Management & E-Commerce

Problem-Solving Methods

Knowledge Representation

Validation, Evaluation and Certification

Methodologies

OIL in a Nutshell

D. Fensel[1], I. Horrocks[2], F. Van Harmelen[1,3], S. Decker[4], M. Erdmann[4], and M. Klein[1]

[1] Vrije Universiteit Amsterdam, Holland, {dieter, frankh, mcaklein}@cs.vu.nl

[2] Department of Computer Science, University of Manchester, UK, horrocks@cs.man.ac.uk

[3] AIdministrator, Amersfoort, Nederland

[4] AIFB, University of Karlsruhe, {sde, mer}@aifb.uni-karlsruhe.de

Abstract. Currently computers are changing from single isolated devices into entry points into a worldwide network of information exchange and business transactions. Support in data, information, and knowledge exchange is becoming the key issue in current computer technology. Ontologies will play a major role in supporting information exchange processes in various areas. A prerequisite for such a role is the development of a joint standard for specifying and exchanging ontologies. The purpose of the paper is precisely concerned with this necessity. We will present *OIL*, which is a proposal for such a standard. It is based on existing proposals such as OKBC, XOL and RDF schema, enriching them with necessary features for expressing ontologies. The paper sketches the main ideas of OIL.

1 Introduction

Currently, we are on the brink of the second Web generation. The Web started with mainly handwritten HTML pages; then the step was made to machine generated and often active HTML pages. This first generation of the Web was designed for direct human processing (reading, browsing, form-filling, etc.). The second generation Web, that we could call the "Knowledgeable Web", aims at the machine processable interpretation of information. This coincides with the vision that Tim Berners-Lee calls the Semantic Web in his recent book "Weaving the Web", and for which he uses the slogan "Bringing the Web to its full potential". The Knowledgeable Web will enable intelligent services such as information brokers, search agents, information filters etc. Ontologies will play a crucial role in enabling the processing and sharing of knowledge between programs on the Web.

Ontologies are a popular research topic in various communities, such as knowledge engineering, natural language processing, cooperative information systems, intelligent information integration, and knowledge management. They provide a shared and common understanding of a domain that can be communicated between people and application systems. They have been developed in Artificial Intelligence to facilitate knowledge sharing and reuse. Ontologies are generally defined as a "representation of a shared conceptualisation of a particular domain". Recent articles covering various

R. Dieng and O. Corby (Eds.): EKAW 2000, LNAI 1937, pp. 1–16, 2000.

aspects of ontologies can be found in [43], [26], [22], [14].

The On-To-Knowledge[1] project will develop methods and tools to employ the full power of the ontological approach to facilitate Web-based knowledge use, knowledge access and knowledge management. The On-To-Knowledge tools will help knowledge workers who are not IT specialists to access company-wide information repositories in an efficient, natural and intuitive way. The technical backbone of On-To-Knowledge is the use of ontologies for the various tasks of information integration and mediation. The first major spin-off from the On-To-Knowledge project is OIL (the *Ontology Inference Layer*)[2]. OIL is a Web-based representation and inference layer for ontologies, which combines the widely used modeling primitives from frame-based languages with the formal semantics and reasoning services provided by description logics. Furthermore, OIL is the first ontology representation language that is properly grounded in W3C standards such as RDF/RDF-schema and XML/XML-schema.

It is envisaged that this core language will be extended in the future with sets of additional primitives. A more detailed discussion of OIL, including formal semantics and syntax definitions in RDF and XML, is provided in [28].

The content of this paper is organized as follows. Section 2 provides the underlying rationales of OIL. Section 3 provides the language primitives of OIL and discusses tool support. We also sketch possible directions in extending OIL. Section 4 compares OIL with other ontology languages and web standards. Finally, a short summary is provided in Section 5.

2 OIL = *O*ur *I*deas of a *L*anguage

In this Section, we will first explain the three roots upon which OIL was based. Then we will show why the existing proposal for an ontology exchange language (Ontolingua, [24], [13]) is not very well-defined. Then the relationships of OIL with OKBC and RDF are sketched out. These are discussed further in Section 4.

2.1 The three roots of OIL

OIL unifies three important aspects provided by different communities (see Figure 1): Formal semantics and efficient reasoning support as provided by Description Logics, epistemological rich modeling primitives as provided by the Frame community, and a standard proposal for syntactical exchange notations as provided by the Web community.

Description Logics (DL). DLs describe knowledge in terms of concepts and role restrictions that are used to automatically derive classification taxonomies. The main effort of research in knowledge representation is in providing theories and systems for expressing structured knowledge, for accessing it and reasoning with it in a principled way. DLs (cf. [7], [2]), also known as terminological logics, form an important and powerful class of logic-based knowledge representation languages.[3] They result from early work on semantic networks and define a formal and operational semantics for

1. www.ontoknowledge.org
2. www.ontoknowledge.org/oil

them. DLs try to find a fragment of first-order logic with high expressive power which still has a decidable and efficient inference procedure (cf. [38]). Implemented systems include BACK, CLASSIC, CRACK, FLEX, K-REP, KL-ONE, KRIS, LOOM, and YAK.[4] A distinguishing feature of DLs is that classes (usually called concepts) can be defined intensionally in terms of descriptions that specify the properties that objects must satisfy in order to belong to the concept. These descriptions are expressed using a language that allows the construction of composite descriptions, including restrictions on the binary relationships (usually called roles) connecting objects. Various studies examine extensions of the expressive power for such languages and the trade-off in computational complexity for deriving is-a relationships between concepts in such a logic (and also, although less commonly, the complexity of deriving instance-of relationships between individuals and concepts). In spite of discouraging theoretical complexity results, there are now efficient implementations for DL languages (cf. [6], [35], [29]), see for example DLP[5] and the FaCT system.[6] OIL inherits from Description Logic its *formal semantics* and the *efficient reasoning support* developed for these languages. In OIL, *subsumption* is decidable and with FaCT we can provide an efficient reasoner for this. In general, subsumption is only one of several reasoning tasks for working with an ontology. Others are: instance classification, query subsumption and query answering over classes and instances, navigation through ontologies, etc. However, many of them can be reformulated in terms of subsumption checking. Others may lead to different super- and subsets of the current OIL language version. The current version of OIL can be seen as a starting point for exploring the space of possible choices in designing Ontology exchange languages and characterizing them in terms of their pros and cons.

Frame-based systems. The central modeling primitive of predicate logic are

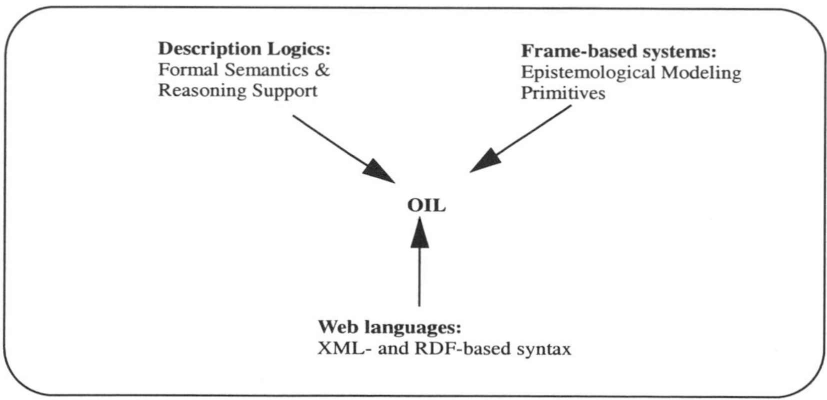

Fig 1. The three roots of OIL.

3. http://dl.kr.org/. Here links to most papers, project, and research events in this area can be found.

4. http://www.research.att.com/sw/tools/classic/imp-systems.html

5. http://www.bell-labs.com/user/pfps/

6. http://www.cs.man.ac.uk/~horrocks/software.html We will discuss later in the paper the use of FaCT as an inference engine for OIL.

predicates. Frame-based and object-oriented approaches take a different approach. Their central modeling primitive are classes (i.e., frames) with certain properties called attributes. These attributes do not have a global scope but are only applicable to the classes they are defined for (they are typed) and the "same" attribute (i.e., the same attribute name) may be associated with different range and value restrictions when defined for different classes. A frame provides a certain context for modeling one aspect of a domain. Many other additional refinements of these modeling constructs have been developed, and this has contributed to the incredible success of this modeling paradigm. Many frame-based systems and languages have been developed, and under the name object-orientation it has conquered the software engineering community. Therefore, OIL incorporates the *essential modeling primitives* of frame-based systems into its language. OIL is based on the notion of a class and the definition of its superclasses and attributes. Relations can also be defined not as attributes of a class but as an independent entities having a certain domain and range. Like classes, relations can be arranged in a hierarchy. We will explain the difference between OIL and pure Description Logics using their different treatment of attributes. In DLs, roles are not defined for concepts. Actually, concepts are defined as subclasses of role restriction. One could rephrase this in a frame context as follows: a class is a subclass of its attribute definitions (i.e., all instances of the class must fulfil the restrictions defined for the attributes). However, asking which roles could be applied to a class does not make much sense for a DL as nearly all slots can be applied to a class. With frame-based modeling one makes the implicit assumption that only those attributes can be applied to a class that are defined for this class.

Web standards: XML and RDF. Modeling primitives and their semantics are one aspect of an Ontology Exchange Language. In addition, you have to decide about its syntax. Given the current dominance and importance of the WWW, a syntax of an ontology exchange language must be formulated using existing web standards for information representation. As already proven with XOL[7] (cf. [30], [34]), XML can be used as a serial syntax definition language for an ontology exchange language. The BioOntology Core Group[8] recommends the use of a frame-based language with an XML syntax for the exchange of ontologies for molecular biology. The proposed language is called XOL. The ontology definitions that XOL is designed to encode include both schema information (meta-data), such as class definitions from object databases, as well as non-schema information (ground facts), such as object definitions from object databases. The syntax of XOL is based on XML, and the modeling primitives and semantics of XOL are based on OKBC-Lite. OIL is closely related to XOL and can be seen as an extension of XOL. For example, XOL allows only necessary but not sufficient class definitions (i.e., a new class is always a sub-class of and not equal to its specification) and only class names, but not class expressions (except for the limited form of expression provided by slots and their facets) can be used in defining classes. The XML syntax of OIL was mainly defined as an extension of XOL, although, as we said above for OKBC, we omit some of the original language primitives. More details on the XML syntax of OIL (defined as a DTD and in XML schema) can be found

7. http://www.ai.sri.com/pkarp/xol/.
8. http://smi-web.stanford.edu/projects/bio-ontology/

in[28] and [31].

Other candidates for a web-based syntax for OIL are RDF and RDFS. The Resource Description Framework (RDF)[9] (cf. [36], [32]) provides a means for adding semantics to a document without making any assumptions about the structure of the document. RDF is an infrastructure that enables the encoding, exchange and reuse of structured metadata. RDF schemes (RDFS) [8] provide a basic type schema for RDF. Objects, Classes, and Properties can be described. Predefined properties can be used to model instance of and subclass of relationships as well as domain restrictions and range restrictions of attributes. In regard to ontologies, RDF provides two important contributions: a standardized syntax for writing ontologies and a standard set of modeling primitives, like instance of and subclass of relationships.

2.2 Why not Ontolingua?

Ontolingua[10] (cf. [24], [13]) is an existing proposal for a ontology exchange language. It was designed to support the design and specification of ontologies with a clear logical semantics based on KIF[11]. Ontolingua extends KIF with additional syntax to capture intuitive bundling of axioms into definitional forms with ontological significance; and a Frame Ontology to define object-oriented and frame-language terms.[12] The set of KIF expressions that Ontolingua allows is defined in an ontology, called the Frame Ontology. The Frame Ontology specifies in a declarative form the representation primitives that are often supported with special-purpose syntax and code in object-centered representation systems (e.g., classes, instances, slot constraints, etc.). Ontolingua definitions are Lisp-style forms that associate a symbol with an argument list, a documentation string, and a set of KIF sentences labeled by keywords. An Ontolingua ontology is made up of definitions of classes, relations, functions, objects distinguished, and axioms that relate these terms.

The problem with Ontolingua is its high expressive power that is provided without any means to control it. Not surprisingly, no reasoning support has ever been provided for Ontolingua. OIL takes the opposite approach. We start with a very simple and limited core language. The web has proven that restriction of initial complexity and controlled extension when required is a very successful strategy. OIL takes this lesson to heart. We already mentioned that the focus on different reasoning tasks may lead to different extensions. We also showed in [18] serious shortcomings in the expressiveness of OIL. This process may finally lead to one version of OIL with similar expressiveness as Ontolingua. Still we would have had a process of rational reconstruction that makes certain choices with their pros and cons explicitly. Second, we would still have versions with smaller expressive power for cases they can be applied to.

---

9. http://www.w3c.org/Metadata/

10. http://ontolingua.stanford.edu/

11. The **Knowledge Interchange Format KIF** ([20], [21]) is a language designed for use in the interchange of knowledge among disparate computer systems. KIF is based on predicate logic but provides a Lisp-oriented syntax for it.

12. The Ontolingua Server as described in [13] has extended the original language by providing explicit support for building ontological modules that can be assembled, extended, and refined in a new ontology.

In general there are two strategies to achieve a standard: Defining a "small" set of modeling primitives that are consensus in the community and define a proper semantics for them; or defining a "large" set of modeling primitives that are present in some of the approaches in a community and glue them together. Both may lead to success. The first approach can be illustrated with HTML. Its first version was very simple and limited but therefore allowed the Web to catch on and become a world wide standard. Meanwhile we have HTML version 4, XHTML, and XML. So beginning with a core set and successively refining and extending them has proven to be successful strategy. The second approach has been taken by the UML community by designing a model that is broad enough to cover all modeling concepts of a community. This leads to ambiguity and redundancy in modeling primitives and sometimes a precise semantic definition is lacking. However, UML has been adopted by Software industry as one of the major approaches, and is therefore a success too. Obviously these two opposed approaches to standardization may both work successfully. We have chosen the first approach in developing OIL. This stems from the purpose OIL is designed for. It should provide machine understandable semantics of domain theories. This will be used in the Web context to provide machine processable semantics of information sources helping the make true Tim Berners-Lee's vision of a semantic web. Therefore clear definitions of semantics and reasoning support is essential.

2.3 OIL and OKBC

A simple and well-defined semantics is of great importance for an ontology exchange language because it is used to transfer knowledge from one context to another. There already exists an ontology exchange standard for frame-based systems, the Open Knowledge Base Connectivity (OKBC)[13] ([9], [10]). OKBC is an API (application program interface) for accessing frame-based knowledge representation systems. Its knowledge model supports features most commonly found in frame-based knowledge representation systems, object databases, and relational databases. OKBC-Lite extracts most of the essential features of OKBC, while not including some of its more complex aspects. OKBC has also been chosen by FIPA[14] as an exchange standard for ontologies (cf. FIPA 98 Specification, Part 12: Ontology Service [19]). OIL shares many features with OKBC and defines a clear semantics and XML-oriented syntax for them. A detailed comparison is made later in this document.

2.4 OIL and RDF

In the same way that OIL provides an extension to OKBC (and is therefore downward compatible with OKBC) it also provides an extension to RDF and RDFS. Based on its RDF syntax, ontologies written in OIL are valid RDF documents. OIL extends the schema definition of RDFS by adding additional language primitives not yet present in RDFS. Based on these extensions an ontology in OIL can be expressed in RDFS.

13. http://www.ai.sri.com/~okbc/
14. http://www.fipa.org

3 The OIL Language

This section provide an informal description of the modeling primitives, its tool environment, and a discussion of future extensions of OIL. The semantics of OIL is described in [28].

3.1 An informal description of OIL

An OIL ontology is a structure made up of several components, some of which may themselves be structures, some of which are optional, and some of which may be repeated. We will write **component**$^{?}$ to indicate an optional component, **component**$^{+}$ to indicate a component that may be repeated one or more times (i.e., that must occur at least once) and **component*** to indicate a component that may be repeated zero or more times (i.e., that may be completely omitted).

When describing ontologies in OIL we have to distinguish three different layers:

- The object level where concrete instances of an ontology are described. We do *not* deal with this level in this paper. The exchange of application-specific information on instances is currently beyond the scope of OIL.
- The first metalevel, where the actual ontological definitions are provided. Here we define the terminology that may be populated at the object level. OIL is mainly concerned with this level. It is a means for describing a structured vocabulary with well-defined semantics. The main contribution of OIL is in regard to this level.
- The second metalevel (i.e., the meta-metalevel) is concerned with describing features of such an ontology like author, name, subject, etc. For representing metadata of ontologies we make use of the DublinCore Meta data Element Set (Version 1.1) [11] standard. The Dublin Core is a meta-data element set intended to facilitate the discovery of electronic resources. Originally conceived for author-generated descriptions of web resources, it is now widely used and has attracted the attention of resource description communities such as museums, libraries, government agencies, and commercial organizations.

OIL is concerned with the first and second metalevels. The former is called *ontology definition* and the latter is called *ontology container*. We will discuss both elements of an ontology specification in OIL. We start with the ontology container and will then discuss the backbone of OIL, the ontology definition.

Ontology Container: We adopt the components as defined by Dublin Core Meta data Element Set, Version 1.1 for the *ontology container* part of OIL. Although every element is optional and repeatable in the Dublin Core set, in OIL some elements are required or have a predefined value. Required elements are written as element^{+}. Some of the elements can be specialized with a *qualifier*, which refines the meaning of that element. In our shorthand notation we will write element.qualifier. The precise syntax based on RDF is given in [37].

Apart from various header fields encapsulated in its container, an OIL ontology consists of a **set of definitions**:

- **import**$^{?}$ A list of references to other OIL modules that are to be included in this ontology. XML schemas and OIL provide the same (limited) means for composing specifications. You can include specifications and the underlying assumption is that names of different specifications are different (via different prefixes).

- **rule-base?** A list of rules (sometimes called axioms or global constraints) that apply to the ontology. At present, the structure of these rules is not defined (they could be horn clauses, DL style axioms etcetera), and they have no semantic significance. The rule base consists simply of a **type** (a string) followed by the unstructured rules (a string).
- **class and slot definitions** Zero or more class definitions **(class-def)** and slot definitions **(slot-def)**, the structure of which will be described below.

A class definition **(class-def)** associates a class name with a class description. A **class-def** consists of the following components:

- **type?** The type of definition. This can be either **primitive** or **defined**; if omitted, the type defaults to **primitive**. When a class is **primitive**, its definition (i.e., the combination of the following **subclass-of** and **slot-constraint** components) is taken to be a necessary but not sufficient condition for membership of the class.
- **name** The name of the class (a string).
- **documentation** Some documentation describing the class (a string).
- **subclass-of?** A list of one or more **class-expressio**ns, the structure of which will be described below. The class being defined in this **class-def** must be a sub-class of each of the class-expressions in the list.
- **slot-constraints** Zero or more **slot-constraints**, the structure of which will be described below. The class being defined in this **class-def** must be a sub-class of each of the slot-constraints in the list.

A **class-expression** can be either a class name, a **slot-constrain**t, or a boolean combination of class expressions using the operators **AND**, **OR** or **NOT**. Note that class expressions are recursively defined, so that arbitrarily complex expressions can be formed.

A **slot-constraint** (a slot may also be called a *role* or an *attribute*) is a list of one or more constraints (restrictions) applied to a **slo**t. A slot is a binary relation (i.e., its instances are pairs of individuals), but a slot-constraint is actually a class definition—its instances are those individuals that satisfy the constraint(s). A **slot-constraint** consists of the following components:

- **name** A slot name (a string). The slot is a binary relation that may or may not be defined in the ontology. If it is not defined it is assumed to be a binary relation with no globally applicable constraints, i.e., any pair of individuals could be an instance of the slot.
- **has-value?** A list of one or more **class-expressions**. Every instance of the class defined by the slot-constraint must be related via the slot relation to an instance of each **class-expression** in the list. For example, the **value** constraint:

  slot-constraint *eats*
  has-value zebra, wildebeest

  defines the class each instance of which *eats* some instance of the class zebra and some instance of the class wildebeest. Note that this does not mean that instances of the slot-constraint eat *only* zebra and wildebeest: they may also be partial to a little gazelle when they can get it. **Has-value** *expresses the existential quantifier of Predicate logic and a necessary condition.* An instance of a class must have at most one value for this slot that fulfils its range restriction.

- **value-type?** A list of one or more **class-expressions**. If an instance of the class defined by the slot-constraint is related via the slot relation to some individual x, then x must be an instance of each **class-expression** in the list. For example, the **value-type** constraint:

  slot-constraint *eats*
  value-type meat

  defines the class each instance of which *eats* nothing that is not meat. Note that this does not mean that instances of the slot-constraint eat anything at all. **value-type** *expresses the all quantifier of Predicate logic and a sufficient condition.* If an instance of a class has a value for this slot, then it must fulfil its range restriction.
- **max-cardinality?** A non-negative integer *n* followed by a **class-expression**. An instance of the class defined by the slot-constraint can be related to at most *n* distinct instances of the **class-expression** via the slot relation.
- **min-cardinality?** A non-negative integer *n* followed by a **class-expression**. An instance of the class defined by the slot-constraint must be related to at least *n* distinct instances of the **class-expression** via the slot relation.

A slot definition (**slot-def**) associates a slot name with a slot description. A slot description specifies global constraints that apply to the slot relation, for example that it is a transitive relation. A **slot-def** consists of the following components:

- **name** The name of the slot (a string).
- **documentation?** Some documentation describing the slot (a string).
- **subslot-of?** A list of one or more **slot**s. The slot being defined in this **slot-def** must be a sub-slot of each of the slots in the list. For example,

  slot-def *daughter*
  subslot-of *child*

  defines a slot *daughter* that is a subslot of *child*, i.e., every pair of individuals that is an instance of *daughter* must also be an instance of *child*.
- **domain?** A list of one or more **class-expressions**. If the pair (*x*,*y*) is an instance of the slot relation, then *x* must be an instance of each **class-expression** in the list.
- **range?** A list of one or more **class-expressions**. If the pair (*x*,*y*) is an instance of the slot relation, then *y* must be an instance of each **class-expression** in the list.
- **inverse?** The name of a slot *S* that is the inverse of the slot being defined. If the pair (*x*,*y*) is an instance of the slot S, then (*y*,*x*) must be an instance of the slot being defined. For example,

  slot-def *eats*
  inverse *eaten-by*

  defines the inverse of the slot *eats* to be the slot *eaten-by*, i.e., if *x eats y* then *y* is *eaten-by x*.
- **properties?** A list of one or more properties of the slot. Valid properties are: **transitive** and **symmetric**.

3.2 Current Limitations of OIL

Our starting point has been to define a decidable core language, with the intention that additional (and possibly important) features be defined as a set of extensions (still with clearly defined semantics). Modelers will be free to use these language extensions, but it will be clear that this may compromise decidability and reasoning support. This seems to us a cleaner solution than trying to define a single "all things to all men" language.

In this section we briefly discuss a number of features which are available in other ontology modeling languages and which are not or not yet included in OIL. For each of these features, we briefly motivate our choice, and mention future prospects where relevant.

Default reasoning: Although OIL does provide a mechanism for inheriting values from super-classes, such values cannot be overwritten. As a result, such values cannot be used for the purpose of modeling default values. Combining defaults with a well defined semantics and reasoning support is known to be problematical.

Rules/Axioms: As discussed above, only a fixed number of algebraic properties of slots can be expressed in OIL. There is no facility for describing arbitrary axioms that must hold for all items in the ontology. Such a powerful feature is undoubtedly useful and may be added to the core language.

Modules: We 3.1 presented a very simple construction to modularize ontologies in OIL. In fact, this mechanism is identical to the namespace mechanism in XML. It amounts to a textual inclusion of the imported module, where name-clashes are avoided by prefixing every imported symbol with a unique prefix indicating its original location. Future extensions would concern parameterized modules, signature mappings between modules, and restricted export interfaces for modules.

Using instances in class definitions: Results from research in description and modal logics show that the computational complexity of such logics changes dramatically for the worse when reasoning with domain-instances is allowed (cf. [1]). For this reason OIL does not currently allow the use of instances in slot-values, or extensional definitions of classes (i.e., class definitions by enumerating the class instances).

Concrete domains: OIL currently does not support concrete domains (e.g., integers, strings, etc.). This would seem to be a serious limitation for a realistic ontology exchange language, and extensions of OIL in this direction are probably necessary. The theory of concrete domains is well understood [3], and it should be possible to add some restricted form of concrete domains without sacrificing reasoning support.

Limited Second-order expressivity: Many existing languages for ontologies (KIF, CycL, Ontolingua) include some form of reification mechanism in the language, which allows us to treat statements of the language as objects in their own right, thereby making it possible to express statements about these statements. A full second order extension would be clearly undesirable (even unification is undecidable in full 2nd order logic). However, much weaker second order constructions already provide much if not all of the required expressivity without causing any computational problem (in effect, they are simply 2nd order syntactic sugar for what are essentially first order constructions).

3.3 Tools

OIL makes use of the **FaCT (Fast Classification of Terminologies)** system in order to provide reasoning support for ontology design, integration and verification. FaCT is a Description Logic classifier that can also be used for consistency checking in modal and other similar logics. FaCT's most interesting features are its expressive logic (in particular the *SHIQ* reasoner), its optimized tableaux implementation (which has now become the standard for DL systems), and its CORBA based client-server architecture. FaCT's optimizations are specifically aimed at improving the system's performance when classifying realistic ontologies, and this results in performance improvements of several orders of magnitude when compared with older DL systems. This performance improvement is often so great that it is impossible to measure precisely as unoptimised systems are virtually non-terminating with ontologies that FaCT is easily able to deal with [29]. Taking a large medical terminology ontology developed in the GALEN project [40] as an example, FaCT is able to check the consistency of all 2,740 classes and determine the complete class hierarchy in about 60 seconds of (450MHz Pentium III) CPU time.[15] In contrast, the KRIS system [4] had been unable to complete the same task after several weeks of CPU time.

4 Comparing OIL with other approaches

This section compares OIL with other frame-based approaches and with the arising web standards RDF and RDFS.

4.1 OIL and other frame-oriented approaches

The modeling primitives of OIL are based on those of XOL (cf. [30]). OIL extends XOL so as to make it more suitable for capturing ontologies defined using a logic-based approach (such as used in DLs) in addition to the frame-based ontologies for which XOL (and OKBC [10]) were designed. The extensions are designed so that most valid XOL ontologies should also be valid OIL ontologies. The exceptions are due to the omission of constructs for which reasoning support (e.g., for class consistency and subsumption checking) could not be provided from OIL, either because their semantics are unclear or because their inclusion would lead to the language being undecidable.

How OIL extends XOL

It is the frame structure itself that restricts the way language primitives can be combined to define a class. In XOL, class definitions consist of the specification of zero or more parent classes (from which characteristics are inherited) and zero or more slots—binary relations whose characteristics can be additionally restricted using slot *facets* (e.g., the range of the relation can be restricted using the **value-type** facet). Viewed from a logical perspective, each slot (with its associated facets) defines a class (e.g., a slot *eats* with the **value-type** junk-food defines the class of individuals who eat nothing but junk food), and the frame is implicitly[16] the class formed from the conjunction of all the slots

15. Adding single classes and checking both their consistency and their position in the class hierarchy is virtually instantaneous.

16. The OKBC semantics (on which XOL relies) are less than clear on this and on several other important points.

and all the parent classes. Consequently, every class must be defined by a conjunction of slots (which themselves have a very restricted form) and other named classes. In contrast, DLs usually allow language primitives to be combined in arbitrary boolean expressions (i.e., using conjunction, disjunction and negation) and allow class definitions to be used recursively wherever a class name might appear. Moreover, XOL only provides one form of class definition statement. It is not clear whether the resulting class is meant to be primitive or non-primitive: we will assume that it is primitive.[17]

In our view, this very restricted form of class definition makes XOL (and indeed OKBC) unsuitable as an ontology exchange language: it makes it impossible to capture even quite basic DL ontologies and precludes some very simple and intuitive kinds of class definition. For example, it is impossible to define the class of vegetarian as the subclass of person such that everything they eat is neither meat nor fish. On the one hand, the value of the **value-type** facet of the slot *eats* cannot be an expression such as "**not** (meat **or** fish)". On the other hand, because vegetarian must be primitive, there could be individuals of type person who eat neither meat nor fish but who are not classified as vegetarians.[18] Another serious weakness of XOL class definitions (and those of OKBC) is that there is no mechanism for specifying disjointness of classes, a basic modeling primitive that can be captured even by many conceptual modeling formalisms used for database schema design.[19] This makes it impossible to capture the fact that the class male is disjoint from the class female. This is easy for a DL, where the class female can simply be made a subclass of "**not** male".

Another weakness of XOL (and OKBC) is that slots (relations) are very much second class citizens when compared to classes. In particular, there is no support for a slot hierarchy and only restricted kinds of properties that can be specified for relations. For example, it is not possible to define the slot *has-parent* as a subslot of the *has-ancestor*, nor is it possible to specify that *has-ancestor* is a transitive relation. The specification of this kind of slot hierarchy including transitive and non-transitive relations is essential in ontologies dealing with complex physically composed domains such as human anatomy [41] and engineering [42].

How OIL restricts XOL

As mentioned above, OIL also restricts XOL in some respects: Initially, only conceptual modeling will be supported, i.e., individuals are not supported. The slot constraints **numeric-minimum** and **numeric-maximum** are not supported. Again, future extensions of OIL may support concrete data types (including numbers and numeric ranges). Collection types other than **set** are not supported. Slot **inverse** can only be specified in global slot definitions: naming the inverse of a relation only seems to make sense when applied globally.

4.2 OIL and RDF

The **Resource Description Framework (RDF)** [32] is a recommendation of the World Wide Web Consortium (W3C) for representing meta-data in the Web. RDF data

17. In contrast, OKBC supports the definition of both primitive and non-primitive classes.
18. This aspect of the definition can be captured in OKBC as non-primitive classes are supported.
19. For example extended entity relationship (EER) modeling.

represents resources and attached attribute/value pairs. Since RDF does not define any particular vocabularies for authoring of data, a schema language with appropriate primitives is needed. For this purpose the RDF-Schema specification was createdn (cf. [8]). RDF-schema is a simple ontology language able to define basic vocabularies which covers the simplest parts a of a knowledge model like OKBC (classes, properties, domain and range restrictions, instance-of, subclass-of and subproperty-of relationships).

The relationship between OIL and RDF/RDFS is very close because RDF/RDFS was meant to capture meaning in the manner of semantic nets. In the same way, as RDF-Schema is used to define itself it can be used to define other ontology languages. We define a syntax for OIL by giving an RDF-Schema for the core of OIL and proposing related RDF-Schemas that could complement this core to cover further aspects. To ensure maximal compatibility with existing RDF/RDFS-applications and vocabularies the integration of OIL with the resources defined in RDF-Schema has been a main focus in designing the RDF-model for OIL (for more details see [28]). In a nutshell, RDFS relies on RDF and defines a new name space called RDFS. Some of the OIL primitives can directly be expressed in this name space. Others require a refinement of the RDFS primitives in an additional OIL name space.

5 Summary

In this paper, we sketched out both the syntax and semantics of an ontology exchange language called OIL. One of our main motivations while defining this language has been to ensure that it has a clear and well defined semantics—an agreed common syntax is useless without an agreement as to what it all means.

The core we have currently defined can be justified from a pragmatic and a theoretical point of view. From a pragmatic point of view, OIL covers consensual modeling primitives of Frame systems and Description Logics. From a theoretical point of view it seems quite natural to us to limit the expressiveness of this version so that subsumption is decidable. This defines a well-understood subfragment of first-order logic. However, it is important to note that we are open to further discussions that may influence the final design of an ontology exchange language.

We are currently evaluating the use of OIL in the two running IST projects: On-to-knowledge[20] and Ibrow[21]. In On-to-knowledge, OIL will be extended to become a full-fledged environment for knowledge management in large intranets. Unstructured and semi-structured data will be annotated automatically and agent-based user interface techniques and visualization tools will help users to navigate and query the information space. Here On-to-knowledge continues a line of research that was set up with SHOE (cf. [33], [27]) and Ontobroker (cf. [15], [17]): using ontologies to model and annotate the semantics of information in a machine processable manner. In Ibrow, we are

20. *On-To-Knowledge: Content-driven Knowledge-Management Tools through Evolving Ontologies*. http://www.ontoknowledge.com

21. *IBROW* started with a preliminary phase under the 4th European Framework and has been a full-fledged Information Society Technologies (IST) project under the 5th European Framework Program since February 2000. http://www.swi.psy.uva.nl/projects/ibrow/home.html

currently investigating the usefulness of OIL for software component description, based on its integration with UPML (cf. [18]).

Acknowledgment. We thank J. Broekstra, Monica Crubezy, W. Grosso, Carole Goble, Peter Karp, Robin McEntire, Enrico Motta, Mark Musen, Steffen Staab, Guus Schreiber, Rudi Studer, and the anonymous reviewers for helpful comments on drafts of this paper, and Jeff Butler for correcting our English.

References

[1] C. Areces, P. Blackburn, and M. Marx: A road-map on complexity for hybrid logics. In *Proc. of CSL'99*, number 1683 in LNCS, pages 307–321. Springer-Verlag, 1999.

[2] F. Baader, H.-J. Heinsohn, B. Hollunder, J. Muller, B. Nebel, W. Nutt, and H.-J. Profitlich: Terminological knowledge representation: A proposal for a terminological logic. Technical Memo TM-90-04, Deutsches Forschungszentrum für Künstliche Intelligenz GmbH (DFKI), 1991.

[3] F. Baader and P. Hanschke: A Scheme for Integrating Concrete Domains into Concept Languages. In *Proceddings IJCAI91*, 1991: 452–457.

[4] F. Baader and B. Hollunder: KRIS: Knowledge representation and inference system. *SIGART Bulletin*, 2(3):8–14, 1991.

[5] S. Bechhofer, I. Horrocks, P. F. Patel-Schneider, and S. Tessaris: A proposal for a description logic interface. In *Proc. of DL'99*, pages 33–36, 1999.

[6] A. Borgida and P. F. Patel-Schneider: A semantics and complete algorithm for subsumption in the CLASSIC description logic. *J. of Artificial Intelligence Research*, 1:277–308, 1994.

[7] R. J. Brachman and J. G. Schmolze: An overview of the KL-ONE knowledge representation system. *Cognitive Science*, 9(2):171–216, 1985.

[8] D. Brickley and R.V. Guha: Resource Description Framework (RDF) Schema Specification 1.0, W3C Candidate Recommendation 27 March 2000. http://www.w3.org/TR/2000/CR-rdf-schema-20000327.

[9] V. K. Chaudhri, A. Farquhar, R. Fikes, P. D. Karp, and J. P. Rice: Open knowledge base connectivity 2.0. Technical Report KSL-98-06, Knowledge Systems Laboratory, Stanford, 1997.

[10] V. K. Chaudhri, A. Farquhar, R. Fikes, P. D. Karp, and J. P. Rice: OKBC: A programmatic foundation for knowledge base interoperability. In *Proceedings of the 15th National Conference on Artificial Intelligence (AAAI-98) and of the 10th Conference on Innovative Applications of Artificial Intelligence (IAAI-98)*, pages 600–607. AAAI Press, 1998.

[11] http://purl.oclc.org/dc/

[12] H. Eriksson, R. W. Fergerson, Y. Shahar, and M. A. Musen: Automated Generation of Ontology Editors. In *Proceedings of the Twelfth Workshop on Knowledge Acquisition, Modeling and Management (KAW99)*, Banff, Alberta, Canada, October 16-21, 1999.

[13] A. Farquhar, R. Fikes, and J. Rice: The ontolingua server: A tool for collaborative ontology construction. *Journal of Human-Computer Studies*, 46:707–728, 1997.

[14] D. Fensel. *Ontologies: Silver Bullet for Knowledge Management and Electronic Commerce*. Springer-Verlag, to appear.

[15] D. Fensel, S. Decker, M. Erdmann und R. Studer: Ontobroker: The Very High Idea. In *Proceedings of the 11th International Flairs Conference (FLAIRS-98)*, Sanibal Island, Florida, USA, 131-135, Mai 1998.

[16] D. Fensel, J. Angele, and R. Studer: The Knowledge Acquisition And Representation Language KARL, *IEEE Transactions on Knowledge and Data Engineering*, 10(4):527-550, 1998.

[17] D. Fensel, J. Angele, S. Decker, M. Erdmann, H.-P. Schnurr, S. Staab, R. Studer, and A. Witt: On2broker: Semantic-Based Access to Information Sources at the WWW. In *Proceedings of the World Conference on the WWW and Internet (WebNet 99),* Honolulu, Hawaii, USA, October 25-30, 1999.

[18] D. Fensel, M. Crubezy, F. van Harmelen, and M. I. Horrocks: OIL & UPML: A Unifying Framework for the Knowledge Web. In *Proceedings of the Workshop on Applications of Ontologies and Problem-solving Methods, 14th European Conference on Artificial Intelligence ECAI'00*, Berlin, Germany August 20-25, 2000.

[19] Foundation for Intelligent Physical Agents (FIPA): *FIPA 98 Specificatio*n, 1998.

[20] M. R. Genesereth: Knowledge interchange format. In J. Allen, R. Fikes, and E. Sandewall, editors, *Principles of Knowledge Representation and Reasoning: Proceedings of the Second International Conference (KR'91*). Morgan Kaufmann Publishers, San Francisco, California, 1991.

[21] M.R. Genesereth and R.E. Fikes: Knowledge interchange format, version 3.0, reference manual. Technical Report Logic-92-1, Computer Science Dept., Stanford University, 1992.

[22] A. Gomez Perez and V. R. Benjamins: Applications of ontologies and problem-solving methods. *AI-Magazin*e, 20(1):119–122, 1999.

[23] W. E. Grosso, H. Eriksson, R. W. Fergerson, H. Gennari, S. W. Tu, and M. A. Musen: Knowledge Modeling at the Millennium (The Design and Evolution of Protégé-2000). In *Proceedings of the Twelfth Workshop on Knowledge Acquisition, Modeling and Management (KAW99)*, Banff, Alberta, Canada, October 16-21, 1999.

[24] T. R. Gruber: A translation approach to portable ontology specifications. *Knowledge Acquisitio*n, 5(2), 1993.

[25] R. Guenther: Type Working Group List of Resource Types 1999-08-05. http://purl.org/DC/documents/wd-typelist.htm

[26] G. van Heijst, A. Th. Schreiber, and B. J. Wielinga: Using explicit ontologies in KBS development. *International Journal of Human-Computer Studie*s, 46(2/3):183–292, 1997.

[27] J. Heflin, J. Hendler, and S. Luke: SHOE: A Knowledge Representation Language for Internet Applications. Technical Report, CS-TR-4078 (UMIACS TR-99-71), Dept. of Computer Science, University of Maryland at College Park. 1999.

[28] I. Horrocks, D. Fensel, J. Broekstra, S. Decker, M. Erdmann, C. Goble, F. Van Harmelen, M. Klein, S. Staab, and R. Studer: The Ontology Inference Layer OIL. http://www.ontoknowledge.org/oil.

[29] I. Horrocks and P. F. Patel-Schneider: Optimising description logic subsumption. *Journal of Logic and Computatio*n, 9(3):267–293, 1999.

[30] P. D. Karp, V. K. Chaudhri, and J. Thomere: XOL: An XML-based ontology exchange language. Version 0.3, 1999.

[31] M. Klein, D. Fensel, F. van Harmelen, and I. Horrocks: The Relation between Ontologies and Schema-Languages: Translating OIL-Specifications to XML-Schema. In *Proceedings of the Workshop on Applications of Ontologies and Problem-solving Methods, 14th European Conference on Artificial Intelligence ECAI'00*, Berlin, Germany August 20-25, 2000.

[32] O. Lassila and R. Swick: Resource description framework (RDF). W3C recommendation. http://www.w3c.org/TR/WD-rdf-syntax, 1999.

[33] S. Luke, L. Spector, and D. Rager: Ontology-Based Knowledge Discovery on the World-Wide Web. In *Working Notes of the Workshop on Internet-Based Information Systems at the 13th National Conference on Artificial Intelligence (AAAI96)*, 1996.

[34] R. McEntire, P. Karp, N. Abernethy, F. Olken, R. E. Kent, M. DeJongh, P. Tarczy-Hornoch, D. Benton, D. Pathak, G. Helt, S. Lewis, A. Kosky, E. Neumann, D. Hodnett, L. Tolda, and T. Topaloglou: An evaluation of ontology exchange languages for bioinformatics, 1999.

[35] R. M. MacGregor: A description classifier for the predicate calculus. In *Proceedings of the Twelfth National Conference on Artificial Intelligence*, pages 213–220, Seattle, Washington, USA, 1994.

[36] E. Miller: An introduction to the resource description framework. *D-Lib Magazine*, 1998.

[37] E. Miller, P. Miller, and D. Brickley: Guidance on expressing the Dublin Core within the Resource Description Framework (RDF). http://www.ukoln.ac.uk/metadata/resources/dc/datamodel/WD-dc-rdf.

[38] B. Nebel: Artificial intelligence: A computational perspective. In G. Brewka, editor, *Principles of Knowledge Representation*, Studies in Logic, Language and Information. CSLI publications, Stanford, 1996.

[39] P. F. Patel-Schneider and B. Swartout: Description logic specification from the KRSS effort, 1993.

[40] A. L. Rector, W A Nowlan, and A Glowinski: Goals for concept representation in the GALEN project. In *Proceedings of the 17th Annual Symposium on Computer Applications in Medical Care (SCAMC'93)*, pages 414–418, Washington DC, USA, 1993.

[41] A. Rector, S. Bechhofer, C. A. Goble, I. Horrocks, W. A. Nowlan, and W. D. Solomon: The GRAIL concept modelling language for medical terminology. *Artificial Intelligence in Medicine*, 9:139–171, 1997.

[42] U. Sattler: A concept language for engineering applications with part–whole relations. In *Proceedings of the International Conference on Description Logics—DL'95*, pages 119–123, Roma, Italy, 1995.

[43] M. Uschold and M. Grüninger: Ontologies: Principles, methods and applications. *Knowledge Engineering Review*, 11(2), 1996.

The Knowledge Model of Protégé-2000: Combining Interoperability and Flexibility

Natalya Fridman Noy, Ray W. Fergerson, Mark A. Musen

Stanford Medical Informatics, Stanford University, Stanford, CA 94305-5479
{noy, fergerson, musen}@smi.stanford.edu

Abstract. Knowledge-based systems have become ubiquitous in recent years. Knowledge-base developers need to be able to share and reuse knowledge bases that they build. Therefore, interoperability among different knowledge-representation systems is essential. The Open Knowledge-Base Connectivity protocol (OKBC) is a common query and construction interface for frame-based systems that facilitates this interoperability. Protégé-2000 is an OKBC-compatible knowledge-base–editing environment developed in our laboratory. We describe Protégé-2000 knowledge model that makes the import and export of knowledge bases from and to other knowledge-base servers easy. We discuss how the requirements of being a usable and configurable knowledge-acquisition tool affected our decisions in the knowledge-model design. Protégé-2000 also has a flexible metaclass architecture which provides configurable templates for new classes in the knowledge base. The use of metaclasses makes Protégé-2000 easily extensible and enables its use with other knowledge models. We demonstrate that we can resolve many of the differences between the knowledge models of Protégé-2000 and Resource Description Framework (RDF)—a system for annotating Web pages with knowledge elements—by defining a new metaclass set. Resolving the differences between the knowledge models in declarative way enables easy adaptation of Protégé-2000 as an editor for other knowledge-representation systems.

1 The Trade-off between Interoperability and Usability

In recent years, knowledge sharing and reuse has become one of the primary goals of the knowledge-based–systems research community [9]. Enabling interoperability among knowledge-representation systems is a crucial step in achieving this goal. The Open Knowledge-Base Connectivity (OKBC) protocol [2, 6] facilitates this interoperability by providing an application-programming interface (API) that serves as a common query and construction interface for frame-based systems. A number of OKBC-compatible knowledge-representation systems are currently available including Ontolingua [4], Loom [8], and Protégé-2000 [5], which was developed in our laboratory.

Protégé-2000 is the latest component-based and platform-independent generation of the Protégé toolset [5]. Two goals have driven the design and development of Protégé-2000: (1) being an easy-to-use and configurable knowledge-acquisition tool and (2) achieving interoperability with other knowledge-representation systems. We achieve the interoperability by making the knowledge model of Protégé-2000 compatible with OKBC (Section 2). As a result, Protégé-2000 users can import ontologies from other

R. Dieng and O. Corby (Eds.): EKAW 2000, LNAI 1937, pp. 17–32, 2000.

OKBC-compatible servers and export their ontologies to other OKBC knowledge servers. Protégé-2000 uses the freedom allowed by the OKBC specification to maintain the model of structured knowledge acquisition that was present in all the generations of the Protégé tools (Section 3) and to achieve the design goal of being a usable and extensible tool.

To function effectively as an access layer for many different knowledge-representation systems, it was important for OKBC to have an extremely general knowledge model. The set of representational commitments in the OKBC knowledge model is minimal and OKBC allows knowledge-representation systems to define their own behavior for many aspects of the knowledge model (e.g., default values). Protégé-2000 *restricts* the OKBC knowledge model in the following two ways (Section 4):

1. If implementing a general feature caused significant changes to the way that knowledge acquisition is performed in Protégé and if OKBC allowed restricting the feature and still remain OKBC-compatible, Protégé-2000 did that.
2. If OKBC did not specify the behavior of a knowledge-model component at all, Protégé-2000 specified the behavior explicitly.

Protégé-2000 also *extends* some features of the OKBC knowledge model in a way that is not prohibited by OKBC. The Protégé-2000 metaclass architecture is one such extension (Section 5). A *metaclass* is a template that is used to define new classes in an ontology. The use of metaclasses allows us to apply the knowledge-acquisition approach that we use to acquire instance data to the ontology-editing process itself. Protégé-2000 uses metaclasses widely and it implements the internal structure of its own knowledge model in a metaclass architecture.

The metaclass architecture in Protégé-2000 along with its component-based approach also enables developers to use Protégé-2000 as an editor for knowledge-representation systems with knowledge models different from that of Protégé-2000. We have demonstrated this flexibility by defining a knowledge model of Resource Description Framework (RDF) [10] as a new metaclass set in Protégé-2000. RDF, developed by the World-Wide Web consortium, is an emerging standard for defining metadata for encoding machine-readable semantics in Web documents. The knowledge model underlying RDF—RDF Schema [1]—is different from the Protégé-2000 knowledge model. However, it is possible to define the main elements of the RDF knowledge model by defining metaclasses that will add RDF-specific features to the templates used to create new classes and slots (Section 6). This definition enables the use of Protégé-2000 as an editor for RDF documents. Our collaborators have implemented an independent Protégé-2000 component that translates the RDF knowledge base created in Protégé-2000 into standard RDF syntax effectively making Protégé-2000 an editor for RDF documents.

2 Protégé-2000 Knowledge Model

The knowledge model of Protégé-2000 is frame-based: frames are the principal building blocks of a knowledge base. A Protégé *ontology* consists of classes, slots, facets, and axioms. *Classes* are concepts in the domain of discourse. *Slots* describe properties or attributes of classes. *Facets* describe properties of slots. *Axioms* specify additional constraints. A Protégé-2000 *knowledge base* includes the ontology and individual *instances* of classes with specific values for slots. The distinction between classes and instances is not an absolute one, however, as we will discuss shortly.

We will use the task of modeling the knowledge about a newspaper-publishing company as an example throughout the paper.[1] This model must include such notions as employees and authors of a newspaper, the newspaper itself, different newspaper sections, layout of issues for each day of the week, and so on.[2] In this domain, we can define a *class* `Newspaper`, where we will store the general information of what a newspaper is and what properties it may have. The January 1, 2000 issue of the *New York Times* will then be an individual *instance* of the class `Newspaper`.

2.1 Classes and Instances

Classes in Protégé-2000 constitute a taxonomic hierarchy. If a class `A` is a subclass of a class `B` then every instance of `A` is also an instance of `B`. For example, a class representing newspaper `Editors` is a subclass of the `Employee` class (Fig. 1). Protégé-2000 visualizes the subclass relation in a tree. Protégé supports multiple inheritance: one class can have more than one superclass. For example, `Editor` is a subclass of both `Employee` and `Author`, since a newspaper editor is both an employee and an author of the newspaper. The root of the class hierarchy in Protégé-2000 (and in OKBC) is the built-in class `:THING`.

In Protégé-2000, both individuals and classes themselves can be *instances* of classes. A *metaclass* is a class whose instances are themselves classes (see Section 5).

2.2 Slots

Slots in Protégé-2000 describe properties of classes and instances, such as contents of a newspaper, or the name of an author. A slot itself is a frame. In Protégé, as in OKBC, slots are first-class objects: Slots are defined independently of any class. When a slot is *attached* to a frame in the user's ontology, it describes properties of that particular frame. For example, we can define a slot `name` and attach it both to the class `Newspaper` and to the class `Author` to represent the name of a newspaper and the name of an author respectively. When a slot is attached to a frame it can have a *value*. For example, the `name` slot for a specific issue of a newspaper (instance of the `Newspaper` class) may have a string "New York Times" as the value.

2.3 Facets

We can specify *constraints* on allowed slot values through *facets*. The constraints specified using facets include cardinality of a slot (how many values a slot can have), restrictions on the value type of a slot (for example, integer, string, instance of a class), minimum and maximum value for a numeric slot, and so on. For example, a slot `salary` can have a type `Float` and a minimum value of `15,000`. When the

---

[1] You can browse the complete example of the newspaper ontology at the Protégé-2000 Web site: http://www.smi.stanford.edu/projects/protege/protege-2000/doc/users_guide/index.html

[2] We do not attempt to build a comprehensive model of this domain.

slot `salary` is attached to the class `Editor`, we can increase the minimum value to `30,000`.

2.4 Template and Own Slots

A slot can be attached to a frame in one of two ways: as a *template slot* or as an *own slot*. An own slot attached to a frame describes properties of an object represented by that frame (an individual or a class). Own slots attached to a class do not get inherited to its subclasses or propagated to its instances. Template slots can be attached only to class frames. A template slot describes properties of the class instances. A template slot attached to a class is inherited by its subclasses. In addition, a template slot on a class becomes an own slot on the instances of that class (Fig. 2).

For example, a slot containing a name of a specific editor—a `name` slot attached to a frame representing that individual instance of the class `Editor`—is an *own slot* attached to that frame (Fig. 3). All the other slots in the instance frame—`salary`, `date hired`, and so on—are also own slots attached to this instance.

Classes can have own slots as well. For example, `documentation` for a class is an own slot attached to that class since it describes the class itself rather than instances of that class. If we represented synonyms for each class name, then the `synonyms` slot would also be an own slot for a class: "Source" is a synonym for the class name `Author` in the newspaper context, but it is not a synonym for John—a specific instance of the class `Author`. Since both `documentation` and `synonyms` in this example are own slots for a class, these slots and their values do not get inherited by

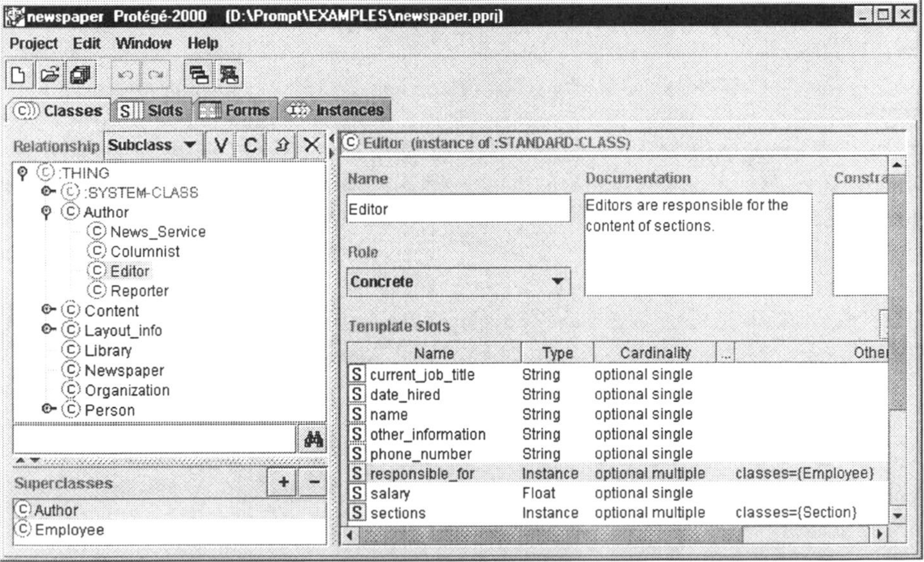

Fig. 1. A representation of an ontology in Protégé-2000. The left-hand panel contains the class hierarchy. The selected class `Editor` is a subclass of two classes: `Employee` and `Author`. The right-hand panel is the form for the class `Editor` containing the own slots for the class and their values and the template slots attached to the class along with their value restrictions—facets.

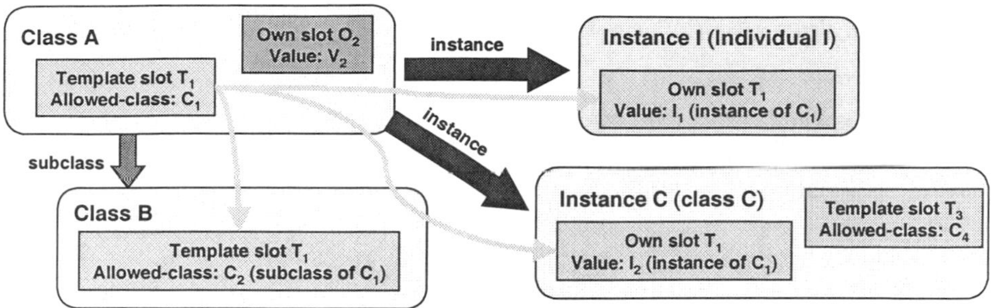

Fig. 2 Propagation of template and own slots through the `subclass-of` and `instance-of` relations.

subclasses. Indeed, synonyms of the class name `Author` are not related to the synonyms for the class name `Columnist`—a subclass of `Author`.

Template slots describe properties that an instance of a class shall have. For example, instances of the class `Editor`—individual editors themselves—have names, dates when they were hired, newspaper sections for which they are responsible, and so on. The slots `name`, `date hired`, and `sections` are template slots for the class `Editor` (Fig. 1). Every instance of the class `Editor` has these slots as own slots with specific values (Fig. 3). Any subclass of `Editor` also will inherit these template slots. In fact, the class `Editor` inherited most of its template slots from its superclasses: `Author` and `Employee` (see Fig. 1).

To summarize, own slots describe a property of a (class or individual) frame itself rather than properties of instances of that frame. Template slots describe properties of instances of a class. Own slots do not propagate to either subclasses or instances of the frame to which they are attached. Template slots get inherited as template slots to the subclasses, and they become own slots for instances.

Protégé-2000 does not allow direct attachment of own slots to classes or instances (we explain why in Section 4). An individual instance can acquire own slots only by being an instance of a class that has those slots as template slots and a class can acquire own slots only by being an instance of a metaclass that has those slots as template slots.

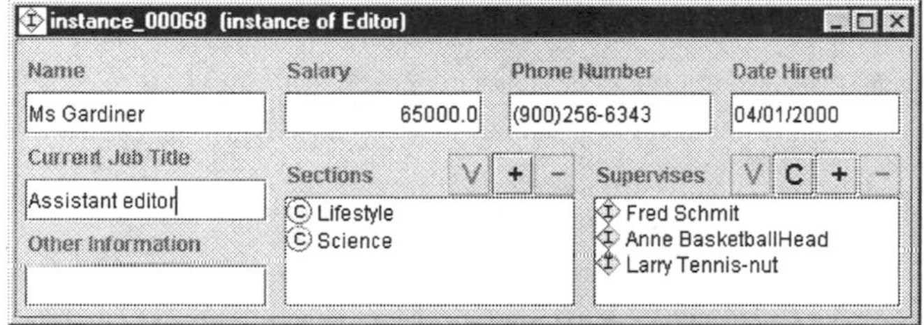

Fig. 3 An instance of a class `Editor`. All the slots on the form are own slots

3 Knowledge-Acquisition Forms

In Protégé-2000, *structured data entry* allows users to enter information about instances quickly and easily and to verify the entered information directly. Protégé-2000 enables structured data entry by using knowledge-acquisition *forms* to acquire instances information. The form-based interface is one of the central user-interface metaphors in Protégé. When a user defines a class and attaches template slots to it, Protégé automatically generates a form to acquire instances of that class. The slots for the class, their cardinality and value type determine the default layout and the content of the form. For example, Protégé-2000 uses a text field as a default way to display and acquire a value of a single-cardinality slot of type `string`. It uses a pull-down menu for a slot whose values are limited to a set of symbols. It represents a boolean slot with a checkbox. It uses a list for slots that have multiple values.

Users can customize the standard form that Protégé-2000 automatically generates for each class to suit the requirements of the specific class better. Customization includes changing the layout of the form components by moving the "important" information to the top of the form, changing labels for the form fields, and choosing different ways of displaying and acquiring slot values. For example, we can use a text field (with the appropriate validation) to acquire an integer value or we can use a slider to set the value instead (Fig. 4). The component-based architecture of Protégé-2000 enables developers to write their own domain-specific and task-specific components to acquire and display slot values.

The current knowledge-acquisition process in Protégé-2000 therefore consists of three steps: (1) define a class and its template slots; (2) lay out the form that will be used to acquire instances of that class; (3) acquire instance of the class. Therefore, there is a form associated with each class and this form is used to acquire instances of

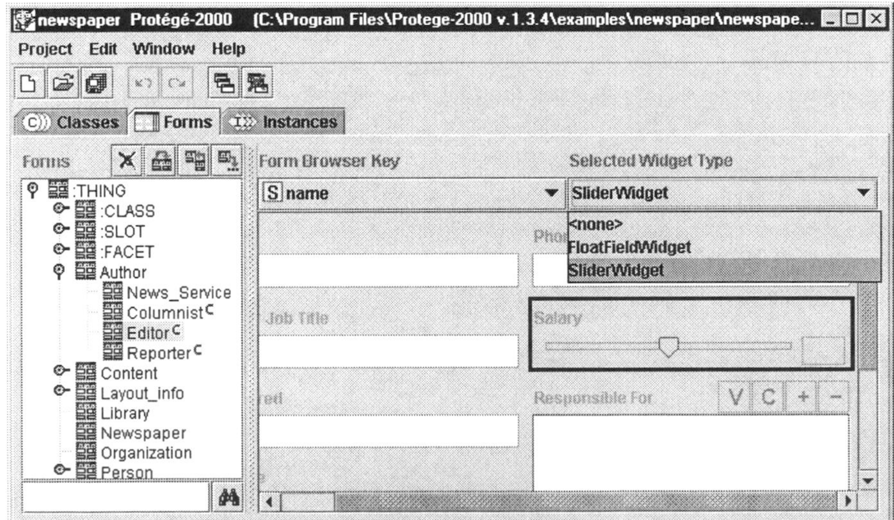

Fig. 4. Customizing the form for class `Editor`. We choose to use a slider to acquire the numeric value for the `salary` slot instead of a text field used in the form in Fig. 1

that class. This user-interface approach resulted in some restrictions in our support of the OKBC knowledge model. We discuss these restrictions in the next section.

4 OKBC and Protégé-2000 Knowledge Models

Protégé-2000 uses the OKBC knowledge model [2] as the basis for its own knowledge model. The main goal of the OKBC developers was to ensure maximum generality and interoperability among knowledge-representation systems. Therefore the OKBC knowledge model makes minimal knowledge-representation commitments and it is extremely general. OKBC attempts to incorporate all the features of the basic approaches to frame-based systems. To allow maximum flexibility, when incompatibility between two features arose, the OKBC designers often *allowed* both features without *requiring* the OKBC-compatible systems to implement either of them.[3] In some cases, OKBC did not specify the behavior at all leaving the implementation up to the knowledge-representation systems completely. This approach—allowing as many features as possible, requiring as few features as possible, and leaving some features underspecified—is perhaps the best approach for a common-access protocol, but designers of individual systems must make some design choices that restrict this generality.

The Protégé-2000 knowledge model is completely compatible with OKBC: Protégé implements everything that the OKBC knowledge model requires and everything in the Protégé-2000 knowledge model is logically consistent with OKBC. For the features where OKBC allows flexibility, Protégé-2000 preserves as much of the OKBC generality as possible and restricts the OKBC model only when the current Protégé user-interface paradigm requires it. Table 1 summarizes differences between the Protégé-2000 and the OKBC knowledge model. Table 1 does not include all the differences between the knowledge models of Protégé-2000 and OKBC. The exhaustive discussion of features where Protégé-2000 knowledge model diverges from the OKBC one, such as own facets and template-slot values, is beyond the scope of this paper.

We made the design choices in Protégé-2000 to enable optimal knowledge acquisitions. As with any evolving system, the decisions may change if we no longer believe that they are justified by the knowledge-acquisition requirements.

The first for items in Table 1 result from the Protégé approach to modeling and knowledge acquisition: Protégé generates a knowledge-acquisition interface based on the users' specification of the objects that they need to acquire. This specification includes defining a class of objects to acquire, having Protégé generate a knowledge-acquisition form based on the class definition, and, if necessary, custom-tailoring the form to acquire that class of objects (Section 3). This approach to knowledge acquisition requires that there is always a way to specify and to custom-tailor a form for acquiring information for any instance. The first four items in Table 1 ensure that there is indeed a class form associated with every instance. If a frame is an instance of more than one class, there is no single place where the form can be laid out, since different own slots for the instance come from different classes. Similarly, if an own slot is

[3] The OKBC protocol enables the knowledge-based systems to specify their design choices.

attached directly to an instance and it does not come from a template slot, there is no place where the user can customize how the values of the slot should be acquired. The same problem is true if a frame is not an instance of *any* class: all the own slots need to be attached to it directly and there is no place where the form can be laid out before the slot values for the instance are acquired.

Currently, the Protégé-2000 user interface is centered around frames and forms to acquire values for slots. Therefore only primitive data types—numbers, strings, symbols, and so on—do not have to be represented as frames. All the user-defined entities are frames. This requirement is less general than the OKBC approach where objects do not have to be frames. For example, a set {1, 2, 3, 4} can be a class.

The sets of classes, slots, and facets are disjoint in Protégé-2000. An object can be either a class, or a slot, or a facet. Protégé imposes this requirement because the three types of frames play inherently different roles in the knowledge acquisition process. In summary, we used the flexibility that OKBC allows to restrict some of the features of the extremely general knowledge model and thereby maintain the uniform knowledge-acquisition interface. There are aspects of a knowledge-representation system for which OKBC allows alternative behaviors or does not specify the behavior at all. We utilized the latter flexibility to implement the Protégé metaclass architecture described in the next section.

5 Metaclasses

The Protégé-2000 metaclass architecture enables us to extend the knowledge-acquisition approach that we use to acquire instance data to the ontology-editing process itself. We can customize and lay out the forms for specifying classes and slots in exactly the same way that we customize and lay out forms for acquiring instances (Section 3). The metaclass architecture in Protégé-2000 also enables developers to use Protégé-2000 as an editor for knowledge-representation systems with knowledge models different from that of Protégé-2000. For example, in Section 6 we describe an example implementation of an editor for Resource Description Framework schema and instance data in Protégé-2000. The Protégé-2000 metaclass architecture is modeled after the metaobject protocol [7] in the Common Lisp Object System.

Table 1. Summary of differences between the knowledge models of OKBC and Protégé-2000

	OKBC	Protégé-2000
1	A frame can be an instance of multiple classes	A frame can be an instance of only one class
2	An own slot can be attached directly to any frame	An own slot is always derived from the corresponding template slot
3	A frame does not have to be an instance of any class	A frame is always an instance of a class
4	Classes, slots, facets, and individuals do not have to be frames	Every class, slot, facet, and individual is a frame
5	A frame can be a class, a slot, and a facet at the same time	A frame is either a class, or a slot, or a facet

A *metaclass* is a class whose instances are themselves classes. Every frame in Protégé-2000 is an instance of a class (see Table 1). Since classes are also frames, every Protégé-2000 class is an instance of another class. Therefore, every class has a dual identity: It is a *subclass* of a class in the class hierarchy—its superclass,—and it is an *instance* of another class—its metaclass. In this section, we will describe how metaclasses work in Protégé-2000, give examples of how metaclasses can be used in knowledge modeling and describe the metaclass architecture of the Protégé-2000 knowledge model itself.

5.1 What is a Metaclass

Metaclass is a *template* for classes that are its instances. A metaclass describes how a class that instantiates this template will look: namely, which own slots it will have and what are the constraints for the values of these slots. Similarly, a traditional class describes how instances of that class will look: which own slots the instances will have and what are the constraints for the values of these slots.

Own slots for a class—the slots that the class acquires from its metaclass—describe the properties of the class itself and not of its instances. For example, a class's `documentation` is a free-form description of the class. It describes the class itself and not the class' subclasses or instances.

In Protégé (and in OKBC) all metaclasses are subclasses of the system class `:CLASS`. By default, each class in Protégé is an instance of the `:STANDARD-CLASS` metaclass, which is a subclass of `:CLASS`. The `:STANDARD-CLASS` metaclass has template slots to store a class's name, documentation, a list of template slots, a list of constraints, and so on (Fig. 7). These slots then become own slots for each of the newly created classes—instances of `:STANDARD-CLASS`. We will discuss `:STANDARD-CLASS` in more detail in Section 5.3. The form that Protégé uses to acquire the class information (for example, the form on the right-hand side in Fig. 1) is in fact the knowledge-acquisition form that corresponds to the `:STANDARD-CLASS` class. Users can customize this form in exactly the same manner as they customize forms for other classes.

Protégé-2000 allows users to define their own metaclasses and to define new classes as instances of these user-defined metaclasses. They can then customize the forms to acquire instances of these metaclasses, which are new classes in the ontology, effectively creating new ontology editors [3].

5.2 User-Defined Metaclasses

Consider the earlier example of defining a newspaper ontology. Suppose we wanted to record the recommended minimum and maximum salary for different employee positions as well as whether or not a particular position is at the management level. For example, the recommended minimum salary for an editor is $30,000 and the recommended maximum salary is $60,000. An editor is a management position. Since the two numbers are only the *recommended* minimum and maximum, we cannot encode them as the minimum and maximum constraints for the `salary` slot: our model should allow a very good editor to earn more than $60,000. Also, we consider all editors to be managers and we should not have to specify this fact for each new instance of the `Editor` class. These three slots—the recommended minimum and maximum salary and whether or not the position is a management position—are in fact own slots for the class `Editor`: the values of these slots define properties of the `Editor` class, but not the properties of their corresponding instances.

We will use metaclasses to implement this model. We define an `Employee metaclass` class which we will then use as a template for the class `Employee` and all of its subclasses. Protégé-2000 requires that all metaclasses be subclasses of the system class `:CLASS`. In practice, most metaclasses are subclasses of `:STANDARD-CLASS`, since all the metaclasses usually include the slots defined in `:STANDARD-CLASS` (see Section 5.1). We create additional template slots for the `Employee metaclass` (Fig. 5): the `minimum recommended salary` and `maximum recommended salary` slots have the value type `Integer` and cardinality `Single`; the `management position` slot has the value type `Boolean`.

We define the `Employee` class and its subclasses as instances of the `Employee metaclass`. These classes then have the three new slots as their own slots. The `Editor` class in Fig. 1 was an instance of the `:STANDARD-CLASS` metaclass and did not have these domain-specific own slots. Fig. 6 shows the definition of the class `Editor` as an instance of `Employee metaclass`. Before defining the `Editor` class, we laid out the form for the `Employee metaclass` class in a manner similar to the one demonstrated in Fig. 4. Protégé-2000 uses this form to acquire instances of the `Employee metaclass` class such as the `Editor` class.

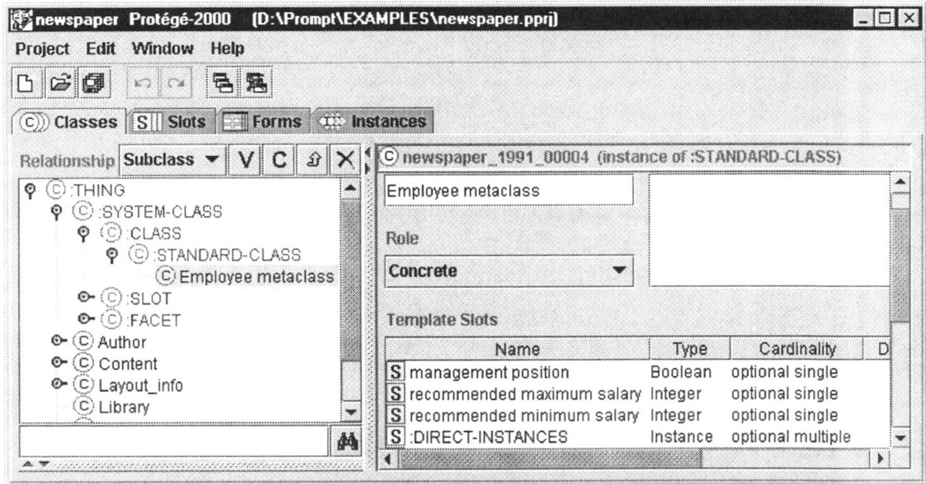

Fig. 5 Definition of the class `Employee metaclass`. The template slots defined here will become own slots for classes that are instances of this metaclass

5.3 Protégé-2000 Built-in Metaclass Architecture

Protégé-2000 uses the metaclass mechanism to implement its own internal class structure. Metaclasses define the representation of all the frames in the system—classes, slots, facets, and individuals. All the information about a class, from its name and documentation to a list of its template slots and superclasses, is stored in its own slots. In other words, Protégé uses its own class structure to store the information about itself. The users of Protégé-2000 do not need to see this internal information (and very few users do indeed see it) unless they decide to explore the ontology describing the Protégé-2000 knowledge model. The three system classes—`:CLASS`, `:SLOT`, `:FACET`—serve as types for all the Protégé-2000 classes, slots, and facets respectively. These classes do not have any template slots attached to them. This feature allows Protégé-2000 developers to implement their own knowledge models in Protégé-2000 without making the same knowledge-model assumptions that Protégé-2000 does. The Protégé-2000 knowledge model itself is implemented using the three standard subclasses of these classes: `:STANDARD-CLASS`, `:STANDARD-SLOT`, and `:STANDARD-FACET`. These three classes have the template slots that define the structure of their instances—the Protégé-2000 classes, slots, and facets respectively.

`:STANDARD-CLASS` defines the default metaclass for Protégé-2000 classes.

- Template slots of `:STANDARD-CLASS` (Fig. 7) define the standard own slots for classes in Protégé-2000. The slots store the class name, documentation, direct subclasses, direct superclasses, and direct template slots for the class. Usually, all the user-defined metaclasses will be subclasses of `:STANDARD-CLASS`. The `:STANDARD-CLASS` is an instance of itself and therefore has the same sets of slots attached to it twice: once as own slots with values and once as template slots with value-type restrictions in the form of facets.

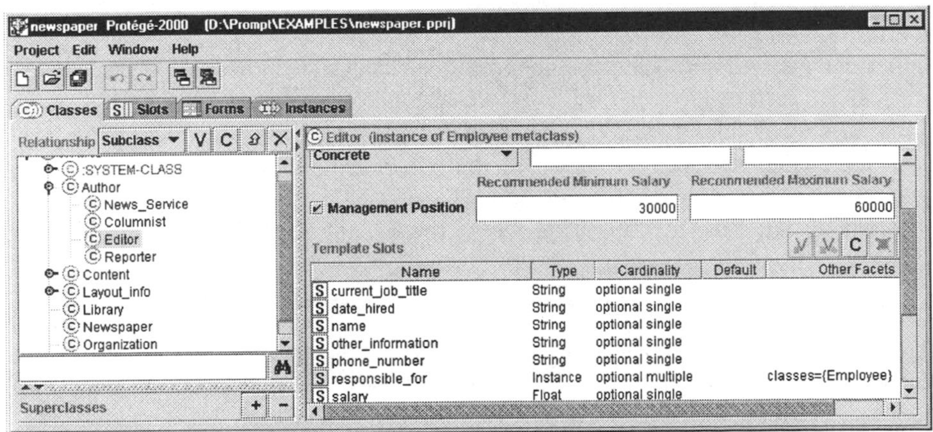

Fig. 6 The definition of the `Editor` class as an instance of the `Employee` metaclass. The definition has the additional own slots with the corresponding values. The `Editor` class in Fig. 1 was an instance of `:STANDARD-CLASS` and did not have these own slots.

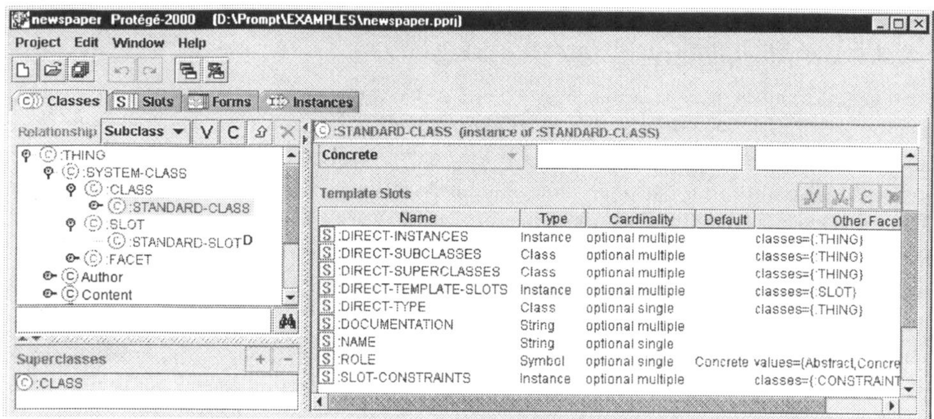

Fig. 7 Definition of the `:STANDARD-CLASS` metaclass. Protégé-2000 uses the slots attached to this class to store the information about all its classes

- `:STANDARD-SLOT` defines the default metaslot in Protégé-2000. Template slots of `:STANDARD-SLOT` such as `:SLOT-DEFAULTS`, `:SLOT-VALUE-TYPE` and so on define the standard own slots for slot frames in Protégé-2000. These slots store the slot name, its documentation, value type, default values, cardinality, and so on. User-defined metaslots are subclasses of `:STANDARD-SLOT`.
- `:STANDARD-FACET` defines the class to which all the built-in and user-defined facets belong. Currently there are no required slots for facets.

We can use the Protégé-2000 form mechanism to customize the forms for acquiring data for instances of these metaclasses. For example, if a customized version of the system does not need to have the constraint slot on the class form, the user can simply customize the form for `:STANDARD-CLASS` to remove the elements acquiring constraints from the form.

To summarize, the metaclass architecture in Protégé-2000 enables users to adapt and change the system to suit the requirements of their domain and task. This adaptation can be performed in two ways: (1) custom-tailoring the knowledge-acquisition forms for class definitions and (2) changing the knowledge model by defining a new metaclass architecture.

In the next section we demonstrate how we can use the Protégé-2000 metaclass architecture to implement a different knowledge model in Protégé-2000—that of RDF.

6 Adapting to a Different Knowledge Model—RDF

The combination of (1) the metaclass architecture, (2) the ability to define specialized user-interface components to display and acquire slot values, and (3) the ability to implement additional persistence layers as components in Protégé-2000 allows Protégé-2000 users to adapt the tool to create and edit knowledge bases with knowledge models that are different from the Protégé-2000 knowledge model.

With our collaborators, we have recently adapted Protégé-2000 to become an editor for Resource Description Framework (RDF) Schema and instance data. RDF is an evolving knowledge-representation standard being defined by the WWW Consortium

[10]. The main goal for RDF is to make Web-based pages not only *human-readable* but also *machine-readable* enabling computer agents to use the information. Currently, HTML enables Web-site developers to encode how the document is going to appear on the page. RDF takes the representation further, allowing semantics to be encoded as well. For example, two Web sites may describe the same movie: the Internet Movie Database has a list of all the characters, awards, technical details, and so on. Amazon.com has the information on purchasing the videotape. If the two sites represent the information formally and use a shared ontology to do so, an agent can link the two databases and can answer requests that require the knowledge of both. The RDF Schema specification defines the knowledge model that will be used to express ontologies in RDF [1].

Adapting Protégé-2000 to become an editor for RDF Schema and instance data requires bridging the gap between the two knowledge models. We now describe what the differences are and how we can resolve many of the differences by defining specialized classes and metaclasses in Protégé-2000. We then discuss which differences we cannot resolve declaratively and describe how they can be solved as part of the RDF persistence layer—a Protégé-2000 component that translates between the Protégé-2000 internal representation of classes and the RDF serialization format.

6.1 Summary of the RDF Knowledge Model

RDF is a model for describing *resources*. Anything can be a resource. An RDF document describes resources and relations among resources. An RDF Schema defines what classes of resources exist, how resources are related to one another and what restrictions on those relations exist.

In RDF, *classes* of concepts constitute a hierarchy with multiple inheritance. Classes have instances and a resource can be an instance of more than class. Resources have *properties* associated with them. Properties describe attributes of a resource or a relation of a resource to another resource. A property is represented as a predicate–subject–object triple: *predicate* is the property, *object* and *subject* are resources related by the property. For example, a statement "John is a father of Alice" can be represent as a triple consisting of the predicate `father`, subject `John`, and object `Alice`. A property can be a specialization of another property. The RDF schema defines *domain* of a property—resources that can be subjects of the property—and *range* of a property—resources that can be objects of the property. For example, the property `father` may have a class `Person` both as its domain and as its range.

RDF defines a set of core properties. For example, the `rdfs:seeAlso` property specifies another resource containing information about the subject resource and the `rdfs:isDefinedBy` property indicates the resource defining the subject resource.

Therefore, a class (in the sense of frame-based languages) is defined by a resource and all the properties describing the resource (all the properties where the resource is the domain). The following are the core classes in RDF:

- `rdfs:Resource`: the class containing all resources—the superclass for all RDF classes

- `rdfs:Class`: the class containing all classes as its instances—the metaclass for all RDF classes
- `rdf:Property`: the class containing all properties—the metaslot for all RDF properties

6.2 Core RDF Classes and Metaclasses in Protégé-2000

Both RDF and Protégé-2000 are based on a frame-based paradigm and their knowledge models have a lot in common. The notion of classes is the same. Classes are organized in a taxonomic hierarchy in both cases. Classes can have instances. *Properties* in RDF are *slots* in Protégé. Both properties and slots are first-class objects describing attributes of classes and instances and relations among them.

We start by defining in Protégé-2000 the core RDF classes described in the Section 6.1 (Fig. 8). The Protégé-2000 class `rdfs:Resource` is the root of the hierarchy of classes defined in an RDF schema. This class has three template slots: `resource uri` to store a Uniform Resource Identifier and the core properties `rdfs:seeAlso` and `rdfs:isDefinedBy`, which are required by each resource. All the classes that are subclasses of `rdfs:Resource` inherit these slots.

The class `rdfs:Class` is a default metaclass for all the newly defined classes in the RDF project. It is also a subclass of `rdfs:Resource`. Therefore, `rdfs:Class` inherits the three template slots attached to `rdfs:Resource`. These template slots become own slots for instances of `rdfs:Class`—all the classes in the RDF project. The `rdfs:Resource` and `rdfs:Class` are themselves instances of `rdfs:Class` and therefore they have these standard slots as their own slots as well.

The class `rdf:Property` is a default metaslot in the RDF project. It is the template for all newly defined slots. The metaslot `rdf:Property` is a subclass of both `rdfs:Resource` and `:STANDARD-SLOT`. As a result all slots—properties—have these own slots: `resource uri`, `rdfs:seeAlso`, and `rdfs:isDefinedBy`.

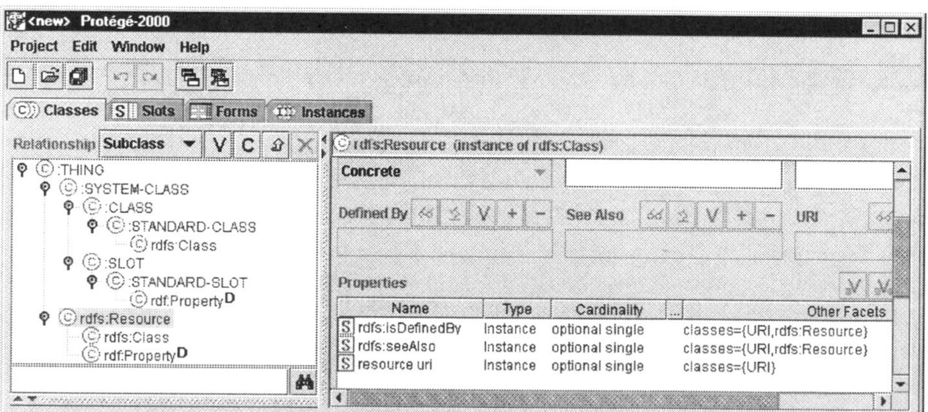

Fig. 8 The RDF project: definition of the `rdfs:Resource` class. The template slots attached to this class will propagate to all the classes and instances in the project.

Table 2. Summary of differences between the knowledge models of Protégé-2000 and RDF

	Protégé-2000	RDF and RDF Schema
1	A frame can be an *instance of only one class*	A resource can be an *instance of multiple classes*
2	A value of a slot can be a value of a primitive type or an instance of a class. There can be *one or more* classes that constrain the value	The *range* of a property is a *single class* which constraints the objects of the property to instances of that class
3	*A slot* in an individual instance and *cannot be a subclass* of another slot	A property *can be a specialization of another property*

6.3 Differences between the Protégé-2000 and RDF Knowledge Models

Defining the RDF metaclass structure cannot resolve all the differences between the Protégé-2000 and RDF knowledge models. The implementation of the RDF persistence layer—a Protégé-2000 component that translates the knowledge base betwee the internal Protégé-2000 representation and RDF documents—can resolve the differences between the knowledge models that could not be resolved by defining the metaclass structure. The RDF persistence layer enables the direct import and export of RDF documents making Protégé-2000 an editor for RDF documents. Our collaborators have implemented one such component.

Table 2 presents some of the differences between the Protégé-2000 and the RDF knowledge models that the persistence layer must resolve. As in OKBC, resources in RDF can be instances of more than one class. In Protégé-2000 each instance is a member of only one class. However, *multiple inheritance* enables Protégé-2000 to simulate the multi-class membership. If an imported RDF schema has an instance `I` that belongs to several classes, $C_1, \ldots, C_n$, the persistence layer can create a new class `C` that is a subclass of all of $C_1, \ldots, C_n$. The instance `I` will then be an instance of the class `C` and, by inheritance, it will be an instance of all the original classes $C_1, \ldots, C_n$.

In RDF Schema, the range of a property is constrained to a single class. That is, the objects of a property must be instances of that single class. In Protégé-2000, slot range can be a primitive data type, can be constrained to instances of several classes ("allowed classes" for the slot), or can be constrained to subclasses of several classes ("allowed parents" for the slot). If a Protégé-2000 slot has multiple allowed classes, the RDF persistence layer can create a new class that is a superclass of all of the intended allowed classes and use the new class as the range for the RDF property.

The RDF Schema allows specializing properties. For example, the `father` property is a specialization of the more general `parent` property: If John is a `father` of Alice, then John is also a `parent` of Alice. In Protégé-2000, all slots are individual instances and therefore cannot form a subclass–superclass hierarchy. If a domain model requires a hierarchy of properties, the properties can be reified to become regular classes in the class hierarchy.

To summarize, we extended the Protégé-2000 built-in metaclass architecture to implement the structure of RDF Schema declaratively and the RDF persistence layer can use the knowledge structures to hide or repair other differences programmatically.

6 Conclusions

We have presented the knowledge model of Protégé-2000—an ontology-editing and knowledge-acquisition environment. The OKBC-compatibility of the knowledge model enables the interoperability between Protégé-2000 and other OKBC-compatible systems. We have discussed how the knowledge model was affected by the requirements for structured knowledge acquisition. The Protégé-2000 metaclass architecture enables elegant and powerful knowledge modeling as well as allows us to implement the internal structure of Protégé-2000 explicitly in the ontology. We have described how Protégé-2000 uses its own metaclasses to describe itself. The flexibility of the knowledge model and the component architecture of Protégé-2000 make it easy to adapt the tool to work as an editor for other knowledge-representation systems. We demonstrated how Protégé-2000 can be adapted to become an editor for RDF.

Acknowledgments

Henrik Eriksson both inspired and was instrumental in the design of the Protégé-2000 metaclass architecture. Stefan Decker and William Grosso implemented the RDF persistence layer. We would also like to thank William Grosso for comments on the paper. This work was supported in part by the grants 5T16 LM0733 and 892154 from the National Library of Medicine, by a grant from Spawar, and by a grant from FastTrack Systems, Inc.

References

1. Brickley, D. and Guha, R.V., *Resource Description Framework (RDF) Schema Specification*, World Wide Web Consortium, 1999.
2. Chaudhri, V.K., Farquhar, A., Fikes, R., Karp, P.D. and Rice, J.P., *Open Knowledge Base Connectivity 2.0.3.*, 1998.
3. Eriksson, H., Fergerson, R.W., Shahar, Y. and Musen, M.A. Automatic generation of ontology editors. In: *Twelfth Banff Workshop on Knowledge Acquisition, Modeling, and Management.* Banff, Alberta, 1999.
4. Farquhar, A., Fikes, R. and Rice, J., The Ontolingua server: a tool for collaborative ontology construction. *International Journal of Human-Computer Studies.* **46**: p. 707-727, 1997.
5. Grosso, W.E., Eriksson, H., Fergerson, R.W., Gennari, J.H., Tu, S.W. and Musen, M.A. Knowledge modeling at the millennium (the design and evolution of Protégé-2000). In: *Twelfth Banff Workshop on Knowledge Acquisition, Modeling, and Management.* Banff, Alberta, 1999.
6. Karp, P., Chaudhri, V. and Paley, S., A Collaborative Environment for Authoring Large Knowledge Bases. *Journal of Intelligent Information Systems* 2000.
7. Kiczales, G., des Rivieres, J. and Bobrow, D.G., *The Art of the Metaobject Protocol.* Cambridge, MA: The MIT Press, 1991.
8. MacGregor, R., *Retrospective on Loom*, USC ISI, 1999.
9. Musen, M.A., Dimensions of knowledge sharing and reuse. *Computers and Biomedical Research.* **25**: p. 435-467, 1992.
10. W3C, *Resource Description Framework (RDF)*, World-Wide Web Consortium, http://www.w3.org/RDF/, 2000.

A Case Study in Using Protégé-2000 as a Tool for CommonKADS

Guus Schreiber[1], Monica Crubézy[2], and Mark Musen[2]

[1] University of Amsterdam, Social Science Informatics
Roetersstraat 15, NL-1018 WB Amsterdam, The Netherlands
schreiber@swi.psy.uva.nl

[2] Stanford University, School of Medicine, Stanford Medical Informatics
251 Campus Drive, MSOB X-215, Stanford, CA 94305-5479, USA
{crubezy,musen}@smi.stanford.edu

Abstract. This article describes a case study in which Protégé-2000 was used to build a tool for constructing CommonKADS knowledge models. The case study tries to capitalize on the strong points of both approaches in the tool-support and modeling areas. We specify the CommonKADS knowledge model as an ontology in the Protégé specification formalism, and define a number of visualizations for the resulting types. The study shows that this type of usage of Protégé-2000 as a "metaCASE" tool is to a large extent feasible. In particular, the flexible class/instance distinction in Protégé is a feature that is needed for undertaking such a metamodeling exercise. The case study revealed a number of problems, such as the representation of rule types. The study also led to a set of new tool requirements, such as extended expressivity of the Protégé forms. Finally, this experience shows how the concrete, operational approach of Protégé and the highly methodological approach of CommonKADS can be combined successfully to provide the middle-ground tool that reduces the gap between a conceptual model and a usable knowledge model.

1 Introduction and Approach

Knowledge engineering has matured and KE techniques are used increasingly not just for knowledge-system development but also for knowledge analysis and structuring in knowledge management in general. However, the availability of adequate tool support is crucial for a wider adoption of these techniques. In this paper we describe a case study in which we used the Protégé-2000 tool to build a "knowledge-model editor" for CommonKADS. This editor should support analysts and (to a limited extent) domain specialists in modeling a knowledge-intensive task using the CommonKADS knowledge-modeling framework [11]. The aim was to create an editor that adheres as much as possible to the distinctions made in the CommonKADS knowledge model.

This case study tries to capitalize on the strong points of both approaches. Traditionally, Protégé has put an emphasis on providing configurable and usable knowledge-engineering tools [10]. In CommonKADS the main focus of attention has always been on the modeling side, more or less assuming that support tools would become available in due time. This case study was triggered by the observation that the Protégé-2000 tool

R. Dieng and O. Corby (Eds.): EKAW 2000, LNAI 1937, pp. 33–48, 2000.

is capable of supporting metamodeling. This recent addition to Protégé extends its scope to creating customized editors for knowledge representation systems with different knowledge models [5]. Another interesting feature of Protégé-2000 is the possibility to save the results as RDF [8]. Finally, the authors thought it would be a sign of maturity of the knowledge-engineering field if two leading methodologies could be linked in this fashion.

Tool requirements. In this case study we look at the usability of Protégé-2000 from the perspective of three different types of users:

1. The *tool builder*: the person constructing the knowledge-model editor.
2. The *knowledge engineer*: the person using the editor to create and maintain a knowledge model. Also, the knowledge engineer should be able to define a domain-knowledge editor to be used by the domain specialist.
3. The *domain specialist*: the person editing and updating the actual domain knowledge of the application.

These three types of users have different requirements. For the tool builder the main requirement is expressivity: can she define the required modeling constructs and visualizations without losing information or clarity? The question whether the interface is easy to use is less important for this type of user, as a high level of expertise in this area is required anyway. The knowledge engineer needs a tool that enables a convenient and consistent environment for defining a knowledge model. For her it is important that there be no specification redundancy and that consistency and completeness checks for model verification be available. Also, she should be able to include and adapt predefined model parts, such as the catalog of CommonKADS task templates. The domain specialist will especially be interested in a simple and intuitive interface for updating knowledge bases. Early Protégé research has shown that this requires the use of a domain-specific vocabulary in the user interface [9].

Of course, these requirements are related, as the tool created by the tool builder has a strong influence on the functionality offered to the knowledge engineer. The same holds for the domain specialist, who has to use the knowledge-elicitation interface defined by the knowledge engineer. Still, we view these three users as useful perspectives for evaluating the usability of Protégé-2000.

Related work. Over the years, a number of tools have been developed for knowledge modeling with CommonKADS. An early example is the Shelley workbench [1]. PC-PACK[1] is a contemporary tool with similar aims. PC-PACK focuses on the early phases of knowledge acquisition. It provides functionality for annotating and structuring expertise data such as domain texts, interviews, and self reports. Examples of the use of PC-PACK can be found in various publications [11,13]. Although PC-PACK offers some support for knowledge-model specification through the GDM grammar [14], the tool can best be seen as complementary to a knowledge model editor. The main area in which

[1] `http://www.epistemics.co.uk/products/pcpack/`

functionality overlaps concerns the interface for the domain specialist. WebCokace[2] is an interactive web editor for CommonKADS knowledge models [4]. It uses an earlier version of the CommonKADS CML language to represent knowledge models. The tool is targeted at the knowledge engineer and provides facilities for reusing model elements from catalogs, such as existing task templates and ontologies. KADS-22[3] is also targeted at the knowledge engineer and supports the knowledge-model editing using the CML version used in the CommonKADS textbook [11]. The tool includes graphical editors and can produce "pretty-prints" of the knowledge model, for exale in HTML format.

CASE tools also need to be compared with "low-level" tools, in particular dedicated drawing tools. A CASE tool needs to have a marked advantage in functionality for users to prefer it above such baseline tools. A good example of a baseline tool is ModelDraw[4], developed by Wielemaker. In an evaluation study one would typically want to compare a "heavy" CASE tool with such a light-weight drawing tool.

Paper overview. In Sec. 2 we briefly summarize the main features of Protégé-2000 and of CommonKADS. Sec. 3 reports on the tool construction process and shows examples of usage of the tool. In Sec. 4 we discuss the experiences gathered during this case study, taking also the different user perspectives into account. Throughout this paper we use examples from an assessment application. This application is concerned with the problem of assessing whether people who applied for a certain (rental) residence conform to the criteria set out for this residence. A full knowledge model of this application can be found in the CommonKADS textbook [11, Ch. 10]. The code of the tool including the example can be downloaded from the Protégé-2000 website.[5]

2 Background

2.1 Protégé-2000

Protégé-2000 is the latest incarnation of the series of tools developed for many years by researchers at SMI to provide efficient support in knowledge modeling and knowledge acquisition [7]. Protégé-2000 is platform-independent and offers a component-based architecture, which is extensible through its API. Protégé was recently adapted to support the creation and editing of RDF Schema ontologies and the acquisition of RDF instance data (see [5] for more details). In the rest of this article we use the shorthand "Protégé" to refer to Protégé-2000.

Frame-based knowledge model. Protégé is a frame-based environment for knowledge-based system development. Its knowledge model has been re-factored to meet the requirements of the recent OKBC standard [3]. An ontology in Protégé consists of classes, slots, facets and axioms [5]:

[2] `http://www-sop.inria.fr/acacia/Cokace/index-eng.html`

[3] `http://www.swi.psy.uva.nl/projects/kads22/index.html`

[4] `http://www.commonkads.uva.nl/`, see the tools section

[5] `http://smi.stanford.edu/projects/protege/`

- Class frames specify domain concepts and are organized in a subsumption hierarchy, that allows for multiple inheritance. Classes are templates for individual instance frames.
- Slots are special frames that can be attached to classes to define their attributes, with specific value type restrictions. **Own** slots define intrinsic properties of class or individual instance frames. **Template** slots are attached to class frames to define attributes of their instances, which in turn define specific values for slots. Slots in Protégé are first-class objects. They can be specified both globally for the ontology and locally as attached to classes, where their properties are overridden.
- Facets are properties of slots, which specify constraints on their allowed values. Examples are the cardinality of a slot value, its type (primitive, such as string or integer, or complex, such as instance of a class), range and default values, etc.
- Axioms are additional constraints that can be defined on frames, for example to link the values of a group of template slots attached to a class. As a very recent addition to Protégé, a constraint language enables developers to represent constraints throughout an ontology as sentences expressed in KIF-based [6] predicate logic. Protégé defines a set of built-in predicates and functions that can be used to express constraints. Protégé also provides functionality to evaluate the constraints and check that the individual instances in a knowledge base conform to those constraints. Examples of constraints are given in Sec. 3.3.

Configurable forms for knowledge acquisition. Protégé-2000 perpetuates the support for structured and customizable knowledge entry that has always been fundamental to the Protégé tools. It achieves that goal by providing a configurable user interface for all steps in the process of modeling and acquiring domain- and task-specific knowledge. The graphical user interface of Protégé allows users to define and visualize classes and their slots, to customize a corresponding set of forms for acquiring instances of the classes, and to acquire instances themselves.

The central metaphor for knowledge acquisition in Protégé is the notion of a *form* composed of a set of graphical entry fields ("widgets"). A form is attached to a class to display and acquire its instances. Specific widgets facilitate and locally verify the entry of slot values on instances. Based on the specification of the classes in an ontology, such as the value-type restrictions on their template slots, Protégé automatically generates a form for each class, with a default layout and set of widgets (text fields for string slots, pull-down menus for enumerated symbolic slots, etc.). Tool builders and knowledge engineers can customize the generated forms to meet domain-specific requirements on knowledge entry and checking. They can rearrange the layout and configure the widget components on the forms, or provide their own pluggable widget.

A special kind of knowledge acquisition metaphor that Protégé offers is the notion of a diagram, which provides a means for the synthetic display and acquisition of complex structures defined by a set of related classes in the ontology. Protégé's support for diagrams comes with a special-purpose ontology of metaclasses and classes representing diagrammatic components, that the user extends to create domain-specific diagram templates. The user defines the nodes of the diagram, that refer to domain classes in the ontology and the types of connectors that can link nodes together. Forms are generated for each diagram construct, that not only take care of graphical layout and navigation but also handle consistency and partially automatic filling of the instances and slot values being acquired through this metaphor. The user is also able to fill-in additional details of instances by zooming into the nodes and connectors.

Flexible class/instance distinction. Protégé also provides a flexible class/instance distinction based on the notion of metaclasses. A metaclass is a class whose instances are classes themselves. Thus, metaclasses are templates to create new classes and slots in an ontology. They define template slots that are propagated to their instance classes as own slots. Examples are the role and documentation own slots on standard classes.

The metaclass mechanism is described in detail elsewhere [5]. The mechanism implements the internal structure of the Protégé knowledge model itself with a set of built-in metaclasses for classes, slots and facets. The metaclass mechanism also enables developers to tailor the underlying knowledge model of their ontology, by defining their own domain- or task-specific metaclasses. Forms for the metaclasses can be customized and instances (new classes and slots in the ontology) can be acquired, similarly to traditional classes and instances. Therefore, this approach extends the scope of modeling possibilities to metamodeling: Developers can use Protégé as an editor for knowledge representation systems with different knowledge models.

The case study that we describe in this paper can be seen as using Protégé to build a specific editor for CommonKADS knowledge bases. As we show in the next section, we made heavily use of the metamodeling constructs offered by Protégé to define the CommonKADS knowledge model.

2.2 CommonKADS

Details about the CommonKADS approach can be found in the recent CommonKADS textbook [11]. CommonKADS is centered around a so-called "model suite", which takes different perspectives on a knowledge-intensive task. The central model is the knowledge model. The use of CommonKADS in this case study is limited to this model. A synopsis of the main constructs in a knowledge model can be found in Table. 1.

Most constructs are well known from previous CommonKADS publications, e.g. [12]. A relatively recent addition is the notion of **rule type** in the domain knowledge. A rule type is used to model a set of rules that share a similar structure. For example, in the assessment application we distinguish three rule types: (1) *abstraction rules* that are used to abstract case values (e.g., the age category of an applicant can be derived from the age), (2) *requirements* describing the way in which case values determine truth or falsehood of an assessment criterion such as RentFitsIncome, and (3) *decision rules* that link a boolean combination of criterion values to a particular decision (eligible or not). Although intuitively the notion of rule type can be easily understood, from a formal point of view it is in fact quite complex. We will see later on that the rule type was the "hardest nut to crack" when constructing the tool.

Category	Construct	Description
Task knowledge	*task*	a problem statement of what needs to be achieved; specifies also input and output
	task method	a way to achieve a task by decomposing it into subtasks, inferences and transfer functions; also defines a control regimen over the decomposition
Inference knowledge	*inference*	a primitive reasoning function that uses a part of the domain knowledge to achieve a basic problem-solving step
	dynamic role	input or output of an inference; signifies a place holder and an abstract name for domain objects "playing" the role
	static role	the static knowledge used by an inference, also defined as a placeholder for domain objects (e.g., a rule set)
	transfer function	a primitive function needed to that interact with the outside world
Domain knowledge	*domain schema*	a set of domain-type definitions; a domain schema can be imported into other schemata
	concept	a group of "things"with shared features; cf. "object class" or "entity"
	relation	a set of tuples that relate "things"to each other; cf. "association", ER-type relationship
	rule type	expressions about concepts/relations in an antecedent/consequent form
	knowledge base	a set of domain-type instances (usually rule instances) that can be used as static knowledge by one or more inferences

Table 1. Constructs in the CommonKADS knowledge model

3 Constructing the Protégé-CK Tool

3.1 Architectural Considerations

In order to build a tool for specifying a CommonKADS knowledge model we need to define the knowledge-model constructs as classes and slots in Protégé. For example, a **task** can be represented as a class with slots pointing to the input and output roles, the method that realizes it, etc. Actual tasks will then be instances of **task**. The same can be done for all task and inference constructs listed in Table. 1, i.e., inferences, roles, methods and transfer functions.

However, this approach presents a problem when we come to the domain types. We have three abstraction levels here which we like to represent:

1. Domain-modeling constructs: **concept**, **relation**, **rule type**.
2. Domain-specific types: concept applicant, rule type abstraction-rule.
3. Domain-specific instances: a particular applicant or a particular abstraction rule.

This problem is typical of metamodeling in general. What seems to be an instance from one level, behaves as a class at a lower level. To handle this we can make use of the flexible class/instance distinction made by Protégé. We can define a class as being an instance of a custom metaclass. The resulting class can both be used as an instance (filling in slot values for the slots defined on the metaclass) and as a class (defining template slots for its own instances as well as constraints that should hold). Note that this use of metaclasses is different from approaches in which a metaclass is nothing more than an abstract superclass.

By way of the metaclass architecture we were able to model the three-level approach of the CommonKADS knowledge model. For example, we defined a domain-type metaclass as a template for all domain type classes with an additional template slot rolesPlayed to denote the knowledge role of its instances in the domain. We represented domain-modeling constructs as instance classes of DomainTypeMetaClass, with a root class DomainType. We then modeled domain-specific types as subclasses of the domain modeling classes (thus also instances of DomainTypeMetaClass) with specific values for their rolesPlayed slot. Finally, domain-specific individuals can be acquired as instances of the domain-specific classes. In Sec. 3.3 this approach is illustrated in Fig. 3, where we see its usage in defining the CommonKADS domain-schema constructs.

3.2 Task and Inference Knowledge

As outlined above, the task- and inference-knowledge constructs were modeled as Protégé classes. An example class definition is shown in Fig. 1 for a task method. The slots correspond to the information that needs to be specified for a task method in the CommonKADS knowledge-modeling language [11, Appendix].

To represent the CommonKADS task-method decomposition and inference diagrams, we configured two specialized diagrammatic classes in our ontology, as well as their associated forms, along the lines described in Sec. 2.1.[6] For example, we defined the InferenceStructureDiagram class with nodes (inferenceStructureNodes) to be instances of the TransferFunction, KnowledgeRole and Inference classes (and subclasses) and connectors to be instances of special-purpose connector classes. For example, the HasInputRole connector links a DynamicRole (subclass of KnowledgeRole) node to a Inference or TransferFunction node. This way, when we create an instance of the InferenceStructureDiagram (see Fig. 2), we can add or create instances of the nodes, for example an inference abstract and a dynamic role case description, and link them with an instance of HasInputRole connector. Based on the definition of HasInputRole, the diagram automatically fills-in the slot inputRoles of the Abstract instance with the instance value case description.

The use of the diagrams gave rise to a large set of small problems and requirements with respect to their usage (symbol availability, user-interface behavior, etc.). We can see some small graphical differences (e.g., rounded rectangles, no border) when we compare the inference structure in Fig. 2 with the original figure in the CommonKADS textbook [11, p. 136]. However, the basic mechanisms for form specification suited our purposes well.

[6] For details, see the Protege tutorial on the use of the "diagram widget" at `http://smi-web.stanford.edu/projects/protege/protege-2000/doc/tutorial/diagrams/index.html`

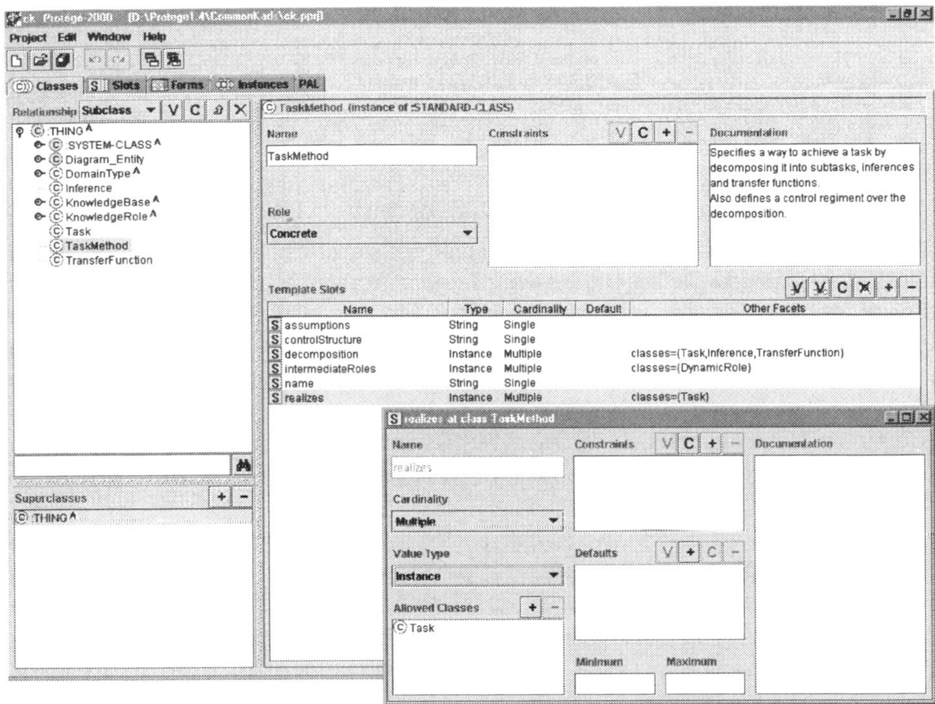

Fig. 1. Specification of the class TaskMethod. At the left, part of the hierarchy of classes is shown. TaskMethod is a root class (i.e., a subclass of :THING, see lower-left). At the right, the class definition is shown. The own slot role indicates whether the class is concrete (can have direct instances) or abstract (no direct instances). Abstract classes are marked with an "A" in the class hierarchy. In the lower-right area the template slots of TaskMethod instances are defined. Each slot has a value range, a cardinality constraint (single or multiple), and a possible value restriction (e.g. the slot realizes can only be filled by instances of the class Task, as shown in the pop-up slot definition window).

3.3 Domain Schema

In principle, one can specify several different domain schemata in a knowledge model. For the moment we have limited the tool to a single schema. A schema contains a set of definitions of concepts, relations and rule types. A **concept** is represented as a class. The attributes of the concept (which in CommonKADS, as in UML, always point to atomic values, and not to other concepts) are modelled as slots.

To ensure that the attributes of a concept are atomic, we defined a constraint on the DomainTypeMetaClass metaclass, which is the template for all domain-modeling constructs such as the class Concept (see below). The constraint specifies that all subclasses of Concept (which define domain-specific types, such as Applicant) should have their template slots restricted to primitive (atomic) value types, such as string, boolean or integer. The following formula is the constraint expressed using the language provided in Protégé:

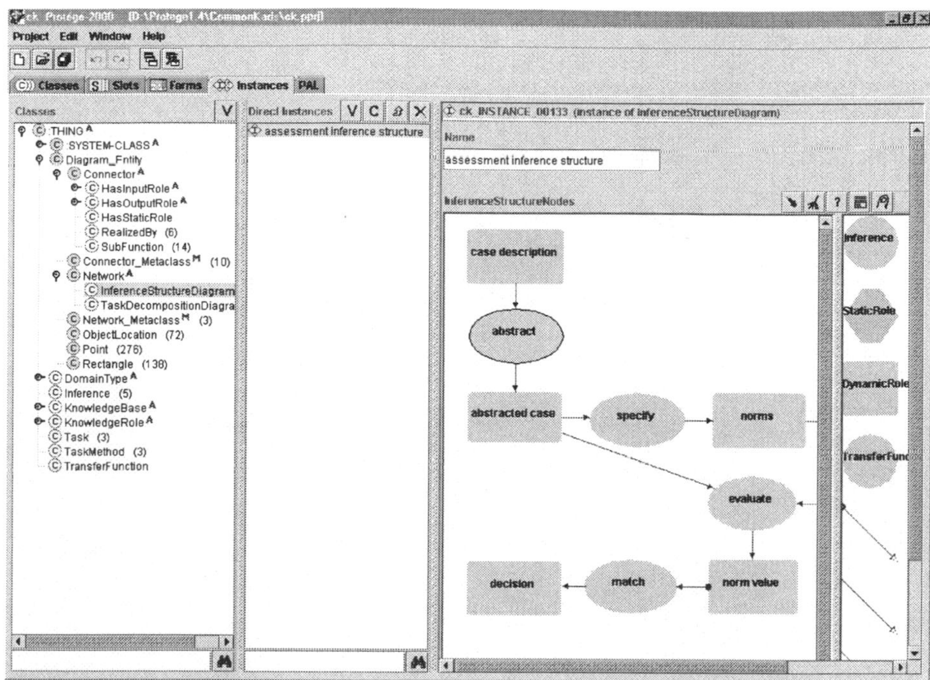

Fig. 2. Instance of an inference structure diagram for assessment. We defined the specific InferenceStructureDiagram as a subclass of the NetworkClass, thus also an instance of the NetworkMetaclass, that has additional slots to hold nodes and connectors. Our specific connectors are subclasses of ConnectorClass and instances of the ConnectorMetaclass. At the right, the form for acquiring an inference structure shows the instance created for an assessment task. It includes a palette of graphical elements from which the diagram can be constructed.

```
(defrange ?dtype :FRAME DomainTypeMetaClass)
(defrange ?att   :FRAME :STANDARD-SLOT)

(forall ?dtype (forall ?att
   (=> (and (subclass-of ?dtype Concept)
            (template-slot-of ?att ?dtype))
       (allowed-slot-value-type ?dtype ?att :PRIMITIVE-TYPE))))
```

Fig. 3 shows an example concept Applicant, i.e a person applying for a house. The slots describe attributes of the applicant that can be used for assessment purposes. In Fig. 3 we can also see the class-instance issue discussed in Sec. 3.1. The class Applicant is at the same time a subclass of Concept and an instance of the metaclass DomainTypeMetaClass. This metaclass has a slot rolesPlayed. The fillers of this slot are the knowledge roles that refer to this domain type (here: case description and abstracted case).

A **relation** in CommonKADS is a "first-class citizen", meaning that it can have attributes. As explained in Sec. 2.1, slots in Protégé-2000 are also first-class objects, that are instances of a metaslot class. However, slot frames cannot form a slot hierar-

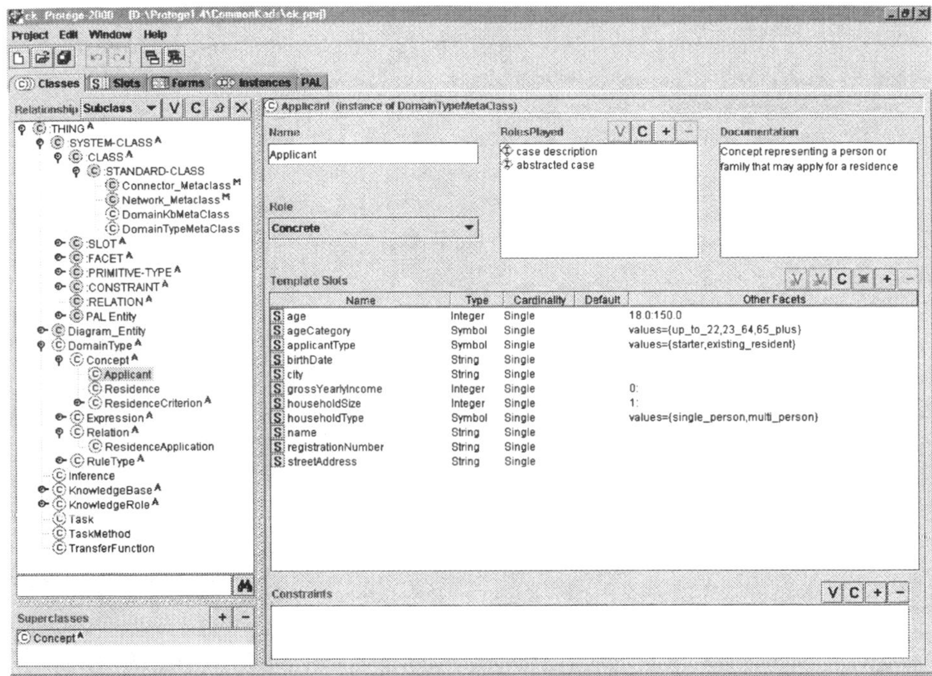

Fig. 3. Specification of the concept Applicant. The figure illustrates the three-level specification of the CommonKADS knowledge model. The domain-specific class Applicant is both a subclass of the domain-modeling construct Concept, and an instance of the special-purpose DomainType-MetaClass metaclass (shown in the :CLASS subtree). Therefore it has an additional own slot rolesPlayed that can be filled-in in the right hand form. Also, it only defines slots of primitive value type. Individual applicants are instances of Applicant class, that have specific values for the template slots age, name, etc.

chy. Therefore, we do not model relations as slots but as domain classes (instances of DomainTypeMetaClass). Each "relation" class should have at least two slots that point to the object types being related (the relation "arguments"). These object types can be concepts and relations, meaning that higher-order relations are allowed (cf. the notion of "association class" in UML). The name of the slot pointing to the argument defines the role the argument plays in the relation. Other slots may be added to define attributes of the relation.

The representation of a **rule type** is more complex. Rule types model relations between *expressions about* concept/relation slots. Therefore, we first have to define the notion of "expression". We decided to model an expression as a class with four slots:

1. The concept/relation involved in the expression.
2. The possible slots involved. This should be existing slots of the concepts/relations involved.
3. An operator such as `equal`, `not-equal`, `greater`. The set of legal operators depends on the slot involved in the expression.

4. The value: this should be a legal value for the slot involved.

With this expression construct we can define a class ApplicantExpression. An example instance of this expression could have the following slot values:

```
class = Applicant, slot = age, operand = greater, value = 22
```

The intended interpretation of the expression instance is that "the age of the applicant should be higher than 22".

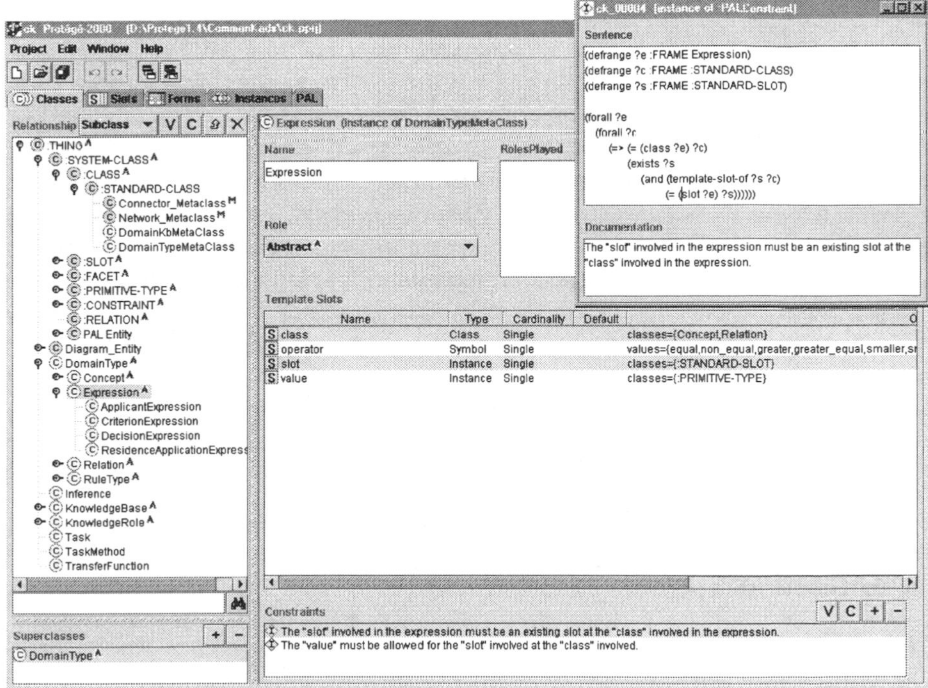

Fig. 4. Definition of the class Expression as an instance of DomainTypeMetaClass. The four slots that are attached to it have additional constraints on their value (bottom right). First, the slot slot involved in the expression should be an existing slot of the class involved. The KIF-based formula for this constraint is displayed in the pop-up window: it defines the range for the variables and the actual sentence of the constraint. A second constraint specifies that the value involved in the expression should be a valid value for the slot attached to the class involved.

Fig. 4 shows the definition of the Expression class. Besides the usual value-type restrictions on slots we specified constraints to express the above definition of an expression. We defined a first constraint to restrict the value of the slot involved in an expression (the value of the slot slot) to existing template slots of the class involved (the class value of the class slot). We defined a second constraint to ensure that the value involved in an expression (the value slot) is legal for the slot involved (the slot value of the slot slot at the class value of the class class). Constraints can subsequently be used to check the validity of expression instances (example omitted for reasons of space). A special-purpose constraint checking tab can be plugged in to Protégé user interface and enable the user to trigger the constraint-checking engine on the knowledge base and view violations.

We can now model a rule type as a relation between a set of expressions which form the antecedent of the rule and a set of expressions which constitute the consequent. For example, we defined the rule type ApplicantAbstraction as a subclass of RuleType, and specialized its inherited slots antecedent and consequent so that their value type is restricted to instances of ApplicantExpression. In the next subsection we see examples of the actual rule instances, and how we can define specialized forms for entering rules of a particular type.

3.4 Knowledge Bases

In CommonKADS there is not one large knowledge base. Instead, several knowledge bases are defined. Each knowledge base contains instances of a designated set of domain types. Most commonly, knowledge bases contain instances of rule types, i.e. the actual "rules". Knowledge bases are modelled as classes with a slot pointing to the rule types or other instances to be included in the knowledge base. Fig. 5 shows an instance of a knowledge base AbstractionRuleSet. This particular knowledge base contains two rules, both concerning a simple abstraction in the sample application. Using Protégé's set of built-in user interface elements in a customized way, we defined a specialized form for acquiring instances of KnowledgeBase classes, shown in Fig. 5. This enables the user to browse and create knowledge bases in a synthetic way, acquiring their rules and the expressions that form the rules immediately from the same form.

4 Discussion

This case study does not provide us with a formal evaluation. Still, a number of remarks can be made. It should be noted that the remarks are made from the perspective of using Protégé as a "metaCASE" tool. This typically requires stretching the possibilities of a tool to its limits. A standard case study using Protégé only directly as an ontology-editing tool would have given rise to different remarks. In the discussion below on the strong and weak points of Protégé we refer back to the three user types mentioned in the introduction: tool builder, knowledge engineer, and domain specialist.

Strong points. The main strong point of Protégé is that it supports at the same time tool builders, knowledge engineers and domain specialists. This is the main difference with existing tools, which are typically targeted at the knowledge engineer and lack flexibility for metamodeling. This latter feature makes it easier to adapt Protégé to new requirements and/or changes in the model structure.

For the tool builder Protégé combines an expressive framework with a consistent way of generating editor interfaces (the forms). As mentioned, the metaclass mechanism in which classes can be modelled as "real" instances of metaclasses is an indispensable

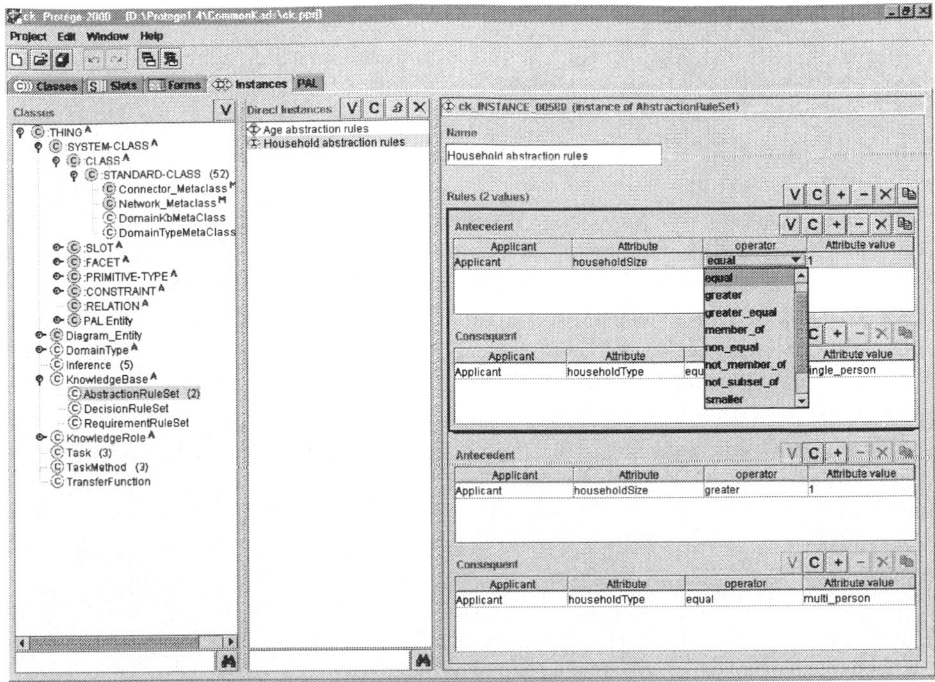

Fig. 5. Example knowledge base with two abstraction rules. The form for acquiring instances of KnowledgeBase has been highly customized to present a synthetic view of the rules contained in a knowledge base by way of container and table graphical elements. First, we customized the form for acquiring RuleType instances to display its antecedent and consequent slots as rows that enable in-place editing of slot values. Then, we "included" this RuleType form in the form for KnowledgeBase instances.

feature. Also, the fact that classes (as opposed to instances) can serve as the range of a slot is a useful feature (although this is also common in other languages). Another positive point is the time required to build a tool. Constructing a first version is a matter of a few hours. In this case study a number of revisions were made, but this is more or less intrinsic to the complexity of metamodeling in general.

Although still preliminary in terms of scope and user interface, an important feature for the tool builder is the possibility to define constraints on the classes and slots being defined. This provides a means for the knowledge engineer to check model completeness and correctness. In the context of this case study we specified a subset of the constraints for CommonKADS knowledge models, but it should be straightforward to generate a full set. In particular, we will express the third constraint on expressions (see Sec. 3.3), to ensure that the set of legal operators offered on a certain type of expression (subclass of Expression) is suitable for the type of slot involved in the expression.

It is to note that during construction the models are *by definition* incomplete or even inconsistent. Therefore, a verification mechanism should preferably be explicitly invoked by a knowledge engineer, and not be done automatically by the tool. The fact that the tool offers this approach of decoupling the acquisition phase from the constraint checking phase is a strong point. It goes further in enabling the check constraints step by step, for example locally to a class. The constraints we created in our modeling study range over class seen as instances of metaclasses (e.g., Expression, Concept) and restrict or bind the value-type of slots (rather than the value itself). That is again an important aspect of metamodeling.

A nice feature for the knowledge engineer is that it proved possible to generate diagrammatic editors close to the representation used in CommonKADS. The additional requirements here are really on a very detailed, uninteresting level, having to do with the availability of particular graphical symbols, labels, etc. Also, the RDF support is potentially a positive feature of Protégé, because it makes import into and export from the tool feasible in a standard format. This is traditionally problematic for CASE tools supporting only a proprietary format.

Finally, it should also be noted, that the fact that the tool never crashed during this case study also greatly helped in creating user confidence (especially with the first author).

Weak points and opportunities for improvement. Currently, Protégé only has a simple inclusion mechanism for importing definitions. In order to make use of libraries of existing partial models that the user can specialize and adapt, a more refined import/export mechanism for sets of class/form/instance definitions is required.

Another drawback is the fact that a single interface is used for all types of users. In particular for the domain specialist, it should be possible to create a stand-alone interface with just the forms for entering domain knowledge. This ensures that the domain specialist does not get confused by modeling details. The same could hold, to a lesser extent, for the knowledge engineer.

At the time of this case study, Protégé was not able to handle the automatic filling of inverse slot relationships, for example the domainMapping and rolesPlayed slots of respectively knowledge roles and domain types. This would be a useful extension, as it prevents redundancy and omissions in the interface for the knowledge engineer (in fact, it is now being implemented).

The expressiveness of the predefined forms could be extended in a number of ways. For example, the diagram widget could be extended to enable the creation of UML-type diagrams [2]. For CommonKADS this would open the possibility to create domain-schema diagrams, which use the UML conventions. It could also be a powerful way to set and visualize constraint links among classes. Another advantage would be that it makes Protégé potentially usable as a CASE tool for object-oriented analysis.

Rule types proved to be difficult to represent. The negative effect is mainly felt in the knowledge-elicitation interface created for the domain specialist. The somewhat contrived way of representing rule types diminishes the naturalness of the interface for entering rule instances in a knowledge base, as we saw in Sec. 3.4. It would be worthwhile to study more in detail the user-interface requirements for editing this type of expertise data, and adapt the tool accordingly. We could define a custom user interface component that would be more intuitive and synthetic to acquire rule bases, and would also check constraints on expressions locally.

Protégé and CommonKADS. Beyond the engineering details of the tool, we can draw conclusions from this case study about Protégé, CommonKADS, and their relationship. CommonKADS-type modeling is a highly abstract activity. Protégé helps to represent it in an understandable way, to focus users' attention on certain parts of it, and to constrain it. The self-contained expression of the (meta-)model makes it easier to understand it and to instantiate it. More is needed in terms of knowledge-elicitation metaphors to guide users in building a knowledge model following certain steps. As mentioned before, UML diagrammatic notation and full support in translating it to CommonKADS models would also narrow the cognitive gap between Protégé and CommonKADS. Also, inclusion and reuse of model templates from catalogs would significantly augment the tool's usefulness.

Protégé and CommonKADS target different levels/ways of modeling. CommonKADS has a clearly identified methodology divided in different models and modeling steps, powerful but complex to embrace and instantiate. Protégé's methodology is very straightforward (a cycle of metaclass/class definition, form customization, and instance acquisition). It is completely independent of any given application or domain, and makes no assumption on what it is used for (besides the frame-based conceptualization of a domain). Therefore it enables concrete and immediately usable systems to be built. Protégé-based knowledge models are storable in different electronic formats, therefore can be queried and used in different applications. So the main benefit that Protégé brings to CommonKADS lies in the way the metamodel can itself be modeled in Protégé and in the way the acquisition of models and application instances can be customized and constrained. The tool that we have built in this case study provides a uniform framework that embraces the three-level approach of modeling a KBS using one representation formalism.

We limited this case study to the central knowledge model of CommonKADS with only one domain schema. Building a full CASE tool for CommonKADS would require extending the Protégé-CK tool with the other CommonKADS models, following the same principles. We would also need to specify the interaction links among those models in the form of inter-model constraints.

Finally, this case study shows how important metamodeling constructs are in specifying ontologies. Simple class/instance distinctions are insufficient for describing real-life conceptualizations. It is high time this requirement is taken seriously in ontology-specification research.

Some final remarks. We plan to use the resulting CASE tool in an experiment in which a group of students in knowledge engineering at the University of Amsterdam uses the tool to construct knowledge models. The experiment is planned for the end of 2000. We will divide the students into two groups, one working with a baseline drawing tool, the other group with the knowledge-engineering interface of the Protégé-CommonKADS tool. This experiment will hopefully provide us with more precise data on usability.

Acknowledgments. We thank the developers of the Protégé-2000 software tools, Ray Fergerson and William Grosso, for their valuable help and their promptness in implementing user requirements. Richard Benjamins contributed to the discussion on the setup of the tool. We thank the three anonymous reviewers for their helpful comments. This work is partly supported by the ICES-MIA project funded by the Dutch government and by a grant from Spawar.

References

1. A. Anjewierden, J. Wielemaker, and C. Toussaint. Shelley - computer aided knowledge engineering. *Knowledge Acquisition*, 4(1), 1992.
2. G. Booch, J. Rumbaugh, and I. Jacobson. *The Unified Modelling Language User Guide*. Addison-Wesley, Reading, MA, 1998.
3. V.K. Chaudhri, A. Farquhar, R. Fikes, P.D. Karp, and J.P. Rice. OKBC: A programmatic foundation for knowledge base interoperability. In *Proceedings 15th National Conference on Artificial Intelligence (AAAI-98). Madison, Wisconsin*. AAAI Press/MIT Press, 1998.
4. O. Corby and R. Dieng. The WebCokace knowledge server. *IEEE Internet Computing*, 3(6):38–43, November/December 1999.
5. N. Fridman Noy, R. W. Fergerson, and M. A. Musen. The knowledge model of Protégé-2000: combining interoperability and flexibility. In *Proceedings of EKAW'2000*. Springer-Verlag, 2000. This volume. Also as: Technical Report Stanford University, School of Medicine, SMI-2000-0830.
6. M. R. Genesereth and R. E. Fikes. Knowledge interchange format version 3.0 reference manual. Report Logic 92-1, Logic Group, Stanford University, California, 1992.
7. W. E. Grosso, H. Eriksson, R. W. Fergerson, J. H. Gennari, S. W. Tu, and M. A. Musen. Knowledge modeling at the millennium: The design and evolution of Protégé-2000. In *12th Banff Workshop on Knowledge Acquisition, Modeling, and Management. Banff, Alberta*, 1999.
8. O. Lassila and R. R. Swick. Resource description framework (RDF) model and specification. W3C recommendation, W3C Consortium, 22 February 1999. URL: http://www.w4.org/TR/1999/REC-rdf-syntax-19990222.
9. Mark A. Musen, L. M. Fagan, D. M. Combs, and E. H. Shortliffe. Use of a domain-model to drive an interactive knowledge-editing tool. *Int. J. Man-Machine Studies*, 26:105–121, 1987.
10. A. R. Puerta, J. Egar, S. Tu, and M. Musen. A multiple-method shell for the automatic generation of knowledge acquisition tools. *Knowledge Acquisition*, 4:171–196, 1992.
11. A. Th. Schreiber, J. M. Akkermans, A. A. Anjewierden, R. de Hoog, N. R. Shadbolt, W. Van de Velde, and B. J. Wielinga. *Knowledge Engineering and Management: The CommonKADS Methodology*. MIT Press, Cambridge, MA, 1999.
12. A. Th. Schreiber, B. J. Wielinga, R. de Hoog, J. M. Akkermans, and W. Van de Velde. CommonKADS: A comprehensive methodology for KBS development. *IEEE Expert*, 9(6):28–37, December 1994.
13. P. Speel, N. R. Shadbolt, W. de Vries, P. van Dam, and K. O'Hara. Knowledge mapping for industrial purposes. In *Proc Twelfth Workshop on Knowledge Acquisition, Modelling Management (KAW'99)*, 1999.
14. G. van Heijst, P. Terpstra, B. J. Wielinga, and N. Shadbolt. Using generalised directive models in knowledge acquisition. In Th. Wetter, K. D. Althoff, J. Boose, B. Gaines, M. Linster, and F. Schmalhofer, editors, *Current Developments in Knowledge Acquisition: EKAW-92*, Berlin, Germany, 1992. Springer-Verlag.

The MOKA Modelling Language

Richard Brimble[1], Florence Sellini[2]

[1] BAE SYSTEMS, Advanced Technology Centre Sowerby, AIP Dept, CASDAM,
PO Box 5, Filton, Bristol BSIZ 7QW, UK
Richard.Brimble@src.bae.co.uk

[2] PSA Peugeot Citroën, Knowledge Management, 18 rue des Fauvelles
92250 La Garenne Colombes, France
Florence.Sellini@wanadoo.fr

Abstract. Development and maintenance of knowledge intensive software applications is a complex and expensive activity. By employing a systematic approach long term risk can be reduced. The ESPRIT-IV funded project called MOKA, (No. 25418), defined a methodology for Knowledge Based Engineering (KBE) application development. Results include a modelling language, called the MOKA Modelling Language (MML), dedicated to KBE application development that models engineering product and process knowledge at one level of abstraction above application code. MML is based on the Unified Modelling Language (UML). This paper describes the philosophy of MML, how it is related to UML and provides examples of its use.

1. Introduction

Engineering knowledge is complex, diverse, and interrelated, involving implicit knowledge, tacit knowledge, background knowledge and underlying assumptions. How to manage knowledge effectively is a key issue in many companies today. They wish to capture and reuse, to reduce the time to find solutions, to build products "right first time" and to retain best practice.

Knowledge Based Engineering (KBE) automates engineering design tasks by embedding engineering knowledge within software applications. Leading industrial companies exploiting KBE have shown dramatic return on investment. BAE SYSTEMS for example has achieved dramatic results automating wing box design tasks on the Airbus A340-600 aircraft.

Development and maintenance of complex KBE applications requires both Knowledge Engineering and Software Engineering techniques. Knowledge must be captured, represented, validated and maintained. Software must be specified, designed, coded and tested. The scarce skills needed to perform all these tasks, encourages the use of a systematic approach within large development teams to facilitate long-term maintenance and re-use.

R. Dieng and O. Corby (Eds.): EKAW 2000, LNAI 1937, pp. 49–56, 2000.

The ESPRIT funded project called MOKA, (EP 25418), has defined a methodology to capture and formalise engineering knowledge, allowing it to be retained and exploited, for example within KBE applications. This paper discusses part of that methodology, namely the MOKA Modelling Language (MML), a Unified Modelling Language (UML) extension used to formally model engineering knowledge at one level above KBE application code.

2. Requirements for a KBE formal modelling language

MOKA identified two engineering knowledge models as key artefacts in the KBE application development lifecycle [1].

Informal Model	Structured, natural language representation using pre-defined forms [4]
Formal Model	Graphical, object-oriented at one level of abstraction above application code [2].

The language must be capable of formalising all useful knowledge. It must provide a mediating language between experts, knowledge engineers and software developers, simple yet expressive and preferably graphical. Formal enough to support code generation. User extensible and customisable to capture best practice within an organisation and allow models to be organised according to local style.

3. The MOKA Modelling Language

UML exhibits most of the characteristics required by MOKA; it is graphical, object-oriented, extensible, etc. It is however general-purpose and a more dedicated language was created that more readily supports the KBE domain. This is the MOKA Modelling Language [2].

MML plays an advisory role within KBE development. It is not rigid in its definition, nor is it to be rigidly applied. MML captures best practice by pre-defining classes, associations and attributes and offering these elements to MML users in a structured and logical way. The aim is to provide a framework and guidance to the modeller, to enable organisations to build and capture modelling experience, not to dictate what can and cannot be modelled. It is an extension of UML and users are free to model at the UML level as required. Alternatively, users may extend the core MML definition to tailor it to their particular concern. MML is achieved by providing and organising the following :

- **Pre-defined views** - provide different perspectives on the underlying model and consequently an expected content for diagrams. The core MML definition is presented through *Functional*, *Structural* and a *Behaviour* views.

- **Pre-defined classes** - represent meta-classes identifying the type of classes expected to be created by users. For example, a <Part> is a pre-defined class and users are expected to create classes of type <Part>.
- **Pre-defined class attributes** - capture commonly used attributes for a particular type of class. For example, the meta-class *Assembly* has a pre-defined attribute called *Assembly_Operation*.

4. MML Product Modelling

The MOKA Product Model represents a family of products by building *product model diagrams*, defining *product model classes* and maintaining a *product model constraint table*. Product model classes identify and describe generic product family components - e.g. chassis, body, brakes - where instantiating a class produces an object in the final *product model instance*.

4.1 Product Model Views

The core MML definition has the following views; Structure, Function, Behaviour, Technology and Representation. Users are encouraged to consider these as a basis for building their own product model. As an illustration, the functional view is described here (see Fig. 1).

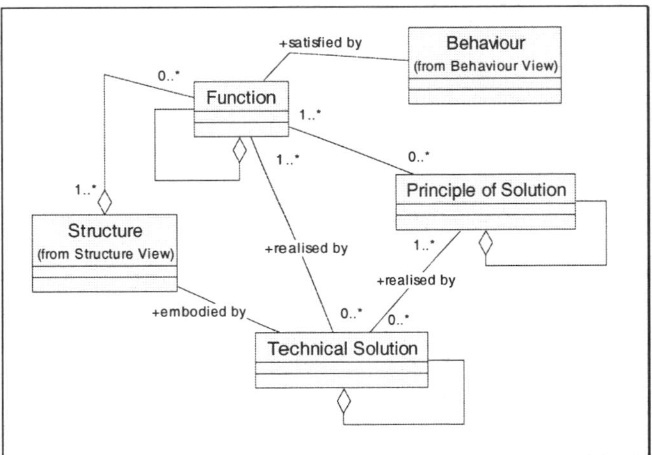

Fig. 1 : The Functional view

A *Function* is something that the product must do in order to be successful. A product may be required to generate heat, or to amplify a signal. Top-level functions are derived from higher level objectives - e.g. *the product must keep its occupants warm* - and subsequently decomposed into sub-functions until they are directly solvable by either a *technical solution* or a *principle of solution.*

4.2 Product Model Constraints

Constraints represent generic design restrictions that must be satisfied. For example, the dimensions of a component are often constrained by the dimensions of another. MML classifies product model constraints according to the way they are modelled within MML product model diagrams:

Attribute-Bound	Constraints scoped within the boundaries of an attribute; e.g. $X < 10$
Class-Bound	Constraints scoped within the boundaries of the class; e.g. $ClassA.X < ClassA.Y$
Association-Bound	Constraints scoped by association links between classes ; e.g. $ClassA.X < ClassB.Y$
Existence constraints	Constraints related to the existence of objects within the final product model instance.

5. MML Process Modelling

The MOKA design process describes how a Product Model Instance is derived from a Product Model. It describes how to resolve product choices, subject to product constraints, and the order in which steps are executed and decisions made.

An MML design process model can be presented to users in different ways. The preferred approach is to use extended UML Activity Diagrams, though current software support can limit users to using UML class diagrams.

5.1 Static and Dynamic Processes

Design activity sequencing is not always fixed and different strategies, giving different execution orders, can be adopted depending on runtime conditions. Consequently, MOKA makes a distinction between *static* and *dynamic* design processes :

- A static design process is one where the activity order is pre-defined.
- A dynamic design process is one where the order of execution is determined at runtime.

The MOKA design process model captures activity decomposition, serial and parallel execution flow, branching, synchronisation, static and dynamic processes. To accommodate this, the UML Activity Model is extended to include two new classes; *Compound Activity* and *Elementary Activity*.

6. MOKA Formal Model Examples

This section shows a modelling example developed during the MOKA project extracted from the *Aerospatiale* test case *on Fuselage design* (see Fig. 3). The main function of the panel is a structural element of the aircraft section. There are different principles of solution, one of these is to stiffen the panel. There are two sub-principles of solution to this, either stiffeners (stringers) are fastened to the panel, or the panels are designed in such a way that they integrate the stiffeners. A technical solution to fasten the stiffeners is to use riveting. The technical solution "riveting" requires fasteners and holes in the panel and in the stringers. Those are *Features* type classes defined within the *Structure* view.

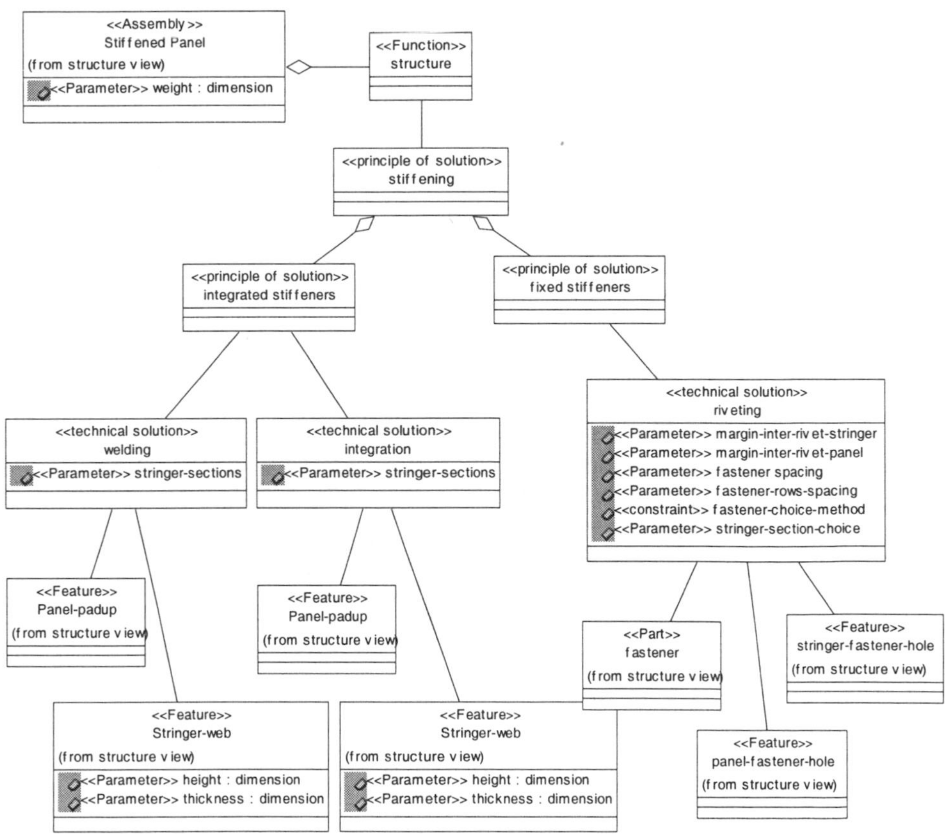

Fig. 2 : Function view example

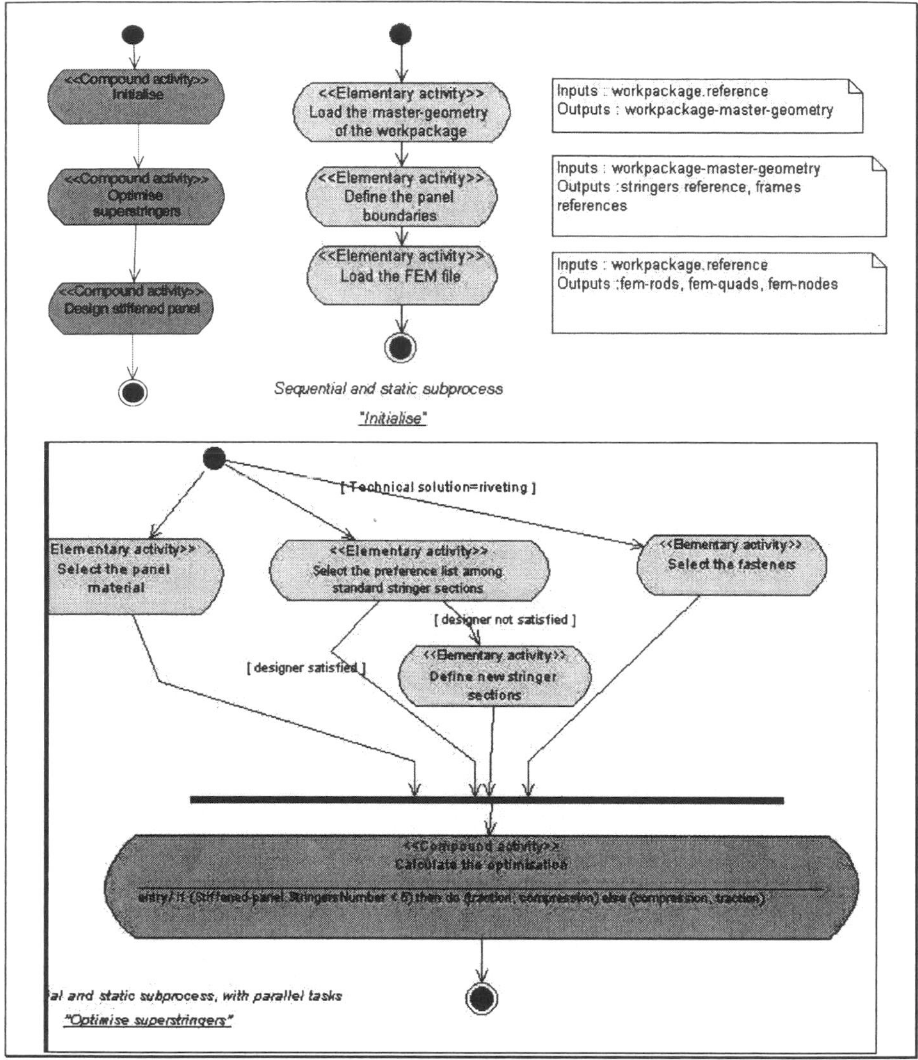

Fig. 3 : Design Process Model Example

7. Discussion

To build a formal model, developers require a *modelling language*. As described in [4], there are various methodological approaches available :

- CommonKADS [6] or the comparable approach KARL [7] as a methodology of knowledge-based systems.

- KIF/Ontolingua , formal ontology based knowledge representation [8], [10].
- General object oriented modelling techniques like UML [3].

Each of these provides valuable input to a methodology of knowledge-based engineering, but none is powerful enough to immediately fulfil all the needs.

CommonKADS is based on a general classification of knowledge and is more or less a de facto knowledge-based methodology standard today. The knowledge representation and problem-solving requirements in KBE applications tend to be not so demanding. More complicated problem-solving methods as needed in many engineering applications and the flexibility which is necessary in order to support user interactions are major open research issues in this field.

KIF/Ontolingua is a very expressive knowledge representation approach, with good examples of ontologies including engineering relevant domains. However, experiences show that the approach is currently underdeveloped for industrial application. Research question include determining the right granularity of model representation and comprehensible representation of the many relevant and interrelated aspects.

Object oriented methods like UML have shown increasing popularity because of their expressiveness, flexibility, and ease of use. However, these are general-purpose and within a particular domain this is a weakness; object orientation alone does not provide the necessary clear semantics. The main advantage of modelling engineering knowledge in UML – as shown in our test cases studies [9] – is the expressiveness of the language, the possibility to customise and the graphical support available during modelling.

MOKA has chosen to extend UML, using standard UML mechanisms, to target it towards the engineering domain. The resulting extension is called the MOKA Modelling Language (MML), a graphical object-oriented modelling language, used to represent engineering design knowledge at a user level for deployment in KBE applications. There are still unanswered questions, including the granularity of MML and its applicability to non-KBE knowledge engineering activities.

Acknowledgement

This research is a result of the MOKA European project (No. 25 418) conducted within the ESPRIT-IV framework. Partners involved within MOKA are : BAE SYSTEMS (UK), Aerospatiale-Matra (F), Daimler-Chrysler (G), PSA Peugeot Citroën (F), DECAN-Ingenia (F), KTI (F), The Coventry University (UK). Special thanks go to Aerospatiale-Matra for allowing us to use diagrams from their test case.

References

1. Callot, M., Oldham, K., Kneebone, S., Murton, A., and Brimble, R., 1998, "MOKA", Proceedings of the Conference on Integration in Manufacturing, Goteborg, Sweden, IOS Press, Amsterdam, 1998, pp 198-207. (see also http://www.kbe.coventry.ac.uk/MOKA).
2. MOKA consortium, 2000, "MOKA Modelling Language, Core Definition", v1.0, June 2000.
3. Rumbaugh, J., Jacobson, I., Booch, G., 1999, "The Unified Modeling Language Reference Manual", Addison Wesley, 1999.
4. Coventry University, 1998, "State of the Art Study of Current Methodologies", MOKA/COV/TK1.1/DL/D1.1/3/CC/SUB, 21 May 1998.
5. Pahl, Beitz, 1995, "Engineering Design", Springer-Verlag, ISBN 3-540-19917-9
6. Schreiber, A. Th., et al., 1999, "The CommonKADS Book", MIT Press, Boston, 1999.
7. Fensel, D., Angele, J., and Studer, R., 1998, "The Knowledge Acquisition and Representation Language KARL", IEEE Transactions on Knowledge and Data Engineering, 10/4, 527-550, 1998.
8. Genesereth, M. R. and R. E. Fikes, 1992, "Knowledge Interchange Format", Version 3.0 Reference Manual. Computer Science Department, Stanford University, 1992.
9. MOKA consortium, 1999, "Report on Testing the MOKA Methodology", Deliverable 3.2, January 1999
10. Ontolingua (online) Reference Manual, http://ai-www.aist-nara.ac.jp/doc/documents/modules/ontolingua/doc/reference-manual/index.html

$Md_{\omega\varsigma}$: A Modelling Language to Build a Formal Ontology in Either Description Logics or Conceptual Graphs

Jérôme Nobécourt and Brigitte Biébow

Université de Paris-Nord,
Laboratoire d'Informatique de Paris-Nord (LIPN) - UPRES-A 7030
Av. J.B. Clément 93430 Villetaneuse (France),
{Jerome.Nobecourt,Brigitte.Biebow}@lipn.univ-paris13.fr
tel: +33 (0)1 49 40 36 09 fax: +33 (0)1 48 26 07 12

Abstract. $Md_{\omega\varsigma}$ is a semi-formal modelling language allowing to model graphically static knowledge of a domain under the form of a conceptual network. It makes easier the model translation into a representation formalism as description logics and conceptual graphs. $Md_{\omega\varsigma}$ is part of a more general method designed to build domain ontologies from French texts. The approach has been proposed in the context of an industrial application concerning the supervision of telecom networks. Using $Md_{\omega\varsigma}$ implies modelling before formal representation in order to avoid the pitfalls of direct representation. Choice of a formalism and its implementation is allowed to be postponed until the representation needs are better known.

1 Introduction

This paper presents the results of an industrial experiment concerning the supervision of complex telecom networks[1]. The initial purpose of our study concerned the comparison of knowledge representation formalisms such as description logics or conceptual graphs (DL and CG in what follows). Although these formalisms are not totally equivalent [5], our objective was to compare their usability. These formalisms allow the representation of static and generic knowledge which correspond to a domain model. Problem solving knowledge can only be represented outside these formalisms and have not been considered.

The representation of real-world knowledge shows that the trouble of representation into a formalism is due not only to the expressiveness of the formalism and from the skill of the knowledge engineer, but also mainly from the difficulty of conceptualisation. Direct representation is a difficult and dangerous endeavour, which leads to poor systems. Both DL and CG are among the most widely used formalisms in knowledge representation, but formal problems are only taken into account and the modelling problem is never tackled per se. The well

[1] Granted by CNET/CNRS cognisciences, Centre National d'Études des Télécommunications

R. Dieng and O. Corby (Eds.): EKAW 2000, LNAI 1937, pp. 57–64, 2000.

known problem in knowledge engineering is not how represent knowledge, but how model it. Nevertheless, some recent studies on ontology building stress that direct representation is still common and comes up against known problems in knowledge engineering [2]. Thus formalisms are not directly usable, it is necessary to build up a model and then to translate it into the formalisms. To compare CG and DL usability does not come down to confront the representation in one language to the other; protocol is based on a common model and compare the consequences of the translation of each piece of the model into each formalism.

We have therefore defined $Md_{\omega\varsigma}$, a modelling language translate the resulting model into either one formalism or the other, by using some rules governing the translation. Its use postpones the choice of a formalism and its implementation until the representation needs are better known. With this language, modelling uses semantic network. $Md_{\omega\varsigma}$ generalises the expressive power of both of the formalisms. It is semi-formal language: syntax is rigorously defined as well as some semantic rules to avoid some bad uses of the language. $Md_{\omega\varsigma}$ is coupled together with a graphical tool that controls the syntax and the semantic rules.

In our telecom application, the domain knowledge have to be discovered from texts. Therefore, a corpus has been build and linguistically analysed using principles proposed by the French TIA[2] group. Terms with their description in natural language have been extracted. Our work comes within the scope of the current trends in knowledge acquisition from texts which involves terminology and natural language processing (NLP). These recent works allow the acquisition of terminological knowledge by applying NLP-tools to a corpus. The first results lead to the definition of a "terminological knowledge base" [1]. Among the most recent works, [4] propose a method for building formal ontologies from a linguistic analysis of texts.

We design a method to help a knowledge engineer to model and represent knowledge from texts. This method guides the extraction of the conceptual primitives of the domain from the set of terms resulting from the linguistic analysis, as well as their modelling under $Md_{\omega\varsigma}$ schemata. All these models form a domain ontology that can be formalised in CG as well as in DL using some translation rules. The tool supporting $Md_{\omega\varsigma}$ offers a graphical modelling by successive refinement from the text study to the formalisation, keeping the link to the text. The language offers a user-friendly touch with its graphical syntax and the links to the texts then it avoids the pitfalls of direct representation. Language and method are implemented in Java.

A longer version of this paper with a comprehensive state of the art may be found at [8]. Section 2 presents the $Md_{\omega\varsigma}$ language. Section 3 describes the method, the language and the tool on an example taken from the telecom application. Some general translation rules are explicited there.

2 $Md_{\omega\varsigma}$: A Modelling Language for CG and DL

We describe now the language objects. Building an ontology in $Md_{\omega\varsigma}$ starts with the constitution of a corpus, a set of documents which describe the domain and

[2] the Terminologie et Intelligence Artificielle group is a working group of the AFIA, French Association for Artificial Intelligence.

the application. Then, the conceptual primitives (CPs in what follows), basic items of modelling, have to be extracted from this corpus. A CP is for us an expression which corresponds either to a term or to a relation between terms or between relations.

2.1 The Objects of the Language

The language includes three types of objects, concepts and properties, which correspond to CPs, and schemata. Some comments, which may be text or attributes, are attached to concepts and properties.

Concept A concept is described by its name and by the set of properties that relate it to other concepts, in some schema. Each concept is associated with a level, a state and a nature. The level is the depth of the concept into the ontology. The state indicates the progress of the modelling of the primitive. The nature specifies the origin and the role that the primitive plays in the modelling. This information makes the modelling and the maintenance easier.

1. *Concept level*: The level is useful when modifying a concept : the closest the concept is to the top of the ontology, the most important would be the consequences on the whole ontology.
2. *Concept state*: Modelling is a long phase, it is usual to give a partial model of a primitive. States may have one of four values *TopConcept*, *State0*, *State1*, *State2*. The *TopConcept* is the highest one in the specialisation hierarchy, only described by its name. A concept is *State2*, if its description is completed, i.e. all its properties have been described with schemata. So, it cannot be modified any more. In all other cases, a concept is under modelling, *State0* with only hierarchy properties in its description, *State1* with other kind of properties.
3. *Concept nature*: There is two kinds of nature, a structural and a linguistic one. The structural nature explains the role of the concept in the modelling, it may have the values *grouping*, *structural*, *auxiliary*. A concept r has value *grouping*, if its properties are included in the properties of a set of concepts already described, which are thus more specialised than r. A concept has value *auxiliary*, if it is only introduced to describe more easily a CP. In all other cases, the concept has value *structural*. The structure of a concept plays a part in case of modification. So when modifying a grouping concept, it is important to take care of the coherence of the factorisation of properties.
   The linguistic nature specifies the link of the primitive with the corpus, it may have the values *terminological*, *pre-terminological*, *not terminological*. A terminological nature expresses that the primitive comes from the corpus, its description corresponds to the definition of a term. A pre-terminological nature expresses that there is no agreement, among the experts of the domain, on an expression that may describe the primitive. In all other cases, the nature is said not terminological. When a concept is created, its nature by default is the couple (structural,not terminological).

Property A property is described by its name, its type, its nature, by the set S of CPs that are source of the corresponding link and by the set C of CPs that are target of this link. The arity of a property is the sum of the cardinality of S and C. A property may have a cardinality; the most used property is specialisation, of concept or property.

1. *Property type*: It is a couple of binary values, which is deduced from the property description: *simple* vs *calculated*, and *basic* vs *specialised*.
   A property is said *simple* if its description includes only concepts as its source or as its target; it is said *calculated* if its description needs another property as its source or as its target.
   A property is said *basic* if it is not more specific than any other property, it is *specialised* in the opposite case.
2. *Property nature*: The nature of a property is only linguistic, it takes the same values as a concept.
3. *Property cardinality* : In case of binary link, a [min,max] couple can be associated with the property. Min and max are two integers that represent the minimum and the maximum numbers of objects that can be the target of the property for any given source concept. The default cardinality is [0,n].
4. *Specialisation*: The specialisation of a concept is a binary basic and simple property used to structure the ontology. Its name is omitted on the schemata.
   The specialisation of a property may concern its target or source CPs as its cardinality. The specialisation of a property is an example of calculated property where the target is a more generic property, and the source a more specialised one.
5. *Calculated property*: A calculated property expresses some complex process between heterogeneous CPs, it is annotated to describe the calculation that it models.

Annotation of conceptual primitive An annotation is a comment attached to a primitive; it may consist of text, or of an attribute with its value. Some comments are compulsory, as the attributes giving the name, state, type and nature of the primitive. These comments are represented graphically on the schemata by labels, colors or specific forms. The text does not appear on the schemata but on an hyper-text document to keep the schema legibility; it includes:

1. the reference term if the primitive nature is terminological;
2. some information on the choices made for modelling the primitive;
3. the links to the corpus, when the nature is terminological or pre-terminological;
4. the cardinality of a property;
5. the explanation to compute a calculated property.

Schema A schema is a semantic network which models one or several primitives. The name, state, type and nature of a primitive are the same in all schemata. A schema is a part of the ontology which is formed of the set of all the schemata.

2.2 Control in $Md_{\omega\varsigma}$

$Md_{\omega\varsigma}$ is also a modelling tool which controls the correctness of the schemata relatively to the previous definitions and the respect of some semantic rules. When a user's action does not obey some rule, the action is not realised and the user is warned. These rules characterise the semi-formal feature of $Md_{\omega\varsigma}$:

1. Unicity of the name of a CP: The name of a primitive is the same in every schema, but the same name may be given to a property and to its specialisations.
2. Compatibility of cardinality of property: In case of specialisation of property, the cardinality of a simple binary property must be less or equal to the one it specialises.

3. Constraints on specialisations: A concept inherits the description of each concept it specialises. Its properties may either be basic, or specialise a more generic property of a concept that it specialises.
4. Constraints on the state and nature of a concept: The state and nature of a concept are the same in all the schemata. A concept in State2 cannot be modified anymore, it cannot be source of a new property. There exists one and only one TopConcept.

3 Method

We present the language and tool on some examples coming from an industrial experiment concerning the supervision of telecom networks (see [6]).

3.1 The Supervision Domain

Supervision consists in making a real-time diagnosis of the incidents that happen in a complex telecom network, the diagnosis being based on the observation of the state of the network. A network is composed of equipments connected together, mainly beams and switches. When some incident happens on the network, several indicators are positioned (lights, messages, curves...). These indicators give information on switches, beams, and traffic. Then, an operator provides a diagnosis concerning the type of the incident. With this diagnosis, he/she should perform some action to inhibit the consequences of this incident on the network. Our job concerned building an ontology to allow a description of every incident from the alarms, which appear in the supervision room. Having no access to the site, we had to build the ontology from the various documents put at our disposal. Nevertheless, an expert could validate our results.

3.2 Modelling Phase

First, a corpus has to be defined relatively to the objective. A candidate-term extractor [3] allows the automatic extraction and further expert validation of the main terms of the domain. This gives a list of CPs. During the modelling, the name given to the primitive should remind of the associate term. From this first and often very long list, the knowledge engineer looks for primitives that describe the main sub-domains of the ontology. These primitives structure the ontology, they are modelled as concepts and they form the initial list of modelling CPs (LMCP). In the application, it is the case of "alarm", "incident" (figure 1).

Each primitive of LMCP is described in natural language. This description is considered as a new document, from which a new list of conceptual primitives is created. The knowledge engineer looks in this list for:

1. CPs that express a relation between high-level concepts,
2. primitives already present in the initial list,
3. new primitives only present in this list.

In our application, the first case leads to define basic properties between high-level concepts, like "toBeDisclosedBy" or "toBeAbout" (figure 1). Cases 2 and 3 give new high-level concepts like "cause" (figure 2) and so allow to build up the LMCP.

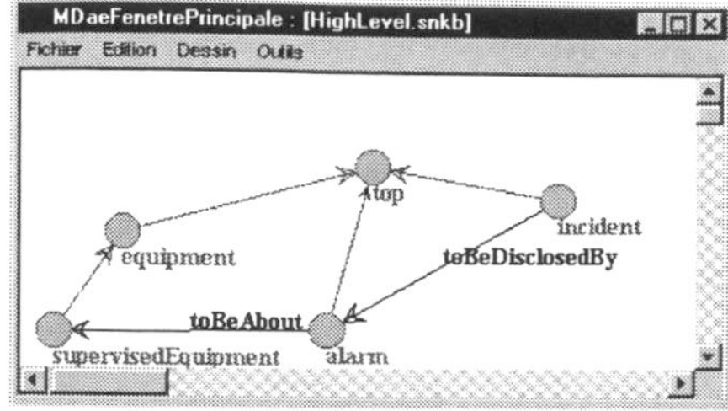

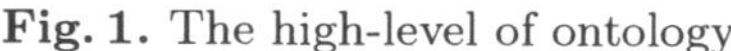
Fig. 1. The high-level of ontology

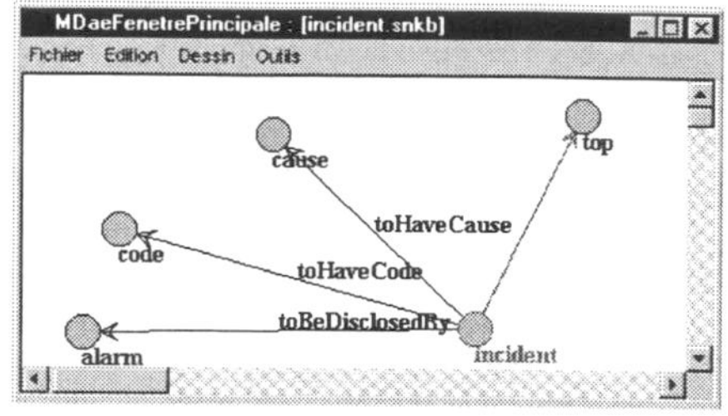

Fig. 2. Adding new concepts

The method is therefore based on a process of successive refinements of the CPs initially selected.

At each iteration, new schemata are created and the previous are updated; especially, the state and nature of a concept may change. An expert must as soon as possible validate the schema of the high-level ontology to stabilize the different sub-ontologies. Once a stable state is reached, the other primitives of the initial list are gradually modelled and added to the LMCP.

Let us suppose that the CPs on equipment, incidents and actions, are already modelled, and let us apply this process to the term "duplex stop incident". Present in numerous technical documents, this primitive, that will be called "duplexStop", is described as follows: *"A duplex stop incident is disclosed by one simplex stop alarm, one or more overloading alarms and at least three null efficiency alarms. The alarms of type simplex stop are alarm events on switches. The alarms of type overloading and the alarms of type null efficiency provide information on the state of the beams"*. This description includes many CPs, among which "duplexStop" (incident of type duplex stop), "simplexStop" (simplex stop alarm), "overloading" (alarm of type overloading of beams), "nullEfficiency" (alarm of type null efficiency) are not yet modelled. The table 1 presents the LMCP before inserting these new primitives; it tells for each primitive if it is modelled by a concept or by a property, and gives the level of concepts or the type of properties (Basic or Specialised).

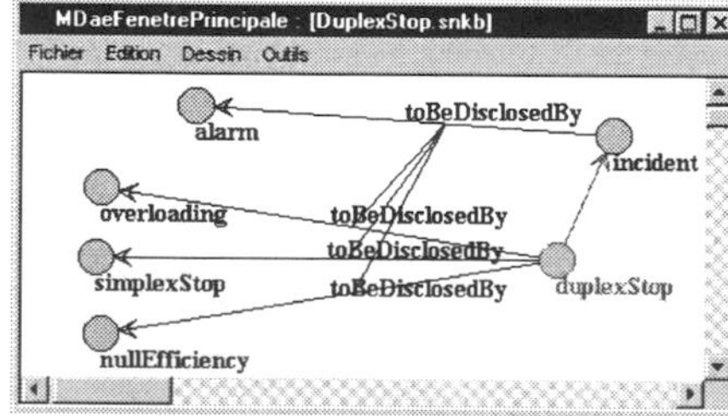

Fig. 3. Use of calculated property

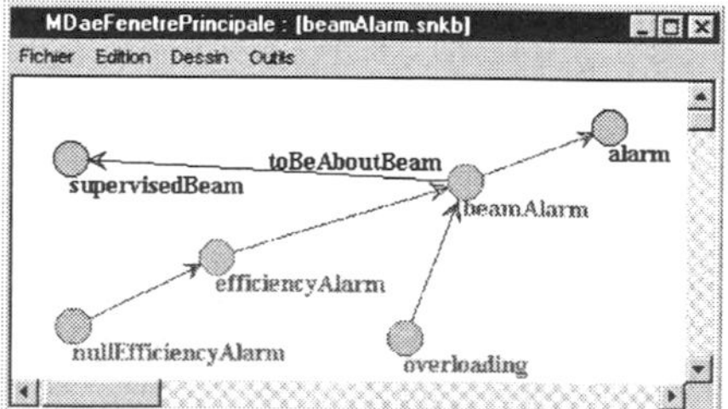

Fig. 4. Example of grouping concept

Table 1. Example of conceptual primitives

Conceptual primitives (Concept)	Level	Conceptual primitives (Concept)	Level
alarm	1	simplexStop	3
beam	3	switchAlarm	2
cause	1	supervisedEquipement	2
efficiencyAlarm	3	switch	3
incident	1		
Conceptual primitives (Property)	**Type**	**Conceptual primitives (Property)**	**Type**
toBeDisclosedBy	B	toBeAboutBeam	S
toBeAbout	B	toBeAboutSwitch	S

Among the new CPs, some specialise already existing concepts, for example "duplexStop" is kind of "incident" (figure 3). These primitives are modelled as specialising concepts. Their structural nature is structural, and their linguistic nature is terminological or pre-terminological depending on the fact that the primitive corresponds more or less to a domain term. The description of these primitives lead to specialise some properties. Here, "duplexStop" is disclosed by three types of alarms that are modelled (figure 3) by three specialisations of "toBeDisclosedBy".

When some properties are shared by more than one concept, the knowledge engineer may add a grouping concept, like "beamAlarm" (figure 4) which is added with the couple (State1,(grouping, not terminological)). Indeed, the label of "beamAlarm" concept does appear neither like a term, nor like a complex expression in the documents. The final modelling gives:

1. the three properties "toBeDisclosedBy" are properties of the type (simple, specialised) with a terminological nature,
2. concept "duplexStop" is State1 with nature (structural, terminological),
3. concepts "overloading", "nullEfficiencyAlarm" and "simplexAlarm" are State0 with nature (structural, terminological).

3.3 Representation Phase

The representation is the translation of the modelling schemata into an object formalism like CG or like DL, for which some general rules are provided:

1. The translation of a $Md_{\omega\varsigma}$ concept must be clearly defined into the formalism. It is not obvious at all that a direct translation would be possible even if the formalism shelters a primitive called *concept*. This concerns in particular the TopConcept.
2. The translation of basic properties must also receive a properly defined representation, and it is necessary to tell whether their translation can modify the description of the concepts that use it.
3. The specialisation of properties must then be defined in the formalism and here again, it must be clear whether they may entail modifications of some concept descriptions or of some property descriptions.
4. Finally, case by case, each calculated property should be represented. The corresponding computation has to be represented by special-purpose operators, inferences rules or algorithms. Their translation is generally the most difficult problem.

We have shown in [7] that a chain of binary properties can sometimes be translated only into an inference mechanism.

These general guidelines have to be made explicit for each target formalism, in a way detailed in [6].

4 Conclusion

$Md_{\omega\varsigma}$ aims to facilitate the representation of domain ontology in a formalism like DL and CG. $Md_{\omega\varsigma}$ satisfies the needs of smoothness and legibility of the modelling and offers verification facilities without too rigorous semantic constraints. The language is based on a method for acquiring knowledge from texts, which aims to keep the link between words in text and CPs in model so that understand and maintain the model and its formalisation would be easier.

We have illustrated the modelling steps from texts to a semi-formal terminological ontology in $Md_{\omega\varsigma}$ with examples taken from an industrial application. We have presented some translation rules from the semi-formal ontology to a formal one in CG and DL.

References

[1] N. Aussenac-Gilles, D. Bourigault, A. Condamines, and C. Gros. How can knowledge acquisition benefit from terminology ? In *Proceedings of KAW'95*, 1995.

[2] M. Blázquez, M. Fernández, J.M. García-Pinar, and A. Gómez-Pérez. Building ontologies at the knowledge level using the ontology design environment. In *Proceedings of KAW'98*, 1998.

[3] D. Bourigault. Lexter, a natural language processing tool for terminology extraction. In *Proceedings of the 7th EURALEX International Congress*, Goteborg, 1996.

[4] B. Biébow and S. Szulman. Terminae : A linguistics-based tool for building of a domain ontology. In D. Fensel and R. Studer, editors, *Proceedings of EKAW'99*, LNAI, 1621, pages 49–66. Springer-Verlag, 1999.

[5] P. Coupey and C. Faron. Toward correspondences between conceptual graphs and description logics. In M.L. Mugnier and M. Chein, editors, *Proceedings of ICCS'98*, LNAI, 1453, pages 165–178. Springer-Verlag, 1998.

[6] J. Nobécourt. *De la modélisation à la représentation : $Md_{\omega\varsigma}$ un exemple de langage de modélisation multi-formalismes.* PhD thesis, Université Paris-Nord, Villetaneuse, France, 1999.

[7] J. Nobécourt. Représenter la notion de propriété dans les graphes conceptuels et les logiques de description. In J. Charlet, M. Zacklad, G. Kassel, and D. Bourigault, editors, *Ingénierie des connaissances : Evolutions récentes et nouveaux défis*, pages 177–194. Eyrolles, 2000.

[8] URL: http://www-lipn.univ-paris13.fr/~nobecourt.

Ontology's Crossed Life Cycles

Mariano Fernández López, Asunción Gómez Pérez, and María Dolores Rojas Amaya

Facultad de Informática
Universidad Politécnica de Madrid
Campus de Montegancedo s/n
Boadilla del Monte, 28660. Madrid. Spain.
Tel: +34 91 3367439, Fax: +34 91 3367412

email: {mfernand, mrojas}@delicias.dia.fi.upm.es,
asun@fi.upm.es

Abstract. This paper presents the idea that the life cycle of an ontology is highly impacted as a result of the process of reusing it for building another ontology. One of the more important results of the experiment presented is how the different activities to be carried out during the development of a specific ontology may involve performing other types of activities on other ontologies already built or under construction. We identify in that paper new intra-dependencies between activities carried out inside the same otology and inter-dependencies between activities carried out in different ontologies. The interrelation between life cycles of several ontologies provokes that integration has to be approached globally rather than as a mere integration of out implementation.

1 Introduction

A lot of ontologies have been developed in recent years in different domains and for all sorts of applications. Many of these ontologies were built from scratch, that is, without reusing definitions from other existing ontologies. Furthermore, the reuse of other ontologies has been confined to the implementation phase, and the most commonly used software environments today [2],[3], [13] admit integration of code. Additionally, there is hardly any information or documentation describing the development *process* followed to build the ontologies. In other words, the community was more interested in the end product than providing information about the Ontology Development Process (ODP), that is, the activities carried out when building ontologies in a given domain. As consequence of this situation, not many ontology development methodologies have been developed to date.

Uschold and King's methodology [14] and Grüninger and Fox [10] methodologies start by setting out the need and purpose for building the ontology. Having acquired a significant amount of domain knowledge, they propose direct codification in special-purpose ontology implementation languages. The main drawbacks of this approach are: a) conceptual models are implicit in the implementation codes; b) Domain experts and human end users have no undesrtanding of formal ontologies codified in ontology languages; c) direct coding of the knowledge acquisition result is too abrupt

R. Dieng and O. Corby (Eds.): EKAW 2000, LNAI 1937, pp. 65-79, 2000.

a step, especially for complex ontologies. So, ontologists should think simoultaneously on the analysis of the knowledge and the technology to implement such knowledge; and d) ontology-developer preferences in a given languages condition the notation and implementation of the acquired knowledge.

Methontology [4], [5], however, provides guidelines for specifying ontologies at the knowledge level as a conceptualisation that is independent of the ontology implementation languages. Methontology includes the definition of the ODP, which is based on the IEEE Standard 1074-1995 [11] for software development process; a life cycle based on evolving prototypes [5]; and the techniques that encompasses the activities identified in the ODP. Three kind of activities are identified in Methontology are [5]: *Project Management Activities* include: Planning, Control and Quality Assurance; *Development-Oriented Activities* include: Specification, Conceptualization, Formalization, Implementation and Maintenance; and *Support Activities* include: Knowledge Acquisition, Integration, Evaluation [8], Documentation and Configuration Management. The ontology life cycle identifies the set of stages through which the ontology moves during its life time, describes what activities are to be performed in each stage and how the activities are related (relation of precedence, return, etc.).

ODE [4] is an environment that gives technical support to Methontology. Ontologies can be conceptualised in ODE using tables and graphs. Ontologies are also evaluated at the conceptual level, and the translators generate the computable code. Thus, domain experts can use this approach to conceptualise new ontologies and validate domain ontologies, leading to cuts in the time spent on and resources invested in the knowledge acquisition and evaluation activities.

With the purpose of identifying new activities and obtaining new techniques, we have developed ontologies in different domains and with different representation needs. One of the more interesting ontologies, from the viewpoint of the methodological results, is the Monatomic Ions (MI) ontology. During its development, not only *intra-dependencies* inside the activities of its ODP were found, but also *inter-dependencies* between the MI ontology and activities in some of the ontologies reused by the MI ontology. By intra-dependences we refer to the relationships between activities carried out inside the same ontology, for example, the relationship between knowledge acquisition and conceptualisation in Monatomic Ions. That is, intra-dependences define the ontology life cycle. By inter-dependences we refer to the relationships between activities carried out in different ontologies. For example, the MI development involved the performance of reengineering, merge, evaluation and configuration management on other ontologies, concretely, standard-units (SU) and chemical-elements (CE) (which were existing ontologies). In this paper, we describe some results about intra-dependencies, but our attention is mainly focused in inter-dependencies.

2 Need of Environmental Ontologies

Experts in several domains, including biology, geology, chemistry, law, computing, etc., work in the field of the environmental sciences. Each expert uses a vocabulary related to one of the areas of this science, and there is neither a common terminology nor any standard to support the accurate use of each term.

There are many potential ontologies in that domain, but we have centred on environmental pollutants. An ontology of this kind must include the methods for detecting all the pollutant components in several media (water, soil, air, etc.) and the maximum permitted concentration of these components, taking into account the legislation (European and Spanish) in force. The components of pollutants are ionic. Therefore, ions are the primary entities to be taken into account, as they are indicators of environmental pollution, deterioration, etc. Background knowledge of the elements in their pure state and their properties, as well as the units of measure of some properties, are needed to represent knowledge on ionic concentrations. The ontology of pollutants aims to output a unified, complete and consistent terminology that can be used precisely, non-ambiguously and consistently in environmental applications that employ the maximum permitted concentration to detect alterations in the above-mentioned media.

3 Monatomic Ions Ontology Development Process

The MI ontology was developed within the Methontology framework and using ODE. Methontology proposes that the ontology be specified after having started knowledge acquisition. Fig. 1 presents in continuous line the *intradependencies* between the activities of the MI ontology. While knowledge is being acquired, the ontology developer builds the conceptual model, integrates the selected ontologies, evaluate the ontology under development, as well as generate the associated documentation. Note that many of these activities take place at the same time. Having completed the conceptualisation, the system would be formalised and implemented. In our framework ontologies are not formalised, as ODE has a module that maps the conceptual model to a computable model using its translators to Ontolingua, OCML and Flogic.

Related to the *interdependencies* between the activities of different ontologies (see discontinuous lines at Fig. 1), they emerged at the specification and integration activities of the monatomic ion ontology. First, at the specification of the MI ontology, we looked for candidate ontologies at the Ontolingua Server, at the Cyc server and ODE. Then, we made a preliminary evaluation the content and suitability of the candidate ontologies, and we selected the Ontolingua ontologies, which are more suitable for our purposes.

The second interdependency emerged during the MI ontology integration activity. The selected ontologies (Standard Units and Chemical Elements) (SU and CE) were reviewed in depth to assure their correctness and completeness before their integration in the MI ontology. We performed reengineering of SU, and merge, evaluation and configuration management on CE. The aim behind this was to assure that these ontologies provided a solid basis on which to incrementally develop new ontologies.

3.1 Requirements Specification

The purpose of the specification phase is to output a document that includes the purpose, level of formality and scope of the ontology, including other significant information. The starting point of the MI ontology are the ions, both anionic and

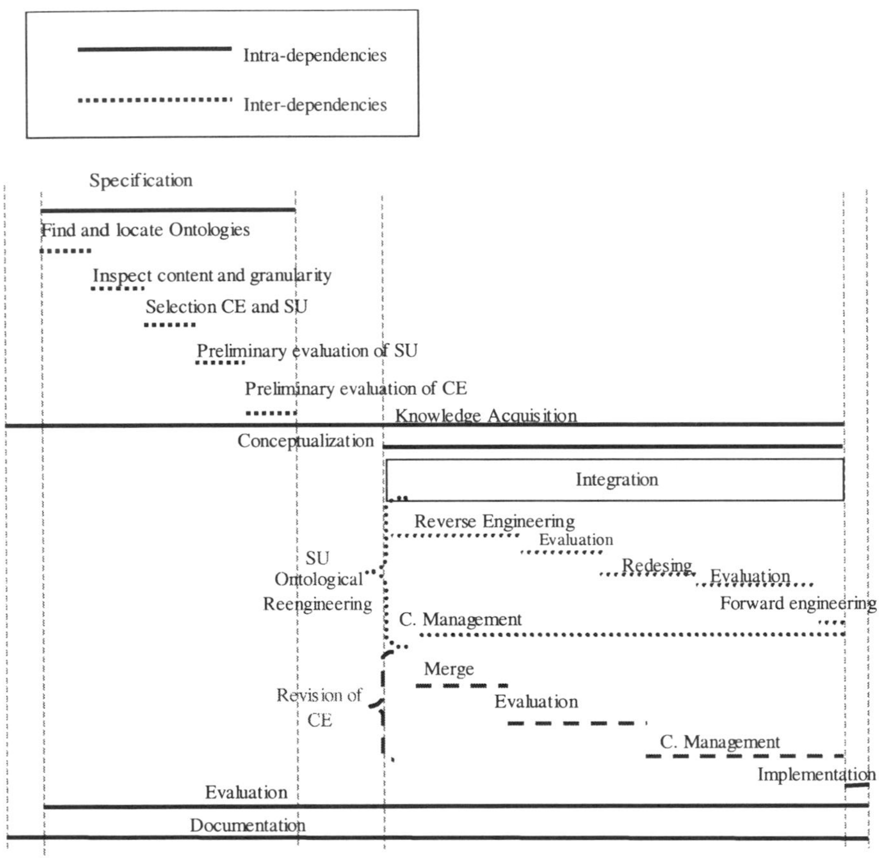

Fig. 1. Inter and intra dependencies between activities of the Monatomic Ions ODP

cationic, addressed from the viewpoint of inorganic chemistry and, also, analyzed with a view of standardization in the soil and waterfields within the physical environment and in terms of human health. From the environmental viewpoint, the monatonic ions detected in the physical variables –water, soil and air- are defined, specifying the methods of detection and maximum permitted concentrations.

It is important to mention here that at the requirements specification phase of the MI ontology we started the integration process with other ontologies. The initial activities we performed were:

- To find and locate candidate ontologies to be reused. We located the SU ontology [9], which defines the basic units of measure at the Ontolingua Server, and CE [4], which defines the chemical elements of the periodic system in their pure state, at ODE and its Ontolingua code at the Ontolingua Server. At the Cyc server, we found some units of measure and chemical entities (atom, ion, molecule and radical).
- To inspect the content and granularity of the candidate ontologies. The SU ontology at the Ontolingua Server includes for each unit: a natural language definition, its physical quantity and factors of conversion to other units of the same quantity, whereas the Cyc ontology included only a natural language definition.
- We selected the ODE and Ontolingua Server ontologies, and we used Cyc ontologies for reference purposes. Fig. 2 shows how all these ontologies, and the ontologies included by the SU and CE ontologies are related at the Ontolingua Server. Ontologies at the top include the ontologies at the bottom.
- Ontologits did a preliminar evaluation of SU from the knowledge representation point of view. As described in [7], several problems were found at the SU ontology

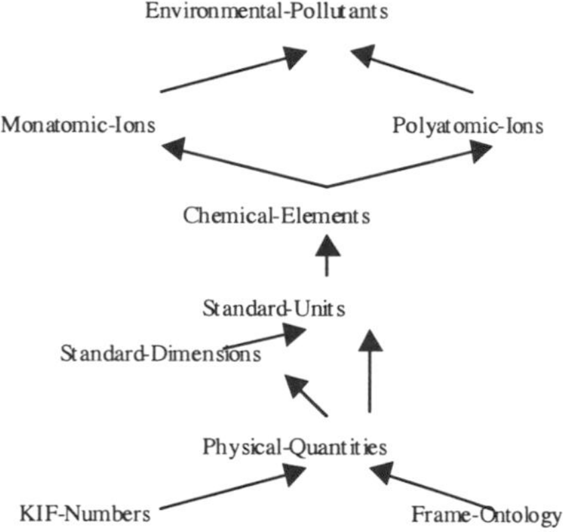

Fig. 2. Relationships between the ontologies

and CE. The most important problem in SU was the lack of taxonomic organization since all the instances were of the root class. The review process in CE showed that different versions of the ontology needed to be merged to output a new unified and corrected ontology with which could be extended before being included in the MI ontology.

- Simoultaneously with the previous evaluation, domain experts also did a preliminar evaluation of CE ontology since its conceptual model was available in ODE and was understandable for the experts. However, we have postponed SU domain experts evaluation since domain experts were unable to understand Ontolingua code.

Thus, the need of the SU preliminar evaluation forces the SU reverse engineering for obtaining its conceptual model, and the presence of several versions on CE forces its merge, evaluation and configuration management.

3.2 Knowledge Acquisition

Knowledge acquisition was performed using techniques recommended in Knowledge Engineering for developing Knowledge-Based Systems. So, two open interviews (which output a preliminary classification of ions) and six structured interviews (to get the final classification of ions, concepts, attributes, etc.) were held and informal text analysis and table analysis was conducted.

3.3 Conceptualisation

As we have already said, the conceptualisation was performed, following Methontology and using ODE. The Methontology intermediate representations used were: glossary of terms, concept classification trees, relationship diagram, table of relationships, concept dictionary, class attribute tables, logical axiom tables, and constants table. Other intermediate representations, like instance attribute tables, formula tables and instance tables, have not been used, because this ontology does not have any instance. Of all the representations, the Concept Classification Tree (CCT) deserves a special mention. Only one CCT was built from the concepts identified in the GT, which means that we have only one ontology.

Four criteria were applied when building the CCT. First, the chosen model must be easily understandable and must accurately reflect the knowledge specified by the experts. Second, the ontology must be easily extendible. Third, the ontology must be easily integrated with other ontologies. Fourth, it must be possible to select only part of the ontology for use in other ontologies or applications.

According to these objectives, ions can evidently be studied from more than one viewpoint: from the general viewpoint, which is concerned with specifying the name and symbol of the ion among other properties; from the chemical viewpoint, which is concerned with defining chemical properties; from the viewpoint of the physical environment. Any taxonomy built should enable an ion defined from the chemical viewpoint to inherit the name and the symbol that are defined for that ion from the general viewpoint. The CCT designed takes into account all these considerations. As shown in Fig. 3, the CCT is actually a graph. The benefits of this classification are:

- As the ions are defined from more than one viewpoint, it is possible to *reuse part of the knowledge gathered by the ontology*. Thus, if an application is defined strictly in the domain of chemistry, it is possible to reuse only the knowledge present in the Chemical Ion subhierarchy.
- If the water pollutant ions are required, the water ions will be selected (e.g., Cadmium (+II) in Water), as well as all the classes that link each ion to the

hierarchy root class. Note that apart from classes related to environmental ions, classes such as Cadmium (+II) and General Ion will also be included, thus making it possible to access properties which are associated with the ion in its pure state, irrespective of the viewpoint used.

- All the knowledge can be reused if it is *integrated into a higher level ontology*.
- The *ontology can be easily extended to other media and variables*, such as the human or social environment.
- *New definitions of ions can be entered from any viewpoint*. For example, if a future directive were to include any additional ion as a possible pollutant of the physical medium water, it would be easy to define this new ion and enter it as new knowledge into the ontology.

  It is just as straightforward to enter new ions from the chemical viewpoint, where all you have to do is to correctly select the group to which the above ion belongs and get the attribute values identified for the other ions from any of the referenced knowledge sources.
- By using *inheritance*, an ion in water has the properties defined for the ion and will inherit the properties defined for the above ion in the physical medium and from the general viewpoint.
- *New properties can be easily included* if required by any individual application.

The concept classification tree was verified to assure that: (a) No concepts are repeated and there are no synonyms, which rules out redundancies in the conceptual model, (b) There are no cycles [6] among concepts, (c) There are no isolated subtrees for concepts that should be related, and (d) All the concepts represented in the tree are in the glossary of terms and vice versa.

3.4 Formalisation and Implementation

No formalisation was performed, as ODE has a module that maps the conceptual model to a computable model automatically using translators.

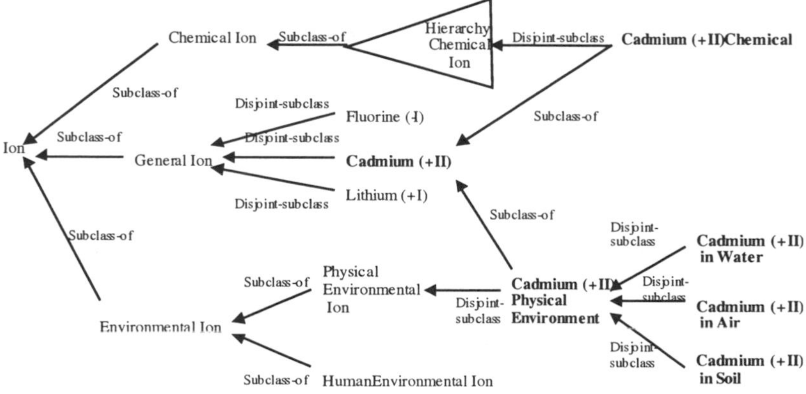

Fig. 3. CCT of thonatomic ion ontology

3.5 Integration

The objective of integration is to build an ontology by reusing definitions of knowledge present in other ontologies. Before they were reused, the following activities were carried out: reengineering on SU, and merge, evaluation and configuration management on CE. It is mainly in this integration activity where the main and stronger interdependencies appear. These *interdependencies* are shown in Fig. 1. As we said before, the main reason for reengineering the SU ontology were: (a) domain experts and human end users have no understanding of formal ontologies codified in ontology languages. So, they can not validate the content of these ontologies; and (b) the lack of taxonomic organisation and conversion factor between some units of the SU ontology. Here, we also present the process for reviewing CE to assure their suitability.

3.5.1 Ontological Reengineering on Standard Units

Ontological reengineering [7] is the process of retrieving and mapping a conceptual model of an implemented ontology to another, more suitable conceptual model, which

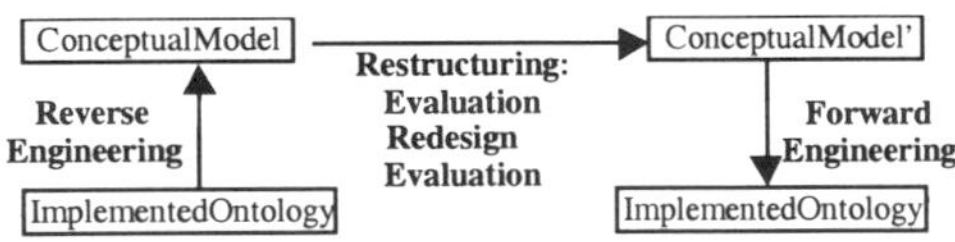

Fig. 4. Ontological reenginering process

is re-implemented. The method for reengineering ontologies is presented in Fig. 4 and adapts Chikofsky's software reengineering schema [1] to the ontology domain. Three main activities were identified: reverse engineering, restructuring and forward engineering. Fig. 5 pictures in detail an organizational chart showing the activities performed during the reengineering process and the documents generated in each step. The goal of the processes described at Fig. 4 are:

Step 1. **Reverse Engineering**. Its objetive is to output a possible conceptual model on the basis of the code in which the ontology is implemented. SU was analyzed on the basis of its Ontolingua implementation.

Step 2. **Restructuring**. The goal of restructuring is to reorganized this initial conceptual model into a new conceptual model which is built bearing in mind the use of the restructured ontology by the ontology/application that reuses it. As presented in [7], the restructuring activity contains two phases: analysis and synthesis. The analysis phase includes evaluation (steps 2 to 5 of Fig. 5), whose general aim is to evaluate the ontology, that is, to check that the hierarchy of the ontology and its classes, instances, relations and functions are complete, consistent (there are no contradictions), concise (there are no explicit and implicit redundancies) and syntactically correct. The synthesis phase (step 6 of Fig. 5) seeks to correct the ontology after the analysis phase and document any changes made. So, activities related with **configuration management** arise in that context, which goal is to keep a record of ontology evolution and strict change control.

SU was restructured bearing in mind its future use by the CE and MI ontologies. Since the reverse engineering phase provided a possible conceptual model, domain experts can now validate the SU ontology. The evaluation they performed at the conceptual model were if all the units to be used at the MI ontology were already defined at the SU ontology, as well as the factor conversions needed between the

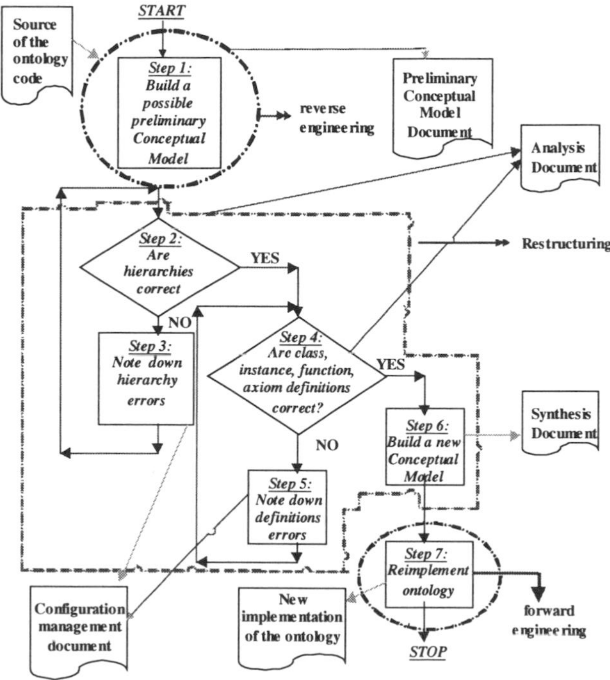

Fig. 5. Ontological reenginering activities

units. It is important to stress here that this restructuring is guided by the ontology that is to reuse the knowledge, which means that there is no way of assuring that the restructured ontology will be a hundred per cent valid for ontologies that reuse the restructured knowledge.

Step 3. **Forward Engineering**. The objective of this step is to output a new implementation of the ontology on the basis of the new conceptual model. The implementation of the new conceptual model of SU was carried out using ODE translators. Note that after doing reengineering on SU, there exist two versions of that ontology, the old version at the Ontolingua Server, and the new version in ODE.

Finally, to keep control of the changes made, we performed **configuration management** during the whole process. It is defined in software engineering as [12]: „Activity that is applied throughout the software engineering process for the following purposes: establish and maintain the integrity of the products generated, evaluate and control the system changes and provide product visibility". Adapting the idea of configuration management from Software Engineering into the ontological engineering field, on the Methontology framework, we recommend the following activities:

CM.1. **Identification of the elements to be controlled**. These elements include not only the documents related with the development of the ontology (requirement specification document, the sources used in Knowledge acquisition, conceptual models, implementation, integration documents, ontologies reused by this ontology, etc.) but also management activities (plan, quality assurance and control) and the software used to develop the ontology. To identify which are the elements to be controlled you can think what are your needs if the project stops and you re-start the project sometime later. We controlled the previous elements in CE and the mechanisms used to identify them was the concatenation of: the name of the ontology, the name of the element within the ontology, the version identifier, etc.

CM.2. **Control of changes**. Adapting Software Engineering steps to Ontological Engineering, and for each of the changes request, we propose that the Change control starts with a petition for change, followed by the classification and registration of request; approval or rejection of the change petition; report on how the change is to be made and what implications it has; order to make the change; making of change; performance of the change and certification that the change was made correctly. It ends when the result is reported to the person who proposed the change.

CM.3. **Generation of status reports**. We distinguish in that section the daily documentation generated about each configuration element and also general reports by demand (i.e., a report requested on the latest changes made to the ontology).

For the purpose of assuring information about the evolution of the Standard-Units ontology, a rigorous change control has been performed throughout the restructuring phase. The goal is to have all the changes documented, detailing the changes made, their causes and effects. It is important to perform proficient change control of both definitions and taxonomies. In this manner, any ontologist who needs to use part of or the entire ontology can easily understand its evolution. Even if an ontology has not been fully developed, provided it is well documented, it could be finished off by another developer using the existing documentation. The configuration management documents can rule out incorrect decision making, if they state the courses of action to be taken at any time, and justify the choice of one rather than another. Change control also helps end users to determine which version of the ontology they require for their system or for the new ontology they are to develop.

Consequently, although the reengineering activity and configuration management of the SU ontology would belong to the life cycle of that ontology, the MI integration activity forces the realisation of that activity on a "stable" ontology. Besides, although the SU reengineering process provokes the SU evaluation and configuration management, we stress that these activities make sense *per se*. For more information on the re-engineering process, see [7].

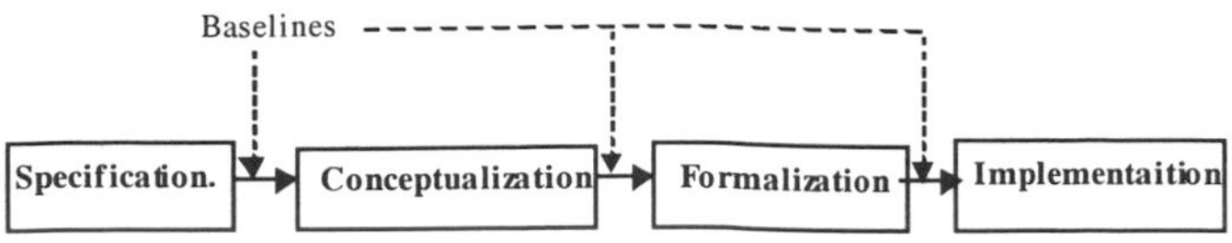

Fig. 6. Points where configuration elements are approve

3.5.2 Review of Chemical-Elements (CE)

CE is also a stable ontology whose conceptual model is available in ODE. It is also available at the Ontolingua Server. Again, the experts wanted to review the ontology before reusing it. The review process revealed that there were different versions of this ontology, which needed to be merged prior to any extension. The review process was divided into the three following activities (see Fig. 1):

- **Merging.** Chemicals started to be developed in June 1995, and the first stable version was built in December 1996. New versions of this ontology have been created since then to be used in different ontologies. Therefore, it was necessary to group all the conceptual models into one, which includes all the improvements made to the ontology.
- **Evaluation**. The knowledge present in the resulting conceptual model after merging was evaluated with the experts in order to assure that the knowledge was correct and complete, and to detect omissions.
- **Configuration Management.** Configuration management was carried out according to the guidelines described previously to make this new version of CE easier to understand for users and also to keep records of all the versions of the CE ontology.

  Configuration management activities had a strong relationship with evaluation activities. There are two reasons. First, evaluation has to be run at least after each of the phases of the ontology development process, since configuration elements can be used as a basis in the following phases of the ontology development process. Second the changes performed as a consequence of the evaluation activity need to be controlled. Fig. 6 presents the baselines on the ontology development process.

Again, although the merge, evaluation and configuration management activities belong to the life cycle of CE ontology, the MI integration activity forces the realisation of those activities on a "stable" ontology.

3.6 Evaluation

The MI ontology was evaluated by the experts throughout the entire life cycle and, especially, in the conceptualisation using ODE evaluation module.

3.7 Documentation

Documentation has been carried out throughout the whole ODP. The previous activities output: a requirements specification document; a knowledge acquisition document; the conceptual model, composed of a set of intermediate representations; an integration document; the configuration management reports, and the evaluation document.

4 Crossed Life Cycles

In the previous section we have presented the main activities carried out during the development of the MI ontology, the order of execution of such activities as well as the interdependencies with other activities that were performed in other ontologies prior to their integration on the MI ontology.

In that section we present the idea that when an ontology reuses definition of other ontologies, the ontology life cycle of the first crosses with the life cycle of the second and provokes some changes on its life cycle.

The main intersections between the life cycles of the SU, CE and MI ontologies are shown in Fig. 7. Note that the SU ontology was built at the beginning of the last decade and, probably, several applications have already used its definitions. The SU ontology life cycle was "latent" or "hibernate". That is, since the SU ontology was built, nobody has changed its definitions at the Ontolingua Server and ontologies and applications reuse that ontology as it is. When we developed CE [4], we identified some units of measures that did not appear at SU, and we added them to the SU ontology at the Ontolingua Server. We updated that ontology with the new units but we did not performed big changes in its structure and on its content. Consequently, these updates could be seen as *maintenance* activities on the SU ontology. We can really say that the life cycle of the SU "wakes up" when SU is going to be reused on the MI ontology and the reengineering process over the SU ontology starts. At this point, the SU life cycle is alive since we modified its structure and its content.

Another interesting observation in Fig. 7 is that the life cycle of the SU branches in two. So, two SU ontologies -the Ontology Server SU and the reengineered SU- were available after running a reengineering process on SU. The opposite occurs with CE, where several ontologies exist, each one with its life cycle, and they meet with the new life cycle of the merged CE ontology after the merging process.

These confluences and forking of life cycles call for a global management of ontologies. We claim that, the configuration management of each ontology must not be carried out separately from the others in which are integrated. Configuration management must be global and simultaneously affect all the ontologies handled by the group.

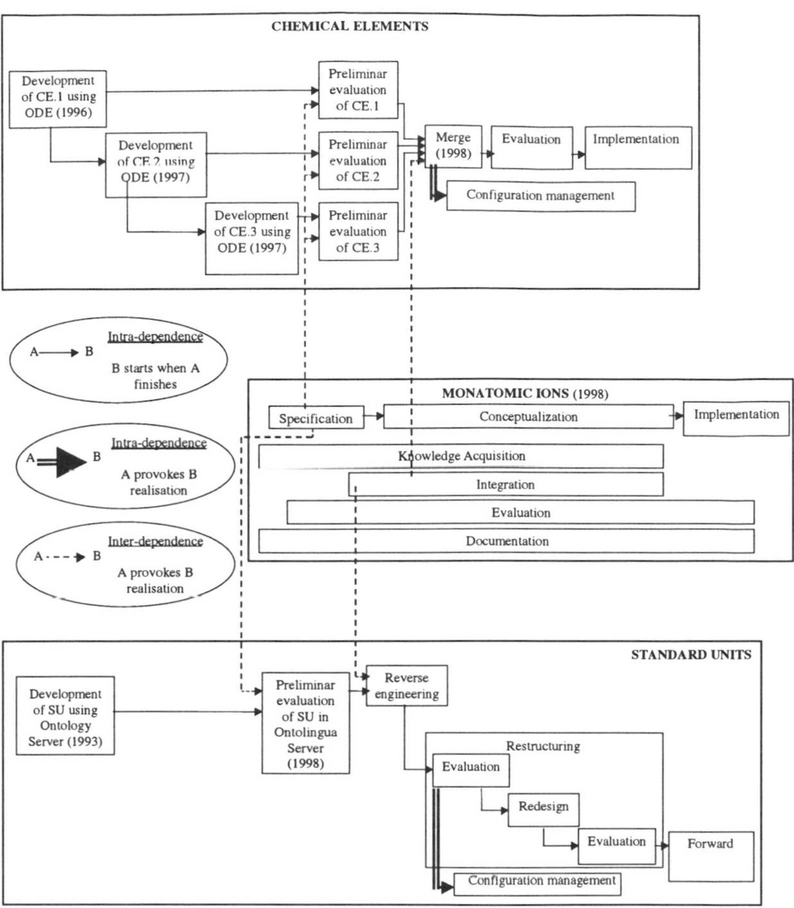

Fig. 7. Crossed life cycles of Standard Units, Chemical and Monatomic Ions

5 Conclusions

In this paper we present how the different activities to be carried out during the development of a specific ontology may involve performing other types of activities on other ontologies already built or under construction. Such activities include: reengineering, merge, technical evaluation and configuration management. So, neither integration at the implementation level nor at the knowledge level is sufficient. There is also a need to unify ontology development management policies and to integrate products output throughout the development of ontologies whose development processes are interrelated. Therefore, the life cycle of an ontology should always be documented and accessible.

We have presented the intradependencies between the activities (specification, knowledge acquisition, conceptualization, formalization, integration, implementation, evaluation, documentation) of the MI ODP. We have also presented how the different activities to be performed during the development of a concrete ontology (i.e., specification and integration activities in MI) may involve performing other activities (reengineering, evaluation, configuration managemnent) on other ontologies already built (SU and CE ontologies). The idea to consider the activities on each ontology as separate and dependant life cycles helps to understand clearly the complementarity between knowledge reuse and knowledge modelling of domain specific knowledge. Below, an assessment is given of each activity performed, specifying the contributions made from the methodological viewpoint. Also, the results obtained in each of the following areas are evaluated:

- **Knowledge reuse.** This paper presents a clear example of an ontology that reuses knowledge from other ontologies. In this case, the reuse and integration of ontologies led to the reengineering of SU and the merge, evaluation and configuration management of CE.
- **Ontology evaluation.** Three ontologies were evaluated, each by means of a different process:
  a. **Standard Units**. It is done during the restructuring phase of the ontological reengineering process.
  b. **Chemicals**. This ontology passed three evaluations. The first was a technical judgement throughout its ODP, that is, when it was built [4]. The second was the evaluation after the merging process. The third is the assessment by the experts to determine the compliance with the new MI ontology.
  c. **Monatomic Ions**. The ontology was evaluated throughout the ODP to assure that: the requirements specification was met, the knowledge represented was comparable with reality, the content of the ontology was consistent, complete and concise, etc.
- **Configuration management.** Configuration management was conducted on SU and CE as a supplementary activity to reengineering, merge and evaluation. It is important to control de changes because an ontology developer who needs to reuse that ontology (in full or in part) can easily understand its evolution.
- **Development of the MI ontology.** The conceptual model finally developed, in which MI is studied from several viewpoints, assures that the definitions are independent of the end use of the ontology. For proving this with the experience, ontologies reusing MI are been developed at present. Additionally, this ontology can be totally or partially reused in other ontologies or applications. In fact, an important purpose that we have with the development of MI and other environmental ontologies is to prove that it is possible to build reusable and usable ontologies incrementaly.

To refine the reengineering process showed in this paper, it should be desirable to apply this process to more complex ontologies than SU. However, MI is an ontology that has need several month of work, and its ODP has required not only development activities, but also management, control and support activities. Besides, for some activities (for example, evaluation), we had former experience based on the development of others ontologies. So, the more likely is that the most techniques and processes showed in this paper will need a minor refinement for being applicable to other developments.

We are scaling up the method making the necessary changes for adapting it to the development of other ontologies in the environmental field. Normally, when a new ontology is built, there are less modifications on the method than the necessary modifications for former ontologies, so there should be a moment in which the method is general enough to be applied to the development of a large quantity of ontologies.

Acknowledgements. This research is funded by the Polytechnic University of Madrid, under the multidisciplinary research and development project grants programme, reference no. AM-9819. Thanks to the experts, Almudena Galán and Rosario García. Thanks to Oscar Corcho for their technical comments.

References

1. Chikofsky, E.J.; Cross II, J.H. „Reverse Engineering and design recovery: A taxonomy." Software Magazine. January 1990. PP:13-17.
2. Domingue, J. „Tadzebao and WebOnto: Discussing, Browsing, and Editing Ontologies on the Web". Knowledge Acquisition Workshop (KAW). Banff (Canadá). 1998.
3. Farquhar A., Fikes R., Rice J., The Ontolingua Server: A Tool for Collaborative Ontology Construction, KAW'96. PP. 44.1-44.19, 1996.
4. Fernández, M.; Gómez-Pérez, A.; Pazos, J.; Pazos, A. Building a Chemical Ontology using methontology and the ontology design environment. IEEE Intelligent Systems and their applications. Vol.4 (1):37-45. 1999.
5. Fernández, M., Gómez-Pérez, A. Juristo, N. METHONTOLOGY: From Ontological Art Toward Ontological Engineering. Spring Symposium Series on Ontological Engineering. AAAI97.
6. Gómez Pérez, A. „Evaluation of Taxonomic Knowledge in Ontologies and Problem Solving Methods". 12th Banff Conference on Knowledge Acquisition for Knowledge Based Systems. 1999.
7. Gómez-Pérez, A.; Rojas-Amaya, M.D. Ontological Reengineering for Reuse. Knowledge Acquisition Modeling and Management. EKAW'99. pp. 139-156.
8. Gómez-Pérez, A. A Framework to Verify Knowledge Sharing Technology. Expert Systems with Application. Vol. 11, N. 4. 1996. PP: 519-529.
9. Gruber, T.;Olsen, G. „An ontology for Engineering Mathematics". Fourth International Conference on Principles of Knowledge Representation and Reasoning. Doyle, Torasso y Sandewall (eds.) Morgan Kaufmann. 1994.
10. Gruninger M., Fox M., Methodology for the Design and Evaluation of Ontologies, Proceedings of IJCAI95's Workshop on Basic Ontological Issues in Knowledge Sharing, 1995.
11. „IEEE Standard for Developing Software Life Cycle Processes". IEEE Computer Society. New York (USA). April 26, 1996.
12. Pressman, R.S. „Ingeniería del Software. Un enfoque práctico." Mac-Graw Hill. 1993.
13. Swartout, B.; Ramesh P.; Knight, K.; Russ, T. „Toward distributed use of large-scale ontologies". Symposium on Ontological Engineering. American Association for Artificial Intelligence (AAAI). Stanford (California). Marzo 1997.
14. Uschold M., Grüninger M., ONTOLOGIES: Principles, Methods and Applications, Knowledge Engineering Review, Vol. 11, N. 2, June 1996.

A Roadmap to Ontology Specification Languages

Oscar Corcho[1] and Asunción Gómez-Pérez[1]

[1]Facultad de Informática, Universidad Politécnica de Madrid. Campus de Montegancedo s/n. Boadilla del Monte, 28660. Madrid. Spain.

ocorcho@delicias.dia.fi.upm.es, asun@fi.upm.es

Abstract. The interchange of ontologies across the World Wide Web (WWW) and the cooperation among heterogeneous agents placed on it is the main reason for the development of a new set of ontology specification languages, based on new web standards such as XML or RDF. These languages (SHOE, XOL, RDF, OIL, etc) aim to represent the knowledge contained in an ontology in a simple and human-readable way, as well as allow for the interchange of ontologies across the web. In this paper, we establish a common framework to compare the expressiveness and reasoning capabilities of „traditional" ontology languages (Ontolingua, OKBC, OCML, FLogic, LOOM) and „web-based" ontology languages, and conclude with the results of applying this framework to the selected languages.

1 Introduction

In the past years, a set of languages have been used for implementing ontologies. Ontolingua [6] is perhaps the most representative of all of them. Other languages have also been used for specifying ontologies: LOOM [16], OCML [17], FLogic [12], etc. Protocols such as OKBC[4] have been also developed to access KR systems. KR paradigms underlying these languages and protocols are diverse: frame-based, description logic, first (and second) order predicate calculus and object-oriented.

In the recent years, new languages for the web have been created -XML [2], RDF [13] and RDF Schema [3]- and are still in a development phase. Other languages for the specification of ontologies, based on the previous ones, have also emerged: SHOE [15], XOL [11] and OIL [10]. Preliminary studies exist on the use of web-based languages for representing ontologies. In [9], an analysis is shown on the role of HTML, XML and RDF when providing semantics for documents on the Web.

The purpose of this paper is to analyse the tradeoff between expressiveness (*what can be said*) and inference (*what can be obtained from the information represented*) in traditional and web-based ontology languages. In Section 2, we will present a framework for evaluating the expressiveness and inference mechanisms of ontology specification languages. Section 3 will describe both the *so-called* traditional ontology languages and the web-based ontology languages. As a conclusion, section 4 presents a discussion on the results of the study.

R. Dieng and O. Corby (Eds.): EKAW 2000, LNAI 1937, pp. 80-96, 2000.

2 Evaluation Framework

The goal of this section is to set up a framework for comparing the expressiveness and inference mechanisms of potential ontology languages. We use in our analysis the CommonKADS framework [18], which distinguishes between domain knowledge and inference knowledge. Figure 1 summarises the relationship between the KR components and the reasoning mechanisms of languages.

2.1 Domain Knowledge

The *domain knowledge* describes the main static information and knowledge objects in an application domain [18]. We identify the main kind of components used to describe domain knowledge in ontologies. Accordingly to Gruber [8], knowledge in ontologies can be specified using five kind of components: concepts, relations, functions, axioms and instances. Concepts in the ontology are usually organised in taxonomies. Sometimes the notion of ontology is somewhat diluted, in the sense that taxonomies are considered to be full ontologies [19]. Other components like procedures and rules are also identified in some ontology languages (i.e., OCML). For each one of the components outlined before (except for procedures, as it is very difficult to find common characteristics for them in all languages) we will select a set of features that we consider relevant.

Concepts [18], also known as classes, are used in a broad sense. They can be abstract or concrete, elementary or composite, real or fictious. In short, a concept can be anything about which something is said, and, therefore, could also be the description of a task, function, action, strategy, reasoning process, etc. The following questions identify the expressiveness of a language when defining classes:

- Is it possible to define **metaclasses** (classes as instances of other ones)? They are important in case that a KR ontology exists for the language.
- Is it possible to define **partitions** (sets of disjoint classes)?
- Does the language provide mechanisms to define **slots/attributes**? For example:
    - **Local attributes**. Attributes which belong to a specific concept. For instance, attribute *age* belongs to concept *Person*.
    - **Instance attributes (template slots)**. Attributes whose value may be different for each instance of the concept.
    - **Class attributes (own slots)**. Attributes whose value must be the same for all instances of the concept.
    - **Polymorph attributes**. Attributes (slots) with the same name and different behaviour for different concepts. For instance, the attribute *author* for concept *Thesis* is different from the attribute *author* for concept *Book*. Its type for *Thesis* is *Student*, and its type for *Book* is *Person*.
- Does the language provide the following **predefined facets** for attributes?
    - **Default slot value**, which will be used to assign a value to the attribute in case there is no explicit value defined for it.

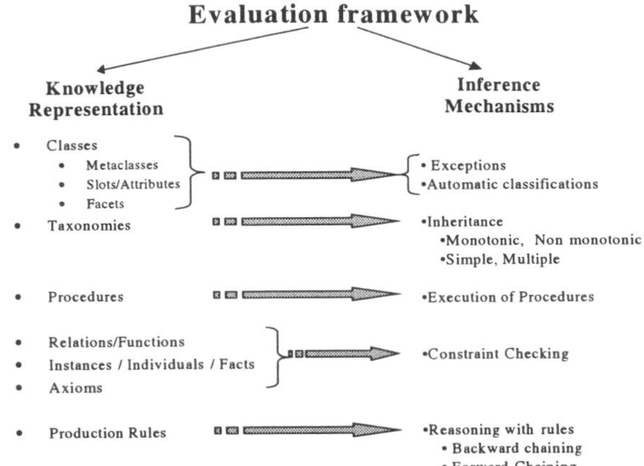

Fig. 1. Evaluation Framework

- **Type**, which will be used to constrain the type of the attribute.

- **Cardinality constraints**, which will be used to constrain the minimum and maximum number of values of the attribute.
- **Documentation**, which could include a natural language definition for it.
- **Operational definition**, which could include the definition or selection of a formula, a rule, etc to be used, for instance, when obtaining a value for that attribute.
- May **new facets** be created for attributes?

Taxonomies. They are widely used to organise ontological knowledge in the domain using generalisation/specialisation relationships through which simple/multiple inheritance could be applied. Since there exists some confusion regarding the primitives used to build taxonomies, we propose to analyse whether or not the following primitives (which are based on the definitions provided by the frame ontology at Ontolingua) are predefined in the languages.

- **Subclass of** specialises general concepts in more specific concepts.
- **Disjoint decompositions** define a partition as subclass of a class. The classification does not necessarily have to be complete (there may be instances of the parent class that are not included in any of the subclasses of the partition).
- **Exhaustive subclass decompositions** define a partition as subclass of a class. The parent class is the union of all the classes that make up the partition.
- **Not subclass of** may be used to state that a class is not a specialisation of another class. This kind of knowledge is usually represented using the denial of the *subclass of* primitive.

Some languages have a formal semantics for those primitives, and others must define their semantics by using axioms or rules.

Relations [8] represent a type of interaction between concepts of the domain. They are formally defined as any subset of a product of n sets. First, we consider the relationship between relations and other components in the ontology. We will ask if concepts and attributes are considered, respectively, as unary and binary relations. **Functions** [8] are considered as a special kind of relations where the value of the last argument is unique for a list of values of the n-1 preceding arguments.

Second, we focus on the arguments (both in relations and functions):

- Is it possible to define **arbitrary n-ary relations/functions**? If this is not possible, which is the maximum number of arguments?
- May the type of arguments be constrained?
- Is it possible to define **integrity constraints** in order to check the correctness of the arguments' value?
- Is it possible to define **operational definitions** to infer values of arguments with procedures, formulas and rules, or to define its semantic using axioms or rules?

Axioms [8] model sentences that are always true. They are included in an ontology for several purposes, such as constraining its information, verifying its correctness or deducting new information. We will focus on the next characteristics:

- Does the language support building axioms in **first order logic**?
- And **second order logic** axioms?
- Are axioms defined as independent elements in the ontology (**named axioms**) or must they be included inside the definition of other elements, such as relations, concepts, etc? This feature improves readability and maintenance of ontologies.

Instances/Individuals/Facts/Claims. All these terms are used to represent elements in the domain. **Instances** [8] represent elements of a given concept. **Facts** [17] represent a relation which holds between elements. **Individuals** [6] refer to any element in the domain which is not a class (both instances and facts). **Claims** [15] represent assertions of a fact by an instance. It is important to highlight the inclusion of claims, since people on internet can make whatever claims they want. Hence, agents shouldn't interpret them as facts of knowledge, but as claims being made by a particular instance about itself or about other instances or data, which may prove to be inconsistent with others [15]. The following questions will be asked in this section:

- Is it possible to define **instances of concepts**?
- Is it possible to define instances of relations (**facts**)?
- Does the language provide special mechanisms to define **claims**?

Production rules. Production rules [16], which follow the structure *If ... Then ...*, are used to express sets of actions and heuristics which can be represented independently from the way they will be used. A set of questions will be asked about them:

- Is it possible to define disjunctive and conjunctive premises?
- May the **chaining mechanism** be defined declaratively?
- Is it possible to define **truth values** or **certainty values** attached to the rule?

- May **procedures** be included **in the consequent**? They are commonly used to change the values of attributes of a concept, add information to the KB, etc.
- Does the language support **updates of the KB**, performed by adding or removing facts or claims?

2.2 Inference Mechanisms

This dimension describes how the static structures represented in the *domain knowledge* can be used to carry out a reasoning process [18]. There is a strong relationship between both dimensions, as the structures used for representing knowledge are the basis for the reasoning process, as seen in Figure 1. We analyse whether the language supports the following features or not:

- Does the language provide an **inference engine** that reasons with the knowledge represented using the language? Is it **sound**? And **complete**?
- Does the inference engine perform **automatic classifications**?
- Does the inference engine deal with **exceptions**? Exceptions are considered when attribute Attribute1 is defined for concept C1 and concept C2, being C1 subclass of C2 and we analyse whether the definition of Attribute1 in concept C1 overrides the definition of Attribute1 in concept C2 or not.
- Is it possible to use **monotonic**, **non-monotonic**, **simple** and/or **multiple inheritance?**
- Are **procedures** executable?
- Do axioms perform any kind of **constraint checking**?
- When reasoning with rules, does the language allow **forward and backward chaining**?

3 Ontology Specification Languages

In this section, we show an analysis of ontology specification languages which have been and are widely used by the ontology community (Ontolingua, OKBC, OCML, FLogic and LOOM), other languages created in the context of Internet, which are recommendations of the W3C (XML, RDF and RDFS) and, finally, other new languages for the specification of ontologies (XOL, SHOE and OIL).

3.1 Traditional Ontology Specification Languages

Ontolingua [6] is a language based on KIF [7] and on the Frame Ontology (FO) [6], and it is the ontology-building language used by the Ontolingua Server [6].

KIF (Knowledge Interchange Format) was developed to solve the problem of heterogeneity of languages for knowledge representation. It provides for the definition of objects, functions and relations. KIF has declarative semantics and it is based on first-order predicate calculus, with a prefix notation. It also provides for the representation of meta-knowledge and non-monotonic reasoning rules.

As KIF is an interchange format, it is tedious to use for specification of ontologies per se. The FO, built on top of KIF, is a knowledge representation ontology that allows an ontology to be specified following the paradigm of frames, providing terms such as *class*, *instance*, *subclass-of*, *instance-of*, etc. The FO does not allow to express axioms; therefore, Ontolingua allows to include KIF expressions inside of definitions based on the FO. Summarizing, Ontolingua allows to build ontologies in any of the following three manners: (1) using exclusively the FO vocabulary (axioms cannot be represented); (2) using KIF expressions; (3) using both languages simultaneously.

Currently, an inference engine is being developed for Ontolingua. The OKBC API must be used in case we want to develop a customized one.

OKBC Protocol [4] is an acronym for *Open Knowledge Base Connectivity*, previously known as *Generic Frame Protocol*. It specifies a protocol (not a language). The protocol makes assumptions about the underlying KR system (frames), and it is complementary to language specifications developed to support knowledge sharing.

The GFP Knowledge Model, which is the implicit representation formalism underlying OKBC, supports an object-centered representation of knowledge and provides a set of representational constructs commonly found in frame representation systems: constants, frames, slots, facets, classes, individuals and knowledge bases.

It also defines a complete *tell&ask* interface for knowledge bases accessed using OKBC protocol, and procedures (with a Lisp-like syntax) in order to describe complex operations to perform in a knowledge base when accessing it over a network.

Eventually it has been developed the *OKBC-Ontology* for Ontolingua, which is fully compatible with the OKBC protocol.

In this study, when referring to OKBC we will mean the API, together with the maximum expressiveness permitted.

OCML [17] stands for *Operational Conceptual Modeling Language*, and was originally developed in the context of the VITAL project.

OCML is a frame-based language that provides mechanisms for expressing items such as relations, functions, rules (with backward and forward chaining), classes and instances. In order to make the execution of the language more efficient, it also adds some extra logical mechanisms for efficient reasoning, such as procedural attachments. A general tell&ask interface is also implemented, as a mechanism to assert facts and/or examine the contents of an OCML model.

Several pragmatic considerations were taken into account in the development of OCML. One of them is the compatibility with standards, such as Ontolingua, so that OCML can be considered as a kind of „operational Ontolingua“, providing theorem proving and function evaluation facilities for its constructs.

FLogic [12] is an acronym for *Frame Logic*. FLogic integrates frame-based languages and first-order predicate calculus. It accounts in a clean and declarative fashion for most of the structural aspects of object-oriented and frame-based languages, such as object identity, complex objects, inheritance, polymorphic types, query methods, encapsulation, and others. In a sense, FLogic stands in the same relationship to the object-oriented paradigm as classical predicate calculus stands to relational programming.

FLogic has a model-theoretic semantics and a sound and complete resolution-based proof theory.

Applications of FLogic go from object-oriented and deductive databases to ontologies, and it can be combined with other specialized logics (HiLog, Transaction Logic), to improve the reasoning with information in the ontologies.

LOOM [16] is a high-level programming language and environment intended for use in constructing expert systems and other intelligent application programs. It is a descendent of the KL-ONE family and it is based in description logic, achieving a tight integration between rule-based and frame-based paradigms.

LOOM supports a "description" language for modeling objects and relationships, and an „assertion“ language for specifying constraints on concepts and relations, and to assert facts about individuals. Procedural programming is supported through pattern-directed methods, while production-based and classification-based inference capabilities support a powerful deductive reasoning (in the form of an inference engine: the classifier).

It is important to focus on the description logic approach to ontology modeling, which differs from the frame-based approach of the previously described languages. Definitions written using this approach try to exploit the existence of a powerful classifier in the language, specifying concepts by using a set of restrictions on them.

3.2 Web Standards and Recommendations

XML [2] stands for *eXtended Markup Language* deriving from SGML (*Standard General Markup Language*). It is being developed by the XML Working Group of the World Wide Web Consortium (W3C), and it is next to become a standard.

As a language for the World Wide Web, its main advantages are: it is easy to parse, its syntax is well defined and it is human readable. There are also many software tools for parsing and manipulating XML. It allows users to define their own tags and attributes, define data structures (nesting them), extract data from documents and develop applications which test the structural validity of a XML document.

When using XML as the basis for an ontology specification language, its main ***advantages*** are:

- The definition of a common syntactic specification by means of a DTD (*Document Type Definition*).
- Information coded in XML is easily readable for humans.

- It can be used to represent distributed knowledge across several web-pages, as it can be embedded in them.

XML also presents some ***disadvantages*** which influence on ontology specification:

- It is defined in order to allow the lack of structure of information inside XML tags. This makes it difficult to find the components of an ontology insidc the document.
- Standard tools are available for parsing and manipulating XML documents, but not for making inferences. These tools must be created in order to allow inferences with languages which are based on XML.

XML itself has no special features for the specification of ontologies, as it just offers a simple but powerful way to specify a syntax for an ontology specification language (this is the reason why XML is not included in the comparison of section 5). Besides, it can be used for covering ontology exchange needs, exploiting the communication facilities of the WWW.

RDF [13] stands for *Resource Description Framework*. It is being developed by the W3C for the creation of metadata describing Web resources. Examples of the use of RDF in ontological engineering may be analyzed in [1] and [20].

A strong relationship stands between RDF and XML. In fact, they are defined as complementary: one of the goals of RDF is to make it possible to specify semantics for data based on XML in a standardized, interoperable manner. The goal of RDF is to define a mechanism for describing resources that makes no assumptions about a particular application domain nor the structure of a document containing information.

The data model of RDF (which is based in semantic networks) consists of three types: **resources** (subjects), entities that can be referred to by an address at the WWW; **properties** (predicates), which define specific aspects, characteristics, attributes or relations used to describe a resource; and **statements** (objects), which assign a value for a property in a specific resource.

RDF Schema [3] (RDFS) is a declarative language used for the definition of RDF schemas. The RDFS data model (which is based on frames) provides mechanisms for defining the relationships between properties (attributes) and resources. Core classes are *class*, *resource* and *property*; hierarchies and type constraints can be defined (core properties are *type*, *subclassOf*, *subPropertyOf*, *seeAlso* and *isDefinedBy*). Some core constraints are also defined.

3.3 Web-Based Ontology Specification Languages

XOL. [11] stands for *XML-Based Ontology Exchange Language*. It was designed to provide a format for exchanging ontology definitions among a set of interested parties. Therefore, it is not intended to be used for the development of ontologies, but as an intermediate language for transferring ontologies among different database systems, ontology-development tools or application programs.

XOL allows to define in a XML syntax a subset of OKBC, called OKBC-Lite. As OKBC defines a protocol for accessing frame-based representation systems, XOL may be suitable for exchanging information between different systems, via the WWW. The main handicap is that frames (defined in OKBC) are excluded from this language, and only classes (and their hierarchies), slots and facets can be defined.

Many XML editing tools are available which allow to generate XOL documents.

SHOE [15] stands for *Simple HTML Ontology Extension.* It was developed first as an extension of HTML, with the aim of incorporating machine-readable semantic knowledge in HTML or other WWW documents. Recently, it has been adapted in order to be XML compliant. The intent of this language is to make it possible for agents to gather meaningful information about web pages and documents, improving search mechanisms and knowledge-gathering. The two-phase process to achieve it consists of: (1) defining an ontology describing valid classifications of objects and valid relationship between them; (2) annotating HTML pages to describe themselves, other pages, etc.

In SHOE, an ontology is an ISA hierarchy of classes (called categories), plus a set of atomic relations between them, and inferential rules in the form of simplified horn clauses. Therefore, classes, relations and inferential rules can be defined. An important feature included in SHOE is the ability to make claims about information, as discussed in section 2.

OIL [10], *Ontology Interchange Language*, is a proposal for a joint standard for describing and exchanging ontologies. It is still in an early development phase, and has been designed to provide most of the modelling primitives commonly used in frame-based and description logic ontologies (it is based on existing proposals, such as OKBC , XOL and RDF), with a simple, clean and well defined semantics, and an automated reasoning support.

In OIL, an ontology is a structure made up of several components, organized in three layers: the object level (which deals with instances), the first meta level or ontology definition (which contains the ontology definitions) and the second meta level or ontology container (which contains information about features of the ontology, such as its author). Concepts, relations and functions and axioms can be defined in OIL. The syntax of instances, rules and axioms has not yet been defined.

4 Results and Comparison of Languages

The results of applying the evaluation framework described in section 2 are presented in this section. It is worth mentioning that a common evaluation framework has been used for different knowledge representation languages (and different knowledge representation paradigms, such as frame-based, description logic and object-centered), and that the results have been achieved taking into account the experience of coding, in all the selected languages, an ontology for electronic commerce, which is not shown here due to the lack of space.

The trade-off between the degree of expressiveness and the inference engine of a language (the more expressive, the less inference capabilities) makes it difficult to establish a scoring of languages. Moreover, we claim that different needs in KR exist nowadays for applications, and some languages are more suitable than others for the specific needs of a given application.

When developing domain ontologies for an application, it is not only necessary to study the KR and reasoning needs for the application, but also the KR and reasoning capabilities provided by the languages. This framework will avoid the developer of ontologies taking blind decisions on the selection of the ontology language(s) to use.

Information in tables of the next sections will be filled using '+' to indicate that it is a supported feature in the language, '-' for non supported features, '+/-' for non supported features, but could manage to support it by doing something, '?' when no information is available and 'N.D.' for features which are not restricted, but could be implemented in order to support them. The contents of tables represent the present situation of languages[1] and may change because of the evolution of them.

4.1 Domain Knowledge

Table 1 shows at first glance the main components of the ontology specification languages selected for this study.

Concepts, n-ary relations and instances can be defined easily in almost all languages. In OKBC and FLogic, which are frame-based languages, relations can be represented by using frames, but not as special elements provided by the language. In OKBC, axioms are only supported in the tell&ask part of the API, although neither deductive nor storage guarantees are made for all OKBC implementations.

Table 1. Definition of the main components of domain knowledge

	Onto	OKBC	OCML	LOOM	FLogic	XOL	SHOE	RDF(S)	OIL
Concepts	+	+	+	+	+	+	+	+	+
n-ary relations	+	+/-	+	+	+/-	-	+	+	+
Functions	+	+/-	+	+	+/-	-	-	-	+
Procedures	+	+	+	+	-	-	-	-	-
Instances	+	+	+	+	+	+	+	+	ND
Axioms	+	+/-	+	+	+	-	-	-	ND
Production Rules	-	-	+	+	-	-	-	-	ND
Formal semantics	+	+	+	+	+	+	-	-	-

Functions, procedures and axioms cannot be defined using web-based languages, except for some restricted forms of axioms, such as deductive rules, which are definable in SHOE.

[1] 'Onto' will be used to refer to Ontolingua. RDF(S) is the acronym used to refer to the combination of RDF and RDFS.

It is worth mentioning that procedures are only definable in Lisp-based languages, and production rules are just definable in OCML and LOOM.

An additional row has been added to the table, analysing the presence of a formal semantics: some web-based languages, such as SHOE, RDF(S) and OIL lack of it, whereas traditional languages and XOL provide it.

Concepts. Table 2 summarizes the most important features to be analyzed when describing concepts in an ontology. It is divided in 4 sections: metaclasses, partitions, definition of attributes and definitions of properties of attributes (facets).

Table 2. Definition of concepts

CONCEPTS	Onto	OKBC	OCML	LOOM	FLogic	XOL	SHOE	RDF(S)	OIL
Metaclasses	+	+	+	+	+	+	-	+	-
Partitions	+	-	-	+	-	-	-	-	-
ATTRIBUTES									
Template (instance attrs)	+	+	+	+	+	+	+	+	+
Own (class attrs.)	+	+	+	+	+	+	-	+	+/-
Polymorphic	+	+	+	+	+	-	-	-	+
Local scope	+	+	+	+	+	+	+	+	+
FACETS									
Default slot value	-	+	+	+	+	+	-	-	-
Type constraint	+	+	+	+	+	+	+	+	+
Cardinality constraints	+	+	+	+	+/-	+	-	-	+
Documentation	+	+	+	+	-	+	+	-	+
Procedural knowledge	-	-	+	+	-	-	-	-	-
Adding new facets	+	+	-	+	-	-	-	-	-

Only SHOE and OIL do not allow to define metaclasses, and partitions can only be defined in Ontolingua and LOOM.

Instance attributes and type constraints for attributes can be defined using any of the chosen languages. The results of the rest of the values depend on the languages, although a glance at the table shows us that traditional ontology languages allow us, again, to define more features than web-based languages.

Procedural knowledge inside the definition of attributes is only supported by OCML and LOOM, due to their operational behavior. It must be included in the definition of the OCML´s attributes by means of special keywords, such as *:prove-by* or *:lisp-fun*, not as simple facets, or in the definition of the LOOM's attributes by means of keywords such as :sufficient, :is, :is-primitive or :implies.

FLogic just allows to define the maximum cardinality for slots as 1 or N, while the minimum cardinality is always set to 0.

Table 3. Definition of taxonomies

TAXONOMIES	Onto	OKBC	OCML	LOOM	FLogic	XOL	SHOE	RDF(S)	OIL
Subclass of	+	+	+	+	+	+	+	+	+
Exhaustive subclass partitions	+	-	+/-	+	+/-	-	-	-	-
Disjoint Decompositions	+	-	+/-	+	+/-	-	-	-	+/-
Not subclass of	+/-	-	-	+/-	-	-	-	-	+

Taxonomies. When defining taxonomies, there is just one primitive predefined in all languages and correctly handled by them: *subclass of*. Ontolingua and LOOM are the only languages which have the rest of primitives (except for *not subclass of*, which must be declared using the denial of primitve *subclass-of*). These primitives can be defined as relations in the rest of languages, but as a consequence, there is no special treatment for them. In FLogic, axioms must be defined in order to provide the semantics for them. OIL allows to define the primitive *not subclass-of*; hence it is also possible to define disjoint decompositions.

Relations and Functions. Relations are very important components in an ontology (hence they are supported by almost all the ontology languages), but not every desirable characteristic of relations is implemented in all languages. Functions are not included in some languages.

Table 4. Definition of relations and functions

RELATIONS FUNCTIONS	Onto	OKBC	OCML	LOOM	FLogic	XOL	SHOE	RDF(S)	OIL
Functions as relations	+	+	-	+	+	-	-	-	+
Concepts: unary rels.	+	+	+	+	-	-	+	-	+
Slots: binary rels.	+	+	+	+	-	+	+	+	+
n-ary rels./functs.	+	+/-	+	+	+/-	-	+	+	+/-
Type constraints	+	+	+	+	+	-	+	+	+
Integrity constraints	+	+	+	+	+	-	-	-	-
Operational defs.	-	-	+	+	+	-	-	-	-

Many languages represent concepts as unary relations. Attributes are usually considered as binary relations, except for FLogic, where they are considered as ternary ones.

Great semantic differences are found when analysing the role that functions play in different languages. Some languages, such as KIF (and consequently, Ontolingua), consider functions as a special case of relations in which the nth element of the relation is unique for the n-1 preceding elements. LOOM consider functions as relations where the result can be calculated given the domain arguments. In OCML, functions are considered as modelling elements which play a role which is completely different to the one of relations. In FLogic, functions are considered as methods which are defined inside a concept. Their value is calculated by using a deductive rule associated to the method previously declared.

FLogic, OKBC, RDF(S) and OIL cannot define n-ary relations directly. They must define them as associative classes or by means of several binary relations.

All languages allow the definition of type constraints for arguments, and the main differences among traditional and web-based ontology languages lay on the definition of integrity constraints (the last ones don't allow to define them).

The last comments are on operational definitions for relations: just OCML, LOOM and FLogic allow to define operations inside relations, although there is a difference between them: while LOOM provides operational definitions just for an inferential purpose, OCML also provides non-operational definitions which can be used for representational purposes [17]. In FLogic, this kind of operations must be defined by using axioms, which are defined apart. Ontolingua does not support user-defined Lisp lambda bodies for relations, but it has certain relations that have procedural attachments which are activated by the tell&ask interface (for instance, asking *(+ 3 2 ?x)* will reply with a single binding of *5* for *?x*).

Instances. Instances of concepts and of relations (facts) are supported by all the languages. Claims, however, are just allowed in some of the web-based ontology languages. This is due to the fact that the management of information which comes from different sources is an intrinsic characteristic of the web environment and so these languages have specialised ways to treat this information.

Table 5. Definition of instances

INSTANCES	Onto	OKBC	OCML	LOOM	FLogic	XOL	SHOE	RDF(S)	OIL
Instances of concepts	+	+	+	+	+	+	+	+	ND
Facts	+	+	+	+	+	+	+	+	ND
Claims	-	-	-	-	-	-	+	+	ND

Axioms. This is a good measure of expressiveness. The richest the axioms defined, the more expressive the language is. Ontolingua allows the definition of first-order and second-order logic axioms. OCML and FLogic also allow to define first-order logic axioms independently of the rest of components of the ontology.

LOOM just allows to define first-order logic axioms inside the definitions of relations, concepts and functions.

The rest of languages, except for XOL, only allow restricted types of axioms. So, OKBC just supports a subset of the axioms which can be represented with KIF (and they must be included as a frame or by using the tell&ask interface), and SHOE just allows to define deductive rules. In OIL, the syntax of axioms has not yet been defined, while in RDF(S) several studies are currently trying to specify the syntax and semantics for the most commonly used axioms.

Table 6. Definition of axioms

AXIOMS	Onto	OKBC	OCML	LOOM	FLogic	XOL	SHOE	RDF(S)	OIL
1st-order logic	+	+/-	+	+	+	-	+/-	+/-	ND
2nd order logic	+	+/-	-	-	-	-	-	-	-
Named axioms	+	+	+	-	-	-	-	-	-

Production rules. Production rules are components of an ontology in OCML and LOOM. LOOM distinguishes between purely deductive rules and side-effecting, procedural rules (production rules). OCML makes the same distinction, defining „backward" and „forward" ones. Therefore, OCML and LOOM allow to define the chaining when performing the reasoning with knowledge defined in the ontology.

As far as OIL is concerned, rules are just a weak form of general inclusion axioms.

Finally, SHOE does not allow to define production rules, but inference rules, as stated in the previous section.

Table 7. Definition of rules

PRODUCTION RULES	Onto	OKBC	OCML	LOOM	FLogic	XOL	SHOE	RDF(S)	OIL
PREMISES									
Conjunctive	-	-	+	+	-	-	-	-	ND
Disjunctive	-	-	+	+	-	-	-	-	ND
CONSEQUENT									
Truth values	-	-	-	-	-	-	-	-	ND
Execution of procedures	-	-	+/-	+	-	-	-	-	ND
Updating the KB	-	-	+	+	-	-	-	-	ND

4.2 Reasoning

A clear distinction between KR and reasoning exists for all languages, except for OCML. For instance, Ontolingua is maybe the most expressive of all the languages chosen for this study, but there is no inference engine implemented for it. OCML allows to define some features concerning reasoning inside representational elements (for instance, rules can be defined as backward rules or forward ones, so that the chaining is explicitly defined).

Just FLogic and OIL inference engines are sound and complete, which is a desirable feature, although it can make representation in the language more difficult.

Automatic classifications are performed by description logic-based languages (LOOM and OIL).

The exception handling mechanism is not addressed, in general, by language developers (FLogic is the only one handling exceptions). Works have been carried out in other languages, such as LOOM, to support them.

Table 8. Reasoning mechanisms of the language

REASONING	Onto	OKBC	OCML	LOOM	FLogic	XOL	SHOE	RDF(S)	OIL
INFERENCE ENG.									
Sound	-	-	+	+	+	-	-	-	+
Complete	-	-	-	-	+	-	-	-	+
CLASSIFICATION									
Automatic classif.	-	-	-	+	-	-	-	-	+
EXCEPTIONS									
Exception handling	-	-	-	-	+	-	-	-	-
INHERITANCE									
Monotonic	+	+	+	+	+	ND	+	ND	+
Non-monotonic	+/-	+	+/-	+	+	ND	-	ND	-
Single Inheritance	+	+	+	+	+	ND	+	+	+
Multiple inheritance	+	+	+	+	+	ND	+	+	+
PROCEDURES									
Execution of procedures	+	+	+	+	-	-	-	-	-
CONSTRAINTS									
Constraint checking	+	+	+	+	+	-	-	-	-
CHAINING									
Forward	-	-	+	+	+	-	ND	-	-
Backward	-	-	+	+	+	-	ND	-	-

Single and multiple inheritance is also supported by most of the languages (except for XOL), but conflicts in multiple inheritance are not resolved. All languages are basically monotonic, although they usually include some non-monotonic capabilities.

For instance, the only non-monotonic capabilities present in both Ontolingua and OCML are related to default values for slots and facets. In XOL and RDF specifications there is no explicit definition of the behaviour of inherited values.

All the languages which allow to define procedures, allow to execute them.

Constraint checking is performed in all the traditional ontology languages. Information about constraint checking in XOL is not available. In OKBC, constraint checking is guaranteed to be included in all implementations of it. However, it can be parameterised and even switched off. Constraint checking in SHOE is not performed because conflicts are thought to be frequent in the Web, and resolving them will be problematic. However, type constraint checking is performed when necessary.

Chaining used in SHOE is not defined in the language: freedom exists so that each implementation may choose between any of them. OCML allows to define the chaining of rules when defining them, although default chaining used is the backward one. LOOM performs both kinds of chaining, and FLogic's one is in between.

5 Future Works

Future works in this area will try to identify factors to choose among a set of languages when building a domain ontology for an application. Different needs in KR and reasoning exist, and some languages are more suitable than others. We recommend:

- Web based languages for the interchange of ontologies on the web.
- Traditional languages for the representation – modeling – of ontologies with high expressiveness needs. However, if ontologies are considered just as taxonomies, the use of web-based languages is not a problem.
- For performing reasoning inside agents, XML-based languages do not provide inference engines. However, some of the traditional ontology languages not only provide them but also translators to other computable languages.

Besides, an analysis of the existing tools for editing, managing, integrating and translating ontologies (which would extend the one described in [5]) will be useful for determining the most suitable language for our needs, and studies on the treatment of namespaces in different languages will be also interesting to analyse the easiness of integrating and scaling up ontologies.

Finally, the analysis on how components are codified in each language will also help to face up to the translation problem.

Acknowledgements. This paper would not be possible without comments and feedback of developers and users of the mentioned languages who verified our tables: V. K. Chaudhri (XOL), Stefan Decker (FLogic), Belén Díaz (LOOM), Yolanda Gil (LOOM), Jeff Heflin (SHOE), Ian Horrocks (OIL), Enrico Motta (OCML), James Rice (Ontolingua and OKBC) and Tom Russ (LOOM).

References

1. Amann, B., Fundulaki, I. *Integrating Ontologies and Thesauri to Build RDF Schemas*. 1999.
2. Bray, T., Paoli, J., Sperberg, C. *Extensible Markup Language (XML) 1.0*. W3C Recommendation. Feb 1998. http://www.w3.org/TR/REC-xml.
3. Brickley, D., Guha, R.V. *Resource Description Framework (RDF) Schema Specification*. W3C Proposed Recommendation. March, 1999. http://www.w3.org/TR/PR-rdf-schema.
4. Chaudhri, V., Farquhar, A, Fikes, R., Karp, P., Rice, J. *The Generic Frame Protocol 2.0*. July, 1997.
5. Duineveld, A., Studer, R., Weiden, M, Kenepa, B., Benjamis, R. *WonderTools? A comparative study of ontological engineering tools*. Proceedings of KAW99. Banff. 1999.
6. Farquhar, A., Fikes, R., Rice, J. *The Ontolingua Server: A Tool for Collaborative Ontology Construction*. Proceedings of KAW96. Banff, Canada, 1996.
7. Genesereth, M., *Fikes*, R. *Knowledge Interchange Format*. Technical Report. Computer Science Department. Stanford University. Logic-92-1. 1992.
8. Gruber, R. *A translation approach to portable ontology specification*. Knowledge Acquisition. #5: 199-220. 1993.
9. van Harmelen, F., Fensel, D. *Surveying notations for machine-processable semantics of Web sources*. Proceedings of the IJCAI'99 Workshop on Ontologies & PSMs. 1999.
10. Horrocks, I., Fensel, D., Harmelen, F., Decker, S., Erdmann, M, Klein, M. *OIL in a Nutshell*. Proceedings of the ECAI'00 Workshop on Application of Ontologies and PSMs. Berlin. Germany. August, 2000.
11. Karp, R., Chaudhri, V., Thomere, J. *XOL: An XML-Based Ontology Exchange Language*. July, 1999.
12. Kifer, M., Lausen, G., Wu, J. *Logical Foundations of Object-Oriented and Frame-Based Languages*. Journal of the ACM. 1995.
13. Lassila, O., Swick, R. *Resource Description Framework (RDF) Model and Syntax Specification*. W3C Recommendation. January, 99. http://www.w3.org/TR/PR-rdf-syntax.
14. Lenat, D.B., Guha, R.V. *Building Large Knowledge-based systems. Representation and Inference in the Cyc Project*. Addison-Wesley. *Reading*. Massachusetts. 1990.
15. Luke S., Heflin J. *SHOE 1.01. Proposed Specification*. SHOE Project. February, 2000. http://www.cs.umd.edu/projects/plus/SHOE/spec1.01.htm
16. MacGregor, R. *Inside the LOOM clasifier*. SIGART bulletin. #2(3):70-76. June, 1991.
17. Motta, E. Reusable Components for Knowledge Modelling. IOS Press. Amsterdam. 1999.
18. Schreiber, G., Akkermans, H., Anjewierden, A. *Knowledge engineering and management. The CommonKADS Methodology*. MIT press, Massachussets. 1999.
19. Studer, R., Benjamins, R., Fensel, D. *Knowledge Engineering: Principles and Methods*. DKE 25(1-2).pp:161-197. 1998
20. *Using Protégé-2000 to Edit RDF*. Technical Report. Knowledge Modelling Group. Stanford University. February, 2000. http://www.smi.Stanford.edu/projects/protege/protege-rdf/protege-rdf.html

A Formal Ontology of Properties

Nicola Guarino and Christopher Welty[†]

LADSEB-CNR

Padova, Italy
{guarino,welty}@ladseb.pd.cnr.it
http://www.ladseb.pd.cnr.it/infor/ontology/ontology.html
† on sabbatical from Vassar College, Poughkeepsie, NY

Abstract. A common problem of ontologies is that their taxonomic structure is often poor and confusing. This is typically exemplified by the unrestrained use of subsumption to accomplish a varicty of tasks. In this paper we show how a formal ontology of unary properties can help using the subsumption relation in a disciplined way. This formal ontology is based on some meta-properties built around the fundamental philosophical notions of *identity, unity, essence,* and *dependence*. These meta-properties impose some constraints on the subsumption relation that clarify many misconceptions about taxonomies, facilitating their understanding, comparison and integration.

1 Introduction

Ontologies are becoming increasingly popular in practice, but a principled methodology for building them is still lacking. Perhaps the most common problem we have seen in practice with ontologies is that, while they are expected to bring order and structure to information, their taxonomic structure is often poor and confusing. This is typically exemplified by the unrestrained use of subsumption to accomplish a variety of reasoning and representation tasks. For example, in previous work [5] several unclear uses of the *is-a* relation in existing ontologies were identified, such as:

1. a physical object is an amount of matter (Pangloss)
2. an amount of matter is a physical object (WordNet)

This striking dissimilarity poses a difficult integration problem, since the standard approach of generalizing overlapping concepts would not work, and shows that even the most experienced modelers need some guidance for using subsumption consistently.

Our answer to problems like this lies in a better understanding of the nature of the properties corresponding to taxonomic nodes. To facilitate this understanding, we first introduce some meta-properties resulting from a revisitation of the fundamental philosophical notions of *identity*, *unity, essence*, and *dependence*, and we show how they impose some natural constraints on taxonomic structure that facilitate ontology understanding, comparison and integration. We then explore in a systematic way how these meta-properties can be combined to form different *kinds* of properties. The result of this analysis is a meta-level ontology of properties, which helps to make explicit the meaning every property has within a certain conceptualization.

R. Dieng and O. Corby (Eds.): EKAW 2000, LNAI 1937, pp. 97–112, 2000.

Our formal ontology of properties is part of a methodology for *ontology-driven conceptual analysis* which combines the established tradition of *formal ontology* in Philosophy with the needs of information systems design [4]. An more detailed overview of the methodology can be found in [7].

2 Background

This section provides an overview of previous work, intuitive descriptions of the basic meta-properties used to form our ontology of properties, and a discussion of related notions from other information systems fields.

2.1 Previous Work

The need of distinguishing among different kinds of property is recognized only sporadically in the vast literature on knowledge representation, knowledge engineering, database conceptual modeling, and object oriented modeling.

We briefly discuss in this section a few papers belonging to the knowledge engineering and knowledge representation area. A more complete treatment of previous and related work can be found in [7].

Uschold and Gruninger [17] describe their methodology as a skeleton, acknowledge places in which "flesh" needs to be added. In our experience, one such place is in the area of organizing principles for taxonomies: there are in general a multitude of ways to represent the same knowledge, and there exists very little guidance for judging when one approach is better than another.

Some effort to accomplish this was made several years ago by the IDEF group in establishing the IDEF5 ontology capture method [1]. Of particular relevance to this paper, the IDEF5 method attempts to clarify the difference between *kinds, classes, types, attributes,* and *properties*. The specified differences, however, become vague and confused in a number of places. For example,

> "[Kinds] should not be identified with types or classes. [They share characteristics that are, however] distinguishing features of what are typically called *properties*. Because properties are already a part of [IDEF5], it will ... be convenient to take kinds to be properties of a certain distinguished sort." (p. 16).

This definition still leaves completely open the question of *how* to distinguish kinds from other properties. The authors are clearly aware of subtle differences here, but did not precisely specify what those differences are. We have attempted to do this by first identifying the formal tools required to make such distinctions, and placing these distinctions within our methodology.

A first attempt to draw some formal distinctions among properties for knowledge engineering purposes was made in [2], and later in [3]. The present work can be seen as a radical extension and refinement of the latter paper, with a better account on the underlying philosophical notions (especially identity), a complete combinatorial analysis of the space of property kinds, and more emphasis on the impact of these distinctions on a general methodology for ontological analysis.

One particular kind of property we discuss here, namely *roles*, is discussed in great detail in a recent paper [15].

2.2 The Basic Notions

At the core of our methodology are three fundamental – and yet intimately related - philosophical notions: *identity*, *unity*, and *essence* (a fourth notion, *dependence*, will be discussed later). The notion of identity we adopt here is based on intuitions about how we, as cognitive agents, in general interact with (and in particular recognize) individual entities in the world around us. It fits therefore the paradigm of *descriptive metaphysics* [16], whose goal is to provide a framework in which the world *as perceived by us* can be analyzed and described. Despite its fundamental importance in Philosophy, it has been slow in making its way into the practice of conceptual modeling for information systems, where the goals of analyzing and describing the world are ostensibly the same.

The first step in understanding the intuitions behind identity requires considering the distinctions and similarities between *identity* and *unity*. These notions are different, albeit closely related and often confused under a generic notion of identity. Strictly speaking, identity is related to the problem of distinguishing a specific instance of a certain class from other instances of that class by means of a *characteristic property*, which is unique for *it* (that *whole* instance). Unity, on the other hand, is related to the problem of distinguishing the *parts* of an instance from the rest of the world by means of a *unifying relation* that binds them together (not involving anything else). For example, asking "Is that my dog?" would be a problem of identity, whereas asking "is the collar part of my dog?" would be a problem of unity.

Both notions encounter problems when time is involved. The classical one is that of *identity through change*: in order to account for common sense, we need to admit that an individual may remain *the same* while exhibiting different properties at different times. But which properties can change, and which must not? And how can we reidentify an instance of a certain property after some time? The former issue leads to the notion of an *essential property*, on which we base the definition of *rigidity*, discussed below, while the latter is related to the distinction between *synchronic* and *diachronic* identity. An extensive analysis of these issues in the context of conceptual modeling has been made elsewhere [6], and further development of meta-properties based on unity which are used by other parts of our methodology can be found in [8].

Finally, it is important to note that our identity judgements ultimately depend on our *conceptualization* of the world [4]. This means that, while we shall use examples to clarify the notions central to our analysis, *the examples themselves will not be the point of this paper*. For example, the decision as to whether a cat remains the same cat after it loses its tail, or whether a statue is identical with the marble it is made of, are ultimately the result of our sensory system, our culture, etc. The aim of the present analysis is to clarify the formal tools that can both make such assumptions explicit, and reveal the logical consequences of them. When we say, e.g. that "having the same fingerprint" may be considered an identity criterion for *PERSON*, we do *not* mean to claim this is the universal identity criterion for *PERSON*s, but that *if this were* to be taken as an identity criterion in some conceptualization, what would that mean for the property, for its instances, and its relationships to other properties?

2.3 Related Notions

Identity has many analogies in conceptual modeling for databases, knowledge bases, object-oriented, and classical information systems, however none of them completely captures the notion we present here. We discuss some of these cases below.

2.3.1 Membership conditions.

In description logics, conceptual models usually focus on the sufficient and necessary criteria for class *membership*, that is, recognizing instances of certain classes. This is not identity, however, as it does not describe how instances of the same class are to be told apart. This is a common confusion that is important to keep clear: membership conditions determine when an entity is an instance of a class, i.e. they can be used to answer the question, "Is that *a* dog?" but not, "Is that *my* dog?"

2.3.2 Globally Unique IDs.

In object-oriented systems, uniquely identifying an object (as a collection of data) is critical, in particular when data is persistent or can be distributed [18]. In databases, *globally unique id's* have been introduced into most commercial systems to address this issue. These solutions provide a notion of identity for the descriptions, for the units of data (objects or records), but not for the entities they describe. It still leaves open the possibility that two (or more) descriptions may refer to the same *entity*, and it is this entity that our notion of identity is concerned with. In other words, globally unique IDs can be used to answer, "Is this the same description of a dog?" but not, "Is this my dog."

2.3.3 Primary Keys.

Some object-oriented languages provide a facility for overloading or locally defining the equality predicate for a class. In standard database analysis, introducing new tables requires finding unique keys either as single fields or combinations of fields in a record. These two similar notions very closely approach our notion of identity as they do offer evidence towards determining when two descriptions refer to the same entity. There is a very subtle difference, however, which we will attempt to briefly describe here and which should become more clear with the examples at the end of the paper.

Understanding this subtle difference first requires understanding the difference between what we will call *intrinsic* and *extrinsic* properties. An intrinsic property is typically something inherent to an individual, not dependent on other individuals, such as having a heart or having a fingerprint. Extrinsic properties are not inherent, and they have a relational nature, like "being a friend of John". Among these, there are some that are typically assigned by external agents or agencies, such as having a specific social security number, having a specific customer i.d., even having a specific name.

Primary (and candidate) keys and overloaded equality operators are typically based on the latter kind of extrinsic properties that are required by a system to be unique. In many cases, information systems designers add these extrinsic properties simply as an escape from solving (often very difficult) identity problems. Our notion of identity is based mainly on intrinsic properties—we are interested in analyzing the inherent nature of entities and believe this is important for understanding a domain.

This is not to say that the former type of analysis never uses intrinsic properties, nor that the latter never uses extrinsic ones – it is merely a question of emphasis. Furthermore, our analysis is often based on information which *may not be represented in the implemented system*, whereas the primary key notion can never use such information. For example, we may claim as part of our analysis that people are uniquely identified by their brain, but this information would not appear in the final system we are designing.

Our notion of identity and the notion of primary keys are not incompatible, nor are they disjoint, and in practice conceptual modelers will often need both.

3 The Formal Tools of Ontological Analysis

In this section we shall present a formal analysis of the basic notions discussed above, and we shall introduce a set of *meta-properties* that represent the behaviour of a property with respect to these notions. Our goal is to show how these meta-properties impose some constraints on the way subsumption is used to model a domain.

Our analysis relies on certain fairly standard conventions and notations in logic and modal logic, which are described in more detail in [8]. It is important to note that our use of *meta-properties* does not require second-order reasoning, and this is also explained further in [8].

We shall denote primitive meta-properties by bold letters preceded by the sign "+", "-","¬" or "~" which will be described for each meta-property. We use the notation $\phi^{\mathbf{M}}$ to indicate that the property ϕ has the meta-property **M**.

3.1 Rigidity

A rigid property was defined in [3] as follows:

Definition 1 A *rigid property* is a property that is essential to *all* its instances, i.e. $\forall x\, \phi(x) \rightarrow \Box\, \phi(x)$.

from this it trivially follows through negation that

Definition 2 A *non-rigid property* is a property that is not essential to *some* of its instances, i.e. $\exists x\, \phi(x) \wedge \neg\Box\, \phi(x)$.

For example, we normally think of *PERSON* as rigid; if *x* is an instance of *PERSON*, it must be an instance of *PERSON* in every possible world. The *STUDENT* property, on the other hand, is normally not rigid; we can easily imagine an entity moving in and out of the *STUDENT* property while being the same individual. This notion was later refined in [4]:

Definition 3 An anti-rigid property is a property that is not essential to *all* its instances, i.e. $\forall x\, \phi(x) \rightarrow \neg\Box\, \phi(x)$.

Definition 4 A *semi-rigid property* is a property that is non-rigid but not anti-rigid.

Rigid properties are marked with the meta-property **+R**, anti-rigid with **~R**, non-rigid with **-R**, semi-rigid with **¬R**.

The notion of anti-rigidity was added to gain a further restriction. The **~R** meta-property is subsumed by **–R**, but is stronger, as the former constrains all instances of a property and the latter, as the simple negation of **+R**, constrains at least one instance.

Anti-rigidity attempts to capture the intuition that all instances of certain properties must possibly not be instances of that property. Consider the property *STUDENT*, for example: in its normal usage, every instance of student is not necessarily so.

Rigidity as a meta-property is not "inherited" by sub-properties of properties that carry it, e.g. if we have $PERSON^{+R}$ and $\forall x\, STUDENT(x) \rightarrow PERSON(x)$ then we know that all instances of *STUDENT* are necessarily instances of *PERSON*, but not *necessarily* (in the modal sense) instances of *STUDENT*, and we furthermore may assert $STUDENT^{\sim R}$. In simpler terms, an instance of *STUDENT* can cease to be a student but may not cease to be a person.

3.2 Identity

In the philosophical literature, an *identity condition* (IC) for a arbitrary property ϕ is usually defined as a suitable relation ρ satisfying the following formula:

$$\phi(x) \wedge \phi(y) \rightarrow (\rho(x, y) \leftrightarrow x = y) \tag{1}$$

Since identity is an equivalence relation, it follows that ρ restricted to ϕ must also be an equivalence relation. For example, the property *PERSON* can be seen as carrying an IC if relations like *having-the-same-SSN* or *having-the-same-fingerprints* are assumed to satisfy (1).

As discussed in more detail elsewhere [6], the above formulation has some problems, in our opinion. The first problem is related to the need of distinguishing between *supplying* an IC and simply *carrying* an IC: it seems that non-rigid properties like *STUDENT* can only carry their ICs, inheriting those supplied by their subsuming rigid properties like *PERSON*. The intuition behind this is that, since the same person can be a student at different times in different schools, an IC allegedly supplied by *STUDENT* (say, having the same registration number) may be only local, within a certain studenthood experience. It would not supply therefore a "global" condition for identity, satisfying (1) only as a sufficient condition, not as a necessary one.

The second problem regards the nature of the ρ relation: what makes it an IC, and how can we index it with respect to time to account for the difference between *synchronic* and *diachronic* identity?

Finally, deciding whether a property carries an IC may be difficult, since finding a ρ that is both necessary *and* sufficient for identity is often hard, especially for natural kinds and artifacts.

For these reasons, we introduce below a notion of identity conditions that have the following characteristics: i) they can only be supplied by rigid properties; ii) they reformulate the ρ relation above in terms of a formula that explicitly takes two different times into account, allowing the distinction between synchronic (same time) and diachronic (different times) identity; iii) they can be only sufficient or only necessary.

Definition 5 A rigid property ϕ *carries the necessary IC* $\Gamma(x,y,t,t')$ if Γ contains x,y,t,t' as the only free variables, and:

$$\neg\forall xytt'(\Gamma(x,y,t,t') \leftrightarrow x=y) \tag{2}$$

$$E(x,t) \wedge \phi(x,t) \wedge E(y,t') \wedge \phi(y,t') \wedge x=y \rightarrow \Gamma(x,y,t,t') \tag{3}$$

$$\neg\forall xy(\mathrm{E}(x,t) \wedge \phi(x,t) \wedge \mathrm{E}(y,t) \wedge \phi(y,t') \rightarrow \Gamma(x,y,t,t')) \tag{4}$$

Definition 6 A rigid property ϕ *carries the sufficient IC* $\Gamma(x,y,t,t')$ if Γ contains x,y,t,t' as the only free variables, satisfies (2), and:

$$\mathrm{E}(x,t) \wedge \phi(x,t) \wedge \mathrm{E}(y,t') \wedge \phi(y,t') \wedge \Gamma(x,y,t,t') \rightarrow x=y \tag{5}$$

$$\exists xytt'\, \Gamma(x,y,t,t'). \tag{6}$$

In the formulas above, E is a predicate for *actual existence* at time t (see [8] for further clarification of our usage, which is based on [9]), (2) guarantees that Γ is bound to identity under a certain sortal, and not to arbitrary identity, (4) is needed to guarantee that the last conjunct in (3) is relevant and not tautological, and (6) ensures that Γ is not trivially false.

ICs are "inherited" along a hierarchy of properties, in the sense that, if $\phi(x) \rightarrow \varphi(x)$ and, for example, Γ is a necessary IC for φ, then (3) above will hold for ϕ replacing φ.

Definition 7 A non-rigid property *carries* an IC Γ iff it is subsumed by a rigid property carrying Γ.

Any property carrying an IC is marked with the meta-property **+I** (**-I** otherwise).

Definition 8 A property ϕ *supplies* an IC Γ iff i) it is rigid; ii) it carries Γ; and iii) Γ is not carried by *all* the properties subsuming ϕ. This means that, if ϕ inherits different (but compatible) ICs from multiple properties, it still counts as supplying an IC.

Any property supplying an IC is marked with the meta-property **+O** (**-O** otherwise). The letter "O" is a mnemonic for "own identity".

From the above definitions, it is obvious that **+O** implies **+I** and **+R**. For example, both *PERSON* and *STUDENT* do carry identity (they are therefore **+I**), but only the former *supplies* it (**+O**).

Definition 9 Any property carrying an IC (**+I**) is called a *sortal* [16].

Notice that to recognize that a property is a sortal we are not forced to know *which* IC it carries: as we shall see, distinguishing between sortals and non-sortals is often enough to start bringing order to taxonomies.

3.3 Dependence

The final meta-property we employ as a formal ontological tool is based on the notion of dependence. This is a very general notion, whose various forms and variations are discussed in detail in [14]. We shall introduce here a specific kind of dependence, based on Simons' *notional dependence:*

Definition 10 A property ϕ is *externally dependent* on a property ψ if, for all its instances x, necessarily some instance of ψ must exist, which is not a part nor a constituent of x:

$$\forall x \Box (\phi(x) \rightarrow \exists y\, \psi(y) \wedge \neg P(y,x) \wedge \neg C(y,x)) \tag{7}$$

The part and constituent relations are discussed further in [8]. An externally dependent property is marked with the meta-property **+D** (**-D** otherwise).

Intuitively, we say that, for example, *PARENT* is externally dependent on *CHILD* (one can not be a parent without having a child), but *PERSON* is not externally dependent on heart nor on body (because any person has a heart as a part and is constituted of a body).

In addition to excluding parts and constituents, a more rigorous definition must exclude qualities (such as colors), things which necessarily exist (such as the universe), and cases where ψ is subsumed by ϕ (since this would make ϕ dependent on itself).

4 Constraints and Assumptions

Let us now discuss the constraints that follow from our definitions, which are largely overlooked in many practical cases [5]. In the following, we take ϕ and ψ to be arbitrary properties.

$$\phi^{\sim R} \text{ can't subsume } \psi^{+R} \tag{8}$$

This constraint follows immediately from Definitions 1-3. As we shall see, this means that if *PERSON*$^{+R}$ and *AGENT*$^{\sim R}$, the latter cannot subsume the former.

$$\phi^{+I} \text{ can't subsume } \psi^{-I} \tag{9}$$

$$\text{Properties with incompatible ICs are disjoint.} \tag{10}$$

(9) follows immediately from our definitions, while (10) deserves some comment. An important point is the difference between *different* and *incompatible* ICs, related to the fact that they can be inherited and specialized along taxonomies. Consider the domain of abstract geometrical figures, for example, where the property *POLYGON* subsumes *TRIANGLE*. A necessary and sufficient IC for polygons is, “Having the same edges and the same angles”. On the other hand, an *additional* necessary and sufficient IC for triangles is, “Having two edges and their internal angle in common” (note that this condition is only-necessary for polygons). So the two properties have *different* ICs (although they have one IC in common), but their extensions are not disjoint. On the other hand, consider *AMOUNT OF MATTER* and *PERSON*. If we admit mereological extensionality for the former but not for the latter (since persons can replace their parts), they have *incompatible* ICs, so they must be disjoint (in this case, we can’t say that a person is an amount of matter).

$$\phi^{+D} \text{ can't subsume } \psi^{-D} \tag{11}$$

This constraint trivially follows from our definitions.

Finally, we make the following assumptions regarding identity, adapted from [12]:

- *Sortal Individuation.* Every domain element must instantiate some property carrying an IC (**+I**). In this way we satisfy Quine’s dictum “No entity without identity” [13].

- *Sortal Expandability.* If two entities (instances of different properties) are the same, they must be instances of a single property carrying a condition for their identity. In other words, every entity must instantiate at least one rigid property.

5 Property Kinds

We now explore the various combinations of meta-properties discussed in the previous section in order to characterize some basic kinds of properties that usually appear in taxonomies.

5.1 A systematic analysis

Analyzing properties based exclusively on the meta-properties discussed in the previous section gives us 24 potential categories (**I, O, D** are boolean, **R** partitions into three cases, **+R**, **~R**, **¬R**). Since **+O→+I** and **+O→+R** we reduce the number to 14, shown in Table 1, that collapse into the 8 relevant classes of properties discussed below. Each class is labelled with what we consider as the prototypical kind of property belonging to that class. In some cases (for the non-rigid properties), these labels may not be precise, in the sense that further investigation is needed to understand the nature of non-prototypical properties belonging to a certain class.

Table 1: Formal ontological property classifications.

<table>
<tr><td rowspan="2">+O</td><td rowspan="2">+I</td><td rowspan="2">+R</td><td>+D</td><td rowspan="2">Type</td><td rowspan="8">Sortal</td></tr>
<tr><td>-D</td></tr>
<tr><td rowspan="2">-O</td><td rowspan="2">+I</td><td rowspan="2">+R</td><td>+D</td><td rowspan="2">Quasi-type</td></tr>
<tr><td>-D</td></tr>
<tr><td>-O</td><td>+I</td><td>~R</td><td>+D</td><td>Material role</td></tr>
<tr><td>-O</td><td>+I</td><td>~R</td><td>-D</td><td>Phased sortal</td></tr>
<tr><td rowspan="2">-O</td><td rowspan="2">+I</td><td rowspan="2">¬R</td><td>+D</td><td rowspan="2">Mixin</td></tr>
<tr><td>-D</td></tr>
<tr><td rowspan="2">-O</td><td rowspan="2">-I</td><td rowspan="2">+R</td><td>+D</td><td rowspan="2">Category</td><td rowspan="5">Non-sortal</td></tr>
<tr><td>-D</td></tr>
<tr><td>-O</td><td>-I</td><td>~R</td><td>+D</td><td>Formal Role</td></tr>
<tr><td rowspan="4">-O</td><td rowspan="4">-I</td><td>~R</td><td>-D</td><td rowspan="4">Attribution</td></tr>
<tr><td rowspan="2">¬R</td><td>+D</td></tr>
<tr><td>-D</td><td></td></tr>
<tr><td rowspan="3">+O</td><td>-I</td><td></td><td></td><td rowspan="3">incoherent</td><td rowspan="3"></td></tr>
<tr><td rowspan="2">+I</td><td>~R</td><td rowspan="2"></td></tr>
<tr><td>-R</td></tr>
</table>

The taxonomic structure of these classifications is shown in Figure 1. At the top level (the left), we distinguish between *sortal* and *non-sortal* properties, based on the presence or absence of ICs (the meta-property **+I**). *Roles* group together anti-rigid, dependent properties (**~R+D**), and split into *formal roles* (**-I**) and *material roles* (**+I**). Sortals are divided into *rigid* (+**R**) and *non-rigid* (-**R**), and non-rigid sortals have a further specialization for *anti-rigid* (~**R**). This taxonomy refines and extends the work presented in [2] and [3].

The next sections describe the meta-properties of each of the classes above, as well as the intuitive definition, where properties of that kind should appear in a taxonomy (see Figure 2), and examples of the property kind.

5.1.1 Categories

Categories are properties that are rigid but do not carry identity. Since they can not be subsumed by sortals, categories are normally the highest level properties in an ontology. They carve the domain into useful segments, and they are often primitive, in the sense that no necessary and sufficient membership conditions can be defined for them.

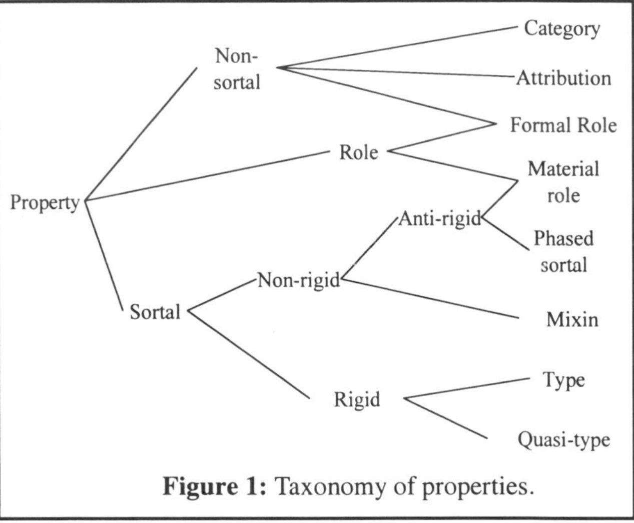

Figure 1: Taxonomy of properties.

According to our constraints, categories can be subsumed by other categories and attributions, and they can subsume any other kind of property. In our experience, categories tend naturally to form a tree. We recommend that at least the topmost categories be disjoint. The archetypal category may be *ENTITY*, other examples may be *CONCRETE ENTITY* and *ABSTRACT ENTITY*.

5.1.2 Types

Types are rigid properties that supply their own identity. They are the most important properties in an ontology, being the only ones that *supply* identity (+**O**), and as a consequence of the Sortal Individuation assumption, *every domain element must instantiate at least one type*. Intuitively, types should be used to represent the main properties in an ontology – not the highest level nor the lowest, simply the properties that will be used the most when describing the domain.

Types can only be subsumed by categories, other types, quasi-types, and attributions. They can subsume any kind of sortal property, and can not subsume any non-sortal properties. We recommend that types by subsumed by at least one category.

Types in general should represent the major properties in an ontology, in our methodology we recommend starting by enumerating the types in a system, since again they should account for every entity. Examples may be *PERSON*, *CAT*, and *WATER*.

Top-types are types that are directly subsumed by categories, and are therefore the highest level (most general) properties that supply identity. We recommend that top-types be subsumed *only* by categories, and furthermore that all top-types be disjoint to the degree possible. Examples may be *LIVING-BEING* or *AMOUNT-OF-MATTER*.

5.1.3 Quasi-Types

Quasi-types are sortals that do not *supply* identity, but nevertheless carry it and are rigid. They often serve a highly organizational purpose by grouping entities based on useful combinations of properties that do no affect identity. Often they tend to introduce new necessary and sufficient *membership* conditions (see the Related Notions section).

Quasi-types can be subsumed by categories, types, attributions, and mixins, and they must be subsumed by at least one type (in order to inherit identity). Quasi-types can subsume any sortal property, and can not subsume non-sortal properties. Like types, we do not recommend subsuming quasi-types by mixins, and recommend minimizing the subsumption of quasi-types by attributions. Examples may be *INVERTEBRATE-ANIMAL*, or *HERBIVORE*.

5.1.4 Backbone Properties

Collectively, the rigid properties in an ontology (categories, types, and quasi-types) form what we call the *backbone taxonomy*. This is of high organizational importance in any ontology, since it identifies the properties that can not change. Backbone properties are also considerable value in understanding a ontology, as they form a subset of all the properties in the ontology and carry a relevant structural information. The backbone carves the domain into useful segments through the categories, identifies every kind of entity in the domain through the types, and contains the most useful groupings of entities through the quasi-types.

5.1.5 Formal Roles

In general, roles are properties expressing the *part played* by one entity in an event, often exemplifying a particular relationship between two or more entities. All roles are anti-rigid and dependent (compare this with [2]). In addition, *formal* roles do not carry identity, and intuitively represent the most generic roles that may form the top level of role hierarchies. For example, the property of being the *PATIENT* of an action is a formal role, since there are no common identity criteria for recipients in general (they may be objects, people, etc.).

Formal roles can be subsumed only by other formal roles, attributions, or categories, and can subsume any non-rigid dependent property, therefore dependent attributions, dependent mixins, and material roles. We recommend that formal roles be used only to organize role taxonomies, i.e. that they not subsume mixins or attributions. Examples include *PATIENT* and *INSTRUMENT*.

To capture our intuitions about formal roles (and roles in general) we may need more than the simple combinations of meta-properties presented here. There might be properties like *BEING LOVED BY JOHN* that seem to belong to the same class as formal roles, without sharing their intuitions. A precise characterization of roles is probably still an open issue (see [2], [15]).

5.1.6 Material Roles

Material roles are anti-rigid and dependent, but inherit identity conditions from some type. Material roles represent roles that are constrained to particular kinds of entities. Intuitively, when a property is recognized to be a role, there should be some event that the role corresponds to.

Material roles can be subsumed by anything, and must be subsumed by at least one type (to inherit identity). They can subsume other material roles, and dependent mixins. We recommend that material roles only subsume other material roles, and that they be subsumed only by roles and backbone properties.

The prototypical material role is *STUDENT,* which would be subsumed by *PERSON* and corresponds to the event *enroll*, other examples may be *MARRIED*, and *FOOD*.

5.1.7 Phased Sortals

Phased sortals [19] are an interesting kind of property that come from combining a requirement for carrying identity with anti-rigidity and independence. Although they do not supply a *global* IC, they supply a *local* IC, corresponding to a certain temporal phase of their instances. Intuitively, they account for entities which naturally, yet fundamentally, change some of their identity criteria over time and in discrete phases. For example, an individual may at one time be a *CATERPILLAR* and at another time be a *BUTTERFLY*. Some local ICs change across these phases, but it is still the same entity and this fact should be reflected in some global ICs.

Phased sortals can be subsumed by anything independent, and can subsume anything non-rigid. According to the Sortal Expandability principle, we have that phased sortals must be subsumed by a type, because it must be possible to determine that they are the same entity at these two times. We recommend that phased sortals be subsumed by backbone properties and that they subsume other phased sortals and material roles. Furthermore we strongly recommend that all the phases of a phased sortal be subsumed by a type or quasi-type that subsumes only them.

Phased sortal properties should never appear alone, each phased sortal must have at least one other phase into which it changes, but note that this does not make it dependent –the properties for each phase will not be instantiated by different entities.

The prototypical examples of phased sortals are *CATERPILLAR* and *BUTTERFLY*. True phased sortals seem rare outside of biology, and often properties classified as phased sortals are single properties into which multiple meanings have been collapsed (see for instance the example of *COUNTRY* discussed in (7), which might be–mistakenly–classified as **~R** thinking that a region may become a country and cease to be a country, while a further analysis reveals that geographical regions and countries are disjoint–although related–entities).

Other properties that belong to the same class as phased sortals might be those resulting from a conjunction of attributions and types, like for instance *RED APPLE:* despite *RED* is usually conceived as semi-rigid (since it may be essential for some instances but not for all), it seems plausible to assume that its restriction to *APPLE* becomes anti-rigid (because every red apple might become brown, for instance). In this case, *RED APPLE* is **~R +I -D**, being therefore a phased sortal.

5.1.8 Attributions

Attributions are the most relevant example of non-sortal properties that are either semi-rigid, or anti-rigid and independent. They intuitively represent values of *attributes* (or *qualities*) like *color, shape,* etc.

The possibility exists that attributions should be always anti-rigid, but we have left it open for now, pending further analysis of cases where types have attributions as essential properties. One might say that e.g. instances of the type *HAMMER* necessarily have the property *HARD*, whereas other types such as *SPONGE* have the property conditionally (a dry sponge is hard, a wet sponge is soft).

Attributions can subsume anything, and can be subsumed by any non-sortal properties. We recommend that attributions subsume only mixins, discussed below, or other attributions, and that they be subsumed only by categories.

Examples include *RED, TRIANGULAR,* and *MALE* (assuming that it is possible to change sex).

5.1.9 Mixins

We generically call *mixins* all the properties that carry identity and are semi-rigid. These properties intuitively represent various combinations (disjunctions or conjunctions) of rigid and non-rigid properties.

Mixins can be subsumed by anything, and can subsume any sortal property. They must be subsumed by at least one sortal. We recommend that mixins not subsume rigid properties. In a sense, mixins should "hang off" the backbone.

Mixins are a difficult kind of property because they are so weakly constrained by our meta-properties. For example, the property *CAT-OR-WEAPON*, subsuming the type *CAT* and the role *WEAPON*, is semi-rigid; some of its instances (instances of *CAT*) are necessarily so, others (instances of *WEAPON* and not *CAT*) are not. We strongly discourage the use of these artificial properties, and in general recommend minimizing the use of mixins. While they may seem useful in large ontologies for organization, we have found unrestrained proliferation of this kind of property to generate confusion more than order.

6 Methodology

Our methodology at the moment focuses mainly on precisely describing properties and clarifying their taxonomic structure. One result of this analysis is what we believe to be "cleaner" taxonomies. In this section we briefly discuss the part played by the formal ontology of properties in the methodology, and then present a short example that uses our meta-property analysis to "clean" a taxonomy.

6.1 The Role of Property Kinds

In general, the ideal structure of a clean taxonomy based on our property kinds is shown in Figure 2. The intuition presented here is that non-rigid properties should "hang off" the backbone taxonomy, and should not subsume anything in the backbone. This makes it possible to easily view the rigid properties without the non-rigid ones, offering a simplified view that still describes every entity in the domain. This structure is not always possible to achieve strictly, but approaching it is desirable.

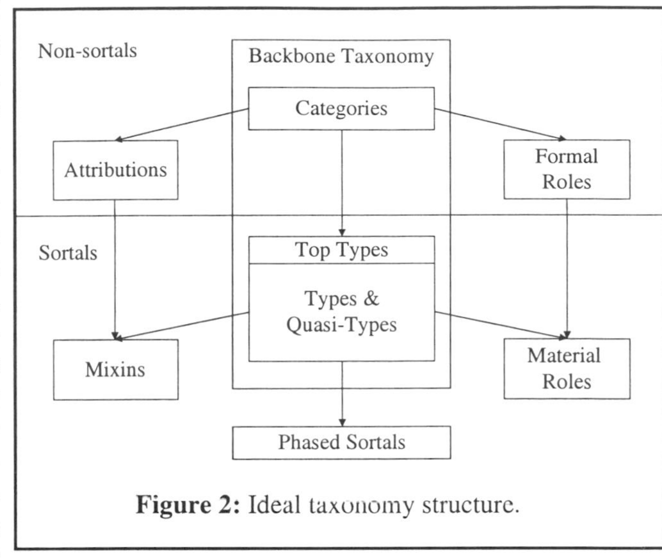

Figure 2: Ideal taxonomy structure.

In addition to providing this idealized structure, our formal ontology of properties also adds to a modeler's ability to specify the meaning of properties in an ontology, since the definition of each property kind includes an intuitive and domain-independent description of what part that kind of property should play in an ontology.

7 Conclusions

We have presented here the basic steps of a methodology for ontology design founded on a formal ontology of properties, which is itself built on a core set of meta properties. These meta-properties are formalizations of the basic notions of identity, rigidity, and dependence. We have seen how a rigorous analysis based on these notions offers two main advantages to the knowledge engineer:

- It results in a cleaner taxonomy, due to the semantic constraints imposed on the *is-a* relation;
- The backbone taxonomy is identified.
- It forces the analyst to make ontological commitments explicit, clarifying the intended meaning of the concepts used and producing therefore a more reusable ontology.

8 Acknowledgments

We are indebted to Bill Andersen, Massimiliano Carrara, Pierdaniele Giaretta, Dario Maguolo, Claudio Masolo, Chris Partridge, and Mike Uschold for their useful comments on earlier versions of this paper.

References

1. Benjamin, P. C., Menzel, C. P., Mayer, R. J., Fillion, F., Futrell, M. T., deWitte, P. S., and Lingineni, M. 1994. IDEF5 Method Report. Knowledge Based Systems, Inc., September 21, 1994.
2. Guarino, N. 1992. Concepts, Attributes and Arbitrary Relations: Some Linguistic and Ontological Criteria for Structuring Knowledge Bases. Data & Knowledge Engineering, 8(2): 249-261.
3. Guarino, N., Carrara, M., and Giaretta, P. 1994. An Ontology of Meta-Level Categories. *Principles of Knowledge Representation and Reasoning: Proceedings of the Fourth International Conference (KR94).* Morgan Kaufmann.
4. Guarino, N. 1998. Some Ontological Principles for Designing Upper Level Lexical Resources. *Proceedings of LREC-98.*
5. Guarino, N. 1999. The Role of Identity Conditions in Ontology Design. In *Proceedings of IJCAI-99 workshop on Ontologies and Problem-Solving Methods: Lessons Learned and Future Trends*. Stockholm, Sweden, IJCAI, Inc.: 2-1 2-7.
6. Guarino, N., and Welty, C. 2000a. Identity, Unity, and Individuality: Towards a Formal Toolkit for Ontological Analysis. In *Proceedings of ECAI-2000.* IOS Press, Amsterdam. Available from http://www.ladseb.pd.cnr.it/infor/ontology/Papers/OntologyPapers.html.
7. Guarino, N., and Welty, C. 2000b. Ontological Analysis of Taxonomic Relationships. In *Proceedings of ER-2000: The Conference on Conceptual Modeling.* Available from http://www.ladseb.pd.cnr.it/infor/ontology/Papers/OntologyPapers.html.
8. Guarino, N., and Welty, C. 2000c. Towards a methodology for ontology-based model engineering. In *Proceedings of the ECOOP-2000 Workshop on Model Engineering.* Available from http://www.ladseb.pd.cnr.it/infor/ontology/Papers/OntologyPapers.html.
9. Hirst, G. 1991. Existence Assumptions in Knowledge Representation. *Artificial Intelligence*, 49: 199-242.
10. Huitt, R., and Wilde, N. 1992. Maintenance Support for Object-Oriented Programs. *IEEE Transactions on Software Engineering*. **18**(12).
11. Lewis, D. 1983. New Work for a Theory of Universals. *Australasian Journal of Philosophy*, **61**(4).
12. Lowe, E. J. 1989. *Kinds of Being. A Study of Individuation, Identity and the Logic of Sortal Terms.* Basil Blackwell, Oxford.
13. Quine, W. V. O. 1969. *Ontological Relativity and Other Essays*. Columbia University Press, New York, London.
14. Simons, P. 1987. *Parts: a Study in Ontology.* Clarendon Press, Oxford.
15. Steimann, F. 2000. On the Representation of Roles in OBject-Oriented and Conceptual Modelling. *Data and Knowledge Engineering* (to appear).
16. Strawson, P. F. 1959. *Individuals. An Essay in Descriptive Metaphysics.* Routledge, London and New York.
17. Uschold, M. and Gruninger, M. 1996. Ontologies: Principles, Methods and Applications. *The Knowledge Engineering Review*, 11(2): 93-136.

18. Wieringa, R., De Jonge, W., and Spruit, P. 1994. Roles and dynamic subclasses: a modal logic approach. In *Proceedings of European Conference on Object-Oriented Programming*. Bologna.
19. Wiggins, D. 1980. *Sameness and Substance.* Blackwell, Oxford.

Construction and Deployment of a Plant Ontology

Riichiro Mizoguchi, Kouji Kozaki, Toshinobu Sano, and Yoshinobu Kitamura

ISIR, Osaka University
8-1 Mihogaoka, Ibaraki, Osaka, 567-0047 Japan
{miz, kozaki, sanop, kita}@ei.sanken.osaka-u.ac.jp

Abstract. Although the necessity of an ontology and ontological engineering is well-understood, there has been few success stories about ontology construction and its deployment to date. This paper presents an activity of ontology construction and its deployment in an interface system for an oil-refinery plant operation which has been done under the umbrella of Human-Media Project for four years. It also describes the reasons why we need an ontology, what ontology we built, what environment we used for building the ontology and how the ontology is used in the system. The interface has been developed intended to establish a sophisticated technology for advanced interface for plant operators and consists of several agents. The system has been implemented and preliminary evaluation has been done successfully.

Introduction

Ontological engineering [1] is a successor of knowledge engineering which has been considered as a technology for building knowledge-intensive systems. Although knowledge engineering has contributed to eliciting expertise, organizing it into a computational structure, and building knowledge bases, AI researchers have noticed the necessity of a more robust and theoretically sound engineering which enables knowledge sharing/reuse and formulation of the problem solving process itself. Knowledge engineering has thus developed into "ontological engineering" where "ontology" is the key concept to investigate.

Although the necessity of an ontology and ontological engineering is well-understood, there has been few success stories about ontology construction and its deployment to date. This paper presents an activity of ontology construction and its deployment in Oil-refinery plant which has been done under the umbrella of Human-Media Project for four years.

Human Media project, which is a MITI(Japanese Ministry of International Trade and Industries) funded national project, is intended to invent an innovative media technology for happier human life in the coming information society in 21st century. It is something an integration of the three representative media such as Knowledge media, Virtual media and Kansei media. "Kansei" is a Japanese term which roughly means the sixth or seventh sense sensing for satisfaction, comfort, beauty, softness, etc. Our ontology construction activities have been done in the project named "Development of a human interface for the next generation plant operation" running as a subproject of Human Media project.

R. Dieng and O. Corby (Eds.): EKAW 2000, LNAI 1937, pp. 113-128, 2000.

The interface for oil-refinery plant operation has been developed intended to establish a sophisticated technology for advanced interface for plant operators and consists of Interface agent: IA, Virtual plant agent: VPA, Semantic information presentation agent: SIA, Ontology server: OS and Distributed collaboration infrastructure: DCI. The last two are mainly for issues related to system building, while the first three are related directly to interface issues. OS has been developed employing ontological engineering as a key knowledge media technology[2].

This paper presents the reasons why we need an ontology, what ontology we built, what environment we used for building the ontology and how the ontology is used in the system. The next section discusses a short introduction to ontology. Section 3 explains the role of the plant ontology. Detailed description of the plant ontology we built is given in Section 4. Section 5 presents the explanation of its use in the entire interface system we are developing. Section 6 describes an ontology development environment, Hozo, we developed and used for building the plant ontology. Hozo has been extensively used in many other projects in our group and the next version is being developed based on our experience and uses' feedback. Section 7 discusses the related work followed by conclusion.

What Is Ontological Engineering and What Is an Ontology?

Roughly speaking, ontologies consist of **task ontology**[3][4] which characterizes the computational architecture of a knowledge- based system which performs a task and **domain ontology** which characterizes the domain knowledge where the task is performed. By a task, we mean a process like diagnosis, monitoring, scheduling, design, and so on. In our context, operation is a task. The idea of task ontology which serves as a theory of vocabulary/concepts used as building blocks for knowledge-based systems[3][4][5][6] might provide us with an effective methodology and vocabulary for both analyzing and synthesizing knowledge-based systems. An ontology is understood to serve as a kernel theory and building blocks for content-oriented research.

Why ontology instead of knowledge? Knowledge is domain-dependent, and hence knowledge engineering which directly investigates such knowledge has been suffering from rather serious difficulties, such as domain-specificity and diversity. Further, much of the knowledge dealt with in expert systems has been heuristics domain experts have, which makes knowledge manipulation more difficult. However, in ontological engineering, we investigate knowledge in terms of its origin and elements from which knowledge is constructed. An ontology reflects what exists out there in the world of interest or represents what we should think exists there. Hierarchical structure of concepts and decomposability of knowledge enable us to identify portions of concepts sharable among people. Exploitation of such characteristics makes it possible to avoid the difficulties knowledge engineering has faced with. The following is an enumeration of the merits we can enjoy from an ontology:

1. *A common vocabulary.* The description of the target world needs a vocabulary agreed among people involved.
2. *Explication* of what has been often left implicit. In all of the human activities, we find presuppositions/assumptions which usually are left implicit. Any knowledge

base built is based on a conceptualization possessed by the builder and is usually implicit. An ontology is an explication of the very implicit knowledge. Such an explicit representation of assumptions and conceptualization is more than a simple explication.

3. *Systematization* of knowledge. Knowledge systematization requires well-established vocabulary/concepts in terms people use to describe phenomena, theories and target things under consideration. An ontology thus contributes to providing a backbone for the systematization of knowledge.
4. *Standardization.* The common vocabulary and knowledge systematization bring us more or less standardized terms/concepts.
5. *Meta-model functionality.* A model is usually built in the computer as an abstraction of the real target. And, an ontology provides us with concepts and relations among them which are used as building blocks of the model. Thus, an ontology specifies the models to build by giving guidelines and constraints which should be satisfied. This function is viewed as that at the metalevel.

The Role of a Plant Ontology

Any intelligent system needs a considerable amount of domain knowledge to be useful in a domain. The amount of knowledge necessary often goes large, which sometimes causes difficulties in the initial construction and maintenance phases. As described above, one of the methods we adopted to cope with such problems is ontological engineering. The plant ontology makes contributions in our system in many respects described above. Roughly speaking, the essential contribution of an ontology is making shared commitment to the target plant explicit, and hence terminology is standardized within the community of agents. By agents, we also mean human agents, operators, to share such a fundamental understanding about the plant. This enables the system to communicate with operators using the terms stored in Ontology server: OS. It is the second major role of OS in the current implementation of the interface system which is discussed below in Section 4.

In message generation, we need to pay maximal attention to word selection to make operators' cognitive load minimum in message understanding. After an intensive interview with domain experts, we found human operators use different terms to denote the same thing depending on context. When we first noticed this fact, domain experts apologized for this seemingly random fluctuation of word usage, since they did not know the reason why they use terms that way and they were used to collaboration with computer engineers who do not like neat adaptation and tend to compel their idea of "this is what a computer can do, so accept it". They kindly declared that they would soon determine a unique label for each thing. But, we were different from such computer engineers. Instead of accepting their proposal, we carefully analyzed the way of their word usage and finally came up with that it is not random except a few cases. Many of the wording have good justifications which have to be taken care of in the message generation. The way of doing so is described in 5.2.

The reasons why we employed distributed collaboration architecture with multiple agents include making the whole system robust and easy to maintain. As is well known, however, these merits are not free. We need a well-designed vocabulary for describing message content as well as a powerful negotiation protocol. Although the latter is of importance, it is out of the scope of this paper.

DCI is responsible for enabling collaborative problem solving by multiple agents with the help of OS. It is one of the key factors that domain-dependent knowledge be isolated in OS so that DCI can be as general as possible.

Plant Ontology

We built a plant ontology which consists of several hierarchical organizations of concepts such as *operation task ontology*, *plant components, plant objects, basic attributes* and *ordinary attribute*. The key issue in design of an ontology is clear distinction essential categories from peripheral or view-dependent concepts.

Operation Task Ontology

The major constituents of a task ontology are concepts of action done by the task performer, operators in our case, and concepts of the role which domain objects play in the task performance. This is the key issue of task ontology. That is, a task ontology reveals the problem solving context in a task of interest to specify the roles the domain objects play. Without this, it is left implicit that how domain concepts should be organized under a specific task.

Activity Concepts: Operation of a plant consists of monitoring the behavior of the plant, diagnosing abnormal states if any and operating devices to recover from such states. Thus, the three actions, ***monitor***, ***diagnose*** and ***operate*** are the top level category of action part. Under these, we also identified ***enumerate, list up, decide, predict, etc.***

There are two kinds of hierarchies of concepts organization. *is-a* hierarchy and *part-of* hierarchy. For example, sub-concepts of ***operate*** in the *part-of* hierarchy would be ***recognize***(the state), ***predict***(the near future), ***identify***(the causes), and ***decide*** (operation to take). On the other hand, sub-concepts of ***reason*** in the *is-a* hierarchy, are ***predict and retrospectively reason*** and its super is ***think.*** In the *is-a* hierarchy case, properties of the super concepts are inherited to the sub-concepts. In ***reason*** case, its [input : output] roles, [state : state], are inherited by ***predict and retrospectively reason*** but specialized to [current state : future state] and [current state : causal state].

Role Concepts: Major task-specific role concepts include state of operation, ***abnormal state, candidate cause, countermeasure operation*** etc. When a state of operation is recognized as abnormal, then it comes to be called ***abnormal state***. ***Near future state*** is a state predicted from an ***abnormal state*** as the ***current state***. A ***cause*** of a fault has its sub-states: a ***candidate cause*** which is an inferred causal state and a cause which is a real cause.

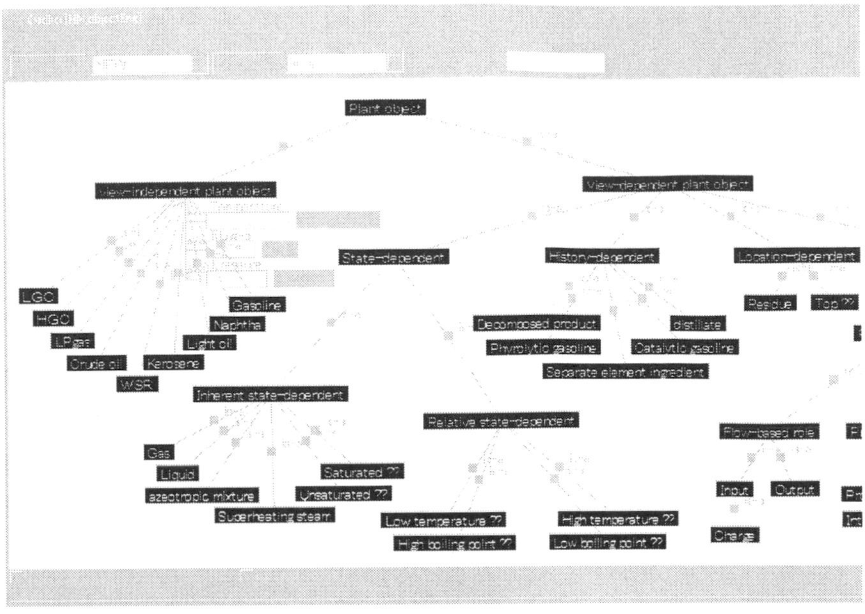

Fig. 1. A Portion of Plant Object is-a Hierarchy in the Plant Domain Ontology

Domain Ontology

There exist two major things in the plant domain: ***Plant components(devices)*** and ***plant objects*** to be processed by the ***devices***. Domain concepts also have role concepts like task ontology. To say precisely, many of the domain concepts are role concepts. The first things we have to do when designing a domain ontology is discrimination of roles concepts from essential categories(or basic concepts), i.e., view- or context-independent concepts. Let us first take ***plant object***. The top-level categories of ***plant object*** are ***view-independent object*** and ***view-dependent object***. The former includes LP gas, gasoline, naphtha, etc. which are categories persistent in any situation. The latter includes ***tower-head ingredient, liquid, distillate, input, intermediate product, raw material, fuel***, etc. All are view- or context-dependent. The major task needed was categorization of such dependency. Fig. 1 shows a portion of ***plant object*** *is-a* hierarchy. The top-level categories of ***view-dependent plant object*** are ***state-dependent, location-dependent, history-dependent and role-dependent*** objects. ***state-dependent*** objects has ***inherent state-dependent*** and ***relative state-dependent*** objects as its sub-concepts. The former includes ***liquid, gas, superheating steam*** etc. and the latter ***low temperature ingredient***, ***low boiling point ingredient***, etc.

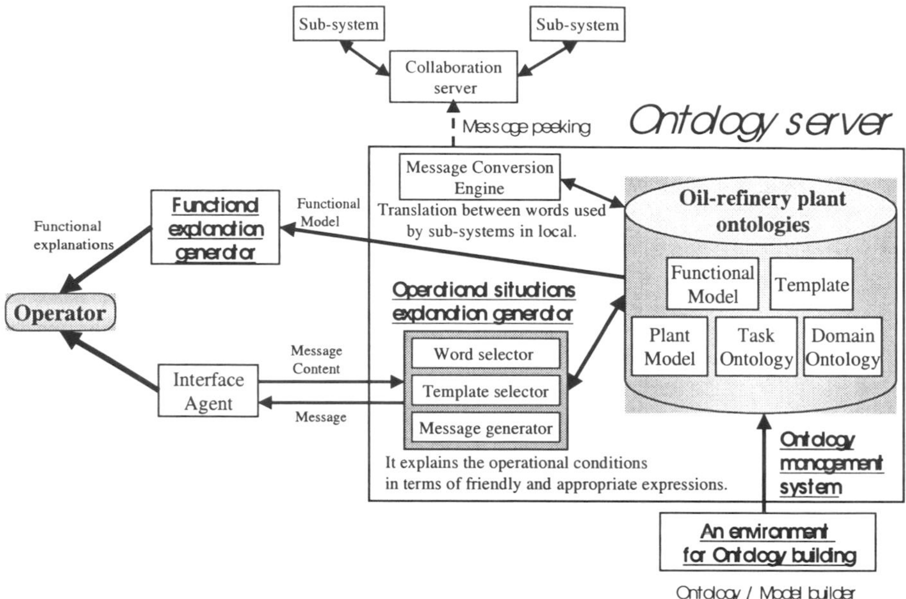

Fig. 2. Block diagram of Ontology server

Attribute also needs careful treatment. Most of the attributes people think so are not true attribute but ***role attribute***. Let us take an example of ***height***. It is a ***role attribute*** whose ***basic attribute*** is ***length. Height, depth, width*** and ***distance*** are ***role attributes.*** Just like a man is called a husband when he has got married. The true attribute is called ***basic attribute***. Examples of ***basic attribute*** include ***length, area, mass, temperature, pressure, volt, etc***. Role attribute includes ***height, depth, input pressure, maximum weight, area of cross section, etc.*** Needless to say, these attributes are also decomposed into several sub-concepts.

We finally built an ontology which contains about 500 concepts which are approved by the domain experts and the coverage is around the normal pressure fractionator of a full-scale refinery plant.

Another kind of domain ontology is necessary to build a model of a plant as an active artifact. That is an ontology of function and behavior which is task-independent. This ontology is used for deeper understanding of the dynamic characteristics of an artifact. Although it is interesting, it is omitted in this paper because of the space limitation [8][9].

Use of the Ontology

System Overview of Ontology Server: OS

Ontology server has several functions in the interface system.
(1) To store the plant ontology for use of representing message contents.
(2) To build a model of the target plant shared by other agents
(3) To generate natural language messages presented to operators according to appropriate word selection
(4) To answer questions about the structure of the plant
(5) To translate among vocabularies local to each of the agents.

In general, the major contribution of OS to the whole system is to standardize concepts about the target plant each agent has as well as vocabulary used by them. Fig. 2 shows the block diagram of OS where several types of plant ontologies are stored and two functional modules such as explanation generator and message generator are also shown. OS has a stylized application protocol interface supported by DCI, by which any agent can communicate with OS and can inspect the ontology in it.

Appropriate Word Selection

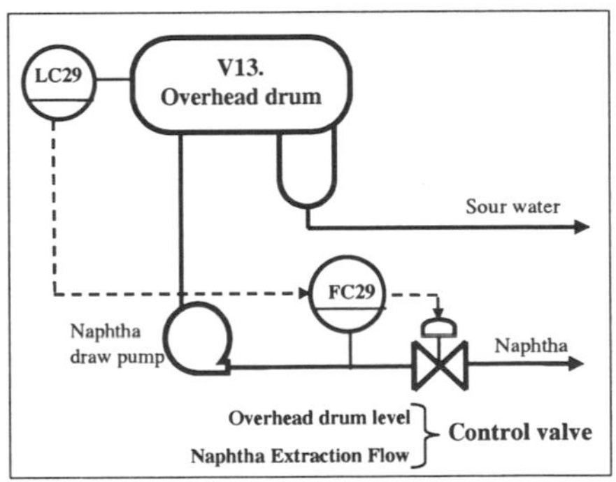

Fig. 3. Cascaded control of LC and FC

After intensive discussion with domain experts, we found a remarkable fact that they sometimes use multiple names to denote the same entity. Let us take an example shown in Fig. 3 in which two controllers exist: Level controller (LC29) and flow controller (FC29). Both controllers use the same control valve as an actuator. It is a typical example of cascaded control. LC29 takes care of the liquid level of the overhead drum which contains reflux(Naphtha). And FC29 is in charge of controlling the flow of Naphtha coming out of the overhead drum. The control valve is called "Level adjustment control valve" and "Naphtha extraction flow control valve" depending on which controller the operator focuses on. The problem, however, is that the focused controller is seldom explicit. So, the system has to infer where is the focus on and to trace the focus shifts during the course of operation. Further, the system has to know the term generation mechanism to attain the maximal flexibility of the system. Concerning the labels of each concept, we only ask the model builder of the target plant to write the default name of things appearing in the plant. The role name which will be attached to things are basically generated by the system according to the context identified. This makes system building easier. Especially, plant objects have various role names which the objects play from the viewpoint of the device which processes them. For example, ***input material*** is a typical role name which many of the plant objects could play.

The system has two kinds of rules such as **Focus tracing rules** and **Role name generation rules.** The former is for tracing the focal point to identify the context and the latter for "name" generation of the target entity. The philosophy of name generation is to associate a default name with each entity and rules are invoked when names other than the default one should be used. Note that roles names are generated adaptively to the topological structure of the plant.

While the rule application, knowledge about each concept/term is obtained by consulting the ontology and the plant model which has been built by connecting components generated by instantiation of corresponding concepts in the ontology.

Focus Tracing Rules

Assume the system is asked to choose an appropriate term for things(attributes, name, etc.) of an object identified by its unique identifier. Let us call the object CO: Current Object. The rule are divided into four cases according to what things of CO is:

Case 1: An attribute of a plant object(not a device)

(a) If CO is input or output of the device focused previously, then the focused device is the same as the last focused device.
(b) If the last focused device is either a controller or a control valve and CO is equal to that the controller measures, then the device the controller measures is the new focused device.
(c) If the task is decision of countermeasure, then the new focused device is the entire plant.
(d) Otherwise, no focused device exists.

Case 2: An attribute of a device

(a) If a controller which measures the attributes exists, then the new focused device is the controller.
(b) Otherwise, the new focused device is the same as the last focused device.

Case 3: A control valve(CO is a control valve itself)

(a) If CO is the same as the target object of the last focused device, the focused device is the same as the last focused device.
(b) Otherwise, the device which operates CO is the new focused device.

Case 4: others

(a) In all cases where device names are concerned other than the cases (2) and (3), CO is the new focused device.

Role Name Generation Rules

The philosophy is to associate a default name with each thing and rules are invoked when names other than the default one should be used.

(1) For plant objects
 (a) If there is a focused device, then

(a-1) if the focused device has role names of its input/output objects, then CO name is the role name of the input/output object of the focused device.
(a-2) otherwise, the CO name is "<focused device> input/output".
(b) Otherwise, default name of CO is used.

(2) For a controller and a control valve
(a) If the focused device measures an attribute of another device, then the name of the CO is "<the device which focused device controls>" + "<the attribute>" + ["control valve" or "controller"](e.g., overhead drum level controller).
(b) If the focused device measures an attribute of a plant object and if the device controlled by the focused device has a role name of its input/output object, then CO name is "<the role name>" + "<the attribute>" + ["control valve" or "controller"]. If there is no role name, then the CO name is "<the controlled device>" + ["inlet" or "outlet"] + "<the attribute>" + ["control valve" or "controller"](e.g., desalter inlet temperature controller).

(3) For a thing other than a control valve or a controller
(a) If an attribute of CO is concerned, then return "<the object which the focused device measures>" + "<the attribute>".
(b) Otherwise, CO name is the name of the focused device.

Template Design of Messages

A message should be easily understood by operators in any situation. So, its syntactic form should be highly stylized and cannot be long. We collected a lot of sample messages with the help of domain experts and classified the syntactic forms into the following seven types:

(1) Warning
(2) Near future prediction
(3) Candidate cause presentation
(4) Diagnosis result presentation
(5) Justification of decisions
(6) Countermeasure presentation
(7) Justification of countermeasures

Each type has a few templates for covering a small amount of variations. Each template is specified using concepts in the ontology. Message construction algorithm can be simple for the above reason. In fact, a simple blank filling method is employed. Templates are described in terms of intermediate categories contained in the ontology

Example: OS receives a message content from Interface Agent which monitors the plant. A message content is represented in a list as follows: (<Template type> <non-terminal symbols>*)

J: [警告 [VFC29, MV] 全開]
E: [Warning [VFC29, MV] full throttle]

J: 警告:ナフサ抜き出し流量コントロールバルブが全開です
E: Warning: Naphtha extraction flow control valve is in full throttle.
J: [原因候補1 [VFC29] スティック]
E: [Candidate cause1 [VFC29] stick]

J: 原因候補:リフラックスドラム液レベルコントロールバルブがスティック
E: Plausible cause: Reflux drum level control valve sticks.

Implementation and Evaluation

OS has been implemented in Java and Lisp. The ontology developed has been implemented in Ontology editor discussed in Section 6. The number of concepts in the ontology is about 500. We did a full-scale experiment to evaluate the system. Domain experts developed seven scenarios of various faults with countermeasures for them and many types of messages to operators. The templates we built cover all the messages. We picked up all of the messages to evaluate the word selection and message generation functions of OS and confirmed all of the message contents sent from IA through LAN were successfully translated into the desirable messages in terms of appropriate terms. Fig. 4 shows an example screen dump of the prototype system . The lower half is a portion of the plant model we built and the left upper window is a window of IA and right one is of OS. The window configuration is arranged for demonstration. The plant model generated using the ontology is shared by all the agents. The domain experts evaluated the performance of the system favorably.

An Environment for Ontology Development and Its Use

The environment, named “Hozo”, used for building the plant ontology and model, is composed of graphical interface, editor and ontology/model server in a Client-Server architecture. It is implemented in Java and editor is implemented as Java applet so that it can work as a client through the Internet. Hozo manages ontologies and models for each of the developers. Users can read and copy all the ontologies and models stored in Hozo, but cannot modify any developed by others. Models are built by choosing and instantiating concepts in an ontology and by connecting the instances. After consistency checking of the model using axioms defined in the ontology, the model is ready for use by other agents. The model built is available in a Lisp format which is sound and machine interpretable.

Editor

The editor interface is composed of the following five parts:

1. **Browsing panel** displays an ontology/model graphically
2. **Definition panel** where definition of concepts and relations is done.
3. **Term list panel** lists all the concepts contained in the ontology alphabetically and is used for concept retrieval.
4. **Menu bar** for selecting tools
5. **Tool bar** for selecting commands

The editor can be viewed as a kind of two-dimensional language in the sense that users can develop an ontology by defining concepts with appropriate relations such as *is-a*, *part-of*, etc. in the browsing panel. User can define their own relations. Consistency of the ontology and of the model built from the ontology is automatically guaranteed in terms of the subsumption and *instance-of* relations. Attributes are defined in the definition panel for each concept with the visible inheritance history.

Browsing panel

Browsing panel has two modes: Tree mode and Network mode. The former

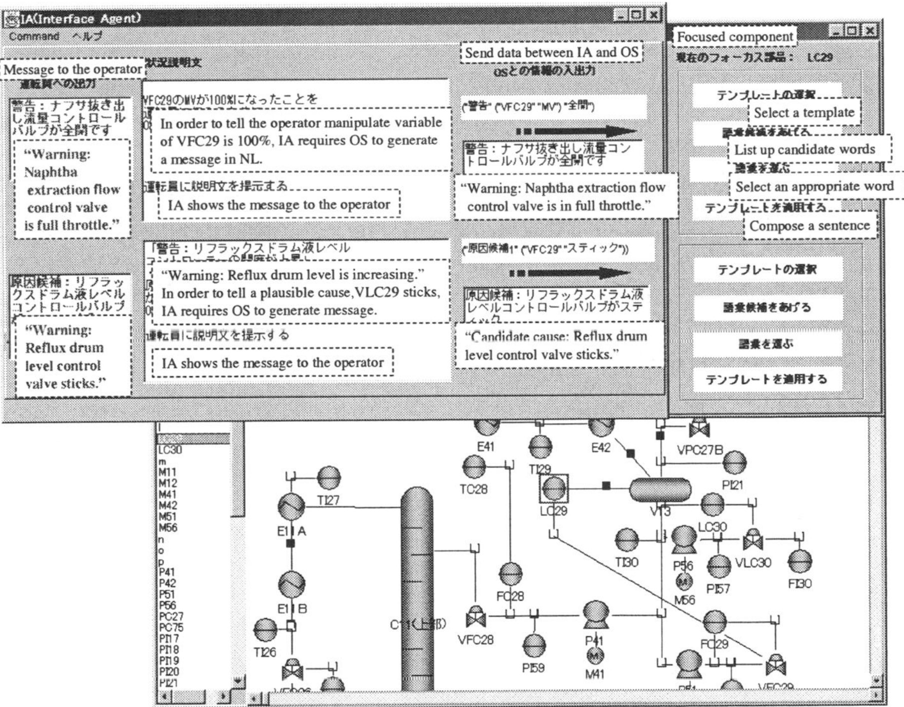

Fig. 4. Screen dump of a message generation demonstration

displays the ontology in a hierarchical structure using only *is-a* relations between concepts. In the latter mode, all the relations including those user defined are shown in a network structure. In the both modes, slots of a concept, usually representing its attributes and parts, can be shown by request. A number of mouse operations for manipulating trees and networks are available.

Definition panel

Definition panel allows users to read and define concepts and relations they designate in the Browsing panel. Items for edition are as follows:

label: It denotes a label denoting the concept being defined.
axiom: Constraints which has to be satisfied by all of its instances.
def: Informal definition in natural language
slot:(kind, name(label), class constraint, value)

"kind" denotes kinds of content of the slot such as *attribute* and *part* etc. "name" is a label of the slot, "class constraint" denotes what class should the "value" belong to and "value" is a value in the case that "kind" is *attribute* or a *part* in the case that "kind" is *part*. These are used for consistency checking by the server, and hence, property inheritance and consistency between subsumption and *instance-of* relations are checked by the server.

Model construction

A model is built using the ontology developed and is used by other agents. As described in the above, Hozo guarantees the compliance of the model with the ontology. All the necessary operations such as instance making, connecting them, deletion/ addition of instances, etc. for building and manipulating a model are done by built-in mouse operations in the browsing panel. During the model construction, users are given all the classes defined in the ontology to instantiate. So, the browser works as a model browser/editor. When the user selects a class to instantiate, its definition is displayed in the class-browsing panel. All the instances built properly inherit properties of all of their super-concepts. In fact, the model used in OS has been built like this and shared by all of the other agents as an ontology-compliant model.

Other Functions

Managing and overriding inheritance

Managing *is-a* inheritance is done by Hozo automatically. When necessary, overriding the inherited value is allowed to specialize it more.

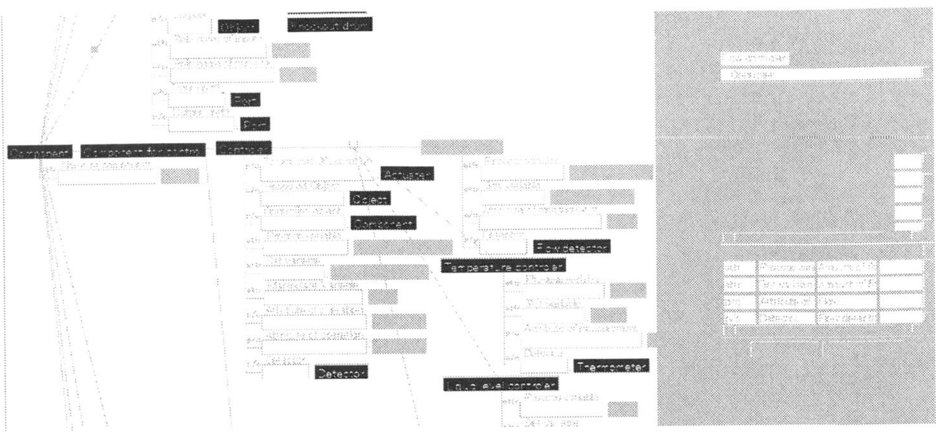

Fig. 5. A snapshot of the plant ontology definition

GIF attachment

A node, which denotes concept(class and instance), is usually displayed as a square. If necessary, GIF can be attached to it to make the instances real just like we did in our project which is shown in Fig. 4.

Output in a text format

The ontology and model can be output not only in a Lisp format for computer interpretation but also in a text format with indentation. XML version will be ready soon.

Implementation

The current version of Hozo has been implemented in Java(JDK1.1) and been used for two years not only by our lab members but also by some researchers outside. The following are some example ontologies developed thus far:

1. Ontology for Learning support systems
2. Ontology for Authoring systems
3. Ontology for Instructional design
4. Ontology of fault in diagnostic tasks
5. Ontology of function in artifact design

Fig. 5 shows a snapshot of the plant ontology definition about *Component* in a Network view mode. A node has its super concept to its left and has several slots for attribute and its part definition. Components are classified according to their functions because function is an essential property of them. Controller inherits "control function" from its super concept "Component for control" and has specialized information such as its "control object is an instance of actuator" is written in the slot. While a slot is defined as "PV(Process Variable) takes a "value" in "Controller", that of its sub-concept, "Flow controller", is defined as "PV takes a "value of amount of flow" by overriding it.

Hozo is available at the URL: http://www.ei.sanken.osaka-u.ac.jp/oe/oe.html

Future Work

We have identified some room to improve Hozo through its extensive use. The first topic is about effective guidelines for ontology development that is badly needed by developers. Because many of the existing guidelines are those similar to Software development guidelines, we need neater one, that is, one which can help users distinguish between classes and roles, identify appropriate relations and build a proper abstraction hierarchy of classes. Although this topic is the most important, it is out of the scope of this paper.

Other topics include basic functions which support neat representation of an ontology. Especially, we extended Hozo with respect to treatment of "Relation" and "Role" concepts. The following is the summary of extension:

- On the basis of that most of the things are composed of parts and that those parts are connected by a specific relation to form the whole, we introduced "Wholeness concept" and "Relation concept". The former is a conceptualization of the whole and the latter of the relation. Typical example is "married couple(fufu in Japanese)" and "fufu relation". Hozo will provide functions to manage the correspondence between these two different conceptualizations of the same entity. Needless to say, Hozo gives an identity to every relation.
- Description framework of roles: Role is specified in various ways. One of the typical way is specification in a *part-of* relation, like "husband" in "fufu", that is, husband is a role in a wholeness concept of a married couple(fufu).
- Sophisticated display of *part-of* relations and its editing
  The current Hozo has only one *part-of* relation which is transitive, but the next version will introduce several *part-of* relations some of which are not transitive.
- Augmentation of the axiom definition and the language

The latest version of Hozo has been currently implemented and will be open soon. Compatibility to existing ontology representation method like OIL[10] will be considered.

Related Work

ONTOGENERATION[11] explains the content of ontology in Spanish based on two kinds of ontologies: domain and linguistic ontologies. Message generation in our system is not special. Templates are designed by observing sample messages provided by the domain experts. Sentence structure of the message is highly stylized because of the small number of templates. Its unique feature exists in context-sensitive word selection rather than sentence generation itself.

Our view of an ontology is based mainly on its use in building a well-founded model, that is, we think meta-model functionality is of the most important. This contrasts well with that of Guarino's idea of top-level ontology design[7]. The idea of task ontology shares a lot with Common KADS[4][5].

Several ontology development methodologies have been proposed[12][14]. Both of them present users guidelines to follow together with sophisticated tools like those employed in the conventional knowledge acquisition process. Most of the tools are based on a frame-based knowledge representation language with an additional functionality for writing axioms. Hozo is similar to them in that sense, but is different from them in some respects: (1) It is essentially a GUI-based language. An ontology is defined through the graphical interface based on *is-a* and *part-of* hierarchies. (2) It has special functionalities for ontology design such as treatment of role concepts whose instatiation is done differently from that of a basic concept. (3) Clear discrimination among, **role**(husband role), **role-holder**(husband) and **basic concept**(man) is done to treat "Role" properly. (4) In the next version of Hozo, several kinds of *part-of* relations are to be introduced such as *component-part-of* which is the most common *part-of* relation, *material-part-of*, and so on[13]. (5) It does not allow multiple inheritance because most of the use of multiple inheritance in knowledge representation are inappropriate from ontology point of view.

Hozo shares an idea of ODE of METHONTOLOGY[14] in that it generates machine code of the ontology defined in a more informal way.

Conclusion

Plant ontology and its roles in the interface system for oil-refinery plant operation have been discussed. The plant ontology design has been almost completed and its utility has been demonstrated in message generation with appropriate word selection. The future work until the end of the project, March in 2001 includes design of a negotiation ontology for use of flexible and powerful collaboration among agents through sophisticated negotiation. Task ontology will be used for specifying functionality of each agent and hence for helping negotiation task ontology design. This topic is one of the main topics in our research plan.

We also discussed an environment for ontology development, Hozo, used for the development of our plant ontology. It was informally evaluated by domain experts and they gave favorable comments. They found utility of Hozo in making their knowledge explicit and in operationalizing it and want to use it in the daily activity. Hozo has been extensively used in many projects to develop various ontologies. Its revised version will be ready soon.

Acknowledgement

This paper was prepared under an Entrustment Contract with the Laboratories of Image Information Science and Technology (LIST) from the New Energy and Industrial Technology Development Organization (NEDO) in concern with the Human Media Research and Development Project under the Industrial Science and Technology Frontier (ISTF) program of the Ministry of International Trade and Industry (MITI) of Japan.

References

[1] Mizoguchi, R. A Step towards Ontological Engineering, National Conference on AI of JSAI, AI-L13, 1998, http://www.ei.sanken.osaka-u.ac.jp/english/step-onteng.html.

[2] R. Mizoguchi, A. Gofuku, Y. Matsuura Y. Sakashita, M. Tokunaga, Human Media Interface System for the Next Generation Plant Operation, Proc. of 1999 IEEE Int'l Conf. On SMC, Tokyo, October, pp.630-635, 1999.

[3] R. Mizoguchi, et al., Task Ontology for Reuse of Problem Solving Knowledge. KB&KS '95, pp.46-59, 1995

[4] V. R. Benjamins, B. Wielinga, J. Wielemaker, and D. Fensel : Brokering Problem-Solving, Knowledge at the Internet. In Knowledge Acquisition, Modeling, and Management, Proceedings of the European Knowledge Acquisition Workshop (EKAW-99), D. Fensel et al. (eds.), Lecture Notes in Artificial Intelligence, LNAI 1621, Springer-Verlag, May 1999

[5] G. van Heijst, A. Th. Schreiber, and B. J. Wielinga: Using explicit ontologies in KBS development. International Journal of Human-Computer Studies, 46(2/3):183–292, 1997.

[6] B. Chandrasekaran, J. R. Josephson, and R. Benjamins, What are ontologies, and why do we need them?, IEEE Intelligent Systems, Vol.14, No.1, pp.20-26, 1999

[7] Guarino, Nicola: Some Ontological Principles for Designing Upper Level Lexical Resources. Proc. of the First International Conference on Lexical Resources and Evaluation, Granada, Spain, 28-30 May 1998.

[8] M. Sasajima, Y. Kitamura, M. Ikeda, and R. Mizoguchi, FBRL:A Function and Behavior Representation Language, Proc. of IJCAI'95, pp.1830-1836, 1995.

[9] Y. Kitamura and R. Mizoguchi, Meta-Functions of Artifacts, The Thirteenth International Workshop on Qualitative Reasoning (QR-99), Scotland, June 6-9 1999.

[10] I. Horrocks, D. Fensel, J. Broekstra, S. Decker, M. Erdmann, C. Goble, F. Van Harmelen, M. Klein, S. Staab, and R. Studer: OIL: The Ontology Inference Layer, to appear. http://www.ontoknowledge.com/oil.

[11] G. Aguado, et al., ONTOGENERATION; Reusing domain and linguistic ontologies for Spanish generation, Proc. of the ECAI 98 Workshop on Applications of ontologies and problem-solving methods, pp.1-10, 1998.

[12] M. Uschold and M. Gruninger, ONTOLOGIES: Principles, Methos and Applications, J. of Knowledge Engineering Review, Vol.11, No.2, 1996.

[13] Mizoguchi, R. et al., Foundation of ontological engineering – An ontological theory of semantic links, classes, relations and roles --, J. of JSAI, Vol. 14, No.6, pp.1019-1032, 1999(in Japanese).

[14] Lopez, M.F., Gomez-Perex, A. et al., Building a chemical ontology using Methontology and the ontology design environment, IEEE Intelligent Systems, Vol.14, No.1, pp.37-46, 1999.

The Role of Ontologies for an Effective and Unambiguous Dissemination of Clinical Guidelines

Domenico M. Pisanelli, Aldo Gangemi, and Geri Steve

CNR, Istituto di Tecnologie Biomediche
Viale Marx 15, 00137 Roma, Italy

{pisanelli, gangemi, steve} @itbm.rm.cnr.it
http://saussure.irmkant.rm.cnr.it

Abstract. Guidelines for clinical practice are being introduced in an extensive way in more and more different fields of medicine They have the potential to improve the quality and cost-efficiency of care in a complex health care delivery environment. Computerization may increase the effectiveness of both the information retrieval of guidelines and the management of guideline-based care. The scenario is evolving from stand-alone workstations to telematics applications that enable guidelines development and dissemination. However, such a knowledge sharing requires the definition of formal models for guidelines representation. The models should have a clear semantics in order to avoid ambiguities. The role of ontologies is that of making explicit the conceptualizations behind a model. In this paper we present our library of generic and domain ontologies and point out its role for integrating existing guideline models and defining standard representations. In particular, we stress the distinction –often collapsed within existing guideline models– between the conceptualization of actual procedures, the conceptualization of planning, and the conceptualization behind the diagrammatic representation of plans.

1. Introduction

Guidelines for clinical practice are being introduced in an extensive way in more and more different fields of medicine [1][2]. They have the goal of indicating the most appropriate decisional and procedural behavior optimizing health outcomes, costs and clinical decisions.

Guidelines can be expressed in a textual way as recommendations or in a more formal and rigid way as protocols or flow diagrams. In different contexts they can be either a loose indication for a preferred set of choices or they can be considered a normative set of rules.

Clinical practice guidelines are seen as a tool for improving the quality and cost-efficiency of care in an increasingly complex health care delivery environment. It has been proved that adherence to plans may reduce cost of care up to 25% [3].

However the overwhelming number of guidelines available makes it difficult to select the right one. Just to give an idea of the figures, it is reported that there are 855 different guidelines for British GPs ranging from a single page to small booklets of more than 15 pages [4].

R. Dieng and O. Corby (Eds.): EKAW 2000, LNAI 1937, pp. 129-139, 2000.

Computerization may increase the effectiveness of both the information retrieval of guidelines and the delivery of guideline-based care. In an optimal scenario they are integrated with the information systems operational at the point of care. The full potentialities of computerized systems can be exploited in such an environment where different processes are executed in parallel on several patients. In this context such systems must be able to retrieve the updated situation of every patient, as well as to give an overall report on the ward, freeing the physicians to concentrate more on clinical decisions. Keeping track of the parallel activities performed, they should avoid unnecessary duplication of tasks and prevent possible omissions.

Several research projects deal with the computer representation and implementation of guidelines. In the next paragraph we review some of the most relevant ones. The scenario is evolving from stand-alone workstations to telematics applications that - utilizing e.g. the Internet - not only support the use of guidelines, but also enable their development and dissemination.

Such a knowledge sharing requires the definition of formal models for guidelines representation. The models should have a clear semantics in order to avoid ambiguities. The role of ontologies is that of making explicit the conceptualizations behind a model. In particular an ontology contains the formal description of the entities to which a model makes a commitment and of the relations holding among the entities.

In this paper we present our library of ontologies and point out its role for integrating existing guideline models and defining standard representations.

2 Applications of Clinical Guidelines

Many efforts have been devoted in the last few years in realizing computerized tools for guidelines management (see for example: Vissers and co-workers [5] and Ertle and co-workers [6]).

The European PRESTIGE project (Guidelines for healthcare: faster implementation of health care standards) is mainly dedicated to supplying information and modelling technology to guidelines in the context of the IV Framework Programme (1994-1999) [7]. PRESTIGE aims to produce telematic applications for a faster implementation of new standards of quality in clinical practice in Europe. It is therefore directed more towards the clinical part, neglecting the organisational and administrative components.

The PRO*forma* knowledge representation language and associated software tools are designed to support the dissemination of medical knowledge by means of electronic publishing [8]. It is also a method for specifying clinical guidelines and protocols in a form which can be executed by a computer in order to support the management of medical procedures and clinical decision making.

Web based tools for supporting clinical care are becoming increasingly popular (see for example [9-11]). The system SMART allows users to access its database - storing information on patients following a guideline-based care - by means of the Internet [12].

COLLATE is a WWW-enabled workgroup environment designed to support dispersed collaborative groups throughout the complete guideline development cycle [13]. COLLATE supports document management, collaborative authoring and editing over the Internet, and provides methods for accessing and browsing multimedia databases of systematic literature reviews and guideline documents, and can provide links to external applications such as on-line bibliographic database packages.

Recently, increasing attention has been paid to formal model of guidelines and protocols. For instance, EON is a computational model of treatment protocols [14]. The EON framework consists of three different components: the domain knowledge base of medical concepts that will specify the application and temporal-abstraction knowledge necessary for reasoning, one or more applications that use problem-solving methods formulated as collections of CORBA objects and the Tzolkin subsystem that performs temporal abstraction and temporal pattern matching.

This model was the basis for implementing the protocol-based decision-support module for the already existing T-HELPER system [15]. This system was originally aimed at supporting AIDS care, but, because its architecture was domain independent, it was possible to substitute the AIDS knowledge base with another one regarding breast cancer. The Protégé-II tool was employed to create an ontology of concepts related to the management of breast cancer [16]. Such a reuse of knowledge allowed the Stanford researchers to implement their prototype system in less than one week.

The successful experience of the EON model demonstrates that knowledge-based systems cannot be constructed in isolation from development in the software-engineering community. Their approach, oriented to modularity and to the definition of ontologies, facilitated knowledge re-use.

3 An Excerpt of Our Ontology Library

Ontologies not only make knowledge re-use easier, they are also the foundation of standardization efforts since they make explicit the conceptualizations behind a terminology or a model. The actual demand is not for a unique conceptualization, but for an unambiguous communication of complex and detailed concepts (possibly expressed in different languages), leaving each user free to make explicit his/her conceptualization.

We developed ONIONS, a methodology for integrating domain terminologies by exploiting a library of generic theories [17]. By means of this methodology we realized the library of ontologies ON9.2 (available in Ontolingua at: http://saussure.irmkant.rm.cnr.it), including both general and domain specific ontologies [18]. The ontologies related to guidelines, which we will sketch out in the next paragraph, are part of this library. Figure 1 reports a fragment of the library architecture. Each oval represents an ontology, i.e. a module which embodies the formal definition of related concepts and relationships.

Arrows denote inclusion between ontologies: the specific one includes the generic one (e.g. "medical procedures" includes "procedures").

"Clinical activities" is one ontology included by "guidelines", meaning that its concepts and relationships are used by the former one. It consists of the main types of entities involved in clinical activities, including: "patient", "patient group", "health care operator", "medical device", "health care structure", "medical sign" and "health condition", and some actor-like relations that divide into: 1) treatment relations, i.e. "treats" (between a "health care operator" and a "health condition"), and other composed relations (i.e. chaining "treats" with other relations) that account for different senses of "treats", e.g. "treatment-device" (between a "medical device" and a "health condition"); 2) diagnosis relations, i.e. "diagnoses" (between a "health care operator" and a "health condition"), and some composed relations; 3) care relations, i.e. "cares for" (holding between a "health care operator" and a "patient" or "patient group"), and some composed relations.

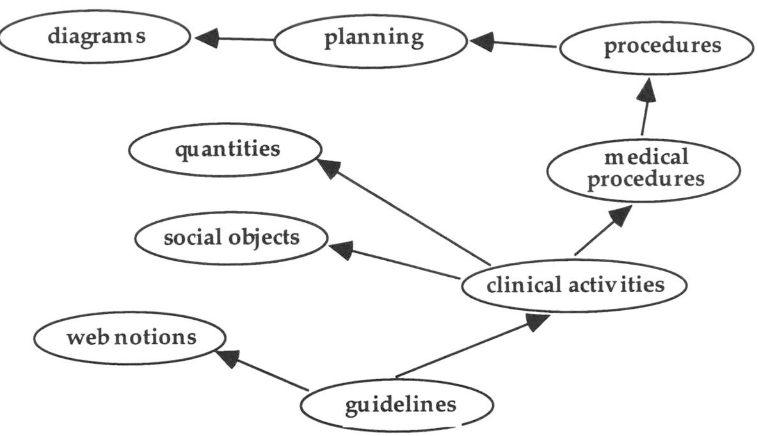

Fig. 1. An excerpt from the ontology library ON 9.2, showing the included theories nearest to the guidelines theory.

"Medical procedures" contains the definition of the main types of medical procedures, deriving from the integration of the UMLS Semantic Network [19] and the types defined by the Institute of Medicine. A medical procedure is a procedure having health-care activities as temporal parts. Five main kinds of medical procedures are defined: 1) screening and prevention procedures; 2) surgical procedures; 3) care of clinical conditions procedures; 4) diagnostic procedures; 5) laboratory procedures.

Procedures 1) to 3) share the need for some "bearer" patient or patient group, some pharmacologic resource, and some medical device; 4) are characterized by a patient or patient-group "target" and by their "diagnostic action" carried out on clinical conditions; 5) are characterized by the fact that they "analyze" some chemical or body substance, possibly assessing their effect. Relations such as: "bearer", "target", "analyzes", and "diagnostic action" are defined according to the generic ontology "actors", which describes the relations holding between the entities participating in processes and situations with a particular role (e.g. "performer", "embodier", "instrument", "goal", etc.).

To implement our ontology we adopted both Ontolingua [20], which is a very expressive language, and the Loom knowledge representation system [21] which supports automatic classification and semantic consistency check. Both languages allow HTML translation and browsing facilities. In particular the Ontosaurus [22], an interface to Loom through the CL-HTTP server, is appropriate for allowing collaborative development of ontologies [23].

What is peculiar to our library is its integration of medical domain and generic (domain-independent) ontologies. Examples of generic ontologies include: "mereology" or theory of parts, "topology" or theory of wholes and connexity, "morphology", or theory of form and congruence, "localization", "time", "actors", "planning", etc.

The relevance of generic theories to the development of ontologies is not always recognized. There are a number of significant experiences showing that an ontological analysis can profit from theories which are philosophically and linguistically grounded [24]. Our position is that generic theories are essential to the development of ontologies and to a rigorous conceptual integration of heterogeneous models [25].

For example, available formal models of guidelines make commitments to various entities and relations associated with guideline specification: plans, diagrammatic charting, information requests, actions, decisions, situations, tasks, etc.

These formal models do not sort out the entities by means of their ontological nature, but only on the basis of system design and efficiency issues.

For example, the Asbru model defines some guideline properties, but it splits them in two sets: one (plan status) includes "rejected", "ready", etc., another (plan state) includes "aborted", "completed", etc. [26] .

Understanding such properties within an ontological framework requires at least understanding the difference between a plan and a procedure: a plan is an abstract entity (a "script") which acts as the method of a procedure, which is a process actually occurring in the real world.

Such distinction can be drawn with the use of some generic theories that define a "plan" as a special kind of "abstract entity", a "procedure" as a special kind of "process", a "method" relation as a special kind of "actor" relation, and so on.

Once plan and procedure are kept disjoint in our ontology, one can easily infer why the two sets of Asbru properties actually draw that distinction: only a plan can be "rejected", and only a procedure can be "aborted".

If one disagrees with the plan/procedure distinction only has to dismiss the commitment to the generic theories mentioned, possibly providing other theories that support a different conceptualization.

4 The Ontology of Guidelines

In this paragraph we present the main features of the "guidelines" ontology and related concepts.

Guidelines are distinguished in "paper guidelines" and "web guidelines". Some common concepts - like "author" - pertain to both of them, whereas "URL" and "last-checked" are peculiar of the web guidelines.

They are also categorized in five different kinds, as defined in the Guideline Interchange Format standard (GLIF) [27]: "guideline for care of clinical condition", "screening and prevention", "diagnosis and prediagnosis management of patients", "indications for use of surgical procedures", "appropriate use of specific technologies and tests".

Such classification is furtherly specialized by us: for example a "guideline for care of clinical condition" may be a "therapy assessment", a "pharmacologic therapy" or a "disease management".

Figure 2 shows the relations among the basic concepts concerning guidelines. More specific concepts inherit these relations holding at general level. As an example, let us consider "diabetic patients" (concept more specific than "group", defined as any collection of individuals that carry a diabetic health condition). Such patients are the "scattered location" (this is a special location relation accounting for naïve localization holding between distributed object, defined in the generic ontology "localization") of "diabetes" (a "health condition"), which is the "target" of "diabetes therapy" (a "medical procedure") which "has method" a given guideline.

As far as the formal representation of guidelines is concerned, our ontology integrates some of the most relevant modeling efforts so far produced: notably PROforma [8], EON [14], Asbru [26] and GLIF [27]. It is also an evolution of a model previously defined in the context of the SMART system [12].

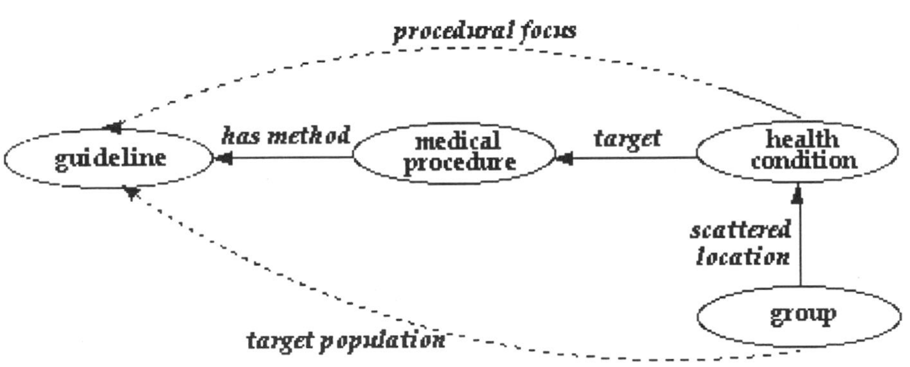

Fig. 2. The relations among basic concepts concerning guidelines (grey arrows stand for composite relations); concepts belong to different ontologies in the ontology library.

A "guideline" is a kind of "plan" which is a method of a "procedure", and it is represented by a "flowchart" (fig. 3).

The concept of "flowchart" pertains to the "diagrams" ontology. It is defined as a set of nodes and edges like an ordinary graph with some restrictions. Every flowchart has a first and a last node, only four kinds of nodes are allowed: single nodes, branching nodes, synch nodes and cycle nodes. Moreover the flowchart ontology allows for recursion, i.e. a node may be expanded into a flowchart.

This ontology accounts for the structural part of a guideline, but no semantics for actions is attached to it. The semantics for the actions involved pertains to the *planning* ontology, where simple nodes represent elementary actions and branching nodes enquiries and decisions. The recursion allowed in the flowchart domain, where a node of a flowchart may be expanded into a flowchart, is isomorph to the planning ontology, where an elementary action may be refined into a plan.

We believe that in our model it is appropriate to capture the distinction between the structural part of a guideline, represented by the flowchart, and its action semantics, represented by the plan. A third level is that of the procedure, i.e. what is actually performed.

Figure 4 reports an excerpt from the *planning* ontology (the representation language is Loom). Such an approach can put in evidence - at formal level - the equivalences among the various modeling approaches. We defined the *GL-mapping* ontology in order to account for such equivalences (figure 5).

Therefore this ontology integrates some of the most relevant work in the guideline modeling field. It is GLIF-compliant, i.e. each concept defined in GLIF is represented in it (e.g. the "synch" node after parallelization of activities). It takes into account the ProForma task ontology which categorizes tasks into: actions, enquiries and decisions and allows recursive definition of them (a plan is made of tasks, a task may be a plan).

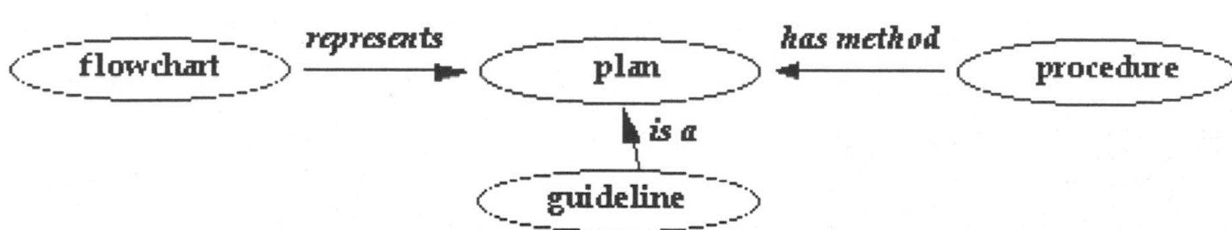

Fig. 3. The main concepts concerning a guideline. A guideline is a plan, and planning should be kept distinct from both diagrammatic representation and reference to actual procedures.

5 Conclusions

It has been proven that the introduction of guidelines can significantly decrease the costs of care and this make them a "hot topic" in the agenda of health care professionals.

Guidelines are mushrooming and computers can help in retrieving them and can give assistance during their execution. However such a widespread diffusion poses new problems, not only in terms of credibility and acceptability, but also concerning non-ambiguity in knowledge dissemination. Formal models with a clear semantics should be defined in order to represent guidelines and facilitate their diffusion.

The definition of ontologies - i.e. the formal description of the entities to which a model makes a commitment and of the relations holding among the entities - is the groundwork for making a standard model acceptable and sharable. An ontology library is not normative, but allows an inter-subjective, explicit and formal agreement on the semantics of the primitives of a model, by referring to more generic primitives (generic theories).

In this paper we presented our work in terms of the definition of an ontology of guidelines which is part of a larger ontology library containing both domain and generic theories. We believe that such an approach can facilitate the standardization process by allowing an explicit mapping in a formal ontology of the concepts represented in the heterogeneous models proposed so far.

References

1. Woolf SH. Practice Guidelines, a New Reality in Medicine: Impact on Patient Care. *Arch Intern Med,* 1993; 153: 2646-2655.
2. Grimshaw JM, Russell IT. Effect of Clinical Guidelines on Medical Practice: a Systematic Review of Rigorous Evaluations. *Lancet,* 1993; 342: 1317-1322.
3. Clayton PD, Hripcsak G. Decision support in healthcare. *Int. J. of Bio-Medical Computing,* 1995; 39: 59-66.
4. Hibble A., Kanka D., Penheon D., Pooles F: Guidelines in general practice: The new Tower of Babel? *British Medical Journal,* 1998; 317: 862-3.
5. Vissers MC, Hasman A, van der Linden CJ. Protocol Processing System (ProtoVIEW) to Support Residents at the Emergency Ward. *Proc. MIE 94,* 1994: 138-143.
6. Ertle AR, Campbell EM, Hersh WR. Automated Application of Clinical Practice Guidelines for Asthma Management. *Proc. AMIA 96,* 1996: 552-556.
7. Gordon CJ et al. Telematics for Clinical Guidelines: A Conceptual Modeling Approach. *Proc MIE 97,* 1997.
8. Fox J, Johns N, Rahmanzadeh A. Disseminating Medical Knowledge: The PROforma Approach *Artificial Intelligence in Medicine,* 1998; 14.
9. Barnes M, Barnett GO. An Architecture for a Distributed Guideline Server.*Proc. 19th SCAMC,* 1995: 233-237.
10. Cimino JJ, Socratous SA. Automated Guidelines Implemented via the World Wide Web.*Proc. 19th SCAMC,* 1995: 941.
11. Liem EB, Obeid JS, Shareck EP, Sato L, Greenes RA. Representation of Clinical Practice Guidelines through an Interactive World-Wide-Web Interface.*Proc. 19th SCAMC,* 1995.
12. Pisanelli DM, Consorti F, Merialdo P. SMART: A System Supporting Medical Activities in Real Time, *Proc. MIE 97,* 1997. .
13. http://antipodes.cec.fr/collate/co-home.nsf
14. Musen MA, Tu SW, Das AK, Shahar Y. EON: A component-based approach to automation of protocol-directed therapy. *JAMIA,* 1996; 3.
15. Musen MA, Carlson CW, Fagan LM et al. T-HELPER: Automated support for community-based clinical research. *Proc. 16th SCAMC,* 1992.
16. Gennari JH, Altman RB, Musen MA. Reuse with Protégé-II. Proceedings of the Symposium on Software Reuse, Seattle, 1995.
17. Steve G, Gangemi A, Pisanelli DM, "Integrating Medical Terminologies with ONIONS Methodology", in: *Info.Modelling and Knowledge Bases VIII,* Amsterdam, IOS Press 1998.
18. Pisanelli DM, Gangemi A, Steve G, "A Medical Ontology Library that integrates the UMLS Metathesaurus", *Proc. AI in Medicine,* 1999.

19. National Library of Medicine, *UMLS Knowledge Sources,* 1998 edition, available from the NLM, Bethesda, Maryland.
20. Gruber TR, "A translation approach to portable ontology specification", *Knowledge Acquisition,* 5 (2), 1993: 199-220.
21. MacGregor RM, "A Description Classifier for the Predicate Calculus" *Proceedings of AAAI 94, Conference,* 1994.
22. Swartout B, Patil R, Knight K, Russ T, "Toward Distributed Use of Large-Scale Ontologies", *Proceedings of Knowledge Acquisition Workshop,* Banff, participants edition, 1996.
23. Pisanelli DM, Gangemi A, Steve G, "WWW-available Conceptual Integration of Medical Terminologies", *Proc. AMIA 97,* 1997.
24. Guarino N, Carrara M, Giaretta P, An Ontology of Meta-Level Categories. *Proc. of KR94.* San Mateo, CA, Morgan Kaufmannn, 1994.
25. Pisanelli DM, Gangemi A, Steve G, "An Ontological Analysis of the UMLS Metathesaurus", *Proc. AMIA 98,* 1998.
26. Shahar Y, Miksch S, Johnson P. The Asgaard project, *Artificial Intelligence in Medicine,* 1998; 14.
27. Ohno-Machado L et al. The Guideline Interchange Format, *JAMIA,* 1998; 6.

```
(defcontext planning
  :theory (unrestricted-time diagrams meronymy))

(defconcept generic-plan
  :annotations ((DOCUMENTATION "A generic plan is a script that
contains the method for executing or performing a procedure or
a stage of a procedure."))
    :is-primitive (:and script
                   (:all method
                     (:or procedure procedures^stage)))
    :implies (:and (:some represented-by document)
               (:some has-component generic-plan)
               (:all component generic-plan)
               (:all serial-value serial-value-filler)
                (:all has-title symbolic-string)
               (:all has-precondition situation)
                (:all authored-by plan-author)
               (:all duration-value number)
                (:all has-description symbolic-string)
               (:all has-postcondition situation))
    :partitions $generic-plan$)

  (defconcept elementary-plan
  :annotations ((DOCUMENTATION "A plan that does not contain
compacted plans (ie, subplans represented by a simple node that
can be expanded into a flow-chart)."))
    :is-primitive
     (:and generic-plan
      (:all has-component Incoherent generic-plan)))

  (defconcept complex-plan
    :is (:and generic-plan
              (:at-least 2 has-component generic-plan)))

  (defconcept branching-plan
    :annotations ((DOCUMENTATION "A plan that subdivides in a
set of plans."))
    :is-primitive
     (:and elementary-plan
      (:at-least 2 plan-direct-predecessor))
    :implies (:and (:some represented-by fork-node)
                   (:some method planning-transition))
    :in-partition $generic-plan$)

  (defconcept case-plan
    :annotations ((DOCUMENTATION "A plan branched to a set of
plans not executable in parallel."))
    :is-primitive
     (:and branching-plan
      (:at-least 2 plan-direct-predecessor
       (:and generic-plan
        (:at-least 1 has-precondition)
        (:all co-exist Incoherent generic-plan))))
    :implies (:some represented-by fork-node))
```

Fig. 4. An excerpt from the *planning* ontology.

```
(defcontext  GL-Mapping  :theory (guidelines))

(defrelation  maps
  :is-primitive  extrinsic-structuring-relation)

(defrelation  mapped-by
  :is (:inverse  maps))

(defrelation  equimaps
  :is-primitive maps)

(defrelation  equimapped-by
  :is (:inverse  equimaps))

(defrelation  partly-maps
  :is-primitive  maps)

(defrelation  partly-mapped-by
  :is (:inverse  partly-maps))

;;;ProForma
(defconcept  Proforma-entity
  :is-primitive  (:and  document
                        (:some mapped-by  document)))

(defconcept  Proforma-task
  :is-primitive  (:and  Proforma-entity
                   (:the  equimapped-by  generic-plan)))

(defconcept  Proforma-plan
  :is (:and  Proforma-task
             (:the equimapped-by  complex-plan)))

(defconcept  Proforma-action-task
  :is-primitive
   (:and Proforma-task
    (:the subsumapped-by  elementary-plan)
    (:all has-description  symbolic-string)))

;;;GLIF
(defconcept  Glif-step
 :is-primitive  (:and  Glif-entity
                  (:the equimapped-by  generic-plan)))

(defconcept  Glif-guideline-step
  :is (:and Glif-entity
            (:the equimapped-by  complex-plan)
            (:all has-description  symbolic-string)))

(defconcept  Glif-action-step
  :is-primitive  (:and  Glif-step
                   (:the subsumapped-by  elementary-plan))
  :implies
   (:some has-description  Glif-action-specification))
```

Fig. 5. An excerpt from the *GL-mapping* ontology.

Supporting Inheritance Mechanisms in Ontology Representation

Valentina A.M. Tamma and Trevor J.M. Bench-Capon

Department of Computer Science
The University of Liverpool
Chadwick Building
Peach Street
Liverpool L69 7ZF
United Kingdom
{valli,tbc}@csc.liv.ac.uk

Abstract. Research in the ontology engineering field is becoming increasingly important, especially in the area of knowledge sharing. Many research efforts aim to reuse and integrate ontologies that have already been developed for different purposes. This gives rise to the need for suitable architectures for knowledge sharing. This paper analyses a specific aspect of knowledge sharing; that is the integration of ontologies in a way such that different inheritance mechanisms within the ontology are supported, and focuses on conflicts due to multiple inheritance. We first illustrate the problems that inheritance can cause within ontologies together with different approaches presented in the literature to deal with multiple inheritance conflicts and then propose a semi-automatic approach to deal with such conflicts.

1 Introduction

Ontologies have become increasingly important in sharing and reusing knowledge. In [26] an architecture of multiple shared ontologies for knowledge sharing was presented. In this architecture, resources no longer commit to a single comprehensive ontology but instead are clustered together on the basis of the similarities they show in the way they conceptualise the common domain: each cluster sharing an ontology. Ontology clusters are then organised in a hierarchical fashion thus permitting concepts to be described at different levels of abstraction. Since different siblings can extend their parent cluster concepts in different ways the cluster hierarchy permits the co-existence of heterogeneous (sibling) ontologies. This approach has the advantage of minimising the information loss when performing translations between resources, since they communicate using the least abstract ontology common to them.

The proposed structure of multiple shared ontologies is based on inheritance mechanisms. From studies on inheritance [2], [24] it has emerged that anomalies might arise when dealing with inheritance mechanisms; research efforts in *non-monotonic reasoning* have focused on these anomalies [15], [19], [13]. This paper

R. Dieng and O. Corby (Eds.): EKAW 2000, LNAI 1937, pp. 140–155, 2000.

analyses how inheritance problems can affect ontologies and proposes a methodology to deal, in a semi-automatic fashion, with the conflicts caused by the use of inheritance mechanisms, following the approach proposed by Goldszmidt and Pearl [9].

The proposal is to represent ontologies by an "enriched" frame-based language where the set of the slot's facets has been extended to encompass additional information required for a full understanding of a concept. Understanding a concept involves a number of things. First it involves knowing what can sensibly be said of a thing falling under that concept. This can be represented by associating *attributes* with the concept, and possible values that these attributes can take when applied to things of that type. Thus it is important to know that some birds fly and others do not. A full understanding of a concept involves more than this, however: it is important to know also what is true of a *prototypical* [22] instance of a concept, to know that the prototypical bird flies. There are, however differences in how confident we can be that an arbitrary instance of a concept conforms to the prototype: it is a very rare mammal that lays eggs, whereas many types of well known birds do not fly. Understanding a concept also involves understanding how and which attribute values change over time: people may have eyes of various colours, but they do not change over time, whereas hair colour does. This dynamic behaviour also forms part of the domain conceptualisation. We believe that this additional information needs to form part of the ontology. In this paper we concentrate on prototypical values, but also mention, in passing, one method of dealing with dynamic values.

Representation of concepts within the ontology should be enriched by information concerning the *degree of strength* associated with some properties and some measures of how is likely that a value is associated to an attribute. We take these measures to be qualitative rather than numeric. This additional information enables us to deal with conflicts and inconsistencies due to inheritance mechanisms, as rules with a higher degree of strength and ranking can be given precedence. Other facets are introduced to represent how the attribute's value can change over time; this is based on the intuition that attributes can change their values either regularly in time or if an event occurs and that these changes contribute to enrich the attribute description.

The remainder of the paper is organised as follows: section 2 describes problems caused by different inheritance mechanisms, while section 3 presents Goldzsmidt and Pearl's nonmonotonic approach which is the theoretical framework we follow to deal with inheritance problems and section 4 highlights the problems arising when supporting multiple inheritance in the ontology representation. Section 5 illustrates the extended knowledge model used to apply the Goldzsmidt and Pearl's approach, while section 6 sketches the framework used to deal with inheritance conflicts and section 7 applies this framework to a classical artificial intelligence example of inheritance problem: the Nixon diamond. Finally, section 8 draws conclusions and presents future work.

2 Providing a Motivation for the Additional Facets

Representing knowledge about the world means representing the objects presumed or hypothesised to exist and to be relevant in the world and their relationships. It has been argued that a knowledge representation is a surrogate [5], a stand-in, for what is in the world. Like any surrogate it is not completely *accurate*; it will necessarily contain simplifying assumptions because of the complexity of the natural world. Indeed even restricting to a subset of the natural world is still overwhelmingly complex. In this respect, a knowledge representation is also a set of *ontological commitments.* Ontological commitments determine not only the objects of the world but also what are the features of these objects that are relevant for the knowledge representation task.

Objects correspond to *classes*: all the member of a class share some common properties. Classes represent *concepts* (the terms can be used as synonyms).

The set of relevant concepts and the relationships holding between them form the *conceptualisation* [8] used to represent the world. When selecting a conceptualisation of the world some decisions have to be made in order to establish what concepts to describe and how to describe them. Concepts are identified by sets of attribute-value pairs, where the attributes are those deemed important for the knowledge representation task and the values associated with them permit us to distinguish one concept from another. Usually in the conceptualisation are also represented properties that are *generally* true for that concept, that is the conceptualisation usually describes a prototypical member of that class [22]. This gives rise to an important issue in knowledge representation: properties that are true for a class prototype are not necessarily true for all members of the class represented by the concept. Examples of such cases are frequent in everyday life; *Almost all* mammals give birth to live young, but three highly unusual mammals (monotreme) do not. Analogously, the ability of birds to fly is a property that is *generally* true; it is a property describing the prototypical bird. This type of information on the descriptive strength of properties should be encompassed in the conceptualisation of the domain and thus in the ontologies derived from it.

An ontology is *"an explicit specification of a conceptualisation"* according to Gruber [10]. That is, the conceptualisation refers to an abstract model of some phenomenon in the world by identifying the concepts that are relevant to that phenomenon; in the ontology, the type of concepts used to describe the phenomenon and the constraints on their use are *explicitly* defined [23]. Ontology representations should include ways to represent how generally a property is shared among the members of a class. The ability of ontologies to distinguish not only between *hard* statements like "Elephants are animals" and *soft* ones like "Birds fly", but also between degrees of "softness", is crucial for reasoning about the knowledge represented in the ontology. This reasoning can prove helpful in dealing with problems arising from of the hierarchical organisation of concepts in ontologies. Concepts in ontologies are hierarchically organised through an IS-A relationship, with a partial order relation that is the ontology's main structure and that is further enriched by attributes, and by relationships or functions relating concepts. The IS-A relationship introduces also the powerful notion of *inheritance of properties.* Properties are shared by concepts either in their original form or modified in order to give the inheriting class, known as *subclass*, a more restrictive definition than that provided by the parent concept. Furthermore other properties can be added to form more specialised concepts.

Anomalies arising from inheritance mechanisms have been illustrated in the literature ([2] and [24]), where a distinction is made between *single inheritance* and *multiple inheritance.* The former permits a concept to inherit properties from one parent only and can cause *default conflicts* while the latter permits a concept to inherit properties from more than one parent and can cause inconsistencies in inherited attribute values. In [3], default values are defined as a way to deduce information about a concept if the information is consistent with what is already known about the concept. Reasoning about defaults can became extremely problematic when only *strict inheritance* is allowed, that is when the IS-A link amounts to logical implication or set inclusion. Then, more specific information cannot overrule information obtained from more general classes thus causing wrong conclusions to be inferred. A *defeasible* approach [24] permits the more specific information to overrule the more general one" thus solving the conflict.

Other kind of conflicts can arise when multiple inheritance is supported and conflicting information is inherited from two or more general concepts. In this case a choice has to be made about which value has to be associated with the attribute. This choice can be made by knowledge engineers, or the value can be (semi) automatically provided by determining the property's degree of "softness". The same inconsistency problems caused by supporting multiple inheritance can be encountered when trying to integrate ontologies developed for different purposes (the word *integration* is used here to summarise all the possible meanings that the term takes in the ontological engineering field, and that are illustrated in [20]). In fact, with ontology integration an attempt is made to relate concepts in different ontologies. Concepts to relate can be described by the same attributes, but inconsistent values may be associated with them. So, when integrating ontologies, a crucial issue is to choose, among the inconsistent candidates, the value to associate with an attribute. An example of problems encountered while trying to integrate two or more ontologies can be found in [7] and [6]. Once again, the choice is made by the knowledge engineers performing the integration who can be assisted by some tool that (semi) automatically chooses the most promising attribute's value among a set of candidates.

Before proceeding with the discussion, we would like to clarify a point: most of the classical example of default inconsistencies, such as Tweety the penguin or the Nixon diamond concern *instances* instead of concepts. However, all the considerations that have been made for the instances still hold true also for classes, as we can semantically overload the IS-A relationship with the meaning of *Instance-of relation.* We are aware that such an attitude has been strongly criticised in the literature [27], but we deem that such a difference can be disregarded when considering multiple inheritance.

It is interesting to note that the conflicts do not only arise when the IS-A relationship is explicitly stated; in fact conflicts as the Tweety triangle can as well occur in cases of feature inheritance. The Tweety triangle can be easily reformulated as *Concept*: ***Bird***, *Feature*: **Flier** =" yes" etc.; in this case also the conflict for Tweety arises.

Other kind of conflicts can arise when the knowledge representation system allows multiple inheritance and conflicting information is inherited from two or more concepts. The typical example of such a situation is the *Nixon diamond*. In this case, however, we are not able to infer any conclusion, not even the wrong one.

3 Reasoning with Conflicts

Both inheritance with exceptions and multiple inheritance default conflicts have been widely investigated in the literature concerning *inheritance networks*. Several approaches have tried to infer a reasonable conclusion (if not the right one) from conflicting premises. Horty in [12] divides theories of inheritance into *direct* and *translational* theories. Direct theories are those where the properties and the features of the inheritance networks (such as consistency) along with the set of conclusions that can be inferred from the premises are analysed and characterised in terms of the networks formalism itself. Examples of direct theories can be found in [24], [13], and [12].

Translational theories are those where the meaning of an inheritance network is specified in terms of some type of logical language, either classical first order logic, or some nonmonotonic logic such as Circumscription [15], or Default Logic [21]. This section focuses mainly on direct approaches. Among the direct approaches here we mention the approach by Pearl [19] and lately by Goldszmidt and Pearl [9] as being particularly relevant for dealing with multiple inheritance within ontologies. The main idea of this approach is that knowledge from an inheritance network can be associated with a probability expressing the degree of (dis)belief associated with that bit of knowledge. This measure of the degree of belief permits the approach to handle more complex default interactions (such as inheritance with exceptions) correctly, as pointed out in [1].

More formally, given the language L of the inheritance network (that for Pearl is the language of propositional formulas), every sentence in L corresponds to a set of possible *worlds*, where a world is a conjunction of all the properties describing a typical individual in the domain. As some worlds are definitely more typical than others it is necessary to express the differences between all the possible worlds. This is obtained by weighing every world by assigning it a probability ε, which defines a probability distribution P over L. All the inheritance rules such as $Elephant(x) \rightarrow Animal(x)$ impose restriction conditions on P in the form of extreme conditional probability infinitesimally close either to 0 or to 1, where the closer to 1 the probability, the higher the number of subclasses (and eventually individuals) inheriting the property. So, if we consider the inheritance rule $Mammal(x) \rightarrow Gives\text{-}birth\text{-}to\text{-}live\text{-}young(x)$, this means

P(Gives-birth-to-live-young(x)|Mammal(x)) $\geq 1 - \varepsilon$ that for ε arbitrarily small is close to 1, meaning that if all is known is that x is a mammal, than x almost certainly inherits the property of giving birth to live young.

However, the full precision provided from this framework is not necessary for taking decisions on inheriting conflicting default values. Under this assumption Goldszmidt and Pearl measure the degree of belief not in the continuous interval $[0, 1]$ but rather on a logarithmic scale and they consider beliefs that map into two different values as being of different order of magnitude.

Let $P(\omega)$ be the probability distribution defined over a set Ω of possible worlds; if we write the probability $P(\omega)$ as a polynomial in ε (that is $P_\varepsilon(\omega) = 1 - c_1\varepsilon$, or $\varepsilon^2 - c_2\varepsilon^4$ and so on) then the ranking function $\kappa(\omega)$ is defined as the power of the most significant ε-term in $P_\varepsilon(\omega)$. That is the ranking $P(\omega)$ is expressed as some power of a parameter ε which plays only the role of linking the defaults together. Letting $\varepsilon \to 0$ means that the defaults tend to be certain.

The ranking κ permits to reason about both "hard" and "soft" statements; "Birds fly" is, for instance, a soft one because it is **typically** true for most of the subclasses of the class Birds. The rank κ roughly corresponds to linguistic quantifiers such as *believable*, *unlikely*, *very rare* etc. In fact for $\kappa(\phi) = 0$ it means that both ϕ and $\neg\phi$ are equally possible, for $\kappa(\phi) = 1$ it means that $\neg\phi$ is believed, for $\kappa(\phi) = 2$ it means that $\neg\phi$ is ***strongly*** believed, for $\kappa(\phi) = 3$ it means that $\neg\phi$ is ***very strongly*** believed and so on.

An inference system (*Z-system*) based on the ranking of probabilities has been developed in [9]. The Z-system is able to draw plausible conclusions in most of the cases by a technique known as *z-entailment*, [9] which guarantees that conclusions in inheritance rules will receive high probabilities whenever the premises receive sufficiently high probabilities. This system can compute the priorities of inheritance rules and provides also consistency checks. Unfortunately, one of the main drawbacks of the z-entailment is that it cannot sanction the inheritance property from classes to subclasses with exceptions. This happens because the z-entailment labels all the classes with exceptions as exceptional in all respects, so that they become unable to inherit any of the properties that are typical of their parent class. To overcome this drawback the authors introduce the capabilities for a Z-system to handle variable-strengths thus allowing some defaults to be stated "more strongly" than others.

The *system* $- Z^+$ [9] extends the specification of the inheritance rules by associating with each rule a parameter δ which expresses the *degree of strength* of the rule. Inheritance rules are now ordered on the grounds of a *priority function* Z^+, which is computed as function of both the ranking associated with an inheritance rule and the degree of strength δ; each of them reflects different considerations to be taken into account when drawing conclusions about inheriting properties. The degree of strength δ_i associated with an inheritance rule $r_i = \phi_i \to \psi_i$ establishes the relative strength with which ψ_i is committed to be accepted in the context of ϕ_i while the priority $Z^+(r_i)$ expresses the degree of surprise concerning the finding of a world that violates r_i, which includes also the degree of surprise associated with ϕ_i. Again all the consistency considerations hold also for the $system - Z^+$. Therefore now for each rule $r_i = \phi_i \rightarrow \psi_i$ the Z^+ ordering is determined by both the degree of strength and the ranking function. This type of ordering guarantees that features of more specific contexts override conflicting features of a less specific order, thus allowing the well known Tweety the Penguin problem to be solved. Furthermore, whenever the ranking functions associated with the rules do not permit us to distinguish between inheritance rules, because no specificity consideration is made, the Z^+ ordering depends on the degree of strength alone, therefore permitting preference of one inheritance rule over the other(s). In this way the system can deal with types of conflicts such as the Nixon diamond.

4 Ontologies and Multiple Inheritance

Latest research on inheritance has focused on extending the basic framework of single inheritance without exceptions to inheritance with exceptions and multiple inheritance. However, research on these issues has mainly been confined to academia, giving the impression that problems such as multiple inheritance and inheritance with exceptions are quite rare in real applications [18].

Research in the ontology field has not yet considered any of the problems due to the inheritance of conflicting default values. Indeed many languages to represent ontologies support either multiple inheritance or inheritance with exceptions, but often they do not have any mechanism to deal with the problems caused by these formalisms. Possibly, the problem of handling conflicts has not been regarded as such because ontologies have been usually written from scratch whenever they were needed. This trend in the ontology field has been changing recently, mainly due to research in ontology engineering, which has stressed the importance of building ontologies that are reusable and sharable.

When trying to integrate ontologies developed for different purposes, inconsistencies can arise ([7] and [6]). In fact, one concept can have different parents in different ontologies, and those parents can be described in terms of conflicting attributes. The situation can be even more complicated because inconsistencies can be implicit. Inheritance literature has not been extensively discussed in this context although it is extremely relevant in ontology merging. Indeed, it is likely that ontologies built for different purposes and then merged represent concepts in terms of attributes that are semantically equivalent although with mismatches in the names [25]. Morgenstern [18] has modified the Touretzky's Nixon diamond [24] to show how inconsistencies can be also implicit. The new Nixon's diamond example is shown in figure 1.

The two concepts ***Quaker*** and ***Republican*** are described by two attributes **Pacifist** and **Hawk** that have different names but are semantically related (one is the opposite of the other), as they both describe someone's attitude towards going to war. The proposed framework, illustrated in the next section, deals with such types of inconsistencies.

From the inheritance network viewpoint, ontologies are mixed inheritance networks, where both strict and defeasible paths are allowed, therefore, when

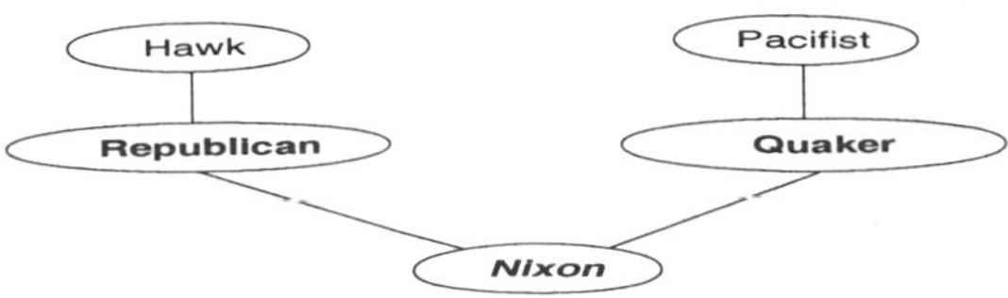

Fig. 1. The modified Nixon diamond

trying to reason with the knowledge expressed in the ontology, an inference method that is able to deal with both types of path is needed. Unfortunately most of the ontologies are based on frames representation systems such as the Generic Frame Protocol [4] where no slot's facet is used to distinguish between these paths. This is the reason why we propose to augment the typical facets of a slot by introducing some additional pieces of information which are useful in dealing with default and inheritance problems: the ranking associated with the inheritance rule, a degree of strength associated with the attribute and facets about how the attribute's value can change over time. The ranking expresses the degree of belief which is associated with the inheritance rule expressed by the attribute, that is how surprising is to find out that, for the concept that is being described, the attribute takes a particular value. In our approach the degree of strength is associated with the attribute (and therefore with the inheritance rule) by the knowledge engineers who are either writing or merging the ontologies, as these people should be familiar with the domain and should therefore be able to weight inference rules. The degree of strength not only distinguishes between strict and defeasible links, but can also be used to measure the degree of defeasibility. Moreover, it permits us to establish preferences among defaults when no specificity considerations are available. If we consider the Nixon diamond example, both facts A: "Quakers are pacifists" and B: "Republicans are not pacifists" are absolutely true, but they might be evaluated differently depending on the domain and even on specific circumstances. A degree of strength can be associated with both these rules. Let us assume that the knowledge engineer believes that religious convictions carry more weight than political affiliations, than the degree of strength associated with A, δ_A is greater then the degree of belief associated with B δ_B. So when the value of the attribute Pacifist is determined for the object Nixon, whenever no specific information on the object is available, the degree of strength makes it infer that Nixon is a pacifist.

Although the degree of strength is decided by the knowledge engineer, it can be affected by specific events that can change the status of an attribute. The intuition behind this is that nonmonotonicity is either time dependent or event dependent, meaning that the value of an attribute can change regularly in time or it can change if a particular event occurs. Therefore, in case of conflicting default values the choice among the possible values should be made by taking into account the regularity in time or the occurrence of one of the modifying events. Going back to the Nixon example, one of the events that can change the status of the attribute Pacifist is the declaration of a war: as president of the United States, although maybe personally inclined to be pacifist, Nixon would tend to protect the interests of his country in the event of a conflict, and so in such a scenario he would not act as a pacifist. This can also mean that until a war is not declared we can assume that the degree of strength associated with the religious conviction is stronger than the one associated with the political conviction, but in case of war this would be no longer true.

Finally, it is interesting to note that many problems with multiple inheritance could be solved by a more careful design of ontologies as pointed out by Guarino [11]. This is due to the fact that in many cases the IS-A relationship is used to represent many other specialised links such as reduction of sense, overgeneralisation, confusion of senses, clash of senses, and sometimes some kind of type-to-role links.

5 The Extended Knowledge Model

So far, all the efforts to deal with inconsistencies have been performed by hand by a knowledge engineer who is expert in the domain that is being described, and who can thus associate the correct default value with an attribute. Choosing between several conflicting defaults requires an extremely rich semantics. For this reason performing the choice automatically is quite unrealistic, but a more realistic possibility is a semi-automatic approach, where an inferential system presents the knowledge engineer with a list of sound alternatives (according to the inference process), but leaves the actual choice to the knowledge engineer.

The model of knowledge used to represent the ontology plays a crucial role in the framework proposed in this paper, as it provides the elements necessary to apply the Goldszmidt and Pearl inference process. The proposed knowledge model is frame-based [17]. Our model is based on *classes*, *slots*, and *facets*. *Classes* correspond to concepts and are collections of objects sharing the same properties, hierarchically organised into a multiple inheritance hierarchy, linked by *IS-A* links. Classes are described in terms of *slots*, or attributes, that can either be sets or single values. A slot is described by a name, a domain, a value type and by a set of additional constraints, here called *facets*. Facets can contain the documentation for a slot, constrain the value type or the cardinality of a slot, and provide further information concerning the slot and the way in which the slot is to be inherited by the subclasses. Our framework suggests the introduction of a set of facets that describes in detail the attribute and its behaviour in the concept description to accommodate different inheritance mechanisms, both within and between ontologies, and changes over time. This additional information is to be used in case of inconsistencies as a guide towards the most reasonable and informed suggestion to be presented to the domain expert, who will than validate such suggestion. The facets we introduce are:

- **Value**: There are three possibilities:
  - If the concept that is being defined is very high in the hierarchy (so high that any distinction based on the attribute's value is not possible), then **Value** is equal to **Domain**;
  - If the concept is still general, but it is possible to determine that it can have different attribute values for its children then **Value** is set equal to **Sub-domain** $\subset$ **Domain**;
  - If the concept is defined in terms of a specific value for an attribute then **Value** is set $v \in$ **Domain**.

  For the *third case* only, further information about the type of value (see next item) or the degree of strength (see item below) can be added;
- **Type of value**: {*Necessary, Prototypical, Inherited, Distinguishing*}. An attribute's value is a *Necessary* one if the value is true for all concept's children. It describes necessary conditions in the concept's description. An attribute's value is a *Prototypical* one if the value is generally true for any children of the concept that is being defined, that is the value is generally true for any prototypical instance of the concept, but exceptions are permitted with a degree of softness expressed by the facet *Ranking*. An attribute's value can be *Inherited* from some super concept or it can be a *Distinguishing* value, that is a value that differentiates among siblings;
- **Degree of strength**: a number describing how relevant is, in the concept's description, the property represented by the attribute. For example, to reason about birds ability to fly, the attribute *species* is more relevant than the attribute *feather colour*. In merging ontologies this facet represents the weight associated with the inheritance rule corresponding to the attribute;
- **Ranking**: an integer describing the probability ranking associated to the fact that the attribute takes the value specified in the facet **Value**. The possible values for this facet are 1: *All*, 2: *Almost all*, 3: *Most*, 4: *Possible*, 5: *A Few*, 6: *Almost none*, 7: *None*. So, to represent the soft statement *Birds fly* we could describe the concept *Bird* by a slot, **Fly** that takes value *Yes* with *Ranking* equal to "Most";
- **Change frequency**: {*Regular*, *Once only*, *Volatile*}. This facet describes how often an attribute's value changes. If the information is set equal to *Regular* it means that the value changes at regular time intervals; if set equal to *Once only* it indicates that only one change is possible, and finally *Volatile* indicates that the attribute's value can change more than once. If the change frequency is *Regular* then the time interval is specified otherwise the event causing the attribute to change is specified;
- **Time interval**: This information can either be empty (if the change frequency is not *Regular*) or it contains the time interval between two changes;
- **Event**: This facet is either empty (if the change frequency is *Regular* and the time interval is set) or it is the set of events $\boldsymbol{E}$ that causes a change in the attribute's value. The logical theory chosen to reason about events is the

Event Calculus [14], and the information **Event**$=e_i$ is interpreted as one of the following Event calculus expressions:

1. *Hold(before(*e_i*, P))* that is, the property P holds *BEFORE* the event e_i;
2. *Hold(after(*e_i*, P))* that is, the property P holds *AFTER* the event e_i;

where the interpretation is decided on the information **Event Validity** (see below). For each event $e_i \in \boldsymbol{E}$ we specify also the *Event Property* and the *Event Validity* facets as follows:

- **Event Property**: $\{V\}$. This facet describes the value taken by the attribute before or after the event E. If this bit of information is empty it means that the event E causes a change in the attribute's value that cannot be specified, possibly because the value can be identified only by considering the instances of the concept;
- **Event Validity**: $\{$*Before, After*$\}$. It states whether the property V specified in the item above holds before the event E or after the event E.

The above facets describe how crucial the slot is in characterising a class, and what conditions determine a change in the value of the slot for that class. These changing conditions are used to query the knowledge engineer while solving default inconsistencies to try to associate with a slot a value as close to the true one as possible. These facets could also be used by knowledge engineers to learn more about the attribute they are dealing with.

6 The Framework to Deal with Inheritance Conflicts

When dealing with heterogeneous resources, mismatches in the names of concepts and attributes might occur [25], [6]. The first step of our framework consists of resolving name mismatches following [7]. This is necessary to avoid cases of implicit inconsistencies, where attributes describing two parent concepts are denoted with different names, while describing the same property. Then the attempt to relate the concepts in the ontologies composing the structure can begin.

In the remainder we present the steps composing this framework, explaining how a system can resolve inconsistencies when trying to build multiple shared ontologies. Ontologies are assumed to be represented by the knowledge model illustrated above. The knowledge engineer **KE** interacts with the system in several steps:

- The first step of our framework consists of scanning both the class names and the slot names in all the ontologies to find possible synonyms. Synonyms are evaluated intensionally, selecting them on the basis of a general thesaurus such as WordNet [16]. For the attributes, however, also an extensional check is performed, by checking the similarity in the attribute's domains.
- Once the name mismatches are resolved, the system proceeds both bottom-up and top down trying to relate classes. When it finds two or more classes

that are suitable parents for the class the system is handling, then a consistency check is performed, according to the technique by Goldszmidt and Pearl [9];

- If an inconsistency is detected then the *priority functions* (see section 3) for the inheritance rules are computed on the grounds of both the *rankings* of probabilities and the *degrees of strength*. These facets permit to solve both default conflicts and inconsistencies due to either multiple inheritance or to the integration of diverse ontologies. The slot's facets encompassing information about the events that can cause the attribute to change are taken into account too, as this information is presented to the **KE** who is requested to validate the events. The system should have now everything necessary to compute the priority function: if so it proceeds to the next step, otherwise if either the ranking or the degree of strength are missing, the systems asks the **KE** to insert them. The value of the inserted facet is decided on the grounds of the information regarding the attribute's changes over time.
- After all the priority functions are computed and ordered, the system presents the **KE** with the slot's value with the best scores.
- The **KE** decides whether to accept the system suggestion or to ask the system to present the list of possible choices in rank order.

7 Applying the Framework to the Nixon Diamond Problem

To explain more clearly how the proposed approach works let us consider the following example, which is an extension of the Nixon diamond. Let us suppose that we need to model the beliefs of the US population from two different viewpoints: political affiliations and religious convictions. The two ontologies describing these viewpoints are partially illustrated in figure 2. These different viewpoints do not

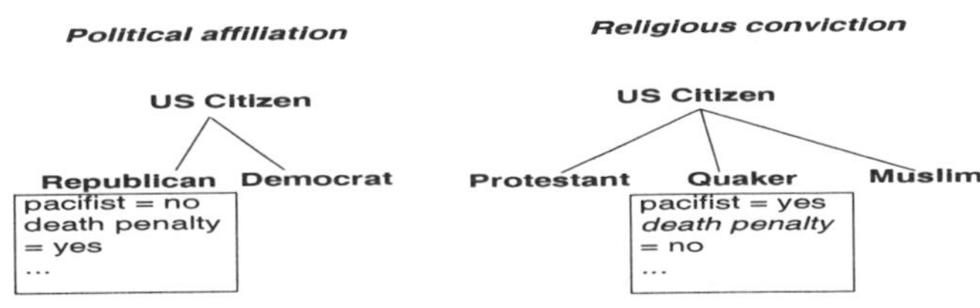

Fig. 2. Sections of the two ontologies modeling the beliefs of the US population

always contrast in the process of taking decisions because one of them often prevails, depending on the matter: political affiliations usually determine people's positions on issues such as welfare and economics whereas religious convictions affect moral issues. However there are some controversial issues that have also a strong moral component, therefore both viewpoints contribute to the process of decision making. In such cases the two viewpoints can either agree or contrast so in this latter case a choice is necessary.

In this example we consider two ontologies, one modeling the political affiliations of US citizens and the other the religious convictions: the two ontologies need to be merged to use this knowledge in order to take decisions about public interest issues that can be considered from both a political and a moral viewpoint.

In merging the two ontologies the following inheritance rules hold for the class "Nixon":

r_1: *"quakers are pacifists with strength δ_1"*, $q \xrightarrow{\delta_1} p$

r_2: *"republicans are non pacifists with strength δ_2"*, $r \xrightarrow{\delta_2} \neg p$

r_3: *"quakers are against death penalty with strength δ_3"*, $q \xrightarrow{\delta_3} \neg d$

r_4: *"republicans support death penalty with strength δ_4"*, $r \xrightarrow{\delta_4} d$

Let us suppose we want to use the knowledge in these two ontologies to infer what would be the position of Nixon in two different situations: going to war and voting on the death penalty. These are decisions that might be taken on the grounds of both political and religious beliefs. Therefore we try to apply the algorithm sketched in the previous section to merge the two ontologies in this two cases. Let us start from the situation in which Nixon has to decide whether the US should go to war. In both these examples we are not concerned with problems due to name mismatches, so we assume that the first step of the procedure is executed successfully. Then the system attempts to relate classes; it finds the class Nixon in both ontologies and with a different parent in each ontology, so the system considers the class Nixon as child of both the class Quaker and Republican, thus inheriting attributes from both of them. At this point the system detects an inconsistency, therefore it tries to resolve it by considering the rankings of probability and the degrees of strength associated with rules r_1 and r_2.

In such a case, as also pointed out by Goldszmidt and Pearl [9], the Z^+ system is not able to decide which rule to prefer on the grounds of the ordering alone, because the priority functions associated to the rules by the Z^+ system are: $Z^+(r_1) = \delta_1$ and $Z^+(r_2) = \delta_2$. In fact in this case the decision to prefer one rule over the other does not depend on specificity considerations but rather on the weight that is associated with each inheritance rule and that *depends on the task at hand.* In problems such as the Nixon diamond it is likely to find that the degree of strength associated with the inheritance rule is is left as choice to knowledge engineers. Knowledge engineers use their knowledge of the domain to assign a value with the degree of strength for each inheritance rule. However, the facets concerning the events causing the attribute's value to change can provide additional information to the process of making a decision. In this specific case the event causing the attribute *Pacifist* to take value *No* for any child of the concept *Republican* in the "Political Affiliation" ontology is the threat of a war against the USA, that is in terms of event logic *Hold(after(War-Against-USA, Pacifist=No))*. So, when the knowledge engineers merging the two ontologies decide the values of the degrees of strength, the choice is made on the grounds of the available information. Since it is in the "Political Affiliation" ontology that the attribute which is being handled is described as changing its value if a war occurs, then this inheritance rule prevails. So, knowledge engineers set $\delta_2 > \delta_1$. The system returns the Z^+ ordering r_2, r_1, thus solving the conflict by preferring the rule *republicans are non pacifists* over the rule *quakers are pacifists*.

In the other situation, that is deciding over death penalty, the algorithm works pretty much in the same way. In this case the class "Nixon" inherits both the rules r_3 and r_4, thus the system detects an inconsistency. In this case no event is specified as able to change either attribute's values: in general the position taken on the death penalty is a fixed opinion. However, for this example the probability of finding that a quaker is against death penalty is higher then the probability of finding that a republican is against it, since it is *always* true that a quaker does not approve death penalty whereas it is only *likely* that a republican approves it. This difference is reflected by the Z^+ ordering of the two rules, which is: $Z^+(r_3) > Z^+(r_4)$. Moreover, if knowledge engineers wish to encompass the information that, in case of death penalty, Nixon's religious conviction carry more weight than Nixon's political affiliation, they might set $\delta_3 > \delta_4$. The system returns in any case the Z^+ ordering of the rules, which is r_3, r_4, thus solving the conflict by preferring the rule *quakers are against death penalty*, as considerations on the degree of belief prevail in this case.

8 Conclusion and Future Work

This paper has presented a semi-automatic framework to deal with multiple inheritance inconsistencies while integrating ontologies. After analysing the problems that are classically proposed in the multiple inheritance literature, we have presented a formal approach to deal with inconsistencies. This approach has been chosen to deal with inconsistencies in the ontology representation. Inconsistencies in ontologies can be more subtle than the ones in semantic networks because diverse ontologies can use different names for the same concept or attributes, so that some inconsistencies can be implicit.

This framework is based on a knowledge model that extends the usual frame-based model in order to associate with each attribute a degree of strength and other information concerning the behaviour of the attribute. By means of this framework knowledge engineers trying to integrate different ontologies are now provided with a tool that checks the inconsistencies and presents them with a list of suggestions that are evaluated according to a priority function, instead of having to check inconsistencies by hand and resolve them. The final choice is always left to the knowledge engineers, but the system provides them with a set of possible choices and with information concerning how and when the attribute changes.

One crucial issue is the choice of the degree of strength to be associated with a slot. At the moment the choice on the degree of strength for inheritance rules is left to the knowledge engineer, although the possibility of increasing the degree of strength of a slot if an event causing the attribute to change occurs will be investigated. Future work will concentrate on extending the framework by introducing some form of temporal reasoning based on event logics that extend the facets.

Acknowledgment

This research is conducted as part of a PhD project funded by BT. The authors wish to thank Floriana Grasso and Dean Jones.

References

[1] R.A. Bourne and S. Parsons. Maximum entropy and variable strength defaults. In T. Dean, editor, *Proceedings of the Sixteenth International Joint Conference on Artificial Intelligence (IJCAI)*, pages 50–55. Morgan Kaufmann Publishers Inc., 1999.

[2] R.J. Brachman. On the epistemological status of semantic networks. In R.J. Brachman and H.J. Levesque, editors, *Readings in Knowledge Representation*, pages 191–215. Morgan Kaufmann, Los Altos, CA, 1985.

[3] B. Carpenter. Skeptical and credulous default unification with application to templates and inheritance. In T. Briscoe, A. Copestake, and V. de Paiva, editors, *Default reasoning and Lexical Organization.* Cambridge University Press, 1993.

[4] V.K. Chaudhri, A. Farquhar, R. Fikes, P.D. Karp, and J.P. Rice. The generic frame protocol 2.0. Technical report, Stanford University, 1997.

[5] R. Davis, H. Shrobe, and P. Szolovits. What is a knowledge representation? *AI Magazine*, 14(1):17–33, 1993.

[6] R. Dieng and S. Hug. Comparison of ≪personal ontologies≫ represented trough conceptual graphs. In H. Prade, editor, *Proceedings of the 13th European Conference of Artificial Intelligence (ECAI)*, pages 341–345. John Wiley & Sons, 1998.

[7] N. Friedman Noy and M.A. Musen. SMART: Automated support for ontology merging and alignment. In *Proceedings of the 12th Workshop on Knowledge Acquisition, Modeling and Management (KAW)*, Banff, Canada, 1999.

[8] M.R. Genesereth and N.J. Nillson. *Logical foundations of Artificial Intelligence.* Morgan Kauffman, 1987.

[9] M. Goldszmidt and J. Pearl. Qualitative probabilistic for default reasoning, belief revision, and causal modelling. *Artificial Intelligence*, 84(1-2):57–112, 1996.

[10] T. R. Gruber. A translation approach to portable ontology specifications. *Knowledge Acquisition*, 5(2):199–220, 1993.

[11] N. Guarino. The role of identity conditions in ontology design. In V.R. Benjamins, editor, *Proceedings of the IJCAI'99 Workshop on Ontology and Problem-Solving Methods: Lesson learned and Future Trends*, volume 18, Amsterdam, 1999. CEUR Publications.

[12] J.F. Horty. Some direct theories of nonmonotonic inheritance. In D. Gabbay, C. Hogger, and J. Robinson, editors, *Handbook of Logics in Artificial intelligence and Logic Programming, Vol. 3: Nonmonotonic Reasoning and Uncertain Reasoning*, pages 111–187. Oxford University Press, Oxford, 1994.

[13] J.F. Horty, R.H. Thomason, and D.S. Touretzky. A skeptical theory of inheritance in nonmonotonic semantic networks. *Artificial intelligence*, 42:311–348, 1990.

[14] R. Kowalski and M. Sergot. A logic-based calculus of events. *New Generation Computing*, 4:67–95, 1986.

[15] J. McCarthy. Applications of circumscription to formalizing common sense knowledge. *Artificial Intelligence*, 28:89–116, 1986.

[16] G.A. Miller. Nouns in WordNet: a lexical inheritance system. *International Journal of Lexicography*, 3(4):245–264, 1990.

[17] M. Minsky. A framework for representing knowledge. In A. Collins and E.H. Smith, editors, *Cognitive Science*, pages 191–215. Morgan Kaufmann, Los Altos, CA, 1992.

[18] L. Morgenstern. Inheritance comes of age: Applying nonmonotonic techniques to problems in industry. *Artificial Intelligence*, 103:1–34, 1998.

[19] J. Pearl. *Probabilistic Reasoning in Intelligent Systems: Networks of Plausible Inference*. Morgan Kauffman, San Mateo, CA, revised second printing edition, 1988.

[20] H.S. Pinto, A. Gómez-Pérez, and J.P. Martins. Some issues on ontology integration. In V.R. Benjamins, editor, *Proceedings of the IJCAI'99 Workshop on Ontology and Problem-Solving Methods: Lesson learned and Future Trends*, volume 18, pages 7.1–7.11, Amsterdam, 1999. CEUR Publications.

[21] R. Reiter. A logic for default reasoning. *Artificial Intelligence*, 13:81–132, 1980.

[22] E.H. Rosch. Cognitive representations of semantic categories. *Journal of Experimental Psychology: General*, 104:192–233, 1975.

[23] R. Studer, V.R. Benjamins, and D. Fensel. Knowledge engineering, principles and methods. *Data and Knowledge Engineering*, 25(1-2):161–197, 1998.

[24] D.S. Touretzky. *The Mathematics of Inheritance Systems*. Morgan Kaufmann, 1986.

[25] P.R.S. Visser, D.M. Jones, T.J.M. Bench-Capon, and M.J.R. Shave. Assessing heterogeneity by classifying ontology mismatches. In N. Guarino, editor, *Formal Ontology in Information Systems. Proceedings FOIS'98, Trento, Italy*, pages 148–162, Amsterdam, The Netherlands, 1998. IOS Press.

[26] P.R.S. Visser and V.A.M. Tamma. An experience with ontology-based agent clustering. In V.R. Benjamins, editor, *Proceedings of the IJCAI'99 Workshop on Ontology and Problem-Solving Methods: Lesson learned and Future Trends*, volume 18, pages 12.1–12.13, Amsterdam, 1999. CEUR Publications.

[27] W.A. Woods. What's in a link: Foundations for semantic networks. In D. G. Bobrow and A. Collins, editors, *Representation and Understanding*, pages 35–82. Academic Press, New York, 1975.

Conflict Resolution in the Collaborative Design of Terminological Knowledge Bases

Gilles Falquet, Claire-Lise Mottaz Jiang

Centre universitaire d'informatique, University of Geneva[1]
24, rue du Général-Dufour, CH-1211 Genève 4, Switzerland
{Gilles.Falquet, Claire-Lise.Mottaz}@cui.unige.ch

Abstract. Designing a terminological knowledge base consists in collecting terms and associating them to their definition. Our objective is to define a process model to support this design task in a collaborative work environment. The proposed concept model is based on terminological logic and the issue-based model IBIS. The terminological logic part is intended to formally express definitions and associate them to terms and points of view. The process model we define is based on a cyclic conflict resolution process. It includes a formal concept comparison operation, to highlight definition conflicts and their nature, and other operations (derivation, intersection, union, etc.) to solve the detected conflicts. The IBIS part of the model enable users to express and record issues, positions, arguments and endorsements that occur during conflict resolution.

1 Introduction

1.1 Background

Terminology is about identifying, describing and naming a field's concepts. Terminology's basic elements are: concepts, terms, definitions and fields. A concept is described by a definition and is named by a term. As a rule, a term can only refer to a single concept within a field. The elaboration of terminological dictionaries and concept bases is generally intended to make translators' job easier or to ensure a better communication between field's specialists. In the recent years it has become obvious that this terminological work is crucial in information systems design and particularly in knowledge management.

Everyone has his own perception of real world's objects. Thus, when a group of people is building up a concept base or an information system, its members often don't agree on the meaning of the terms, i.e. there are vocabulary conflicts. Surprisingly, although there are many types of concept bases, none of them allows, as far as we know, to store and manage multiple, not necessarily coherent, points of view for a concept's definition. As a result, the choice of a definition or a term must usually be done before it can be inserted into the concept base. So we can say that concept models only allow to store the conceptualization's result but don't directly support the conceptualization process.

---

1. This work is a part of a joint project between the CUI and the ETI (School of Translation and Interpretation) at the University of Geneva

R. Dieng and O. Corby (Eds.): EKAW 2000, LNAI 1937, pp. 156–171, 2000.

1.2 Related Work

Traditional terminology banks, such as Eurodicautom (European Union), Termium (Canada), Lingua-PC (Switzerland, Canton of Bern) or BD-TERM (University of Geneva) [7], [15] represent a first type of concept bases. Concepts are described using textual definitions and other terminological descriptors (synonym, context, source, note). In these terminology banks it could be possible (even if it is not usually done) to store multiple points of view, for instance several definitions for a concept, because the record associated with each term is typically stored as formatted text. But as concept representations are not formalized, it is difficult to apply automatic processing on them.

In terminological knowledge representation systems, (KL-ONE [2], ALCNR [4], etc.) concepts are characterized by a a set of roles which link them to other concepts in the base. In this case, definitions are not textual but formalized, thus allowing some automatic processing. Nevertheless, in this case we have to face the opposite problem: it is not possible, with this kind of formalism, to handle several definitions for a single concept.

The ConcepTerm model [1], [17] is relatively close to classic terminological knowledge representation systems. Concepts are defined by a set of pairs <characteristic; value>. The goal of ConcepTerm was to enable the search for equivalent terms in different languages by comparing related concepts' definitions. This can give interesting suggestions on how to compare concepts, but this model does not allow to store several definitions for a concept.

The Co4 system [9] suggests an interesting approach for the collaborative building of a consensual knowledge base from several individual bases. The bases are organized in a tree in which leaves are the individual bases and each node represents the consensual base of the subtree. The tree's root is the global consensual base. With Co4, the rule is: before inserting a piece of knowledge into a consensual base, one must be sure that all the bases of the subtree agree with it. Co4 is a kind of multi point of view system: knowledge in a consensual base is not the same as knowledge in individual bases. It is however difficult to have a global view, since the different points of view are dispersed in several bases.

Collaboratively designing and building a concept base can also be seen as a decision making process: for each concept and each point of view it is necessary to choose one definition among those which are suggested by the group members. There exist several models for decision making support in an argumentative environment, such as IBIS [5], [6], [12], [13] QOC and DRL [3], [18]. This kind of models will give us a basis for the creation of a multi point of view concept model.

When several points of view are available, it could help to have tools for comparing and manipulating them. So, as we are mainly interested in managing multiple points of view for concepts definitions, we have to quote the works of Shaw and Gaines on conceptual systems comparisons [16]. Since the method of Gaines and Shaw aims at comparing two or more different conceptual systems, it takes into account object names, attributes and values. For instance, it can compare attributes values even if the attributes names do not match.

Table 1. explains some of the terms that we will use later. It is excerpted from [16] and indicates the possible situations resulting from the comparison of two ore more conceptual systems.

Table 1. Conceptual Systems Comparison Results (excerpted from [16])

		Terms	
		Same	**Different**
Concepts	**Same**	**Consensus** People use the same terms to name the same concepts	**Correspondence** People use different terms to name the same concepts
	Different	**Conflict** People use the same terms to name different concepts	**Contrast** People use different terms to name different concepts

One can remark that Shaw and Gaines' method is meant to compare two or more different conceptual systems, whereas our main preoccupation is what to do with one incoherent system, build collaboratively. Their method will nevertheless give us suggestions on how to define our concepts comparison operation. These remarks are also applicable to the method presented by Dieng [8] for modeling knowledge of multiple experts. (This method is based on the comparison of conceptual graphs.) It is also worth noticing that using differents terminologies doesn't inevitably imply a contrast: maybe people just have a different level of abstraction.

1.3 Multiple Points-of-View

The KRL, LOOPS, ROME, VIEWS and TROPES [14] models propose different kinds of solutions for the management of multiple points of view. However, these models all rely on the hypothesis that points of view are partial representations of a unique coherent set of objects. We focus on another situation: when building the concept base, each person (or group of people) has his own incomplete perception of the field; the sum of all individual perception giving an incoherent representation of that field. This difference between basic hypothesis stems from the fact that the model we are presenting in this paper is meant to support group knowledge acquisition and building whereas the others are more adapted to a collective use of already build knowledge.

We consider point of view as a mean to solve definition conflicts. Namely, when two definitions are proposed for the same term, the multi point of view approach allows to keep both definitions, provided they belong to different points of view. For example, it would be easy to accept that a cashier and a mathematician do not define the concept of addition in the same way. Since we do not consider points of view as partial representation of a unique definition, we can even accept definitions which are not completely compatible. This is to reflect the fact that there is generally no strict border to the extension of a concept. For instance, where is the border between red objects and brown objects? Nevertheless, it is clear that the definition must not be contradictory. In addition, points of view are not intended to hide the conflicts and to please each participant, they must in fact correspond to a real application (e.g. sales, engineering, accounting) or group of users of the knowledge base.

1.4 Organization of this Paper

The rest of this paper is organized as follows. Section 2 presents the ConceptIBIS model. Section 3 introduces the concept comparison and derivation operations which will be used in the conflict resolution process. Section 4 presents the conflict resolution process. And finally, section 5 gives a conclusion.

2 The ConceptIBIS Model

When building a terminological concept base, two essential yet reciprocal problems occur: How to define the concept corresponding to a term? What term to use to name a concept with this or that definition? When a group of people is building a terminological concept base, it can lead to several situations corresponding to these two types of problems. Specifically, there can be:

- several different definitions for a single term
- several different terms for a single definition

The main goal of the ConceptIBIS model is to provide a background for 1) highlighting the above-mentioned situations and 2) solving these situations in a multi point of view context. The resolution of a definition conflict can lead to several situations: the two definitions are accepted and each one is linked to a different point of view; or one tries to create a single definition from the two conflicting ones; or one accepts that there are in fact two different concepts (for instance if the definitions are contradictory).

2.1 Structure of the Model

ConceptIBIS is based on ConcepTerm. An argumentative part based on IBIS has been added to enable the management of multiple points of view. The purely terminological part of the model consists of *concepts*, *terms*, *definitions*, *fields*, and *points of view*. A concept definition comprises a set of characteristics with their respective values, the structure of a definition will be detailed in the next section.

Since a concept is an abstraction, a mental representation of real object, it doesn't have a material existence. Thus it must always be associated to either a term of a definition that represent it. This fact is represented in the model by associations between the classes *Concept* and *Term*, and *Concept* and *Definition*. In order to implement the multi point of view approach, each definition must be attached to at least one point of view on the concept's field. Furthermore, two definition may be associated with the same concept only if they belong to different points of view. Violation of this rule means that there is a definition conflict.

In IBIS, there are three types of elements: issues, positions, and arguments. A position can be seen as a way to solve a given issue, and an argument may be in favor or against a position. In ConceptIBIS, we use the IBIS model to formalize and keep track of the conflict resolution process. Definition conflicts are the issues; a position corresponds to the choice of an operation in the conflict resolution process (defined in section 4); and arguments are in favor or against choices. Each operation is related to its operands which are objects of the model (definitions, points of view, concepts, etc.). For instance, the operands of an operation "associate definition *d* with point of view *v*" has two operands of type *Definition* and *Point of view* respectively. Since the concept base construction process involves modifying definitions, it is necessary to keep all the versions of a definition which have been involved in a conflict resolution operation. Thus each definition version is linked to the previous version. Finally, an endorsement is a recognition by some authority that a given definition - concept - term association is valid. Fig. 1. shows a formal definition of the structure of ConceptIBIS (using a UML-like notation)

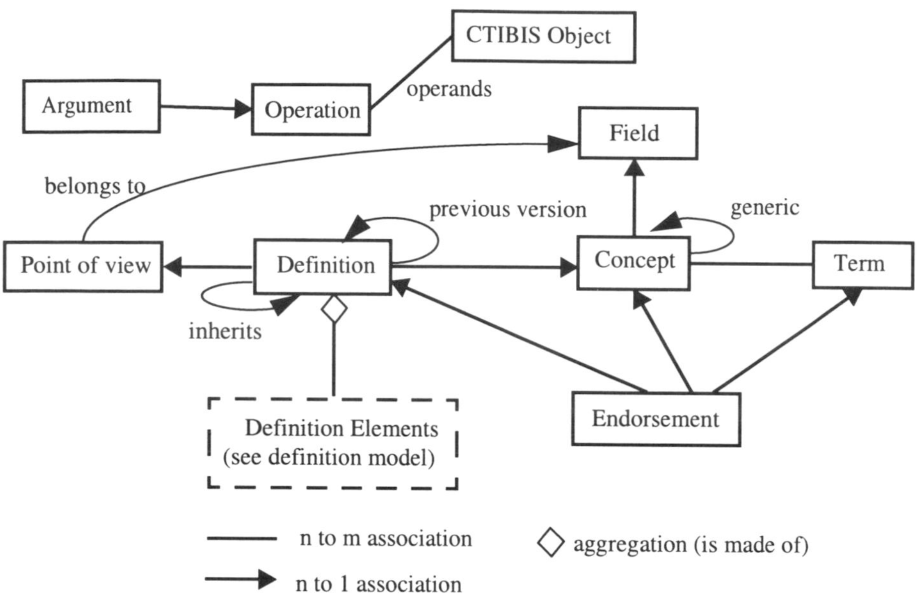

Fig. 1. The ConceptIBIS model in UML

The *generic* association between definitions is a syntactic relationship which means that a definition inherits definition elements from another one. The *generic* association between concepts is semantic one, meaning that the generic concept has a wider interpretation (set of instances). The notion of synonym is implemented by connecting two terms to the same concept.

2.2 Definition Model

We use the definition model that was developed for the creation of multilingual concept bases in the ConcepTerm project [1]. The model we use here is a slight extension of the model presented in [11]. The extension consists in introducing number constraints as a separate construct instead of using "number" characteristics[1].

A definition is a specialization of a more general definition: it is composed of a set of characteristics. A characteristic has a name, a quantifier or a number restriction and a value definitions. A value definition is itself a definition, it specifies which object categories are allowed for a given characteristic. Formally, a concept definition is a statement which follows the following syntax:

ConceptDefinition ::=

definition DefinitionId **generic** DefinitionId **characteristics** Characteristic*

1. This extension was dictated by early results we obtained with the comparison algorithm. It is intended to reduce the relative importance of having equalities on number restrictions when comparing concepts.

Characteristic ::= [**all** | NumberRestriction] CharacteristicName ":" Value
NumberRestriction ::= "<" PositiveNumber "," NonNullPositiveNumber ">"
PositiveNumber ::= "0" | "1" | "2" | ... | "*"
NonNullPositiveNumber ::= "1" | "2" | ... | "*"
Value ::= [**not**] Term | Disjunction | Conjunction | Characteristic
Disjunction ::= "{" Value* "}"
Conjunction ::= "(" Value* ")"

Where * denotes 0, 1 or several occurrences of an element; [] denotes 0 or 1 occurrences and | denotes alternative.

Example. A definition for the concept [wardrobe][1]

definition wardrobe
generic storage_furniture
characteristics
Dimension : big,
Part : (type : door)
Part : <2, *> (type : shelf)
Part : (type : body)
all Main_Use : (verb : store, object : {linen ; clothes})

Terms which appear in a definition indicate predefined concepts, i.e. concepts for which there is not an explicit definition in the concept base (atomic concepts). The atomicity of a concept is not an absolute notion, it is relative to a field. For instance, *wood* can be regarded as atomic within the furniture field whereas it will be explicitly defined when talking about building materials.

It is sometimes useful to view a concept definition as a syntax tree with each arc representing a characteristic. In particular, we will define the definition comparison operation in terms of tree transformation. The following figure shows the tree representation of the previous example (wardrobe).

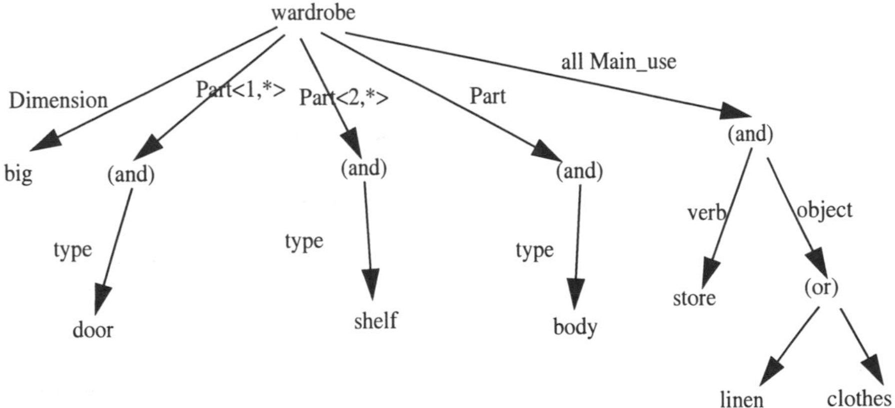

Fig. 2. A definition in tree form

1. from the "Furniture" concept base of ConcepTerm project

The semantics of a definition is a subset of an interpretation domain. This subset corresponds to the extension a concept. A knowledge base is a set of definitions. An interpretation I of a knowledge base (KB) is composed of

- a set Δ^I (the interpretation domain)
- for each elementary concept e (designated by a term), an interpretation $e^I \subseteq \Delta^I$
- for each characteristic R, a relation $R^I \subseteq \Delta^I \times \Delta^I$

The interpretation of a definition is obtained by applying the following rules :

$$
\begin{aligned}
\mathrm{I}(\textbf{generic}\ \mathrm{G}\ \textbf{characteristics}\ \mathrm{K}_1\ \mathrm{K}_2, \ldots\ \mathrm{K}_n) &= \mathrm{I}(\mathrm{G}) \cap \mathrm{I}(\mathrm{K}_2) \cap \ldots \cap \mathrm{I}(\mathrm{K}_n) \\
\mathrm{I}(\mathrm{R}\text{: <min, max> V}) &= \{\ o \mid \min \leq \mathrm{card}\{p \in \mathrm{I}(\mathrm{V}) \mid (o, p) \in \mathrm{R}^I\} \leq \max\} \\
\mathrm{I}(\textbf{all}\ \mathrm{R}\text{: V}) &= \{\ o \mid \forall\ p.\ (o, p) \in \mathrm{R}^I \Rightarrow p \in \mathrm{I}(\mathrm{V})\ \} \\
\mathrm{I}(\ (\mathrm{C}_1, \mathrm{C}_2, \ldots, \mathrm{C}_n)\ ) &= \mathrm{I}(\mathrm{C}_1) \cap \mathrm{I}(\mathrm{C}_2) \cap \ldots \cap \mathrm{I}(\mathrm{C}_n) \\
\mathrm{I}(\ \{\mathrm{C}_1, \mathrm{C}_2, \ldots, \mathrm{C}_n\}\ ) &= \mathrm{I}(\mathrm{C}_1) \cup \mathrm{I}(\mathrm{C}_2) \cup \ldots \cup \mathrm{I}(\mathrm{C}_n) \\
\mathrm{I}(\mathrm{term}) &= \mathrm{term}^I, \\
\mathrm{I}(\textbf{not}\ \mathrm{term}) &= \Delta^I \setminus \mathrm{term}^I,
\end{aligned}
$$

Commutativity and associativity of the union and the intersection imply that the order in which the elements of a concept definition appear has no importance (interpretation remains unchanged under element permutation).

This model and its semantics are close to the terminological knowledge representation model *ALCNR* [4]. The main difference lies in the number restriction construct. In *ALCNR* a number restriction applies to a role ($\leq$ *n Role* and $\geq$ *n Role*) while in ConcepTerm it applies to a role and a value (*Role*: *<min, max>Value*), meaning that an instance of this concept must be linked to at least *min* and at most *max* instances of *Value* through *Role*. If there are several characteristics with the same name, an equivalent *ALCNR* definition can be obtained by introducing new role names.

In terms of concept base, a definition is represented by objects of the classes and associations shown in Fig. 3.. In the ConceptIBIS system, definitions are actually stored under this form.

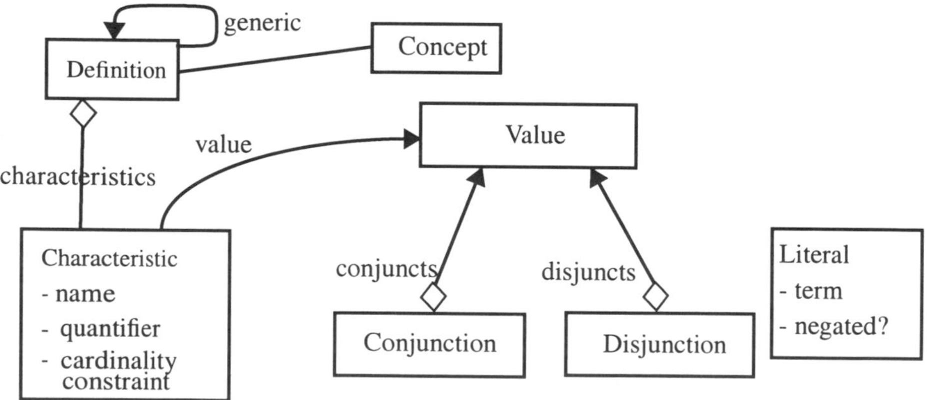

Fig. 3. Structure of a definition in UML-like notation

3 Operations for Collaborative Work

The main operations of the ConceptIBIS model are the definition comparison (to detect conflicts), and definition derivations (to help the resolution process.)

3.1 Definitions Comparison

Comparison is the basic operation to identify consensus and divergence, identify synonyms, etc. It is central in a process of collaborative building of concept bases. The comparison of two definitions is done by comparing their respective sets of characteristics. For this operation to be useful, it must indicate precisely the differences that exist between two definitions. A boolean comparison is not enough (A is equal to B or A is different from B); neither is a comparison that calculates a distance between two concepts and only gives a positive real number (whatever the sophistication of the calculation). One should also note that the n-dimensional distance is not applicable since characteristics may be multivaluated.

Our approach, which is mostly syntactic consists in expressing the difference between two definitions C1 and C2 as modifications. A *modification* of a definitions C1, regarded as a tree, is a labeled tree which is an extension of C1. Arcs coming from C1 may remain unlabeled (unchanged) or be labeled with [–] to indicate subtree removal. Added subtrees are labeled with [+] on their to level arcs. Similarly, number constraints may be added and removed. A difference between definitions C1 and C2 is a modification of C1 which, when evaluated, yields C2, and has minimal complexity.

C1 =
generic storage_furniture
characteristics
    Dimension: big
    Part: <1,*> (type: door),
    Part: <1,*> (type: shelf),
    Part: <1,*> (type: body)
    Main_Use : <1,1> (verb: store,
        object: {linen; clothes})

C2 =
generic storage_furniture
characteristics
    Part: <0,*>(type: door,
        material: (type: pane)),
    Part: <2,*>(type: shelf)
    Main_Use:
        <1,1> (verb: store, object:books)

Fig. 4. Two concept definitions

Example. Let C1 and C2 be the definitions shown on Fig. 4.. The following expression is a modification of C1 that yields C2:

[+] Dimension: big
    Part: [-]<1,*>[+]<0,*>(type: door, [+] material: (type: pane)),
    Part: [-]<1,*>[+]<2, *>(type: shelf),
[-] Part: <1,*>(type: body)
    Main_Use: (verb: store, object: {[-] linen; [-] clothes; [+] books})

The complexity of a modification depends on the number of modification labels it has and the depth at which these labels occur. A modification label at level n has weight $1/p^n$, where p is an integer parameter greater than 2.

If a modification is composed of characteristics $K_1, \ldots, K_n$, its complexity $\chi(M)$ is defined as the mean of the characteristics' complexities:

$$\chi(M) = (\chi(K_1) + \ldots + \chi(K_n))/n$$

The complexity of a labeled characteristic is recursively defined by the following rules:

adding/removing a characteristic

$$\chi([\ ]\ R \langle \mathit{min}, \mathit{max}\rangle : V) = \chi([\ ]\ \text{all}\ R : V) = 1$$

modification of a number constaint

$$\chi(R : [-]\langle \mathit{min}, \mathit{max}\rangle\ [+]\langle \mathit{min}', \mathit{max}'\rangle\ V)$$

$$= b_{comp} + 1/p\ \chi(V) \text{ if } \langle \mathit{min}, \mathit{max}\rangle \text{ et } \langle \mathit{min}', \mathit{max}'\rangle \text{ are compatible}$$

$$= b_{incomp} + 1/p\ \chi(V) \text{ if } \langle \mathit{min}, \mathit{max}\rangle \text{ et } \langle \mathit{min}', \mathit{max}'\rangle \text{ are incompatible}$$

(Constraints are incompatible if the set of integer they define have an empty intersection, b_{comp} and b_{incomp} are real number parameters satisfying $b_{comp} < b_{incomp}$ and $b_{incomp} + 1/p \leq 1$.)

modification of the values (values may be characteristics, conjuctions, disjunctions, or literals)

$$\chi(R \langle \mathit{min}, \mathit{max}\rangle : V) = \chi(\text{ all } R : V) = 1/p\ \chi(V)$$

adding or removing a conjunction, a disjunction, or a literal

$$\chi([\ ](V_1, \ldots, V_n)) = \chi([\ ]\{V_1; \ldots; V_n\}) = \chi([\ ]\textbf{not}\ [-]\ \text{term}\ [+]\ \text{term}') = 1$$

adding or removing an element within a conjunction or a disjunction

$$\chi((V_1, \ldots, V_n)) = \chi(V_1) + \ldots + \chi(V_n))/n$$

$$\chi(\{V_1; \ldots; V_n\}) = \chi(V_1) + \ldots + \chi(V_n))/n$$

Formal definitions of the notions of modification and difference, as well as a discussion on the computational and semantic properties of the difference can be found in [11].

It is important to note that this notion of difference is essentially syntactic. However, when the complexity of a difference is null, we are sure that both definitions have the same interpretation, but the converse is not true. In fact, computing a semantic distance would require to know the interpretation of each predefined term, which is not the case in the bases we consider. As mentioned before, what is most important for conflict resolution is to have a clear view of what makes two definitions different. In addition, we are interested in finding syntactic differences even if they have no semantic effect. This is typically what happens when two designers have used different characteristic names to mean the same thing. Since we consider this situation as a conflict, it must be detected when computing differences.

The complexity of the distance and difference calculation is exponential, because in all cases of (and), (or) and multivaluated characteristics (several characteristics with the same name), one needs to try all possible permutations to find which one minimizes complexity. However, in the real cases that we met, the size of the permutations was limited.

3.2 Manipulation Operations: Derivation

Once comparison has been carried out, one needs a few manipulation operations in order to make further steps towards consensus. Basically, manipulation operations should enable the modification of existing definitions. But as endorsements refer to terms and definitions, modifying a definition could invalidate an endorsement. Similarly, conflict resolution arguments refer to operations and operands and could be invalidated by definition changes. To avoid this situation, it is forbidden to change definitions that are referenced from an endorsement or argument. Every operation must be done either on a new version of an existing definition or on a completely new definition (both are basically a copy of the original definition).

In other words, one can say that all manipulation operations are grouped under the "derivation" label. A *derivation* is a new definition which is created from an existing definition by either

- modifying the name and/or the value of one or more of its characteristics, or
- adding one or several new characteristics, or
- removing one or several characteristics.

A derivation can either be considerated as a new version of the original definition or as a completely new definition. (A new version of a definition still refers to the same concept, whereas a new definition corresponds to a new concept.). The following two operations are intended to automatically produce derivations that can help in the resolution process.

Definitions Intersection

The intersection of two definitions A and B is a new definition that possesses only their common parts. This operation depends on the difference between A and B that is chosen. If D is a difference (labeled tree) from A to B, the intersection corresponding to D is obtained by removing all the [–] or [+] labeled subtrees that belong to a conjunction (including the top-level characteristics); retaining all the subtrees that belong to a disjunction; and removing all the [–] or [+] labeled cardinality constraints and universal quantifiers. One can see that the intersection creates a definition that is more general than the intersected definitions (i.e. its interpretation will always contain the interpretation of each intersected definition).

Definitions Union

The union is the dual of the intersection operation. It retains all the characteristics of both definitions which are in a conjunction and retains only the common characteristics in disjunctions. It creates a definition whose interpretation is included in each one of the original definition interpretation.

Although these two operations do not automatically solve definition conflicts, they produce different alternatives that can be examined by the designers. This corresponds to the well known conflict resolution technique which consists in generating and proposing new alternatives.

4 Conflict Analysis and Resolution

In ConceptIBIS, we use the term "conflict" when:

- two (or more) terms designate the same concept,
- in a given field, two (or more) definitions describe the same concept and they belong to the same point of view.

The first type of conflict can be solved by answering to the question: "Are those two terms synonyms?". In the case of a positive answer, a synonymy link is created between them. Otherwise, it is necessary either to remove one term, or to create a new concept for one of these terms. Solving definition conflicts will be the main topic of this section. We will first situate the conflict resolution task within the terminological knowledge base building process. Then we will show what can be done automatically to analyze definition conflicts and indicate which operations can be used to resolve them.

4.1 The Collective Creation Process

The collaborative building of a terminological concept base with ConceptIBIS is an iterative process. We can see three main phases:

1) Free creation of terms, definitions and concepts.
2) Deliberations: participant can show their agreement or disagreement with the definitions by creating positive or negative endorsements.
3) Conflict analysis and resolution

The conflict analysis and resolution phase can be applied locally to a part of the knowledge base, while the other parts remain in phase 1 and 2. Moreover, it is not compulsory to resolve all the conflicts to return to phase one. The idea is that the knowledge base is built progressively and also becomes gradually more consistent.

4.2 Using Comparisons to Analyze Conflicts

Testing Generalizations and Specializations

If there exist a path F from D1 to D2 which only contains [+] in conjunctions and [-] in disjunctions and which only restricts cardinality constraints and adds universal quantifiers, then it is sure that the interpretation of D1 will contain the interpretation of D2 (this is true because there are no negations outside literals and also because the <0,0> cardinality constraint is forbidden and replaced by a universal quantifier). One will then say that F proves that D2 is a specialization of D1. If D2 is a specialization of D1.

Testing Compatibility

D1 and D2 are incompatible if no object can fulfil both definitions at the same time. With the analysis of differences between D1 and D2 it is possible to prove some cases of incompatibility. However, one can not prove every incompatibility case because it would require a precise knowledge of concepts corresponding to terms used in literals. One can enumerate a set of inference rules which allow to discover some incompatibilities between definitions. (incoherent concept detection in CLASSIC [2])

A difference F between two concepts definitions or between two value definitions proves the incompatibility of two definitions in the following cases:

Replacement of a Literal by its Negation,

F contains: [+] term [-] not term or [-] term [+] not term

Replacement by an Incompatible Cardinality Constraint

F contains: R [–] <min, max>[+]<min', max'>: D
where <min, max> and <min', max'> are incompatible and D only contains operations corresponding to a generalization or a specialization.

Incompatibility between an Existential Characteristic and an Universal Characteristic

If one can prove the incompatibility between D and D' (by analysing their differences) and F contains: [+] all R : D and [–] R : D' (or the opposite).

Conjunction

if one can prove that D_i and D_j are incompatible and F contains: (D_1, ..., [+] D_i, ..., [–] D_j, ..., D_n).

Disjunction

if for $1 \leq i \leq n$ and $1 \leq j \leq m$ one can prove that D_i is incompatible with E_j and F contains : {[+]D_1; ...; [+]D_n; [–]E_1; ...; [–]E_m}.

Compatibility is independent from distance (the complexity of a difference) between definitions. For example, if two definitions have no common characteristic, they will be perfectly compatible even if the distance is large. The compatibility of two definitions does not necessarily imply that they represent the same concept. A human intervention is required to complete the diagnostic, that is to identify semantic incompatibilities that difference analysis can not detect. Compatibility should be regarded as a constraint rule that the knowledge base must validate in order to be in a coherent state. For the knowledge base to be in a coherent state, two definitions of a same concept, must be compatible and belong to different points of view. However, during the development of the base, incompatibilities are allowed.

4.3 The Resolution Process

The concept base is in a *coherent* state if, for each concept, there is at most one current definition per point of view, and if all these definitions are compatible. When a definition conflict occurs, there are three possibilities to solve it:

- Consensus: only one definition is kept. For that purpose, one can either remove one of them or merge the two basic definitions, with the union operation for example.
- Contrast: one decides that the two definitions correspond to two different concepts. One can then either create a new concept and a new term for one of the definitions, or create a new concept, keep the same term and link to another field.
- Different points of view: the two definitions are kept but each one is linked to a different point of view.

Remark: We use the terms: “conflict”, “consensus”, “correspondence” and “contrast” in the same way as Shaw and Gaines [16] (see table in section 1.2)

Table 2. D1 is a generalization (specialization) of D2

		Possible operations and typical arguments (arg)
D1 and D2 compatible	**1** same concept	keep both D1 and D2 + link them to different points of view argument: the specific characteristics of D2 are useful for a point of view and useless for the other or remove one of them + choose a point of view *argument*: D1 is incomplete / D2 is hyperspecific (some of its characteristics are redundant) *Remark*: union(D1,D2)=D2 / intersection(D1,D2)=D1 so it is useless to suggest a merge operation
	2 different concepts	create a new concept + create a new term for one of the definition. + create an inheritance link between D1 and D2. *argument*: the characteristics of D2 that are not in D1 make the specificity of D2.

Table 3. D1 is not a generalization (specialization) of D2

		Possible operations and typical arguments
D1 and D2 compatible	**3** same concept	keep both D1 and D2 + link them to different points of view or remove one of them *argument*: D1 and D2 are similar or create a new definition by combining D1 and D2, for example by using union(D1, D2) or intersection(D1,D2) *argument*: (for union) D1 and D2 are incomplete (not specific enough) or keep both + create a new definition by combining D1 and D2 + link to different points of view *argument*: D1 and D2 are both interesting, but it would also be useful to have a more "general" definition
	4 different concept	create a new concept + create a new term or create a new concept + keep the same term + link to another field argument: D1 and D2 are homonyms

Table 3. D1 is not a generalization (specialization) of D2

D1 and D2 incompatible	**5** same concept	same as 3 *Remarks*: union(D1,D2) is incoherent (empty interpretation) In this case, keeping both D1 and D2 and linking them to different points of view is not a completely satisfying solution, because the knowledge base stays in an incoherent state.
	6 different concept	same as 4

We can see that conflicts can be solved using simple operations, for example: create a new concept, associate definition to different points of view, "merge" definitions, delete a definition. The choice of an operation must be justified by an argument. In Table 2. and Table 3., we enumerate possible operations to apply in each situation, with examples of typical arguments Of course, the proposed resolution process does not automatically lead to an acceptable solution. So, designers may decide to suspend the resolution of a particular conflict and to wait for some new versions of a conflicting definition, as shown in Fig. 5..

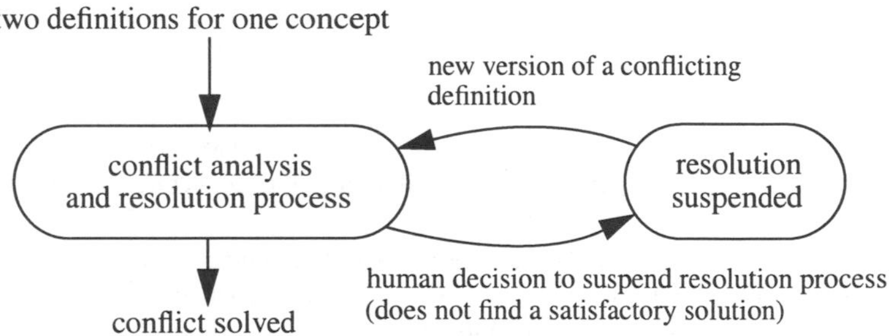

Fig. 5. the conflict resolution process

Keeping Track of the Decisions: Arguments and Endorsements

Storing the arguments underlying each operation together with terminological knowledge allows to remember how "final" definitions were chosen, thus avoiding to repeat past reflection. Arguments represent informal knowledge (in the sense of Conklin [6]). Arguments are informal knowledge that give a background to operations.

Endorsements act as "checkpoints" in the process. They "mark" situations which are approved by some authority. Even if the knowledge base continues to evolve, they form references. From an end-user point of view, the most interesting definitions are probably not the latest versions but the latest approved versions.

5 Conclusion

In this paper we have presented ConceptIBIS, a formal concept model which is aimed at the collaborative building of terminological knowledge bases. ConceptIBIS provides a multi point of view management support. In addition to its formal part, this model also enables to store informal knowledge that gives information on how the terminological knowledge is built.

Then we described a process to resolve the conflicts that inevitably occur when a group of people is involved in the building of a concept base. This process includes:

- semi-automatic conflict analysis with the help of the concept comparison operation and its resulting differences
- operations to resolve conflicts
- memorization of arguments to justify the choice of an particular resolution operation
- endorsement to express agreement on definitions

We are currently testing the comparison operation, as well as other operations, on a multilingual concept base in the field of furniture. The results obtained so far are encouraging.

Meanwhile, we are developing a collaborative system, with a Web interface, for translators and terminologists to easily exchange terminological knowledge. This system currently deals with textual definitions. We are now working on the integration of this ConceptIBIS in this system.

References

1. Berthet D., Bonjour M., De Bessé B., Falquet G., Léonard M, Sinayamaze J., ConcepTerm "Construction de dictionnaires encyclopédiques multilingues et informatisés", CUI technical report, University of Geneva, 1994
2. Brachman, R., McGuinness, D., Patel-Schneider, P., Borgida, A. and Resnick, L. Living with CLASSIC: When and How to Use a KL-ONE-Like Language, in Principles of Semantic Networks. Morgan Kaufman. Pp. 401-456. May, 1991.
3. Buckingham Shum S., Representing Hard-to-Formalise, Contextualised, Multidisciplinary, Organisational Knowledge, in AIKM'97 Proceedings
4. Buchheit M., Donini F. M., Schaerf A., Decidable Reasoning in Terminological Knowledge Representation Systems, Journal of Artificial Intelligence Research, 1993
5. Conklin J., Begeman M., gIBIS: A Tool for All Reasons, Journal of the American Society for Information Science, 40, pp 200-213, 1989
6. Conklin J., Designing Organizational Memory: Preserving Intellectual Assets in a Knowledge Economy, Group Decision Support Systems, 1996
7. De Bessé B., Pulitano D., BD-TERM, un logiciel de gestion terminologique, ETI, Université de Genève,1989
8. Dieng R., Comparison of Conceptual Graphs for Modelling Knowledge of Multiple Experts: Application to Traffic Accident Analysis, Rapport de Recherche n°3161, INRIA Sophia Antipolis, Projet Acacia, 1997

9. Euzenat J., Corporate memory through cooperative creation of knowledge bases and hyper-documents, in Proceedings of the Tenth Knowledge Acquisition for Knowledge-Based Systems Workshop (KAW '96)
10. Falquet G., Sindayamaze J., Bonjour M., Leonard M., F2Concept, un modèle intégrant la description de la compréhension et l'extension des classes d'objets, CUI, Université de Genève, 1991
11. Falquet G. Mottaz C.-L., A Model for the Collaborative Design of Multi-Point-of-View Terminological Knowledge Bases, Proceedings of the Knowledge Management and Organizational Memory workshop of the International Joint Conference on Artificial Intelligence, Stockholm, 1999
12. Group Decision Support Systems, The IBIS Manual: A Short Course in IBIS Methodology, http://www.gdss.com/IBIS.htm
13. Kuntz W., Rittel H., Issues as elements of information systems, Working Paper No 131, Institute of Urban and Regional Development, University of California at Berkeley, 1972
14. Mariño Drew O., Raisonnement classificatoire dans une représentation à objets multi-points de vue, thèse de doctorat, Université Joseph Fourier, Grenoble, 1993
15. Pulitano D., Création d'une banque de terminologie à l'Ecole de traduction et d'interprétation de l'Université de Genève : BD-TERM, ETI, Université de Genève, 1988
16. Shaw M. L. G., Gaines B. R., Comparing Conceptual Structures; Consensus, Conflict, Correspondance and Contrast, Knowledge Science Institute, University of Calgary, 1989
17. Sindayamaze J., Prise en compte de la compréhension dans les bases de données, thèse de doctorat, Université de Genève
18. Stumpf S, Argumentation-based Design Rationale - The Sharpest Tools in the box, Working Paper IN/98/01, University College London

Revisiting Ontology Design: A Method Based on Corpus Analysis

Nathalie Aussenac-Gilles[1], Brigitte Biébow[2], and Sylvie Szulman[2]

[1] Université Toulouse 3, Institut de Recherche en Informatique de Toulouse(IRIT)
118 route de Narbonne, 31062 TOULOUSE Cedex 4 (France)
Nathalie.Aussenac-Gilles@irit.fr

[2] Université de Paris-Nord, Laboratoire d'Informatique de Paris-Nord(LIPN)
Av. J.B. Clément, 93430 VILLETANEUSE (France)
{Brigitte.Biebow,Sylvie.Szulman}@lipn.univ-paris13.fr

Abstract We promote a new approach for knowledge modelling based on knowledge elicitation from technical documents. It benefits of the increasing amount of available electronic texts and of the maturity of natural language processing tools. The approach defines a framework where the knowledge engineer selects the appropriate tools, combines their use and interprets their results to build up a domain model. The paper presents the method and reports an on-going application to design an ontology of knowledge engineering tools in French.

1 Introduction

Ontology design has been a very active field of investigations in knowledge engineering (KE) over the last 10 years. Recently, studies have focused on either reuse as a solution to ontology building, or automatic knowledge acquisition using learning techniques and data mining, or integration with problem solving models. However many basic problems still remain unsolved [6] [36]. For example, concept definitions, selecting the right properties, defining the semantics of relations or even proper grouping of concepts are barely mentioned. In the best cases, guidelines propose to organize terms into a taxinomy, to gather synonyms into clusters and to define concepts from them [18]. But too little is said on which criteria may guide the knowledge engineer during knowledge structuring.

This leads us to advocate a different method based on linguistics and to give a central role to texts. Such an approach takes its roots in the early French works of knowledge acquisition with the KOD method and the K-station workbench [37]. It was the first attempt to consider texts as main knowledge repositories, and approaches in linguistics and terminology as the proper way to explore them. About 10 years after, both convergent theoretical problems and sufficient maturity led the French KE, AI, Terminology and Linguistics communities to cooperate into the TIA (Terminology and Artificial Intelligence) working group. TIA group's major statements are to start from texts to acquire knowledge, to connect source texts to conceptual models, to explore texts by applying natural language processing tools and techniques based on results in linguistics.

R. Dieng and O. Corby (Eds.): EKAW 2000, LNAI 1937, pp. 172–188, 2000.

Several states of the art in ontology design show that texts are hardly used or, at least, they aren't explicitly mentionned as knowledge sources. When used, texts are read and manually explored without any precise indication of the applied techniques. In fact, knowledge reuse is much preferred and studied as an acute problem, often to the detriment of the ontology actual usability in the current application [26], [6]. The relation between ontologies and texts gains interest with the development of the Internet and with the generalisation of electronic documents. Ontologies look like a promising ressource to improve information retrieval in documents, to index them [35] or to make them easily available among a community of readers [14]. Ontologies and texts may be connected in two ways: either concepts are used as semantic tags added to documents, or texts are connected to some concept instances in the ontology. Even in these cases, the documents themselves are not used as input of the modelling.

In this article, we present our method for domain knowledge elicitation and modelling from texts. First, we describe the approach characteristics with regard to other trends in knowledge acquisition from texts. We go on with a review of the approach, its main stages and their intermediary outputs. To end with, we report the early stage of an experiment where we applied it to organize the concepts describing KE tools in France from French documents.

2 Recent Trends in Knowledge Acquisition from Texts

2.1 Classical KA from Texts

Since the early 80's, researchers in knowledge acquisition (KA) are interested in text analysis to make acquisition easier. Two major trends, presented in [7], were tools for the automatic translation of texts into a knowledge base and hypertext editors. This classification remains valid today.

Automatic transfer tools. Based on linguistics, they usually combine a text parser with a knowledge analyser that tries to represent knowledge into a formal linguistic language. This representation is then translated into logics in the knowledge base. The knowledge analyser may also be a classifier or an inductive generalizer [28]. Most of these systems have the ambitious goal to extract any kind of knowledge from natural language texts, whereas some specialize on specific knowledge (such as taxonomic knowledge [17] or causal knowledge). Most of them refer to general relation types and ontological classes to start the process and to organise concepts. They set high expectations on the performance of the parser, whereas it is doubtful to get an efficient parser for any natural language. We agree with Bourigault's severe evaluation of these tools: they carry out costly, hazardous and, worst, often useless analyses. Other automatic tranfer tools learn concepts from a statistical clustering of terms (like co-occurring terms) that should identify concept classes. These systems cannot give information to help to judge the quality of their analyses [20].

Automatic transfer tools still form part of a language understanding chain. Improvements in text parsers by enriching the semantic analysers (for instance with recent results about verb constructions) turned SNOWY-BIOS, a new version of SNOWY, into a powerful tool to answer questions about biographical texts [22]. Hahn's view relies on the same basic goal to automate text understanding as a prerequisite for KA. Automation in his system [20] is a two-step process: the parser generates concept hypotheses, that are later on evaluated by a qualifier. This qualifier is a set of quality evaluation meta-rules, which contain general linguistic knowledge. The meta-reasonner classifies the various hypotheses which guides the KE to decide to which class add an instance in the concept hierarchy. The rules can be tuned in keeping with the application, which makes the tool more powerful. It must be underlined that automatic transfer tools are rarely used outside their development team, which points out their immaturity.

Hypertext systems. They guide text exploration and analysis, and include text browsers and devices to connect conceptual structures to natural language phrases underlined in texts. In the most powerful systems, the text decomposition into units (sentences, paragraphs or word lists) is model driven [30]. Hypertext capabilities to browse expertise documents such as transcripts of interviews are still a basic device in KA plat-forms. PC-PACK, the knowledge elicitation tool of the CommonKads method [31], includes such functionnalities.

2.2 A New Proposal

A new trend appeared recently, born from a major evolution of Terminology. It mixes up acquisition tools based on linguistics with browsing and modelling tools keeping links between models and texts. This evolution is due to new Natural Language Processing (NLP) tools which are corpus oriented and have gained efficiency from valuable collaborations between linguists, terminologists and knowledge engineers. This trend is less ambitious that the automatic transfert approach: NLP tools are seen as helps for the knowledge engineer who selects and combines their results to build up the model. Moreover these linguistic tools are of a different kind. Instead of general language understanding parsers, they deliver specific kinds of linguistic ressources. They are all the more efficient as they can be adapted to each application.

Exploring corpora to identify thesauri, terminologies or even ontologies require to define new methods and techniques [3], which rely on a novating theoretical framework in Linguistics [34]. This linguistic theory is an interpretative, linguistic and textual semantics: its object is the attested text, the meanings are described through linguistic paraphrases, and the interpretation provides the meanings. Moreover, a concept is a normalized meaning, which results from a work of restriction with respect to the corpus and the application. The method follows some precise steps: a corpus is set up, then terms and lexical relations of the domain can be extracted automatically. The designer builds concepts and semantic relations from studying the use of the corresponding words in the texts. The target conceptual model is more than an intermediate data, it is a result in itself. It can be used later as a knowledge source, for instance to define indexes, glossaries or thesauri. Conceptual models usually set apart static domain knowledge from problem solving knowledge. Depending on the type of text, a text analysis can bear on any of them. For instance, procedure guidelines are relevant to acquire reasoning knowledge. Until now, only domain knowledge (concept descriptions and their organization) is considered.

The method we propose in this trend emphasizes the purpose of the final model. Right from the start of the elicitation process, the task is one of the filtering criteria to look for knowledge in texts, select it and set it in the model. This model is later translated into a formal concept description in a terminological logics so that its consistency and validity could be automatically checked. Moreover, our method fulfills basic engineering principles and suggests to start any project by a precise study of the needs to be met by the model. In the following, the domain is bound to the task, the selected corpus and domain specialists. Our proposal promotes to study the domain after breaking it into sub-domains. It classically suggests to reuse existing resources such as model or domain ontologies, terminologies, thesauri or indexes and so on.

In the next section, we present the main stages of our method.

3 Methodological Framework

This method is general, and independent of the language used in texts. It defines a framework where some technical and methodological choices are left to the knowledge engineer, depending on different factors: the application requirements; available technical documents; elements of existing models (ontologies, terminological ressources like thesauri or glossaries); human expertise; available NLP tools (which depend on the language used in texts.

The designer who follows the method is more or less qualified in linguistics, in knowledge modelling and in formalization. At every step, he/she must decide which techniques must be used depending on the previous factors and his/her own ability. To use the method, he/she needs a specific software to manage a great amount of information (terms, concepts and relations), to describe it, to organize it and to formally represent it. Such an environment must allow an easy access to the terms and the lexical relations, the texts from which they are extracted and the model in which they will be inserted.

We have already developed Terminae [5] and Géditerm [2] for this purpose. Terminae offers to consult a corpus and to integrate the results of the Lexter extractor of term-candidates [1]. The designer extracts terms from the list of term-candidates and defines notions from term meanings. In Terminae, a notion refers to a concept under modelling, whereas a concept is formal. These notions are then structured and differentiated, to be finally formalized as concepts (keeping the link to the corpus). In Terminae, the formal language is close to terminological

[1] A term-candidate is a syntagm extracted from texts that may become a term if validated by an expert.

logics. The link is kept between each formal concept, the notion, its associated terms and their occurrences in the corpus. Géditerm assists the first steps to select terms. The term/concept link is justified by the occurrences of the terms in the corpus. Terminae and Géditerm both may take as input the list of term-candidates given by Lexter. Géditerm does not allow the resulting conceptual network to be formalized but it provides tools for a better management and visualization of the conceptual network before its formalization.
In what follows the methodological framework is presented, focusing firstly on the nature of the data used and produced during the process, from the corpus to a domain model. Then the main stages of the process itself are described.

3.1 From Texts to a Formal Model

The method applies on technical documents and ends to a formal domain model. It differentiates terms from concepts, and lexical relations from semantic relations. Terms and lexical relations are syntagms occurring in the corpus and regarded as important in the domain. Lexical clustering puts together syntagms which occur in some similar contexts. The syntagms are interpreted in a local context (sentence or paragraph) then in a global one (text or whole corpus). If they are considered as terms, they give rise to concepts and semantic relations that they label. The set of concepts and relations makes up a semantic network, informal but understandable by the designer. Then concepts and relations are formalized into a terminological language close to description logics: concepts and roles are structured into an inheritance hierarchy. The concepts are characterized following two dimensions, a linguistic one to express how close to a syntagm in the corpus a concept is, and a pragmatic one, reflecting the reasons why the concept has been integrated into the formal model. This information makes both the model and the knowledge base easier to understand and to maintain [4].

3.2 Used Natural Language Processing Tools

We have selected the most frequently used tools in the French TIA community. We differentiate tools dedicated to terminological knowledge acquisition (TKA) from texts, and particularly terminological extractors, from classic linguistic tools for NLP.

Terminological extractors. Term-candidate extractors extract from a corpus a list of terms that must be validated. They return a great amount of data often with some noise; so a long and boring selection must be made that requires both a good domain expertise and a good anticipation of the way terms will be used. These tools can be based on syntactic principles, as Lexter [8] and Nomino [13], or on statistic principles as Ana [15] and Startex [29]. Their use does not imply a great competence in linguistics.

Relation extractors are usually based on linguistic patterns such as Prométhée [25] or Caméléon [32]. Some of these tools need first to be provided with general linguistic relation patterns like "X IS INDEFINITE_ARTICLE Y" for the hyperonymy relation (kindOf). Patterns are applied on the corpus in order to visualize the pieces of texts where the lexical relation appears. Other tools require couples of related forms as input, from which specific patterns are identified. Starting from some predefined patterns their application onto the corpus rises up terms from which domain specific patterns may be created for new lexical relations. The use of these tools requires some linguistic skills but gives significant information for structuring the domain.

Term and relation extractors may be used in a separate or complementary way. If a term extractor is firstly used, then relations between terms may be searched for by exploring their contexts. If a relation extractor is firstly used, then projecting the relations onto the corpus may rise up related terms. These tools usually offer an environment to browse their results.

Other terminological tools. Some TKA tools are more oriented towards concept discovery. Conceptual clustering tools like Zellig [19] or Lexiclass [1] put together noun phrases that share syntactic dependency relations. The resulting clusters must be manually analyzed to define semantic classes. Results interpretation is difficult but term structuring and concept definition is made easier. Asium [16] uses learning techniques to propose term clusters. Each cluster must be manually validated before defining concepts. Synoterm [21] offers potentially synonym clusters, that can be also considered as concept-candidates. Lexis [27] finds names in a corpus, which may be useful to find some class instances.

An example of sophisticated acquisition tool working in English is KAWB (Knowledge Acquisition WorkBench) [24]. It acquires some semantic classes of a domain from large text corpora. It uses various methods from computational linguistics, information retrieval and KE. A data extraction module includes word class identification based on linguistic annotation of texts, statistical word clustering, with access to external linguistic and semantic sources. A pattern finder collects word collocations, searches for regularities and proposes lexico-semantic patterns for a conceptual characterization to the user. An analysis and refinement module helps the user to test patterns which represent his/her hypotheses, groups together the cases and generalizes them to ask the user for a final decision.

Classic linguistic tools. Some simple and very easy to use linguistic tools have been available for many years now, like concordancers and KWIC tools. KWIC (KeyWord In Context) tools bring into vertical alignment along a given word or phrase all the sentences of a corpus in which this word occurs. This is very practical to study all its contexts, its linguistic behaviour and, first of all, to get an idea of its meaning from the way it is used. Concordancers offer a similar assistance: they look into the corpus for every occurrence of any user given syntagm. They are more powerful than KWIC tools because these syntagms may be characterized by syntactic or semantic properties, not only by giving explicit nouns phrases or verbs. So concordancers result very practical to apply and test some patterns on a corpus, study their occurring contexts and compare them.

Generic tools for text analysis, such as Sato [12] offer a variety of options, which range from research of occurrences and text alignment to syntactic analysis and corpus tagging, including statistics on word frequency, disambiguation at a syntactic or sometimes semantic level. They may be useful for extracting and structuring knowledge when looking for very specific information.

3.3 Detailed Description of the Method Steps

The modelling process is detailed below from setting up the corpus along to designing the formal model.

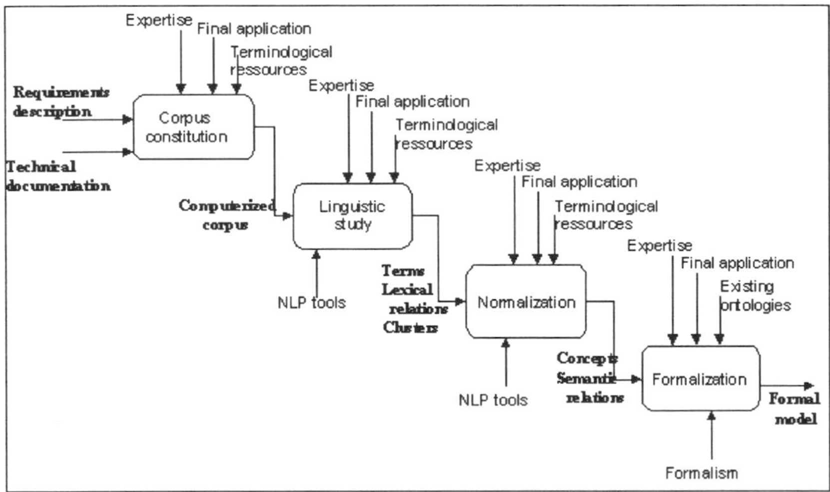

Figure 1. Steps of the modelling process from text according to our approach

Setting up the corpus. From the requirements that explain the objectives underlying the model development, the designer selects texts among the available technical documentation. He must be an expert about texts in this domain to characterize their type and their content. The corpus has to cover the entire domain specified by the application. A glossary, if it exists, is useful to determine sub-domains and to verify that they are well covered. The corpus is then digitalized if it was not. Beginning the modelling may lead to reconsider the corpus.

Linguistic analysis. This step consists in selecting adequate linguistic tools and techniques and in applying them to the text. Their results are sifted and a first linguistic based elicitation is made. The objective is to allow the selection of the terms and lexical relations that will be modelled. The results of this stage are quite raw and will be further refined.

Normalization. Normalization is a particular conceptualization process based on corpus analysis, in line with [10] in contrast with expert introspection. The expertise and the target system influence concept definitions in a second time. Indeed, the restricted meaning of concepts is mainly derived from the study of term occurrences in texts. These terms become concept labels. Thus concepts are described thanks to the use of their label together with the other terms in the corpus. So, the corpus plays an important role during normalization. Linguistic study and normalization are closely intertwined and cyclic activities. At any time of the normalization process, we use linguistic tools and principles to explore the text and to decide whether a concept, an attribute or a relation should be defined or not.

Normalization includes two parts: the first one is still linguistic, it refines the previous lexical results; the second one concerns the semantic interpretation to structure concepts and semantic relations. The modelling goes from terminological analysis to conceptual analysis, that means from term to concepts and from lexical relations to semantic ones. During normalization, the amount of data to be studied is gradually restricted.

During the linguistic step, among the set of terms and lexical relations, the designer has to choose those that will be modelled. This choice is mainly subjective, the terms and relations are kept when they seem important both in the domain and for the application. Because of this subjectivity the selection is rather large. Then, from the study of each syntagm occurrences, the designer writes in natural language a definition that remains close to the texts. In the same time, he determines for each term and relation if it has one or several meanings in the domain. In case of polysemy, he decides which meanings attested by the corpus have to be kept because they are relevant.

The second step is conceptual modelling. Concepts and semantic relations are defined in a normalized form using the labels of the concepts and relations already defined. These definitions may be less close to the text as long as they must be relevant for the task for which the model is built. These descriptions are structured into a semantic network, with a strong emphasis on the hierarchical relations (kindOf, partOf). Only the rigor of the work and perhaps the modelling environment may guarantee the coherence of this semi-formal ontology.

Formalization. The formalization step includes building and validating the ontology. Some existing ontologies may help to build the highest levels and to structure it into large sub-domains. Then semantic concepts and relations are translated into formal concepts and roles and inserted in the ontology. This may imply to restructure the ontology or to define additional concepts, so that the inheritance constraints on the subsumption links are correct. Inserting a new concept triggers a local verification to guarantee the syntactic correctness of the added description. A global validation of the formal model is performed once the ontology reaches a quite stable state to verify its coherence.

4 Applying This Method to Describe KE Tools

To test our tools and refine our approach, we applied it to build an ontology of KE tools from a corpus of selected texts in French. For the time being, our study is restricted to the tools currently used and developed in France for KE. We present the context of the experiment in the section below. Then, we detail how we manage the linguistic study and the normalization steps. As long as these tasks are performed in a cyclic way, we differenciate the early sifting of the row results provided by the linguistic tools from further concept identification and clustering, where linguistic tools are used for specific goals. We finally present our preliminary results.

4.1 Context of the Experiment

Final application. The ontology aims to help researchers in KE to compare and describe their own tools with respect to existing ones. Before developing a new tool, one may want to know which ones exist with similar functionalities.

The expertise. The model designers are not linguists but they are specialists in KE. As such, they alternatively behave as knowledge engineers or as experts.

The corpus. We use a corpus built up by the French TIA group for creating a thesaurus to index Web pages and documents in KE. The kernel of this corpus, described in [9], consists of 34 selected papers published in the KE French conferences during the last 3 years and gathered in a synthesis book [11]. The first term studies showed that the corpus did not cover the whole domain. Moreover, it contained too few definitions of domain concepts. In order to cope with these limitations, it has been enriched with 4 general papers presenting KE. The corpus volume raised by 30%, reaching now 207.000 words.

NLP tools. We use two linguistic tools, a term extractor (Lexter [8]) and a relation extractor (Caméléon [33]), and a modelling tool (Terminae). Terminae provides convenient modules to validate and to display results from Lexter, as well as to organize the terms and to build an informal ontology. We use the Terminae concept structure as if it were informal. Each concept is documented by a comment. A classifier checks the validity of the insertion of a concept and gives warnings to the designer if some mistakes or redundancies are found. As previously said, concepts are characterized along a linguistic dimension. Terminological concepts are built from the corpus study, and they correspond to one or several domain terms, one of them being the concept label. These concepts are linked to their term occurrences in the corpus. Pre-terminological concepts correspond to several phrases, sometimes as large as sentences, none of them being more frequently used than the others. Their label is not in the corpus. Non-terminological concepts do not correspond to any term or phrase in the domain. It also happens that a concept is needed to structure the ontology and that a domain term corresponds to it, but this term is not attested in the corpus. In such a case the concept will be defined as terminological but not attested.

4.2 Linguistic Study

The early sifting work consists in exploring the row data provided by the linguistic tools from the corpus analysis. These lists of term and relation hypotheses help to quickly read the corpus according to the major domain concepts.

We could start this work in two different ways: (a) focus on terms and then look for relations between these terms or (b) identify lexical relations that help to select domain terms. We choose the first way because the aim is to build an ontology on KE tools:

Term study We have two methods to approach corpus analysis, according to the weight given to names. Firstly, compound term-candidates including the word "outil" (*tool*) indicate potential sub-classes of the corresponding concept OUTIL. Lexter extracts 26 349 term-candidates, but only 109 of them begin with the word "outil". Secondly the names of specific tools are easily collectable and directly identifiable when written in capitals.

Relation identification Many relations could be easily identified by reading term occurrences. However, this practice is as costly and time consuming as reading the whole corpus. The number of occurrences to be read is restricted by using Caméléon [32]. Caméléon suggests hypotheses of partOf and kindOf relations between domain terms. It finds them by applying general linguistic patterns that are stored in the system. For this project, we define only two new patterns for the kindOf relation like (*X is a Y which*), which are small variations of general patterns. For each concept in the model, we browse the Caméléon hypotheses and read their occurrences. Caméléon found about 2 to 10 relations for concepts under OUTIL, and about 50 relations for OUTIL, the third of which have been validated.

4.3 Normalization

After sifting through the results of linguistic tools, we have in hand a first list of terms. From this list, we have to model concepts and to structure them. Each occurrence of each term is closely studied. We decide to suppress terms when not suitable for the application, such as "outil de bureautique" (*office automation tool*). We also associate various terms to the same notion either because they are judged synonyms in the corpus, or because they are not worth being distinguished for the application. We are able to evaluate term synonymies because we know the application domain. If it were not the case, we would rely on linguistic criteria, like similar uses of these terms in different occurrences.

Conceptual clustering consists in bringing terms together to form a concept, and in defining synonyms. By exploring and comparing all the occurrences of some terms, synonymy relations may be observed. Another way to find synonyms is to explore the syntactic relations that bind co-occuring terms.

Examples of synonymy detection by exploring occurrences.

- From reading the occurrences of the terms "outil textuel" (*textual tool*), "outil d'analyse de textes" (*text analysis tool*), "outil linguistique" (*linguistic tool*), "outil d'analyse de corpus" (*corpus analysis tool*), we decide to group these terms under a single concept "outil d'analyse de corpus" (*corpus analysis tool*) (Figure 2).
- The term "outil anthropotechnique" (*anthropotechnical tool*) will be rejected because it is used with the meaning of "outil de génie cognitif" (*knowledge enginering tool*) and it is not worth being distinguished for this application.

Synonymy detection thanks to co-occurrences. For each couple of terms which we know as experts that they label related concepts, we look for their co-occurrences within a window of one sentence using a Terminae module. Several criteria guide us to structure the concepts, as illustrated in the following:

- The terms "outil" and "méthode" (*method*) are often bound by the coordinating conjunction *and*, from which we consider they are not synonyms. Another relation between "outil" and "méthode" is the relation "utilise"(*uses*): a *method* "utilise" a *tool* or a *tool* "utilise" a *method.* There are as many sentences of both types, which stresses the ambiguity of the relation label "utilise". Two relations types with different labels are distinguished.
- There is no co-occurrence of "outil" and "algorithme", only one of "outil" and "formalisme" in which a *formalism* is defined as a conceptual *tool.*
- The 25 co-occurrences of "outil" and "système" put forward two kinds of relations: identity(*the SATO system is a top-down tool*) and inclusion (*tools of the information system*). Inclusion may occur in the two directions (a tool includes a specific system or a system consists of several tools), which confirms the terms synonymy.

4.4 First Results of the Structuration

Our work is at its very beginning, only the kindOf relation has been deeply studied. We have to investigate other relations like partOf, "sert-à" (*to be useful for*), "utilise" (*uses*) or "auteur" (*author*) to continue the structuration.

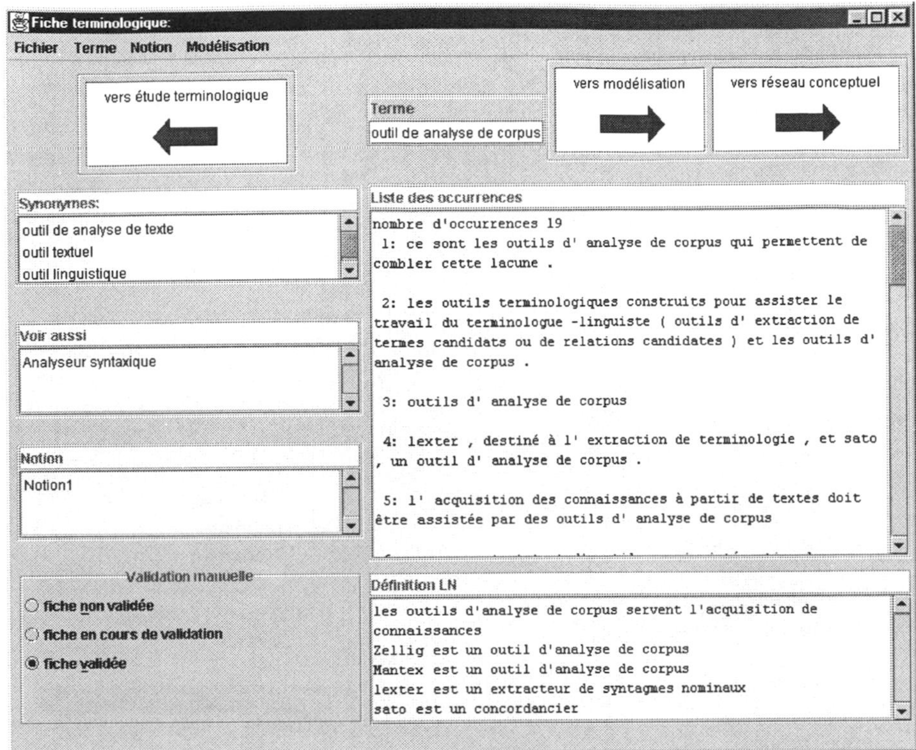

Figure 2. First stage of the normalization of a concept: *corpus analysis tool*

As long as we focus on KE tools, we first define the concept OUTIL. Several semantic relations such as *author*, corresponding to lexical relations, describe this concept. We organize most of the concepts around OUTIL. From the relations presented in 4.3, we distinguish conceptual tools (method, formalism, algorithm, model) from software tools. From our expertise and after reading occurrences of specific tools, we decide to differenciate two kinds of software tools: results of an engineering process and software for system development, which can be either KE tools (OUTIL D'INGÉNIERIE DES CONNAISSANCES) or software engineering tools (OUTIL DE GÉNIE LOGICIEL).

Thus we create under OUTIL two terminological concepts: OUTILLOGICIEL (*software tool*) and OUTILCONCEPTUEL (*conceptual tool*). Figure 3 [2] shows the hierarchy under OUTIL, the next lower concepts (*software tool* and *conceptual tool*), and the lower levels.

Only OUTILINGÉNIERIECONNAISSANCES and OUTILVALIDATION are terminological not attested (TNA) concepts (c.f. 4.1). The terminological concept OUTILAIDE gathers all the concepts corresponding to terms which begin with

[2] In the figures showing parts of the ontology, terminological concepts are in italic, individual concepts which correspond to a specific tool have a capital first letter.

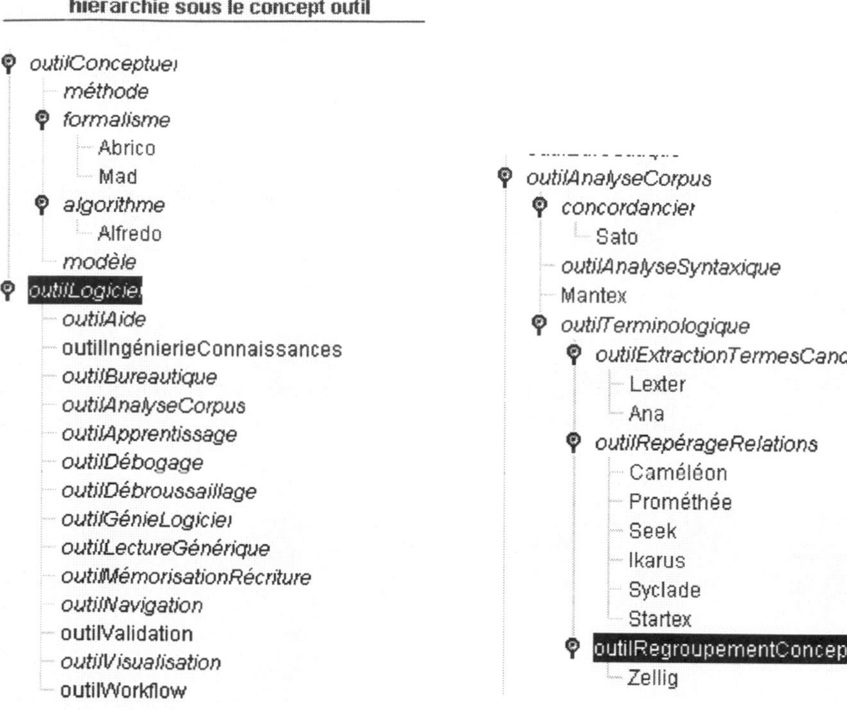

Figure 3. Hierarchy under OUTIL

Figure 4. Hierarchy under OUTILANALYSECORPUS

"outil d'aide" (*front-end tool*). We identify linguistic tools, a particular kind of software tools, described in the corpus. Figure 4 presents the concepts under OUTILANALYSECORPUS. We define OUTILEXTRACTIONTERMESCANDIDATS (*term-candidate extractor*) and OUTILREPERAGERELATIONS (*relation locating tool*) as subclasses of OUTILTERMINOLOGIQUE.

4.5 Experiment Report and Evaluation

We have focused on knowledge extraction from texts. But we actually take into account other knowledge ressources, domain expertise, additional information as existing ontologies, databases,... Several criteria guide data selection among these various sources: the expertise in the domain and the target application and users. These criteria may be contradictory. Priority is given to the relevance for the application and to the expertise, which may bias what the text says. For instance, ASTREE, a specific tool, is described in a text as a *KE tool*, which is not precise enough in an ontology that should help to compare and characterize KE tools. If we read further this text, we understand that ASTREE is a tool that assists the design of a conceptual model. So we decide to define OUTILAIDEMODÉLISATION as a concept and ASTREE as one of its son concepts.

To validate our model, we plan to try to add new tools and evaluate whether it is easy or not to describe them in the ontology. These tools wil be described by a small text in a demonstration form-sheet. We will consider our ontology as valid if we can set these new specific tools as concept instances in the ontology. This means that either we'll be able to characterise them conveniently with existing properties, or it will be easy to distinguish new sub-classes by taking into account new concept properties. The second case will lead to re-organize part of the taxinomy in the model.

5 Conclusion

In this article we have presented a method to create a domain model from a corpus analysis, by using NLP tools. We also have reported an experiment where we applied it to build an ontology of the French tools of the KE domain. In the future this work may be compared to the European project $(KA)^2$ and to the team project of [23]. It is also close to the EuroKnowledge project [36] which describes the English terminology about "modelling at the knowledge level" for a didactic book to be used as a reference.

To experiment our method on an application shows up all its capacities but also all the pratical, methodological and even theoretical queries left to be answered. It is obvious that we have not yet exploited the whole complementarity of the different types of analyses that can be made on the corpus. For instance, term and relation studies are still used in different environments. We have not used all the tools which exist today, especially because they are research tools and neither easily available nor usable. But the results obtained thanks to our approach are still of a good quality and promising. They have to be completed and evaluated in the next step of the project. Additional investigations are also needed to extend the approach to other languages than French.

A list of criteria of effectiveness is presented in the CommonKADS book [31]. For each one of them, we are convinced that KA from texts as we presented it is a good way to go one step further. Unlike the authors of the CommonKADS book, we assert that the previously presented techniques will minimize the effort spent in gathering, transcribing, and analyzing the knowledge required by the target application. Exploring texts minimizes the time spent with expensive and scarce domain experts. The direct connection between texts and models is a means to maximize the yield of usable knowledge. NLP tools and linguistics based techniques tend to make elicitation techniques a systematic process. We assume that these techniques are reliable and mature enough to make the process more robust as a whole. For instance, each choice must be justified and many references towards texts form a track that improve the model readability. The experiment reported in this paper is currently being carried on and we hope the final results will give precise measures of the method effectiveness.

References

1. H. Assadi. Construction of a regional ontology from text and its use within a documentary system. In N. Guarino, editor, *Proc. of the 1st International Conference on Formal Ontology and Information System (FOIS'98))*, pages 236–249. IOS Press, 1998.
2. N. Aussenac-Gilles. Gediterm, un logiciel de gestion de bases de connaissances terminologiques. *Terminologies Nouvelles*, 19:111–123, 1999.
3. N. Aussenac-Gilles, D. Bourigault, A. Condamines, and C. Gros. How can knowledge acquisition benefit from terminology ? In *Proc. of the 9th Knowledge Acquisition for Knowledge Based Systems Workshop (Banff'95)*, 1995.
4. B. Biébow and S. Szulman. Terminae : A linguistics-based tool for building of a domain ontology. In D. Fensel and R. Studer, editors, *Proc. of the 11th European Workshop (EKAW'99)*, LNAI 1621, pages 49–66. Springer-Verlag, 1999.
5. B. Biébow and S. Szulman. Terminae: une approche terminologique pour la construction d'ontologies du domaine à partir de textes. In *Proc. of Reconnaissance des Formes et Intelligence Artificielle (RFIA'2000)*, volume II, pages 81–90, 2000.
6. M. Blázquez, M. Fernández, J.M. García-Pinar, and A. Gómez-Pérez. Building ontologies at the knowledge level using the ontology design environment. In *Proc. of the 11th Knowledge Acquisition Workshop (KAW'98)*, Banff, Canada, 1998.
7. D. Bourigault. *Lexter, un Logiciel d'EXtraction de TERminologie, Application à l'acquisition des connaissances à partir de textes.* PhD thesis, Ecole des Hautes Etudes en Sciences Sociales, Paris, France, 1994.
8. D. Bourigault. Lexter, a natural language processing tool for terminology extraction. In *Proc. of the 7th EURALEX International Congress*, Goteborg, 1996.
9. D. Bourigault and J. Charlet. Construction d'un index thématique de l'ingénierie des connaissances. In *Proc. of Ingénierie des Connaissances (IC'99)*, pages 107–118, Paris, 1999.
10. J. Charlet and B. Bachimont. De l'acquisition à l'ingénierie des connaissances: Applications et perspectives. In *Actes des Assises Nationales 1998 du PRC-I3*, http://www.irit.fr/ACTIVITES/EQ_SMI/GRACQ/index-commf.html, 1998.
11. J. Charlet, M. Zacklad, G. Kassel, and D. Bourigault, editors. *Ingénierie des Connaissances, évolutions récentes et nouveaux défis.* Eyrolles, 2000.
12. F. Daoust. *Système d'Analyse de Textes par Ordinateur.* Centre ATO, Université du Québec à Montréal, 1992.
13. S. David and P. Plante. *Termino version 1.0.* Centre d'Analyse de Textes par Ordinateur, Université du Québec à Montréal, 1990.
14. J. Domingue and E. Motta. A knowledge-based news server supporting ontology-driven story enrichment and knowledge retrivial. In D. Fensel and R. Studer, editors, *Proc. of the 11th European Workshop (EKAW'99)*, LNAI 1621, pages 103–120. Springer-Verlag, 1999.
15. C. Enguehard and L. Pantéra. Automatic natural acquisition of terminology. *Journal of Quantitative Linguistics*, 2/1:27–32, 1995.
16. D. Faure and C. Nedellec. Knowledge acquisition of predicate argument structures from technical texts using machine learning: The system ASIUM. In D. Fensel and R. Studer, editors, *Proc. of the 11th European Workshop (EKAW'99)*, LNAI 1621, pages 329–334. Springer-Verlag, 1999.
17. F. Gomez. Acquiring knowledge about the habitats of animals from encyclopedic texts. In *Proc. of the Workshop on Knowledge Acquisition for Knowledge-Based Systems (KAW'95)*, volume 1, pages 6.1–6.22, 1995.

18. A. Gómez-Pérez. Knowledge sharing and reuse. *Hand-book of Expert Systems - CRC*, 1997.
19. B. Habert, E. Naulleau, and A. Nazarenko. Symbolic word clustering formedium-size corpora. In *Proc. of the 16th International Conference on Computational Linguistics (COLING'96)*, pages 490–495, Copenhagen, 1996.
20. U. Hahn, M. Klenner, and K. Schnattinger. Automated knowledge acquisition meets metareasoning: Incremental quality assessment of concept hypotheses during texts understanding. In *Proc. of the Workshop on Knowledge Acquisition for Knowledge-Based Systems (KAW'98)*, 1998.
21. T. Hamon, A. Nazareko, and C. Gros. A step towards the detection of semantic variants of terms in technical documents. In *Proc. of the 36th Annual Meeting of the Association for Computational Linguistics and 17th International Conference on Computational Linguistics (COLING-ACL'98))*, pages 498–504. Morgan Kaufmann, 1998.
22. R. Hull and F. Gomez. Automatic acquistion of historical knowledge from encyclopedic texts. In *Proc. of the Workshop on Knowledge Acquisition for Knowledge-Based Systems (KAW'98)*, 1998.
23. G. Kassel, M.-H. Abel, C. Barry, P. Boulitreau, C. Irastorza, and S. Perpette. Construction et exploitation d'une ontologie pour la gestion des connaissances d'une équipe de recherche. In *Proc. of Ingénierie des Connaissances (IC'2000)*, pages 251–259, Toulouse, 2000.
24. A. Mikheev and S. Finch. A workbench for acquisition of ontological knowledge from natural language. In *Proc. of the 9th Banff Knowledge Acquisition for Knowledge-Based Systems Workshop (KAW'95)*, 1995.
25. E. Morin. Acquisition de patrons lexico-syntaxiques caractéristiques d'une relation sémantique. *TAL (Traitement Automatique des Langues)*, 40/1:143–166, 1999.
26. N. Fredman Noy and C. Hafner. The state of the art in ontology design : a survey and comparative review. *Artificial Intelligence Magazine*, pages 53–74, 1997.
27. T. Poibeau. Repérage des entités nommées : un enjeu pour les système de veille. *Terminologies Nouvelles*, 19:43–51, 1999.
28. U. Reimer. Automatic knowledge acquisition from texts: Learning terminological knowledge via text understanding and inductive generalization. In *Proc. of the Workshop on Knowledge Acquisition for Knowledge-Based Systems (KAW'90)*, pages 27.1–27.16, 1990.
29. F. Rousselot, P. Frath, and R. Oueslati. Extracting concepts and relations from corpora. In *Proc. of the 12th European Conference on Artificial Intelligence (ECAI'96)*, 1996.
30. G. Schmidt and F. Schmalhofer. Case-oriented knowledge acquisition from texts. In B. Wielinga, J. Boose, B. Gaines, G. Schreiber, and M. Van Someren, editors, *Proc. of the 4th European Workshop (EKAW'90)*. IOS Press, 1990.
31. G. Schreiber, H. Akkermans, A. Anjewierden, R. de Hoog, N. Shadbolt, W. Van de Velde, and B. Wielinga, editors. *Knowledge Engineering and Management: The CommonKADS Methodology*. MIT Press, 1999.
32. P. Séguéla. Adaptation semi-automatique d'une base de marqueurs de relations sémantiques sur des corpus spécialisés. *Terminologies Nouvelles*, 19:52–60, 1999.
33. P. Séguéla and N. Aussenac. Extraction de relations sémantiques entre termes et enrichissement de modèles du domaine. In *Proc. of Ingénierie des Connaissances (IC'99)*, pages 79–88, Paris, 1999.
34. M. Slodzian. Comment revisiter la doctrine terminologique aujourd'hui? *La Banque des Mots*, 7/95:11–18, 1995.

35. URL: http://imat.swi.psy.uva.nl/ofi/ofi.html.
36. M. Uschold. Knowledge level modelling: concepts and terminology. *The knowledge engineering review*, 13/1:5–29, 1998.
37. C. Vogel. *Génie cognitif*. Masson, Paris, 1988.

Mining Ontologies from Text

Alexander Maedche and Steffen Staab

AIFB, Univ. Karlsruhe, D-76128 Karlsruhe, Germany
{maedche, staab}@aifb.uni-karlsruhe.de
http://www.aifb.uni-karlsruhe.de/WBS

Abstract. Ontologies have become an important means for structuring knowledge and building knowledge-intensive systems. For this purpose, efforts have been made to facilitate the ontology engineering process, in particular the acquisition of ontologies from domain texts. We present a general architecture for discovering conceptual structures and engineering ontologies. Based on our generic architecture we describe a case study for mining ontologies from text using methods based on dictionaries and natural language text. The case study has been carried out in the telecommunications domain. Supporting the overall text ontology engineering process, our comprehensive approach combines dictionary parsing mechanisms for acquiring a domain-specific concept taxonomy with a discovery mechanism for the acquisition of non-taxonomic conceptual relations.

1 Introduction

Ontologies[1] have shown their usefulness in application areas such as intelligent information integration [23], information brokering [20] and natural-language processing [21], to name but a few. However, their wide-spread usage is still hindered by ontology engineering being rather time-consuming and, hence, expensive. A number of proposals have been made to facilitate ontological engineering through automatic discovery from domain data, domain-specific natural language texts in particular (cf. [1,3,5,13,14,16,24]). However, most approaches have "only" tackled one step in the overall ontology engineering process, e.g. the acquisition of concepts, the establishment of a concept taxonomy or the discovering of non-taxonomic conceptual relationships, whereas one must consider the overall process when building real-world applications.

In this paper we describe a case study for mining ontologies from textual resources, *viz.* from technical dictionaries and from domain texts, where we consider all three before-mentioned steps. For this purpose we combine existing techniques for the acquisition of concepts and a concept taxonomy with a new

[1] We restrict our attention in this paper to *domain ontologies* that describe a particular small model of of the world as relevant to applications, in contrast to *top-level ontologies* and *representational ontologies* that aim at the description of generally applicable conceptual structures and meta-structures, respectively, and that are mostly based on philosophical and logical point of views rather than focused on applications.

R. Dieng and O. Corby (Eds.): EKAW 2000, LNAI 1937, pp. 189–202, 2000.

approach for mining non-taxonomic conceptual relationships from natural language in an integrated framework for manual and semi-automatic ontology engineering.

The remainder of the paper is as follows. In Section 2 we will give an overview of the overall system architecture, in particular about which linguistic processing has been done and how discovered conceptual structures are added to the ontology using a graphical ontology engineering environment. Subsequently, we will focus on the techniques for acquiring concepts and concept hierarchies which are an essential part for the algorithm discovering non-taxonomic conceptual relations. This algorithm will be presented in Section 4. An example will show some promising results we obtained applying our mechanisms for mining ontologies from text. Before we conclude we give an overview of related work in Section 5.

2 Architecture

The purpose of this section is to give an overview of the architecture of our approach. The process of semi-automatic ontology acquisition is embedded in an application that comprises several core features described as a kind of pipeline in the following. Nevertheless, the reader may bear in mind that the overall development of ontologies remains a cyclic process (cf. [12]). In fact, we provide a broad set of interactions such that the engineer may start with primitive methods first. These methods require very little or even no background knowledge, but they may also be restricted to return only simple hints, like term frequencies. While the knowledge model matures during the semi-automatic engineering process, the engineer may turn towards more advanced and more knowledge-intensive algorithms, such as our mechanism for discovering generalized relations.

2.1 Text & Processing Management Component

The ontology engineer uses the Text & Processing Management component to select domain resources (dictionaries, domain texts, ...) exploited in the further discovery process. She chooses among a set of text (pre-)processing methods available on the Text Processing Server and among a set of algorithms available at the Learning & Discovering component. The former module returns text that is annotated by XML and this XML-tagged text is fed to the Learning & Discovering component described in subsection 2.3.

2.2 Text Processing Server

The Text Processing Server comprises a broad set of different methods. In our case, it contains a shallow text processor based on the core system SMES (Saarbrücken Message Extraction System; cf. [15]). SMES is a system that performs syntactic analysis on natural language documents. In general, the Text Processing Server is organized in modules, such as a tokenizer, morphological and lexical processing, and chunk parsing that use lexical resources to produce

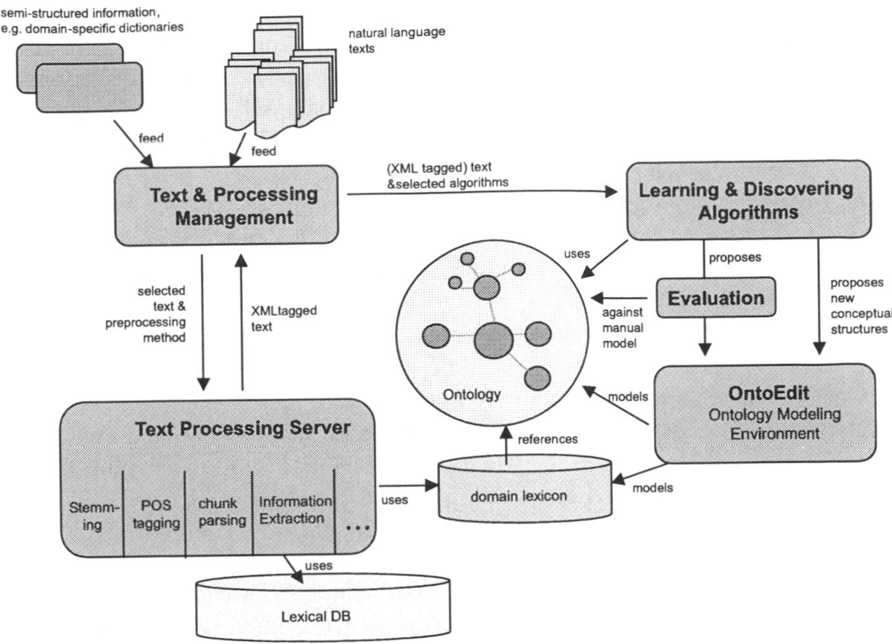

Fig. 1. Architecture of the Ontology Learning Environment

mixed syntactic/semantic information. The results of text processing are stored in annotations using XML-tagged text.

SMES is a generic component that adheres to several principles that are crucial for our objectives. *(i)*, it is fast fast and robust, *(ii)*, it yields "normalized" terms, and, *(iii)*, it returns pairs of concepts the coupling of which is motivated through *linguistic* constraints on the corresponding textual terms. In addition, we made some minor changes such that principle *(iv)*, linguistic processing delivering a high recall on the number of dependency relations occuring in a text, is also guaranteed.

The Architecture of SMES comprises a *tokenizer* based on regular expressions, a *lexical analysis* component including a word and a domain *lexicon*, and a *chunk parser*.

Tokenizer. Its main task is to scan the text in order to identify boundaries of words and complex expressions like "$20.00" or "Baden-Wuerttemberg"[2], and to expand abbreviations.

Lexicon. The lexicon contains more than 120.000 stem entries and more than 12,000 subcategorization frames describing information used for lexical analysis and chunk parsing. Furthermore, the domain-specific part of the lexicon associates word stems with concepts that are available in the concept taxonomy.

[2] Baden-Wuerttemberg is a region in the south west of Germany.

The reader may note that at the beginning there are no or only few mappings from word stems to (some few, domain-independent) concepts available in the domain lexicon. Only with the extension of the ontology the domain-specific part of the lexicon is augmented, too.[3] At the beginning the ontology engineer uses simple means, e.g. word counts, in order to establish new concepts and their linkages to word stems. By doing so, she leverages the linguistic processing and, thus, the further knowledge discovery process in subsequent stages.
Lexical Analysis uses the lexicon to perform, *(1)*, morphological analysis, *i.e.*, the identification of the canonical common stem of a set of related word forms and the analysis of compounds, *(2)*, recognition of name entities, *(3)*, retrieval of domain-specific information, and, *(4)*, part-of-speech tagging:

1. In German compounds are extremely frequent and, hence, their analysis into their parts, e.g. "database" becoming "data" and "base", is crucial and may yield interesting relationships between concepts. Furthermore, morphological analysis returns possible readings for the words concerned, e.g. the noun and the verb reading for a word like "man" in "The old man the boats."
2. Processing of named entities includes the recognition of proper and company names like "Deutsche Telekom AG" as single, complex entities, as well as the recognition and transformation of complex time and date expressions into a canonical format, e.g. "January 1st, 2000" becomes "1/1/2000".
3. The next step associates single words or complex expressions with a concept from the ontology if a corresponding entry in the domain-specific part of the lexicon exists. E.g., the expression "Deutsche Telekom AG" is associated with the concept TKCompany.
4. Finally, part-of-speech tagging disambiguates the reading returned from morphological analysis of words or complex expressions using the local context.

Lexical analysis is the first of two primary outputs from SMES that we exploit. It returns "normalized" readings for different word forms (e.g., singular vs. plural) that we want to abstract from in order to add a corresponding concept to the ontology.
Chunk Parser. SMES uses weighted finite state transducers to efficiently process phrasal and sentential patterns. The parser works on the phrasal level, before it analyzes the overall sentence. Grammatical functions (such as subject, direct-object) are determined for each dependency-based sentential structure on the basis of subcategorizations frames in the lexicon.

The chunk parser of SMES returnes the second primary output that we use, *viz. dependency relations* [9] found through lexical analysis (compound processing) and through parsing at the phrase and sentential level. We take advantage of the fact that syntactic dependency relations coincide rather closely with semantic relations holding between the very same entities (cf. [6]). Thus, we consider syntactic results as the signposts that points our discovery algorithms into the direction of semantic relationships. We feed those conceptual pairs to

[3] In the future, we also want to extend the lexicon proper during domain adaptation.

the learning algorithm the corresponding terms of which are dependentially related. Thereby, the grammatical dependency relation need not even hold directly between two conceptually meaningful entities. For instance, once we have the linkages between "France Telecom" and "Paris" denoting instances of Company and City, respectively, in example (1), we may conjecture a semantic relationship between Company and City. The motivation is derived from the dependential relationships between "France Telecom", "in", and "Paris". The preposition "in" acts as a mediator that incurs the conceptual pairing of Company with City (cf. [17] for a comprehensive survey of mediated conceptual relationships).

(1) *France Telecom* in *Paris* offers the new DSL technology.

Heuristics. Chunk parsing such as performed by SMES still returns many phrasal entities that are not related within or across sentence boundaries. This however means that our approach would be doomed to miss many relations that often occur in the corpus, but that may not be detected due to the limited capabilities of SMES. For instance, it does not attach prepositional phrases in any way and it does not handle anaphora, to name but two desiderata. We have decided that we needed a high recall of the linguistic dependency relations involved, even if that would incur a loss of linguistic precision. The motivation is that with a low recall of dependency relations the subsequent algorithm may learn only very little, while with less precision the learning algorithm may still sort out part of the noise. Therefore, the SMES output has been extended to include heuristic correlations beside linguistics-based dependency relations:

- The *NP-PP-heuristic* attaches all prepositional phrases to adjacent noun phrases.
- The *sentence-heuristic* relates all concepts contained in one sentence if other criteria fail. This is a crude heuristic that needs further refinement. However, we found that it yielded many interesting relations, e.g. for enumerations, which could not be parsed successfully.

Thus, these heuristics complement the output produced by the chunk parser. **To sum up**, linguistic processing outputs "normalized" terms and sets of concept pairs, $CP := \{(a_{i,1}, a_{i,2}) | a_{i,j} \in C\}$. Normalization is based on lexical analysis and the coupling of concepts is motivated through various direct and mediated linguistic constraints or by several general or domain-specific heuristic strategies.

2.3 Learning & Discovering Component

The Learning & Discovering component uses various algorithms on the annotated texts:

1. Conventional term extraction mechanisms are applied to extract relevant terms from the corpus.
2. An approach for mining a concept taxonomy from a dictionary, which is based on regular expression-based pattern matching algorithms, described in further detail in Section 3

3. An approach for mining non-taxonomic relations, that uses the learning algorithm for discovering generalized association rules described in Section 4.

Conceptual structures that exist at learning time (e.g. concepts or a concept taxonomy) may be incorporated into the learning algorithms as background knowledge. The evaluation of the applied algorithms such as described in [13] is performed in a submodule based on the results of the learning algorithm.

2.4 Ontology Engineering Environment OntoEdit

The Ontology Engineering Environment OntoEdit, a submodule of the Ontology Learning Environment "Text-To-Onto" (cf. Figure 2), supports the ontology engineer in semi-automatically adding newly discovered conceptual structures to the ontology.[4] In addition to core capabilities for structuring the ontology, the engineering environment provides some additional features for the purpose of documentation, maintenance, and ontology exchange. OntoEdit internally stores ontologies using an XML serialization of the ontology model. OntoEdit accesses an inference engine that is based on Frame-Logic.[5]

2.5 System Wrap-Up

The principle idea of our framework is based on applications of knowledge discovery techniques based on input from linguistic processing in a semi-automatic bootstrapping approach. The learning mechanisms in our system do not determine the complete structure, but they are only meant to help the ontology engineer with building a domain ontology by giving recommendations for adding concepts or relations. The system is also not intended to be used in a pipeline fashion, but rather we conceive that simple methods should be exploited first in order to determine the scope of the ontology and the set of relevant concepts. With the extension of the ontology, conceptual *and* linguistic resources are augmented and, thus, they nourish more complex and fruitful linguistic processing and knowledge discovery in subsequent passes through the ontology learning and engineering cycle.

3 Mining a Concept Taxonomy from a Telecommunications Dictionary

In order to provide a starting set of concepts and their taxonomic relations for the domain ontology of our case study, we have exploited the structuring of a

[4] A comprehensive description of the ontology engineering system OntoEdit and the underlying methodology is given in [22].

[5] F-Logic is a frame-logic representation language conceived by [10]. In the implementation by Angele and Decker that we use, F-Logic is a proper subset of first-order predicate logic. Concepts and relations are reified and, hence, may be treated as first-order objects over which quantification is possible. For efficient processing, F-Logic is translated into a datalog-style representation (*cf.* [11,2]).

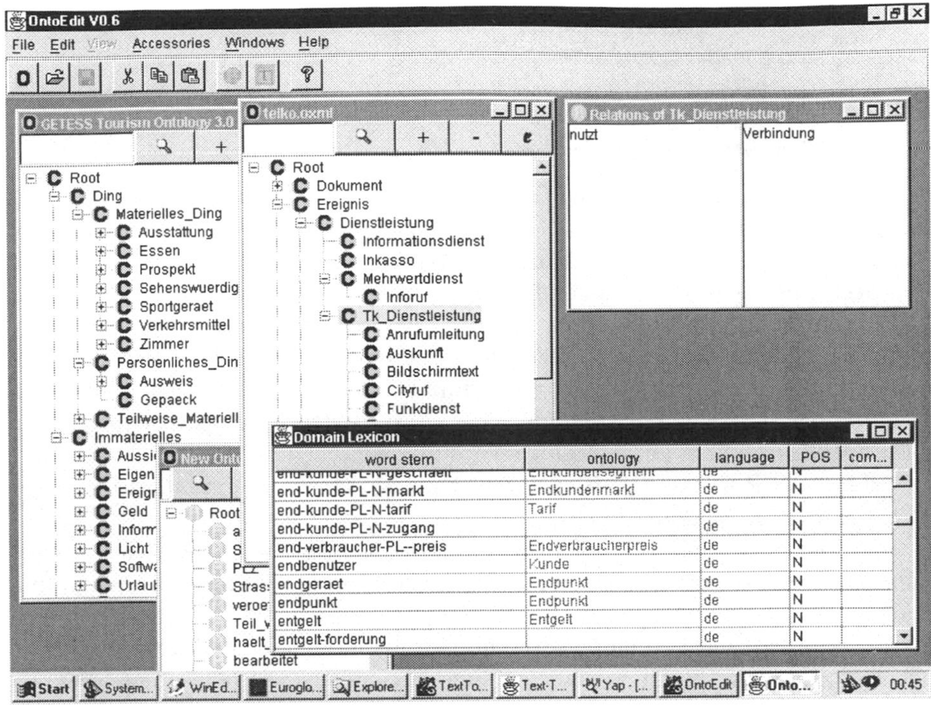

Fig. 2. OntoEdit

freely available dictionary from the telecommunications domain in the first step. In order to make use of the resulting ontology as input for the discovery of further conceptual relations (cf. Section 4), we also had to acquire the mapping between concepts and words.

Example

A dictionary containing natural-language definitions of terms in the telecommunications domain, which is freely available at *http://www.interest.de/online/tkglossar/index.html*, served as a good starting point for the case study. The given 1465 HTML pages were downloaded and transformed into our predefined XML representation for dictionaries, such as given in the following small example:

```
<termEntry>
   <admin>
      <entrynumber>1328</entrynumber>
   </admin>
   <term lang='Deutsch'> Kommunikationsserver
         <description type='Definition'>
           <descriptionText>
              Zentrale Funktionseinheit, welche fuer
```

```
                mehrere Benutzer Kommunikationsdienste erbringt.
              </descriptionText>
            </description>
        </term>
    </termEntry>
```

Every entry has been defined as a concept and a corresponding domain lexicon entry of this concept (reduced to its word stem) has been generated using the Text Processing Server lexical analysis. The definitions of the terms have also been processed using the Text Processing Server.

Similar to the work described in [8,14], we have defined several lexico-syntactic patterns in the form of regular expressions for extracting ISA relations between concepts on the given processed and normalized dictionary definitions. In our small example above the following simple pattern, which is expressed in natural language here for ease of presentation, matched:

"the last NP of the definition before the last comma represents a hypernym of the concept to be defined"

The patterns have resulted in ISA relations, such as between the concept Kommunikationsserver (engl. communication server) and Funktionseinheit (engl. functional unit).

However, we have to emphasize that for building a representative domain ontology, the described dictionary parsing mechanisms are not sufficient. Typically, domain-specific dictionaries describe terms only at a very detailed technical level focusing on the leaf concepts of the taxonomy. For instance, the above mentioned dictionary lacked many important concepts, such as private customer and business customer. For this reason, we have also applied term extraction mechanisms based on the tfidf measure [18] on the given corpus in order to propose frequent terms as candidate concepts. These concepts were then added manually to the domain ontology.

This mixed approach using a combination of automatic extraction mechanisms and user modeling resulted in an core ontology with 265 concepts connected through 312 ISA relations. Additionally, 620 domain lexicon entries mapping words to concepts have been brought into the system.

4 Mining Generic Relations from Text

Our text mining mechanism for discovering relations between concepts is based on the algorithm for discovering generalized association rules proposed by Srikant and Agrawal [19]. Their algorithm is used for well-known applications of data mining, viz. finding associations that occur between items, e.g. supermarket products, in a set of transactions, e.g. customers' purchases. The algorithm aims at descriptions at the appropriate level of abstraction, e.g. "snacks are purchased together with drinks" rather than "chips are purchased with beer" and "peanuts are purchased with soda". The basic association rule algorithm is provided with a set of transactions $T := \{t_i | i = 1 \dots n\}$, where each transaction t_i consists of a set of items $t_i := \{a_{i,j} | j = 1 \dots m_i, a_{i,j} \in C\}$ and each item $a_{i,j}$ is from a set of concepts C. The algorithm computes *association rules* $X_k \Rightarrow Y_k$ ($X_k, Y_k \subset C, X_k \cap Y_k = \{\}$) such that measures for *support* and *confidence* exceed user-defined thresholds. Thereby, support of a rule $X_k \Rightarrow Y_k$ is the percentage of transactions that contain $X_k \cup Y_k$ as a subset, and confidence for $X_k \Rightarrow Y_k$ is defined as the percentage of transactions that Y_k is seen when X_k appears in a transaction, *viz.*

$$(2)\ \text{support}(X_k \Rightarrow Y_k) = \frac{|\{t_i | X_k \cup Y_k \subseteq t_i\}|}{n}$$

$$(3)\ \text{confidence}(X_k \Rightarrow Y_k) = \frac{|\{t_i | X_k \cup Y_k \subseteq t_i\}|}{|\{t_i | X_k \subseteq t_i\}|}$$

Srikant and Agrawal have extended this basic mechanism to determine associations at the right level of a *taxonomy*, formally given by a taxonomic relation $H \subset C \times C$. For this purpose, they first extend each transaction t_i to also include each ancestor of a particular item $a_{i,j}$, i.e. $t'_i := t_i \cup \{a_{i,l} | (a_{i,j}, a_{i,l}) \in H\}$. Then, they compute confidence and support for all possible association rules $X_k \Rightarrow Y_k$ where Y_k does not contain an ancestor of X_k as this would be a trivially valid association. Finally, they prune all those association rules $X_k \Rightarrow Y_k$ that are subsumed by an "ancestral" rule $\hat{X}_k \Rightarrow \hat{Y}_k$, the itemsets $\hat{X}_k, \hat{Y}_k$ of which only contain ancestors or identical items of their corresponding itemset in $X_k \Rightarrow Y_k$.

For the discovery of conceptual relations we may directly build on their scheme, as described in the following four steps that summarize our learning module:

1. Determine $T := \{\{a_{i,1}, a_{i,2}, \ldots, a_{i,m'_i}\} | (a_{i,1}, a_{i,2}) \in CP \wedge$ $l \geq 3 \rightarrow ((a_{i,1}, a_{i,l}) \in H \vee (a_{i,2}, a_{i,l}) \in H)\}$.
2. Determine support for all association rules $X_k \Rightarrow Y_k$, where $|X_k| = |Y_k| = 1$.
3. Determine confidence for all association rules $X_k \Rightarrow Y_k$ that exceed user-defined support in step 2.
4. Output association rules that exceed user-defined confidence in step 3 and that are not pruned by ancestral rules with higher or equal confidence and support.

The reader may note that we here have chosen a baseline approach considering the determination of the set of transactions T. Actually, one may conceive of many strategies that cluster multiple concept pairs into one transaction.

For instance, let us assume a set of 100 texts each describing a particular client in detail. Each private client might come with an address, but it might also have an elaborate description of the different types of private telecomunication services and different calling types resulting in 10,000 concept pairs returned from linguistic processing. Our baseline choice considers each concept pair as a transaction. Then support for the rule {PrivateClient}⇒{Address} is equal or, much more probably, (far) less than 1%, while rules about telecommunication services and different calling types might achieve ratings of several percentage points. This means that an important relationship between {PrivateClient} and {Address} might get lost among other conceptual relationships. In contrast, if one considers complete texts to constitute transactions, an ideal linguistic processor might lead to more balanced support measures for {PrivateClient}⇒{Address} and {Service}⇒{CallingType} of up to 100% each.

Thus, discovery might benefit when background knowledge about the domain texts is exploited for compiling transactions. In the future, we will have to further investigate the effects of different strategies.

Example

For the purpose of illustration, we here give a comprehensive example, which is based on our actual experiments. We have generated a text corpus by crawling texts from several WWW providers for telecommunications information (URL: http://www.TK-news.de/). The corpus describes actual objects, like telecommunication companies, new technologies, telecommunication services, and trends, such as given in the following example sentences.

(4) a. France Telecom bietet als erster Telekommunikationsdienstleister das *DSL-Netz* mit maximaler *Uebertragungsgeschwindigkeit*.
b. Die *Swiss Telekom Beteiligungsgesellschaften* erschweren den Fortschritt.
c. Laut interner Information wird *France Telecom* mit der *BCDM AG* mergen.
d. Alle *Basisanschluesse* sind mit *Kabel*, *Telefon* und *PC-Karte* ausgestattet.

Processing the example sentences (4a) and (4b), SMES (Section 2) outputs dependency relations between the terms, which are indicated in *slanted fonts* (and some more). In sentences (4c) and (4d) the heuristic for prepositional phrase-attachment and the sentence heuristic relate pairs of terms (marked by *slanted fonts*), respectively. Thus, four concept pairs – among many others – are derived with knowledge from the domain lexicon (cf. Table 1).

Table 1. Examples for linguistically related pairs of concepts

Term_1	$a_{i,1}$	Term_2	$a_{i,2}$
DSL-Netz	DSLNetz	*Ueb.geschwindigkeit*	Uebgeschwindigkeit
Swiss Telekom	TKCompany	*Bet.gesellschaft*	Bet.gesellschaft
France Telecom	TKCompany	*BCDM AG*	TKCompany
Basisanschluss	Basisanschluss	*Kabel*	Kabel

The algorithm for learning generalized association rules (cf. Section 4) uses our semi-automatically generated domain taxonomy, an excerpt of which is depicted in Figure 3, and the concept pairs from above (among many other concept pairs). In our actual experiments, it discovered a large number of interesting and important non-taxonomic conceptual relations.

A few of them are listed in Table 2. Note that in this table we also list a conceptual pair, viz. (private client, city), that is not presented to the user, but which is pruned. The reason is that there is an ancestral association rule, viz. (client, city), with higher confidence and support measures.

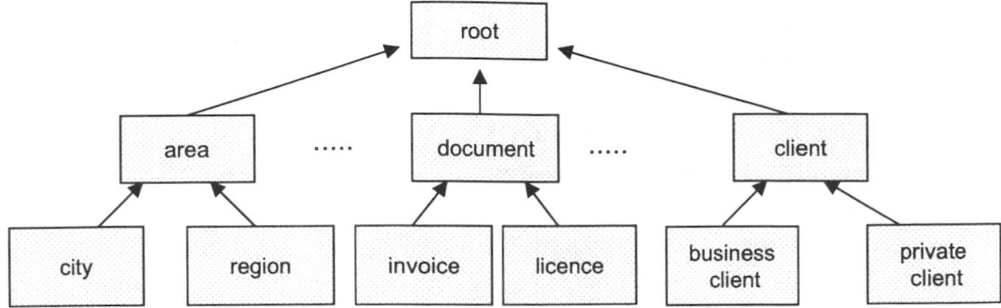

Fig. 3. An example scenario

Table 2. Examples of discovered relations

Discovered relation	Confidence	Support
(market, tariff)	0.38	0.04
(connection, price)	0.39	0.03
(TKCompany, TKCompany)	0.5	0.1
(client, city)	0.39	0.03
~~(private client, city)~~	~~0.29~~	~~0.02~~

5 Related Work

The objective of our framework is to facilitate ontology engineering from texts in real-world settings through several information extraction and learning approaches. Thus, we had to face (i) the discovery of relevant concepts, (ii) their organization in a taxonomy, and (iii) the non-taxonomic relationsships between concepts.

In our actual case study, we have employed a three-step approach. We have exploited some fairly well-known methods for concept discovery and organization, such as standard statistics-based approaches for term extraction [18] and the use of lexico-syntactic patterns on machine-readable dictionaries [8,14].

Based on the concept hierarchy from the first two steps, we have set a new method for the discovery of non-taxonomic relations on top. Regarding this part of our work, we want to give a more detailed survey of related work.

Most researchers in the area of discovering conceptual relations have "only" considered the learning of taxonomic relations. To mention but a few, we refer to some fairly recent work, e.g., by Hahn & Schnattinger [5] and Morin [14] who used lexico-syntactic patterns with and without background knowledge, respectively, in order to acquire taxonomic knowledge.

For purposes of natural language processing, several researchers have looked into the acquisition of verb meaning, subcategorizations of verb frames in particular. Resnik [16] has done some of the earliest work in this category. His model is based on the distribution of predicates and their arguments in order to find selectional constraints and, hence, to reject semantically illegitimate propositions like "The number 2 is blue." His approach combines information-theoretic measures with background knowledge of a hierarchy given by the WordNet taxonomy. He is able to partially account for the appropriate level of relations within the taxonomy by trading off a marginal class probability against a conditional class probability. He considers the question of finding appropriate levels of generalization within a taxonomy to be very intriguing and concedes that further research is required on this topic (cf. p. 123f in [16]) .

Faure and Nedellec [3] have presented an interactive machine learning system called ASIUM, which is able to acquire taxonomic relations and subcategorization frames of verbs based on syntactic input. The ASIUM system hierarchically clusters nouns based on the verbs that they co-occur with and *vice versa.*

Wiemer-Hastings *et al.* [24] aim beyond the learning of selectional constraints, as they report about inferring the meanings of unknown verbs from context. Using WordNet as background knowledge, their system, Camille, generates hypotheses for verb meanings from linguistic and conceptual evidence. A statistical analysis identifies relevant syntactic and semantic cues that characterize the semantic meaning of a verb, e.g. a terrorist actor and a human direct object are both diagnostic for the word “kidnap”.

The proposal by Byrd and Ravin [1] comes closest to our own work. They extract named relations when they find particular syntactic patterns, such as an appositive phrase. They derive unnamed relations from concepts that co-occur by calculating the measure for mutual information between terms — rather similar as we do. Eventually, however, it is hard to assess their approach, as their description is rather high-level and lacks concise definitions.

To contrast our approach with the research just cited, we want to mention that all the verb-centered approaches may miss important conceptual relations not mediated by verbs. All of the cited approaches except [16] neglect the importance of the appropriate level of abstraction.

6 Conclusion

In this paper we have presented an approach towards mining ontologies from natural language. We have considered a domain-specific dictionary as well documents taken from the telecommunications domain as relevant resources for the difficult task of ontology learning.

For the future much work remains to be done. First, we need to investigate what specific types of linguistic and heuristic output are best suited to optimize performance. Maybe chunk parsing does not even help so much, but noun phrase recognition does, or *vice versa.* Second, we are planning a study to investigate our defined evaluation and similarity measures precision, recall, and $\overline{\text{RLA}}$ described in [13] for that human modelers achieve when they are given the same task as our discovery mechanism. Third, we will have to investigate the influence of different transaction definitions (cf. Section 4). Fourth, several existing ontologies such as WordNet [4] and the german counterpart GermaNet [7] have to be integrated as a core resource into the cyclic approach and mechanisms for pruning ontologies to the relevant domain have to be developed. Finally, and probably the most intricate, we want to approach not only the learning of the existence of relations, but also their names and types.

Acknowledgments. The research presented in this paper has been partially funded by BMBF under grant number 01IN802 (project "GETESS"). We thank our student Raphael Volz who implemented large parts of the learning algorithm and our project partners, in particular Günter Neumann, from DFKI, language technology group, who supported us in using their SMES system.

References

1. R. Byrd and Y. Ravin. Identifying and extracting relations from text. In *NLDB'99 — 4th International Conference on Applications of Natural Language to Information Systems*, 1999.
2. S. Decker. On domain-specific declarative knowledge representation and database languages. In A. Borgida, V. Chaudri, and M. Staudt, editors, *KRDB-98 — Proceedings of the 5th Workshop Knowledge Representation meets DataBases, Seattle, WA, 31-May-1998*, 1998.
3. D. Faure and C. Nedellec. A corpus-based conceptual clustering method for verb frames and ontology acquisition. In *LREC workshop on adapting lexical and corpus resources to sublanguages and applications*, Granada, Spain, 1998.
4. Christiane Fellbaum. *WordNet – An electronic lexical database.* MIT Press, Cambridge, Massachusetts and London, England, 1998.
5. U. Hahn and K. Schnattinger. Towards text knowledge engineering. In *Proc. of AAAI '98*, pages 129–144, 1998.
6. E. Hajicova. Linguistic meaning as related to syntax and to semantic interpretation. In M. Nagao, editor, *Language and Artificial Intelligence. Proceedings of an International Symposium on Language and Artificial Intelligence*, pages 327–351, Amsterdam, 1987. North-Holland.
7. B. Hamp and H. Feldweg. Germanet - a lexical-semantic net for german. In *Proceedings of* ACL *workshop Automatic Information Extraction and Building of Lexical Semantic Resources for* NLP *Applications, Madrid.*, 1997.
8. M.A. Hearst. Automatic acquisition of hyponyms from large text corpora. In *Proceedings of the 14th International Conference on Computational Linguistics. Nantes, France*, 1992.
9. R. Hudson. *English Word Grammar.* Basil Blackwell, Oxford, 1990.
10. M. Kifer, G. Lausen, and J. Wu. Logical foundations of object-oriented and frame-based languages. *Journal of the ACM*, 42, 1995.
11. J. W. Lloyd and R. W. Topor. Making Prolog more expressive. *Journal of Logic Programming*, 1(3), 1984.
12. A. Maedche, H.-P. Schnurr, S. Staab, and R. Studer. Representation language-neutral modeling of ontologies. In Frank, editor, *Proceedings of the German Workshop "Modellierung-2000". Koblenz, Germany, April, 5-7, 2000.* Fölbach-Verlag, 2000.
13. A. Maedche and S. Staab. Discovering conceptual relations from text. In *Proceedings of ECAI-2000.* IOS Press, Amsterdam, 2000.
14. E. Morin. Automatic acquisition of semantic relations between terms from technical corpora. In *Proc. of the Fifth International Congress on Terminology and Knowledge Engineering - TKE'99*, 1999.

15. G. Neumann, R. Backofen, J. Baur, M. Becker, and C. Braun. An information extraction core system for real world german text processing. In *ANLP'97 — Proceedings of the Conference on Applied Natural Language Processing*, pages 208–215, Washington, USA, 1997.
16. P. Resnik. *Selection and Information: A Class-based Approach to Lexical Relationships.* PhD thesis, University of Pennsylania, 1993.
17. M. Romacker, M. Markert, and U. Hahn. Lean semantic interpretation. In *Proc. of IJCAI-99*, pages 868–875, 1999.
18. K. Sparck-Jones and P. Willett, editors. *Readings in Information Retrieval.* Morgan Kaufmann, 1997.
19. R. Srikant and R. Agrawal. Mining generalized association rules. In *Proc. of VLDB '95*, pages 407–419, 1995.
20. S. Staab, J. Angele, S. Decker, M. Erdmann, A. Hotho, A. Maedche, H.-P. Schnurr, R. Studer, and Y. Sure. Semantic community web portals. In *WWW9 - Proceedings of the 9th International World Wide Web Conference, Amsterdam, The Netherlands, May, 15-19, 2000.* Elsevier, 2000.
21. S. Staab, C. Braun, I. Bruder, A. Düsterhöft, A. Heuer, M. Klettke, G. Neumann, B. Prager, J. Pretzel, H.-P. Schnurr, R. Studer, H. Uszkoreit, and B. Wrenger. Getess - searching the web exploiting german texts. In *CIA '99 - Proceedings of the 3rd international Workshop on Cooperating Information Agents. Upsala, Sweden, July 31-August 2, 1999*, LNAI 1652, pages 113–124. Springer, 1999.
22. S. Staab and A. Maedche. Ontology engineering beyond the modeling of concepts and relations. In *Proceedings of the ECAI'2000 Workshop on Application of Ontologies and Problem-Solving Methods*, 2000.
23. G. Wiederhold and M. Genesereth. The conceptual basis for mediation services. *IEEE Expert / Intelligent Systems*, 12(5):38–47, September/October 1997.
24. P. Wiemer-Hastings, A. Graesser, and K. Wiemer-Hastings. Inferring the meaning of verbs from context. In *Proceedings of the Twentieth Annual Conference of the Cognitive Science Society*, 1998.

SVETLAN'
Or
How to Classify Words Using Their Context

Gaël De Chalendar and Brigitte Grau

LIMSI/CNRS
BP 133, 91 403 Orsay Cedex, France
{gael,grau}@limsi.fr

Abstract. Using semantic knowledge in NLP applications always improves their competence. Broad lexicons have been developed, but there are few resources which contain semantic information available for words and which are non-dedicated to specialized domains. In order to build such a base, we designed a system, SVETLAN', able to learn categories of nouns from texts, whatever their domain. In order to avoid general classes mixing all the meanings of words, they are learned taking into account the contextual use of words.

1 Introduction

Improving the competence of NLP applications and Information Research systems requires to develop more and more in-depth analysis of documents in order to capture their meaning more precisely. In NLP, existing techniques correspond to two kinds of approaches, radically different. On one hand, surface analysis of texts is based on the distribution of words and their importance in a corpus. It exploits lexical knowledge on words and, possibly, general semantic information such as the semantic classes of a word and relations between words or concepts, as those found in WordNet [7] or in thesauri. This kind of approach can be applied to large text bases, whatever their subjects. In return, it does not allow these systems to develop a detailed and precise analysis, due to the lack of a precise and structured knowledge base. Even when using WordNet, this problem remains. Words in WordNet are related to a Synset when they are synonymous, however Synsets correspond to large categories, and there exists some shifts of meaning between two synonyms so that when two words belonging to a same Synset are considered within a specific context, they often no longer share a common meaning.

On the other hand, in-depth understanding systems require highly structured semantic knowledge as well as pragmatic knowledge about situations referred in texts (the events, their causal links and characters). These systems aim at developing semantic analysis of sentences and building a representation of the meaning of texts. Their limitation comes from these required resources that are impossible to build except in very limited and well-known domains. The problem we address in this paper is then to improve the first systems, in order to go towards the second ones, but without losing the large coverage of the first ones. This is done by automatically

R. Dieng and O. Corby (Eds.): EKAW 2000, LNAI 1937, pp. 203-216, 2000.

acquiring a more structured knowledge base than the bases presently used. Our goal is to extract knowledge from texts, considering that they contain many examples of word uses. We do not want to model a specialized domain, *a priori* chosen. On the contrary, we want to process "general" language, as opposed to a specialized language, but it is well known that there is no "general language corpus". Each corpus is a subpart of the language that has its own specificity. Thus we use a corpus made of newspaper articles (French *Agence France Presse* (*AFP*) newswires and "*Le Monde*" articles). This corpus covers a wide range of different subjects and so, is close to what would be a "general language corpus", apart from the quite fixed journalistic style.

Automatic processes that extract knowledge from texts belong to statistical or syntactical approaches with a lot of variations between these two extremes. Purely statistical ones, such as [15] often obtain groups of words that characterize a sense of a target word. Other approaches ([1], [6], [10], [11], [14]) are more syntactical and obtain classes of words with similar meanings[1]: ARIOSTO [1] and STARTEX [14] use manual semantic tagging and next classification, but while STARTEX uses not tagged repeated text segments, ARIOSTO uses syntactically parsed text. On the contrary ASIUM [6] applies a cooperative clustering algorithm on classes obtained from syntactically parsed texts. ZELLIG [11] constructs a graph of words linked by their common contexts in elementary noun phrases. By the study of the characteristics of this graph, it builds semantic categories. These three systems are designed to work on specialized languages belonging to a specific domain, whose vocabulary is well defined and generally not very ambiguous. When applied to non-specialized texts, they lead to build large classes, mixing all the meanings of words[2], as shown by Fabre et al. [5] for ZELLIG.

As newspapers articles contain a lot of polysemous words, these approaches cannot be applied directly, because they are more or less based on the assumption that their target corpus is sufficiently specialized to be able to ignore the problem of polysemy. However, when considering these polysemous words in their contextual use, i.e. a segment of text about only one topic, their meaning is no more ambiguous. Thus, our system, SVETLAN', takes advantage of a precise context recognition ability in order to build homogeneous classes of words despite the generality of the corpus. It is based on a distributional approach: nouns playing the same syntactic role with a verb in sentences related to the same topic, i.e. the same domain, are aggregated in the same class. The contextual approach of SVETLAN' relies on knowledge about semantic domains of texts, automatically learned by SEGAPSITH [9]. This is way of focusing the construction of the classes by reference to controlled topics. It allows our system to deal naturally with more general texts while giving classes of words with similar meanings, in comparison with the other approaches which have to process specialized texts or that give more disjoined classes.

---

[1] In the rest of this paper, we use the term 'words with similar meanings' to identify words that refer to concepts with an immediate, or quasi-immediate, ancestor in a conceptual ontology.

[2] Pereira et al. [13] use also syntactically parsed texts and a statistical clustering algorithm but applied to more general texts: Associated Press newswires. Classes obtained do not seem to constitute synonym sets as those of the preceding systems, but they have been used successively on a disambiguation task.

2 Overview of the System

Input data of SVETLAN' (see Fig. 1) are semantic domains with the Thematic Units (TUs) that have given birth to them. TUs are the result of a topic segmentation process relying on lexical cohesion that processes texts such as newspaper articles. Each TU contains the lemmatized content words of a text segment. The domains are automatically learned by aggregating similar thematic units. So, domains are sets of weighted words, relevant to represent a specific topic.

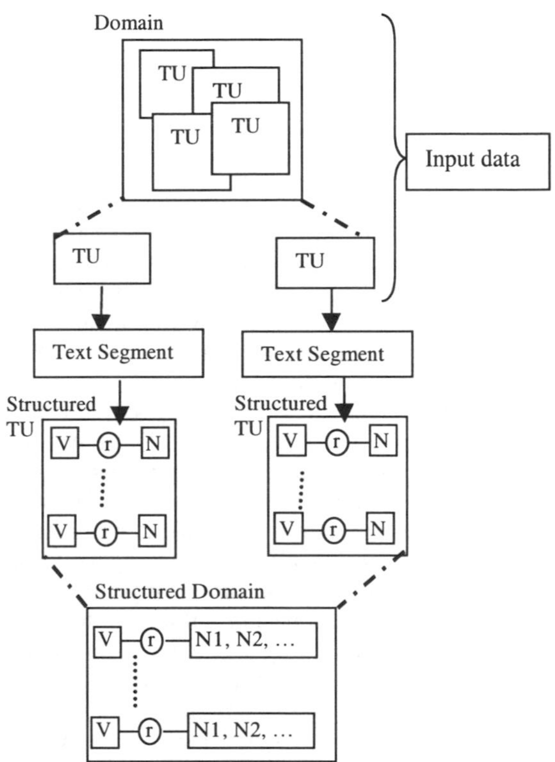

Fig. 1. Schema of structured domain learning

The first step of SVETLAN' consists of retrieving text segments of the original texts associated to the different TUs in order to parse their sentences. SVETLAN' extracts triplets from the parser results, that are constituted by a verb, the head noun of a phrase and its syntactic role. Thus, to each TU corresponds a text segment and a set of triplets we call a structured thematic unit. In order to build classes of nouns according to their contextual use, only the structured thematic units associated to a same semantic domain are aggregated altogether. Aggregation consists of grouping nouns playing the same syntactic role with a same verb. In such an approach, a verb associated to a type of phrase (subject, direct object, ...) constitutes a criterion for building categories. However, one can find words belonging to different semantic categories associated to a same verb and a same type of phrase when the verb is polysemous, as for example *to drive a car* and *to drive a railway*; the same problem occurs with very general verbs, as *to search* for example, that do not entail alone a discrimination among their direct objects. Thus the application of a distributional method without any control coming from the context would lead the system to build heterogeneous categories. SVETLAN' solves this problem by aggregating verb complements within TUs belonging to a same domain. That ensures a better homogeneity of the data and leads SVETLAN' to form context sensitive classes. A last filtering step, based on the weights of the words in their domain, allows the system to eliminate nouns from classes when they are not very relevant in this context. This whole process leads to the formation of structured domains, i.e. semantic domains where each verb is related to categories of nouns that are semantically homogenous.

3 Semantic Domain Learning

We only give here a brief overview of the semantic domain learning module. This one is described more precisely in [9]. This module incrementally builds topic representations, made of weighted words, from discourse segments delimited by SEGCOHLEX [8]. It works without any *a priori* classification or hand-coded pieces of knowledge. Processed texts are typically French newspaper articles coming from *Le Monde* or *AFP*. They are pre-processed to only keep their lemmatized content words (adjectives, single or compound nouns and verbs).

The topic segmentation implemented by SEGCOHLEX is based on a large collocation network, built from 24 months of *Le Monde* newspaper, where a link between two words aims at capturing semantic and pragmatic relations between them. The strength of such a link is evaluated by the mutual information between its two words. The segmentation process relies on these links for computing a cohesion value for each position of a text. It assumes that a discourse segment is a part of text whose words refer to the same topic, that is, words are strongly linked to each other in the collocation network and yield a high cohesion value. On the contrary, low cohesion values indicate topic shifts. After delimiting segments by an automatic analysis of the cohesion graph, only highly cohesive segments, named Thematic Units (TUs), are kept to learn topic representations. This segmentation method entails a text to be decomposed in small thematic units, whose size is equivalent to a paragraph. Discourse segments, even related to the same topic, often develop different points of view. To enrich the particular description given by a text, we add to TUs those words of the collocation network that are particularly linked to the words found in the corresponding segment.

Learning a complete description of a topic consists of merging all successive points of view, i.e. similar TUs, into a single memorized thematic unit, called a semantic domain, or simply a domain. Each aggregation of a new TU increases the system's knowledge about one topic by reinforcing recurrent words and adding new ones. Weights on words represent the importance of each word relative to the topic and are computed from the number of occurrences of these words in the TUs. This method leads SEGAPSITH to learn specific topic representations as opposed to [12] for example whose method builds general topic descriptions as for economy, sport, etc.

mots	words	occ.	weight
juge d'instruction	examining judge	58	0.501
détention	police custody	50	0.442
bien public	public property	46	0.428
charge	charging	49	0.421
emprisonner	to imprison	45	0.417
cour d'appel	court of criminal appeal	47	0.412
recel	receiving stolen goods	42	0.397
supposer	to presume	45	0.382
police judiciaire	criminal investigation department	42	0.381
fraude	fraud	42	0.381

Fig. 2. The most representative words of a domain about justice

We have applied the learning module of SEGAPSITH on one month (May 1994) of *AFP* newswires. Fig. 2 shows an example of a domain about justice that gathers 69 TUs. In all figures displaying examples extracted from our results obtained on French texts, we will put the original data plus their literal English translation.

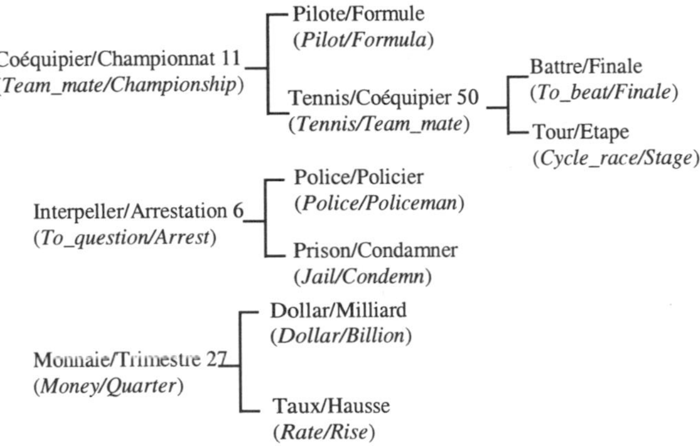

Fig. 3. Three hierarchies of semantic domains

As some of these domains are close and refer to the same general topic, we have applied a hierarchical classification method based on their common words to organize them in separate general topics and to structure them. Fig. 3 shows the hierarchies built about sport, police and stock exchange. Each leaf is a domain, named by its two more weighted words, while their name and their size, i.e. the number of common words found in their children, describe internal nodes.

4 Structured Domains Learning

As in [6], verbs allow us to categorize nouns. Those nouns that play a same role relative to a same verb define a class. In order to learn very homogeneous[3] classes, we only apply this principle on words belonging to a same context, i.e. a domain.

4.1 Syntactic Analysis

In order to find the verbs and their arguments in the texts, we use the syntactic analyzer Sylex [3,4].

```
******************** Phrase 193-466 ***********************************
"L'état de santé critique du pilote autrichien Karl Wendlinger (Sauber-Mercedes), victime d'un grave accident jeudi matin lors des premiers essais du Grand Prix de Monaco de Formule Un, laisse planer une menace sur le déroulement de la course, dimanche en Principauté."
******************** Partie 1 193-466 taux 4 **************************
"L'état de santé critique du pilote autrichien Karl Wendlinger (Sauber-Mercedes), victime d'un grave accident jeudi matin lors des premiers essais du Grand Prix de Monaco de Formule Un, laisse planer une menace sur le déroulement de la course, dimanche en Principauté."
                              <Lexico-Syntactic information>
 193-195 (164) "L'" "le" [gs.1,avn,pdet.1] pdet : singulier elision dmaj
 195-208 (165) "état de santé" "état de santé" [gs.1,nom.1] nom : masculin singulier mot_compose locsw
...<snip>....
 382-388 (203) "laisse" "laisse" [gs.12,nom.1] nom : feminin singulier
 389-395 (204) "planer" "planer" [gs.13,verbe] verbe : infinitif
...<snip>....
 193-195 (16) "L'" "le" [gs.1,avn,pdet.1] pdet : singulier elision dmaj
 195-208 (117) "état de santé" "état de santé" [gs.1,nom.1] nom : masculin singulier mot_compose locsw
...<snip>....
 382-388 (211) "laisse" "laisser" [gs.13,verbe] verbe : singulier autoontif antiontif anontif present indicatif subjonctif imperatif
 389-395 (212) "planer" "planer" [gs.14,verbe] verbe : infinitif
...<snip>....
                              <Syntactic Links>
`L'état de santé critique' (164) ->- cn head ->- `du pilote autrichien' (170)
`planer' (204) ->- a2 head ->- `une menace' (205)
...<snip>....
`planer' (153) ->- a2 head ->- `une menace' (154)
...<snip>....
`planer' (161) ->- a2 head ->- `une menace' (162)
...<snip>....
`planer' (212) ->- a2 head ->- `une menace' (213)
`sur le déroulement' (66) ->- cn head ->- `de la course' (235)
```

Fig. 4. An extract of an analysis of a sentence by Sylex (in French only).

Fig. 4 shows a little part of the results of Sylex for a sentence. The first part exhibits lexico-syntactic information for the words and this for four different interpretations (indicated by the code "**taux 4**" = rate 4) due to the fact that Sylex cannot chose between two interpretations for two words: "*laisse*" between the verb "*laisser*" (to let) and the noun "*laisse*" (leash) and "*critique*" between the verb "*critiquer*" (to criticize) and the adjective "*critique*" (critical). The second part shows the syntactic links found by Sylex. Between parenthesis are references to the words in the preceding analysis. Here Sylex has found four times the same interpretation. In this case, we count one occurrence of the link. But if it finds several times the same relation between a verb and different words, for example several possible subjects, then we keep all the different interpretations. That is because we have no way to

[3] We call homogeneous a class that contains words that have similar meanings, as defined above, in the corresponding domain.

choose between them. We make the reasonable expectation that the false interpretations will have much less occurrences in the corpus and so, will be filtered out during the rest of the processing.

The results of Sylex are very detailed and not easy to parse directly with, say, Perl. Furthermore, we do not need all the information it extracts. In fact, we only need to find the verb with its links and the head nouns arguments of these links. So, we have developed a formal grammar that extracts from these raw analyzes the associations between a verb and its arguments. This grammar extracts links from the results of Sylex in the following format:

i # j   verb # **token1** # *lemma1* # k   rel # **token2** # *lemma2* # l

where i and j are the boundaries of the sentence that contains the link in the corpus; **token1** and *lemma1* are the token and the lemma of the verb respectively; rel is the syntactic relation which can be "subject", "direct object" or a preposition ("to", "from", etc.) ; **token2** and *lemma2* are the token and the lemma of the head noun of the noun phrase pointed by the relation; lastly, *k* and *l* are the indexes in the corpus of **token1** and **token2** respectively. Fig. 5 shows some links that we have extracted.

token 1	*lemme 1*		relation	**token 2**	*lemme 2*
plane	*planer*		sujet	**menace**	*menace*
joue	*jouer*		COD	**coupe**	*coupe*
apprenons	*apprendre*		de	**sources**	*source*

token1	*lemma1*		rel	**token2**	*lemma2*
hang over	*hang over*		subject	**threat**	*threat*
play	*play*		object	**cup**	*cup*
hear	*hear*		of	**sources**	*source*

Fig. 5. Examples of extracted links

Sylex, as other syntactic analyzers, has problems with some constructions and consequently introduces errors that can cause problems to the remaining of the system. Some common errors are the bad interpretation of the passive form that causes a subject to be analyzed as a direct object and conversely, a direct object to be viewed as a subject. Another common error is that it often happens that Sylex does not find any link in a phrase. That is what we call *silence*. We will see in Sect. 5 that we can obtain good results despite these problems thanks to the redundancy needed to validate the links in the next steps of processing. But a consequence of this redundancy need is that the system must use great quantities of texts in order to create classes with a satisfactory size.

Having obtained the syntactic links that were in the texts, we want to group them relatively to the belonging of their text segment to a Thematic Unit. So, we define a structured thematic unit as a set of *<Verb→syntactic relation→Noun>* structures, syntactic relations instantiated with a verb and a noun. We will refer to these structures as instantiated syntactic relations. We are able to put in relation the links extracted from the results of Sylex and the words contained in the domains because each domain in the thematic memory remembers which thematic units have been used to create it. In the same way, each thematic unit remembers the part of text it comes from.

4.2 Aggregation

In order to construct groups of words with very similar meanings, we want to group the nouns appearing with the same syntactic role in relation to a verb inside a domain. Then, a structured domain is a set of <$Verb \rightarrow syntactic\ relation \rightarrow Noun_1, \ldots, Noun_n$> structures, i.e. a set of aggregated instantiated syntactic relation.

Structured thematic units related to a same domain are aggregated altogether to form the structured domains. Aggregating a structured thematic unit within a structured domain consists of:

- aggregating their instantiated syntactic relations that contain a same verb ;
- adding new instantiated syntactic relations, i.e. adding new verbs with their arguments made of a syntactic relation and the lemmatized form of a noun.

Structured Domain source		
to play [4]	object	cup [3], match [1]
	with	ball [1]
to win [2]	subject	player [1]
	object	match [1]
2 Instantiated Syntactic Relations sources		
to play	subject	champion
	object	match
to lose	object	championship

Structured Domain result		
to play [**5**]	object	cup [3], match [**2**]
	with	ball [1]
	subject	**champion [1]**
to win [2]	subject	player [1]
	object	match [1]
to lose [1]	**object**	**championship [1]**

Fig. 6. An example of the aggregation of an instantiated syntactic relation in a structured domain

Fig. 6 shows the aggregation of a structured domain and two instantiated syntactic relations. This example shows all the possible effects of the aggregation. In the figure, bold elements represent new or updated data. Aggregating an instantiated syntactic relation in a structured domain that already contains the verb of the instantiated syntactic relation leads to increment the occurrence number of the verb, as for *play* in the example which occurred 4 times before the aggregation. Similarly, the occurrence number of common nouns related to the verb by the same relation are updated (*match* goes from 1 to 2), and new relations with their associated nouns are added to the verb. In the example, the subject *champion* with an occurrence of 1 is added. An instantiated syntactic relation with a new verb is simply added with an occurrence of 1, as for <to *lose*→ *object*→ *championship*>.

Classes of nouns in the produced structured domains contain a lot of words that disturb their homogeneity. These words often belong to parts of the various TUs at the origin of the structured domain that are not very related to the described topic. They correspond to a meaning of a verb scarcely used in the context defined by the domain. Another possibility is that the instantiated syntactic relation results from an error of Sylex. As these words are weekly weighted in the corresponding domains, the data can be filtered: each noun that possesses a weight lower than a threshold is removed from the class. By this selection, we reinforce learning classes of words according to their contextual use. At this time the threshold is empirically chosen. In the future, we plan to automatically find the threshold. It would be fixed in order to maximize the score of a validation task we outline in Sect. 7. Fig. 7 shows two aggregated links obtained without filtering in its upper part and the filtered counterparts in its lower part. The link for the verb '*to establish*' has been completely removed while the link of the verb '*to answer*' with the preposition '*to*' has been reduced by the removing of '*list*'. We can see on this example that this filtering is efficient: the verb '*to establish*' is not very related to the domain of '*nuclear weapons*' from which this example is taken and the usage of '*to answer to a list*' has a very low probability. More details on the effects of the filtering will be given in the Results section.

établir	*COD*	base, zone
répondre	*à*	document, question, liste
~~**établir**~~	~~*COD*~~	~~base, zone~~
répondre	*à*	document, question, ~~liste~~

to establish	*object*	base, zone
to answer	*to*	document, question, list
~~**to establish**~~	~~*object*~~	~~base, zone~~
to answer	*to*	document, question, ~~list~~

Fig. 7. Two filtered aggregated links in a domain about nuclear weapons

In the principle, the described operations are not very complicated. The difficulties come from the necessity to work with data coming from various tools. Furthermore, for performance and practical reasons, we do not apply the chain of tools text by text. The natural way to see the process would be to:

- read a text,
- extract the TUs from it,
- extract the corresponding structured thematic units,
- add each TU to its domain,
- add each structured thematic unit to its corresponding structured domain.

In fact, each computing step is done on the entire corpus and the results are next aligned. This allows us to save computation time because we do not have to run each one multiple times. But in return we have to deal with dictionaries and indexes for various files and tools.

5 Results

The experiments we realized aim at showing that SVETLAN' lead to learn classes of words which have similar meanings in the domain. To obtain such results we have chosen to run our system on one month of the French version of *AFP* wires, that forms a corpus stylistically coherent but that covers varied subjects with very polysemous and non specific verbs.

The judgements about the quality of the classes obtained are now manual and made by ourselves. We will obviously need a better and more systematic validation approach in the future. We will sketch in Sect. 7 some possibilities we consider.

The one month of *AFP* wires is made of 4,500,000 words and 48,000 sentences in 6,000 texts. The thematic analysis gives 8,000 TUs aggregated in 2,000 domains. More details on these domains can be found in [9]. From these 48,000 sentences, Sylex extracts 117,000 different instantiated syntactic relations. 24,000 of these links concern subject, direct object, or circumstantial complements introduced by a preposition and are integrated in 1,531 structured domains.

After aggregating, but before filtering, the system obtains 431 aggregated links with two or more arguments, equivalent to 431 word classes. Some of them, such as *<to manufacture → direct object → bomb, weapon>* are good. Nevertheless other classes are heterogeneous as *<to return → direct object → territory, strip, context, synagogue>* (here strip comes from the Gaza Strip), or clearly mix different meanings of a verb, like *<to quit → direct object → base, government>* which mixes together the meanings "to leave a place" and "to retire from an institution". For the two latter cases, one can see the interest to take into account the fact that the domains contain words with different weights representing their relevance to this domain. The higher the weight, the higher the relevance of this word in this domain. So we apply the aforesaid filter to our classes and retain only those with weights higher than a threshold. The class *<territory, strip, context, synagogue>* is corrected to *<territory, strip>* and *< base, government>* is removed.

Among the wrong classes, some are due to errors of Sylex, as *<to confer→ direct object → price, actor>* where *actor* should be linked to *to confer* by the preposition *to*. The remaining errors are due to the extensive use of two different meanings of the verb in the same domain, as for: *<to conduct/to manage → direct object → delegation, negotiation>* (in French: "conduire une négociation/une délégation"). This kind of error is inherent to the method we use and should be removed by other means. Note again that the correctness of the links have been manually judged by ourselves.

We have tried two thresholds: 0.05 and 0.1. Fig. 8 details the results for both.

Threshold	Total	Good	Sylex errors	Remaining errors
0.05	73	46	13	14
		63%	18%	19%
0.1	38	27	7	4
		71%	18%	11%

Fig. 8. Results of the filtering for two thresholds

After filtering, a lot of classes are removed but the remaining classes are well founded in most cases. An example of a retained class for both thresholds is:

<to injure→ subject → colonist, soldier>

With a threshold set to 0.1 rather than to 0.05, we retain only 38 links, but we gain

8% in precision. If we ignore the errors due to Sylex, the real precision of SVETLAN' is in the first case 78% and in the second case 87%. It shows the interest there is to choose a good threshold.

Our experiments lead to homogeneous classes containing words having similar meanings, though these classes contain few words. In order to show the efficiency of building classes of words inside a domain, it is interesting to see what kind of classes would be obtained by the merging of all domains, that is to say: creating context-free classes. So, we have applied the same aggregation principle to the same corpus but without taking into account the domains. Just below, we show two classes for the verb "*to replace*". The top one is made context-free and the bottom one is made inside a domain. This verb is very general, virtually everything can be replaced.

remplacer	*COD*	texte, constitution, pantalon, combustible, loi, dinar, barre, film, circulation, juge, saison, appareil, parlement, bataillon, police, président, traité
remplacer	*COD*	combustible, barre
to replace	*object*	text, constitution, trousers, combustible, law, dinar, bar, film, circulation, judge, season, device, parliament, battalion, police, president, treaty
to replace	*object*	combustible, bar

The first group of words merges very different senses while the second class, much more little, is better because it contains words referring to very similar concepts: a bar of uranium is nuclear combustible. Another example is the following, for the verb "*to attribute*":

attribuer	*COD*	parole, prix, décoration, pape, responsabilité, télévision, attentat, lettre, contrat, ministre, jury, fond, autorité, note, bonus, bande, bombardement
attribuer	*COD*	prix, décoration
to attribute	*object*	talk, prize, decoration, pope, responsibility, television, attempt, letter, contract, ministry, jury, funds, authority, note, bonus, band, bombing
to attribute	*object*	prize, decoration

Obtaining meaningful classes with a corpus such as "*AFP*" shows the efficiency of our method. Moreover, we obtain cohesive classes for verbs very general and polysemous.

Words are often polysemous or ambiguous. However, when used in context, they denote one meaning, and moreover this meaning is generally the same in different occurrences of a same context. When building classes according to their context, we avoid mixing all the meanings of a word in a same class. Such a result can be exhibited in the classes (law, constitution) and (law, article, disposition) in the juridical context, for the words "articles", "constitution" and "disposition".

6 Related Works

There is a lot of works dedicated to the formation of classes of words. These classes have very various statuses. They can contain words belonging to the same semantic field or near synonymous. We give here some details about three approaches we cited in the introduction that are good examples of different approaches: manual, statistical and syntactical.

WordNet [7] is a lexical database made by lexicographers. It aims at representing the sense of the bigger part of the lexicon. It is composed of Synsets. A Synset is a set of words that are synonymous. These Synsets are linked by IS A relations. Its coverage is large but this quality is, in a sense, its shortcoming. Indeed, the generality of its contents makes it difficult to use in real sized applications that are often centered on a domain. It rarely can be used without a lot of manual adaptation, even if some authors tried to relate automatically acquired lexical knowledge with it, for example [2].

IMToolset, by Uri Zernik [15], extracts, for a word, several clusters of words from text. Each of these clusters reflects a different meaning of the studied word. This extraction is done by scanning the local contexts of the word, the 10 words surrounding it in the texts. These signatures are statistically analyzed and clustered. The result is groups of words that are similar to our domains but more focused on the sense of a word alone.

We have already stressed out some characteristics of ASIUM by D. Faure and C. Nedellec, but we give here some more details. ASIUM learns subcategorization frames of verbs and ontologies from text using syntactic analysis and a conceptual clustering algorithm. It analyses texts with Sylex and creates basic clusters of words appearing with a same verb and a same syntactic role or preposition, as do SVETLAN'. These basic classes are then clustered to create an ontology by the mean of a cooperative learning algorithm. The main difference with SVETLAN' is this cooperative part: ASIUM critically depends on the expert that has to valid, and possibly split, the clusters made by the algorithm. As a consequence, it has to work on specific technical texts. As a consequence, ASIUM, applied on texts such as our *AFP* wires would certainly not have been able to extract good classes. Indeed, there is a lot of very polysemous words in these texts that take a precise meaning only in a sufficiently focused context, such as our domains. Furthermore, as each word does not occur a lot, the distance measure currently used in ASIUM would not allow grouping any cluster.

7 Future Directions of Work

We envisage two major directions of work that are closely related: the extension of our results and a real validation of them.

At this time, the classes do not contain a lot of words. A way to enlarge them, and the more obvious one, is to process more texts in order to have more data. That will necessitate some modifications of the algorithm of domain building. At this time, we store all the thematic units and all the words in domains, even if they are never aggregated and so have always an occurrence number of one. Thus, the memory usage is too important. We will set up a kind of "garbage collection" process to remove or maybe recycle old and not very aggregated domains. This will allow us to process much more texts and so enlarge classes in two directions: their sizes and the number of occurrences of words inside them.

Another way could be to regroup classes that are related to the same verb, by the same syntactic relation in two domains belonging to the same hierarchy, i.e. a same more general context, assuming the words always have the same meaning. However this method has to be tested on more results in order to prove its reliability. With our results, we would build for example (law, constitution, article, disposition) in the domain of "Law" and (rebel, force, northerner, leader) in the domain of "conflict". This way of enlarging the classes should be studied carefully in a theoretical point of view. Indeed, the originality of our work is the focused context entailed by the use of the domains. That allows us to deal with texts from general language. When we consider domains in the same hierarchy, we enlarge the context and so, we take the risk to have the same problems as other works, discussed in the introduction and Sect. 6, when they are applied to general language: the merging in a same class of different meanings of some words.

Another possibility to enlarge our classes is to generalize them as in ASIUM. ASIUM merges classes independently of the related verbs according to a similarity measure, even if, in our case, this generalization process would operate in a same general domain. Afterwards, as in ASIUM, we would ask an expert to validate its results. The problem would be, again, to find an expert of "general language".

Concerning the validation task, it could be realized by relating our classes to existing classifications, as do [2] with WordNet. Another possibility would be to evaluate the improvement SVETLAN' permits when performing a task. Our group participates to the "Question Answering" track in the TREC evaluations and uses a search engine to find documents able to contain the answers. The questions of the QA track are about various topics from a newspaper corpus. So, we believe that the classes obtained by SVETLAN' could be very useful to extend precisely the requests to the search engine.

8 Conclusion

The system SVETLAN' we propose, in conjunction with SEGAPSITH and the syntactic parser Sylex, extracts classes of words from raw text. Instead of just having sets of weighted words for describing semantic domains, domains are described by a set of verbs related to classes of words by a syntactic link. These classes are created by the gathering of nouns appearing with the same syntactic role after the same verb inside a context. This context is made by the aggregation of text about similar subjects. Besides, we can also view this base as semantic classes, each one being related to its context of interpretation. The first experiments carried out give satisfying results. But they also confirm that a great volume of data is necessary in order to extract a large quantity of lexical knowledge by the analysis of syntactic distributions. Moreover the very low recall of the syntactic parser and its systematic errors on some constructions, for example the passive form, which is very common in the journalistic style of our corpus, reduce the number and size of the classes. To solve this problem, we envisage trying another analyzer or adding a post-processing step to Sylex that detects the passive form by using data already in its output. These adaptations and the study of larger corpora will allow us to obtain a good coverage of numerous semantic domains. So, we will be able to give valuable semantic data useful in a lot of applications as information retrieval systems or word sense disambiguation systems.

References

1. Basili, R., Pazienza, M.T., Velardi, P.: What can be learned from raw texts? Machine Translation, Vol. 8 (1993) 147-173
2. Basili, R., Della Rocca, M., Pazienza, M.T., Velardi, P.: Contexts and Categories: Tuning a General Purpose Verb Classification to Sublanguages. Proceedings of the International Conference on Recent Advances in Natural Language Processing, Tzigov Chark, Bulgaria, (14-16 Sept.1995)
3. Constant, P.: Analyse Syntaxique Par Couches. PhD thesis, École Nationale Supérieure des Télécommunications, (Apr. 1991)
4. Constant, P.: L'analyseur linguistique SYLEX. 5ème école d'été du CNET (1995).
5. Fabre, C., Habert, B., Labbé, D.: La polysémie dans la langue générale et les discours spécialisés. Sémiotiques, number 13 (1997) 15-31
6. Faure, D., Nedellec, C.: ASIUM, Learning subcategorization frames and restrictions of selection. In: Kodratoff, Y. (ed.): Proceedings of the 10th European Conference on Machine Learning – Workshop on text mining (1998)
7. Fellbaum, C. (Ed.): WordNet: an electronic lexical database. The MIT Press (1998)
8. Ferret, O.: How to thematically segment texts by using lexical cohesion? Proceedings of ACL-COLING'98 (student session). Montreal, Canada, (1998) 1481-1483
9. Ferret, O., Grau, B.: A Thematic Segmentation Procedure for Extracting Semantic Domains from Texts. Proceedings of the European Conference on Artificial Intelligence, ECAI'98. Brighton, UK (1998)
10. Greffenstette, G.: Explorations in automatic thesaurus discovery. Kluwer Academic Pub., Boston (1994)
11. Habert, B., Fabre, F.: Elementary dependency trees for identifying corpus-specific semantic classes. Computers and the Humanities, volume 33, number 3 (1999) 207-219
12. Lin, C.-Y.: Robust Automated Topic Identification. Doctoral Dissertation, University of Southern California (1997)
13. Pereira, F., Tishby, N., Lee, L.: Distributional clustering of English words. Proceedings of ACL'93 (1993)
14. Rousselot, F., Frath, P., Oueslati, R.: Extracting concepts and relations from corpora. Proceeding of the Corpus-Oriented Semantic Analysis workshop of the European Conference on Artificial Intelligence, ECAI'96. Budapest, Hungary (1996) 74-78
15. Zernik, U.: TRAIN1 vs. TRAIN2: Tagging Word Senses in Corpus. Proceedings of Recherche d'Informations Assistée par Ordinateur, RIAO'91 (1991)

KIDS: An Iterative Algorithm to Organize Relational Knowledge

Isabelle Bournaud[1], Mélanie Courtine[2], and Jean-Daniel Zucker[2]

[1] LRI, Bat. 490 Université Paris-Sud, Av. du Général de Gaulle, F-91405 Orsay Cedex, France
Isabelle.Bournaud@lri.fr
[2] LIP6, Université Paris VI, 4, place Jussieu
F-75252 Paris Cedex 05, France
{Melanie.Courtine, Jean-Daniel.Zucker}@lip6.fr

Abstract. The goal of conceptual clustering is to build *a* set of embedded classes, which cluster objects based on their similarities. Knowledge organization aims at generating *the* set of most specific classes: the Generalization Space. It has applications in the field of data mining, knowledge indexation or knowledge acquisition. Efficient algorithms have been proposed for data described in <attribute, value> pairs formalism and for taking into account domain knowledge. Our research focuses on the organization of relational knowledge represented using conceptual graphs. In order to avoid the combinatorial explosion due to the relations in the building of the Generalization Space, we progressively introduce the complexity of the relations. The KIDS algorithm is based upon an iterative data reformulation which allows us to use an efficient propositional knowledge organization algorithm. Experiments show that the KIDS algorithm builds an organization of relational concepts but remains with a complexity that grows linearly with the number of considered objects.

1 Introduction

In Artificial Intelligence, the problem of the automatic construction of classifications has been the subject of much researches during the last fifteen years [6], [8], [13]. It consists in searching for similarities between objects which are not pre-classified and structuring them in a hierarchy of classes in which *similar* objects are clustered. A class is also called a *concept* since it is described by an extension (the set of objects clustered) and by an intension (the similarities of the descriptions of the objects clustered). Most of the existing *Conceptual Clustering* approaches defined this task as the search for *a* classification that would best predict unknown features of new objects [5], [7], [8]. This type of construction is guided by heuristics, which allow one to choose the best classes among the possible ones. The developed methods have proved their interest in various fields [6], [8], [9], [13]. In other words, the classifications built do not contain a class for each subset of objects whose descriptions have similarities. More recent researches concern the construction of classifications that *organize* knowledge [3], [15]. In these tasks, the goal is not to build a subset of the possible classes but all the classes clustering similar objects: the *Generalization Space*. In these methods, the process of construction is not based on a numerical distance

R. Dieng and O. Corby (Eds.): EKAW 2000, LNAI 1937, pp. 217-232, 2000.

among descriptions and on a function to be optimized but on a language to describe the similarities among the object descriptions. This language is called the *generalization language*.

Efficient algorithms have been proposed for organizing data described by a set of pairs <attribute, value> [15] and for taking into account domain knowledge [1], [3]. Our research concerns organization of relational data, i.e. data represented in more expressive formalisms (first-order logic, description logic, conceptual graphs ...). To avoid the problem of combinative explosion due to graph matching, we propose to take *gradually* the complexity of graphs into account through a hierarchy of abstraction spaces. The proposed approach, called KIDS, extends the propositional approach of knowledge organization COING [1] to the relational framework. Given a set of objects described using conceptual graphs [17] and domain knowledge represented in a generalization lattice [14], COING builds the Generalization Space of propositional descriptions of the objects. KIDS gradually enriches this space thanks to a generalization language which is made more and more expressive at each step of the algorithm. This idea, inspired from the REMO system [19], consists in increasing gradually the structure of matching. The KIDS algorithm is based upon an iterative reformulation of the data, which allows us to use COING on the reformulated descriptions of the objects.

In the next section, we present the COING propositional algorithm for knowledge organization. Although COING is based upon relational descriptions of data, it does not use the structure of the descriptions in the construction of the Generalization Space. Section 3 introduces the KIDS approach: we describe our method for graph reformulation by abstraction, present the KIDS algorithm and illustrate our approach on an example. In the next section, we evaluate KIDS on a Chinese characters database. These experiments show the feasibility of the proposed approach. Finally, in section 5, we conclude with a brief summary and outline directions for future research.

2 Organization of Relational Knowledge

2.1 A Graphical Representation of Relational Data and Their Generalization

In the automatic construction of classifications, choosing the right language for representing the objects is very important; it has an impact on the efficiency of the algorithms manipulating them. The more expressive a language is, the more complex are the algorithms manipulating it. Objects are structured, and this is true in many fields; they may be decomposed into several parts, and these are then linked together thanks to various relations (for example a *part-of* relation). Attribute-value languages do not allow to easily represent such structure. We use a language based on a higher-order logic and represent relational descriptions of objects in the conceptual graphs formalism. However, this representation is not a limitation of our approach, as it may be applied to any relational data described by graphs.

A *conceptual arc* is a triplet: $[concept_s]$->$(relation)$->$[concept_d]$, where $(relation)$ corresponds to a relation between $[concept_s]$ and [concept$_d$]. A *conceptual graph* is a graph composed of a set of conceptual arcs. For more information about conceptual graphs, the reader should refer to [19] [4].

Figure 1 below presents an example of a house description using conceptual graphs. The triplet `[Window]-> (color) -> [White]` is a conceptual arc. This example is used throughout the article to illustrate the algorithms presented.

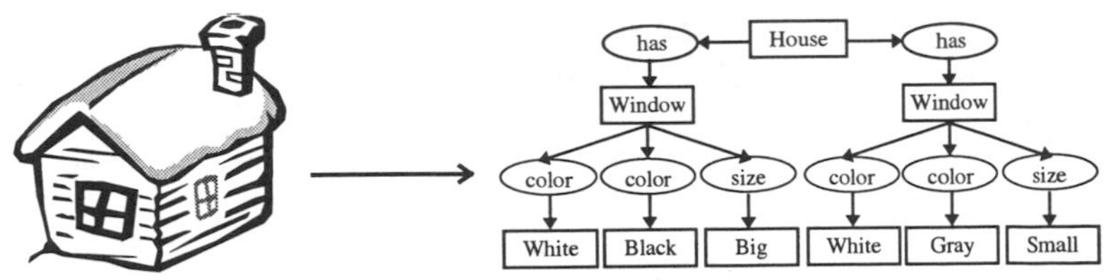

Fig. 1. A house and its description as a conceptual graph.

2.2 Organizing Knowledge in a Generalization Space

Given a set of object descriptions and a generalization language, the associated *Generalization Space* (GS) is the set of the most specific conjunctive concepts generalizing these descriptions. In the GS, a node n_i is a pair (c_i, d_i). The element c_i, called the *coverage* of n_i, is the set of objects covered by n_i; and d_i, called the *description* of n_i, corresponds to the common features (most specific generalization) of the objects of c_i. In the GS, a node corresponds to a cluster of objects described in *intension* by its description d_i and in *extension* by its coverage c_i. Nodes of GS are partially ordered by a subsumption relation between concepts. Given a node n_i with coverage c_i, its ancestors are all the nodes n_j, such that $C_j \supset C_i$. This partial order provided the GS with a *pruned lattice structure*[1], which may be represented by an *inheritance network*. Indeed, GS nodes *inherit* the descriptions of the nodes which are more general.

Figures 4 and 9 present two different Generalization Spaces of the same objects (as explained in the next section, part of their node descriptions come from the use of a generalization lattice over the types). Their differences lie in the expressiveness of the generalization language used to build the GS. In effect, given a set of object descriptions, depending on the language chosen to describe the generalizations (the node descriptions), the nodes of the associated GS will not be the same. The node n'3 in the GS of figure 9 for example does not appear in the GS of figure 4. Moreover, for a given set of objects, nodes belonging to different GS but having the same coverage may have a more or less general description. The node n'2 in the GS of figure 9 and the node n2 in figure 4 have the same coverage on objects ({h2, h3}) but the description of the node n'2 is more specific than that of n2.

---

[1] The Generalization Space may also be defined by the two isomorphic lattices: the Galois lattice of concept descriptions (partially ordered by the subsumption relation) and the lattice of objects (partially ordered by the inclusion relation) [12].

2.3 A Classical Simplification of the Graph Generalization Problem

To avoid the exhaustive analysis of each of the 2^n partitions of n objects, COING adopts a bottom up approach generalizing objects descriptions to incrementally build the GS. In COING, objects are represented using conceptual graphs. In order to deal with the problem of matching graphs which is known to be NP-complete, COING transforms the graph representation into an arc representation. In other words, each graph describing an object is transformed into a set of *independent* arcs. This reformulation has the advantage to limit the complexity of the algorithm (in the worst case quadratic with the number of objects [1]) because, as the arcs are oriented they fully match. However, this restricts the generalization language since relations among arcs are not considered.

The COING principle for building the GS is as follows:

1. *Reformulate* each graph describing the objects to be organized as a set of arcs.
2. *Generalize* each arc describing the objects. COING integrates an efficient method for taking into account domain knowledge in the GS construction [1]. This knowledge, represented in a generalization hierarchy (called the "type lattice" in the conceptual graphs formalism [17]) expresses, for example in the domain of colors, that the type `Black and White` (noted `B&W`) is a generalization of the three types `White, Black` and `Gray`. Figure 2 below presents part of the concept type lattice used for the houses.

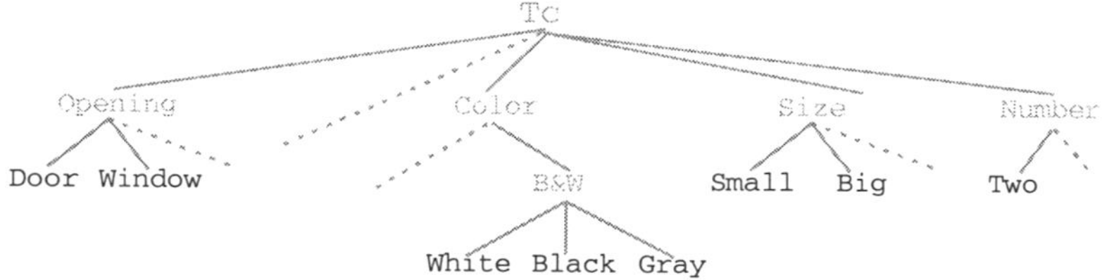

Fig. 2. Part of the concept type lattice used for the houses.

3. *Group* the generalized arcs and initial arcs covering the same set of objects. For example, the arc `[Window]->(color)->[B&W]` is a generalization of the two arcs (thanks to the type lattice above on figure 2): `[Window]->(color)->[Gray]` and `[Window]->(color)->[White]`. This arc will be part of the description of the node covering objects described by one of these arcs.
4. *Filter* the generalized arcs. Indeed, for a given matching there are several possible generalizations. For example, the two arcs `[Window]->(color)->[B&W]` and `[Window]->(color)->[Colour]` are both generalization of the arcs: `[Window]->(color)->[White]` and `[Window]->(color)->[Gray]`. This step considers each set of arcs for a node and chooses the arcs that will form the description of this node in the GS. In constructing the GS, the number of generalizations is limited while considering only the most specific ones. The filtering step thus consists in memorizing only the most specific arcs (on the example above, the arc

[Window]->(color)->[B&W]). As COING is using a propositional language, the most specific generalization is unique.

5. Finally, the nodes are *connected* thanks to the inclusion relation existing among their coverage.

Figure 3 summarizes the principle of the GS construction.

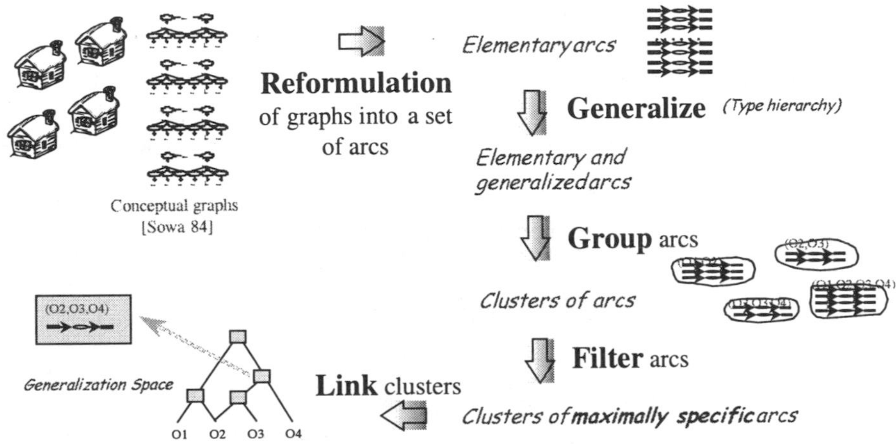

Fig. 3. Principle of the construction of the most specific Generalization Space.

In order to illustrate the COING approach, let us consider the three houses h1, h2 and h3 whose descriptions need to be clustered. These houses are described by their windows which have two proprieties: a color and a size. Figure 4 below presents the GS build by COING for these houses.

This Generalization Space contains two class nodes (n1 and n2) and three object nodes corresponding to the houses (box nodes). The node n2, for example, clusters the houses h2 and h3. Its coverage is {h2, h3} and its description is the arc [Window]->(color)->[Gray]. This class node indicates that h2 and h3 have at least a gray window in common in their descriptions and that this property is not shared by any other object considered. Thanks to the structure of the GS, we may add the description of the root node (n1) to this description. More precisely, we add the arcs from n1 which are not generalizations of arcs from n2, for example the arc [Window]->(Size)->[Big]. Finally, the GS indicates that the two houses h2 and h3 have window(s), which have a size (Small,Big) and a color (Gray and Black).

Let us clarify why the arc [Window]->(color)->[B&W] appears in the root node and why the arc [Window]->(size)->[Size] does not. This explanation will clarify the 3rd step of the COING principle (cf. previous page).

- The arc [Window]->(color)->[B&W] is a generalization of the arc [Window]->(color)->[Black]. As this last arc is more specific and since they have the same coverage on objects ({h1, h2, h3}), the arc [Window]->(color)->[B&W] should not appear. However, this arc is *useful* because its coverage on arcs is bigger than that of [Window]->(color)-

>[Black]: it also covers the arcs [Window]->(color)->[White] and [Window]->(color)->[Gray]. In fact, this arc tells us that there is a window whose color is [B&W].

- Consider now the arc [Window]->(size)->[Size]. It is more general than both the arcs [Window]->(size)->[Small] and [Window]->(size)->[Big]. The coverage on objects of these three arcs is the same ({h1, h2, h3}). The coverage on arcs of [Window]->(size)->[Size] is exactly the union of the coverage on the arcs of the two arcs [Window]->(size)->[Big] and [Window]->(size)->[Small]. The arc [Window]->(size)->[Size] is therefore not useful and not informative; it should not be part of the root node description.

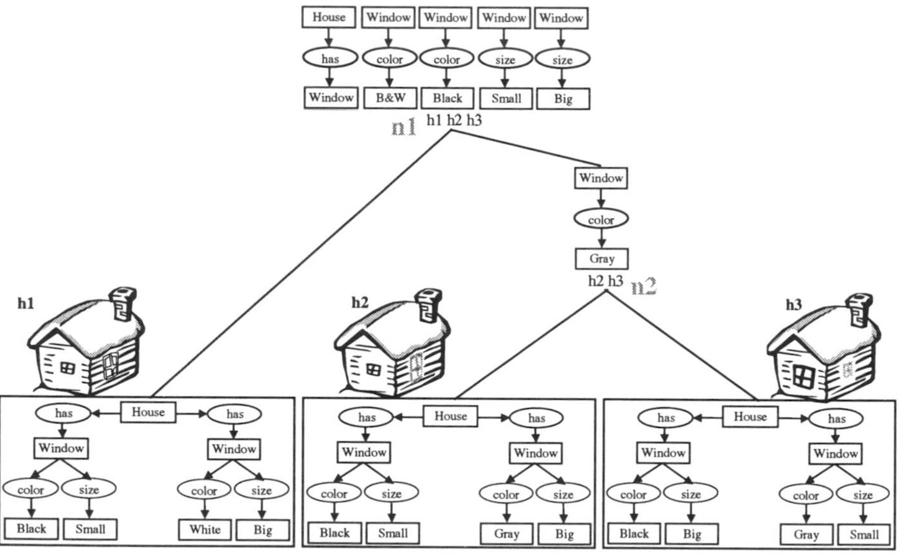

Fig. 4. Generalization Space built by COING.

In order to deal with the traditional knowledge representation tradeoff [11] between an expressive language and an efficient algorithm, COING reformulates conceptual graphs into conceptual arcs. This simplification supplies the COING algorithm with a quadratic complexity in the number of objects, but restricts the generalization language, i.e. the expressiveness of the GS node descriptions. Let us illustrate this point using the house example. The three houses h1, h2 and h3 all have a small window and a black window; for h1 and h2 it is the same window, whereas for h3 it is not. This difference does not appear in the classification built by COING (see fig.4) since it requires representing relations between arcs.

3 Organize Knowledge in a Hierarchy of Generalization Abstraction Spaces

Building an organization of relational descriptions requires to build a Generalization Space whose nodes use a relational representation. Given a set of objects described as graphs in the conceptual graph formalism, each node in the GS would ideally be represented by the graph that is the most specific generalization of the graphs describing the objects it covers. Let us note this Generalization Space as GS_{max}. In fact, due to the complexity of the subsumption relation and the exponential growth of the length of the least general generalization, building GS_{max} directly using an exhaustive method is not practical. The matching curse is also true for the first-order languages used in Inductive Logic Programming (ILP); they define syntactic restrictions on clauses to devise efficient ILP algorithms [16] which are similar to the restrictions on graphs used to devise graph-based algorithms [1], [12].

The solution proposed in this paper is to build an initial GS using a propositional language and then to iteratively enrich this GS. This enrichment consists of refining the descriptions of existing nodes or adding new nodes. We present in the following sections our approach, called KIDS, which is using COING and relies upon the abstraction of relational data.

3.1 KIDS Principle

KIDS is based upon the following property of the GS which allows us to limit the search space at each step of the algorithm:

> *If there exists a sub-graph S_{gn} which generalizes n object descriptions, then there is in the GS built by COING a node whose coverage contains these n objects (and possibly others) and whose description contains all the arcs of the generalizing sub-graph S_{gn}.*

In other words, this property of GS means that to enrich any node of a GS, it is sufficient to restrict the search for richer descriptions only to the objects it covers. This principle simplifies the process of enriching a GS. In effect, the nodes of GS_0 (found by COING) are a subset of the nodes of a GS whose generalization language is richer than the one used in COING and the description of each node of GS_0 is more general than that of GS.

In order to find richer descriptions of GS nodes, our approach consists of *gradually* increasing the matching structure, i.e. the matching structure is made more complex at each step of the algorithm. At each step, the objects descriptions are reformulated based upon this structure into a propositional language. The reformulates descriptions may then be processed by the COING algorithm.

More precisely, KIDS uses sub-graphs to represent the relational nature of the descriptions. In order to reformulate these sub-graphs into a propositional language that may be performed by COING we make an *abstraction*. This abstraction transforms the sub-graphs representation into a representation appropriate to COING : a structure like `[concept-type]->(relation-type)->[concept-type]`. In fact, the relation-type is replaced by an " *abstract relation* " representing the matching structure.

For example, at the 1st level of KIDS (first step of the algorithm), an arc performed by COING is:

```
[House] |-> (has) -> [Window] -> (size) -|> [Small]
```

The triplet *(has)->[Window]->(size)*, which is in the box, is an abstract relation. Figure 5 below presents the general KIDS principle.

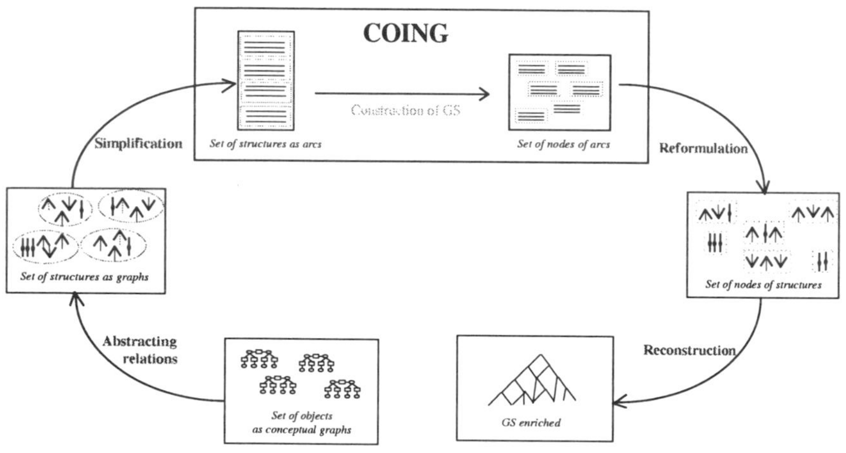

Fig. 5. Principle of KIDS.

3.2 Towards a New Generalization Language

To enrich at each step the matching structure is equivalent to modify at each step the generalization language. KIDS starts with a language of arcs (provided by COING), then it uses at the first step a language of couples of connected arcs, then at the second step a language of triplets of connected arcs, etc.. These successive generalization languages are expressed according to particular connected sub-graphs: *sequence, star* and *hole structures*.

Definition 1: A *sequence* is composed of a succession of arcs, which are connected one-to-another thanks to a common concept. This concept is the origin of the first arc and the target of the other one.

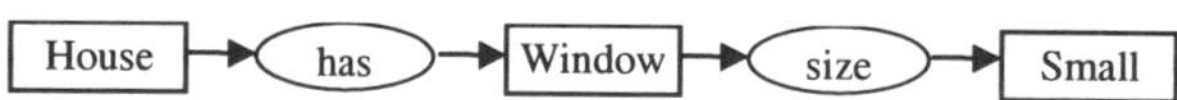

Fig. 6. Example of a sequence-structure composed of two arcs through the common concept of Window

Definition 2: A *star* is composed of a set of conceptual arcs which have the same origin.

Fig. 7. Example of a star-structure composed of two arcs through the concept of House

Definition 3: A *hole-structure* is composed of a set of conceptual arcs which have the same target.

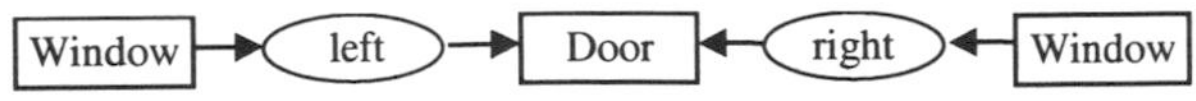

Fig. 8. Example of a hole-structure composed of two arcs

The number of arcs of an abstract relation depends on the level of KIDS (the step of the algorithm): two connected arcs at the 1st level, 3 at the 2nd level, …, i+1 arcs at the ith level. The more the sub-graph structure is complex, the more the matching for the reformulation is expensive. Nevertheless, the specific structure of the GS and the iterative method of KIDS allow us to limit the number of nodes to explore at each step.

3.3 KIDS Algorithm

The principle of the KIDS algorithm is to explore, at the *ith step,* only the nodes which may be enriched, i.e. the nodes whose descriptions potentially contain an ith level structure. In practice, at step (i+1)th, KIDS explores all the nodes which were modified in step i. Indeed, an (i+1)th level structure is the aggregation of an ith structure and *one* arc. We define a *candidate* node for KIDS at step i+1 a node which has been modified in step i. In the first step, KIDS explores all the GS nodes built by COING. The GS enrichment algorithm is as follows (cf. Table 1):

1. For each object covered by a candidate node, determine its ith level description: (i+1) connected arcs. It consists of abstracting the object descriptions using the three structures: sequence, star and hole.
2. Apply COING to the reformulated object descriptions. The result is the addition of new nodes to the GS and/or the modification of the descriptions of existing GS nodes. Notice that the new descriptions found by COING have to be reformulated in terms of sub-graphs. It consists of reformulating the descriptions using the abstract relations.
3. If KIDS modifies the GS at the ith step, then repeat the method from 1) at the (i+1)th level (i+2 connected arcs).

Table 1: KIDS main algorithm

```
KIDS_Algorithm (GS: Generalization Space; l: level)
GS_modified ← false
Nodes_List ← list of GS candidate nodes
for all the nodes n of Nodes_ List do
   Objects_ List ← Description of n's objects at the lth level
   GS_enriched ← COING_Algorithm(Objects _List)
   if GS_enriched modified then GS_modified ← true
   GS ← Add (GS_enriched, GS)
end for
if GS_modified == true then KIDS_ Algorithm(GS,l+1)
```

While the complexity of the matching for generalization is avoided by the use of abstract relations, the complexity of graph matching is not suppressed; it is instead moved to the reformulation of the descriptions. In fact, the more complex the abstract relations are (the higher the KIDS level), the more complex the reformulation is. Nevertheless, the GS's specific structure and KIDS's iterative method allow us to limit the number of nodes to be explored at each step, while exploring only the ones that can be enriched.

However, in order to find all the structural similarities among the descriptions, KIDS needs to be applied up to the level of structure of the maximum level in the objects descriptions. In other words, if there are at least two descriptions including a structure of level l, KIDS will have to be applied up to the l level to assure a search for all the similarities.

KIDS stops either when there is no more candidates node, or when it is not possible to describe the objects at the next level (there is no structures of (i+2) arcs in the descriptions). Experimentally, the time needed to apply the algorithm at the next level may be evaluated from the time needed to build the GS at the previous level. It is possible to approximate the time required for the next level and to stop KIDS if this time is too long. Experiments in section 5 show that in our particular domain, the increase of time required between two successive levels is linear.

3.4 Organizing Relational Data with KIDS

Let us consider again the example of the houses presented in section 2.2 (figure 4) to illustrate KIDS improvement over COING. Figure 9 below presents the enriched GS obtained by KIDS at the 1st level ; the information drawn in black is the result of KIDS and in gray those of COING.

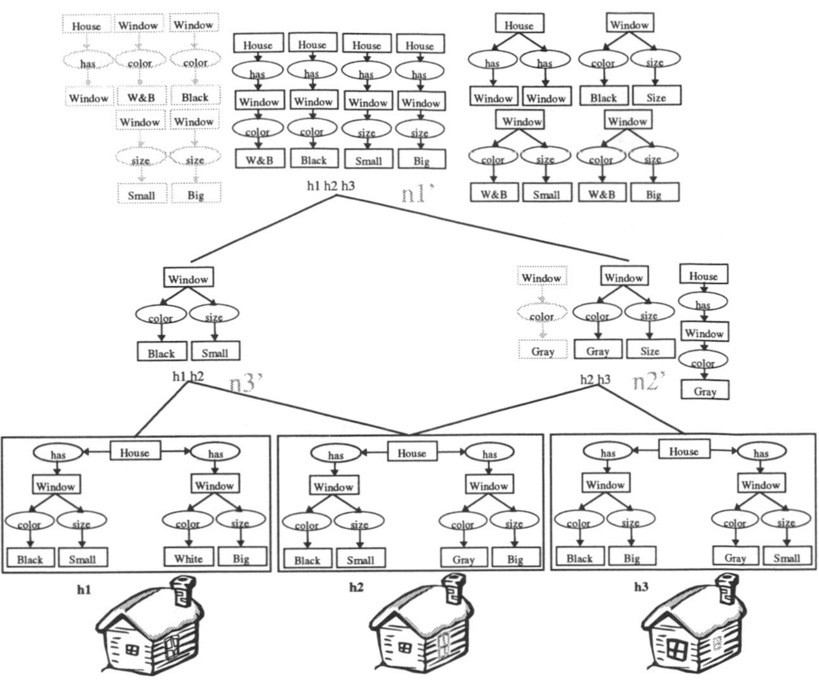

Fig. 9. Generalization Space enriched by KIDS.

The abstraction allows us to discover common substructures between the objects descriptions. At the 1st level, KIDS finds structural descriptions which were not find by COING. For example, COING did not find that all the houses have (at least) two windows and that all these windows have a color (`W&B` or `Black`) and a size (`unknown`, `Small` or `Big`). Furthermore, COING did not find a class clustering h1 and h2 and only these two houses whereas they have a small black window in common and this window does not appear in the description of h3 (even if h3 has a small window and a black window but it is not the same window). This similarity is found by KIDS at the 1st level, because it is a particular composition of two arcs. On this example, KIDS enriched the description of existing nodes and added a new node clustering h1 and h2. From a GS built using a propositional language, KIDS has allowed to give more precise descriptions on the existing similarities between the objects thanks to an abstraction of sub-graphs.

On this example, it is useless to apply KIDS at the 2nd level. Indeed, the stars and sequences of h1, h2 and h3 descriptions are of 1st level, i.e. they connect 2 arcs. Once the descriptions are reformulated using 1st level structures, there is only one way to rebuild the description; the reformulation using first level structures is not ambiguous, nor losses information. Figure 10 illustrates this idea.

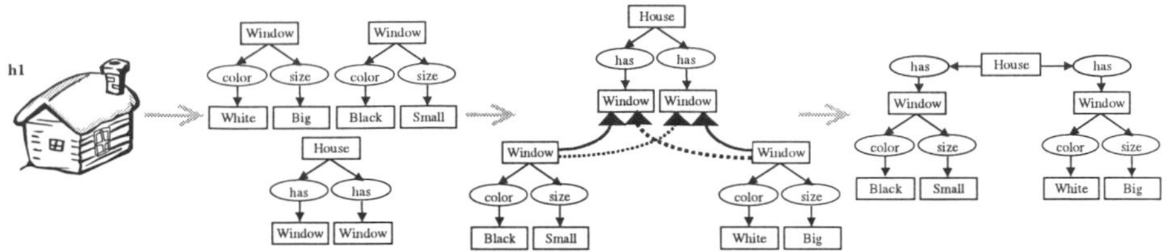

Fig. 10. Rebuilding a graph from its decomposition in structures.

4 Experiments

This section presents an application of the above method in the framework of the construction of a classification of Chinese characters. We briefly remind the context of this work. For more information about this application, the reader should refer to [2]. These experiments aim to show the feasibility of KIDS in terms of complexity and to illustrate its interest for relational data organization.

4.1 Description of the Relational Data

The database considered is a collection of 6780 Chinese characters. Each character is represented by a conceptual graph. Characters are described by : their initial and final pronunciation, the ton of this pronunciation, the components (between 1 and 5) and their relative positions and the key component. For example, the character 情, which is composed of the radicals C5381 and C2843, which is pronounced " qing ", which is in ton 2 and means "feeling", is represented by the conceptual graph of figure 11.

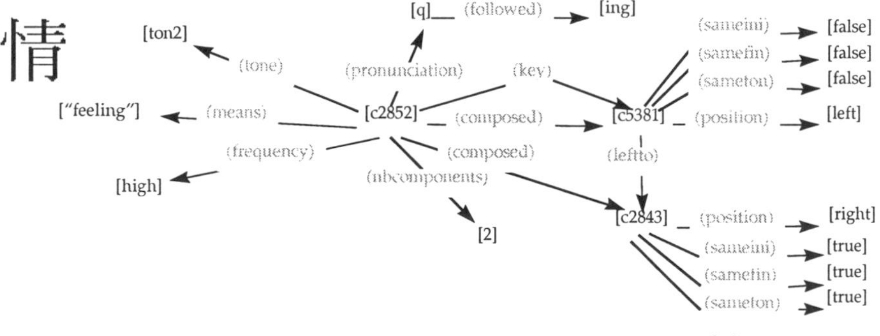

Fig. 11. Conceptual graph describing the character 情.

The type lattices used for the Chinese characters are the following :

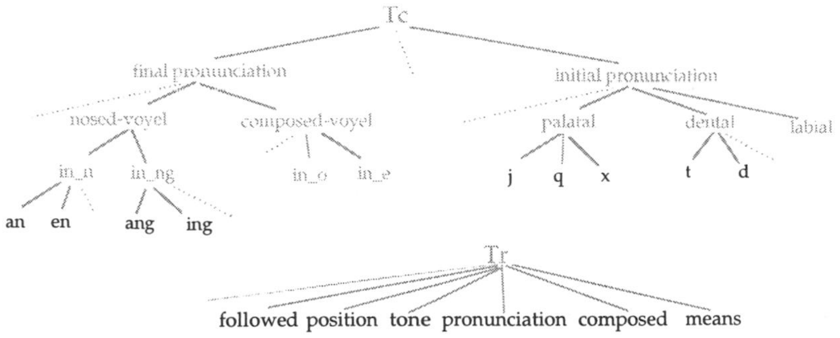

Fig. 12. Part of the type lattices for the Chinese characters.

4.2 Results and Discussion

We evaluated KIDS on several databases of characters composed of 10 to 140 or 416 characters. Figure 13 shows the total time required for generating the GS for 8 of these databases using the COING and the KIDS algorithms.

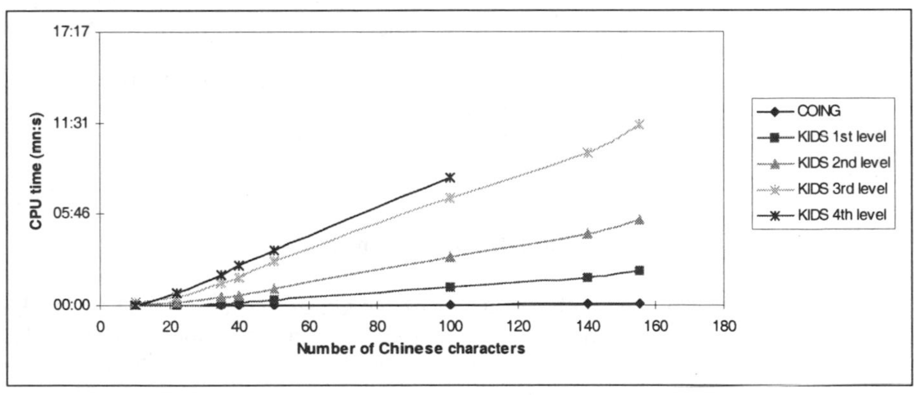

Fig. 13. Average execution time of COING and KIDS on Chinese characters databases.

In practice, the CPU time of the proposed algorithms is linear (it is quadratic in the worst case in COING [1]) with the number of objects. This results may surprise because, as it manipulates sub-graphs, KIDS introduces a complexity factor. However, the combinatorial explosion due to the generalization of sub-graphs is limited since the bigger the level of KIDS is (i.e. the more complex are the graphs to generalize) the less the number of sub-graphs to perform is.

The level introduces a multiplicative factor. The linear growth means that on the average, the time necessary to move to the next level is very close to be constant. Figure 14 illustrates this result.

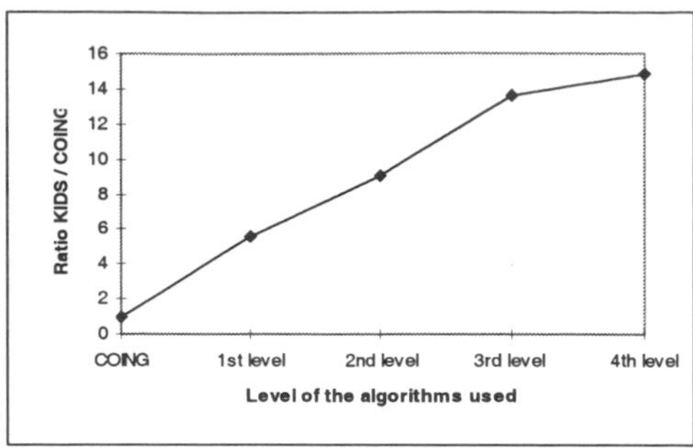

Fig. 14. Evolution of the multiplicative factor as a function of the algorithms used.

During these experiments, we also evaluated the evolution of the number of nodes of the GS as a function of the algorithms used. For COING, this number is in the worst case in O(N) [1]. Figure 15 summarizes these results.

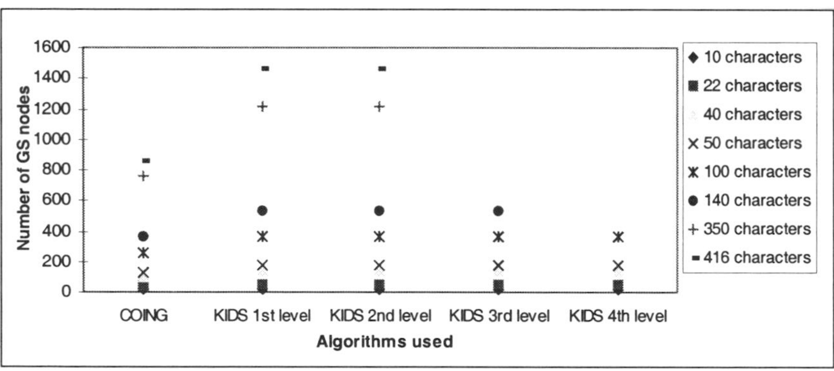

Fig. 15. Evolution of the number of nodes of the GS.

This graph shows that the number of nodes of the GS grows until a specific level – 1st level for the small bases and 2nd level for largest – then it becomes constant. This may be explained by the fact that from a specific level, KIDS does not allow to create new classes, but only to enrich the already existing ones with more complex descriptions.

5 Conclusion

We have presented KIDS, an algorithm for organization of relational data. This algorithm is iterative and is based upon an abstraction of the description. In a first step, it builds the space of the most specific generalizations using a propositional language. Then it uses reformulation to find more complex descriptions. We have implemented and successfully tested our approach. Our experiments suggest that the proposed method provides an organization of relational concepts while keeping a linear complexity in practice with the number of objects. This result is due to the fact that the more complex are the structure, the less are the nodes to explore.

The first perspective of this work is to characterize more precisely the generalized language used in the enriched GS. Indeed, as soon as we work on the o-level structures, there is no longer a unique most specific generalization and GS nodes may be redundant. The characterization of the enriched language of GS allows us to evaluate the usefulness of the sub-graphs and to filter them in order to keep the useful one.

Another possible improvement of the algorithm is to define methods to evaluate the interest of KIDS for a given database. Indeed, when the concepts in the objects of a conceptual graphs database appear only once, it is not necessary to apply KIDS to this database, because the decomposition does not cause a loss of information. In contrast, if a concept appears several times in the objects descriptions (like in the houses), it is not possible to differentiate them. So, we can consider a pre-processing on the data to evaluate the maximal level of KIDS application.

Finally, we plan to extend this method for a more efficient processing of numerical data. Currently, the numerical information contained in descriptions is processed like symbols ; the implicit order existing between numbers is not taken into account. A preprocessing on descriptions would make it possible to determine a hierarchy of generalization of the numerical values. The creation of new values of attributes, as it is the case in constructive induction, would make it possible to better account for the similarities between descriptions [10], [18].

6 References

1. Bournaud I., Ganascia J.-G.: Accounting for Domain Knowledge in the Construction of a Generalization Space. ICCS'97, Lectures Notes in AI n°1257, Springer-Verlag (1997) 446-459.
2. Bournaud I., Zucker J.-D.: Integrating Machine Learning Techniques in a Guided Discovery Tutoring Environment for Chinese Characters. International Journal of Chinese and Oriental Languages Information, Processing Society, 8(2) (1998).
3. Carpineto C., Romano G.: GALOIS: An order-theoretic approach to conceptual clustering. Tenth International Conference on Machine Learning (1993).
4. Chein M., Mugnier M.L.: Conceptual Graphs : Fundamental Notions. Revue d'Intelligence Artificielle, 6(4) (1992) 365-406.
5. Fisher D.: Approaches to conceptual clustering. Ninth International Joint Conference on Artificial Intelligence, Los Angeles, CA, Morgan Kaufmann (1985).
6. Fisher D.: Knowledge Acquisition Via Incremental Conceptual Clustering. In: Michalski, R.S., Carbonell, J., Mitchell, T.(eds.): Machine Learning: An Artificial Intelligence Approach. San Mateo, CA, Morgan Kaufmann. II (1987) 139-172.
7. Fisher D.: Iterative Optimization and Simplification of Hierarchical Clusterings. Journal of Artificial Intelligence Research 4 (1996) 147-179.
8. Gennari J. H., Langley P., Fisher D.: Models of incremental concept formation. Artificial Intelligence 40-1(3) (1989) 11-61.
9. Ketterlin A., Gancarski P., Korczak J.J.: Conceptual clustering in Structured databases : a Practical Approach. Proceedings of the Knowledge Discovery in Databases KDD'95, AAAI Press (1995).
10. Kietz J.U. & Morik K.: A polynomial approach to the constructive induction of structural knowledge. Machine Learning 14(2) (1994) 193-217.

11. Levesque H.J. and Brachman R.J.: A fundamental tradeoff in knowledge representation and reasoning. In: Brachman, R.J, Levesque, H.J. (eds.): Readings in Knowledge Representation. Morgan Kaufmann (1985) 41-70.
12. Liquiere M., Sallantin J.: Structural Machine Learning with Galois Lattice and Graphs. *Fifteen International Conference on Machine Learning (ICML),* (1998).
13. Michalski R. S., Stepp R. E.: An application of AI techniques to structuring objects into an optimal conceptual hierarchy. Seventh International Joint Conference on Artificial Intelligence (1981).
14. Michalski R. S.: A theory and methodology of inductive learning. Machine Learning: An Artificial Intelligence Approach I, Morgan Kaufmann (1983) 83-129.
15. Mineau G., Gecsei J., Godin R.: Structuring knowledge bases using Automatic Learning. Sixth International Conference on Data Engineering, Los Angeles, USA (1990).
16. Muggleton, S., Raedt L. D.: Inductive Logic Programming: Theory and Methods. Journal of Logic Programming 19(20). (1994). 629-679.
17. Sowa J. F.: Conceptual Structures: Information Processing in Mind and Machine. Addisson-Wesley Publishing Company (1984).
18. Wnek J., Michalski R.: Hypothesis-driven constructive induction in AQ17-HCI : a method and experiments. Machine Learning 14(2) (1994) 139-168.
19. Zucker J.-D., Ganascia J.-G.: Changes of Representation for Efficient Learning in Structural Domains. International Conference in Machine Learning, Bari, Italy, Morgan Kaufmann (1996).

Informed Selection of Training Examples for Knowledge Refinement

Nirmalie Wiratunga and Susan Craw

School of Computer and Mathematical Sciences
The Robert Gordon University
St Andrew Street, Aberdeen AB25 1HG
Scotland, UK.

{nw,s.craw}@scms.rgu.ac.uk

Abstract. Knowledge refinement tools rely on a representative set of training examples to identify and repair faults in a knowledge based system (KBS). In real environments it is often difficult to obtain a large set of examples since each problem-solving task must be labelled with the expert's solution. However, it is often somewhat easier to generate unlabelled tasks that cover the expertise of a KBS. This paper investigates ways to select a suitable sample from a set of unlabelled problem-solving tasks, so that only the subset requires to be labelled. The unlabelled examples are clustered according to the way they are solved by the KBS and selection is targeted on these clusters. Experiments in two domains showed that selective sampling reduced the number of training examples used for refinement, and hence requiring to be labelled. Moreover, this reduction was possible without affecting the accuracy of the final refined KBS. A single example selected randomly from each cluster was effective in one domain, but the other required a more informed selection that takes account of potentially conflicting repairs.

1 Introduction

Knowledge refinement is incremental learning, where the learning must adapt existing knowledge in a Knowledge-Based System (KBS). Refinement tools aid knowledge engineers by assisting with the knowledge debugging and maintenance phases in the Knowledge-Based Systems development cycle [1,2,3]. These tools ensure that the KBS's solution is consistent with that of a domain expert for a given task. In common with other learning algorithms, the tasks and the expert's solutions are maintained as training examples. Refinement is triggered when the system's and expert's solution for a given task are inconsistent. Although training examples that indicate faults are useful to drive refinement, access to correctly solved training examples is beneficial, because, they help focus refinement by ensuring that repairs are not too closely fitted to wrongly-solved examples.

The choice of training examples for refinement becomes important when one of the constraints on the refinement process is a limited number of labelled training examples. This is a relatively common problem in a real environment,

R. Dieng and O. Corby (Eds.): EKAW 2000, LNAI 1937, pp. 233–248, 2000.

where labelling many problem-solving tasks with the expert's solution may require significant interaction with a busy expert. Unlabelled training examples are often generated by using domain knowledge already embodied in the KBS or meta-knowledge [4]. Therefore, unlike the labelling task, generating unlabelled examples does not typically require the expert. The goal of the work described in this paper is to perform an informed selection from a set of unlabelled training examples which the expert must subsequently label, thereby reducing the demand on the expert. However, we must ensure that the informed selection of relevant training examples does not hamper the refinement process by omitting examples that uniquely reveal faults.

The problem of unavailability of labelled training examples and sample selection of relevant examples from a set of unlabeled examples falls under the paradigm of active learning and more specifically, selective sampling. Much work has been done in selective sampling mainly related to training classifiers: for nearest neighbour, using a lookahead approach that selects examples based on statistical information about the utility of the resulting classifier [5]; for text classification, using a committee-based approach combined with expectation maximization [6]; and for C4.5 using a probabilistic classifier that selects examples based on class uncertainty [7]. Increasingly, estimation and prediction techniques with roots in statistics are being applied to classifiers with improved accuracy results [8]. However, the use of examples for training classifiers differs from their use for refinement tools:

- in refinement, examples are used to expose faults in an existing KBS and so are employed to refine incomplete concepts and not learn from scratch; and
- examples are used for refining KBSs that model, not only classification tasks but also design tasks [9] and even planning tasks [10].

Direct application of currently available selective sampling methods for learning classifiers to refinement tools is therefore, not straightforward. We adopt the common approach of partitioning the available examples into clusters, but exploit the relationship between the examples and how they are solved by the faulty KBS, in contrast to existing selection techniques that exploit the statistical distribution of examples. As a result our clusters will contain examples that trigger similar problem solving behaviour in the KBS. We then apply various heuristics that help select examples from clusters. However, the presence of interacting faults in a KBS complicates sample selection since they require the selection of more than one example from each cluster. We have developed heuristics that identify those examples that are most likely to demonstrate interacting faults and we propose algorithms that apply these heuristics to example selection. The selected subset of examples is then presented to the expert for labelling. Once labelled, these examples can be used by the refinement tool to drive the refinement process.

Section 2 introduces iterative refinement by describing the process undertaken by a particular family of refinement tools. The selective sampling process in Section 3, firstly, describes a structure that captures problem-solving behaviour of the KBS for a given task, secondly, presents a clustering framework that uses this problem-solving behaviour to determine similarity between unlabelled examples, and thirdly, identifies several heuristics for selecting a suitable number of examples from these clusters. Experimental results from evaluating the selection heuristics on two problem domains which have different problem-solving characteristics is presented in Section 4. Finally, in Sections 5 and 6, we discuss related work in the field and conclude with contributions of this work and implications for future work.

2 Refinement with KRUSTtools

The KRUSTWORKS project has developed a generic knowledge refinement framework. Given a specific rule-base shell, this framework is used to generate a refinement tool, a KRUSTtool, by re-using core refinement modules. These modules are applied to generic knowledge structures which model the behaviour of the rule-base. The structures are formed by translators that work on the specific rules and the associated traces [1]. The currently developed framework is able to deal with faulty KBSs implemented in shells incorporating reasoning strategies that can be forward-chaining, backward-chaining or both.

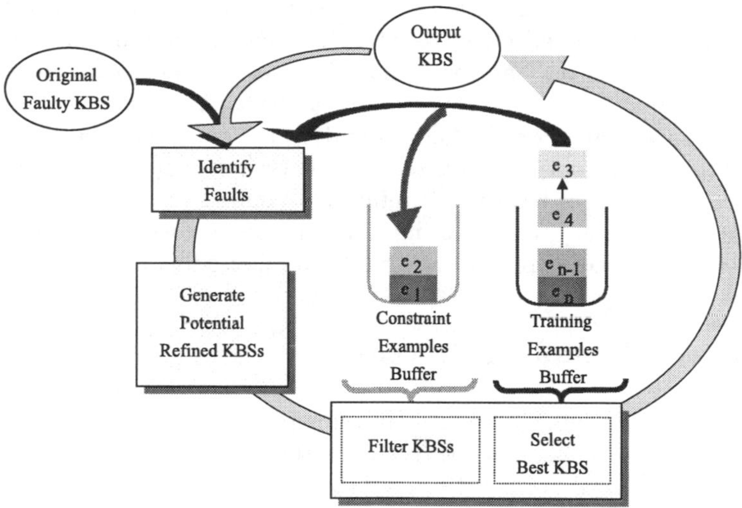

Fig. 1. The KRUSTtool Process.

In common with many refinement tools, KRUSTtools incrementally refine a KBS based on fault evidence provided by labelled training examples. A labelled training example e is a task-solution pair $\langle [f_1, \ldots, f_m], goal \rangle$; the observables $f_1, \ldots, f_m$ are the facts that initialise the problem-solving task, and its solution *goal* is the example's label acquired from the expert. The KRUSTtool's refinement process is iterative with labelled training examples $e_1, \ldots, e_n$, utilized one at a time (Figure 1). The input KBS for each iteration is the best refined output KBS from the previous iteration, or the original faulty KBS in the first iteration. The training examples buffer contains all labelled examples that are yet to be used by the KRUSTtool. For each iteration, the top example in this buffer is chosen as the refinement example and drives that refinement cycle. If the refinement example is correctly solved by the input KBS then refinement is not required, otherwise the fault evidence is employed to allocate blame. The refinement algorithm then identifies various ways by which the required target solution can be attained and generates several potential refinements and implements them as refined KBSs. Once used, the refinement example is then transferred into the constraint examples buffer, which is simply the buffer that keeps track of examples previously solved by the KRUSTtool. However, an important task of this buffer is to help filter refined KBSs, by rejecting those that incorrectly answer any of the examples in it. The filtered refined KBSs are then ranked by their accuracy on the training examples buffer, and the refined KBS with the highest accuracy is the output KBS for this iteration.

Fundamental to the KRUSTtool's successful refinement operation is the availability of labelled examples for its buffers. Availability is often constrained by limited expert interaction and high processing costs. The KRUSTtool should ideally be able to handle such situations by actively selecting training examples from an available set of unlabelled examples. Selected examples must be beneficial for improving the effectiveness and efficiency of the refinement tool. The effectiveness depends on whether or not the tool has had access to examples that are able to expose faults; this requires a mechanism that enables selection of examples that trigger a wide range of faulty problem-solving behaviour in the KBS. Improving efficiency involves selecting fewer refinement examples, thereby reducing the number of refinement iterations required to achieve refined KBSs with improved accuracy; e.g. ensuring that only one incorrectly solved example from a set of examples exposing each fault is processed.

3 Selective Sampling Process

The relevance of training examples for refinement changes as refinement progresses. As the problem-solving behaviour of the KBS is incrementally improved examples that exposed faults before are less likely to expose new faults in future iterations, while examples that did not before may do so in future iterations. Therefore we need selection mechanisms that target examples for refining the KBS given its current problem-solving behaviour. The use of selective sampling for the KRUSTtool encompasses an informed selection of examples, the labelling of these selected examples by the expert, and the refinement of the faulty KBS using the batch of labelled examples. A single iteration of this *select-label-refine* process provides a small batch of labelled examples to use as the initial training examples buffer for the KRUSTtool (see Figure 2). Once the KRUSTtool has incrementally refined the KBS to correctly solve these labelled examples, the next iteration of *select-label-refine* can be triggered. In practice, the *select-label-refine*

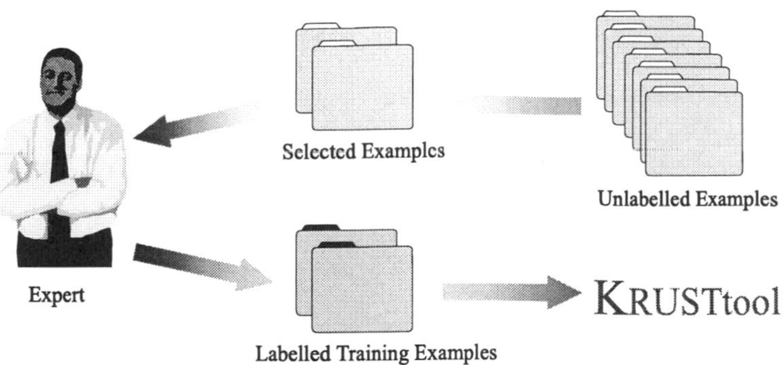

Fig. 2. A single iteration of *select-label-refine.*

process must be repeated until; no further faults are exposed in the KBS hence, no improvement in accuracy; or a limit on the number of examples an expert is willing to label is reached.

3.1 Problem-Solving Behaviour

The KRUSTtool records the problem-solving that is undertaken by a KBS for an example in a structure, the *positive problem graph*[1]. Essentially it records the rule activations and the order in which these activations occur. Figure 3, shows two simple positive problem graphs for a fictitious faulty KBS with rules R_4, R_5, R_7, R_8, R_9 among others. Let us assume that each positive problem graph captures the observed problem solving behaviour of the faulty KBS, as a result of executing each of the two unlabelled examples, A=$\langle [A_1, \ldots, A_4], ? \rangle$ and B=$\langle [B_1, \ldots, B_4], ? \rangle$. With example A, the KBS reasons from the observables by applying leaf rules R_7 and R_4, which together allow a middle rule R_8 to fire, and finally the conclusion of the end rule R_9 provides the system solution, sys_A. A system solution would typically be a class, a design, a formulation or a plan, depending on the type of problem domain. Similar explanations hold for example B's positive problem graph, but notice that reasoning has not progressed beyond the conclusions of leaf rules, R_4 and R_5. Here, we have an intermediate result but no obvious system solution. We shall use the similarity between the positive problem graphs of examples to determine which examples may indicate the same faults in the KBS. The task of establishing similarity in this manner means that we need only be interested in rule activations for examples, regardless of whether or not the system solution is correct. Therefore, more importantly, examples need not be labelled for this task.

3.2 Cluster Formation

To form example clusters we need to define a *similarity metric* which is then utilized by a *clustering technique* that progressively develops the clusters. Since

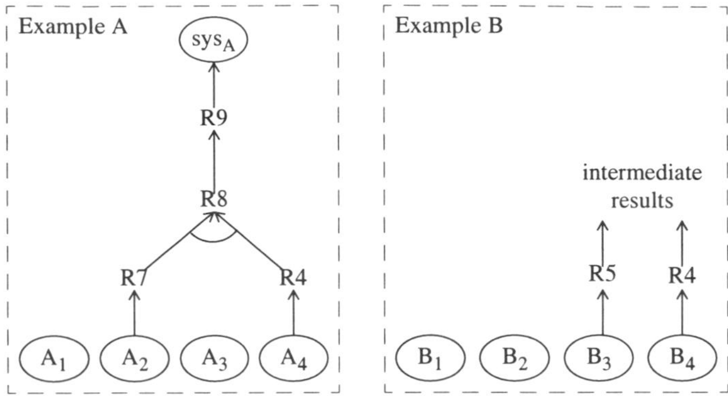

Fig. 3. Positive Problem Graphs for examples A and B.

examples are presented as a vector of observables, an obvious similarity metric compares these vectors. However, in knowledge refinement we are interested in sampling examples with respect to problem-solving behaviour of the faulty KBS and so our similarity metric reflects this by making use of the positive problem graph. Given a KBS containing rules $R_1, \ldots, R_N$, we define a binary valued *rule vector* corresponding to an example e as $\mathbf{r} = (r_1, \ldots, r_N)$, where $r_i = 1$ if R_i appears in the problem graph for e, and $r_i = 0$ otherwise. Thus, the rule vector for the training example A in Figure 3 is (0, 0, 0, 1, 0, 0, 1, 1, 1, 0), where N=10. Here the 1's correspond to rule activations $R4$,$R7$,$R8$ and $R9$.

The similarity measure needs to capture refinement similarity between two unlabelled training examples e_1, e_2. As refinement similarity depends on the similarity in problem solving behaviour, the similarity between e_1, e_2, can be established by comparing their rule vectors $\mathbf{r}_1, \mathbf{r}_2$. For this purpose the Euclidean distance metric may be used, but it can lead to two rule vectors being regarded as highly similar despite them having no common rule activations. Association coefficients [11] avoid this by focusing on the common rule activations and normalizing by the number of rule activations in both rule vectors, thereby ignoring rules that are not activated. We employ the Dice coefficient, a commonly used similarity measure of this type:

$$RefSim(e_1, e_2) = Dice(\mathbf{r}_1, \mathbf{r}_2) = \frac{2\ \mathbf{r}_1 .\ \mathbf{r}_2}{\mathbf{r}_1 .\ \mathbf{r}_1 + \mathbf{r}_2 .\ \mathbf{r}_2}$$

We then use an agglomerative hierarchical clustering technique, where training examples with the greatest similarity are united in small clusters and these clusters are iteratively fused until intra-cluster similarity achieves a predetermined threshold. The decision to fuse clusters is based on the farthest neighbour principle [12], where those two clusters that have the minimum distance between their most dissimilar cluster members are fused. Typically, this form of cluster fusion leads to small, tightly bound clusters, provided that the fusion threshold is low.

3.3 Selecting Examples Using Clusters

Clusters provide information that allows a more informed choice than a random selection of examples. Each cluster represents the problem-solving behaviour pertaining to some part of the faulty KBS, because examples with similar rule activations are clustered together. If we happen to know which area of the KBS is faulty, the task of example selection is reduced to picking the cluster related to that area. However, in most cases the KRUSTtool has no prior knowledge about what parts of the KBS might be faulty, and so we need a more general selection technique that targets all potentially faulty parts of the KBS.

Since each cluster contains examples which are solved in a similar way by the KBS, it might appear reasonable to assume that repairing a fault exposed by a single example from a cluster would correct the rest of the cluster. One selection method CLUSTERREP exploits this assumption by randomly selecting one example from each cluster. Certainly, training examples that activate several rules in common appear in the same cluster and typically are also similar in their observables. However, in some situations examples from a single cluster may not have similar observables, and so may contain a pair of examples where a possible repair for one example introduces a fault into the repaired solution for the other; or result in no obvious repair. Faults of this nature are termed *interacting faults* and the involved pair of examples is termed a *conflict pair*.

3.4 Faults that Interact

To demonstrate the effects of interacting faults on refinement we use 4 Clips rules taken from a corrupted version of a student loans adviser. Of these rules, two have been corrupted by adding extra conditions, highlighted in bold (see Figure 4). Here, $R16$ translates to "if a student has filed for bankruptcy and is enlisted then grant the student a financial deferment", and $R19$ translates to "if a student is disabled and has filed for bankruptcy then grant the student a disability deferment". Assume that the KRUSTtool is attempting to fix these rules based on fault evidence provided by training example x and y in that order.

$$x = \langle [(\texttt{filed\_for\_bankruptcy id}_x), \ldots], (\texttt{eligible\_for\_deferment id}_x)\rangle$$
$$y = \left\langle \left[(\texttt{disabled id}_y), \ldots\right], (\texttt{eligible\_for\_deferment id}_y)\right\rangle$$

Example x concerns a student that has filed for bankruptcy and according to the expert should be eligible for deferment, but when reasoning with the faulty rules the system solution will not match that of the expert's. Therefore, the KRUSTtool will attempt to refine the faulty rules by either generalising $R16$ or $R19$, by deleting condition (*enlist ?Student*), or (*disabled ?Student*), respectively. Let us assume that the KRUSTtool chooses to refine by incorrectly generalising $R19$ (instead of $R16$) and implements this as a new KBS. On proceeding to the next refinement cycle (now with new KBS) the KRUSTtool is presented with fault evidence from training example y, a disabled student who is eligible for deferment. A direct consequence of generalising $R19$ is that the KRUSTtool is now left with no obvious refinement that can fix the fault exposed by y. Consequently, it is forced to re-think its previous refinement choice of generalising $R19$ instead of $R16$, and so faces the prospect of re-starting refinement from a previous state. Notice that if $R19$ and $R16$ were corrupted, but had no common condition that matched observables from either x or y (for instance like `filed_for_bankruptcy`) then the faults exposed by x and y in Figure 4 would not be interacting.

```
(defrule R16
  (filed_for_bankruptcy ?Student) (enlist ?Student)
  => (assert (financial_deferment ?Student)))

(defrule R19
  (disabled ?Student) (filed_for_bankruptcy ?Student)
  => (assert (disable_deferment ?Student)))

(defrule R10
  (financial_deferment ?Student)
  => (assert (eligible_for_deferment ?Student)))

(defrule R12
  (disable_deferment ?Student)
  => (assert (eligible_for_deferment ?Student)))
```

Fig. 4. Some rules taken from a corrupted student loans advisor in Clips.

The presence of interacting faults affects the refinement process, because selecting a non-optimal refined KBS in a previous iteration can cause refinement conflicts in a subsequent iteration. Detecting and resolving these refinement conflicts is important, as we have found that this improves refinement accuracy and guides the search for the best incremental refinements [13]. However, such conflicts can only be detected subject to the availability of fault evidence provided by a pair of examples, a *conflict pair* (such as x and y above). If a cluster contains *conflict pairs* like these, we would want to select further examples from this cluster. In these situations ClusterRep is not sufficient as it randomly selects a single example from each cluster, thereby ignoring all other examples in that cluster, including conflict pairs. A mechanism is needed to identify conflict pairs when they occur in the same cluster so that we ensure that examples exposing interacting faults are chosen. This necessitates an investigation of the problem-solving behaviour of labelled conflict pairs that occur in the same cluster. The aim of such an investigation is to establish criteria that would enable the identification and selection of conflict pairs from a cluster when still unlabelled.

3.5 Characteristics of Conflict Pairs

An analysis of *labelled* conflict pairs revealed that they tend to have overlapping positive problem graphs, yet the best repair choices for the pair are distinguished from each other. Essentially their proofs may exercise similar parts of the KBS but their best repair exercises separate parts. Figure 5 shows the problem-solving for such a pair, C=$\langle[C_1,\ldots,C_6]\,|goal_C\rangle$ and D=$\langle[D_1,\ldots,D_6]\,|goal_D\rangle$. The darkened arrows and bold rule names highlight the positive problem graphs for examples C and D; i.e. the rules that are activated by the observables for each example. Each has resulted in the activation of the same end rule R_3, but the solutions (sys_C and sys_D) might occur with different variable bindings. Invariably a pair like this, with a substantial area of the positive problem graph in common, will be placed in the same cluster, and easily mistaken as representing the same fault.

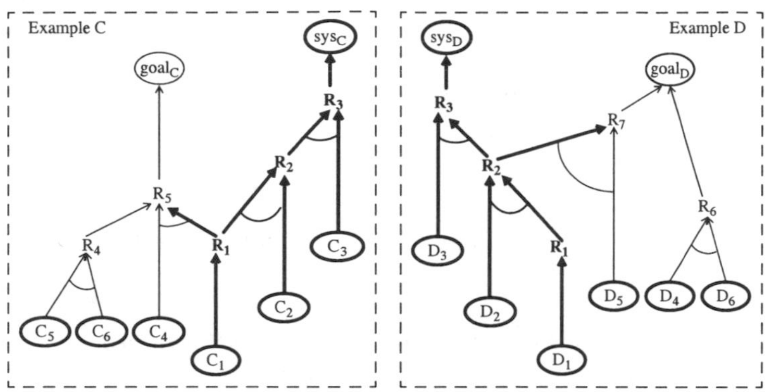

Fig. 5. Illustrating conflict pairs.

Figure 5 also shows all rules that might have concluded each target goal if they had been activated; these (non)activations form the *negative problem graph*. With example C, R_5 is only partially satisfied by R_1's conclusion. The arrow from C_4 is fainter to indicate that this condition in R_5 is not met by the observable without the condition being generalised somehow. The other possible route via R_4 requires both of its conditions to be generalised before being satisfied by C_5 and C_6. Possible repairs attempt to specialise rules in the positive problem graph and generalise those from the negative problem graph[1]. However, specialising R_2 to disallow the proof of sys_C for example C may cause problems when generalising R_7 to allow the proof of $goal_D$, for example D, and vice versa with R_1 and R_5. Essentially, even though conflict pairs are clustered together, a repair for one example will not necessarily repair the other; i.e. their negative problem graphs are fairly disjoint.

[1] For a comprehensive list of KRUSTtool's specialisation and generalisation refinement operators see [14].

3.6 Informed Selection Heuristics

When examples are *unlabelled* we do not know the goals and cannot build the negative problem graphs. Instead we identify potential conflict pairs by formulating an indirect estimate of how overlapping the two negative problem graphs might be. For this purpose we compare their observables since the (non)activations in the negative problem graph depend on them.

We calculate a dissimilarity score for an example $e_i = \langle [f_1^i, \ldots, f_m^i], ?\rangle$, in a cluster $C = e_1, \ldots, e_n$ by summing all pair-wise dissimilarities between example e_i and the remaining examples in C.

$$Dissimilarity(e_i, C) = \sum_{j \neq i} dissimilarity(e_i, e_j)$$

$$dissimilarity(e_i, e_j) = \sqrt{\sum_{k=1}^{m} \delta^2(f_k^i, f_k^j)}$$

$$\delta(x, y) = \begin{cases} 0 & \text{if } x = y \\ \|n_x - n_y\| & \text{if } x, y \text{ are numeric facts}^2 \\ 1 & \text{otherwise} \end{cases}$$

The dissimilarity score of a cluster is the average *Dissimilarity* of its examples. There is some argument for ignoring the influence of observables that have already resulted in activations when calculating the dissimilarity score, however, as the contribution towards dissimilarity from observables associated with activations, compared to those associated with (non) activations is negligible, we have opted for the simpler *dissimilarity* score using all observables.

When a cluster has a high dissimilarity score there is reason to believe that such a cluster may contain conflict pairs, and we want to select it first for refinement. The intuition behind this is that examples clustered together based on similarity of the KBS's problem solving behaviour would normally also be similar in their observables. If observables are dissimilar then it is likely that problem solving behaviour of the KBS for that cluster is faulty and would require the selection of more than one example to fix the faults. We propose several sample selection heuristics that select varying numbers of examples from the cluster with the highest dissimilarity as follows: *DISSIMILAR selects *all* examples; K-DISSIMILAR, selects the K most dissimilar examples; and >DISSIMILAR selects examples with *Dissimilarity* scores above a pre-determined threshold.

4 Experimental Evaluation

Example selection employing CLUSTERREP and the DISSIMILAR family of selection techniques are compared against RANDOM, where refinement examples are

[2] A numeric fact x has a numeric component n_x; e.g., age(fred, 40). $\|n_x - n_y\|$ is the absolute difference normalised by the range of values.

selected randomly. Our experiments test whether selective sampling produces refined KBSs with comparable accuracy but using fewer labelled examples than RANDOM. Furthermore, the performance of these techniques in the presence of interacting and non-interacting faults is also analysed by controlled corruptions of the KBS.

The data set and rule-base for the binary class student loans, and the data set for the multi class soybean was taken from the UCI repository [15]. The student loans data set consisted of 1000 labelled examples. We heavily corrupted the student loans KBS to encourage conflict pairs; by introducing 5 faults to the 20 rules. The soybean data set of 337 labelled examples was formed by merging the large and small soybean data sets and selecting those examples classified in the first 15 classes. A soybean KBS with 44 rules was created by incorporating rule chaining into the rule set generated by `c4.5rules` [16]. This KBS was then corrupted in 7 places, by adding and modifying antecedents in rules covering 4 of the 15 classes. Unlike the student loans corruptions, these faults did not interact, therefore examples from different classes have distinct problem graphs.

For each domain, a set of 100 training examples and a further 100 evaluation examples are randomly selected from the data set. The KRUSTtool is run with increasing subsets of the 100 training examples. Although all examples in the data set are labelled for experimentation purposes, these labels are ignored until examples are selected from the training set for the refinement task. Therefore, the labelling step in the *select-label-refine* iterative process is implicit, and the stop criterion is that the refined KBS has 100% accuracy on the training examples after the refinement step. We note that in practice this criterion is not available, as only selected training examples will be labelled, but that refinement is a continuous process constrained by expert availability. The impact of informed selection on *efficiency* is determined by the percentage of unused (unselected) examples in the training set. The impact on *effectiveness* is determined by the accuracy of the final KBS on the evaluation set. The graphs show results averaged over 10 runs for each training set size. Significance results are based on a 95% confidence level and apply the Kruskal Wallis [17] non-parametric test as some results are not normally distributed. The optimum cluster fusion threshold and the *Dissimilarity* threshold for >DISSIMILAR, with each test domain was ascertained by experimenting with varying thresholds, on a separate subset of examples.

4.1 Student Loans Domain

Experiments indicate that informed selection methods were effective: there was no significant difference in final refined KBS accuracy on the evaluation set, between these methods and RANDOM. Figure 6 shows the graph for unused percentage of examples for each of the methods. We found a significant difference between these selection methods for unused percentage (p=0.005). 3-DISSIMILAR overall has faired best, and on average is three times more efficient than RANDOM or CLUSTERREP. 3-DISSIMILAR and >DISSIMILAR have significantly higher unused percentages compared to $*$DISSIMILAR, suggesting that the subset of most dissimilar examples from the cluster effectively targets the faults highlighted by all the examples in the cluster. All DISSIMILAR methods use significantly fewer training examples compared to CLUSTERREP and RANDOM. CLUSTERREP's poor performance is due to the added complication of interacting faults, and shows that selection of cluster representatives, alone, is not sufficient in these situations. The increase in unused percentage with training set size 10, seen with all methods, is explained by small training sets being insufficient to expose all faults in the KBS. As a result 100% accuracy on the training set is achieved easily, while the accuracy on the evaluation set will be significantly worse when compared to refined KBSs produced from larger training sets.

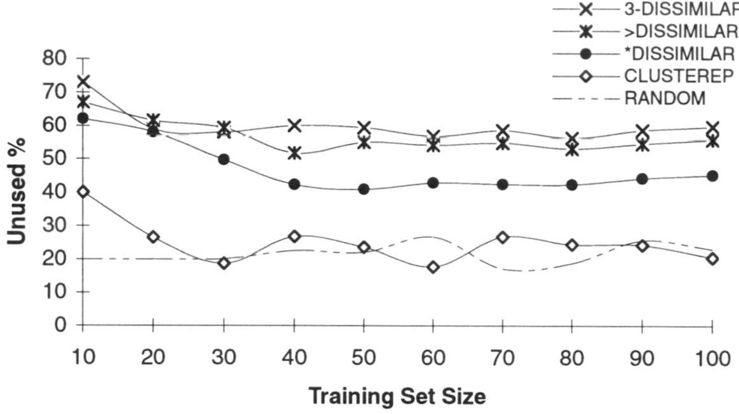

Fig. 6. Unused examples for student loans domain.

4.2 Soybean Disease Domain

Again there was no significant difference in accuracy between the selective methods and RANDOM; while there was a significant difference in unused percentages (p=0.005). From the efficiency view, in this domain, CLUSTERREP, uses significantly fewer examples than ∗DISSIMILAR and RANDOM (see Figure 7). The success of CLUSTERREP and the failure of ∗DISSIMILAR is explained by the absence of interacting faults in this rule base. Furthermore, the performance of CLUSTERREP improves with increased training set sizes, indicating that it was able to target few, yet good, examples. Closer examination of test runs with set sizes 70, 80, 90 and 100, revealed that the number of clusters tends to be constant while the size of clusters increases with the increasing number of examples, therefore, CLUSTERREP selects the same number of examples regardless of the increase in set size. On average CLUSTERREP is three-times more efficient than RANDOM or ∗DISSIMILAR. ∗DISSIMILAR's bad performance with larger training set sizes clearly shows that the absence of an appropriate selection mechanism can result in ultimately using all the unlabelled examples. We have not plotted results for 3-DISSIMILAR and >DISSIMILAR methods as they are derivatives of ∗DISSIMILAR, which has performed poorly.

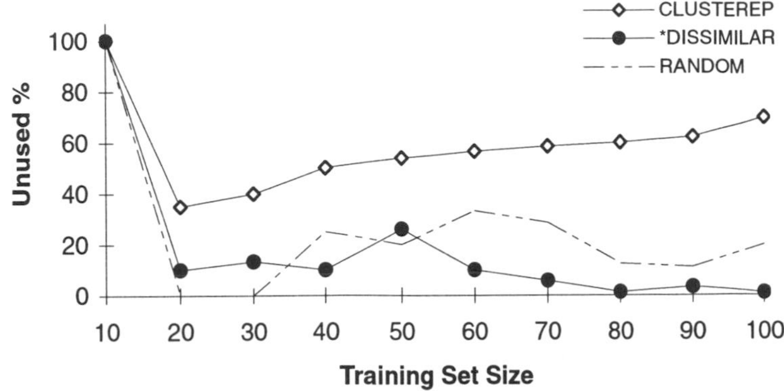

Fig. 7. Unused examples for soybean disease domain.

5 Related Work

The batch version of the refinement tool EITHER also applies incremental learning [18]. It processes batches of examples as they become available, but these examples are not selected for a purpose. Eventually EITHER uses all the examples, and in addition all these examples must be labelled. The use of membership queries and equivalence queries to select examples for learning Horn clauses is presented in [19]. Querying in this manner enables Horn clause learning in polynomial time. However, there is the assumption that labels of examples are known, and more importantly the logic based approach does not adapt well to rule-based systems that have more complex knowledge representation formalisms. EXPO [10] uses selective sampling to filter its proposed plans when the expected outcome of the plan differs from the actual observations. Interestingly EXPO's active selection occurs at plan filtering, analogous to the KRUSTtool's filtering of refined KBSs, and not for actively selecting planning tasks that may trigger learning, hence improving plan formation. This difference with knowledge refinement is possibly explained by the high costs associated with experimentation compared to access to representative planning problems.

Selective sampling employing a neural network for the task of learning a binary concept is discussed in [20]. An example is selected when the most specific and most general network configurations fail to agree on the example's label. With complex concepts the most general network configuration may contain the entire domain, thereby forcing random sampling. Our clustering has similar problems: when the cluster threshold is too high, clusters contain single examples;

when set too low one large cluster contains all examples. With each extreme selective sampling is reduced to RANDOM. Presently, we identify the optimum threshold by experimentation, however, the ability to automatically learn this threshold would be beneficial.

Argamon-Engelson and Dagan in [21] use a query by committee approach to selectively sample training examples for a probabilistic classifier. A committee of classifiers is randomly drawn based on statistics of the labelled sample. Examples are selected according to the degree of disagreement in class labels between the committee members. The committee approach can also be incorporated in knowledge refinement where the generated refined KBSs can vote on the solution for remaining training examples and select examples where the committee was unable to reach consensus. However, a disagreement measure is complicated when the KBS concludes in intermediate results.

Conceptual clustering involves arranging objects into clusters which would then represent certain conceptual classes [22]. However, such techniques require that there is some knowledge about the number of classes or, alternatively, knowledge about the goals of the classification. Usually, with knowledge refinement, there is no prior knowledge about the number of areas of the KBS that are faulty much less the types of faults that need to be addressed. However, our example clustering via rule vectors draws close parallels to classical document clustering in information retrieval where documents are represented as binary term vectors [23]. For information retrieval purposes documents with similar term vectors are grouped together forming a cluster. In document clustering, weights may also be used to indicate the relative importance of terms. We currently assign equal importance to all rule activations. However, a conservative view prefers refinements to rules closer to observables and this might be captured by introducing weights to rule activations.

6 Conclusion

We have presented an initial approach to selective sampling of training examples in the context of knowledge refinement. Experimental results show that selective sampling can significantly reduce the number of examples utilised, without any penalty on final accuracy. The refinement process was able to target particular faults that improved the accuracy of the refined KBS in a way that was effective in general. Not only did this reduce the number of refinement cycles required to achieve a particular level of competence, but it also reduced the demands on the expert's time. The selection was done based on features of the problem-solving task alone and so the expert was consulted about only the selected examples. Once labelled, the selected examples were presented to the refinement tool for processing.

The rule vector representation of the positive problem graph provided a simple similarity measure that created clusters of examples that had been solved by the KBS in a similar way. This clustering was helpful in determining examples that might indicate the same repair. Future work will analyse the implications of rule depth and the sequence of rule activations on similarity and investigate how the similarity measure might be extended to reflect these. Given a clustering, incremental refinement can be visualised by capturing changes in cluster size and cluster membership. We are currently exploiting these dynamic changes for example selection during the refinement filtering stage, where the aim is to identify examples affected by the proposed refinements. We note that this is possible due to our clustering using similarity between, rule vectors rather than feature vectors, as employed by most existing active learning methods.

The difficulty of selecting examples from clusters depends on the level of interaction of the faults in the KBS. Experiments have highlighted the strengths of DISSIMILAR heuristics in the presence of interacting faults and the less informed CLUSTERREP selection heuristic in the presence of non interacting faults. We intend to develop more powerful selection mechanisms that combine these techniques. One possibility would be to choose between selection heuristics CLUSTERREP and a DISSIMILAR method after a clustering has been done: if the maximum intra cluster dissimilarity is large then a DISSIMILAR method is required; if small then CLUSTERREP is sufficient.

Selective sampling is important for knowledge refinement tools whether or not labelled training examples are plentiful. If labels are hard to obtain then it is certainly useful to identify relevant problem-solving tasks that should be labelled by the expert and then used as training examples for refinement. Conversely if there are many labelled training examples then, given that the refinement process is quite computationally expensive, it is convenient to target those examples whose repairs also fix other wrongly solved examples without further refinement, thereby reducing the number of refinement cycles. Selective sampling addresses both these issues by identifying the examples most likely to solve others that indicate the same general fault.

Acknowledgments

The KRUSTWORKS project is supported by EPSRC grant GR/L38387 awarded to Susan Craw. Nirmalie Wiratunga is partially funded by ORS grant 98131005.

References

1. Susan Craw and Robin Boswell. Representing problem-solving for knowledge refinement. In *Proceedings of the Sixteenth National Conference on Artificial Intelligence*, pages 227–234, Menlo Park, California, 1999. AAAI Press.
2. Marcelo Tallis and Yolanda Gil. Designing scripts to guide users in modifying knowledge based systems. In *Proceedings of the Sixteenth National Conference on Artificial Intelligence*, pages 227–234, Menlo Park, California, 1999. AAAI Press.
3. B. Richards and R. Mooney. Automated refinement of first-order horn-clause domain theories. *Machine Learning*, 19:95–131, 1995.
4. N Zlatareva and A Preece. State of the art in automated validation of knowledge-based systems. *Expert Systems with Applications*, 7:151–167, 1994.

5. Dmitry Rusakov Michael Lindenbaum, Shaul Markovich. Selective sampling for nearest neighbor classifiers. In *Proceedings of the Sixteenth National Conference on Artificial Intelligence*, pages 366–371, Menlo Park, California, 1999. AAAI Press.
6. Andrew McCallum and Kamal Nigam. Employing em in pool-based active learning for text classification. In *Proceedings of the Fifteenth International Conference on Machine Learning*, pages 359–367, 1998.
7. David D. Lewis and Jason Catlett. Heterogeneous uncertainty sampling for supervised learning. In William W. Cohen and Haym Hirsh, editors, *Machine Learning: Proceedings of the Eleventh International Conference*, pages 148–156, San Francisco, CA, 1989. Morgan Kauffman.
8. David Cohn, Zoubin Ghahramani, and Michael I. Jordan. Active learning with statistical models. *Journal of Artificial Intelligence Research*, 4:129–145, 1996.
9. Robin Boswell, Susan Craw, and Ray Rowe. Knowledge refinement for a design system. In *Proceedings of the Tenth European Knowledge Acquisition Workshop*, pages 49–64, Sant Feliu de Guixols, Spain, 1997. Springer.
10. Yolanda Gil. Learning from the environment by experimentation: The need for few and informative examples. In *Proceedings of the AAAI Symposium on Active Learning*, MIT, Cambridge, MA, 1995.
11. Peter Willett. Recent trends in hierarchic document clustering: A critical review. *Information Processing and Management*, 24:577–597, 1988.
12. Stephen J. Hanson. Conceptual clustering and categorization. In Y. Kodratoff and R. S. Michalski, editors, *Machine Learning Volume III*, pages 235–268. Morgan Kaufmann, San Mateo, CA, 1990.
13. Nirmalie Wiratunga and Susan Craw. Sequencing training examples for iterative knowledge refinement. In *Proceedings of the Nineteenth SGES International Conference on Knowledge Based Systems and Applied Artificial Intelligence*, pages 41–56, Cambridge, UK, 1999. Springer.
14. Robin Boswell and Susan Craw. Organising Knowledge Refinement Operators In *Validation and Verification of Knowledge Based Systems, Proceedings of the 5th European Symposium on the Validation and Verification of Knowledge Based Systems (EUROVAV'99)*, pages 149–161, Oslo, Norway, 1999. Kluwer.
15. C. Blake, E. Keogh, and C.J. Merz. UCI repository of machine learning databases. http://www.ics.uci.edu/~mlearn/MLRepository.html, 1998.
16. J. R. Quinlan. *C4.5: Programs for Machine Learning*. Morgan Kaufmann, San Mateo, 1993.
17. D. A. Anderson, D. J. Sweeney, and T. A. Williams. *Statistics for Business and Economics*. West Publishing Company, St. Paul, MN, 1990.
18. Raymond J. Mooney. Batch versus incremental theory refinement. In *Proceedings of the AAAI Spring Symposium on Knowledge Assimilation*, Stanford, CA, 1992.
19. Dana Angluin, Michael Frazier, and Leonard Pitt. Learning conjunctions of horn clauses. *Machine Learning*, 9:147–164, 1992.
20. David Cohn, Les Atlas, and Richard Ladner. Improving generalization with active learning. *Machine Learning*, 15:201–221, 1994.
21. Shlomo Argamon-Engelson and Ido Dagan. Committee-based sample selection for probabilistic classifiers. *Journal of Artificial Intelligence Research*, 11:335–360, 1999.
22. R.S. Michalski and R.E. Stepp. Clustering. In S.C. Shapiro, editor, *Encyclopaedia of Artificial Intelligence*, volume 1, pages 103–110. Wiley, 1990.
23. Edie Rasumssen. Clustering algorithms. In W. B. Frakes and R. Baeza-Yates, editors, *Information Retrieval: Data Structures and Algorithms*, pages 419–442. Prentice Hall, London, 1992.

Experiences with a Generic Refinement Toolkit

Robin Boswell and Susan Craw

School of Computer and Mathematical Sciences
The Robert Gordon University
St Andrew Street, Aberdeen AB25 1HG, Scotland, UK.
{rab,s.craw}@scms.rgu.ac.uk

Abstract. Knowledge refinement tools seek to correct faulty knowledge based systems (KBSs). Most current refinement systems are applicable only to a single KBS shell, and typically they ignore the procedural aspects of KBS reasoning. This paper describes the KRUSTWorks framework which refines a number of different shells, and can be extended to new ones. Internal knowledge structures represent rules in the target KBS and their interactions, and generic tools manipulate these structures. In this paper KRUSTWorks is evaluated on two aero-space applications into which various artificial faults have been introduced. KRUSTWorks identifies and fixes these faults, except when the training examples provide insufficient fault evidence. The evaluation demonstrates the effectiveness of KRUSTWorks as a refinement tool, and confirms that it can represent the knowledge and problem-solving in real expert systems.

1 Introduction

Knowledge refinement tools assist in the detection and removal of faults while KBSs are being developed, and in the updating of KBSs whose requirements and specifications change over time. Most current refinement systems are somewhat limited in their applicability, refining KBSs written in a single language or shell, and ignoring procedural features such as rule precedence and conflict resolution strategies. In contrast, the KRUSTWorks framework refines KBSs written in a number of different shells, and can be extended to new shells. Moreover, it represents and reasons about non-logical features of rule execution. It does so by using a set of generic KBS concepts and refinement steps to represent the knowledge and reasoning processes in a variety of KBSs. It has already been shown that KRUSTWorks can represent the knowledge and reasoning processes of different applications [1,2]. In this paper, we describe briefly the KRUSTWorks system and its knowledge representation, and then present the results of an evaluation of KRUSTWorks as applied to two industrial KBSs.

Section 2 presents the KRUSTWorks framework as a set of core refinement techniques, together with a set of toolkits. Section 2.1 describes the knowledge used by KRUSTTools to represent the knowledge in a KBS's rules. Section 2.2 describes the knowledge used to represent the reasoning behaviour of the KBS, which in turn guides the refinement process. Section 3 describes the evaluation

R. Dieng and O. Corby (Eds.): EKAW 2000, LNAI 1937, pp. 249–256, 2000.

of KRUSTWorks using two aero-space applications. Finally, we explore related work and offer our conclusions.

2 The KRUSTWorks Framework

KRUSTWorks is divided into two parts: a set of core KBS-independent refinement routines, and a set of toolkits, such as refinement operators and filters, from which the user selects tools appropriate for a particular application. Here we concentrate on the refinement routines. KRUSTTools apply the standard refinement steps of running the KBS on a particular training example, allocating blame to potentially faulty rules and then proposing repairs that prevent the faulty behaviour (Figure 1). However, KRUSTTools are unusual in generating many repairs and using further training examples to select the best. If several wrongly-solved examples are available, these are used one at a time to drive refinement. Once processed, each example is added to a *constraint* buffer, where it is used to filter subsequent refined KBs.

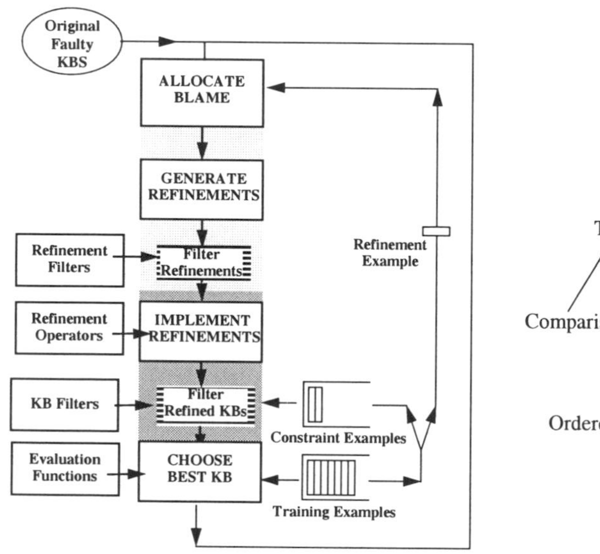

Fig. 1. Iterative refinement by a KRUSTTool

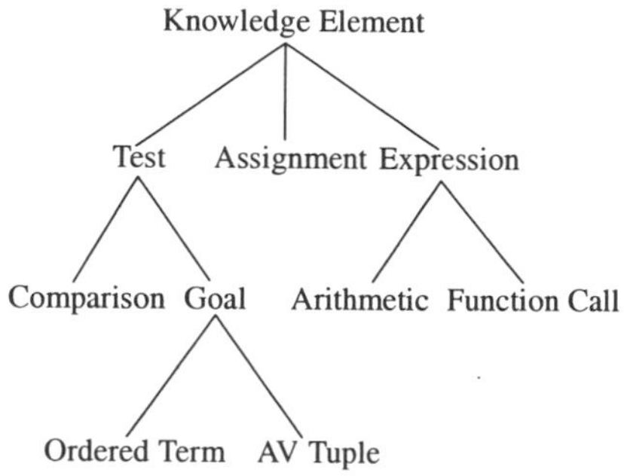

Knowledge Element
Test
Assignment
Expression
Comparison
Goal
Arithmetic
Function Call
Ordered Term
AV Tuple

Fig. 2. Part of the Knowledge Tree

KRUSTWorks uses a common core of refinement procedures applicable to all the KBSs that it refines. It has been possible to create such core procedures because KRUSTWorks represents the knowledge of a KBS in a generic manner, independent of the particular rule language and development environment. This knowledge is divided into two parts: the static knowledge contained in the rules, and a dynamic representation of the ways in which the rules fire for a particular training example. The static knowledge in the rules is known as the *knowledge skeleton*; it forms KRUSTWorks' internal representation of a KBS's rule-base [2]. The dynamic knowledge represents which rules fired, in what order, and how the rules chained [3]. It is known as the *problem graph*, and is a generalised form of proof tree.

2.1 The Knowledge Skeleton

The knowledge skeleton uses a common knowledge representation language (CKRL) [2] to represent the important features in a KB. The CKRL has allowed us to implement a generic set of refinement operators which each KRUSTTool uses to modify the knowledge in the skeleton and so correct faults in the KB. The CKRL is therefore designed to represent the important properties of rule conditions and conclusions. Our experience has shown us that, despite variations in syntax, there are a relatively small number of *types* of rule conditions and conclusions; that is, there are a small number of different roles which conditions and conclusions can perform. Three basic classes of rule elements have been identified, corresponding to the fundamental roles they play in rules. Figure 2 shows how these three classes are broken down into sub-classes. **Tests** can succeed or fail; e.g., retrievals from working memory, or comparisons such as `?Temp` $\leq$ 90 where `?Temp` is a variable name. **Assignments** assign a value to a variable, and always succeed. **Expressions** are rule elements that return a value, and again always succeed; e.g., arithmetical calculations or function calls.

2.2 The Problem Graph

The problem graph represents the KBS's problem-solving for a particular refinement example. Figure 3 shows part of the problem graph generated by a faulty MMU KB (the MMU application is described in section 3). The graph consists of oval nodes representing facts, and rectangular nodes representing rule activations. Nodes with a dotted outline represent knowledge that is currently not derivable but would help to correct the error. In Figure 3 the desired conclusion is `(conclusion cea-failure-side-a)`, but the system is unable to reach any conclusion, though a number of intermediate results are derived. The dotted nodes show alternative ways in which the desired conclusion could be reached.

The solid, or *positive* part of the problem graph, represents knowledge that was applied during problem solving for a particular example. It is constructed by translation from the execution trace. The dotted, or *negative* part of the problem graph, represents knowledge that was *not* applied during problem solving, but which could lead to the desired conclusion.

The problem graph is used by the refinement routines to determine what changes to the rule base will cause it to generate the desired conclusion(s). There are two possible primitive types of refinement: logical refinements, and conflict resolution refinements. These can be combined to form more complex refinements. *Logical refinements* either enable a desired conclusion, as in figure 3,

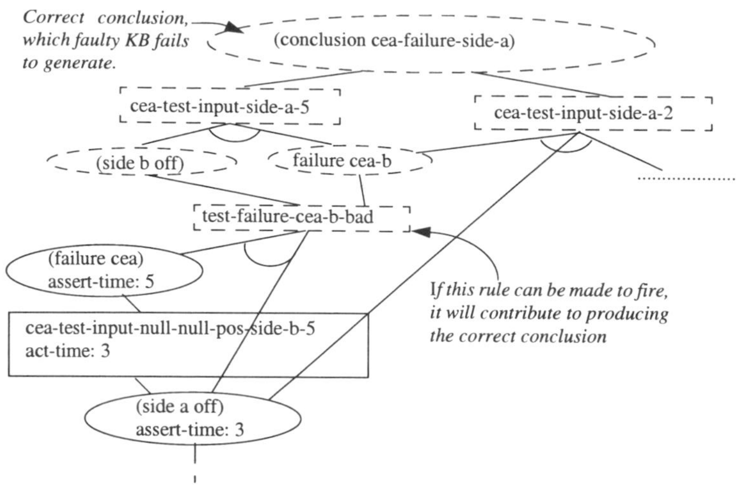

Fig. 3. A Sample Problem Graph

or prevent an undesired conclusion. To enable a conclusion, the KRUSTTool enables any one rule which matches that conclusion. To enable a rule, for each failed antecedent the KRUSTTool either weakens that antecedent so that it is satisfied for the refinement case, or else applies the algorithm recursively, enabling a rule whose conclusion satisfies the failed antecedent. *Conflict resolution refinements* change rule priority, when for example, a rule we wish to fire is activated but then de-activated before firing [3].

3 Evaluation Using Two Applications

KRUSTWorks has been applied to various artificial and real-world KBSs. It has recently been evaluated on two industrial KBSs: AMFESYS and MMU. Here for reasons of space we concentrate on the results from AMFESYS, and refer briefly to the results from MMU. The AMFESYS system was used by the European Space Agency in the control of the Automatic Mirror Furnace payload of the EURECA mission. AMFESYS is written using Intellicorp's POWERMODEL (formerly KAPPA). Much of the system is written in a version of C, but the fault-diagnosis module is written as 67 rules in the Pro-Talk scripting language. It is to these rules that KRUSTWorks was applied. The MMU system performs automatic fault diagnosis, isolation and recovery procedures for the NASA's Manned Maneuvering Unit. It is written entirely in CLIPS, and consists of 104 rules.

For the purposes of our evaluation, we assumed that our copies of AMFESYS and MMU were correct. For each application, we constructed a sample problem set, then used the original KBS as an oracle to generate solutions for these problems. We next created a number of corrupted KBs, and for each KB, performed cross-validation experiments to determine how successful KRUSTWorks is at fixing the faults.

3.1 Construction of Sample Problems and Corrupted KBSs

Applying KRUSTWorks to AMFESYS required some modification to the interface between the diagnostic rules and the rest of AMFESYS. The rules determine the state of the satellite model by accessing object slot values, and by calling functions defined elsewhere in the AMFESYS system. We ran the entire system for a period of time, during which it executed the diagnostic rules in a series of different situations, corresponding to our training examples. We determined the values read by the rules for each example, and then modified the rule interface so that it could be "initialised" to any particular example, after which it would pass the values associated with that example to the diagnostic rules. Applying KRUSTWorks to MMU was more straightforward, since MMU is a stand-alone rule-set.

For each application, five faulty KBs were generated, each constructed by making a single change to the original rule base. These were primitive changes such as: added condition, modified threshold value, modified right-hand side in an equality test, modified CLIPS field constraint, and modified condition in a nested disjunctive structure. For each KB, changes were selected that were applicable to that KB. Further faulty KBs were then generated by combining the single faults into all possible groups of two and three faults. Finally, a KB containing all five faults was constructed. For each application, the faults were numbered 1 through 5, and the corrupted KBs were assigned names indicating the faults they contain; e.g. AMFESYS123 contains faults 1, 2 and 3.

3.2 Refinement Experiments

For each corrupted KB, an n-fold cross-validation was performed. The example set for the application was randomly divided into 5 equal subsets, which were then repeatedly partitioned into training and testing sets in the ratio 3:2, giving 10 experiments. For each experiment, a KRUSTTool was applied iteratively to the training examples as shown in figure 1. Both the initial corrupt KB and the final refined KB were then evaluated on the testing examples. Table 1 shows the results for the two most corrupted KBs: MMU12345 and AMFESYS12345, each with 5 faults. These figures show that a KRUSTTool was able to make considerable improvements to the most corrupt KBs, but could not always reduce the error-rate to zero; and for this particular pair of KBs, the results for MMU are better than for AMFESYS. The reasons for the non-zero error rates are explained in the next section.

3.3 Amfesys Results

The AMFESYS KRUSTTool was almost always able to fix the faults when presented singly, provided that the training examples offered fault evidence. There were three situations in which the tool did not produce the desired improvement in error-rate. First, when none of the examples in the training set exhibited the fault. Second, when none of the examples in the *testing* set exhibited the fault,

Table 1. Error rates before and after refinement

	Error Rates			
	MMU12345		AMFESYS12345	
Run	*Initial KBS*	*Final KBS*	*Initial KBS*	*Final KBS*
1	0.0625	0.0	0.7647	0.1176
2	0.125	0.0	0.8235	0.0588
3	0.125	0.0	0.9375	0.0
4	0.1562	0.0312	0.6471	0.0588
5	0.1562	0.0312	0.75	0.0
6	0.2187	0.0312	0.75	0.0625
7	0.0937	0.0	0.7647	0.0588
8	0.0937	0.0	0.875	0.125
9	0.1562	0.0	0.9375	0.25
10	0.1875	0.0312	0.6875	0.0

so that a fix did not improve the test set's error rate. Third, when an incorrect fix was randomly selected because it performed as well as the correct fix.

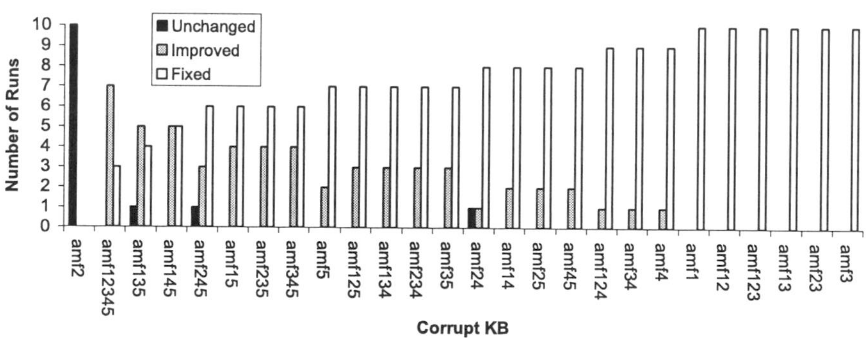

Fig. 4. Improved error rates for AMFESYS KBs

Fault 2 (incorrect threshold value) illustrates the first situation. None of the examples exhibited this fault, so the tool could never fix it. Faults 4 and 5 illustrate the third situation. For both faults, the tool occasionally selected sub-optimal refinements, so that the error rate improved, but not to 0. Figure 4 summarises the results. The bars for each KB represent the number of runs in which the accuracy on the testing set was, respectively, unchanged, improved but not to perfect accuracy, and improved to perfect accuracy. For the multiple-fault KBs, the error rate for the final refined KB was always reduced from the initial corrupt KB. The graph shows that the incorrect refinement selection for faults 4 and 5 already noted was slightly exacerbated by the presence of other faults, so that, for example, the tool performed slightly worse on AMFESYS14 than on AMFESYS4. However, KBs containing combinations of faults 1, 2, and 3 only were always refined to perfect accuracy. For MMU, as with AMFESYS, the KRUSTTool was able to fix the faults when presented singly, provided that the training examples gave evidence of the fault.

3.4 Lessons from the Evaluation

Our experience with AMFESYS showed that it is possible to refine a KB even when it is included as part of a larger system which is not rule-based; the use of a KB in this way is common in industrial expert systems.

Secondly, situations arose when a faulty refined KB disrupted the experiments. For example, some refined MMU KBs ran forever. An ideal solution would have limited the resources allowed when executing a refined KB. In practice, we imposed an extra constraint on the KRUSTTool so that it would not generalise either of the rules which caused this problem when refined. Other refinements caused runtime errors, as illustrated by the following pair of conditions:
`?DiagH != unknown;   ?Delta = ABS(?DiagH-?ModelH);`
If a refinement removes the first condition, a runtime error will occur if the rule is executed with `?DiagH` bound to `unknown`. We therefore modified the KRUSTTool-KBS interface to kill a crashed KBS process and restart it, rejecting the refined KB that caused the error. Thus we can either make KRUSTTools employ complex reasoning to determine in advance whether a KB will generate a run-time error, or else implement a KRUSTTool-KBS interface which recovers from such errors. Because of the difficulty of correctly implementing the predictive approach for all KBS shells, we opt for error-recovery.

4 Related Work

CLIPS-R [4] uses a wider definition of KBS behaviour than other systems, including content of working memory when execution halts, and the order in which actions are performed which display or request information. CLIPS R constructs an explicit representation of the KBS's reasoning in a *trie structure*, which groups together those rule traces which share an initial sequence of rule firings.

Both Etzioni [5] and Smith & Peot [6] create structures similar to our negative problem graph, but in the domain of planning. These structures are built like ours by backward chaining from the final goal, and are used to improve the subsequent performance of the planners. Etzioni uses the *problem space graph* to guide operator use. Smith & Peot's *operator graph* warns which operator conditions have the potential to lead to recursion.

Fensel et al. [7] take a more general approach than the authors so far mentioned, building ontologies for both tasks and problem-solving methods (PSMs). These ontologies state the abilities of each PSM, and the requirements of each task, thus allowing an *adapter* to select a method appropriate for a given task. This approach allows PSMs to be written in a task-independent way, and so to be applied to a range of tasks. KRUSTWorks' refinement operators therefore correspond to the PSMs, and the knowledge hierarchy forms a PSM ontology.

5 Conclusions

Most refinement tools apply to a single KBS environment. We have presented an alternative approach which uses generic representations for the rules, and for the reasoning process of a KBS. This has enabled us to build a set of KBS-independent tools, applicable to a variety of KBS environments. In this paper, we have described an evaluation of these tools as applied to two industrial applications written in the PowerModel and Clips shells. Our experiments have shown that the generic KrustWorks approach to refinement is feasible. The KrustWorks core refinement techniques and toolkit of operators were applicable to two different industrial applications written in two different shells. Secondly, the tools were generally able to identify and fix artificial corruptions in both shells. When the tools were unable to fix faults, the major cause was a lack of fault evidence in the available examples. Our experiences also confirmed that a generic refinement tool should be designed to recover after run-time errors in faulty refined KBS, rather than trying to predict them in advance.

Acknowledgements

This work is supported by EPSRC grant GR/L38387 awarded to Susan Craw. We are also grateful for software donated by ESA and Intellicorp Ltd.

References

1. Robin Boswell, Susan Craw, and Ray Rowe. Knowledge refinement for a design system. In Enric Plaza and Richard Benjamins, editors, *Knowledge Acquisition, Modeling and Management, Proceedings of the 10th European Workshop (EKAW97)*, pages 49–64, Sant Feliu de Guixols, Spain, 1997. Springer.
2. Robin Boswell and Susan Craw. Knowledge modelling for a generic refinement framework. *Knowledge Based Systems*, 12:317–325, 1999. An earlier version appears in Proceedings of the BCS Expert Systems Conference, pages 58–74, Springer, 1998.
3. Susan Craw and Robin Boswell. Representing Problem-Solving for Knowledge Refinement. In *Proceedings of the Sixteenth National Conference on Artificial Intelligence*, pages 227–234, Orlando, FL, 1999. AAAI Press/MIT Press.
4. Patrick M. Murphy and Michael J. Pazzani. Revision of production system rule-bases. In W. W. Cohen and H. Hirsh, editors, *Machine Learning: Proceedings of the 11th International Conference*, pages 199–207, New Brunswick, NJ, 1994. Morgan Kaufmann.
5. Oren Etzioni. Acquiring search-control knowledge via static analysis. *Artificial Intelligence*, 62:255–301, 1993.
6. David E. Smith and Mark A. Peot. Suspending recursion in causal-link planning. In *Proceedings of the Third International Conference on AI Planning Systems*, Edinburgh, Scotland, 1996. AAAI press.
7. Dieter Fensel, Enrico Motta, S. Decker, and Z. Zdrahal. Using ontologies for defining tasks, problem-solving methods and their mappings. In Enric Plaza and Richard Benjamins, editors, *Knowledge Acquisition, Modeling and Management, Proceedings of the 10th European Workshop (EKAW97)*, pages 113–128, Sant Feliu de Guixols, Spain, 1997. Springer.

What's in an Electronic Business Model?

Jaap Gordijn[1,2], Hans Akkermans[1,3], and Hans Van Vliet[1]

[1] Free University Amsterdam
Vuture.net — Amsterdam Centre for Electronic Business Research
De Boelelaan 1081a, NL-1081 LV Amsterdam, The Netherlands
{gordijn,HansAkkermans,hans}@cs.vu.nl

[2] Deloitte & Touche Bakkenist Management Consultants
Wisselwerking 46 NL-1112 XR Diemen, The Netherlands

[3] AKMC Knowledge Management BV
Klareweid 19, NL-1831 BV, Koedijk, The Netherlands

Abstract. An electronic business model is an important baseline for the development of e-commerce system applications. Essentially, it provides the design rationale for e-commerce systems from the business point of view. However, how an e-business model must be defined and specified is a largely open issue. Business decision makers tend to use the notion in a highly informal way, and usually there is a big gap between the business view and that of IT developers. Nevertheless, we show that conceptual modelling techniques from IT provide very useful tools for precisely pinning down what e-business models actually are, as well as for their structured specification. We therefore present a (lightweight) ontology of what should be in an e-business model. The key idea we propose and develop is that an e-business model ontology centers around the core concept of *value*, and expresses how value is created, interpreted and exchanged within a multi-party stakeholder network. Our e-business model ontology is part of a wider methodology for e-business modelling, called $e^3 - value$, that is currently under development. It is based on a variety of industrial applications we are involved in, and it is illustrated by discussing a free Internet access service as an example.

1 Introduction

The design of an electronic commerce application is in our view *not* primarily an IT-oriented activity. Rather, it consists of very different types of design problems [10]. The most important of these is the design of the *e-business model* which highlights the way of doing business. A business model should do so in a very precise way, because stakeholders such as chief executive officers, marketers, and business developers should agree on it, and because it is a crucial bottomline part of the requirements for an electronic commerce system. For example, how do we develop the IT infrastructure and application system for a free Internet service? This cannot be really done without knowing what the underlying business model for the service is in the first place.

Therefore, we propose an *ontology* [3,6] to define from a generic point of view what should be in an e-business model. The key idea we propose and develop in this paper is that an e-business model ontology centers around the core concept of *value*,

R. Dieng and O. Corby (Eds.): EKAW 2000, LNAI 1937, pp. 257–273, 2000.

and expresses how value is created, interpreted and exchanged within a multi-party stakeholder network of (extended) enterprises and customers. It is exactly this notion of value which is currently lacking in information modelling and analysis approaches, including various business-oriented ontologies that have been developed recently.

The present work is part of a broader methodology for e-business development, called e^3*-value*, we are currently developing [10]. It reflects and structures the strategic business decisions that need to be made at the executive level on the e-business model and on business-IT alignment, before one can proceed to the technical design of an electronic commerce system. In Sec. 2, we discuss the need for an e-business model ontology. Sec. 3 describes our e-business model ontology, and we illustrate it by a case study. In Sec. 4 we discuss related work, and we briefly summarize the practical use of the ontology in consultancy and application projects.

2 The Need for a Business Model Ontology

Normally, the design of an electronic commerce system starts with the development of a business model. In most cases, such a business model is written down in natural language, perhaps with some informal sketches. The concepts and their interpretations used to describe a business model vary across different stakeholders, and this leads to important obstacles to achieve business-IT alignment in e-commerce applications. Given the enabling role of IT in electronic commerce, this alignment problem is no longer just an engineering issue: it has a strategic significance.

During the design of a business model, an ontology is therefore useful to prescribe which concepts and relations have to be present in a business model. An ontology should provide a reusable conceptualisation, in this case of the concept of *e-business model*, on which people can agree. By specializing and instantiating concepts and relations of the ontology for a particular case, the ontology can also be used to describe a particular business model in a precise and structured way. In the present context, we are mainly interested in ways to enhance communication between various stakeholders, that is, in shared meaning rather than automated reasoning. Thus, our current goal is to construct a so-called 'lightweight' ontology [16].

Furthermore, a business model ontology shows designers what kind of decisions should be taken during business model development. If stakeholders agree on a particular business model, a number of business decisions have been taken, so that the model serves as a precise set of business requirements for the electronic commerce information system. These requirements are useful for software architects who design the electronic commerce system from a technical point of view.

An ontology for e-business models must be capable of representing a range of business issues. These issues center, and this is our key proposal, around the generic concept of *value*, and how to create and exchange it in a network setting. Value is a central notion emerging from the scientific economic and business literature on e-business. Our practical experience in application projects also shows it to be a natural and useful concept for executives to focus on.

Informally, a business model highlights a network of actors and how they create or consume objects of value. These actors can be private persons, companies or enterprise alliances. Furthermore, a business model represents the services offered by and requested from actors. It should be capable to represent if an actor is willing to exchange an object of value (e.g., the right to listen to a music track) for another object of value (e.g., money). Also, a business model illustrates which actors can have economic transactions with other actors. A transaction is possible if actors offer each other objects of value in which both have a mutual interest. Finally, actors must perform activities to create value; for other actors or even for themselves. The assignment of activities to actors is an important element in e-business models for decision makers. The above business model concepts, which are more formally expressed in our *e^3-value* ontology, originate from scientific studies from a variety of (non-IT) disciplines, in particular marketing [17], axiology [13], business administration [18,19], and emerging e-commerce theory [4,15, 21]. In the next section, we present a lightweight ontology that is capable of representing these business issues to various kinds of stakeholders.

3 An Ontology for E-Commerce Business Models

The *e^3-value* ontology contains concepts, relations, and constraints, to describe actors, alliances between them, the exchange of objects of value, the value-adding activities, and the value interfaces between them. We identify three different views for describing business models for specific business cases. The *global actor* view shows which parties are involved in a business model and which objects of value they exchange. Its main purpose is to explain the overall business model to a wide range of stakeholders. The *detailed actor* view takes a further look at the decomposition aspects. It shows, for actors identified in the global actor view, alliances between parties, for instance virtual enterprises [5]. Finally, the *value activity* view shows the assignment of value-adding activities to actors. The ontology is illustrated by a small case study about a free Internet access service. In The Netherlands, a number of parties are offering such a service. Suppose one is asked to develop the business model of such a service (in actual fact, our example is taken from a real-life case). We show that our ontology can be used to answer such a 'fuzzy' question.

Global actor view. Figure 1 shows the global actor view of a business model for the free Internet access service. Its main purpose is to illustrate the overall business model to all stakeholders. The global actor view shows *actors* involved, such as *surfer* and *free Internet provider*, and the *exchange* of *value objects* between them. A value exchange has a direction, visualized by an arrow, indicating the direction the value object 'flows'. In this case, the *surfer* pays the *free Internet provider*. Value exchange links start and end at *value ports*. These ports are not visualized explicitly at this global level; they are the points connecting the value exchange with actors. Ports are grouped into a *value interface*, modelling the service an actor offers to its environment (also not drawn explicitly at this level). We note that this concept of ports and interfaces actually stems from ontologies relating to systems theory [3]. Some value exchanges relate to each other, for instance *payment* and *Internet access*. This is called an *offering*. In an offering both exchanges need to occur: there is no *Internet access* possible without *payment* and vice versa. Note that, apparently, the free Internet access service is actually not for free at all: a surfer has to pay for the telephone connection.

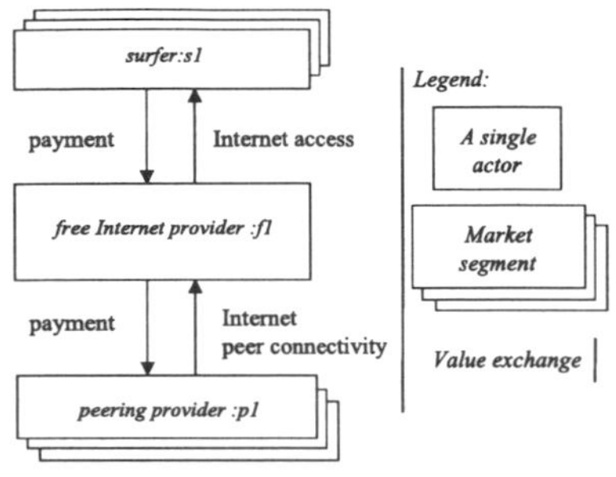

Fig. 1. Business model for the free Internet case: the global actor view.

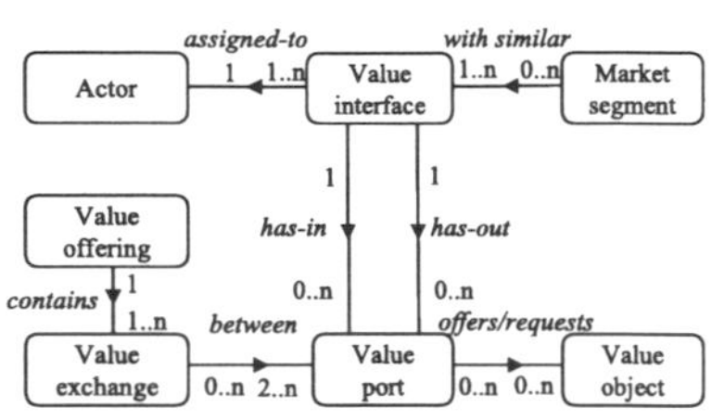

Fig. 2. Core concepts in the e^3*-value* ontology of e-business models (global actor view).

The business model in Figure 1 is a specialization and instantiation of concepts and relations in the e^3*-value* ontology (Figure 2). They are discussed in more depth in this section, and so are the specialization and instantiation of concepts and relations in the ontology for the free Internet access business case. The explanation of our ontology is structured by presenting a description for each concept, properties of the concept, relations with other concepts, constraints, and the visualization in a business model such as depicted in Figure 1. Each concept and relation is illustrated by a practical example.

Actor. An actor is perceived by its environment as an independent economic (and often also legal) entity. Enterprises, strategic business units, and customers are examples of actors.

PROPERTIES. An actor may have a name, e.g. a company name.

EXAMPLE. We identify three specializations of the *actor* concept: (1) the *surfer* actor, (2) the *free Internet provider* actor, and (3) the *peering provider* actor (Figure 3). The *surfer* actor uses the *free Internet provider* to surf the Internet. The *free Internet provider* uses *peering providers* to deliver traffic at the Internet host the *surfer* selected. Peering is necessary for an interconnected network of Internet hosts. Instances of *surfer* (s1, s2,.., sn) , one instance of *free Internet provider* (f1) and a number of instances of *peering provider* (p1, p2,.., pn) are represented in Figure 1. Note that worldwide, a number of free Internet providers exist, but here we are only interested in one.

Value Object. Actors exchange value objects. A value object is a service or product which is of value for the actors. Actors may value an object differently and subjectively, according to their own valuation preferences [13].

PROPERTIES. A value object has one or more valuation properties. A valuation property has a name and a unit which indicates the measuring scale in which the valuation is expressed. In general, the quantification of value has to be done by means of a multi-dimensional utility function [2,9].

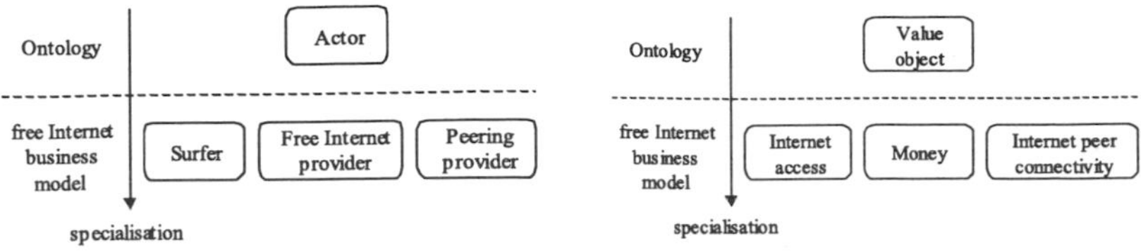

Fig. 3. Specialization of the actor concept.

Fig. 4. Specialization of the value object concept.

EXAMPLE. *Internet access* is a specialization of *value object* and represents the service offered by the *free Internet provider* to *surfers*. *Internet access* is valued in terms of *connection time* which is expressed in seconds and the Committed Information Rate (*CIR*), measured in bits per second. Other value objects are *money* and *Internet peer connectivity* (Figure 4).

Value Port. An actor uses a value port to provide or request value objects to or from its environment. Thus, a value port is used to interconnect actors so that they are able to exchange value objects. The concept of port is important, because it enables to abstract away from the internal business processes, and to focus only on how external actors and other components of the e-business model can be 'plugged in'. This is the value analogue of the separate external interfaces familiar from technical systems theory [3]. Take, for example, a bipolar in+out value multi-port, which is the most characteristic combination occurring in e-business models: an e-service port out and a money port in, or the other way around. Such a bipolar value port combination can be very well compared to an electrical wall outlet. As an external user, you don't want to be involved in what happens behind the wall outlet as long as it gives the right quality of service. The same approach holds for how external parties in an e-business model view the value ports of a service-offering actor: the ports only define how the external connections to other actors should be made.

RELATIONS. Value ports *offer* or *request* value objects. A value object can be requested or offered by multiple value ports.

EXAMPLE. Consider the *Internet access* port, as a specialization of the value port concept. The *offer or request* relation is specialised into a relation between the *Internet access* value port and the *Internet access* value object (Figure 5). The business model (Figure 1) shows two instances of the *Internet access* port. The *surfer* has an in-port and the *free Internet provider* has an out-port.

Value Interface. Actors have one or more value interfaces. A value interface groups individual value ports. (One can see this as a direct analogon to how a wall outlet is an assembly of plug-in ports in a technical system). It shows the value objects an actor is willing to exchange in return for other value objects via its ports.

PROPERTIES. A value interface has a *valuation function*. It expresses, given valuation properties of objects of all in-ports, the required valuation properties of objects on all out-ports, and vice versa. In other words, a valuation function shows if an actor is

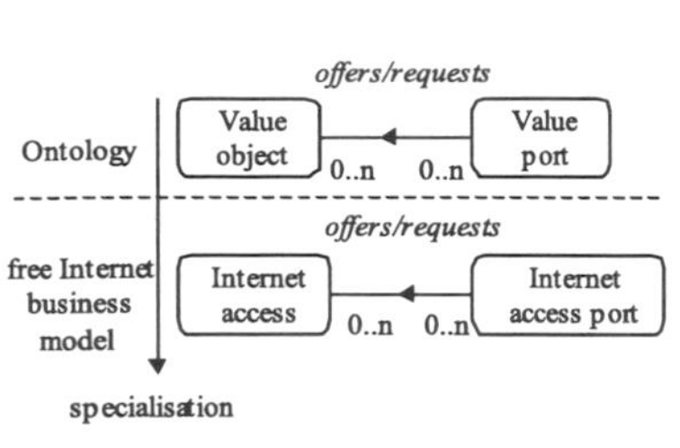

Fig. 5. Specialization of the value port concept and relations.

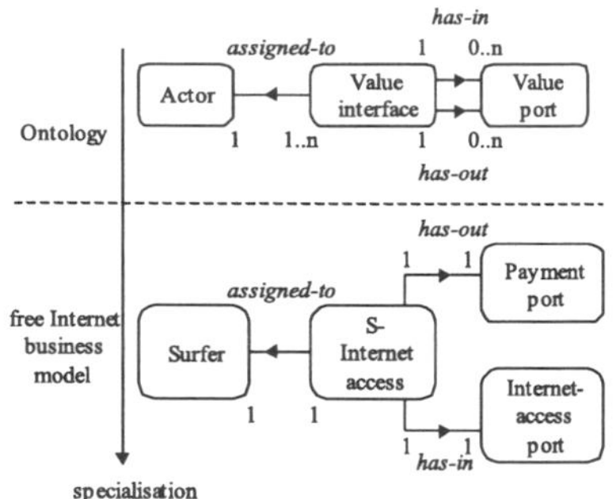

Fig. 6. Specialization of the value interface concept and relations.

willing to exchange value objects in return for other value objects. The valuation of objects depends on a specific actor evaluating the valuation function [13]. The valuation function has a *direction* argument. If the direction is *in*, the valuation function returns the required valuation properties of the value objects on all in-ports. If the direction is *out*, the opposite happens.

Relations. A value interface *is assigned to* one actor and *has* zero or multiple *in* value ports and *has* zero or multiple *out* value ports. A value interface has at least one value port. Multiple value interfaces can be assigned to an actor and a port belongs to exactly one value interface. If an actor has multiple value interfaces, s/he is offering different services to the environment.

Constraints. The exchange of value objects is atomic at the level of the value interface. Either all exchanges occur as specified in the value interface or none at all. For instance, a *surfer* cannot obtain Internet access without paying. The value interface says nothing about the time ordering of objects to be exchanged on its ports. It simply states which value objects are available, in return for some other value objects.

Example. The *surfer* has a specialized value interface called *S-Internet-access* which consists of a *payment* out-port and an *Internet access* in-port. It is important to recognize that the Internet access service is not free at all. The *surfer* has to pay for its telephone connection. The *free Internet provider* has a similar interface, with opposite port directions (Figure 6). Note that cardinality constraints for the *has-out* and *has-in* elations are specified more strictly for the specialization. For example, an *S-Internet-access* value interface consists of exactly one *payment* port and exactly one *Internet-access* port.

Value Exchange. A value exchange represents the trade of a value object between value ports. There are different kinds of value exchanges. First, seen from a port of an actor, value exchanges may occur to other ports of, possibly different, actors (Figure 7(a)). For instance, the port of actor A offering *music* can do so to ports of different actors B and C. This models the situation that multiple actors buy a track of music. Second, it is possible that a number (> 2 ports) are involved in *one particular value exchange*. The following two situations may then occur. Figure 7(b) represents a *split* of the value object, in this case, an amount of money. Actor A pays an amount of money to actor B and C in one value exchange. The situation in Figure 7(c) models *duplication* of a value object. Duplication of a value object is only possible if the marginal costs to create a replica are zero. This may be the case for value objects such as music, video and information. Actor B and C both receive a duplicate of a music track of actor A in one value exchange.

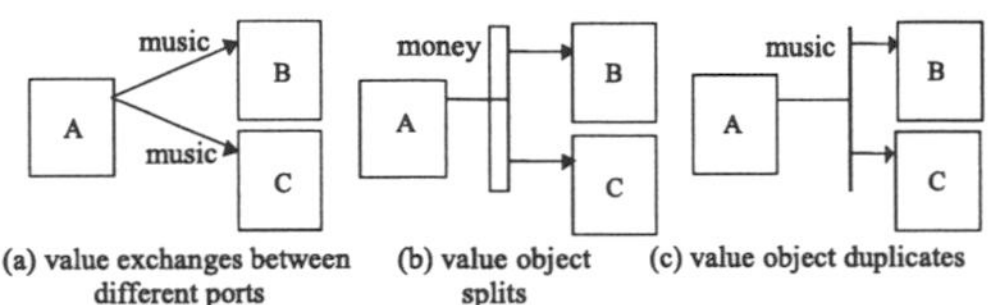

Fig. 7. Different types of value exchanges.

RELATIONS. The value ports involved in a value exchange are represented by the *between* relation. At least two value ports participate in a value exchange. A value port can be in multiple value exchanges.

CONSTRAINTS. A value exchange occurs between ports of opposite directions. A value object flows from an out-port into an in-port. Therefore, at least one in-port and one out-port should be present in a value exchange. Value ports can be seen as the end-points or terminals of a value exchange.

EXAMPLE. An *Internet access* exchange is a specialization of a *value exchange*. In an Internet access value exchange, exactly two value ports participate (Figure 8). Value exchanges occur between *surfers* and the *free Internet provider*.

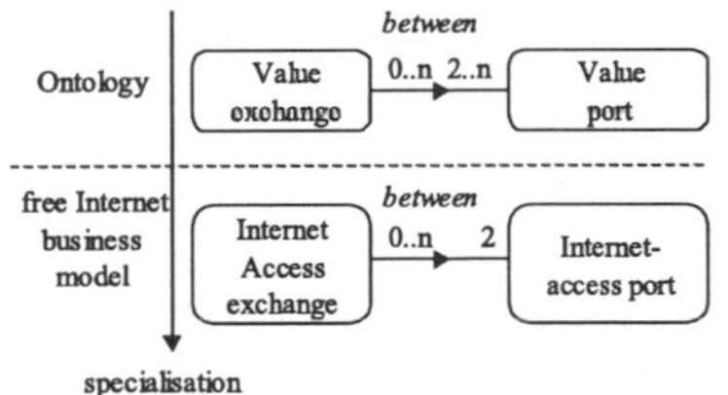

Fig. 8. Specialization of the value exchange concept and relation.

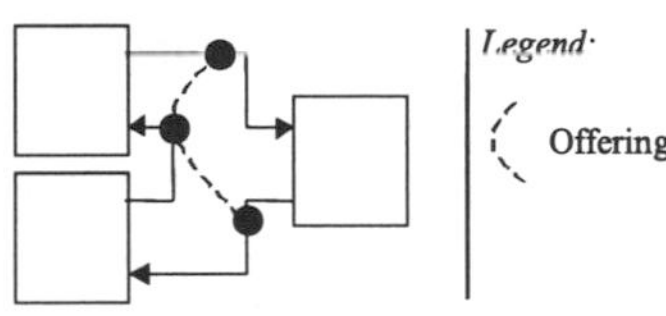

Fig. 9. Ports in an actor's interface connected to ports of two other actors.

Value Offering. A value offering is an assembly of value exchanges. In an offering, value exchanges between multiple actors (≥ 2) can participate.

RELATION. A value offering *contains* a number of value exchanges. A value exchange participates in exactly one value offering.

EXAMPLE. A *free Internet access* offering contains exactly one *Internet-access exchange* and one *payment exchange* (Figurre 10). The two value exchanges between the *free Internet provider f1* and the *surfer s1* clearly are an offering (Figure 1). The same holds for the value exchanges between the *free Internet provider f1* and the *peering provider p1*.

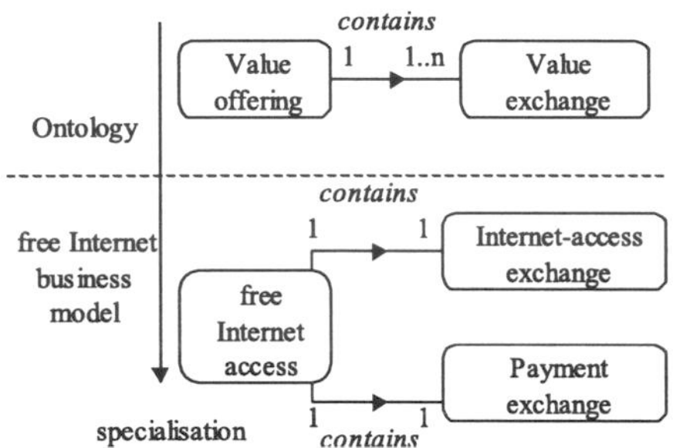

Fig. 10. Specialization of the value offering concept and relation.

Market segment. In the marketing literature [17], a market segment is defined as a concept that breaks a market (consisting of actors) into segments that share common properties. Accordingly, our concept *market segment* shows a set of actors that share a similar valuation function. Consequently, because valuation functions are bound to value interfaces, actors in a segment all have at least one similar value interface. Value exchanges and value offerings drawn to a segment are a shorthand notation for value exchanges and offerings between all actors of the segment, and other actors. Figure 11(a) shows an actor exchanging values with three other actors. Figure 11(b) shows the same but now with the three actors having a similar valuation function.

PROPERTIES. A market segment has a *count*, which indicates the number of actors in the segment. The count can be a number, unbounded, or unknown.

RELATIONS. Value interfaces of actors are *part of* zero or more market segments. A market segment contains one or more value interfaces.

CONSTRAINTS. Value interfaces of actors in a market segment should all have a similar valuation function (shown as a 'stack' of actors). Note that actors in a segment may also have in-similar value interfaces.

EXAMPLE. It is reasonable to expect that, with respect to the valuation function, a number of different *surfers* exist. Some surfers are willing to pay quite some money for high quality Internet access (heavy surfers) while others are only interested in sending low-bandwidth email and want to pay a small amount of money (light surfers). These can be grouped in a *heavy surfer* segment and a *light* segment (Figure 12).

Discussion. The global actor view shows the most important actors in a business model. Furthermore, it shows the objects of value exchanged between these actors, as well as

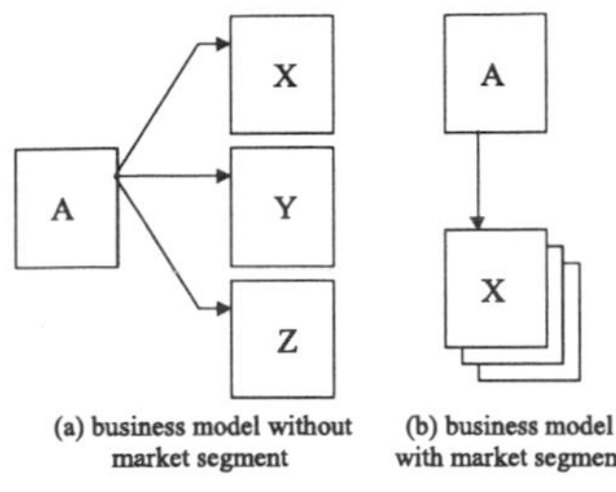

Fig. 11. A business model without and with market segment.

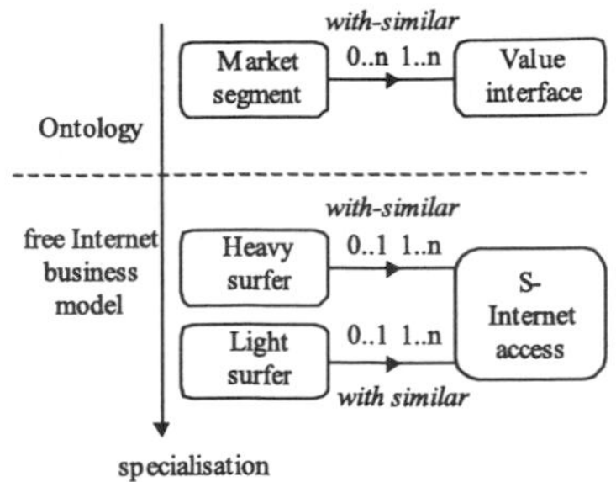

Fig. 12. Specialization of the market segment concept and relation.

offerings. The market segment notion is useful if offerings are of interest to a number of actors who share the same valuation function. The global actor view can easily be constructed in brainstorm sessions and workshops with all key actors. Also, this view can be used to present and explain the overall business model to stakeholders. For the free Internet access service, the global actor view illustrates that the free Internet access service is offered to surfers. However, the service is not for free at all, since the surfer has to transfer money for Internet access. This is due to costs for the telephone connection (a B2B e-business approach known as revenue sharing). Also, this view shows that, to offer an Internet access service, peering services have to be contracted with peering providers.

The detailed actor view: decomposition aspects. The purpose of the *detailed actor view* (Figure 13) is to show alliances between actors. For reasons of space we only show and discuss the detailed actor view for the *free Internet provider*. A detailed actor view can be developed for the *peering provider* as well.

Composite actor and elementary actor. An actor is perceived by its environment as an independent economic (and often also legal) entity. However, for providing a particular service, a number of actors may decide to present themselves, as a single (virtual enterprise) actor to their environment. Such actors decide on one or more common value interfaces to their environment. We call such a group of actors a composite actor. Actors can be composed of other composite actors and/or elementary actors. In the global actor view we do not state explicitly whether an actor is elementary or composite. In the detailed actor view, we refine actors of the global view into their constituents.

RELATIONS. A composite actor *is an* actor. An elementary actor *is an* actor. A composite actor *decomposes into* other actors. Actors may be part of zero or more composite actors.

EXAMPLE. *Telecommunication company* and *free Internet access provider* are specializations of the *elementary actor* concept. A telecommunication actor offers *physical connectivity* for data transport. A free Internet access provider offers *Internet access.* These actors jointly offer a free Internet service, resulting in a composite actor called *free Internet provider* (Figure 14). *TelCo* and *FastNet* (Figure 13) are instances of *Telecommunication company* and *free Internet access provider*, respectively.

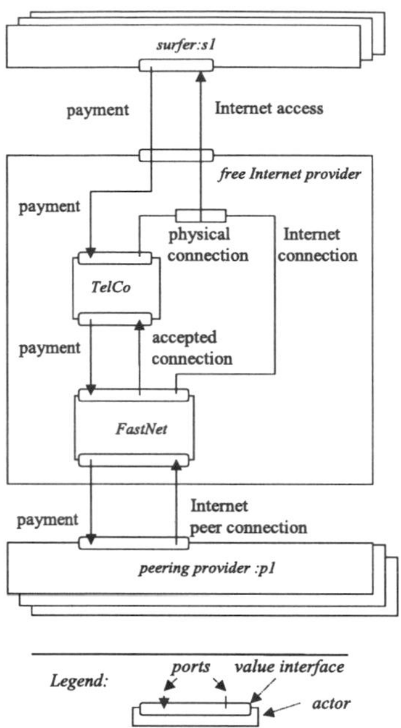

Fig. 13. Business model for the free Internet case: the detailed actor view.

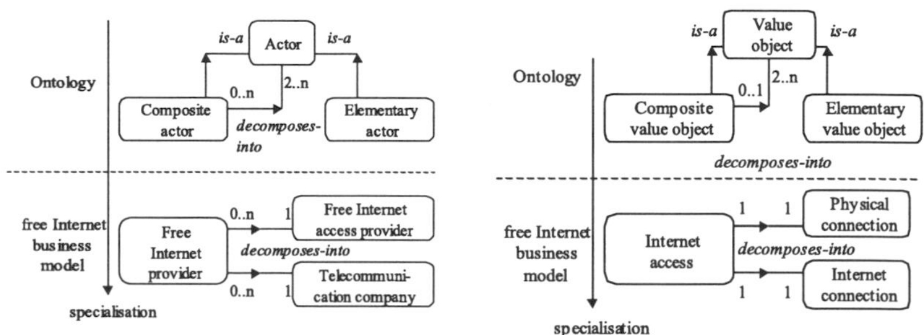

Fig. 14. Specialization and decomposition of the actor concept.

Fig. 15. Specialization and decomposition of the value object concept.

Composite value object and elementary value object. Composite value objects can be decomposed into other value objects. A composite value object can be built from other value objects which may be provided by different actors. *Elementary* value objects cannot be decomposed any further. A value object can be in only one composite value object.

RELATIONS. An elementary value object and a composite value object *is a* value object. A composite value object *decomposes into* other value objects.

EXAMPLE. *Physical connection* and *Internet connection* are specializations of the *elementary value object*. These value objects can be composed to form *Internet Access* (Figure 15).

The exchange of value. A composite actor has a value interface to its environment. However, a value interface of a composite actor must be mapped onto one or more value interfaces of actors which are part of the composite. This mapping is represented by value exchanges and value offerings. To be able to present these mappings accurately, we use a rounded box to visualize a value interface of an actor and an arrow to presents a value port of the value interface. The direction of the arrow indicates whether a value object flows in or out the actor. In Figure 16, a composite actor *a1* is shown, consisting of actors *b1* and *b2*. The ports in the value interface of *a1* are connected using value exchanges with value ports of *b1* and *b2*. On port *p1*, a value object is offered to the environment of actor *a1*. This object is offered by port *p3 or* by port *p5*. Another object of value is requested in return on port *p2*. Internally this object is split in two objects, to port *p4*, and port *p6*.

RELATIONS. The value ports involved in a value exchange are represented in the *between* relation.

CONSTRAINTS. *All* connected ports in value exchange should have direction *in* or *out*.

EXAMPLE. The *free Internet provider* consists of two actors: *Telecommunication company TelCo* and *free Internet access provider FastNet*. These companies are jointly offering an Internet access service. The externally visible value port *Internet access* of the free Internet provider is mapped onto the *physical connection* port of *TelCo* and the *Internet connection* port of *FastNet*. The other externally visible port of the *free Internet provider* is the *payment*. This port is mapped onto the *payment* port of *TelCo* because *TelCo* receives payment of the *surfer*.

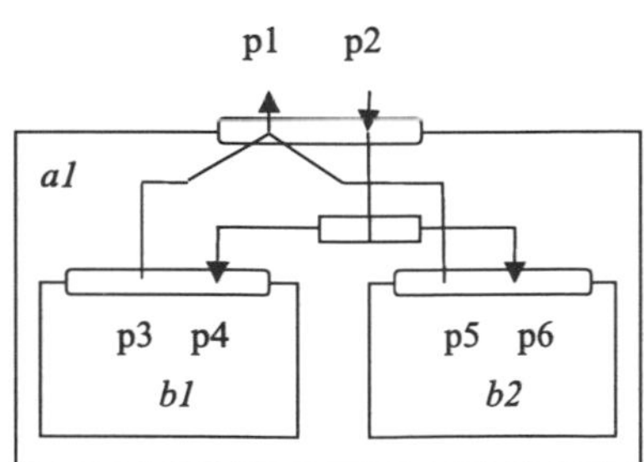

Fig. 16. Value exchanges between a composite actor and its composites.

Discussion. The detailed actor view intends to represent actors jointly offering or requesting a product or service. For each actor in the global actor view, detailed actor views may be considered. Such a detailed view consists of actors sharing a particular value interface to their environment. Furthermore, the detailed actor view shows how the shared value interface is mapped onto value interfaces of the actors themselves. Therefore, in the detailed actor view we make the value interfaces and value ports explicit. Note that *FastNet* and *Telco* jointly only offer the Internet Access service. *FastNet* itself has a value interface for Internet peering; *TelCo* has nothing to do with this.

The value activity view. We now discuss the *value activity* view. Its main purpose is to illustrate the assignment of value-adding activities to actors. Figure 17 shows this view for *TelCo* and *FastNet*. How value-adding activities are assigned to the various possible actors is a free variable that, as a result of the extended enterprise network setting, leads to many design options and choices in e-business models. Hence, this assignment is a key consideration in strategic e-business decision making.

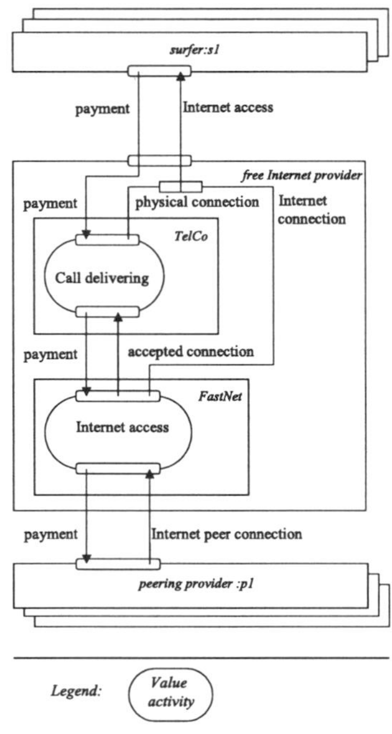

Fig. 17. Business model for the free Internet case: the value activity view.

Value Activity. A value activity is *performed by* an actor and produces objects of value *for* an actor. Both these actors can be different entities but they may also coincide. Consider an actor listening to music s/he bought in order to have a nice experience. In such a case, the actor performs a value activity (listening) and produces an object of value for him/herself (namely, a nice experience: note that what constitutes value may be rather abstract and interpretive). An important issue in e-commerce business model design is the *assignment* of value activities to actors. Therefore, we are interested in the collection of activities which can be assigned as a whole to actors. Such a collection we call a value activity. Therefore, the granularity of value activities should be such that they can be performed economically independent from other value activities [19], *and* they cannot be further decomposed into smaller economic activities that can be assigned to different actors (this gives a decomposition stop rule, which is by the way clearly different from business process or workflow decomposition). Value activities can be assigned to an elementary actor but also to a composite actor. In the latter case, the composite actor is not composed of other actors only (such as a virtual enterprise), but it can perform value activities by itself.

RELATIONS. A value activity *has* one or more value interfaces. A value interface belongs to exactly one value activity. A value activity is *assigned-to* precisely one actor. Multiple value activities can be assigned to an actor.

EXAMPLE. The *value activity* concept is specialized into the *call-delivering* and *Internet access* value activity. A *call-delivering* value activity has two value interfaces: (1) the *connection interface*, modelling a physical connection service which has to be paid for, and (2) an *acceptance interface* which models that a connection should be accepted by someone else, before one can speak of a connection (Figure 18). *FastNet*, which has been assigned the *Internet access value* activity, accepts physical connections for *TelCo*.

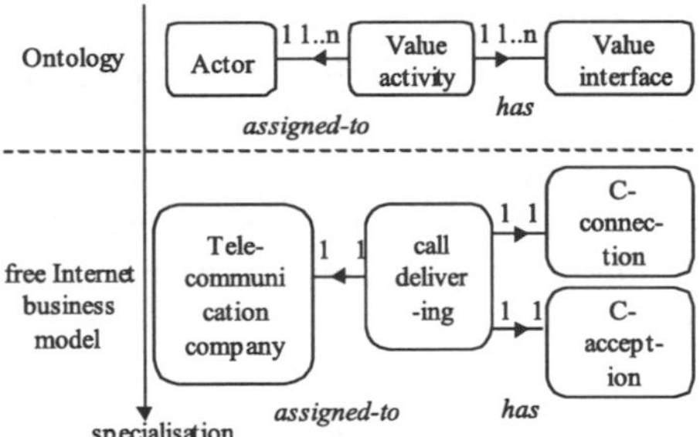

Fig. 18. Specialization of the value activity concept and relations.

Discussion. The value activity view shows which value activities are assigned to specific actors, and how value interfaces of these activities map onto value interfaces of actors. For the free Internet access service, the assignment of value activities is rather arbitrary. However, alternatives, not considered in this paper, are to assign the value activity *Internet access* to *TelCo* also, or to assign the value activities *Internet access* and *call delivering* to a telecommunication company only. Such alternative assignments would also lead to changes in the detailed actor view: they constitute different business models.

4 Discussion and Conclusion

Related work. There are some related business-oriented ontologies, in particular the AIAI enterprise ontology [22] and the TOronto Virtual Enterprise Ontology (TOVE) [7]. The most important difference with our e^3*-value* ontology is that we focus on the notion of value and the way objects of value are created, exchanged and consumed in a stakeholder network, while the enterprise ontology and TOVE concentrate on the enterprise itself, the latter resulting in a business process rather than external value perspective.

AIAI enterprise ontology. The enterprise ontology defines a collection of terms and definitions relevant to business enterprises. Two enterprise ontology concepts relate to our ontology but have a different interpretation: (1) *activity* and (2) *potential sale*. In the enterprise ontology, *activity* is the notion of actually doing something, the how. Our related definition, *value activity*, abstracts from the internal process and in contrast stresses the externally visible outcome in terms of created value, independent from the nature of the operational process. Thus, the defining boundary of what an activity is differs: in the e^3*-value* ontology the decomposition stop rule is to look at economically independent activities; business process or workflow activities have different decomposition rules, as such activities need not be economically independent. The enterprise ontology further defines a *potential sale* as a possible future agreement between two legal entities to exchange one good for another good. In our ontology, the concept of potential sale roughly corresponds to the concept of *offering*. An offering contains *value exchanges*. In the enterprise ontology, only two goods are exchanged in a potential sale. In contrast, in our ontology an offering contains an arbitrary number of value exchanges. This is needed to model a *bundle* of goods that is offered or requested as a whole. Furthermore, our ontology is capable of multi-party offerings. The case study in this paper illustrates the need for such a concept.

Toronto Virtual Enterprise Ontology. The TOVE ontology identifies concepts for the design of an agile enterprise. An agile company integrates its structure, behaviour and information. The TOVE ontology currently spans knowledge of activity, time and causality, resources, cost, quality, organization structure, product and agility. However, the interfaces an enterprise has to its environment are lacking in TOVE. Generally, the notion of the creation, distribution, and consumption of value in a stakeholder network is not present in the TOVE ontology. Hence, the TOVE ontology concentrates on the internal workflow of a company, whereas our ontology captures the outside value exchange network.

System-theoretic ontology. As pointed out earlier in this paper, the e-business ontology reuses several concepts from general and technical systems theory and associated ontologies [3]. In particular, the introduction of the concepts of ports and interfaces of a (network) system help to abstract away from the internal workings of an activity (or subsystem), and to independently specify the connection to the environment (external suubsystems). This is an important advance over what is typically done in business process and workflow modelling [8].

Use of the ontology in e-business development. In summary, this paper is premised on the observation that for the development of electronic commerce systems, e-business models must be specified precisely. Such a clear-cut specification is important for two reasons: (1) to reach agreement between stakeholders involved, and (2) to be able to serve as a specification for designers of the commerce system. The e^3*-value* ontology discussed in this paper specifies which generic concepts have to be present in an e-business model. These concepts are based on the generic and reusable notion of *value*, and are capable of representing creation, exchange, valuation, and consumption of value objects in a network of actors.

Of course, for e-business development an ontology is only one of the necessary tools. It must be embedded in a wider process of e-business modelling and application development. The present paper is rather descriptive in nature, but the ontology has several more dynamic and practical uses in e-business development that are beyond the scope of this paper. In brief:

1. The e^3*-value* ontology gives a baseline of shared concepts with which it is possible to construct e-business models. This baseline is much more rigorous, and therefore more amenable to IT systems follow-up, than value-oriented business approaches such as [18,19]. It is also richer as it handles external value networks and not just value chains — an extension we believe to be essential for e-commerce.
2. It is our practical experience in industry projects that e-business models (on the basis of this ontology, especially the global actor view) can be constructed during workshops or brainstorm sessions with stakeholders such as executive management, and that this type of value analysis is felt as helpful and illuminating. This is similar to experiences with management workshops in knowledge management, see e.g. [1, 20].
3. We have developed a set of steps, business rules and guidelines, and scenario techniques for practitioners (rooted in the ontology concepts) that structure, steer and simplify the *process* of designing and evaluating e-business models. More on this process is found in [10,11].
4. Our ontology has been described in this paper in a graphical and semi-formal way. This is in line with its use as a *lightweight* ontology to enhance communication between different stakeholders [16]. However, tool development is ongoing, and a working Prolog implementation of the ontology has been constructed. There are thus no significant obstacles to formalize e^3*-value* in terms of one of the formal language approaches to ontology [6,14]. Furthermore, it is not difficult to define our graphical notation in terms of UML, using its standard extensions such as stereotyped classes and especially packages with associated icons. As this is straightforward technical labour not adding anything to the semantics, we have not discussed it in this paper.
5. An important further step is to extend the work to a quantitative formulation of the concept of value. This would enable to analyze business scenarios and make choices between business models on quantitative grounds, by linking value analysis to methods and results from utility theory, decision theory and optimization. We are currently researching how to make the transition from qualitative and interpretive customer value notions [13] to quantitative utility analysis. For some application areas we have shown that this indeed can be done, see [9,2] for applications to web

selling of digital music content and to automatic cost-efficient building comfort management, respectively.

6. At the IT level, this provides the basis for agent-based e-business system solutions. Corresponding, extensive and real-life applications where economic agents make local decisions based on utility considerations, are described in some of our other work [23,12,24,2].

Thus, an important virtue of the ontology approach is that it provides a foundation to express and discuss e-business models for specific business cases in a rigorous and structured fashion. This enhances business-IT alignment and smoothens the transition to e-commerce systems engineering.

Acknowledgment. This work has been partly sponsored by the Stichting voor Technische Wetenschappen (STW), project nr VWI.4949.

References

1. J.M. Akkermans, P.-H. Speel, and A. Ratcliffe. Problem, opportunity, and feasibility analysis for knowledge management: An industrial case study. In B. Gaines, R. Cremer, and M. Musen, editors, *Proceedings 12th Int. Workshop on Knowledge Acquisition, Modelling, and Management KAW'99 (16-21 October 1999, Banff, Alberta, Canada)*, volume I, pages 2–1–1 — 2–1–22, Calgary, 1999. University of Calgary, SRDG Publications.
2. E. Boertjes, J.M. Akkermans, R. Gustavsson, and R. Kamphuis. Agents achieving customer satisfaction — the COMFY comfort management system. In *Proceedings 5th Int. Conf. on the Practical Application of Intelligent Agents and Multi-Agent Technology PAAM-2000 (Manchester, UK, 10-12 April 2000)*, pages 75–94, Blackpool, UK, 2000. The Practical Application Company Ltd. ISBN 1-902426-07-X.
3. W.N. Borst, J.M. Akkermans, and J.L. Top. Engineering ontologies. *International Journal of Human-Computer Studies*, 46:365–406, 1997.
4. Soon-Yong Choi, Dale O Stahl, and Andrew B. Whinston. *The economics of doing business in the electronic marketplace*. Macmillan Technical Publishing, Indianapolis, 1997.
5. W.H. Davidow and M.S. Malone. *The virtual corporation - structuring and revitalizing the corporatio for the 21st century*. HarperCollings, New York, 1992.
6. D. Fensel. *Ontologies: Silver Bullet for Knowledge Management and Electronic Commerce*. Springer-Verlag, Berlin, D, 2000. Series LNAI Vol., to appear.
7. M.S. Fox and M. Gruninger. Enterprise modelling. *AI Magazine*, pages 109–121, Fall 1998.
8. J. Gordijn, J.M. Akkermans, and J.C. van Vliet. Business modelling is not proces modelling. 2000. Accepted. Available from http://www.cs.vu.nl/~gordijn.
9. J. Gordijn, J.M. Akkermans, and J.C. van Vliet. Selling bits: A matter of creating consummer value. In *First International Conference on Electronic Commerce and Web Technologies ECWEB-2000 (Greenwich, UK, 4-6 September 2000*, 2000. Accepted for publication. Available from http://www.cs.vu.nl/~gordijn.
10. J. Gordijn, J.M. Akkermans, and J.C. van Vliet. Value-based requirements creation for electronic commerce applications. In *Proceedings of the 33rd Hawaii International Conference on System Sciences (HICSS-33)*, Los Alamitos, CA, January 4-7 2000. IEEE Computer Society. CD-ROM ISSN 0-7695-0493-0/00.

11. J. Gordijn, H. de Bruin, and J.M. Akkermans. Integral design of E-Commerce systems: Aligning the business with software architecture through scenarios. In H. de Bruin, editor, *Proceedings Conference on ICT Architecture in the BeNeLux*, Amsterdam, NL, 1999. Free University and Cap Gemini. Also available from http://www.cs.vu.nl/~gordijn.
12. R. Gustavsson. Agents with power. *Communications of the ACM*, 42:41–47, March 1999.
13. Morris B. Holbrook. *Consumer value: a framework for analysis and research*. Routledge, New York, 1999.
14. I. Horrocks, D. Fensel, J. Broekstra, S. Decker, M. Erdmann, C. Goble, F. van Harmelen, M. Klein, S. Staab, and R. Studer. The ontology-based web inference layer OIL. Technical Report OnToKnowledge EU-IST Project Draft Deliverable, University of Manchester, UK, March 2000. Available from http://www.ontoknowledge.com/oil.
15. J. Hagel III and A.G. Armstrong. *Net Gain - Expanding markets through virtual communities*. Harvard Business School Press, Boston, Massachusetts, 1997.
16. R. Jasper and M. Uschold. A framework for understanding and classifying ontology applications. In B. Gaines, R. Cremer, and M. Musen, editors, *Proceedings 12th Int. Workshop on Knowledge Acquisition, Modelling, and Management KAW'99 (16-21 October 1999, Banff, Alberta, Canada)*, volume I, pages 4–9–1 — 4–9–20, Calgary, 1999. University of Calgary, SRDG Publications.
17. P. Kotler. *Marketing management: analysis, planning, implementation and control*. Prentice Hall, Englewood Cliffs, New Jersey, 1988.
18. R. Normann and R. Ramirez. *Designing interactive strategy - From value chain to value constellation*. John Wiley & Sons Inc., Chichester, 1994.
19. M.E. Porter and V.E. Millar. How information gives you competitive advantage. *Harvard Business Review*, pages 149–160, 1985.
20. A.Th. Schreiber, J.M. Akkermans, A.A. Anjewierden, R. de Hoog, N. Shadbolt, W. Van Der Velde, and B.J Wielinga. *Knowledge Engineering And Management*. The MIT Press, Cambridge, MA, 2000. 455 + xiv pages, ISBN 0-262-19300-0.
21. Carl Shapiro and Hal R. Varian. *Information Rules*. Harvard Business School Press, Boston, Massachusetts, 1999.
22. M. Uschold, M. King, S. Moralee, and Y. Zorgios. The enterprise ontology. *The knowledge engineering review*, 13, 1998.
23. F. Ygge and J.M. Akkermans. Decentralized markets versus central control — a comparative study,. *Journal of Artificial Intelligence Research*, 11:301–333, October 1999. Also available from http://www.jair.org.
24. F. Ygge, J.M. Akkermans, A. Andersson, M. Krejic, and E. Boertjes. The HomeBots system and field test — a multi-commodity market for predictive power load management. In *Proceedings 4th Int. Conf. on the Practical Application of Intelligent Agents and Multi-Agent Technology PAAM-99 (London, UK, 19-21 April 1999)*, pages 363–382, Blackpool, UK, 1999. The Practical Application Company Ltd. ISBN 1-902426-05-3. (Also available from http://www.enersearch.se/ygge).

Chinese Encyclopaedias and Balinese Cockfights - Lessons for Business Process Change and Knowledge Management

Antony Bryant

Professor of Informatics
Leeds Metropolitan University
The Grange, Beckett Park
Leeds LS6 3QS
U K
a.bryant@lmu.ac.uk

Abstract. Two of the main issues that have permeated management thought in the 1990s are Business Process Re-engineering and Knowledge Management. The former rapidly achieved dizzying heights in terms of citations, publications and sales, before equally rapidly falling into disrepute. The latter may be following the same course; and perhaps deservedly so. If this seems to be an injustice to knowledge management, then the precipitous fall of BPR is also undeserved. This paper seeks to stress the strengths and weaknesses of these two trends, offering ways in which they can and should influence our practices. Taking a slightly tangential perspective to each provides the basis for a corrective to any tendency to fall into the trap of a mechanistic or IT-determined orientation; a potential inherent in both. The use of two slightly off-beat examples helps to illustrate the strengths and weaknesses of both phenomena.

1 Problems with BPR and Knowledge Management

For perplexed readers I should start by pointing out that my title is taken from two sources; an essay by Jorge Luis Borges 'The Chinese Encyclopaedia of John Wilkins' and an analysis of Balinese cockfights by the anthropologist Clifford Geertz. I must also stress that unfortunately I have never been to Bali or China; I know very little about cockfighting, other than what I have gleaned from Geertz' writing; and to the best of my knowledge I have never even seen a Chinese encyclopaedia, let alone read any part of one.

What these two sources offer, however, is the opportunity to consider two critical and influential sets of concepts - one already well on the way to near complete dismissal as a management 'fad', the other perhaps just starting on the same path of meteoric rise and equally precipitous decline. In both cases some salvage work and reassessment is required. In the case of BPR it is imperative to move beyond the mechanistic and lax conceptualizations that are usually associated with the term. With

R. Dieng and O. Corby (Eds.): EKAW 2000, LNAI 1937, pp. 274-287, 2000.

knowledge management, at a far earlier phase in its development, there is still a need for clarification of basic tenets, and potential applications.

By the mid-1990s BPR was in sharp decline as practitioners and researchers detailed the severe shortcomings in the organizational and management thinking that surrounded the re-engineering fad. This was particularly warranted with respect to the tendency of BPR towards what might be termed *macho-mechanism*; best exemplified by some of the statements made by Mike Hammer such as those reported in an interview for The Chicago Tribune in 1994. Here Hammer likened BPR to 'a neutron bomb'.

'For Hammer, the message of BPR is that companies must **organize** work around process. That means radically "reinventing" companies, not simply "fixing" them. It means tearing down hundreds, even thousands, of "functional silos" corporations have built. The walls remain standing, says Hammer, but everything inside is nuked ...'[1]

The savage imagery is a trait that Hammer seemed to display with relish. As will be argued below, however, the mechanistic mode of explanation is not limited to BPR; nor is BPR indelibly tainted by such tendencies. Unfortunately the understandable distaste for this mechanistic fallacy contributed to an underestimation of any positive contribution of BPR: Particularly its stress on *process*, both as a concept in itself and as a counter to the overwhelming bias towards *structure* and *function*. Some recent work has sought to accentuate the non-mechanistic aspects that can be found at the centre of BPR, and develop this into a basis for integrated business process management. Combined with developments such as those around the concept of the learning organization, this provides a link to emerging ideas centred on knowledge management.

The term knowledge management does not (yet) seem to suffer from the same negative connotations that beset BPR; but in many respects it is far more problematic. A cynic might view the emergence of knowledge management as a case of 'locking the stable door after horse has bolted': The mass redundancies and down-sizing of the past decade - often done under the guise of BPR - having led to the loss of precisely the *knowledge* and experience - the *know how* - that knowledge management stresses is a key contributory factor to organizational development and even survival.

This apart, at present knowledge management is regarded in a positive light; although it has not suffered from the warp-speed hype that marked the emergence of BPR at the start of the 1990s. But whereas the component terms of BPR were fairly clear, the same does not apply to knowledge management. Many writers on knowledge management understandably seek to distance themselves from epistemology, but the question 'What is 'knowledge'? has still to be asked. Moreover, in the context of information systems, one also has to ask other questions. 'What makes knowledge distinct from 'information'? Is there some basis for thinking that the term 'knowledge' is simply a redressing of the term 'information', given that the latter seems inextricably linked to the electronic gadgetry of computers and communication systems? Furthermore, even if there is some reasonable and workable concept of 'knowledge' in this novel context, what does it mean to '*manage* knowledge'?

2 Information and Knowledge

I do not intend trying to tackle the full intricacies of the distinctions between terms such as 'data', 'information' and 'knowledge'; but the issues and distinctions cannot be evaded completely. I would much rather dispense with the term 'data' altogether. There is unease over its grammatical use - singular or plural? - and continuing dispute regarding the distinction between 'data' and 'information'. The data-information couple lies at the basis of the 'chemical engineering metaphor', where data is regarded as the raw material from which information is extracted. The inadequacies of this have been well documented, but the imagery continues to exert great influence.

If there is any rationale for continuing to use the term *data*, then its only sense seems to be along the lines of 'something that is stored in objects' - both inanimate and animate. Thus books, records, accounts, computer systems, CDs, disks and the like can be thought of as 'containing data'; but then so too do trees, plants, rocks, animals and people. Human beings do not, however, *extract* information from this raw material. As soon as humans turn their attention to any object, we are immediately in the realm of **meaning**. If it/they can be said to exist at all, data is the stuff that human beings are unaware of.

People cannot engage directly in anything to do with data. Scanning a book into a computer is a data process; someone trying to read it - and make sense of it - involves information, because it inevitably involves meaning. Carbon-based entities are information-oriented; silicon-based ones are data-oriented. This is quite a helpful distinction in considering the project of 'artificial intelligence', and dealing with claims that machines can become like humans. Thus one of the key criteria AI might have to fulfil for it to be judged 'successful' would be a revised 'Turing test', where the machine should also be able to distinguish between person and machine.

Information comes about because animate entities - particularly human beings - construct **meaning** and exchange ideas in order to exist as social beings and interact. Meaning construction is a key activity in all human processes. A large amount of misunderstanding about the nature of this process of constructing meaning emanates from the metaphorical imagery in which discussions about this reside. This has been discussed elsewhere, particularly by Schön [2] and Reddy [3]; and has been specifically applied in the field of information systems and software engineering.

The dominance of what Reddy terms the *conduit metaphor*, leads to the presumption that *information flows around a system from source to target*; from sender to receiver. This stresses the action of sending, and implies that receiving is a relatively passive process, at the most calling upon the repertoire of actions required 'merely' for extracting or decoding. This metaphor also obscures the point that what is sent is a series of *signals*: information is created in devising the message and in interpreting it. Reddy makes the distinction between the signals and the selection processes that occur *at both ends of the process*. The thing that is sent is not the message but the signal; the message is what the sender wanted to communicate, and which may or may not correspond to the message derived by the receiver. Sending and receiving each require action and interpretation.

The argument that meaning is continually constructed by social actors has been influentially stated and summarized by Giddens [4] in what he terms the 'theory of structuration'. He distinguishes between *system* and *structure*. Social systems are 'composed of patterns of relationships between actors or collectivities reproduced across time and space' (p26); whereas structures 'have only a "virtual" existence'. This existence has a dual nature - *the duality of structure* - in the sense that the structure 'is both the medium and the outcome of the practices which constitute social systems' (p27).

This is not to say that social actors do this in an arbitrary fashion. On the contrary we continually test and seek to confirm our own sets of meanings. Meaning construction is a social activity, not an individual one. For the most part we do this all the time, without realizing that we are doing so. We only become conscious that we are doing this if someone draws our attention to it - as I am doing here; or if something 'goes wrong', so that our implied or assumed meanings or ascriptions fail to receive support from the context or events. Information is then a human construct that arises from our actions as social beings producing and reproducing social systems against the capacities and constraints afforded by social structures. It also provides a resource for those actions.

Giddens, writing in 1981 did not use the term information, but did talk about 'knowledgeable social actors' and 'stocks of knowledge'. The latter are used by social actors 'in the production and reproduction of interaction', being 'at the same time the source of accounts they may supply of the purposes, reasons and motives of their action.' (p27) This knowledgeability 'is only partly discursive, as it is in part embedded in *practical consciousness*' (stress in original).

2.1 Defining Knowledge

So what does all this imply for the relationship and distinctions between information and knowledge? Many of the likely sources are not helpful. The epistemologists offer a variety of ideas about knowledge, but information is hardly a central focus - although this may change with the encroachment on to their domain that recent work on knowledge management represents.

The knowledge management writers are also evasive on this, and many definitions of 'knowledge management' could just easily be definitions of information management - or even general resource management. For example an article by two researchers based at The Cranfield School of Management in the UK offers a definition of knowledge management as 'the collection of processes that govern the creation, dissemination, and utilisation of knowledge to fulfil organisational objectives' [5]. Replacing both occurrences of the word 'knowledge' with 'information', 'software', 'learning' or a whole host of other terms (e.g. 'coffee-machine') would still result in a meaningful statement, and so begs the question 'what is specific to knowledge that makes its management a specific and critical concern for organizations?' To provide some basis for analysis a definition of knowledge is required, and cannot be avoided.

For Davenport and Prusak [6] knowledge is defined as 'a fluid mix of framed experience, values, contextual information, and expert insight that provides a framework for evaluating and incorporating new experiences and information' (p5). Zack [7] defines knowledge as 'that which we come to believe and value based on some meaningfully organized accumulation of information (messages) through experience, communication or inference'. Demarest [8] somewhat evades the issue by defining what he calls 'commercial knowledge' - an explicitly developed and managed network of imperatives, patterns, rules and scripts, embodied in some aspect of the firm, and distributed throughout the firm, that creates marketplace performances. While Schultze [9] notes that knowledge is an elusive concept, and so offers no definition, preferring Blackler's idea of *knowledge work* - 'i.e. the work of producing and re-producing information and knowledge' (p4) - note the conflation of information and knowledge.

Meehan [10] in his brief survey of definitions of knowledge in the knowledge management literature, argues that definitions like Davenport and Prusak's are heavily slanted towards a 'technical-rational' view; and this can be contrasted with the ideas of Nonaka and Takeuchi [11]. Meehan terms their approach 'Japanese Knowledge Management', and quotes their definition of knowledge approvingly - 'a dynamic human process of justifying personal belief towards the "truth"'. They also distinguish between information and knowledge in terms of 'flows' and 'stocks', so that information is what flows, and adds to knowledge stocks. Meehan points out that the Japanese approach links knowledge to action and subjectivity, and the authors specifically cite the work of social theorists such as Berger and Luckman whose book 'The Social Construction of Reality' anticipates some of the main ideas proposed by Giddens.

Given the range of meanings that can be attributed to the term 'knowledge', and the ramifications these will have on subsequent arguments, the problem of defining the term cannot be evaded, even within the restricted realm of knowledge management. Yet perhaps we are all fooling ourselves by introducing the term. Maybe it is no more than a sophisticated epithet for information; and so any of the achievements around the 'I' word can be readily applied to the 'K' one.

A hint of this can be found in the work of Davenport and Prusak. At the end of their book on knowledge management they note that some organizations are afraid to use the term 'knowledge', and so resort to euphemisms such as 'best practice', 'experience', 'information resource' and so on. They quite rightly point out that this reluctance may well be indicative of an anti-intellectual stance that they term 'know-nothingism'. Using terms related to 'practice' or pragmatics excludes many important aspects of modern processes. They then go on to state that - 'If you call it something related to information, you'll be dragged back to the corporate information systems morass that really involves data' (p174). This is rather a strange statement to find at the end of a book devoted to knowledge management. It really does appear to be something close to an admission that the entire concept of 'knowledge management' has only come about because the term 'information management' is now seen as predominantly or wholly focused on information *technology*. The term knowledge management then appears primarily as a corrective; drawing attention away from the technology towards other aspects - particularly the human and organizational ones. As a minimal basis for focusing on knowledge rather than on information, it seems a sensible solution, although perhaps not exactly what Davenport and Prusak actually had in mind: But at least there is a minimally valid reason to go with the K word. There is, however, always the tendency for technicist reasoning to intrude, and it may not be long before 'knowledge-technology' takes on a role similar to IT, and the 'K-word' has to be replaced by a new euphemism such as 'wisdom', 'experience', or 'intelligence'. (A search across the web indicates that this is already happening.)

So at the very least we can be reconciled to the idea of knowledge in its presently popular embodiment in *knowledge management*. If it moves people's attention away from the technology, and helps them resolve issues at the human, organizational and social level, then this is to be welcomed. There is a problem, however, in linking knowledge to **management**. The term 'management' is not a neutral one; it comes with a set of conceptual baggage that evokes tendencies towards hierarchies, structures, and control: The classic if discredited command-and-control orientation. Management has an inherently mechanistic tendency; the terms and imagery of management writing are slanted towards a rationalistic view of planning, strategy, decision-making, allocations and so on. Management seems wedded to objects - animate and inanimate - and is not very good at dealing with animate 'subjects', meaning and process.

3 The Process Perspective

Taking this as a starting point, many of the management 'fads' of the 1990s can be seen originating in attempts to move away from the mechanistic disposition. TQM, BPR, Process Improvement all stress the concept of 'process' as central; in some cases explicitly moving away from products and objects. But this is not an easy task; people find it far easier to conceptualize and abstract in terms of 'things' or 'objects' than they do in terms of 'processes'. A closer examination of the 'fads' of the last 10-20 years reveals a more complex picture. Many of these 'fashions' really did originate from genuine insights that, if not entirely new, certainly offered a different perspective on key issues. Such insights, however, are always in danger of dissipation once they become re-interpreted in line with older, predominant conceptions. This may be inevitable, since people will always try to understand something new in terms of what they already know. What has been particularly noteworthy with some of the 'innovations' of the 1980s and 1990s is that the originators of the ideas themselves have often been the worst perpetrators of this. Mike Hammer may be the name that everyone associates with BPR; but there is a good case to be made that he was also its worst publicist. He practically admits this in his later work; similarly Davenport's renunciation of BPR [12].

What both Hammer and Davenport have stressed, however, is that the key aspect of the ideas around BPR was **process**. Davenport has sought to develop his approach to knowledge management precisely along the lines of knowledge as a *process*, not as an *object*. Yet he continues to undermine his own position; having confirmed the process nature of knowledge, and defined it in terms of a human quality, Davenport and Prusak state that '[N]ot only can *it* [knowledge] judge new situations and information in the light of what is already known, *it* judges and refines itself in responses to new situations and information' (p11, quoted by Meehan, p5, his stress added). Here is knowledge as a disembodied object; and most definitely not a socially-constructed, human-centred *process*.

I believe that this problem arises because people find *process* abstractions and *process* concepts far more difficult than *product* or *object* ones. This may be a culturally specific disposition, but it certainly seems present in Europe and North America. Some evidence to support this comes from a consideration of object orientation, which was heralded as a conceptual advance on entity modelling because it was allegedly more 'natural' and congruent with the ways in which we think [13]. Objects were seen as a combination of product and process, superseding the data-oriented entity-relationship approaches. Yet the revolution promised by OO never really materialized, although there were some definite benefits. To some extent the

OO enthusiasm of the early 1990s has given way to 'component' development, which is inherently based around *objects* in the tangible sense of the term, and where *process* is still a poor relation.

To substantiate the claims of the previous paragraph I really need to give ground to those with expertize in cognitive psychology. They might be able to offer explanations why humans seem inherently drawn towards object abstractions rather than process ones. For my present purposes, however, I simply wish to state the view that this tendency does seem to exist, and needs to be taken into account when considering how best practice in our field can be put into effect. When we come to look at BPR, knowledge management and so on, it is vital that we continually fight against any inclination towards object-centred, mechanistic and technicist thinking - we might call the tendency *thingking*: And so I want to develop some ideas that might help remedy this - hence my title, which I shall now explain in more detail.

4 Rules, Events, and Dramas

A few years ago I might have had to explain and justify the introduction of the work of anthropologists and cultural theorists to this sort of audience. I will still not take it for granted that my specific sources are 'obvious', but following the work of people such as Boisot, Suchman, and Zuboff [14,15,16], it is perhaps less surprizing to draw upon such work.

The anthropologist Clifford Geertz conducted various fieldwork visits to Bali in the 1950s and 1960s. Some of his findings were published as part of a collection of essays called 'The Interpretation of Cultures', and the essay on cockfighting has become widely read and cited. The full title of the essay is 'Deep Play: Notes on the Balinese Cockfight' [17].

Geertz noted that when he and his wife arrived in a fairly remote village in Bali - 'it was its own world ... we were intruders, professional ones'. The Balinese dealt with us 'as though we were not there ... we were non-persons, spectres'. Their accommodation had been arranged by the provincial government, and was located in an 'extended family compound ... belonging to one of the four major factions in village life'. Apart from the landlord and village chief (the landlord's cousin and brother-in-law) 'everyone ignored us in a way only a Balinese can do ... people seemed to look right through us with a gaze focused several yards behind us'. The villagers knew who they were, but they acted as if the American academics did not exist. Any interaction only occurred if it was absolutely unavoidable, and then was cursory at best - a few short responses to questions or simply non-verbal ones.

The breakthrough came as a result of a cockfight in the village. The cockfight is technically illegal; but in the same way that alcohol was illegal in the US during prohibition; or certain drugs such as marijuana are illegal now. Geertz and his wife go along to watch the fight - although they are still ignored. But during the fight the police arrive and the whole village descends into chaos as people flee the scene to escape questioning and possible arrest. Geertz and his wife join in the flight away from the scene. They follow a man into his compound, where the man's wife magically produces a table and settings for tea, and by the time the police come around they are all sitting drinking as if they had spent the entire afternoon there.

The policeman's attention is taken by the scene of a villager and two obvious foreigners sitting together outside his dwelling. The policeman approaches them and asks what has been going on. The villager, much to the surprize of Geertz and his wife, explains in great detail to the policeman that they are two famous anthropology professors from America, studying Bali with the permission of the local government; and that they have been discussing the local culture with him all afternoon. The policeman retreats, too amazed to utter another word, and a short time later so too do the equally dumbfounded anthropology professors.

The next day brings about a complete change in their position. People speak to them. In fact everyone goes out of their way to engage them in conversation, and ask for a recounting of their experience of the day before. They are asked why they simply did not stay where they were, pull out their papers and protest their innocence and non-involvement. They are treated as members of the village, rather than outsiders. They are complimented for their show of solidarity, although Geertz confides to the reader that their joining with the fleeing spectators was more a result of cowardice than bravado. They are also teased for their inelegant style of running; but for the Balinese being teased is a sign of being accepted.

The parallels between Geertz' position and that of a *knowledge practitioner* (however defined) investigating a new organizational context are readily apparent. They each have a form of authority derived from a hierarchical source, but this does not guarantee acceptance; and even acceptance is hardly sufficient for gaining real insight into the context and characters involved. There is a barrier to any interaction, and a simultaneous stance of complete indifference coupled with intense interest in the nature and characteristics of the outsiders and their objectives. For Mr and Mrs Geertz the barriers were removed in dramatic fashion. The possibility of a series of occurrences such as those that surrounded the cockfight is perhaps rather low in more mundane circumstances, and may not necessarily be very welcome by any of the participants.

What the episode does show, however, is that certain transitions are necessary for 'outsiders' to gain some insight into unfamiliar systems; and that such transitions are not necessarily amenable to 'rational' or 'instrumental' manipulation. Even had Geertz had an inkling of the role of the cockfight in the Balinese context, there was no way that he could have initiated the series of occurrences that took place. Indeed he readily admits that only in the aftermath of the cockfight, and the access this gave him to the village, did he gain a real understanding of the role played by the fight, and more particularly by the betting.

What Geertz' experience does begin to demonstrate is that some form of dramatic incident - or set of incidents - may well illuminate the complexities of a context or system far better than any 'detailed analysis'. This is hardly surprizing since at such points of 'rupture' people will be unguarded or unprepared, and so their responses may well be less inhibited by convention and other constraints - social, cultural, organizational.

Those writers who assume that the nature of business processes and tacit knowledge is simply amenable to rational analysis, discourse and participation between and among all parties fail to account for the sorts of barriers that Geertz encounters. I am not suggesting that similar incidents should be provoked or precipitated, but I do want to suggest that understanding alien systems - village, sub-culture, or organization - takes different forms, and that some levels of understanding may not be amenable to outsiders. *Knowledge practitioners* will have to recognize the limitations of their position, accept the *non-rational* aspects of knowledge contexts, and adapt their practices and analyses accordingly.

To being with, there must be recognition of a range of understanding. This range might be thought of as extending from an analysis of *rules*, *routines*, *regulations* through *events* and *effects* to full scale *dramas*, similar to the one that opened up the Balinese experience to Geertz. Rules, routines, and regulations will tend to provide understanding in terms of structures, with perhaps some hint of function. In general, however, focusing on this level will tend towards a formal and static view of a context. It is also closely related to the idea that intelligence is a matter of following rules: A view associated with Herbert Simon, potently and convincingly dismantled by the critique of Dreyfus and Dreyfus [18]. Contexts cannot be fully grasped simply by studying the rules that actors follow, or say they follow. Again this resonates with Giddens' point about actors using stocks of knowledge to explain their actions, but this is only 'partly discursive', with some aspects being embedded in 'practical consciousness'.

Analysis of events and their accompanying effects provides a less static view; although there is still the danger of lapsing into functional hierarchies; precisely the sorts of functional rigidity that BPR set out to subvert. But it must be pointed out that this sort of analysis and abstraction is often strongly resisted by analysts, as can be seen in their use of methodologies that attempt to provide approaches precisely for this type of model.

A combined study that seeks to account both for rules and events will go some way to reach an understanding; but the Geertz example indicates that more dramatic incidents may ultimately open up far more of a context to an outsider. Only in such *dramas* is there the full richness of a dynamic view of a system; albeit episodic and tending towards anecdote. This may possibly provide a series of interesting narratives, but at an indeterminate level of generalization.

Across the three levels there needs to be a balance between the generic, static and rather formal rule-oriented aspect, and the narrative-based and specific dramatic one. These facets can be seen as ways of gradually coming to an understanding of different levels of a culture, such as those mentioned by Trompenaars and Hampden-Turner [19]. They offer a model of three levels of culture.

- The outer layer - consisting of artefacts and products; the most explicit and amenable of the three;
- the inner layer - constituted from norms and values - 'the mutual sense of what is right and wrong', and what is good and bad;
- the innermost layer - the basic assumptions and core beliefs.

The first two layers are important, and may well be the resources that actors draw upon to explain and justify their actions and accomplishments. Process modelling and knowledge management must focus on these; but this is not sufficient, and the innermost layer must somehow be uncovered and rendered amenable to study. By definition the innermost layer will be resistant to such analysis. The conventional - rationalistic and instrumentalist - techniques simply will not lend themselves to exposing these features in a domain. They may only become amenable at times of crisis or drama, and it is here that much of what the knowledge management writers describe as 'tacit knowledge' - similar to Giddens' *practical consciousness* - may well reside.

Geertz puts the matter succinctly when he states that investigating cultures at this level is a case of *social semantics*, not social mechanics (p448); i.e. we are firmly embedded in the realm of meaning, not mastery. Furthermore he stresses that the narratives around the cockfight show the Balinese telling a story about themselves to themselves; and this aspect is largely omitted from current ideas about knowledge management with its overly and overtly rationalist concept of knowledge about knowledge. To comprehend any context requires the full range of these perspectives, but this is not to argue that 'comprehension' is the same as participation or membership. Geertz does not become a Balinese village member; nor a member of one of the four factions in the village.

It is not being suggested that 'outsiders' have to immerse themselves so completely in the context that they become members or participants. On the other hand, maybe knowledge practitioners need to take more heed of anthropological and other practices - e.g. soft systems and other OR methods - that do indeed stress something along these lines when they talk about becoming one of the 'problem owners', or 'problem-context owners'. It is surely important that there is some recognition of this paradox at the heart of any truly human-centred attempts to gain insight into the *knowledge practices* of others.

What I am stressing is that we have constantly to battle to overcome the tendency to remain at levels of analysis that are based around static structures - looking for rules, regulations, roles. This limitation is not always evident and easy to overcome as our use of language tends to push us in this direction - well it certainly does in English.

In order to draw out the full implications of knowledge management or knowledge *engineering*[1]processes we have constantly to stress the process aspects; and this is not as easy as stressing the structural ones. Models tend to accentuate the static. It is more difficult to model dynamic aspects; and even if a specific person can produce such a model to their satisfaction, it is likely that others will undermine its dynamic aspects in their use or interpretation of the model. DFDs, Petri-nets, State Transition Diagrams, Action diagrams, Use Cases; all have been heralded as breakthroughs in grasping some of these complexities. But in practical application most people fail to construct or use them correctly. CRC cards and scenarios work a little better, and this may well be because they are based on something close to the dramatic aspect mentioned earlier. Perhaps this is why people can often model and communicate around the dynamic/process aspects of a context once they have spent some time looking at it in this fashion.

5 Deep Play

Some of the most interesting aspects that Geertz actually discovers about cockfighting are connected with the gambling and betting that surrounds the activity itself. Indeed he quickly finds that the spectacle of the fight is secondary to the betting. To understand the importance of the betting, Geertz introduces the concept of 'deep play' into his analysis.

---

[1] See [20] for an outline of the argument why 'engineering' may not be an appropriate or useful term in this and related contexts.

'Deep play' is a term used by the 18th century English Utilitarian philosopher Jeremy Bentham in his work 'The Theory of Legislation'. He sought to establish a fully rational basis for legislation, and defined 'deep play' as betting where the stakes are so high that it is actually irrational for anyone to participate. If you bet half of what you own on a bet at odds of 1:1 (evens), then the risk of losing far outweighs any possible gain: Think of doing the same with half of your house.

Bentham actually wanted such 'immoral behaviour' made illegal. Yet Geertz discovers that the Balinese regularly engage in this form of betting - what he calls 'centre betting'. This is because such behaviour is bound up with status, honour, dignity and respect. The money is still important, but it is not the only measure of things. There is an over-riding sense of importance - of **meaningfulness** - to the betting. It is done very publicly. As Geertz notes, the bravado of staking such large amounts is literally 'putting one's cock on the line'; and the word 'cock' in Balinese has the same wide set of meanings as it does in English. The cockfight is actually what Goffman would call 'a status bloodbath'.

What Geertz shows is that if one tries to understand the Balinese practices of betting in a Benthamite (rationalistic) manner, then one will fail to grasp its essential aspects; one has to move from Bentham's realm of 'utility' to Weber's one of 'meaning'. This has such obvious significance for knowledge management, that its ramifications ought to be a central aspect of any associated practices.

The issue is not one of an outsider 'dissecting' a complex set of practices into a base notation of simple actions and beliefs, that can be used as some universal yardstick against which everything can be assessed. We are not in the realm of measurement and mechanism; we are in the realm of meaning, interpretation, dialogue and understanding. This is a critical point to be borne in mind for those of us involved in knowledge management and process analysis.

This point is clearly and forcibly made by Geertz - the involuntary participation in the drama of the Balinese cockfight was indispensable to his later access to the village. We may not always be able to arrange dramas of this kind; and so must always be aware of the partial nature of our 'findings' - partial in the sense both of being incomplete and of being biased or slanted.

6 Chinese Encyclopaedias - From Anthropology to Archaeology

How does all this relate to Chinese encyclopaedias? In his essay 'The Analytical Language of John Wilkins', Borges writes of the encyclopaedia 'discovered' by John Wilkins

> On those remote pages it is written that animals are divided into (a) those that belong to the Emperor, (b) embalmed ones, (c) those that are trained, (d) suckling pigs, (e) mermaids, (f) fabulous ones, (g) stray dogs, (h) those that are included in this classification, (i) those that tremble as if they were mad, (j) innumerable ones, (k) those drawn with a very fine camel's hair

brush, (l) others, (m) those that have just broken a flower vase, (n) those that resemble flies from a distance.[2]

This extract has appeared in the knowledge management literature, used by several authors to make a range of different points. Marc Demarest notes that although it may look bizarre to us, 'it must have worked for the Chinese'. Demarest, like many other writers on knowledge management, tries to circumvent the philosophical issue of 'what constitutes knowledge?' He distinguishes between scientific and philosophical knowledge and commercial knowledge, defining the latter as follows - 'good commercial knowledge is knowledge that works ... Its truth value is incidental to its ability to generate desirable commercial performances' (p3). Demarest stresses that his discussion is only focused on 'commercial knowledge', distinct from scientific and philosophical knowledge, and that this is a form of knowledge that has pragmatic value, with criteria based around *performance* rather than correctness or validity.

Following the extract from Borges, this raises more questions than it answers. If we look closely at the extract from the Chinese Encyclopaedia we can see there is no way that the classification can have 'worked' at a rational level, since it is inherently paradoxical. For instance look at categories (h) and (l). In any case why should the encyclopaedia be classed as commercial knowledge? Surely the concept of commercial knowledge as a distinct category is one that only begins to make some sense to us in the 1990s, and would have been totally alien to the authors of the text itself?

This is not to take some lofty view that consigns the extract and the encyclopaedia to the tray marked 'interesting but not really useful'. Demarest may well be correct to note that the classification was a useful way of ordering things for the people concerned; but that really misses a number of key points.

- Any written text may not accurately represent what was actually 'used' by the people themselves. After all cockfighting was illegal in Bali, but there certainly was a written statute banning it.
- The entry may well summarize what people believed, even though their real actions and underlying assumptions were entirely different. They may not have been dismayed by the paradox and discontinuities, just as people in the UK continue to play the lottery twice a week, even though the odds are so dramatically stacked against them. In fact what they are really doing is paying a highly regressive form of tax.
- Wilkins may have misunderstood what was actually written down in the first place, and/or the process of translation from an ideographic representation to a character-based one may have resulted in a mistaken interpretation of the original. (This is a critical point for IT-based 'solutions' for knowledge management.)
- The 'data' - the Chinese ideographs - may have been drawn with an entirely different set of meanings than those derived by Wilkins or later readers.
- Borges may well have made up the entire extract; quite likely given his genius for imaginative writing. In this case Wilkins may never have existed; or if he did, he may never have discovered such an encyclopaedia. This is not to say that such an

[2]The essay can be found in Borges' collection *Other Inquisitions*; but I have taken the extract directly from Foucault's text, where it is used with out giving the exact reference. I am grateful to Marc Demarest for supplying me with the full reference.

encyclopaedia does not exist - it may well do so; but no-one may actually have discovered it. Here we have an instance where the information exists, but perhaps without any data.
- The logical paradoxes may only exist in particular cognitive systems. In others, categories such as (h) and (l) may happily and consistently co-exist.

All of which means that extracts such as that from Borges are double-edged when introduced into discussions of knowledge management. We have to recognize that Borges' irony can be understood to apply equally to ourselves. Our classifications, so 'obvious' and 'commonplace' that they are hardly noticeable, may appear equally strange and contradictory to others; and if that is the case why should these 'others' only be those from later times and far off places? What do people from other cultures think of our problems with categories of data, information, and knowledge? What might people in future make of such discussions?

Crucially, to what extent are our current debates around 'knowledge' - object, process, technology, social, etc. - critically influenced by the terminology itself? After all in French there are at least two words associated with knowledge and knowing - *savoir* and *connaitre*; German also offers a number of words that are often translated simply as 'knowledge'. Other languages may well exhibit similar ranges of words, and it may be that some of the difficult conceptual issues of knowledge management simply disappear if we move away from the English terminology.

Again, here we have a clear basis for feeling uneasy about mechanistic approaches to knowledge management. Such 'recipes' for knowledge management fail to take account of this 'definite strangeness'. But this should not be taken to mean that knowledge management is an impossibility. On the contrary it locates knowledge management as a critical, social endeavour. Moreover it means that we have to move beyond Davenport and Prusak's concern that we simply distance it from the technology. We must positively move towards existing work in linguistics, philosophy and cultural theory.

Perhaps the most notable use of the extract from Borges was by the cultural theorist Michel Foucault in his book 'Les Mots et Les Choses' - in English published as 'The Order of Things' [21].[3] Foucault argued that the very categories of knowledge were not something that arose from the 'mercy of chance'

> ... what if empirical knowledge, at a given time and in a given culture, *did* possess a well-defined regularity? ... If errors (and truths), the practice of old beliefs, including not only genuine discoveries, but also the most naïve notions, obeyed, at a given moment, the laws of a certain code of knowledge?' (p ix)

Foucault's point is that knowledge is not something that simply grows as extra items are added to an amorphous pile. The imagery of a 'stock of knowledge' is misleading. The way we see things and demarcate between them is culturally bound. The 'things' are themselves part of a far more complex set of cultural cognitive **processes**.

Foucault subtitled his book, 'an archaeology of knowledge', and perhaps the idea of archaeology applied to knowledge artefacts affords a critical insight that might help us guard against the tendency to mechanistic - and technology-centred - views of knowledge management: Instead pushing us firmly towards the social and cultural bases of knowledge. This in turn may cause us to revise or even reject the concept of

[3] This was not a mistranslation, there were already at least two other books in print with the title 'Words and Things'.

knowledge *management*, since our goal becomes one more concerned with achieving insight rather than that of 'making better use of knowledge resources'.[4] The irony is that we may be slowly moving toward the recognition that in order to achieve the latter we really do have to move towards the former, and that quick-fix technological 'solutions' are inadequate and inappropriate. Anthropology and archaeology may well be two of the most important resources for effective knowledge management.

References

1. Adapted from 'Two Separate Tracks for Re-Engineering's Engineers' Ronald E. Yates, Chicago Tribune Knight-Ridder/Tribune Business News
2. Schön, D.A.: 'Generative Metaphor: A perspective on problem setting in social policy, in Ortony, A. (ed): Metaphor and Thought, 2nd edition, CUP, Cambridge (1993)
3. Reddy, M.: 'The conduit Metaphor', in Ortony, A. (ed): see above
4. Giddens, A.: A Contemporary Critique of Historical Materialism, Macmillan, London (1981)
5. Murray, P., and Meyers, A.: 'The Facts About Knowledge', Knowledge Management Survey, www.info-strategy.com (1999)
6. Davenport, T.H., and Prusak, L.: Working Knowledge - How Organizations Manage What They Know, Harvard Business School Press, Cambridge, Mass (1998)
7. Zack, M.H.: 'Managing Explicated Knowledge', www.cba.neu.edu /~mzack/articles/kmarch/kmarch.htm, due to appear in Sloan Management Review, Spring 1999
8. Demarest, M.: 'Knowledge Management: An introduction', www.hevanet.com/demarest/marc (1997)
9. Schultze, U.: 'A Confessional Account of an Ethnography about Knowledge Work', internet version of paper to be published in MIS Quarterly
10. Meehan, J.: 'Knowledge Management: A Case of Quelling the Rebellion?', Critical Management Studies Conference, UMIST July 1999
11. Nonaka, I. and Takeuchi, H.: The Knowledge-Creating Company, OUP, Oxford (1995)
12. Davenport, T.: 'The Fad that Forgot People', Fast Company, (1995)
13. Bryant, A and Evans, A.: 'OO Oversold: Obscure Objects of Desire', Information & Software Technology, volume 36, no 1, (1994)
14. Boisot, M.: Information and Organization: The Manager as Anthropologist, HarperCollins, London (1994)
15. Suchman, L.: Plans and Situated Actions, CUP, Cambridge (1987)
16. Zuboff, S.: In the Age of the Smart Machine, Heinemann, London (1988)
17. Geertz, C.: 'Deep Play - Notes on the Balinese Cockfight', in C Geertz, The Interpretation of Cultures, Basic Books, New York (1975)
18. Dreyfus, H., and Dreyfus, S.: Mind Over Machine, Free Press, (1986)
19. Trompenaars, F., and Hampden-Turner, C.: Brearley, New York (1997)
20. Bryant, A.: 'It's Engineering Jim, but not as we know it: Software Engineering – solution to the software crisis or part of the problem', in Proceedings of 22nd International Conference of Software Engineering, ACM & IEEE, New York (2000), 77-86
21. Foucault, M.: The Order of Things, Tavistock, London (1970)
22. Cilliers, P.: Complexity & Postmodernism, Routledge, London (1998)

[4] This may in some ways parallel the move away from rule-based AI to a network perspective that engages with issues such as complexity and structural aspects of knowledge and meaning - see [22] for an excellent overview of these issues.

Using Problem-Solving Models to Design Efficient Cooperative Knowledge-Management Systems Based on Formalization and Traceability of Argumentation

Myriam Lewkowicz and Manuel Zacklad

Laboratoire Tech-CICO
Université de Technologie de Troyes
12, rue Marie Curie BP 2060
10010 Troyes Cédex
France
myriam.lewkowicz@univ-troyes.fr
manuel.zacklad@univ-troyes.fr

Abstract. We present here a groupware (MEMO-Net) based on a model (DIPA), which uses and simplifies the concepts of Problem-Solving methods. This model comes from a review of Design Rationale formalisms that gave rise to the ABRICo formalism. MEMO-Net enables exchange structuring in order to improve dialog quality and reusability. MEMO-Net prefigures a new KM approach, named "cooperative KM" where we propose virtual work environments for groups that will consist in new "coordination mechanisms".

1. Introduction

In accordance with Zacklad and Grundstein [17], we can classify knowledge management (KM) approaches in three complementary categories: top-down, bottom-up and cooperative. In the first one, models are used with experts to formalize their knowledge (MKSM for example). In the second one, huge corpus are memorized and formalized afterwards (text-mining methods). And in the third one, we consider that organizations' critical knowledge comes within a collective competence that is not enough or badly formalized.

Groupwares generally use two kinds of models to structure interactions and to manage knowledge in organizations: some of these models allow a relationship standardization instead of others that focus on know-how standardization [18].

Among models based on relationship standardization, we can quote the famous Speech-Act theory from Winograd and Flores [15] and its derivative [6]. These models allow a more efficient management of contractual processes in firms. They fit in KM strategies focused on "commitment traceability". On the other hand, models used for decisions' traceability in the scope of know-how standardization are closer to Design Rationale (DR) researches. In these studies, models are decision oriented. We can quote QOC [9] or IBIS [1].

R. Dieng and O. Corby (Eds.): EKAW 2000, LNAI 1937, pp. 288-295, 2000.

In a previous study [8], we came to the conclusion about the difficulty of applying some DR models in complex collective design situations. In this paper we propose to use problem-solving methods to organize the traceability of decision-making processes, particularly in design situations. Problem-solving methods are going to help the formalization of argumentation in collective problem solving situations.

2. CSCW and Knowledge Management

Our approach comes within the scope of cooperative approaches where one considers that crucial knowledge is held by groups. If we want to capitalize on this exchanged knowledge, we have to focus on existing communication processes in the firm. Two approaches are possible faced with this problem: Memorizing all the interactions and then building a thesaurus on the base of the corpus or playing a part during the communication process by a priori structuring information.

The second option is the one that we have chosen. This interest in *a priori* structuring of problem-solving processes in order to guarantee exploitation is not recent. In CSCW (Computer-Supported Cooperative Work) research, several authors [3], [4] have already expressed the wish to switch from a "object-centered paradigm to a "process-centered" paradigm. In the latter, designers' interaction (that is to say questions, decisions and conversations that form the elaboration environment of the objects) would be memorized as well as objects and design process results. This paradigm is the one of DR researches, of which experimentations can be classified in two groups: *A posteriori* DR whose drawbacks are the need of a project memory leader during the project and meetings with all the people of the project after the project [7]. Or DR *following the current*, with tools such as QuestMap for example [10].

Our approach is near the second group although we have shown [8] that DR models are pertinent for some situations but are sometimes far from real design situations in which we construct step by step a solution instead of choosing or sorting several options. Our aim is to propose more realistic models from a cognitive point of view but not too far from concrete design situations which people are confronted with. In order to approach the cognitive dimension of reasoning we propose to use problem-solving method concepts from knowledge engineering.

3. Problem-Solving Models and Design Rationale

Actually, we could say that Design Rationale models have neglected the "information" phase of Simon's decision-making process [13], and have only taken into account the solutions selection phase. Models from Artificial Intelligence do not have this fault. This link with problem-solving methods seems to us a natural evolution in our researches of more realistic Design Rationale models suited to the complexity of real projects.

We have then built a model called DIPA (from the French words Données, Interprétations, Propositions, Accord, meaning facts, interpretations, propositions, agreement) where problem-solving models replace decision-making processes, even complex ones.

The model comes in two forms, according to the situations that lead the actors to give priority to either analysis or synthesis processes (for example as in KADS methodology) [14].

This reference to problem-solving models allows the integration of an important knowledge category that was not taken into account in the two previous models, the "problem data". In the DIPA model, the reasoning progresses in three major steps:

- a problem description step plus collecting of data, considered as symptoms in analysis situations and as needs in synthesis situations
- an abstraction step going from the collecting of problem data to their interpretation corresponding to a possible cause in analysis situations, and to a functionality in synthesis situations;
- an implementation step that going from an interpretation (cause or functionality) to the elaboration of a proposition that is a corrective action removing the symptom's cause (analysis) or the means suitable for the expressed functionality (synthesis)

The fact that we had to present both analysis and synthesis models to designers teams may seem amazing. Actually, it might appear natural at first glance to propose only synthesis models and their variants (routine design, configuration...). But our practical experience of design meetings revealed us that analysis activities are frequent. For example, as soon as a prototype has been developed, its function analysis will give important information that will be reintroduced in the process of solution finding.

These observations are also in accordance with cognitive ergonomic psychology [5] results that teach us that design situations in the organizational sense in fact generate two distinct phases of activity: solution generation and then evaluation of these solutions. The first corresponds to synthesis problems in a KADS sense and is close to design models in this method. The second corresponds to analysis problems whose diagnosis models are well-known.

This idea of a unique model (figure 1) to represent the two types of activity is quite close to some interpretations of the heuristic classification of Clancey [2]. According to Zacklad and Fontaine [16], in both types of situation, there is both exploitation of knowledge from previous solved cases, and construction of an original solution. This solution is a proof or a justification in analysis case and a constraints-compatible approximate solution in synthesis cases.

Whereas, in the DIPA model, the abstraction and implementation inference steps are two symmetrical aspects of the same heuristic reasoning, applicable both in analysis and synthesis. In abstraction cases, for example, the point of view about any one system will change according to whether the symptoms or their causes are considered most important, or even the requirements of internal system functions.

The formalism used to describe DIPA was inspired by KADS [12], [14] but does not strictly follow the KADS conventions as to how to represent inference structures.

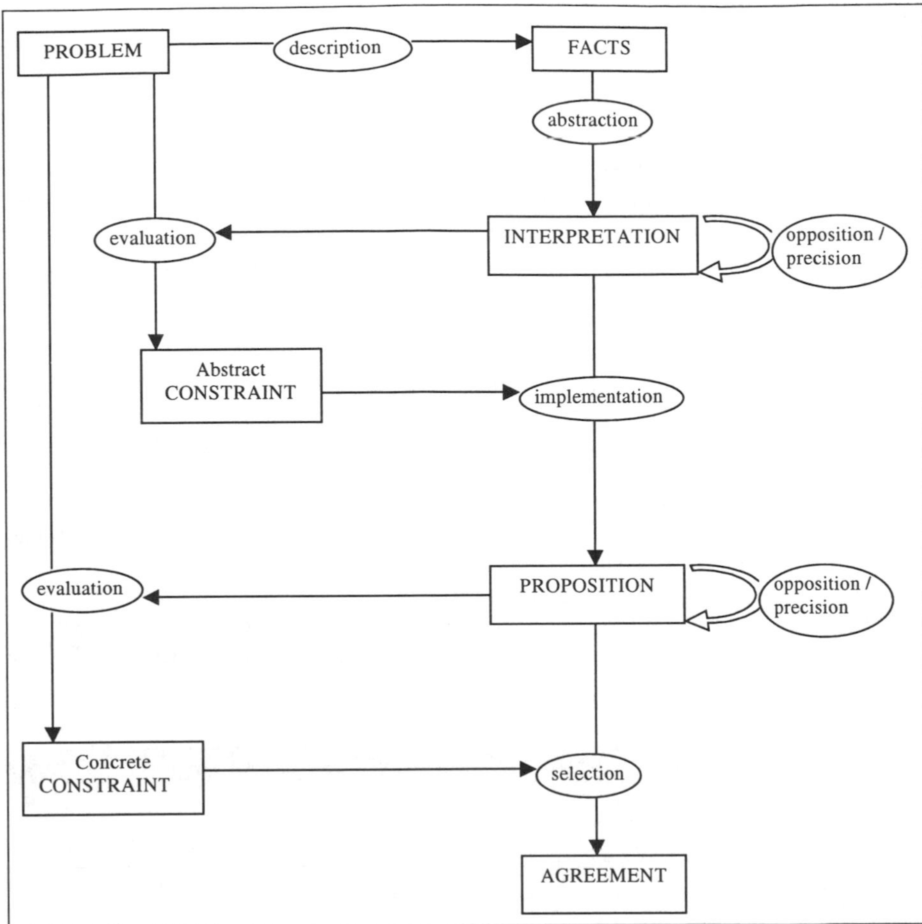

DIPA	DIPA synthesis	DIPA analysis
Problem	Goal	Malfunction
Fact	Requirement	Symptom
Interpretation	Functionality	Cause
Abstract constraint	Constraint	Constraint
Proposition	Means	Corrective action
Concrete constraint	Constraint	Constraint
Agreement	Choice	Choice

Fig.1: DIPA, a heuristic model of design reasoning for analysis and synthesis and its implementation for synthesis and analysis activities (table)

MEMO-Net

Presentation

We implemented the DIPA model to build the MEMO-Net groupware. This system consists of two modules, one for synthesis phases (named "design" in the interface), and the other for analysis phases (named "diagnosis" in the interface). Its goal is to allow a team to solve problems met during meetings by alternating the two types of activity on a cooperative way. The exchange structure allows both to guide the solution process and to organize the arguments, particularly in argument capitalization aspects.

In the diagnosis module (Fig.2), members of the team identify a dysfunction and evoke symptoms, causes or corrective actions. In design (Fig.3), once the goal is known, the actors evoke requirements, functionalities and means. To contribute, people click on signs indicating a malfunction, symptom, cause, and corrective action and then create the corresponding forms.

Contributions are classified chronologically or according to DIPA model categories, or to the authors' names, their roles, or their department.

When users have already discussed a problem, one of their propositions may be submitted to others, in order to collect their opinion and take a decision. This last step corresponds to "selection" inference of DIPA model, which enables a definitive agreement on the best possible solution.

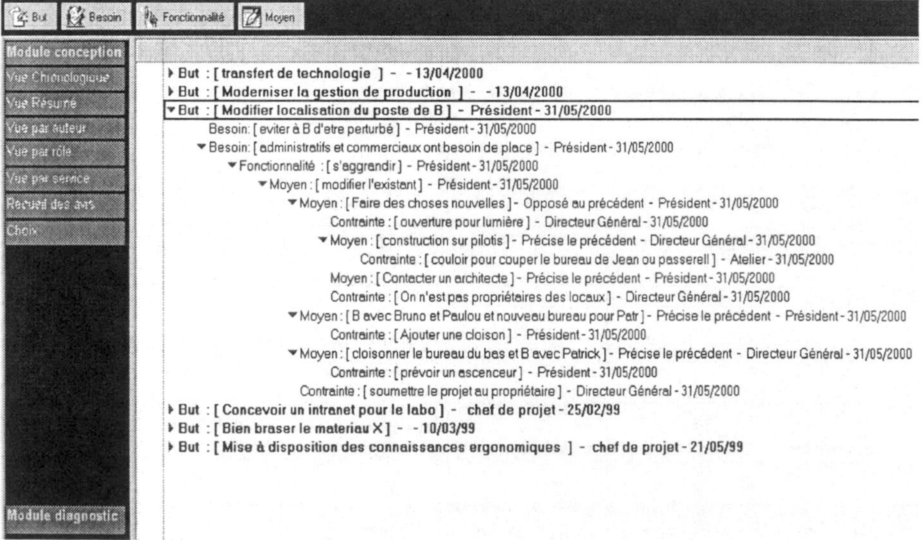

Fig. 2 : A chronological view of a design phase

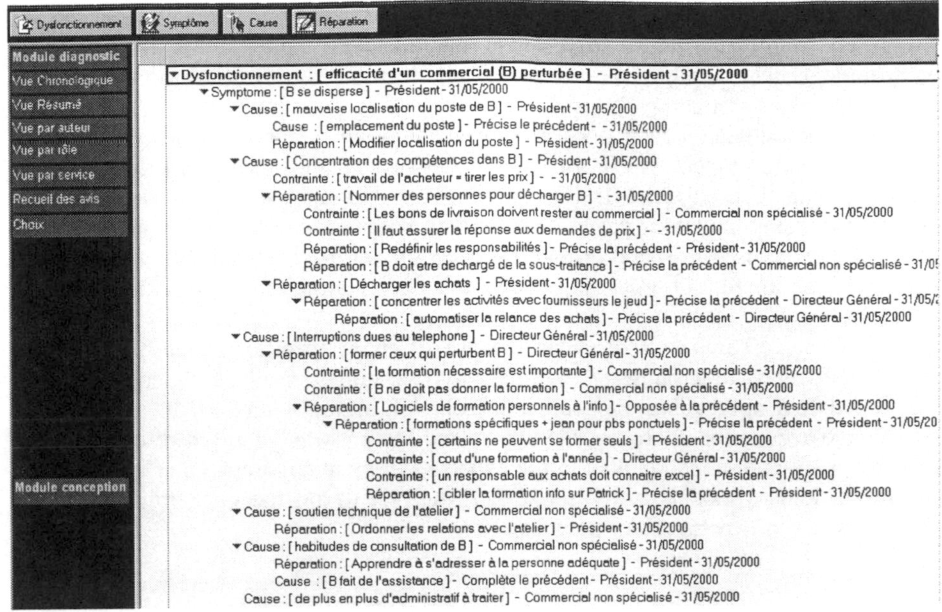

Fig.3 : A chronological view of a diagnosis phase

Experimentations

We have conducted a first experimentation of MEMO-Net with engineer students. They have used MEMO-Net synchronously to solve a familiar problem in their university: the choice of the courses each year. Some groups have solved the problem with a forum and other groups with MEMO-Net. All the students have filled in a questionnaire at the end of the experimentation. We try to prove that MEMO-Net improve collective cognitive performances. That means that the collective building of answers and solutions to a problem with MEMO-Net will be of better quality than with a forum.

We are going to compare the number of proposed solutions and the understanding of the reasoning by experts and to evaluate the quality of the solutions by showing them to experts.

We are also going to experiment soon MEMO-Net in crises meetings where quality experts debate on problems coming from Information System defaults. We will lead the problem solving process by using MEMO-Net.

5. Conclusion

The groupware MEMO-Net prefigures a new KM approach, based on a capture of exchanged arguments during activities following the current. In this approach, named "cooperative KM", we think that the best manner to implement a KM process is to propose virtual work environments that will consist in new "coordination mechanisms" for these groups [11]. These virtual work environments have to be structured to offer a cooperation aid. This aid will incite actors to use these environments. They enable them to trace exchanges and to re-exploit more easily the knowledge when similar problems arise.

When one implements a "cooperative KM" step, an important stake is to identify problem-solving models which will enable the structuring of the work environment for the group. Until then, MEMO-Net used the DIPA model, which was a very general reasoning model (as generic as common KADS models). Future results would confirm that the use of general problem solving models is richer than the use of little-structured forum for the exploration of possible solutions and the re-use of these solutions.

Our future research will focus on the use of more specific models of problem-solving situations in groupware. In this way, we aim to use the synergy between traditional KM approaches and our approach. (cf. figure 4 and 5). In a traditional knowledge acquisition approach, the expert and the knowledge engineer co-construct a problem-solving model applied to the expertise domain (figure 4). Our aim is to re-use these domain models in tools like MEMO-Net to aid the cooperative problem solving between experts and/or novices.

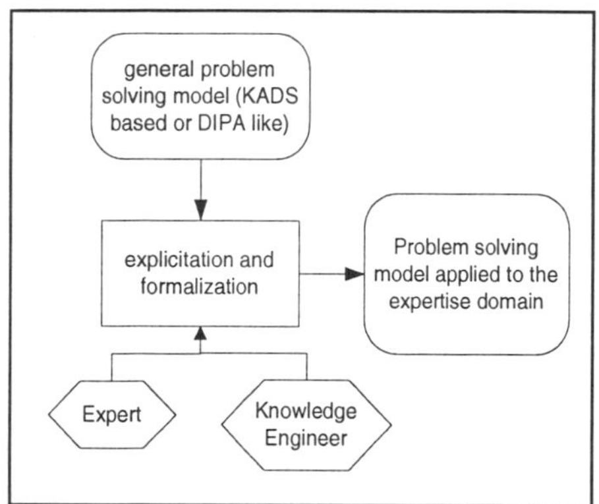

Fig. 4 : traditional KM model

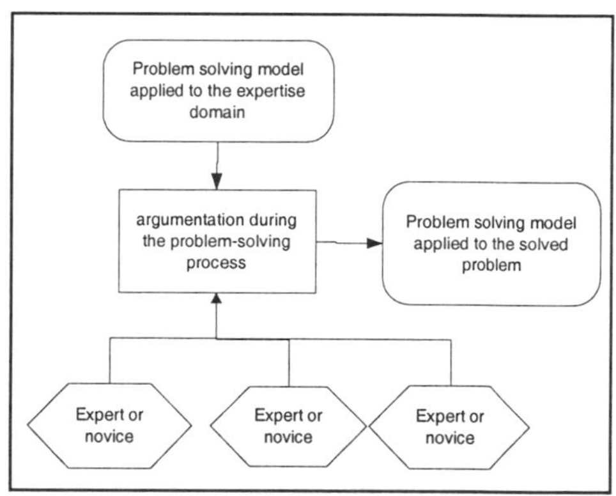

Fig. 5 : cooperative KM model

6. References

1. Burgess-Yakemovic, K.C. and Conklin, E.J. (1990). Report on a Development Project Use of an Issue-Based Information System, in Halasz, F. (Ed.) (1990). *CSCW 90: Proceedings of the Conference on Computer-Supported Cooperative Work*. Los Angeles, Oct. 7-10, 1990. Association for Computing Machinery.
2. Clancey, W. (1985). *Heuristic Classification*, Artificial Intelligence Journal, 27, pp. 289-350, 1985.
3. Conklin, E.J. (1993). Capturing Organizational Memory, in Baecker, R. M. (Ed.) *Readings in Groupware and Computer-Supported Cooperative Work*, Morgan Kaufmann Publishers, Inc.

4. Conklin, E.J. and Burgess-Yakemovic, KC. (1996). A Process-Oriented Approach to Design Rationale, in Moran, T. P. and Carroll, J. M. (Ed.) *Design Rationale Concepts, Techniques and Use*, Lawrence Erlbaum Associates.
5. Darses, F. (1994). *Gestion des contraintes dans la résolution des problèmes de conception*. Thèse de doctorat, Spécialité Psychologie Cognitive. Paris, Université de Paris 8.
6. De Michelis, G. & Grasso, M.A. (1994); Situating conversations within the language/action perspective: the Milan Conversation Model; Proceedings of CSCW'94 Conference, Chapel Hill, Noth Carolina, October 22-26, pp. 89-100.
7. Karcenty, L. (1999), Capitaliser le contexte des décisions en conception : pourquoi et comment ?, in Zacklad, M., Grundstein, M. (Eds.) (1999). *Système d'Information pour la capitalisation des connaissances : tendances récentes et approches industrielles*, Hermès, à paraître.
8. Lewkowicz, M., Zacklad, M. (1998). A formalism for the rationalization of decision-making processes in complex collective design situations, *Procceedings of COOP*. Cannes, may 1998.
9. MacLean, A., Young, R.M., Bellotti, V.M.E., Moran P. (1996). *Questions, Options and Criteria : Elements of Design Space Analysis*, in Moran, T. P. and Carroll, J. M. (Ed.) *Design Rationale Concepts, Techniques and Use*, Lawrence Erlbaum Associates.
10. *QuestMap™*, Group Decision Support Systems, 1000 Thomas Jefferson St. Suite 100, Washington, DC 20007, 1999.
11. Schmidt, K., Simone, C. (1996). Coordination mechanisms : Towards a conceptual foundation of CSCW systems design, JCSCW, vol. 5, no. 2-3.
12. Schreiber, G., Wielinga, B. (1993). *Model Construction*, in Schreiber, G., Wielinga, B., Breuker, J. (Eds.) *KADS a principled approach to knowledge-based system development*, Academic Press.
13. Simon, H.A., (1947) *Administrative Behavior,* trad. Fçse (1983) Administration et processus de décision, Economica.
14. Wielinga, B., Schreiber, G., Breuker, J. (1993). *Modelling Expertise*, in Schreiber, G., Wielinga, B., Breuker, J. (Eds.) *KADS a principled approach to knowledge-based system development*, Academic Press.
15. Winograd, T., Flores, F. (1986) Understanding Computers and Cognition, Addison-Wesley, USA.
16. Zacklad, M., Fontaine, D. (1996). *L'acquisition des connaissances classificatoires pour les systèmes à bases de connaissances*, in Aussenac-Gilles, N., Laublet, P., Reynaud, C. (Eds.) *Acquisition et Ingenierie des Connaissances*, Cepadues-Editions.
17. Zacklad, M., Grundstein, M. (Eds.). *Système d'Information pour la capitalisation des connaissances : tendances récentes et approches industrielles*, Hermès, 1999.
18. Zacklad, M. (2000) *La théorie des transactions intellectuelles : une approche gestionnaire et cognitive pour le traitement du COS,* Intellectica, numéro spécial sur le COS, à paraître.

Integrating Textual Knowledge and Formal Knowledge for Improving Traceability

Farid Cerbah[1] and Jérôme Euzenat[2]

[1] Dassault Aviation - DPR/DESA - 78, quai Marcel Dassault
92552 cedex 300 Saint-Cloud - France
farid.cerbah@dassault-aviation.fr

[2] Inria Rhône-Alpes - 655, avenue de l'Europe
38330 Monbonnot St Martin - France
Jerome.Euzenat@inrialpes.fr – http://www.inrialpes.fr/exmo/

Abstract. Knowledge engineering often concerns the translation of informal knowledge into a formal representation. This translation process requires support for itself and for its traceability. We pretend that inserting a terminological structure between informal textual documents and their formalization serves both of these goals. Modern terminology extraction tools support the formalization process where the terms are a first sketch of formalized concepts. Moreover, the terms can be used for linking the concepts and the pieces of texts. This is exemplified through the presentation of an implemented system.

1 Introduction

Knowledge management is concerned with the relationships between formal and informal knowledge. The informal knowledge is richer and familiar to any user while the formal one is more precise and necessary to the computer. Moreover, translating from informal to formal is a common task of knowledge acquisition and providing traceability information is a major requirement. Therefore, this task requires computational support.

Several attempts were made to provide tools supporting the linking of knowledge sources [8,14,11]. However, they provided only limited computational support. The links had to be established manually and were thus error-prone and time consuming. In the meantime, several works focused on the advantages of using corpus-based terminology extraction for supporting formal knowledge acquisition [3,1,2]. These contributions emphasize the central role of terminological resources in the mapping between informal text sources and formal knowledge bases.

We argue that technical terms can play a key role in traceability too. We put forth an architecture, centered around a terminology extraction and management tool, that enables to generate models from texts and navigate from one to the other through the terminological structure (§2). It has been fully implemented with existing software (§3) and provides high-level hypertext generation, browsing and model generation facilities.

R. Dieng and O. Corby (Eds.): EKAW 2000, LNAI 1937, pp. 296–303, 2000.

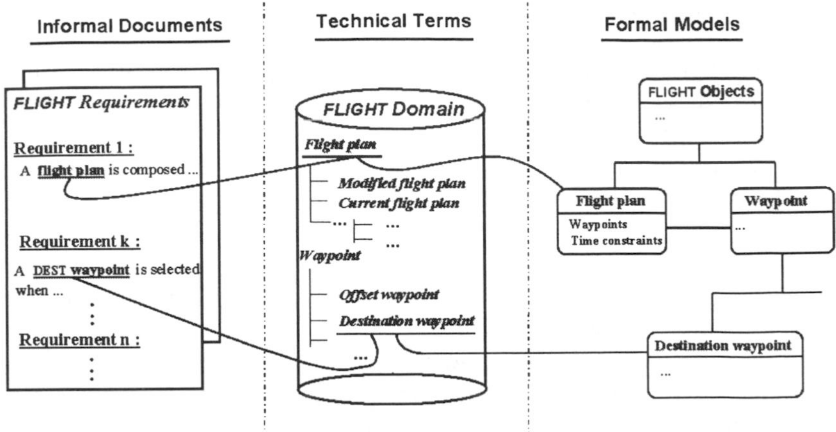

Fig. 1. Using terminological items to link textual requirements and object models

2 An Architecture for Traceability through Terminological Structures

When building a somewhat formal (or at least structured) repository from document sources, the concepts in the formal repository must be linked to their original sources in the texts. These traceability links are useful in many respects:

- Ensuring exhaustiveness: By following traceability links, the user or a program can easily identify the concepts which are not represented in the repository.
- Facilitating change propagation: At any time in the elaboration process, traceability information allows to find out the elements impacted by changes (upstream and downstream).
- Enhancing browsing capabilities of the overall repository, when traceability is established with hyperlinks.

In many information systems where both textual knowledge and formal knowledge are involved to describe related concepts, a terminological structure can play an intermediate role. Some of the technical terms found in the corpora represent concepts which will be subsequently introduced in the formal models. These terms can be seen as an intermediary level between the text found in documents and the formal models. (see figure 1).

In order to achieve both formalization and traceability, a system must articulate the following functions:

Terminology extraction. In technical domains, many precise and highly relevant concepts are linguistically represented by compound nouns. The multiword nature of the technical terms facilitates their automatic identification in texts. Relevant multi-word terms can be easily identified with high accuracy using partial syntactic analysis [3,9] or statistical processing [5] (or even both paradigms [6]). Terminology extraction techniques are used to automatically build term hierarchies that will play the intermediate role between documents and models.

Document and model indexing. The technical terms are used for indexing text fragments in the documents. Fine grained indexing, i.e paragraph level indexing, is required while most indexing systems used in information retrieval work at the document level. Besides, most descriptors used in this kind of indexing are multi-word phrases. The terms are also used for indexing the model fragments (classes, attributes...).

Hyperlink generation. The term-driven indexing of both texts and models with the same terminological structure is the basis of the hyperlink generation mechanisms. However, hyperlink generation should be controlled interactively, in the sense that the user should be able to exclude automatically generated links or add links that have not been proposed by the system.

Model generation. It is quite common that the concept hierarchies mirror the term hierarchies found in the documents. This property can be used to generate model skeletons which will be filled manually.

The integration of these functions within a single process results in a method for helping the acquisition and maintenance of formal knowledge from textual knowledge. It first extracts a terminological structure (which automatically indexes the document fragments). The terminological knowledge must be validated by the users which can generate a class taxonomy (also indexed by the terms).

3 A User Support Tool for Improving Traceability

The functions presented above are implemented by existing components (§3.1 and 3.2) which are linked in the appropriate way (§3.3).

3.1 Terminology Extraction with XTERM

XTERM [4] is a natural language processing tool that performs terminology extraction from French or English documents and offers high level browsing capabilities through the extracted data and the source documents. Starting with a document collection, XTERM scans all document building blocks (paragraphs, titles, figures, notes) in order to extract the text fragments. These word sequences are then prepared for linguistic processing.

The first linguistic processing step is part of speech (POS) tagging. XTERM uses a rule based tagger based on the Multex morphological parser [13]. POS tagging starts with a morphological analysis which assigns to each word its possible morphological realizations. Then, contextual disambiguation rules are applied to choose a unique realization for each word. At the end of this process, each word is unambiguously tagged.

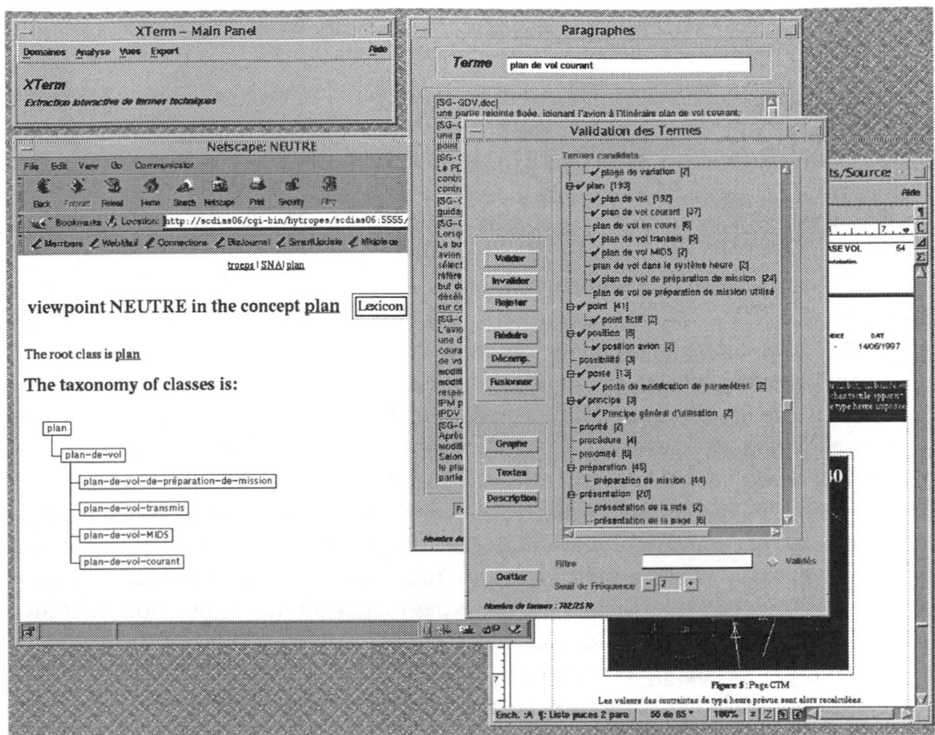

Fig. 2. The integrated system based on XTERM and TROEPS.

As already mentioned, the morpho-syntactic structure of technical terms follows quite regular formation rules which represent a kind of local grammar. For instance, many French terms can be captured with the pattern "*Noun Preposition (Article) Noun*". Such patterns can be formalized with finite state automata, where crossing conditions of the transitions are expressed in terms of morphological properties. To identify the potential terms, the automata are applied on the tagged word sequences. A new potential term is recognized each time a final state is reached. During this step, the extracted terms are organized hierarchically. For example, the term "*flight plan*" ("*plan de vol*" in figure 2) will have the term "*plan*" as parent and "*modified flight plan*" as a child in the hierarchy.

The candidate set obtained after this step is still too large. Additional filtering mechanisms are involved to reduce it, including grouping rules that detect term variants (e.g. "*Waypoint page*" instead of "*page of the waypoints*").

Additionally, XTERM provides the mechanisms for indexing and generating hyperlinks from technical terms to document fragments. Hyperlink generation is a selective process: To avoid overgeneration, the initial set of links systematically established by the system can be reduced by the user.

3.2 Knowledge Modeling with the TROEPS System

TROEPS [10,15] is an object-based knowledge representation system, i.e. a knowledge representation system inspired from both frame-based languages and object-oriented programming languages. It is used here for expressing the models.

An object is a set of field-value pairs associated to an identifier. The value of a field can be known or unknown, it can be an object or a value from a primitive type (e.g. character string, integer, duration) or a set or list of such. The objects are partitioned into disjoint concepts (an object is an instance of one and only one concept) which determine the key and structure of their instances. For example, the "*plan*" concept identifies a plan by its number which is an integer. The fields of a particular "*plan*" are its time constraint which must be a duration and its waypoints which must contain a set of instances of the "*waypoint*" concept.

Object-based knowledge representation provides various facilities for manipulating knowledge including filtering queries (which find objects of a concept satisfying field and attachment constraints), similarity queries (function of field values or attachment classes) involving a distance measure, value inference (through default values, procedural attachment, value passing or filtering), position inference (classification and identification) in which the possible positions of an object or a class in a taxonomy are computed.

TROEPS knowledge bases can be used as HTTP servers delivering the knowledge to the world-wide web. These knowledge servers enable knowledge base browsing and editing from a HTTP client. Moreover, the knowledge is linked to other sources and can be manipulated through knowledge-based operations (e.g. filtering or classification). Lastly, TROEPS offers an XML interface which allows to describe a whole knowledge base or to take specific actions on an existing knowledge base.

3.3 Communication between the Components

The communication between the linguistic processing environment and the model manager is bidirectional: Upon user request, XTERM can call TROEPS to generate class hierarchies from term hierarchies. Conversely, TROEPS can call XTERM to display the textual fragments related to a concept (via a technical term).

For instance, figure 3 illustrates the class generation process from a hierarchy of terms validated by the user (a hierarchy rooted in the term "*Plan*"). The class hierarchy constructed by TROEPS follows the hierarchy of the validated terms.

At the end of the generation process, the created classes are still linked to their corresponding terms, and so the terminology-centered navigation capabilities offered by XTERM are directly available from the TROEPS interface. As illustrated by figure 3, the TROEPS user has access to the multi-document view of the paragraphs where the term "*flight plan*" and its variants occur. From this view, the user can consult the source documents if required.

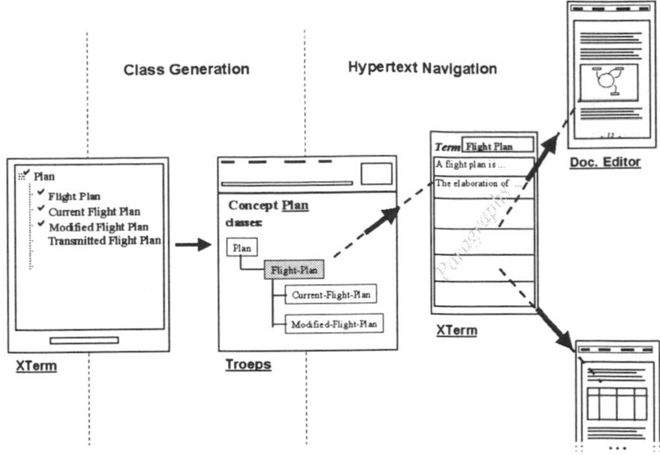

Fig. 3. Class generation and traceability through hyperlinks

Data exchange between XTERM and TROEPS is based on the TROEPS XML interface. XTERM sends to TROEPS short XML statements corresponding to the action performed by the user: creation of a new class or a subclass of an existing class and the annotation of a newly created class with textual elements such as the outlined definition of the term naming the class.

This XML interface has the advantage of covering the complete TROEPS model (thus it is possible to destroy or rename classes as well as adding new attributes to existing classes). Moreover, it is relatively typical of object-based representation languages so that it will be easy to have XTERM generating in other languages (e.g. XMI [12] or Ontolingua) which share the notion of classes and objects.

More details about this approach of XML-based knowledge modeling and exchange can be found in [7].

4 Related Work

Terminology acquisition is one of the most robust language processing technology [3,9,6] and previous works have demonstrated that term extraction tools can help to link informal and formal knowledge. The theoretical apparatus depicted in [3,1,2] provides useful guidelines for integrating terminology extraction tools in knowledge management systems. However, the models and implemented systems suffer from a poor support for traceability, restricted to the use of hyperlinks from concepts and terms to simple text files. On this aspect, our proposal is richer. The system handles real documents, in their original format, and offers various navigation and search services for manipulating "knowledge structures" (i.e., documents, text fragments, terms, concepts...). Moreover, the management services allow users to build their own hypertext network.

With regard to model generation, our system and Terminae [2] provide complementary services. Terminae resort to the terminologist to provide a very precise description of the terms from which a precise formal representation, in description logic, can be generated. In our approach, the system does not require users to provide additional descriptions before performing model generation from term hierarchies. Model generation strictly and thoroughly concentrates on hierarchical structures that can be detected at the linguistic level using term extraction techniques. For example, the hierarchical relation between the terms "*Flight Plan*" and "*Modified Flight Plan*" is identified by XTERM because of the explicit relations that hold between the linguistic structures of the two terms. Hence, such term hierarchies can be exploited for class generation. However, XTERM would be unable to identify the hierarchical relation that holds between the terms "*vehicle*" and "*car*" (which is the kind of relations that Terminae would try to identify in the formal descriptions). As a consequence, the formal description provided by our system is mainly a hierarchy of concepts while that of Terminae is more structural and the subsumption relations is computed by the description logic system.

The transition from informal to formal models is also addressed in [16]. The approach allows users to express the knowledge informally (within texts and hypertexts) and more formally (through semantic networks coupled with an argumentation system). In this modeling framework, knowledge becomes progressively more formal through small increments. The system, called "Hyper-object substrate", provides an active support to users by suggesting formal descriptions of terms. Its integrated nature enables to make suggestions while the users are manipulating the text, and to take advantage of already formalized knowledge to deduce new formalization steps. Our system, whose linguistic processing component is far more developed, could be coherently embedded in this comprehensive modeling framework.

5 Conclusion

We have presented a fully implemented system that produces class hierarchies out of textual documents, taking advantage of term hierarchies automatically built with natural language processing techniques. This system, by integrating document, terminology and knowledge management, provides traceability links through technical terms.

The system is robust but generates only taxonomies. Further work will address the automatic generation of more complex knowledge structures such as attributes and relations between classes.

This work has considered source documents with a low degree of formality: text in paragraphs. Further investigation will adress the problem of link generation from semi-structured sources. Link generation might significantly be improved when the sources are semi-structured. In particular, XML (and SGML) tagging provides useful information about the content structure that allows to accurately identify the potential link anchors.

Acknowledgments This work has been partially realized in the GENIE II program supported by the French ministry of education, research and technology (MENRT) and the DGA/SPAé.

References

1. N. Aussenac-Gilles, D. Bourigault, A. Condamines, and C. Gros. How can knowledge acquisition benefit from terminology ? In *Proceedings of the 9th Knowledge Acquisition for Knowledge Based System Workshop (KAW '95)*, Banff, Canada, 1995.
2. B. Biébow and S. Szulman. Une approche terminologique pour la construction d'ontologie de domaine à partir de textes : TERMINAE. In *Proceedings of 12th RFIA Conference*, pages 81–90, Paris, 2000.
3. D. Bourigault. Lexter, a terminology extraction software for knowledge acquisition from texts. In *Proceedings of the 9th Knowledge Acquisition for Knowledge Based System Workshop (KAW '95)*, Banff, Canada, 1995.
4. F. Cerbah. Acquisition de ressources terminologiques – description technique des composants d'ingénierie linguistique. Technical report, Dassault Aviation, 1999.
5. K. W. Church and P. Hanks. Word association norms, mutual information and lexicography. *Computational Linguistics*, 16(1):22–29, 1990.
6. B. Daille. Study and implementation of combined techniques for automatic extraction of terminology. In J.L. Klavans and P. Resnik, editors, *The Balancing Act: Combining Symbolic and Statistical Approaches to Language.* MIT Press, Cambridge, 1996.
7. J. Euzenat. XML est-il le langage de représentation de connaissance de l'an 2000 ? In *Actes des 6ème journées langages et modèles à objets*, pages 59–74, Mont Saint-Hilaire, CA, 2000.
8. B. Gaines and M. Shaw. Documents as expert systems. In Cambridge University Press, editor, *Proceedings of 9th British society expert systems conference*, pages 331–349, 1992.
9. J. S. Justeson and S. M. Katz. Technical terminology: Some linguistic properties and an algorithm for identification in text. *Natural Language Engineering*, 1(1):9–27, 1995.
10. O. Mariño, F. Rechenmann, and P. Uvietta. Multiple perspectives and classification mechanim in object-oriented representation. In *Proceeding of 9th ECAI*, pages 425–430, Stockholm, 1990.
11. P. Martin. *Exploitation de graphes conceptuels et de documents structurés et hypertextes pour l'acquisition de connaissances et la recherche d'information.* PhD thesis, Université de Nice-Sophia Antipolis, 1996.
12. OMG. XML Metadata Interchange (XMI). Technical report, OMG, 1998.
13. D. Petitpierre and G. Russell. MMORPH – The Multext Morphology Program. Technical report, Multext Deliverable 2.3.1, 1995.
14. F. Rechenmann. Building and sharing large knowledge bases in molecular genetics. In *Proceedings of 1st International Conference on Building and Sharing of Very Large-Scale Knowledge Bases*, pages 291–301, Tokyo, 1993.
15. Projet Sherpa. Troeps 1.2 reference manual. Technical report, Inria, 1998.
16. F. Shipman and R. McCall. Supporting incremental formalization with the hyper-object substrate. *ACM Transactions on information systems*, 17(2):199–227, 1999.

Knowledge Management by Reusing Experience

Sabine Delaître[1] and Sabine Moisan[2]

[1] ENSMP, Pôle Cindyniques, BP 207, F-06904 Sophia Antipolis, France
Sabine.Delaitre@cindy.cma.fr

[2] INRIA, projet Orion, BP 93, F-06902 Sophia Antipolis, France
Sabine.Moisan@sophia.inria.fr

Abstract. The paper presents a study of the use of past experience in emergency management with an application to Forest Fire-Fighting Management. Our objective is the sharing of experience between the emergency managers in order to support the re-planning task, regarded as the relevant task of Forest Fire-Fighting Management. Therefore it is necessary to establish a common working language to facilitate sharing. First, we present the methodology used to determine the key element of this language, which is called a unit of experience. We then introduce a method to capitalize such units. Next, we describe the utilization of units of experience to improve emergency management. The reasoning method provides several levels of support to fire managers.

1 Introduction

This paper studies how reasoning from experience can improve risk management. Risk can be managed by means of different missions [1]. Among them, we are mostly interested in training and in intervention. This paper focuses on intervention like in [2],[3] but by reusing the experience itself which is regarded as a new way to assist emergency management [4]. We put our knowledge management approach into practice in Spain within the Andalusian organization of Forest Fire-Fighting Management (FFFM). The objective is to realize an experience-based support system which allows the fire managers to share their past experience. Among the managers' tasks, we decided to focus on the task of *revising a fighting plan*, or in others words on *re-planning* because it presented the opportunity to exploit past experience. We believe that it is the best choice for validating the contribution of the sharing of experience both in intervention and training. FFFM implies taking into account two essential aspects of forest fire-fighting: the phenomena which govern the fire propagation and the intervention (effect of fighting resources, procedures applied for prevention and fighting, etc.). Interactions between these aspects generate the complexity of FFFM. This complexity must be considered during the constitution of the corporate memory that will be used for sharing and reusing knowledge. The problem is how to capture this complexity without it being detrimental to sharing and reusing of the experience, that we want to favor.

R. Dieng and O. Corby (Eds.): EKAW 2000, LNAI 1937, pp. 304-311, 2000.

Our approach consists of a formalization of the related experience and its capitalization in a corporate memory. Contrary to other knowledge management approaches, we do not store "compiled" experience (e.g., in the form of statistics) but the experience "as is". In our approach the concrete experience from past fire-fighting will be reused, without transformation. Moreover, in order to allow an efficient and sustainable sharing of experience, we propose structuring the experience, to constitute a common working language among fire managers.

The paper first introduces the key element of this language, which is named a *unit of experience*. The second part presents the method to capitalize such units and deals with the different types of decision support which can be provided to forest fire managers. Finally, we describe the construction of a unit of experience and we compare our approach to others in the domain of knowledge management.

2 Unit of Experience

We propose to model the experience of fire managers by a set of so-called *units of experience*, that will constitute the basic elements of the corporate memory about Forest Fire-Fighting Management. The formalization of such units takes into account the previous aspects of forest fire-fighting. Each unit of experience describes a resolved episode of the revision of a fighting plan. We have determined that this is the smallest element of the fire-fighting that preserves the complexity of the re-planning task, while providing useful information for experience sharing. First, a study of the phenomenal aspect enables us to decompose the fire evolution and to define the scope of units of experience. Second, the study of the intervention allows us to identify information relevant to experience used during the re-planning task. We hence specified a structure for units of experience that is easy to understand by managers and easy to process by a system.

2.1 Unit of Experience Scope

In our case, the information on the phenomenal aspect corresponds to an account of fire-fighting given by a manager. FFFM is described by a temporal sequence of situations, each one being the representation of the state of fire-fighting at any one moment. The temporal sequencing of situations is determined by so-called *disruptive events*, which trigger the revision of a plan (*e.g.,* an accident of a fighting resource). The revision starts when the event revokes the current plan, *i.e.* when it revokes at least one of its sub-plans, leading to a new fighting situation. A situation is in turn described by a plan composed of sub-plans. Each sub-plan is associated to one sector, *i.e.* a particular geographic zone, with a given vegetation, topography or infrastructures which necessitate a specific fighting sub-plan. A sub-plan is defined by a set of operations (*e.g.,* "build a break-line") and resources (*e.g.,* fire trucks) to achieve a fighting goal, local to a sector (*e.g.,* "protect a house"). FFFM hence decomposes temporally into situations and spatially into sectors as shown in Figure 1.

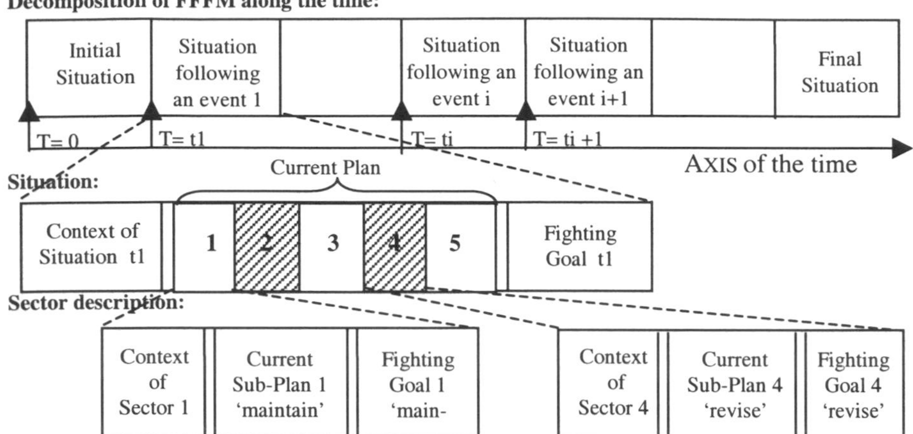

Fig. 1. Twofold decomposition of a Forest Fire-Fighting Management.

This analysis allows us to limit the scope of a unit to a sector of a given situation, where the sub-plan must be 'revised' in response to an event (like sector 4 in Fig.1).

Unit of Experience: Relevant Information and Structure

The knowledge that should be stored in a unit of experience corresponds to the knowledge relevant to the re-planning task of fire-fighting, where the sharing of experience occurs.

UNIT OF EXPERIENCE STRUCTURE	BUILDING STEP	
Problem description, *i.e.*		
- Current plan context (*Environmental context and fighting context*), - Description of the current fighting plan, - Event that lead to a revision,	1	**During FFFM**
- Signature of the problem *(objective of plan revision, parameters relevant to the problem of plan revision, and hints to drive the adaptation process; spot of adaptation).*	2	
Solution description, *i.e.*		
- Description of the revised plan,	3	
- ΔPlan *(actions and decisions that have been taken to apply the modifications on the sub-plan),*		
- Justifications and alternate solutions.	4	**After FFFM**
Outcome, *i.e.*		
- Effects of the modifications, - Global assessment about the new plan *(success or failure).*		

Remark: step 4 gives information about Δplan in order to justify the actions and decisions taken.

Fig. 2. Structure of a unit of experience and identification of its building steps.

First, the context of the current sub-plan is important to store. It consists of the environmental context (topography, vegetation, meteorology), and the fighting context (behavior of the fire, infrastructures and resources available to elaborate the modifications of the sub-plan). Furthermore, the modifications that have been applied and their effects are also stored. They represent the solution to the problem of how to revise a plan and the assessment about this solution. All this information is structured into operational units of experience which model episodes of revision of plans, like cases in case-based planning systems [5]. Their structure captures the previous information in a way that helps the storing and reusing of the experience. During the reasoning of the system the contents of the unit of experience is incremented in four steps (see Fig.2.) which are detailed in figure 4. Each unit of experience gathers all the information representing one cycle of the fire-fighting management (problem, solution, and outcome). That means that it cannot be divided into smaller parts, without losing the complexity of the FFFM otherwise it could not be used anymore for an experience-based support. The unit of experience is the smallest element that encapsulates the relevant experience, at the lowest possible level of complexity.

Reusability of the Approach

Our approach can be adapted to other domains where emergency management applies. We describe a system (in a systemic approach) by a set of concepts: *the phenomena, the behavior of phenomena, and the intervention.* These concepts define an *application ontology* (described in [6] as a framework for both domain knowledge and reasoning method knowledge). A unit of experience describes an episode of plan revision. Therefore it contains information about the previous concepts and it constitutes the essential part of the problem description. This systemic view, and the derived unit of experience notion, are applicable to assist decisions during the re-planning task of intervention in emergency management in general. The concepts of the ontology can be instantiated by domain specific terms. For the FFFM domain, the phenomena is the fire, *i.e.* the parameters which describe the fire (fire perimeter features, propagation, calorific power). The behavior of phenomena is the behavior of the fire *i.e.* the parameters which govern this behavior (vegetation, topography, meteorology) and the intervention is the fire-fighting *i.e.* the components of fighting plans.

2 Management of Units of Experience

We have designed an experience-based decision support system, the reasoning of which is decomposed into four phases : *Initial capitalization, Elaboration* of plan revision in response to an event, *Resolution* and *Final capitalization*.

3.1 Capitalization of Units of Experience

The first and most important step is the collection of information. In Andalusia, the usual tool to collect information about fire development and management was a set of forms. But they did not contain all the relevant information for the needs of units of experience. This lead us to create new forms suitable to promote the sharing of experience for the revision of plans. The new forms fall into two types, corresponding to two types of knowledge acquisition [7]. The first type is filled out during the FFFM and captures the facts and the experience about the fire and the fighting development that are relevant for re-planning purposes. Thus we obtain a description of the concrete experience "as is"; this is the initial capitalization. The forms of second type are filled out after the FFFM and allow the managers to develop a critical point of view based on their experience (*i.e.* to justify their decisions or to propose alternatives). They provide understanding of the FFFM that has been made, *i.e.* they contain a valorization of the concrete experience. They correspond to the final capitalization. The fire management staff, using a real case of fire, validated the new forms.

Reutilization of Units of Experience: Experience-Based Support

The capitalized units of experience are used in a software system to provide support for FFFM. The different levels of proposed support correspond to the different steps of a re-planning task, as summarized in figure 3.

SUPPORT SYSTEM	SUPPORT LEVELS	STEPS OF RE-PLANNING TASK
Definition process (Elaboration)	1. perception support	perception of the problem
Retrieval process (Resolution)	2. analysis support	identification of useful experience
Adaptation process (Resolution)	3. action support	modifications of plan

Fig. 3. Levels of assistance to the re-planning task.

The two important phases, regarding the support levels, are the elaboration and resolution phases. The first phase splits up a problem into sub-problems in order to minimize the revision work. The second phase is divided into two processes (retrieval and adaptation) based on a CBP paradigm [8]; it solves each sub-problem, *i.e.* each 'revised' sub-plan (see Fig.1.). These phases constitute our cycle of plan revision whose specificity, compared to a classical CBP cycle, lies in the additional elaboration phase. This latter phase diagnoses the impact of an event, it corresponds to a dynamic *definition process* which uses inference rules, in order to define the signature of the problem (*i.e.* objective of the plan, relevant parameters and spot of adaptation). Thus, the first level of support is a *perception support*, which proposes explanations on how to interpret the occurring events according to the current fire-fighting plan. The retrieval process of the resolution phase aims to retrieve past units of experience. This process is driven by the objective of plan revision, used to apply a filter, and by the relevant parameters, used to compute a basic similarity measure (an Euclidean distance). After the retrieval process the user could obtain information about past fire-fighting management that has been selected as a useful experience to define a revision. This second level of support is named an *analysis support*. Then, the adaptation process works on past units in order to obtain solutions that may contribute to solving the current problem. The adaptation process, driven by the spot of adaptation, is applied to the retrieved solution plans. For this purpose, we use domain specific methods (following a transformational approach [9]), which are based on the elementary planning actions: insert, remove, reorder, etc. [10]. Some solutions could be suggested to the user. This third level hence proposes an *action support*. However, this last level of support is not always possible because the adaptation process requires a lot of knowledge, which is not always available. Among the support levels, only levels 2 and 3 use past experience, after respectively a selection and a modification. Figure 4 summarizes the support system and presents the way units of experience are built during and after FFFM. The retrieval process2 (see Fig.4.) is a simple request on a unit's identifier (fire and situation identification).

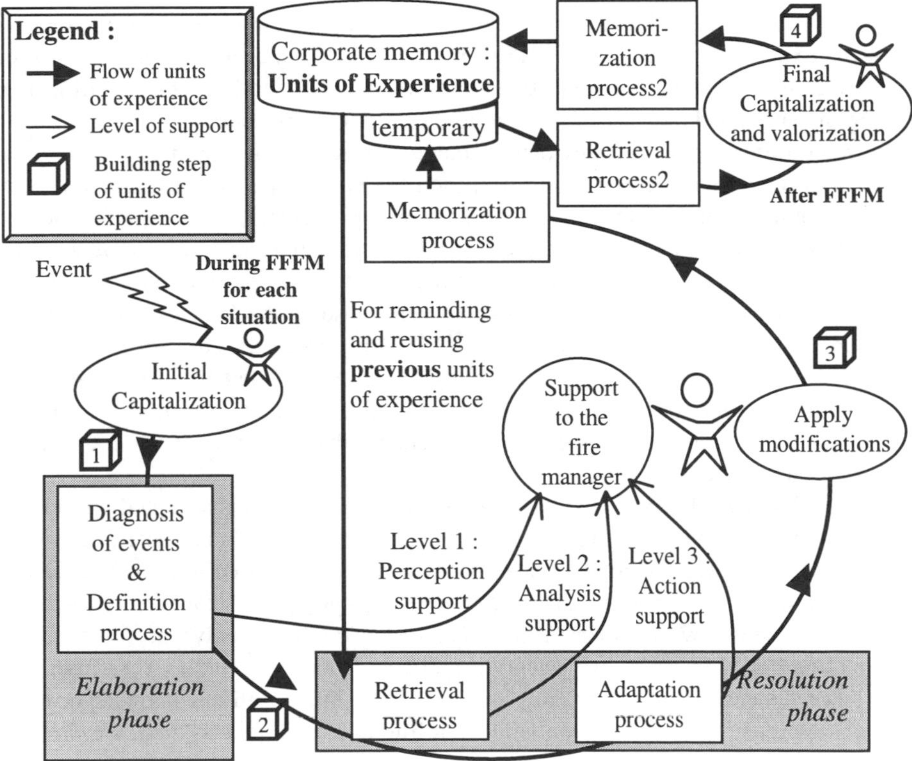

Fig. 4. Construction and reuse of the units of experience in the support system.

Sharing of Units of Experience

The first result of this study is to promote the collecting of information to acquire corporate experience. The model of unit of experience has been accepted by the managers and constitutes a common working language for the description of re-planning tasks. It offers an efficient way to exchange experiences and may constitute in the near future an opportunity to increase the corporate memory with alternate units of experience. One interesting aspect is the identification of "positive experience", which means the proposal of alternate solutions that could have improved this very same situation. These alternate solutions play the same role as the "missed opportunities" mentioned in [11]. The units stored in the corporate memory may also constitute a source of reference cases to favor training, either by working from a single unit to suggest alternate solutions, or from a series of units to build realistic scenarios.

3 Conclusion and Perspectives

Several Knowledge Management methods exist, that are not always supported by software tools, we can cite the MKSM method [12], which covers all aspects of knowledge management. Our objective is more focussed and aims to operationalize the capitalization and reuse of knowledge in the form of experience.

In order to improve emergency management by means of the sharing of experience between different managers, we have proposed the notion of unit of experience. Such a unit is not only a unit of memory, but also a unit of reasoning. The capitalization of units of experience leads to a corporate memory, regarded as an active organizational memory [13] and which constitutes the knowledge base of the reasoning process of our support system. This system follows a cycle close to the feedback life-cycle of experience promoted in the REX method [14]. REX is an experience management method that attempts to capture and reuse the experience. Compared to this method, we provide a second cycle for capitalization and valorization and we offer a computer assisted formalization of "elements of experience", that preserves the initial experience all around the cycle.

The need to learn lessons from past accidents, incidents, etc. is accepted by the risk management community [15],[16]. Debriefing methods promote post-operational evaluations to achieve this aim. In most cases, debriefing is used to define causes of events, but it has also more recently been used to study crisis management and we have adopted this new approach. But, instead of capitalizing only "negative facts", which is generally the case, we integrate and reuse both negative and positive past experience. Indeed, even if debriefing methods have influenced our knowledge management approach, we differ from them according to several points. First, we propose to capitalize not only the facts, but also the experience, and our approach is not only concerned with learning lessons from emergency management but also with understanding and explaining it, because the experience integrates criticisms from the managers themselves about the past fighting. The second point concerns memory organization. Our goal is to build a corporate memory containing the experience of different managers, and which is essential to achieving the sharing of experience. Finally, the third point is related to the sharing of knowledge. Knowledge corresponds to facts in debriefing approaches, while it corresponds to experience in ours. In debriefing methods, the sharing is not achieved because knowledge is not memorized during the debriefing phases. What is more, the analysis process gives as output a computation of facts (*e.g.*, statistics). On the contrary, our approach preserves the experience from the capitalization phase until the sharing phase. The work presented in this paper lead to both an European project and the use of our forms by the training staff.

The presented unit of experience is sufficient to allow the reusing of concrete experience but there are some limits. That is why we intend to use another kind of unit representing schemas (as defined in [17]) or, in other words, plan hierarchies (as used in planning systems [18]). This second kind of unit will not represent an episode of the plan revision, but an abstracted and generalized experience.

References

1. Dykstra, D.P.:Systèmes d'information appliqués à la foresterie. Unasylva 189. Vol. 48, (1997), 10-15.
2. Xanthopoulos, G.: Development of a Decision Support System for water bomber dispatching in Greece. In Proc. 2nd Int. Conf. FFR. Vol. I, A.08, Coimbra, (1994), 139-150.
3. Avesani, P., Perini, A. and Ricci, F.: Combining CBR and Constraint Reasoning in Planning Forest Fire Fighting. EWCBR'93. Springer-Verlag. (1993).
4. Huet, P.: Risques naturels et retour d'expérience: est-ce pour bientôt? Retours d'Expérience, Annales des Ponts et Chaussées. n°91, Septembre, (1999), 54-61.
5. Muñoz-Avila, H., Hendler, J.A. and Aha, D.W.: Towards a Conversational Case-Based Planning Tool. (1998). Review of Applied Expert Systems.
6. Studer, R., Benjamins, R. and Fensel, D.: Knowledge Engineering: Principles and Methods. Data and Knowledge Engineering. 25(1-2), March, (1998).
7. Delaître, S., Mille, A. and Moisan, S.: Instrumentation d'un processus de retour d'expérience pour la gestion des risques. IC2000. May (2000).
8. Hammond, K.J.: CBP - Viewing planning as a memory task. Academic Press Inc. (1989).
9. Carbonell J.G.: Learning by Analogy: Formulating and Generalizing Plans from Past Experience. In Machine Learning: An Artificial Intelligence Approach. (1983), 137-161.
10. Hank, S. and Weld, D.S. : A Domain Independent Algorithm for plan-adaptation. Journal of Artificial Intelligence Research 2, (1995), 319-360.
11. Jarke, M.: Experience-Based Knowledge Management. In A.Solvberg, S.Brinkkemper, E. Lindencrona. (eds.): Information Systems Engineering, Springer-Verlag, June (2000).
12. Ermine, J-L.: Capitaliser et partager les connaissances avec la méthode MKSM. Traité IC2. Volume „ Capitalisation des Connaissances ", Hermès, (2000).
13. Sorli. A., Coll. G.J., Dehli. E., and Tangen. K.: Knowledge Sharing in Distributed Organisations. IJCAI-99 Workshop on KM and Organizational Memories. (1999).
14. Malvache, P., Eichenbaum, C. and Prieur, P.: La maîtrise du retour d'expérience avec la méthode REX. Performances Humaines et Techniques. n°69, Mars-Avril (1994), 6-13.
15. Greenlee, J.: Possible Lesson Learned in Florida. Wildfire. Vol.7, n°11, (1998), 12-14.
16. Gilbert, C.: Premiers éléments de réflexion pour une approche transversale du retour d'expérience. Retours d'Expérience, Annales des Ponts et Chaussées. n°91, (1999), 4-10.
17. Turner, R.M.: Adaptative Reasoning for Real-World Problems : A Schema Based Approach. LEA Publischers, Hillsdale, New Jersey, (1994).
18. Tate, A., Hendler, J. and Drummond, M.: A review of AI Planning Techniques. In Readings in Planning, J. Allen, J. Hendler, and A. Tate. (eds): Morgan Kaufmann Publishers, (1990), 26-49.

Integrating Knowledge-Based Configuration Systems by Sharing Functional Architectures

Alexander Felfernig, Gerhard Friedrich, Dietmar Jannach, and Markus Zanker

Institut für Wirtschaftsinformatik und Anwendungssysteme, Produktionsinformatik, Universitätsstrasse 65-67, A-9020 Klagenfurt, Austria,
email: felfernig@ifi.uni-klu.ac.at
tel. ++43/463/2700/6204

Abstract. Configuration problems are a thriving application area for declarative knowledge representation that experiences a constant increase in size and complexity of knowledge bases. However, today's configurators are designed for solving local configuration problems not providing any distributed configuration problem solving functionality. Consequently the challenges for the construction of configuration systems are the integrated support of configuration knowledge base development and maintenance and the integration of methods that enable distributed configuration problem solving. In this paper we show how to employ a standard design language (Unified Modeling Language - UML) for the construction of configuration knowledge bases (component structure and functional architecture) and automatically translate the resulting models into an executable logic representation which can further be exploited for calculating distributed configurations. Functional architectures are shared among cooperating configuration systems serving as basis for the exchange of requirements between those systems. An example for configuring cars shows the whole process from the design of the configuration model to distributed configuration problem solving.

1 Introduction

Knowledge-based configuration systems have a long history as a successful AI application area and today form the foundation for a thriving industry (e.g. telecommunication systems, automotive industry, computer systems etc.). A configuration task can be characterized through a set of components, a description of their properties (attributes and connection points), and constraints on legal configurations. Given some customer requirements, the result of computing a configuration is a set of components, corresponding attribute valuations, and connections satisfying all constraints and customer requirements.

Here we will employ a scenario where several configuration systems jointly solve such a configuration task. The need for distributed configuration problem solving arises out of an economic necessity. Supply chain integration for complex customizable products and services demands an integration of local configuration systems along the value chain of these products. A centralized approach

R. Dieng and O. Corby (Eds.): EKAW 2000, LNAI 1937, pp. 312–327, 2000.

with a single configurator, that comprises the configuration knowledge of the final product and is additionally capable to configure the supplied parts, is only a theoretical alternative to a cooperative approach. The reasons lie in organizational and corporate security concerns of the involved business entities. As the domain experts are distributed over different manufacturers the maintenance of the configuration knowledge has to happen decentralized within each supplier. Further no supplying organization wants to share her whole configuration knowledge including technical details with the buying manufacturer for reasons of privacy and competition. However current configuration technology [7] encompasses only the solving of local configuration problems, and distributed configuration is still an open research issue.

In this paper we will show how our framework that supports the conceptual design of configuration knowledge bases and the automatic translation of the resulting models into an executable logic representation described in [8] and [9] can be extended in order to support distributed configuration problem solving within our prototype environment. In [8] we present how to employ UML - Unified Modeling Language [23], which is a standard design language widely applied in industrial software development processes, to graphically develop configuration knowledge bases following the component port paradigm described by [16]. We were using the built-in extension mechanism of UML to define configuration domain specific stereotypes based on the work of [25] on a general ontology[1] for configuration modeling. Further we show there how to automatically translate the graphically represented configuration knowledge into a machine executable formal representation. In [9] we give additional translation rules for those complex constraints that cannot be represented with the graphical concepts of UML and have to be formulated with OCL[2] (Object Constraint Language). The acquisition of functional configuration knowledge with our framework is described in [10]. Functional configuration knowledge [3], [4], [16] determines *what* can be realized by a product, i.e. specify the functions a product provides including constraints between those functions and a mapping from functions to components the final product can be built of (*how* the functions are implemented).

Here our approach towards a distributed configuration task is based on the integration of the different configuration models of cooperating business entities by a mechanism of shared functional architectures. This proposed development process for cooperatively solvable configuration tasks is outlined in Figure 1. In the first phase the locally applicable configuration knowledge is modeled and the functional architectures from cooperating configuration systems are integrated, i.e. if a configurator wants to order products from another configurator, it must integrate the functional architecture of the desired product into its local knowledge base (phase 1). The resulting conceptual configuration model is automatically translated into a representation executable by the corresponding

[1] We interpret ontologies in the sense of [5], i.e. ontologies are theories about the sorts of objects, properties of objects, and relations between objects that are possible in a specified domain of knowledge.

[2] The object oriented expression language OCL is part of the UML standard.

configuration system. Since our goal is to support cooperative configuration, the translation process must generate a representation applicable by a distributed problem solving algorithm (phase 2). In the following the configuration system is employed in productive use, i.e. solutions for a distributed configuration task are calculated (phase 3).

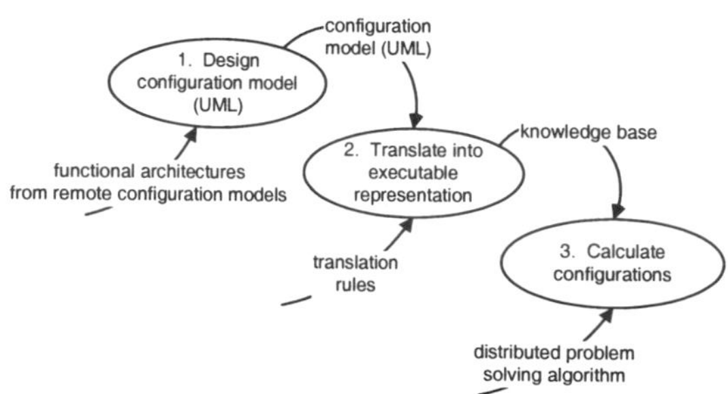

Fig. 1. Configuration system development process

The rest of the paper is organized as follows. First, we sketch the conceptual design of an example configuration model using UML (Section 2). In Section 3 we give a formal definition of a distributed configuration task based on the component port model [16] and show how to translate the example model into this formalism. In Section 4 we show how to share functional architectures between configuration systems and how to organize the local configuration knowledge to be exploited by a distributed problem solving algorithm. Furthermore, we give an example for a distributed car configuration which is realized by three configuration systems (car manufacturer, electric equipment supplier, and motor-unit supplier). In Section 5 we discuss our approach and describe the prototypical implementation of our approach towards cooperative configuration systems using commercial tools. Finally we cite related work followed by general conclusions.

2 A General Configuration Ontology

For presentation purposes we introduce simplified UML models of a car manufacturer (Figure 2), a motor supplier (Figure 3), and an electric equipment supplier (Figure 4) as a working example. These diagrams represent the generic product structure, i.e. all possible variants of the product. The set of possible products is restricted through a set of constraints which relate to customer requirements, technical restrictions, economic factors, and restrictions according to the production process.

A simple scenario for solving a configuration task could be the following. The customer contacts the car manufacturer and communicates requirements concerning the car configuration *(car-body:4door-limo, car-package:standard, engine:55bhp, transmission:manual, front-fog-lights)*. The car configurator calculates a local solution and contacts the motor-unit configurator for configuring a *55-bhp/manual motor-unit.* Furthermore, the car configurator contacts the electric equipment configurator for providing an *electric-equipment* containing *front-fog-lights* which represent optional parts in the configuration model of the electric equipment supplier (see Figure 4). The motor unit configurator contacts the electric equipment configurator for configuring a battery. Finally, the calculation of the distributed configuration is finished and the result is presented to the customer. Note that the customer requirements are related to the configuration model of the car manufacturer as well as to the models of the electric equipment supplier and the motor-unit supplier, i.e. the car manufacturer needs further information from the suppliers in order to provide the relevant information for the customer. In the following we will show how this information is provided by exchanging functional architectures.

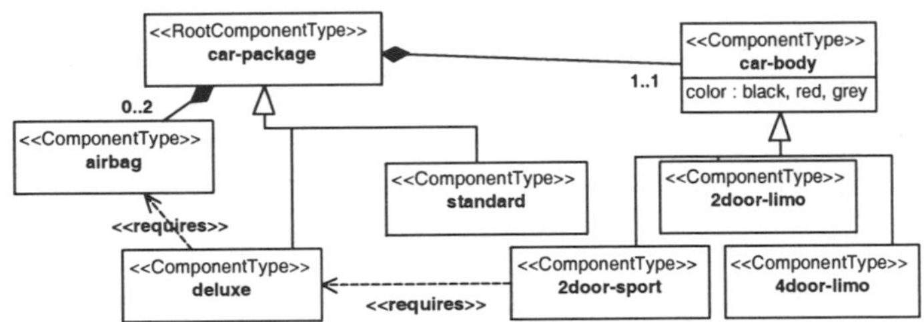

Fig. 2. Component structure of car configurator

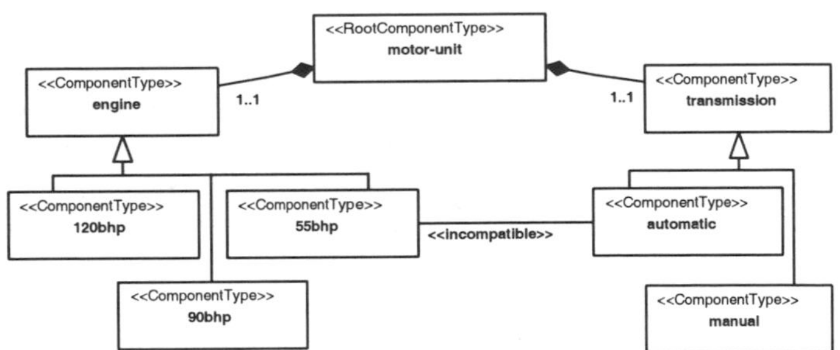

Fig. 3. Component structure of motor configurator

In order to make configuration models executable, we propose a translation into the component port representation, which is well established for modeling and solving configuration problems [16]. In general, consistency-based tools build onto this model can use the logic theory derived from the UML configuration model.

We employ the extension mechanism of UML (stereotypes) to express domain-specific modeling concepts, which has been shown to be a promising approach in other areas [22]. The semantics of the different modeling concepts are formally defined by the mapping of the graphical notation to logical sentences based on

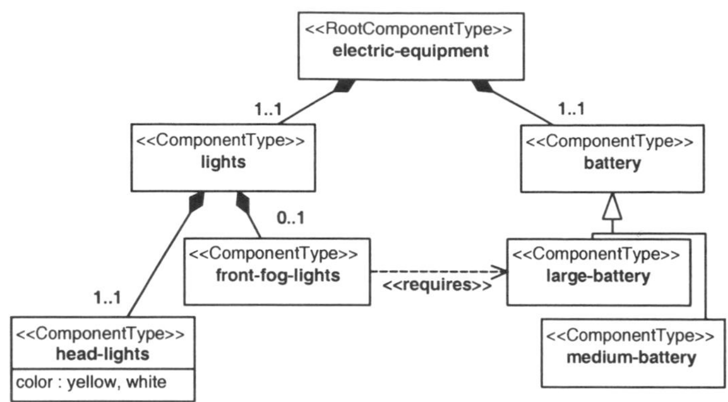

Fig. 4. Component structure of electric equipment configurator

the component port model (see Section 3). The basic structure of the product is modeled using classes, generalization, and aggregation of component types and function types. The following concepts are the basic parts of the ontology employed for designing configuration models [25].

- **Component types** These represent parts the final product can be built of. Component types are characterized by attributes (e.g. *car-body* and *color* in Figure 2).
- **Function types** They are used to model the functional architecture of an artifact, which can be integrated into configuration models of other configurators. Similar to component types they can be characterized by attributes (e.g. *lights-function* in Figure 5).
- **Resources** Parts of a configuration problem can be seen as a resource balancing task, where some of the component (function) types *produce* some resource and others are *consumers*. E.g. the maximum *price* of the car must not exceed a certain limit - in this case the different components (functions) of a configuration represent consumers, the component storing the maximum *price* represents the producer.
- **Generalization** Component (function) types with a similar structure are arranged in a generalization hierarchy (e.g. *engine* in Figure 3).
- **Aggregation** Aggregations between components (functions) represented by part-of structures state a range of how many subparts an aggregate can consist of (e.g. a *transmission* is part of a *motor-unit* - see Figure 3).
- **Connections and ports** In addition to the amount and types of the different components also the product topology may be of interest in a final configuration, i.e. how the components are interconnected with each other (e.g. a *radio power-supply* must be connected to a *battery*).
- **Compatibility and requirements relations** Some types of components (functions) cannot be used in the same final configuration - they are *incompatible* (e.g. *55bhp engine* is *incompatible* with *automatic transmission* - see Figure 3). In other cases, the existence of one component (function) *requires*

the existence of another special type in the configuration (e.g. *front-fog-lights requires large battery* - see Figure 4).

- **Functional architectures** Functional architectures represent exactly those parts of the configuration model, which can be shared between cooperating configurators (e.g. functional architecture *battery-function* in Figure 5). The mapping from functions to components is modeled using the *requires* relations in the simple case. More complex relationships between functions and components can either be represented by additionally defined modeling concepts or OCL (Object Constraint Language) expressions.
- **Additional modeling concepts and constraints** Constraints on the product model, which can not be expressed graphically, are formulated using the language OCL. As it is done for the graphical modeling concepts, OCL expressions are translated into a logical representation executable by the configuration engine. The discussed modeling concepts have shown to cover a wide range of application areas for configuration [21]. Despite this, some application areas may have a need for special modeling concepts not covered so far. To introduce a new modeling concept a new stereotype has to be defined. Its semantics for the configuration domain must be defined by stating the facts and constraints induced to the logic theory when using the concept.

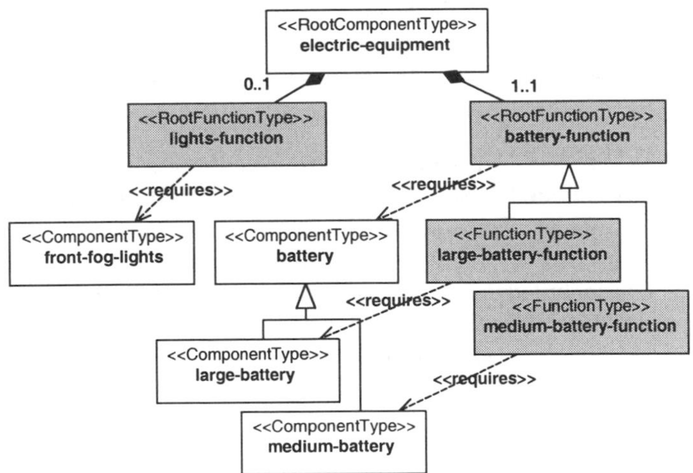

Fig. 5. Functional architectures and component mapping of electric equipment supplier

3 Distributed Configuration Task

In this section we give a formal definition of a distributed configuration task based on the component port model [16], which allows an intuitive definition using configuration domain specific representation concepts.

In practice, configurations are built from a predefined catalog of component types (*types*) of a given application domain. Furthermore, the configuration task is characterized by a set of functional architectures which specify the functional composition of artifacts and constraints on their composition, i.e. a set of necessary and optional functions, and constraints on their composition [12], [16]. The set of functions is further denoted as *functions*. Component types as well as function types are described through a set of properties (*attributes*), and connection points (*ports*) representing logical or physical connections to other components. Both, *attributes* and *ports* have an assigned domain (*dom*).

The domain description (*DD*) of a configuration task contains this information (*types, functions, ports, attributes, dom*) and additional constraints on legal configurations. The actual configuration problem has to be solved according to the set *SRS* (system requirements specification).

The *DD* is derived by translating the component structure as well as the functional architecture(s) and the corresponding constraints (all represented in UML). Based on this characterization of a local configuration task [12], [16] we define a *Distributed Configuration Task* through the following sets of logical sentences.

- $DD = \bigcup DD_i$, where DD_i is the DD of configurator i ($i \in \{1..n\}$ and n is the number of cooperating configurators).
- $SRS = \bigcup SRS_i$.

A configuration result is described through sets of logical sentences *(FUNCS, COMPS, ATTRS, CONNS)*. In these sets the employed functions, components, attribute values, and established connections of a concrete customized product are represented.

- $FUNCS = \bigcup FUNCS_i$, where $FUNCS_i$ represents sets of literals of the form *func(c,t)*. t is included in the set of *functions* defined in DD_i. The constant c represents the identifier of a function.
- $COMPS = \bigcup COMPS_i$, where $COMPS_i$ represents sets of literals of the form *type(c,t)*. t is included in the set of *types* defined in DD_i. The constant c represents the identifier of a component.
- $CONNS = \bigcup CONNS_i$, where $CONNS_i$ represents sets of literals of the form *conn(c1,p1,c2,p2)*. *c1*, *c2* are component (function) identifiers from $COMPS_i$ (FUNCS_i). *p1 (p2)* is a port of the component (function) *c1 (c2)*.
- $ATTRS = \bigcup ATTRS_i$, where $ATTRS_i$ represents sets of literals of the form *val(c,a,v)*, where c is a component (function) identifier, a is an attribute of that component (function), and v is the actual value of the attribute.

The *DD* of the electric equipment supplier (Figure 4, 5) is the following[3] :

types={electric-equipment, lights, battery, front-fog-lights, head-lights,
large-battery, medium-battery}.
functions={lights-function, battery-function,
medium-battery-function, large-battery-function}.
attributes(head-lights)={color}.
dom(head-lights, color)={yellow, white}.
ports(electric-equipment)={lights-port, battery-port,

[3] A detailed discussion on the translation rules can be found in [8].

lights-function-port,battery-function-port}[4].
dom(electric-equipment, lights-port)={*electric-equipment-port*}.
ports(lights)={*electric-equipment-port*}.
ports(battery)={*electric-equipment-port*}.
ports(lights-function)={*electric-equipment-port*}.
ports(battery-function)={*electric-equipment-port*}. ...

The relation *front-fog-lights requires large-battery* (Figure 4) is translated as follows[5]:

type(ID1, front-fog-lights) ∧
conn (ID1, lights-port, ID2, front-fog-lights-port) ∧
conn (ID2, electric-equipment-port, ID3, lights-port) ⇒
∃*(ID4) conn (ID4, electric-equipment-port, ID3, battery-port)*.

The relation *55bhp incompatible automatic* in Figure 3 is translated as follows:

type(ID1, 55bhp) ∧ *conn (ID1, motor-unit-port, ID2, engine-port)* ∧
conn(ID2, transmission-port, ID3, motor-unit-port) ∧
type(ID3, automatic) ⇒ *false*.

An example for a configuration result of the electric equipment supplier is the following:

type(electric-equipment-1, electric-equipment).
type(head-lights-1, head-lights).
type(lights-1, lights).
type(battery-1, medium-battery).
func(battery-function-1, medium-battery-function).
conn(head-lights-1, lights-port, light-1, head-lights-port).
conn(lights-1, electric-equipment-port, electric-equipment-1, lights-port).
conn(battery-1, electric-equipment-port, electric-equipment-1, battery-port).
conn(battery-function-1, electric-equipment-port,
electric-equipment-1, battery-function-port).

The concept of a *Consistent Distributed Configuration* is defined as follows:

Definition 1: Consistent Distributed Configuration. *If (DD, SRS) is a configuration problem and FUNCS, COMPS, CONNS, and ATTRS represent a configuration result, then the configuration is consistent exactly iff DD* ∪ *SRS* ∪ *FUNCS* ∪ *COMPS* ∪ *CONNS* ∪ *ATTRS can be satisfied.*

We specify that *FUNCS* includes all required functions, *COMPS* includes all required components, *CONNS* describes all required connections, and *ATTRS* includes a complete value assignment to all variables in order to achieve a complete distributed configuration[6]. Let AX_{comp} be the additional sentences for completeness purpose.

[4] The *part of* relationships between component and function types are translated into connections between component/function ports in the component port representation.

[5] The form of the sentences is restricted to a subset of range-restricted first-order-logic with set extension and interpreted function symbols. The term-depth is restricted to a fixed number in order to assure decideability. Additionally domain specific axioms are added, e.g. one port can only be connected to exactly one other port.

[6] This is accomplished by additional logical sentences which can be generated using the domain description (see [12] for more details).

In order to assure completeness and correctness of the distributed configuration w.r.t. the overall configuration task the following sentence must hold:

- $DD \cup SRS \cup FUNCS \cup COMPS \cup CONNS \cup ATTRS \cup AX_{comp}$ *is consistent iff* $\forall i : DD_i \cup SRS_i \cup FUNCS \cup COMPS \cup CONNS \cup ATTRS \cup AXcomp$ *is consistent.*

This sentence is fulfilled if we allow in *DD* only sentences using *func, type, conn*, and *val* literals since $FUNCS \cup COMPS \cup CONNS \cup ATTRS \cup AX_{comp}$ is a complete theory w.r.t. these literals. A distributed configuration, which is consistent and complete w.r.t. the domain description and the customer requirements, is called a *Valid Distributed Configuration.*

4 Solving Distributed Configuration Tasks

4.1 Distribution of Functional Architectures

In order to enable effective distributed configuration, the configuration knowledge must be shared between configurators. In the following we will show how knowledge sharing can be realized by exchanging functional architectures.

Definition 2: Functional Architecture. Let FA_{ij} be the *<<RootFunctionType>> j* of configuration model *i*, which is a direct part of the *<<RootComponentType>>* of the configuration model, then FA_{ij} is a *functional architecture*, which includes the *function types* which are directly or transitivly connected with FA_{ij} via generalizations or aggregations, the corresponding *attributes*, and the connected *part-of relations.* Furthermore, all constraints exclusively concerning functions and attributes of FA_{ij}, belong to FA_{ij}. For example, *<<RootFunctionType>> battery-function* represents a functional architecture which is a direct part of *<<RootComponentType>> electric-equipment* (see Figure 5).

Figure 6 shows the configuration model of the motor-unit configurator including an integrated *battery-function* architecture imported from the electric equipment supplier, i.e. the electric equipment supplier transfers the battery configuration task to the motor-unit supplier by providing the configuration information through the functional architecture of the battery.

Furthermore, the electric equipment supplier exports the functional architecture *lights-function* to the car manufacturer, i.e. the car configurator is responsible for communicating requirements concerning lights to the electric equipment supplier. Finally, the functional architecture for configuring a *motor-unit* (*motor-unit-function*) is exported to the car-manufacturer[7]. Figure 7 gives an overview of the distribution of functional architectures between the car manufacturer, electric equipment supplier, and the motor-unit supplier.

[7] Note that the functional architecture of the motor unit supplier exported to the car manufacturer as well as the functional architecture of the car manufacturer "exported" to the customer are not shown in our example models.

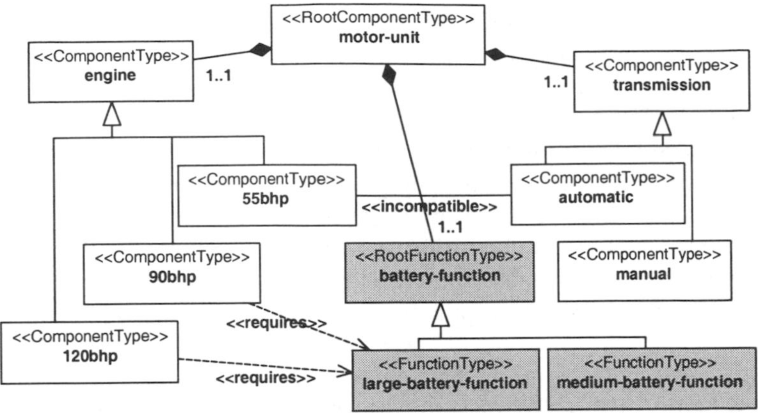

Fig. 6. Imported functional architecture of motor-unit configurator

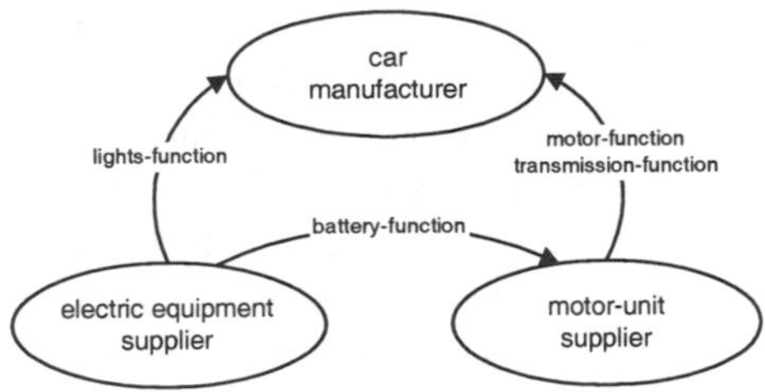

Fig. 7. Distribution of functional architectures

After having distributed the configuration knowledge by exchanging and integrating functional architectures we must define rules for how to organize the local configuration knowledge in order to employ a distributed problem solving algorithm for calculating a solution for a given distributed configuration task.

In the following we sketch the application of *asynchronous backtracking* proposed by [28], which is an algorithm calculating solutions for distributed constraint satisfaction problems (DCSP). In asynchronous backtracking problem variables are distributed among problem solving agents. Constraints concerning shared variables are directed between the agents in the sense that one of the connected agents is the value sending agent (agent, which instantiates the shared variables), the other one is the constraint evaluating agent which informs the value sending agent about inconsistencies of shared variables. Changes of shared variable assignments are communicated to corresponding constraint evaluating agents via *ok?* messages, inconsistent assignments are comunicated to value sending agents via *nogood* messages. Assignments of value sending agents are stored in the local *agent_view* of the constraint evaluating agent, which is used to check the consistency of instantiations of local variables with instantiations of value sending agents. *Nogoods* represent conflicting variable instantiations which are calculated by applying resolution. Value sending agents have a higher priority than connected constraint evaluating agents.

Asynchronous backtracking offers the basis for bounded learning strategies supporting the efficient revision of requirements and design decisions which is of particular interest for configuration systems, since supplier configurators eventually discover conflicting requirements *(nogoods)* which must be communicated back to the requesting configurator. Furthermore, this algorithm can easily be integrated into different configuration systems.

In order to be executeable by asynchronous backtracking the domain description DD_i of each configurator i must be organized conforming the following rules.

1. **Preventing infinite processing loops**[8] **:** If a functional architecture FA_{ij} of configuration model i is exported to configuration model k, no functional architecture from k can be integrated in i. When regarding the resulting configurators, *configurator* i is the supplier configurator and *configurator* k is the consumer configurator, i.e. *configurator* i is the constraint evaluating configurator and *configurator* k is the value sending configurator. Figure 8 shows the communication structure between the three example configurators.
2. **Constraint evaluating configurators:** Let F_j be the set of functions derived from function types of a functional architecture FA_{ij} of configuration model i imported from configuration model k $(k \neq i)$, A_j the set of attributes derived from attributes attached to function types of FA_{ij}, and P_j the set of ports derived from aggregation relations between functions in FA_{ij}. Then each $V \in (F_j \cup A_j \cup P_j)$ has a *constraint evaluating configurator* k, i.e. is represented in the *agent_view* of configurator k.
3. **Value sending configurators:** Let F_j be the set of functions derived from function types of a functional architecture FA_{kj} of configuration model k exported to configuration model i $(i \neq k)$, A_j the set of attributes derived from attributes attached to function types of FA_{kj}, and P_j the set of ports derived from aggregation relations between functions in FA_{kj}. Then each $V \in (F_j \cup A_j \cup P_j)$ is represented in the local *agent_view* of *configurator* k through a copy of V, which is updated by the *value sending configurator* i.

4.2 Example: Distributed Car Configuration

In order to illustrate the concepts discussed so far, we now give an example for solving a distributed configuration task using asynchronous backtracking. The car configurator must configure a car conforming the following functional requirements stemming from customer requirements[9]:

ok?((car-body-function-1,4door-limo-function),(car-package-1,standard-function),
(engine-1,55bhp-function),(transmision-1, manual-function),
(lights-function-1,lights-function)).

[8] Infinite processing loops are prevented in order to guarantee the termination of the algorithm.

[9] In order to keep the example simple, we omit the *conn* predicates describing the connections between the different functions.

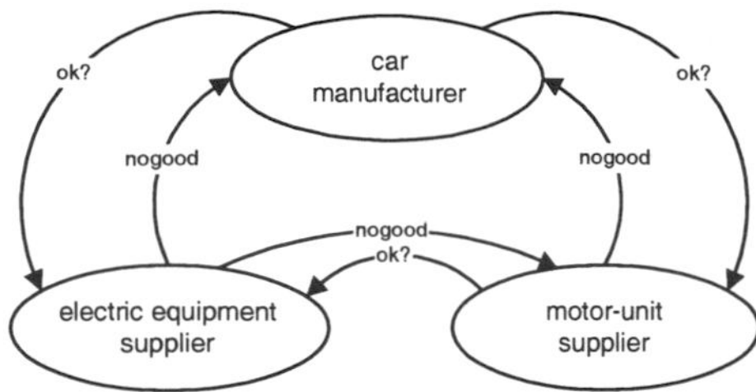

Fig. 8. Communication structure of example configurators

Regarding these functional requirements the car configurator calculates a local solution and propagates the functional requirements to the concerned outgoing configurators. The motor-unit configurator receives the following requirements:

ok?((engine-1,55bhp-function),(transmission-1,manual-function)).

The electric equipment configurator receives the following functional requirements from the car configurator:

ok?((lights-function-1, lights-function)).

The motor-unit configurator calculates a local solution regarding the given functional requirements (chooses a *medium-battery*) and communicates the following functional requirements to the electric equipment configurator:

ok?((battery-function-1,medium-battery-function)).

The electric equipment configurator tries to calculate a local solution and detects a contradiction between *front-fog-lights-function* and *medium-battery-function*, since the *front-fog-lights* component implementing the corresponding function *requires* a *large-battery* component. Consequently a *nogood* message is sent to the motor-unit configurator:

nogood((battery-function-1,medium-battery-function),
(lights-function-1,lights-function)).

The motor-unit configurator locally stores the *nogood* and calculates an alternative solution, i.e. chooses a *large-battery* component with the corresponding *large-battery-function.* The new functional requirements are communicated to the electric equipment configurator. Finally the electric equipment configurator calculates a solution regarding the requirements of the car configurator and the motor-unit configurator.

5 Discussion and Prototype Environment

Our work towards distributed configuration presented in this paper builds on our previous work on knowledge acquisition for configuration systems [8]. This approach differs from previous work on knowledge-engineering methodologies for configuration systems by avoiding the use of proprietary representation concepts. The Unified Modeling Language is a popular standardized conceptual modeling language that uses a graphical notation. This makes the problem domain more comprehensible and eases the communication between the people involved (e.g. domain experts and knowledge engineers). As UML allows to extend the language by defining additional modeling concepts (*stereotypes*), an automated translation from the conceptual model to an executable representation (e.g. logic sentences or constraint representation) is made possible. Thus the configuration knowledge can be maintained on the conceptual level.

When it comes to the design of a distributed configuration problem the task of knowledge sharing among different configuration systems can also be accomplished at an abstract level within our framework. Although for presentation purposes we employed the same constraint satisfaction problem representation for every example configurator, different knowledge representation formalisms resulting from different translation rules for each configuration system are possible. The choice of an algorithm for distributed problem solving depends therefor on the degree of cooperation between the configuration systems. In our example a very close interaction with a distributed backtracking algorithm could be shown, because all participating configurators employed a syntactically and semantically equivalent knowledge representation formalism.

The concepts presented in this paper are implemented in a prototype environment for the construction of cooperative configuration systems. For the design of product configuration models we employ the CASE tool Rational Rose. Our translation tool uses a XMI (XML Metadata Interchange [20]) representation (generated from Rational Rose models) as input and generates e.g. C++ code which includes the ILOG configuration libraries . We have evaluated our approach on real world problems from the domains of private telephone switching systems and automotive industry and noticed a significant reduction of development efforts. An extended version of the distributed car configuration problem presented in this paper is implemented using ILOG configurators which are implemented as CORBA objects. The communication between the configurators is realized using simple KQML [18] performatives. The message content is represented as an XML [27] document containing a set of functional requirements or a set of incompatible requirements.

6 Related Work

There is a long history in developing configuration tools in knowledge-based systems [26]. Progressing from rule-based systems like R1/XCON [1] higher level representation formalisms were developed, i.e. various forms of constraint satisfaction [11], description logics [15], or functional reasoning [24]. [14] propose a resource-based paradigm of configuration where the number of components of a particular type occuring in the configuration depends on the amount of that resource required.

An extensive framework for modeling configuration knowledge and the problem solving behaviour (VITAL methodology) can be found e.g. in [17]. The VITAL approach structures the process of development of a configuration model and an independent description of the problem solving strategy. Therefor this work is complementary to ours, where we start from a conceptual configuration model and translate to different machine executable representations.

The automated generation of logic-based descriptions through translation of domain specific modeling concepts expressed in terms of a standard design language like UML has not been discussed so far. Comparable research has been done in the fields of automated and Knowledge-based Software Engineering [13]. In [2] a formal semantics for object model diagrams based on OMT is defined in order to support the assessment of requirement specifications. We view our work as complementary since our goal is the generation of executable logic descriptions.

An overview on aspects and applications of functional representations is given in [4], where the functional representation of a device is devided into three parts. The intended function, the structure of the device, and a description how the device achieves a function represented through a process description. [16] propose the intergration of functional architectures into the configuration model by defining a matching from functions to key components, which must be part of the configuration if the function should be provided. Exactly this interpretation for the achievement of functions is used in our framework for the integration of configuration systems.

Designing large scale products requires the cooperation of a number of different experts. In the SHADE (Shared Dependency Engineering) project [19] a KIF [18] formalism was used for representing engineering ontologies. Giving an example of a spring construction, the integration of a project engineering agent responsible for the definition of the component hierarchy and basic properties of mechanic components, a spring design agent responsible for the design of the detailed technical structure and an optimization agent is shown. This approach differs from what we did in the sense that no high level design representations are provided to represent the distributed design task, furthermore no strategies for knowledge sharing between the cooperating agents are proposed.

In [6] an agent architecture for solving distributed configuration-design problems is proposed. The whole problem is decomposed into sub-problems of manageable size which are solved by agents. The primary goal of this approach is efficient distributed design problem solving, whereas our concern is to provide effective support of distributed configuration problem solving, where knowledge is distributed between different agents having a restricted view on the whole configuration process.

7 Conclusions

The integration of businesses by internet technologies boosts the demand for distributed problem solving. In particular in knowledge-based configuration we have to move from stand-alone configurators to distributed configuration. In this paper we have proposed a framework for modeling configuration knowledge bases using a standard design language. The representation of (configuration) knowledge on a conceptual level is well suited as basis for the communication with technical experts. Furthermore, the automatic translation of the resulting configuration models significantly reduces the configuration system building effort. Based on these basic concepts we have proposed a framework for the integration of configuration systems based on the sharing of functional architectures which are an integrative part of a configuration model. Furthermore, we have shown how to translate models represented in UML in order to be executable by algorithms based on bounded learning strategies such as asynchronous backtracking. The concepts presented in this paper are an essential part of an integrated environment for the development of cooperative configuration systems.

References

1. V.E. Barker, D.E. O'Connor, J.D. Bachant, and E. Soloway. Expert systems for configuration at Digital: XCON and beyond. *Communications of the ACM*, 32, 3:298–318, 1989.
2. R.H. Bourdeau and B.H.C. Cheng. A formal Semantics for Object Model Diagrams. *IEEE Transactions on Software Engineering*, 21,10:799–821, 1995.
3. B. Chandrasekaran. Functional Representation and Causal Processes. *Advances in Computers*, 38:73–143, 1994.
4. B. Chandrasekaran, A. Goel, and Y. Iwasaki. Functional Representation as Design Rationale. *IEEE Computer, Special Issue on Concurrent Engineering*, pages 48–56, 1993.
5. B. Chandrasekaran, J. Josephson, and R. Benjamins. What Are Ontologies, and Why Do We Need Them? *IEEE Intelligent Systems*, 14,1:20–26, 1999.
6. T.P. Darr and W.P. Birmingham. An Attribute-Space Representation and Algorithm for Concurrent Engineering. *AIEDAM*, 10,1:21–35, 1996.
7. B. Faltings, E. Freuder, and G. Friedrich, editors. Workshop on Configuration. *AAAI Technical Report WS-99-05*, Orlando, Florida, 1999.
8. A. Felfernig, G. Friedrich, and D. Jannach. UML as domain specific language for the construction of knowledge-based configuration systems. In *11th International Conference on Software Engineering and Knowledge Engineering*, pages 337–345, Kaiserslautern, Germany, 1999.
9. A. Felfernig, G. Friedrich, and D. Jannach. Generating product configuration knowledge bases from precise domain extended UML models. In *12th International Conference on Software Engineering and Knowledge Engineering*, Chicago, USA, 2000.
10. A. Felfernig, D. Jannach, and M. Zanker. Diagrammatic Acquisition of Functional Knowledge for Product Configuration Systems with the Unified Modeling Language. In *International Conference on the Theory and Application of Diagrams*, Edinburgh, UK, 2000.
11. G. Fleischanderl, G. Friedrich, A. Haselböck, H. Schreiner, and M. Stumptner. Configuring Large Systems Using Generative Constraint Satisfaction. In E. Freuder B. Faltings, editor, *IEEE Intelligent Systems, Special Issue on Configuration*, volume 13,4, pages 59–68. 1998.
12. G. Friedrich and M. Stumptner. Consistency-Based Configuration. In *AAAI Workshop on Configuration, Technical Report WS-99-05*, pages 35–40, Orlando, Florida, 1999.
13. M. Lowry, A. Philpot, T. Pressburger, and I. Underwood. A Formal Approach to Domain-Oriented Software Design Environments. In *Proceedings 9th Knowledge-Based Software Engineering Conference*, pages 48–57, Montery, CA, USA, 1994.

14. E.W. J ngst M. Heinrich. A resource-based paradigm for the configuring of technical systems from modular components. In *Proc. 7th IEEE Conference on AI applications (CAIA)*, pages 257–264, Miami, FL, USA, 1991.
15. D.L. McGuiness and J.R. Wright. Conceptual Modeling for Configuration: A Description Logic-based Approach. *AIEDAM, Special Issue: Configuration Design*, 12,4:333–344, 1998.
16. S. Mittal and F. Frayman. Towards a Generic Model of Configuration Tasks. In *Proc. of the 11th IJCAI*, pages 1395–1401, Detroit, MI, 1989.
17. E. Motta, A. Stutt, Z. Zdrahal, K. O Hara, and N. Shadbolt. Solving VT in VITAL: a study in model construction and knowledge reuse. *International Journal of Human-Computer Studies*, 44,3/4:333–371, 1996.
18. R. Neches, R. Fikes, T. Finin, T. Gruber, R. Patil, T. Senator, and W. Swartout. Enabling technology for knowledge sharing. *AI Magazine*, 12,3:36–56, 1991.
19. G.R. Olsen, M. Cutkosky, J.M. Tenenbaum, and T.R. Gruber. Collaborative Engineering based on Knowledge Sharing Agreements. In *Proceedings of ACME Database Symposium*, pages 11–14, Minneapolis, MN, USA, 1994.
20. Object Management Group (OMG). XMI Specification. *www.omg.org*, 1999.
21. H. Peltonen, T. M nnist , T. Soininen, J. Tiihonen, A. Martio, and R. Sulonen. Concepts for Modeling Configurable Products. In *Proceedings of European Conference Product Data Technology Days*, pages 189–196, Sandhurst, UK, 1998.
22. J.E. Robbins, N. Medvidovic, D.F. Redmiles, and D.S. Rosenblum. Integrating Architecture Description Languages with a Standard Design Method. In *20th Intl. Conference on Software Engineering*, pages 209–218, Kyoto, Japan, 1998.
23. J. Rumbaugh, I. Jacobson, and G. Booch. *The Unified Modeling Language Reference Manual.* Addison-Wesley, 1998.
24. J.T. Runkel, A. Balkany, and W.P. Birmingham. Generating non-brittle configuration-design tools. *Artificial Intelligence in Design, Kluwer Academic Publisher*, pages 183–200, 1994.
25. T. Soininen, J. Tiihonen, T. M nnist , and R. Sulonen. Towards a General Ontology of Configuration. *AIEDAM, Special Issue: Configuration Design*, 12,4:357–372, 1998.
26. M. Stumptner. An overview of knowledge-based configuration. *AI Communications*, 10(2), June, 1997.
27. W3C. Extensible Markup Language (XML). *www.w3.org*, 1999.
28. M. Yokoo, E.H. Durfee, T. Ishida, and K. Kuwabara. The distributed constraint satisfaction problem. *IEEE Transactions on Knowledge and Data Engineering*, 10,5:673–685, 1998.

The Nature of Knowledge in an Abductive Event Calculus Planner

Leliane Nunes De Barros[1] and Paulo E. Santos[2]

[1] Dept. de Ciência da Computação
Instituto de Estatística e Matemática - Universidade de São Paulo
Rua do Matão, 110 - 05508-900 - São Paulo - Brazil
Phone: (55)(11) 818 6235 FAX: (55)(11) 818 6134
leliane@ime.usp.br

[2] Dept. de Engenharia Elétrica - Escola Politécnica
Universidade de São Paulo
Av. Prof. Luciano Gualberto, travessa 3, n.158
05508-900 - São Paulo - Brazil - Phone: (55)(11) 818 5530
santos@lsi.usp.br

Abstract. There are several works whose goal is to specify complete and sound planning systems based on general purpose theorem provers. Some planners implemented in this way can have a close correspondence with existing partial-ordered planning algorithms. To improve the efficiency of logic-based planners we would like to use some of the results achieved by the AI planning community over the past twenty years in terms of algorithm design. We claim that a *knowledge level* analysis of *problem-solving methods* for planning, can help to identify what is the role of each piece of knowledge in a system and provide a common language to map, classify and compare different systems. In this paper we analyze an abductive event calculus planner using a library of problem-solving methods for planning.

1. Introduction

The main motivation for the construction of logic-based planners is the possibility to specify planning systems in terms of general theories of action and implement them as general purpose theorem provers without worrying about algorithmic concerns. A planning system defined in this way can have a close correspondence between implementation and specification. Although this is a very important feature in the design of a planner the main issue on how to reduce the search space size should still be a concern.

There are several works aiming the construction of sound and complete logic-based planning systems [7] [17] [12] [8]. Moreover, some recent research results [6] demonstrate that, a good theoretical solution can co-exist with a good practical solution despite of contrary widespread belief:

R. Dieng and O. Corby (Eds.): EKAW 2000, LNAI 1937, pp. 328-343, 2000.

> Unfortunately a good theoretical solution does not guarantee a good practical solution ... to make planning practical we need ... to use a special purpose algorithm ... rather than a general-purpose theorem prover to search for a solution. [13] (Russel and Norvig - AIMA, page 342).

In this paper we are going to analyze a particular logic-based planner, named Abductive *Event Calculus Planner* (AEC) [6], which has *Circumscriptive Event Calculus* [16] as the *reasoning about action and change*, with abduction as the inference rule. Within this framework, the work in [6] showed that there is a close correspondence between well known planning algorithms and planning defined as a result of the application of general purpose theorem proving techniques to a general purpose action formalism. In addition, it was also shown that, by adopting theorem proving techniques for planning, the efficiency results of AEC planner was not exponential but comparable to most of the practical planners.

However, we must not neglect results from the past twenty years of research concerning to algorithm design and efficiency. As a matter of fact, there are important lessons we can take from the analysis of hand-coded planners in order to improve the logic-based planners. To find a suitable correspondence between these two planning approaches, we have to bridge the gap between the algorithmic description and the theorem proving technique; in this paper we are going to cross this gap by assuming a common language capable of mapping, classifying and comparing different systems.

We claim that by using a knowledge level planning analysis [1] [25] we may provide an interesting perspective to propose efficiency gains to a planning system. One way to achieve it is by studying the way systems represent and use available knowledge to solve problems; in other words, which *problem-solving* (PSM) methods they use.

In this article we are going to use the results of our previous work related to the construction of a planning library of problem-solving methods available in the AI planning literature [1] [25] (Section 2) in order to guide the process of investigating the correspondence between different planning approaches. We analyze some aspects of Shanahan's Abductive Event Calculus (Section 3) in terms of how the knowledge is represented and used (Section 4) with the purpose of searching for possible improvements on its efficiency (Section 5).

2. A Library of Planning Problem-Solving Methods

Modern approaches to Knowledge Acquisition (KA) stress the importance of having reusable modeling components to support a knowledge engineer in constructing a required system model. These components of knowledge can be organized into a library of problem-solving methods for a *generic task*, e.g. the planning task.

In addition to its standard role as a tool to help in engineering a knowledge-based system, a library of problem-solving methods for planning has another important role: it can be seen as a framework for representing and analyzing planning methods. The library defines a number of components (*knowledge roles* and basic *problem-solving methods*) to describe planning methods in a common language which makes it possible to map, classify and compare different methods.

The methods in the library [25] were obtained by describing planning methods available in the AI planning literature which characterizes our library as *system-derived* as opposed to *domain-derived* libraries [27]. These components adopt a division in two layers CommonKADS [15]. In the domain layer, a set of typical *knowledge roles* characterizes the main types of domain knowledge used in planning methods. They also help in understanding the way knowledge is structured by providing an index to the *domain models* used to play these roles. In the task layer, a *task-method decomposition structure* indexes a set of basic methods by defining in what ways a planning task can be decomposed (what we call *task structures*), and what decomposition results from applying the basic methods to those tasks. Detailed control knowledge is later added to these decompositions by means of *control structures*. The *task-method decomposition structure* proposes a characterization of planning methods in general, as distinct realizations of a basic decomposition of the planning task into three tasks: propose, critique and modify [4]. In order to connect the domain with the task layer, a set of *assumptions* (or *features*) is used to specify when a method is applicable to a domain or a problem, and vice-versa.

A number of versions of (parts of) a library of problem-solving methods for planning were discussed in: [21], where it is discussed in detail the knowledge roles and domain models; in [2], the basic methods and the task-method decomposition structure are presented in detail; in [3], we have focused on the knowledge acquisition benefits of the library, by concentrating on the *assumptions*; in [1] and [25], the problem-solving methods were extended to include control knowledge.

In the next subsections we present a brief description of the components that matter for the discussion in this paper: the knowledge roles and the task-methods for planning. For a more detailed description of the library of problem-solving methods for planning see [25].

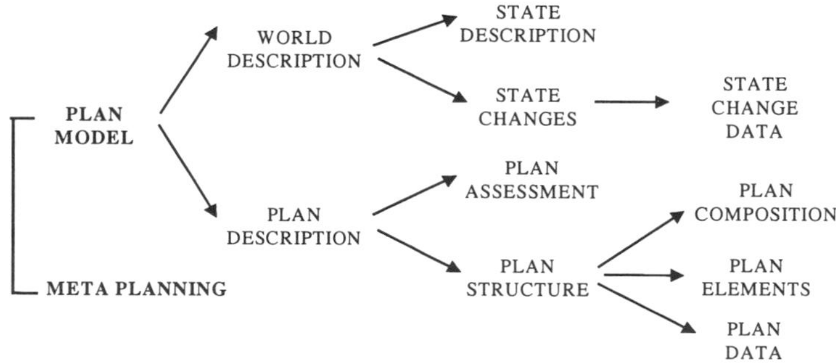

Fig. 1. Hierarchy of static roles in planning

One of the critical elements in the analysis of a planning method is specifying the different *roles* that domain knowledge plays during the planning process. In the planning literature, domain knowledge is defined as static knowledge about the world which is only consulted during planning, but not manipulated. However, from a KA perspective, we must consider how this same knowledge is used by the planner itself in defining its dynamically changing model of the world. Thus, we identify two roles for domain knowledge: static and dynamic [15].

2.1. Static Knowledge Roles in Planning

Figure 1 shows the hierarchical organization of static knowledge roles for planning [1]. The leaves of the hierarchy of static roles arc associated with the types of domain knowledge (domain models) that can play these roles. The plan model role defines what a plan is and what it is made of. It consists of two parts: a world description and a plan description.

The **world description** role describes the world in which planning occurs. It is comprised of two sub-roles. (1) The state description role, which contains the knowledge necessary to represent or describe the state of the world (for example, a set of first order predicates as in STRIPS or a set of fluents from the Situation Calculus [10] or from the Event Calculus [26]). (2) The state changes role explicates the information connected to the specification of changes in the state of the world, i.e., events or actions (e.g., STRIPS-like operators; hierarchical task networks (HTNs) or the wwfs as the event calculus Initiates, Terminates and Releases formulae, that constitute a purely logical description of the effects of actions in a particular domain).

The **plan description** role describes the structure and features of the plan being generated, and comprises two sub-roles: plan structure and the (optional) plan assessment knowledge.

1. The **plan structure** role specifies how the parts of a plan (actions, sub-plans) are assembled together. It has two sub-roles: (a) the plan composition role, which describes whether the plan composition is total or partial order, whether it includes iteration and/or conditional operators, and whether the composition is hierarchical (i.e. whether plans can be recursively decomposed into *sub-plans*); (b) plan elements role describes the components of a plan that can be a state change, a goal or time point; (c) the plan data role contains additional information about the plan, ranging from bookkeeping information, to information about resource use in parts of the plan or yet interval constraints for binding the variables involved in the state changes. Two particularly important resources are agents and time.
2. The **plan assessment knowledge** role determines whether a certain plan (or sub-plan) is valid or whether a plan is better than another, in other words, it defines a theory of actions. A plan is valid if, after executed, it satisfies a list of desirable goals. Based on this knowledge, a plan can be constructed, criticized or modified. An example of plan assessment knowledge is a *rule-based-criterion* which can be used to find out if a condition is true at some (time) point in the plan (as in the *Modal Truth Criterion* (***mtc***) n TWEAK [5] or in the Event Calculus axioms [26]) (in the next sections we will call the *rule-based-criterion* as ***mtc-based***). Another example is the ***causal-link-based*** knowledge, also called *Protection Intervals*, which corresponds to a bookkeeping device for keeping track of the goals that have already been worked on, and thereby avoiding undoing them or working on them multiple times (as in SNLP [9]) The *causal-link based* model contains an explicit causal structure of the plan plus some evaluation criterions [23]. Both types of knowledge representation for the plan assessment role can be used to answer questions about the plan as: is a desired goal *g*

satisfied by the plan? if it is not, what is wrong with the plan? how can we change the plan in order to fix it?

2.2. Dynamic Roles in Planning

Dynamic knowledge roles characterize planning in terms of the relevant variables whose values are constantly updated during the planning process. The dynamic roles include: (1) The **current state** role, which is initially filled by a description of the world at the beginning of the plan, but is subsequently modified to represent intermediary states in the plan. (2) The **goal** role, which describes the active goal or subgoal being worked on by the planner. The content of **goal** can be a set of conditions or a set of actions to be accomplished. Initially, this role is linked to the original goal, and during planning it may be updated with subgoals or decompositions of the original goal. (3) The **conflict** role contains the result of checking the plan for inconsistencies with respect to its conditions. (4) The **plan** role is a composite role consisting of (a) **plan-steps**, (b) **ordering constraints** over the plan-steps, (c) **variable binding constraints**, and (d) **auxiliary constraints** which correspond to a supporting knowledge used by a planner to reason about the construction of a plan and that it is not part of the plan solution. That is the case of **causal-links** or **protected intervals** which represent temporal and truth constraints between plan-steps and conditions.

2.3. The Tasks and Methods for Planning

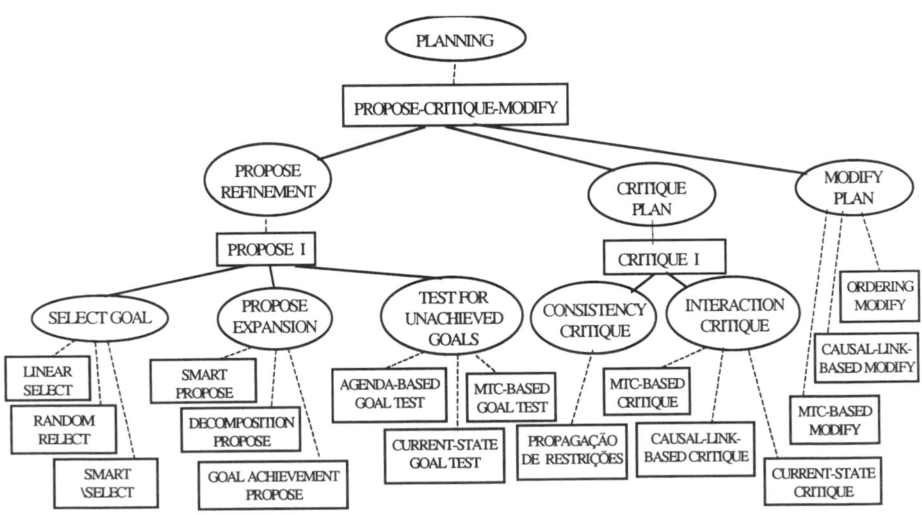

Fig. 2. The task-method decomposition structure for the planning task. Solid lines stand for *executes* (a method executes its subtasks), dashed lines denote *performed-by* (a task can be performed by alternative methods).

Based on an analysis of many classical planning systems, we have identified relevant tasks and problem-solving methods. We organize these into a task-method decomposition structure [11] in Figure 2 (where ellipses represent tasks and rectangles methods). A method *executes* (solid lines) a number of subtasks and a (sub)task can be *performed by* alternative (dashed lines) methods. The leaves of the task-method tree are called *primitive-methods* and the tasks they perform, *primitive-tasks*. Methods have two additional types of knowledge associated with them: control knowledge and suitability criteria [1].

The class of planners we are dealing with share a general, high-level problem-solving method called propose-critique-modify (PCM) [4]. That is, the planners all contain in one way or another these three basic tasks: (i) propose expansion, (ii) critique plan and (iii) modify plan. Planners differ in the problem-solving methods (PSMs) they use to perform these three tasks. These differences also reflect how planning knowledge is represented. For example, in Figure 2, the propose-I method consists of the three subtasks: select goal, propose expansion, and test for unachieved goals. The propose expansion task can, in its turn, be realized by three different methods: smart propose, goal achievement propose, and decomposition propose, and so on. For a detailed description of all tasks and methods involved see [25]. In Section 4 we describe in more details the subtasks/methods realized by the Abductive Event Calculus Planner.

The above framework gives a better understanding of what are the possible choices for a planner design in terms of the nature of the knowledge they use, how they are represented and their choices on control structures.

3. Overview on Abductive Event Calculus Planner

Roughly speaking, abduction is the process of explaining a sentence Γ by finding a set of formulae Δ (called *residue*) such that, given a set of formulae Σ (background theory), Γ is a logical consequence of the conjunction of Σ and Δ [6]. This process of *finding explanations* to goals is applied to a reasoning about actions and state change formalism: *Event Calculus* (EC). Intuitively, Event Calculus, is a temporal (first-order) formalism designed to model and reason about scenarios described as a set of *events* whose occurrences have the effect of starting or terminating the validity of determined properties of the world (the *fluents*). There are many versions of Event Calculi [19]. In this paper we are going to work with the variant of the calculus defined by Shanahan in [16].

3.1. The Event Calculus with Circumscription

Below we briefly present the axiomatization of the Circumscriptive Event Calculus [16] and, in the sequence, we define planning as a process of abduction on this event (action) theory.

The Event Calculus is a 3-sorted first-order language comprising a sort of time points ($t_1, t_2, ..., t_n, t_{n+1}, ...$); a sort of fluents ($f_1, f_2, ..., f_n, f_{n+1}, ...$); and, a sort of event types ($a_1, a_2, ..., a_n, a_{n+1}, ...$). The following are the predicates of the Event Calculus:

HoldsAt(f,t)	Fluent *f* holds at time *t*;
Initially(f)	Fluent *f* holds from time *0*;
Happens(a,t)	Event *a* happens at time *t*;
Initiates(a,f,t)	Fluent *f* holds after the occurrence of an event *a* at time *t*;
Terminates(a,f,t)	Fluent *f* does not hold after the occurrence of an event *a* at time *t*;
Releases(a,f,t)	Fluent *f* is not subject to the common-sense law of inertia after event *a* at time *t*;
Clipped(t_1,f,t_2)	Fluent *f* ceased to hold (or it is released from the common sense law of inertia) in some time point in [t_1, t_2];
Declipped(t_1,f,t_2)	Fluent *f* started to hold (or it is released from the common sense law of inertia) in some time point in [t_1, t_2].

The predicates described above are constrained by the following axioms:

$$HoldsAt(f,t) \leftarrow Initially(f) \wedge \neg\, Clipped(0,f,t) \qquad \text{(EC1)}$$

$$HoldsAt(f,t_2) \leftarrow Happens(a,t_1) \wedge Initiates(a,f,t_1) \wedge t_1 < t_2 \wedge \neg Clipped(t_1,f,t_2) \qquad \text{(EC2)}$$

$$\neg HoldsAt(f,t_2) \leftarrow Happens(a,t_1) \wedge Terminates(a,f,t_1) \wedge t_1 < t_2 \wedge \neg Declipped(t_1,f,t_2) \qquad \text{(EC3)}$$

We have to consider also the following defined notions:

$$Clipped(t_1,f,t_2) \leftrightarrow \exists\, a,t\, [Happens(a,t) \wedge [Terminates(a,f,t) \vee Releases(a,f,t)] \wedge t_1 < t \wedge t < t_2] \qquad \text{(EC4)}$$

$$Declipped(t_1,f,t_2) \leftrightarrow \exists\, a,t\, [Happens(a,t) \wedge [Initiates(a,f,t) \vee Releases(a,f,t)] \wedge t_1 < t \wedge t < t_2] \qquad \text{(EC5)}$$

The frame problem is overcome in this framework using circumscription. Circumscription is a method for default reasoning constructed on classical logic which involves minimizing the extensions of predicates. Intuitively, the circumscription of a property P w.r.t. a certain fact A dictates that the objects that can be shown to have the property P (by reasoning from certain facts A) are all the objects that satisfy P. In other words, as presented by McCarthy [30], circumscription can be used to conjecture that the tuples $<a_1, a_2, ..., a_n>$ which can be shown to satisfy a relation $P(x_1, x_2, ..., x_n)$ are all the tuples satisfying this relation.

In the Event Calculus, circumscription is applied in the following way: given a conjunction Σ of Event Calculus formulae, not including the predicates *Initially* or *Happens*, describing the effects of actions (*domain description*), a conjunction Δ of formulae, not including the predicates *Initiates*, *Terminates* or *Releases*, describing the *narrative* of actions and events, a conjunction Ω of *uniqueness-of-names* axioms for actions and fluents, a conjunction EC of the axioms of the Event Calculus ((EC1) to (EC5)), we have to consider the following formula:

$$\text{CIRC}[\Sigma;\, Initiates, Terminates, Releases] \wedge \text{CIRC}[\Delta;\, Happens] \wedge \text{EC} \wedge \Omega$$

where CIRC[Σ; α, β] means the circumscription of Σ with relation to the predicate symbols α and β. By circumscribing *Initiates*, *Terminates* and *Releases* we are imposing that the known effects of actions are the only effects of actions, and by circumscribing *Happens* we assume that there are no unexpected event occurrences. A more thorough discussion of it can be found in [18].

In a more general setting [19], the axioms of Event Calculus (with Circumscription) are components of a theory denoted by Σ_B, which goal is to handle the events and spatial relations of a mobile robot environment. The relations between the robot and the objects of its environment are described in a theory represented by Σ_E [19].

The central task of this framework is, then, to assimilate sensor data and to construct action sequences (action planning) in order to solve a determined goal. Both sensor data assimilation and action planning are done using abduction w.r.t. the theories Σ_B and Σ_E.

Intuitively, abduction is the process of explaining a sentence Γ by finding a set of formulae Δ such that, given a theory Σ (background theory), Γ is a logical consequence of $\Sigma \cup \Delta$.

In the process of assimilating a stream of sensor data Ψ, the task is to find a logical description of the object's initial locations (Δ_M) using abduction such that

$$\Sigma_B \wedge \Sigma_E \wedge \Delta_N \wedge \Delta_M \models \Psi$$

where Δ_N is a logical description of the movements of the objects, including the robot itself.

Similarly, planning a sequence of actions in order to satisfy a given goal Γ, given the objects initial locations (Δ_M), is the abduction explanation Δ_N such that

$$\Sigma_B \wedge \Sigma_E \wedge \Delta_N \wedge \Delta_M \models \Gamma.$$

It is the analysis of this last feature of Shanahan´s framework that the present paper is concerned.

3.2. Planning in Event Calculus

Restricting this framework to what are our main interests here, planning a sequence of actions in order to satisfy a given goal Γ (given a domain description Σ) is the abduction explanation Δ such that Σ, Δ Æ Γ; which becomes with the circumscription policy stated above:

CIRC[Σ; *Initiates*, *Terminates*, *Releases*] $\wedge$ CIRC[Δ; *Happens*] $\wedge$ EC $\wedge$ Ω Æ Γ,

Δ is a plan that satisfies the goal Γ. In [6] a planning system based in these ideas is presented as a PROLOG meta-interpreter, where each of the EC axioms were encoded in meta-level. In the next sections we will analyze the EC planner based on the planning library. A more thorough discussion of this meta-interpreter can be found in [6].

4. The Nature of Knowledge in the AEC Planner

The Abductive Event Calculus Planner is an abductive theorem prover, coded as a PROLOG meta-interpreter. The job of an abductive meta-interpreter is to construct a *residue* of *abducible* literals that can not be proved from the object-level program [6] which, in the case of a planning task, corresponds to the *plan description*.

4.1. Static Knowledge Roles in the AEC Planner

Table 1 Static knowledge roles in the AEC planner.

Knowledge role	**Domain model**
state description	a set of fluents (f_1, f_2, ..., f_n, f_{n+1}, ...)
state changes	action α is described through a conjunction of event calculus formulae of the form: $Initiates(\alpha,f,t) \leftarrow \Pi$ or $Terminates(\alpha,f,t) \leftarrow \Pi$ or $Releases(\alpha,f,t) \leftarrow \Pi$, where Π is of the form, $(\neg)\ HoldsAt(f_1, t) \wedge .... \wedge (\neg)\ HoldsAt(f_n, t)$
plan composition	partial order plan
plan elements	*happens* (α, t) literals and time points ordered by *before*(t_1,t_2) literals
plan data (causal-links or protected intervals)	negated *clipped* or *declipped* literals
plan assessment knowledge	*1. mtc-based*: the event calculus axioms encoded in the PROLOG meta-interpreter. *2. causal-link-based*: as the process to preserve the list of negated *clipped* or *declipped* literals (causal-links) as part of the abductive process.

Table 1 shows how the planning knowledge roles are fulfilled in the AEC planner. The *state description* role is played by a set of fluent terms of the domain. The *state changes* (actions or events) are played by a conjunction of event calculus formulae involving $Initiates(\alpha,f,t)$, or $Terminates(\alpha,f,t)$ or $Releases(\alpha,f,t)$ of the object level program. Although time points are used as an additional *state change data*, the AEC is not a temporal planner: the time points are used in a similar way as the temporal ordering in classical planning where ordering constraints are imposed over plan-steps. The time points used to describe *state changes* have a similar meaning as in a STRIPS-like action: it is used to describe what are the fluents that must hold ***after*** (effects) or ***before*** (preconditions) the action's execution.

The *plan elements* correspond to the abducible literals *happens* and *before*. Besides of that, time points also play the role of *plan elements*: they will be used to describe the execution ordering of the actions in the plan solution (like the *plan-steps* used in most of non-temporal planning systems [1]).

The *plan composition* is a partial order over the *plan elements* since an order between time points is only imposed when an action is added to be *before* a certain goal or in order to fix a threat in the plan. The *plan data* is played by the literals *clipped* and *declipped* as additional information (bookkeeping information) to be used by the planning tasks.

The *plan assessment knowledge* role is represented in the AEC planner through two different domain models: as a *mtc-based* model and as a *causal-link-based* model. As pointed out by [8], the EC axioms have a close correspondence with Chapman's modal truth criterion [5] and since the theorem prover is a compilation of the event calculus axioms, the *mtc-based* model of the *plan assessment knowledge* role is encoded as meta-clauses of the PROLOG meta-interpreter. On the other hand, the *causal-link-based* model is implemented as the process of preserving the list of negated *clipped* or *declipped* literals (causal-links) as part of the abductive process (as we will se bellow).

Most of the systems from the AI-planning literature represents *plan assessment knowledge* in one way or another way (with the exception of NONLIN [24]). However, there is no harm on having different representations for the same knowledge in a planner.

4.2. Task-Method Decomposition in the AEC Planner

Using the planning library we will characterize the problem-solving method employed by the AEC planner.

```
<Line 1> abdemo ([holds_at (F1,T3)|Gs1],R1,R5,N1,N4) :-
<Line 2>      abresolve (initiates (A,F1,T1),R1,Gs2,R1),
<Line 3>      abresolve (happens (A,T1,T2),R1,[],R2),
<Line 4>      abresolve (before (T2,T3),R2,[],R3),
<Line 5>      append (Gs2,Gs1,Gs3),
<Line 6>      add_neg ([clipped (T1,F1,T3)],N1,N2),
<Line 7>      abdemo_nafs (N2,R3,R4,N2,N3),
<Line 8>      abdemo (Gs3,R4,R5,N3,N4).
```

Fig. 3. The EC2 axiom encoded in meta-level PROLOG program. In order to demonstrate (abductively) that a fluent F1 holds_at time T3, the meta-interpreter has to demonstrate the 7 preconditions of the clause.

Although the specification of a theory of actions (*plan assessment knowledge*) is preserved in the AEC implementation (each meta-level clause correspond to one EC axiom), it is not immediately clear how subtasks and methods are performed unless we

[1] In the EC presented in [6] only one action can occur in the same time point *t*, therefore there is a correspondence between time point and plan-step from classical planning.

make a close analysis of the PROLOG program. Figure 3 shows the *abdemo* clause (standing for abductive demonstration) which is the description of the EC2 axiom in the meta-level.

Table 2 Subtasks and corresponding methods performed by the AEC planner.

Planning subtask	Problem-solving method
select goal	*linear select*
test for unachieved goals	*Agenda-based goal test*
propose expansion	*goal achievement propose*
interaction critique	*Causal-link-based critique*
modify plan	*Causal-link-based modify*

Table 2 shows the five subtasks being executed by the AEC planner and the corresponding methods used to perform them as we will describe bellow:

Select goal This task selects a goal from the set of goals to be accomplished which is performed by the *linear select* method in the AEC planner: it selects the last goal established by its search strategy (goals are added on the beginning of a PROLOG list and are selected as a LIFO goal ordering strategy).

Test for unachieved goals This task checks the current plan for unachieved goals. The method used by the AEC planner to realize this task is the *agenda-based goal test*, i.e., the planner checks if the list of goals is not empty, otherwise the planning task is finished. Only planners that exploit *causal-links* can use this method once they guarantee that the goals already processed are protected by a causal-link. This is because processed goals, that are extracted from the list of goals, can possibly be clobbered during the planning process if the planner do not protect the goals already achieved.

Propose expansion The AEC planner performs this task by a *goal-achievement propose* method, like in most of the partial-order planners. In Figure 3, the PROLOG meta-interpreter clause corresponds to the main part of this method. This task takes the selected goal (Line 1), and proposes a way to accomplish it by selecting an action whose effect includes the goal (Line 2 and Line 3 inserts *happens*(A, T1, T2) in the residue R1 obtaining the residue R2), constraining the place of the action in the plan to be *before* the time point (T3) when the selected goal needs to be valid (Line 4). When a new action is added to the plan, its preconditions are added to the set of goals (Line 5). When there is already a step in the plan that achieves the goal, only the ordering constraint is added to the plan (this is done by a special clause *abresolve* for the *before* predicate (Line 4)). Within this method, planners that protect its goals add a causal-link for the just accomplished goal (Line 6 adds a *clipped*(T1, F1, T3) predicate in a list of facts that can never be satisfied in the proof process). It is interesting to notice that this method has not been characterized in the planning library as *mtc-based* or *causal-link-based*.

Interaction critique This task verifies whether the proposed action for accomplishing the goal would interact with other goals in the plan (e.g., one action might undo (clobber) the precondition of another action). For realizing the interaction critique task, the AEC planner uses the *causal-link-based critique* method, which checks if the proposed plan-step, threats any existent causal-link. Notice that the original EC2 axiom do not define that it is necessary to *protect the interval* defined in between the starting time of the action and the instant in which the fluent hold but only to demonstrate that the interval is not being clobbered by another action, that is, if the negation of *clipped*(T1, F1, T3) holds. The interval protection is done as a part of the abductive process by the meta-predicates *add_neg*([*clipped*(T1,F1,T3)],N1,N2) and *abdemo_nafs*(N2,R3,R4,N2,N3) where the former adds the formula *clipped*(T1,F1,T3) to the list of negated goals, if it is not already there, while the later is only satisfied if there is not any possibility to resolve *clipped*(T1,F1,T3).

Modify plan This task is responsible for modifying the plan with respect to the results of the critique plan subtask (a conflict). A plan modification can be done by adding ordering or variable bindings to the plan until a conflict is solved or avoided. The AEC planner uses the *causal-link-based modify* method, which adds to the plan an ordering constraint (a *before* literal) before or after the protected causal-link (*clipped* literal).

The interaction critique subtask is performed each time the predicate *abdemo_nafs*(N2,R3,R4,N2,N3) is called (Line 7 in Figure 3). This is done by verifying whether any of the elements of the list of negated goals N2 actually fails given R3 (the plan). If not, then there is a threat that should be solved by *promotion* or *demotion* which are additions to the residue to preserve the proof of a previously solved negated clipped goal [6]. This is done by a special clause that defines the *abdemo_nafs* predicate (see [6]).

5. A Lesson Taken from the Analyses of Partial-Order Planning Algorithms

In this section we show that, since we have established a common language to describe planners, we can look at comparative analyses of planning algorithms and try to map its results for the logic based approach, e.g., for the AEC planning. In order to make this map, we use as an example an interesting experimental result pointed out by [22] which investigates the performance of partial-order planning algorithms based on the way they balance the tradeoff between redundancy and systematicity of its search.

5.1. The Tradeoff between Redundancy and Systematicity

There was a belief that by decreasing redundancy it would be possible to improve planning efficiency. Designing a planner that is systematic means that it never visits two equivalent plans, i.e., it does not allow redundancy in its search space [9]. However, Kambhampati in [22] has shown that there is a tradeoff between redundancy elimination and least commitment: redundancy is eliminated at the expense of increasing commitment in the planner. Therefore, the performance of a partial-order

planner is better predicted based on the way it deals with the tradeoff between redundancy and commitment, then on the systematicity of its search as claimed in [9].
In order to show the effects of this tradeoff, Kambhampati starts by choosing two well known planning algorithms named TWEAK [5] and SNLP [9]. They can be characterized as *mtc-based* and *causal-link-based* planners, respectively.

Redundancy in a MTC-based planner TWEAK is a planner achieved by inverting the modal truth criterion [5]. TWEAK does not keep track of which goals were already achieved and which it remains to be achieve, it may achieve and clobber a goal/subgoal arbitrarily many times. Thus, TWEAK turns out to have a lot of redundancy in its search space.

Systematicity in a causal-link based planner SNLP [9] achieves systematicity by keeping track of the causal structures of the plans generated during search, and ensuring that each branch of the search space commits to and protects mutually exclusive causal structures for the partial plans [22]. Such protection corresponds to a strong form of premature commitment, which can increase the amount of backtracking as well as the solution depth, and can have an adverse effect on the performance of the planner.
Kambhampati's experimental analyses shows that there is a spectrum of solutions to the tradeoff between redundancy and commitment in partial-order planning (Figure 4 in [22]) in which the SNLP and TWEAK planners fall in the extremes. He also proposes other planners that can fall in the middle of these two extremes and can have a better performance, for instance, a *multi-contributor causal-link* planner. In the sequence we will discuss how such planner can be implemented using the abductive event calculus approach.

5.2. How the AEC Planner Is Related to TWEAK and SNLP

Kambhampati classifies PO planners as *Causal Link Based* or *Non-Causal Link Based*. Since the AEC planner does bookkeeping of the *clipped* goals, it can be characterized as a causal-link based planner as in SNLP planner (extreme systematic).
On the other hand, the AEC planner uses the *plan assessment knowledge* role modeled as a set of Event Calculus axioms which corresponds to the MTC knowledge in TWEAK (extreme redundant).
The reason why the AEC planner should still be considered a systematic planner (like SNLP) is because in the AEC planner's design a decision was made to add as an *auxiliary constraint* the literal *clipped*(T1, F, T2) in the list of *negative residue*. If instead, the AEC planner added the literals *holds_at*(T1, F, T2) it would become extremely redundant (like in TWEAK).

5.3. An Abductive Event Calculus Planner with *Multi-contributor Causal-Links*

The AEC planner, such as SNLP and NONLIN, uses the traditional single contributor causal-links and fix a threat (conflict) by ordering it to come either before or after the causal-link (demotion or promotion). If none of those conflict resolution methods can be applied, the planner backtracks. On the other hand, a planner bookkeeping *a list of all possible contributors within the causal-links* can reduce premature commitment with a single-contributor causal-link. As showed in [22], this sacrifices systematicity but reduces backtracking.

In the AI planning terminology, a *multi-contributor causal-link* is a 3-tuple <*S, p, w*> where *w* is a plan-step which requires the condition *p* to be true; *S* is a **set of steps** belonging to the plan that satisfy the condition *p*.

We can change the AEC planner into a *multi-contributor causal-link* planner. In order to do so, the abductive meta-interpreter has to look for ***all the actions*** in *happens* that satisfy a fluent *F* and keep a causal-link (*clipped* literal) for each of those actions (for instance, *clipped*(T1, F, T) for a *happens* (A1, T1, Ti) , *clipped*(T2, F, T) for a *happens* (A2, T2, Tj), ... , *clipped*(Tn, F, T) for a *happens* (An, Tn, Tm)).

By keeping this list we will have to make changes in the AEC planner with respect to the way the planner realizes its planning subtasks, i.e., the PSMs. The specification of those methods is out of the scope of the present article.

6. Concluding Remarks

The AI planning community has developed very different planning systems using apparently unrelated data structures and algorithms. Much research has been done to analyze and compare them in terms of efficiency gains and yet in terms of the nature of the knowledge they use.

In previous work we have constructed a library of problem-solving methods for planning [25]. The methods in the library were obtained by describing planning methods available in the AI planning literature. A central knowledge in the planning library is the knowledge role called *plan assessment knowledge* which has been identified to be modeled as: *causal-link-based* or *mtc-based.* The methods used to solve planning subtasks can also be characterized as *causal-link-based* or *mtc-based*, that means, a problem-solving method can use the *plan assessment knowledge* represented as *causal-link-based* or *mtc-based* respectively.

We have analyzed Shanahan´s AEC planner [6] in terms of the knowledge it represents and how it performs the subtasks described in the planning library. We have observed that in the AEC planner, the *plan assessment knowledge* role is represented in both ways: as a *mtc-based* model (a compilation of EC axioms into the clauses of the abductive meta-interpreter) and as a *causal-link-based* model (in the abductive process of preserving the list of negated *clipped* or *declipped* literals (causal-links)).

The interesting feature pointed out by Shanahan [6] is that the planning knowledge components (as conflict, causal-links, promotions and demotions) were not originally designed in the logic programming implementation but rather they were features that naturally arise of the theorem prover's search for a proof. In this paper we have shown that such affirmative can be considered partially true: the idea of having a list of *clipped* goals to be recorded by a bookkeeping procedure do not follow directly from the EC axioms execution but is rather a design choice of the theorem prover implementation (i.e., a choice of what literals will be included in the residue list).
Therefore, the choices on the contents of the residue list can determine whether the planner is *causal-link-based* or *mtc-based* (which in terms of search space characterization means redundant or systematic [22]). If instead of bookkeeping the *clipped* literal in the list of negated residue, the AEC planner had, on the other hand, bookkeeping the *holds-at* literal, the planner would be redundant (like TWEAK [5]). This is still a nice feature of the logic based planner since it shows a clean and simple distinction between the so called *causal-link-based* and *mtc-based* planning methods.
Based on comparative analyses of planning systems [22] we have also proposed a way in which the AEC planner can be changed to become more efficient: bookkeeping *multi-contributors causal-links* in the list of residue. This can be considered a more controlled way to improve efficiency in a logic-based planner instead of inserting a number of *cuts* in the PROLOG program. It also may highlight new ideas on the extension of a theory of action, e.g., the Event Calculus.

References

[1] L. N. Barros, J. Hendler, and V. R. Benjamins. Par-KAP: a knowledge acquisition tool for building practical planning systems. In *Proceedings of the IJCAI-97*, Nagoya, Japan, 1997.

[2] L. N. Barros, A. Valente and V. R. Benjamins. Modeling planning tasks. In *Third International Conference on Artificial Intelligence Planning Systems, AIPS-96,* pages 11-18, 1996.

[3] V. R. Benjamins, L. N. Barros, and A. Valente. Constructing planners through problem-solving methods. In *Knowledge Acquisition Workshop - KAW'96 (Banff)*, 1996.

[4] B. Chandrasekaran. Design problem solving: A task analysis. *AI Magazine,* 11: (59-71), 1990.

[5] D. Chapman. Planning for conjunctive goals. *Artificial Intelligence*, 32:333-377, 1987.

[6] M. Shanahan. An Abductive Event Calculus Planner. To appear. http://www-ics.ee.ic.ac.uk/~mpsha/pubs.html.

[7] K. Eshghi. Abductive planning with event calculus. In *Proceedings of the Fifth International Conference on Logic Programming,* 562-579, 1988.

[8] L. Missiaen, M. Bruyonooghe, and M. Denecker. Chica, a planning system based on event calculus. *The Journal of Logic and Computation,* 5(5): 579-602, 1995.

[9] D. McAllester and D.Rosenblitt. Systematic Nonlinear Planning. In Proceedings of 9th AAAI, 19991.

[10] J. McCarthy and P. J. Hayes. Some philosophical problems from the standpoint of Artificial Intelligence. In *Machine Intelligence 4*, 1969.

[11] K. Orsvärn. Principles for libraries of task decomposition methods - conclusions from a case-study. In N. Shadbolt, K. O'Hara, and G. Schreiber, editors, *Lectures Notes in Artificial Intelligence, 1076, 9th European Knowledge Acquisition Workshop, EKAW-96,* pages 48-65. Springer-Verlag, 1996.

[12] R. Reiter. Knowledge in action: Logical foundations for describing and implementing dynamical systems. Draft of the first eight chapters of the book.

[13] S. Russell and P. Norvig. *Artificial Intelligence: A Modern Approach.* Prentice Hall International, 1995.

[14] P. E. Santos. Formalizing the common sense of a mobile robot. Mol-1998-02, Institute for Logic, Language and Computation, University of Amsterdam, September 1998.

[15] A. Th. Schreiber, B. J. Wielinga, R. de Hoog, J. M Akkermans, and W. Van de Velde. CommonKADS: A comprehensive methodology for KBS development. *IEEE Expert,* 9(6): 28-37, December 1994.

[16] M. Shanahan. A Circumscriptive event calculus. *Artificial Intelligence*, 77:249-284, 1995.

[17] M. Shanahan. Event Calculus planning revised. In *Proceedings of European Conference on Planning,* pages 390-420. Springer-Verlag Lecture notes in Artificial Intelligence 1348, 1997.

[18] M. Shanahan. Solving the frame problem. The MIT press, 1997.

[19] M. Shanahan. A logical account of the common sense information situation for a mobile robot. Linköping Electronic Articles in Computer and Information Science, 1998. http://www.ep.liu.se/ea/cis/1998/.

[20] A. Tate, J.Hendler, and M.Drummond. A review of AI planning techniques. In J. Allen, J. Hendler, and A. Tate, editors, *Readings in Planning,* pages 26-49. Kaufmann, San Mateo, CA, 1990.

[21] A. Valente. Knowledge level analysis of planning. SIGART Bulletin, 6(1): 33-41, 1995.

[22] S. Kambhampati. On the Utility of Systematicity: Understanding Tradeoffs between Redundancy and Commitment in Partial-order Planning. In *Proceedings of IJCAI*, 1991.

[23] S. Kambhampati. Multi-Contributor Causal Structures for Planning: A Formalization and Evaluation. *Artificial Intelligence*, Vol. 69, 1994.

[24] A. Tate. Generating Project Networks. In *Proceedings of IJCAI-77*, pages 888-893, Boston, 1977.

[25] A. Valente, V. R. Benjamins, and L. N. Barros. A library of system-derived problem-solving methods for planning. In *International Journal of Human-Computer Studies 48,* 417-447. Academic Press Limited, 1998.

[26] R. A. Kowalski and M. J. Sergot. A Logic-Based Calculus of Events. In *New Generation Computing*. Vol. 4:67-95, 1986.

[27] H. Cottam and N. Shadbolt.Domain and system influences in problem solving models for planning. In N. Shadbolt, K. O'Hara, and G. Schreiber, editors, *Lectures Notes in Artificial Intelligence, 1076, 9th European Knowledge Acquisition Workshop, EKAW-96,* pages 354-369. Springer-Verlag, 1996.

[28] R. E. Fikes and N. J. Nilsson. STRIPS: a new approach to the application of theorem proving to problem solving. *Artificial Intelligence,* 2:(169-203), 1971.

[29] A. Barret and D. S. Weld. Partial-order planning: evaluating possible efficiency gains. *Artificial Intelligence,* 67: (71-112), 1994.

Adapting Tableaux for Classification

M.G. Jansen[1], A.Th. Schreiber[1], and B.J. Wielinga[1]

University of Amsterdam, Social Science Informatics
Roetersstraat 15, NL-1018 WB Amsterdam, The Netherlands
E-mail: {jansen,schreiber,wielinga}@swi.psy.uva.nl

Abstract. We present an approach for studying logical properties of problem-solving methods (PSMs) for knowledge-intensive tasks. It is based on semantic tableaux (a deduction-style theorem-proving technique). We show how tableaux can be manipulated in a methodical way to formalize non-deductive style PSMs.

1 Introduction

Knowledge-engineering research has delivered an abundance of problem-solving methods (PSMs) for classes of tasks. such as classification, diagnosis, and configuration (see e.g., [2]). These PSMs are used in practical knowledge systems. To get a better understanding of the different PSMs work has been done on the formalization of PSMs, e.g. [4,10,11]. In this paper we describe another approach, in which we adapt semantic tableaux to formalize PSMs. We show that this provides us with a technique for studying the logical properties of PSMs. In particular, we show that this approach allows us to model non-deductive style reasoning. This was a problem with previous formalizations based on first-order logic. We use the classification task as an example.

2 Characterizing Classification

We can characterize a knowledge-intensive task by defining three aspects: (1) the goal of the task, (2) the ontological commitments, and (3) the solution criteria.

Goal The goal is typically an informal description of what the task attempts to achieve. In the case of classification, the goal is to identify to which class a certain object belongs. Example classification tasks are apple classification, rock classification, and art-object classification.

Ontological commitments Ontological commitments describe our assumptions on the representation of the task domain. They provide us with a vocabulary. We can use this vocabulary to define what we mean with classification. Together, the ontological commitments form an ontology for a task. An example of such task ontology is the configuration-design ontology [6]. For classification we base the task ontology on the descriptions of classification given by [9,8].

We define six basic ontological types, namely **attribute**, **object**, **value**, **class**, **feature**, and **observation**. A is a (finite) set of attributes, each of which is associated with a

R. Dieng and O. Corby (Eds.): EKAW 2000, LNAI 1937, pp. 344–351, 2000.

list of possible values. A feature is an admissible attribute-value pair. Objects that need to be classified are described by a finite number of attribute-value (AV) pairs. These AV-pairs are called observations. The set of observations for a particular object is called Obs.

By definition, we assume that an attribute can have only one value at the time. So, if $colour$ is an attribute and $\{red, yellow, blue\}$ is its list of possible values, then an object description can never contain the AV-pairs $colour = red$ and $colour = yellow$ simultaneously. Every attribute with more than two values can be transformed into several attributes which all have binary values. This transformation is performed as follows: For every such AV-pair we take a new attribute with possible values $true$ and $false$. The new attribute has the value $true$ if the original AV-pair holds, and $false$ otherwise.

Note that after having applied such a transformation the exclusion of multiple values for an attribute is no longer guaranteed. In order to maintain this principle every new attribute has the original attribute as it's type. Now we can say that exclusion of multiple values holds for binary AV-pairs of the same type. If one binary attribute has the value true, then all other attributes of the same type have the value false. In this way, each multi-valued attribute can be represented as a set of atomic propositions.

Classes can now be represented as follows:

$$c \rightarrow (a_1 \vee ... \vee a_n) \wedge ... \wedge (b_1 \vee ... \vee b_n)$$

The class name is represented by the proposition c and implies its features (i.e. AV-pairs). Features are here represented as atomic propositions with an index for ease of representation. a_1 represents the feature where a designates the attribute and the index $_1$ a certain value.

Domain knowledge can be represented by assigning meaningful names to such a structure. For example:

$$\begin{array}{l} blackbird \rightarrow \\ (plumage = black) \wedge (bill = yellow) \end{array}$$

The domain theory DT consists of a conjunction of class definitions.

Solution criteria There are several alternative criteria one can formulate with respect to the goal of the classification process. We define two criteria:[1]

Weak classification In weak classification (WC) a candidate solution must be a class c which is consistent with the domain theory DT and the observations Obs made thus far. Formally, this set of candidate solutions S can be expressed by:

$$S = \{c | DT \cup \{c\} \cup Obs \nvdash \bot\}$$

Strong classification In strong classification (SC) a class c is a member of the set of candidate solutions S iff the domain theory together with c explains all observations. That is, we want candidate solutions to be classes which actually possess the properties that have been observed. Formally, the criterion for SC is:

$$S = \{c | DT \cup \{c\} \models Obs\}$$

The criterion of strong classification is stronger in a logical sense than weak classification. If a class is a candidate solution according to SC it is also according to WC. This follows as SC can be formulated as an extension of WC.

[1] In Sec. 4.3 we introduce a third form of classification, namely composite-solution classification.

3 Tableaux

Semantic tableaux were developed in the 50's (see e.g. [3]). Like resolution they form a *refutation* system. In a tableau proof a tree is constructed where nodes are labeled with formulae.[2]

In order to test whether a certain formula φ follows from a set of premises Θ a tableau tree is constructed for $\Theta \cup \{\neg\varphi\}$. Constructing such a binary tree can be seen as checking for (in)consistency of the theory. It is build using reduction rules which determine how the tree is branched. If in any branch, a formula and its negation appear the branch is said to be closed. If all branches close the theory is inconsistent.

Table 1. Rules for the tableau trees

$$\frac{\neg\neg Z}{Z} \quad \frac{\alpha}{\begin{array}{c}\alpha^1\\ \alpha^2\end{array}} \quad \frac{\beta}{\beta^1 \mid \beta^2}$$

Table 1 shows the rules for constructing the tableau tree. The first rule indicates that double negations are redundant. All propositional formulas containing binary connectives can be divided as belonging to two types: True conjunctive formulas (α-type) and true disjunctive formulas (β-type). For example $p \rightarrow q$ can be rewritten to $\neg p \vee q$ and so is a β-formula. The rule for α-type formulas indicates that the conjuncts have to be placed on the same branch of the tree. The β-rule however indicates a branching of the tree.

4 Tableaux for Classification

The general method to use propositional semantic tableaux as a proof procedure for classification proceeds as follows. The solution criterion for the classification task is translated into a consistency formula. Subsequently that formula is expanded into a semantic tableau. If the tableau can be closed or remains partially open, a conclusion can be derived about the solutions of the classification problem. The precise nature of the conclusion depends on the nature of the solution criterion.

The closing rule for tableaux for classification can be specialized on the basis of the ontological commitments described in Sec. 2. Since all features that occur in the domain theory are considered to be typed propositions and since two distinct propositions of the same type exclude each other, any path that contains two different propositions of the same type can be closed. This is equivalent to the addition of formulae of the following type to the domain theory for each feature:

$$a_1 \rightarrow (\neg a_2 \wedge \ldots \wedge \neg a_n)$$

Building this ontological commitment into the proof procedure retains all properties of the general procedure such as soundness and completeness, but is more efficient.

[2] We limit ourselves here to the description of propositional tableaux since this seems sufficient for the description of classification. We follow [5] in this description.

4.1 Weak Classification

In weak classification we assume that the domain theory and the observations together are consistent. This assumption is implicit in the way knowledge is represented and can be viewed as an additional ontological commitment.

Because of this consistency a semantic tableau for $DT \cup Obs$ will have open branches. Fig. 1 shows a tableau for the domain theory $\{c_1 \rightarrow a_1 \wedge d_2, c_2 \rightarrow a_2 \wedge d_3\}$ and the observation d_3. The observation is added to the leaves of the tree for the domain theory.

Now, in order to check which classes are consistent with the observations made up to this point, each class must be individually added to the tableau. If the tree closes the resulting theory is inconsistent and the class is not a candidate. If a new observation is made it must be added to the tree and a check for all remaining candidates has to be made again. Fig. 1 shows class c_1 to be inconsistent with the domain theory together with the observation d_3, as its addition to the tableau would close the tree.

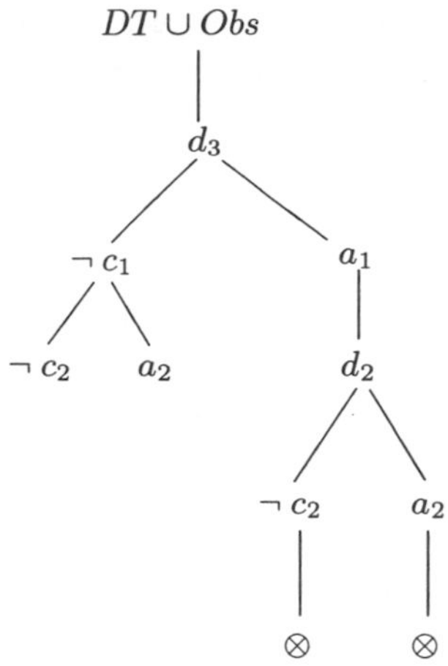

Fig. 1. Tableau for weak classification

This procedure for weak classification with semantic tableaux can be summarized as follows:

```
Procedure WC-1:
  1. Construct a tableau for the observations
     and the domain theory (in this order)
  2. FOR each possible candidate class c DO
       IF c (and c alone) is added to the tableau
          AND the tableau closes
       THEN c is not a possible candidate
       ELSE c remains a possible candidate
  3. When new observations are made:
     a. add observation(s) to top of the tableau
     b. redo step 2}
```

It is interesting to view weak classification in terms of what is actually deduced during the process. In order to prove that a formula follows from a theory with the help of semantic tableaux one has to prove the inconsistency of the negation of the formula together with the theory. In the case of weak classification the aim is to prove the inconsistency of a class together with the domain theory and observations. In terms of consequence this means proving the negation of a class from the domain theory and observations. More formally:

$$DT \cup Obs \cup \{c\} \vdash \perp \Leftrightarrow DT \cup Obs \models \neg c$$

In other words: weak classification only provides negative information about classes. The method is actually more about ruling out candidates than looking for candidates which can explain the observations. This is left to the stronger criterion of strong classification.

The procedure WC-1 is still inefficient since it generates the tableau for the entire domain theory. The ontological commitments about the structure of the knowledge base, i.e. that class definitions are conjunctions of disjunctive feature sets, allow us to specialize the procedure even more. Consequently more efficient procedures can be formulated.

4.2 Strong Classification

We now proceed to describe a procedure for testing whether a candidate class fulfills the SC requirement. If it can be shown for a certain class c that $DT \cup \{c\} \cup \{\neg o_1 \vee \ldots \neg o_n\}$ is inconsistent, the criterion of SC is met with respect to c. In order to show this, first a tableau for DT and the disjunction of negated observations is build. Since this theory is consistent the tree will have open branches. If c is added to the tree and closes the tableau, c is a SC candidate, otherwise it is not. Here we make use of the ontological assumption that $DT \cup \{c\}$ is consistent. An example is given in Fig. 2.

This procedure for SC can be summarized as follows:

```
Procedure SC-1:
  1. Construct a tableau for the domain theory
  2. Add the disjunction of the negation of each
     element of Obs to the leaves of the tableau
     for the domain theory
  3. FOR each possible candidate class c DO
       IF c (and c alone) is added to the tableau
          AND the tableau closes
       THEN c remains a possible candidate
       ELSE c is not a possible candidate
  4. IF new observations become available
     THEN redo step 2 and 3}
```

SC is in general more complex to compute than WC. To infer the observations from the domain theory and a candidate class , the disjunction of all negated observations should be added to the tableau. In contrast to WC, each observation will give rise to a branching of the tree.

The same specializations of the proof procedure that we have described for WC apply to SC.

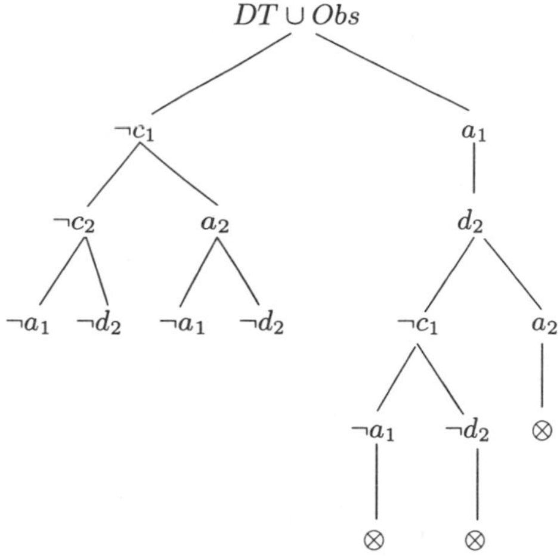

Fig. 2. Tableau for strong classification

4.3 Classification and Abduction

The procedure SC-1 is identical to the way abduction is performed with tableaux as described in [1]. This is intentional. As defined above SC comes down to an abductive method. Abduction is often linked to a style of reasoning which produces causal explanations for observations. Classification is rarely, if ever, considered to be an abductive task. Still the criterion of SC is formally in line with those of abduction, as for example put forward by [7].

In [1] five different styles of abductive reasoning are defined. Given Θ (a theory) and φ (a sentence), α is an abductive explanation (abducible) if:

- Plain: $\Theta, \alpha \models \varphi$
- Consistent: $\Theta, \alpha \models \varphi$ and Θ, α is consistent.
- Explanatory: $\Theta, \alpha \models \varphi$ and $\Theta \not\models \varphi$ and $\alpha \not\models \varphi$
- Minimal: $\Theta, \alpha \models \varphi$ and α is the weakest such explanation.
- Preferential: $\Theta, \alpha \models \varphi$ and α is the best explanation according to some given preferential ordering.

Interestingly enough, SC displays four of these properties of abduction. The "'plain" property follows directly from the solution criterium. Classification is a restricted form of abduction: the only abducibles allowed are atomic class propositions. Since it is an ontological assumption that class definitions are individually consistent with the domain theory (i.e., $DT \cup c$ is consistent), it follows that solutions found by the SC-1 method are consistent. SC is minimal since we restrict the form of abducibles to single classes (atomic propositions) only.

Weak classification does not exhibit any of the properties of abduction, since no formula (φ) is assumed to be entailed by the theory (Θ) and the abducibles (α). Intuitively, WC generates a formula and tests if it is consistent with the current domain theory and observables, but it does not try to explain anything. This makes WC a very different task from SC. This is in line with our earlier observation that WC is a ruling out task rather than an explanation task. From a logical point of view, one could argue that the two forms of classification are rather different ways of reasoning, even though procedurally they are very similar. One could even go as far as considering WC not as a classification task, but as a refutation task.

For the property of minimality, there is a difference between abduction and strong classification. If we decide to allow not only single classes as abducibles but conjunctions of classes as well we end up with a different style of classification. In that case we would get a form of classification in which more than one class explains the observations and counts as a solution. Thus, a conjunction of classes can act as a solution candidate. This is known as composite-solution classification (CSC) [9].

The solution predicate can be formulated as follows:

$$S = \{c_1 \wedge ... \wedge c_n | DT \cup \{c_1 \wedge ... \wedge c_n\} \models Obs\}$$

Note however that we can no longer assume the property of consistency ($DT \cup \{c_1 \wedge ... \wedge c_n\}$), as the simultaneous addition of two or more classes (e.g., a black bird and a white bird) to the tableau of the domain theory may lead to inconsistency. Therefore, the procedure will have to test explicitly for consistency. For example, if $DT = \{c_1 \rightarrow a_1, c_2 \rightarrow a_2\}$, adding the composite solution $\{c_1 \wedge c_2\}$ makes the theory inconsistent, since a_1 and a_2 are regarded as exclusive.

If one allows composite solutions, one could still prefer single solutions. In this case CSC is defined as preferential abduction in the above sense.

5 Discussion

Even though classification is one of the simplest knowledge-intensive tasks in the knowledge-engineering domain, it has been quite hard to prove that certain computational methods satisfy logical competence theories. Similarly, it has been difficult to transform logical competence requirements into an operational method. Problems encountered include: the abductive nature of classificatory reasoning, the incremental nature of observation gathering and the mapping of logical theories onto different computational strategies in classification methods [11]. In this paper we have presented some steps forward towards solving these problems.

A first insight is that strong classification is a special case of abduction. The solution of a classification problem is considered as an abducible of some domain theory and the observed facts. Theories of abduction provide several types of abduction that can be mapped onto different variants of the classification task. However, classification is more specific than abduction in the sense that it restricts the vocabulary of abducibles to a predefined set of classes and that it assumes a particular structure of the domain theory.

Second, it appears that the semantic tableau proof method has some features that makes it suitable to model various forms of classificatory reasoning. Tableaux provide a natural way of handling incrementally growing theories as they often occur in knowledge-based systems, where new facts are incrementally obtained from a user. In classical logical approaches that attempt to formalize classification reasoning, this problem is not easily solved [11]. Tableaux also provide a way of thinking about the search space of possible inferences in a formal context. As we have shown, the ontological commitments of the task restrict the possible expansions and closures of the tableaux. These restrictions can be translated into the proof procedure itself, thus reducing the space of formulae to be processed. This is precisely where knowledge-based systems derive their power from, when compared to general theorem-proving approaches. It can be proven that the specialized proof procedures are equivalent to the normal proof procedure when the ontological commitments are added as axioms to the domain theory.

The third result of our investigation is that PSMs for classification that have been published [9,11] can be mapped onto proof procedures. For example, procedure WC-1 and WC-2 formalize the "pruning" method, which can therefore be characterized as both sound and complete. WC-1 is a "pure" logical method, but computationally not very efficient. In tableau terminology it generates a much larger tableau than WC-2. WC-2 is an optimized method which is in fact close to operational methods used in classification systems. Procedure SC formalizes a generate-and-test method for classification. Here, we can see from the formalization that if the method would terminate after having found one solution (which is often the case in operational methods), the method is sound, but not complete. In short, this type of mapping of PSMs used in knowledge-based systems onto specific tableau proof procedures provides a powerful way of establishing the competence of these methods in logical terms.

References

[1] A. Aliseda-LLera. *Seeking Explanations: Abduction in Logic, Philosophy of Science and Artificial Intelligence*. PhD thesis, ILLC, University of Amsterdam, Amsterdam, The Netherlands, 1997.

[2] V. R. Benjamins and D. Fensel. Problem-solving methods. *Int. J. Human-Computer Studies*, 49(4):305–313, 1998. Editorial special issue.

[3] E.W. Beth. Semantic entailment and formal derivability. In J. Hintikka, editor, *The Philisophy of Mathematics*, pages 9–41. Oxford University Press, 1969.

[4] D. Fensel and R. Groenboom. Specifying knowledge-based systems with reusable components. In *Proceedings of SEKE-97*, 1997.

[5] M. C. Fitting. *First-Order Logic and Automated Theorem Proving*. Springer-Verlag, New York, 1990.

[6] T. R. Gruber, G. R. Olsen, and J. Runkel. The configuration-design ontologies and the VT elevator domain theory. *Int. J. Human-Computer Studies*, 44(3/4):569–598, 1996.

[7] A. C. Kakas, R. A. Kowalski, and M. Toni. Abductive logic programing. *Journal of Logic and Computation*, 2(6):719–770, 1993.

[8] A. Th. Schreiber, J. M. Akkermans, A. A. Anjewierden, R. de Hoog, N. R. Shadbolt, W. Van de Velde, and B. J. Wielinga. *Knowledge Engineering and Management: The CommonKADS Methodology*. MIT Press, Cambrdige, MA, 1999.

[9] M. Stefik. *Introduction to Knowledge Systems*. Los Altos, CA. Morgan Kaufmann, 1993.

[10] F. van Harmelen and A. ten Teije. Characterising problem solving methods by gradual requirements. In *Proceedings of the Eleventh Workshop on Knowledge Acquisition for Knowledge-Based Systems (KAW'98)*, Banff, Alberta, 1998.

[11] B. J. Wielinga, J. M. Akkermans, and A. Th. Schreiber. A competence theory approach to problem-solving method construction. *Int. J. Human-Computer Studies*, 49:315–338, 1998.

Conceptual Information Systems Discussed through an IT-Security Tool

Klaus Becker[1], Gerd Stumme[2], Rudolf Wille[2], Uta Wille[3], and Monika Zickwolff[4]

[1] Entrust Technologies (Switzerland) Ltd liab. Co, Glatt Tower, CH-8301 Glattzentrum, Switzerland; klaus.becker@entrust.com
[2] Technische Universität Darmstadt, Fachbereich Mathematik, D–64289 Darmstadt, Germany; {stumme,wille}@mathematik.tu-darmstadt.de
[3] Jelmoli AG, Information Systems, Postfach 3020, Ch–8021 Zürich, Switzerland; wille_u@jelmoli.ch
[4] NaviCon Gesellschaft für Begriffliche Wissensverarbeitung mbH, Heinrichstrasse 9, 60327 Frankfurt/Main, Germany; zickwolff@navicon.de

Abstract. Conceptual Information Systems are based on a formalization of the concept of 'concept' as it is discussed in traditional philosophical logic. This formalization supports a human-centered approach to the development of Information Systems. We discuss this approach by means of an implemented Conceptual Information System for supporting IT security management in companies and organizations.

Contents

1 Conceptual Information Systems

Information Systems are understood as systems for input, storage, association, processing, analysis, retrieval, and output of information which are designed by organic, technical and organisational principles to support learning and communication processes. Most information systems have the purpose to assist human beings in creating knowledge. Since human knowledge heavily depends on common sense, preknowledge, context and culture, the development of those systems should not only follow a technical understanding of information and knowledge, but also a human-related understanding including meanings, interpretations, purposes etc. Ron Brachman and others have therefore advocated a *human-centered approach* that supports asking, exploring, analyzing, interpreting, and learning in interaction with the information system (cf. [5], [4]). Their

R. Dieng and O. Corby (Eds.): EKAW 2000, LNAI 1937, pp. 352–365, 2000.

claims have been stated as system requirements listed in [25] which we recall with minor modifications:

1. An information system should represent and present to the user the underlying domain in a natural and appropriate fashion. Objects from the domain should be easily incorporated into queries.
2. The domain representation should be extendible by addition of new categories formed from queries; these categories (and their representative individuals) must be usable in subsequent queries.
3. It should be easy to form tentative segmentations of data, to investigate the segments, and to re-segment quickly and easily; there should be a powerful repertoire of viewing and analysis methods, and these methods should be applicable to segments.
4. Users should be supported in recognizing and abstracting common analysis (segmenting and viewing) patterns; it must be easy to apply and modify these patterns.
5. There should be facilities for monitoring changes in classes or categories over time.
6. An information system should increase the transparency of the processes of analysis and retrieval and should document their different stages.
7. Analysis and retrieval tools should take advantage of explicitly represented background knowledge of domain experts, but should also activate the implicit knowledge of experts.
8. An information system should allow highly flexible processes of analysis and retrieval respecting the open and procedural nature of productive human thinking; this means in particular to support intersubjective communication and argumentation.

For fulfilling the listed requirements for a *human-centered development of information systems*, it is promotive to base the formal representation of human knowledge on a broad understanding of knowledge. According to the traditional philosophical logic, knowledge is grounded on the formation of concepts from which humans form their judgments (cf. [30]). Thus, concepts are essential for the creation and representation of knowledge. For human-centered developments of information systems, we therefore suggest to use a formalization of the philosophical understanding of concepts for the formal representation and presentation of knowledge; such a formalization is performed in *Formal Concept Analysis* [7]. We name human-centered information systems developed on the basis of Formal Concept Analysis *"Conceptual Information Systems"*. In the following we discuss the conception of "Conceptual Information Systems" through an example of such system that has been developed to support the security management of information technology [2].

2 IT-Security Management

The task of Information Technology (IT) is to assure the availability, confidentiality, and integrity of the data of an organization. In the past few years the main focus has been on the availability. With an increasing exchange of data via local and public networks the protection of the data against loss of confidentiality and integrity has become a major issue. Reports on damages indicate that it is not sufficient to react on damages once they appear. The management of companies and public organizations needs a systematic support for an effective risk management, such that one can recognize threats well in advance and can prevent them by appropriate safeguards.

The past has shown that individual risk analysis is very costly and often results are not in a reasonable relation to the timely and financial expenses. Furthermore, a major part of the resulting safeguards is independent of the organization, for instance the protection of server or PCs by passwords. A solution is to codify the safeguards which are independent from the individual organization in an IT security management catalogue. Then only the particular aspects of an organization have to undergo an individual risk analysis. The implementation of this IT security catalogue provides an adequate security level for systems with medium-level protection requirements.

For a continuously high security level it is not sufficient to implement a one-time security concept. It is necessary to create processes assuring the continuous interplay of requirement analysis, realisation, and control. The requirement analysis determines the needed security level. It depends on the potential damage and on the value of the objects to be protected. In IT this means before all the value of the processed data. This value is determined by the used IT resource, the IT process, and the organizational unit which applies the IT resource in the particular IT process. For these *IT units*, the needed level of protection is determined in the requirement analysis. An example for an IT unit is the combination of the IT resource 'mailing system', the IT process 'operation', and the organizational unit 'data processing center'.

One of the most important tasks of IT security management is the realisation of the conception, i. e., the assignment of the requirements of the IT security catalogue to the organizational units, as well as the derivation of concrete directives and checklists for the organizational units from the requirements. An important success factor of this task is a high acceptance of the directives by the involved organizational units. This means primarily a suitable structuring with regard to the organizational units:

- Comparable matters of fact should result in comparable requirements (e. g., virus protection for PCs).
- Each IT unit should have assigned to only its specific requirements, since the implementation of the whole catalogue without taking into account the specific security level needed is rarely reasonable. For instance, PCs in the management underly other requirements than PCs in the R&D department.
- Requirements should be ordered by priority. For instance, the protection against breakdown of PCs is more important in production than in marketing departments.

A regular verification of the obtained security level is a core part of IT security management. This includes surveying the application of the directives as well as their adaption to changing requirements or structures.

Requirements to an IT Security Management Tool

Due to the large amount of combinations of IT units and threats, the requirement analysis reaches a high degree of complexity even for small and medium-sized organisations. For realizing the IT security conception, the requirements have to be assigned to the relevant organizational units in an effective and transparent way. The system must support the comparison of typical situations and assigned requirements. In the realisation phase, it must also allow the integration of existing directives and checklists. The verification of the obtained security level requires visualization of the obtained level for different classes of IT units, and support for uncovering inconsistencies. These operative tasks determine directly the requirements for the IT security management tool:

1. The tool has to provide a data model and means of its administration for the requirement analysis, i. e., the construction of IT units and the registration of threats, and for the realization, i. e., the assignment of requirements, directives, and checklists.
2. For revision, the underlying IT security management catalogue must be extendable or replacable.
3. For constitution and maintenance of the data, as well as for the analysis and control of the actual level of security, a graphical user interface is needed.

NaviCon Gesellschaft für Begriffliche Wissensverarbeitung mbH and r^3 *security engineering ag* have developed an IT security management tool to fit these needs. The tool is based on the management system TOSCANA for Conceptual Information Systems which has been developed at the Technische Universität Darmstadt. TOSCANA and its underlying mathematical theory, Formal Concept Analysis, are introduced in the next section. The IT security management tool is presented in Section 4.

3 Formal Concept Analysis and TOSCANA

The philosophical understanding of a concept as a unit of thought constituted by its extension and its intension has been influential to the western culture from the seventeenth century until today (cf. [29]). For instance, the German Industrial Standards DIN 2330 "Begriffe und Benennungen" and DIN 2331 "Begriffsysteme und ihre Darstellung" are based on this understanding of concepts. Let us recall that the extension of a concept comprises all objects belonging to the concept while the intension (comprehension) grasps all attributes (properties, meanings) of those objects.

For allowing a mathematical description of extensions and intensions, Formal Concept Analysis always starts with a *formal context* defined as a triple (G, M, I)

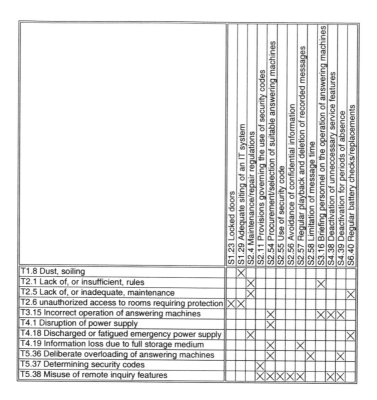

	S1.23 Locked doors	S1.29 Adequate siting of an IT system	S2.4 Maintenance/repair regulations	S2.11 Provisions governing the use of security codes	S2.54 Procurement/selection of suitable answering machines	S2.55 Use of security code	S2.56 Avoidance of confidential information	S2.57 Regular playback and deletion of recorded messages	S2.58 Limitation of message time	S3.16 Briefing personnel on the operation of answering machines	S4.38 Deactivation of unneccessary service features	S4.39 Deactivation for periods of absence	S6.40 Regular battery checks/replacements
T1.8 Dust, soiling		×											
T2.1 Lack of, or insufficient, rules			×							×			
T2.5 Lack of, or inadequate, maintenance			×										×
T2.6 unauthorized access to rooms requiring protection	×	×											
T3.15 Incorrect operation of answering machines					×					×	×	×	
T4.1 Disruption of power supply					×								
T4.18 Discharged or fatigued emergency power supply			×										×
T4.19 Information loss due to full storage medium					×			×					
T5.36 Deliberate overloading of answering machines					×				×			×	
T5.37 Determining security codes				×									
T5.38 Misuse of remote inquiry features				×	×	×	×	×			×	×	

Fig. 1. A formal context concerning a telephone answering machine

where G is a set of *(formal) objects*, M is a set of *(formal) attributes*, and I is a binary relation between G and M (i.e. $I \subseteq G \times M$); in general, gIm ($\Leftrightarrow (g,m) \in I$) is read: "the object g *has* the attribute m"(cf. [7]). In Figure 1, a formal context (taken from [6]) is described by a table in which the crosses represent the binary relation I between the object set G (comprising the threats concerning a telephone answering machine) and the attribute set M (consisting of safeguards to prevent those threats). A *formal concept* of a formal context (G, M, I) is defined as a pair (A, B) with $A \subseteq G$ and $B \subseteq M$ such that (A, B) is maximal with the property $A \times B \subseteq I$; the sets A and B are called the *extent* and the *intent* of the formal concept (A, B). The subconcept-superconcept-relation is formalized by

$$(A_1, B_1) \leq (A_2, B_2) :\Longleftrightarrow A_1 \subseteq A_2 \quad (\Longleftrightarrow B_1 \supseteq B_2).$$

The set of all formal concepts of a formal context (G, M, I) together with the order relation $\leq$ is always a complete lattice, called the *concept lattice* of (G, M, I) and denoted by $\underline{\mathfrak{B}}(G, M, I)$. Figure 2 visualizes the concept lattice by a *(labeled) line diagram.* In a line diagram of a concept lattice, the name of an object g is always attached (from below) to the little circle representing the smallest

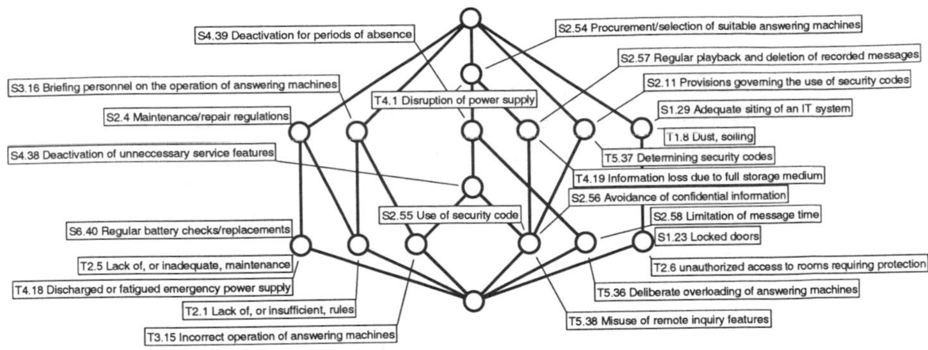

Fig. 2. The concept lattice of the context of Figure 1

concept with g in its extent (denoted by γg); dually, the name of an attribute m is always attached (from above) to the little circle representing the largest concept with m in its intent (denoted by μm). This labelling allows us to read the context relation from the diagram because $gIm \iff \gamma g \leq \mu m$, in words:

the object g has the attribute m if and only if there is an ascending path from the circle representing γg to the circle representing γm.

The extent and intent of each concept (A, B) can also be recognized because

$$A = \{g \in G \mid \gamma g \leq (A, B)\} \text{ and } B = \{m \in M \mid (A, B) \leq \mu m\} \ .$$

For example, the little circle in the line diagram of Figure 2 labelled with *"S4.39 Deactivation of answering machines for periods of absence"* represents the formal concept with the extent {"T3.15 Incorrect operation of answering machines", "T5.36 Deliberate overloading of answering machines", "T.5.38 misuse of remote inquiry features"} and the intent {"S2.54 Procurement/selection of suitable answering machines", "S.4.39 Deactivation of answering machines for periods of absence"}.

Graphically represented concept lattices are useful in discovering and understanding conceptual relationships in given data. Therefore the development of "Conceptual Information Systems" may use concept lattices as query structures for databases. Such interplay of concept lattices and databases has already been designed in the theory of conceptual data systems. A *conceptual data system* consists of a (relational) database and a *conceptual scheme.* A conceptual scheme is a collection of formal contexts, called *conceptual scales,* together with line diagrams of their concept lattices; such systems are implemented with the management system TOSCANA (see [21],[13],[28]). For a chosen conceptual scale, TOSCANA presents a line diagram of the corresponding concept lattice indicating all objects stored in the database in their relationships to the attributes of the scale. For instance, the formal context in Figure 1 is an example of a conceptual scale taken from the data presented in the *IT Baseline Protection Manual* of the Bundesamt für Sicherheit in der Informationstechnik [6]. A TOSCANA system based on the data in [6] (as discussed in [22]) would show, after choosing that scale, the appertaining lattice diagram in Figure 2.

The power of a TOSCANA system lies in the possibility to refine a presented concept lattice by another one so that one obtains either a nested line diagram of a combination of both lattices (see Figure 5 in Section 4) or a line diagram of the second refining a chosen concept of the first. If for instance the study of Figure 2 leads to the assignment of directives and checklists for maintenance and repair regulations (S2.4), it would be advisible to consider maintenance and repair of other facilities such as telecommunication systems; this can be supported by Figure 3 obtained by zooming into the node labelled by S2.4 with the conceptual scale "Telecommunication Systems (Private Branch Exchange)". The concept lattice in Figure 3 indicates how rich the combinations of necessary safeguards are for preventing threats to telecommunication systems against which maintenance and repair is needed. Our small example may give already an idea how conceptual information systems developed with TOSCANA allow highly flexible processes of analysis and retrieval in respecting the open and procedural nature of human thinking (cf. Section 1); these processes are not restricted because the zooming procedure potentially enables to navigate through the whole database (cf. [31]).

4 A Conceptual Information System for IT-Security Management

The IT Baseline Protection Manual of the Bundesamt für Sicherheit in der Informationstechnik provides safeguards against threats for generic components of an IT system. For the implementation of a security concept in an organization or company, the safeguards have to be transformed in more specific directives and checklists. Therefore, NaviCon Gesellschaft für Begriffliche Wissensverarbeitung mbH and r^3 *security engineering ag* have developed an IT security management tool which provides a higher level of detail. Its basic data model is given in Figure 4. The model consists of three major parts: The IT Security Management Catalogue comprises a generic company independent catalogue of threats and related safeguards, which can be extended by company specific facts.

IT Units represent the relationship between the company specific IT processes and the organizational units with regard to the used IT resources. The third part provides directives and checklists which are assigned to the IT units with respect to the requirements.

The data model is implemented in a relational database. Its implementation and maintenance is done via a Graphical User Interface which is based on Anaconda, a preparation tool for Conceptual Information Systems. The data are analysed by the management system TOSCANA. It provides the visualization of relationships between the conceptual scales by nested line diagrams and allows an on-line navigation through the whole database. The conceptual scheme which is needed by TOSCANA is generated and updated by Anaconda.

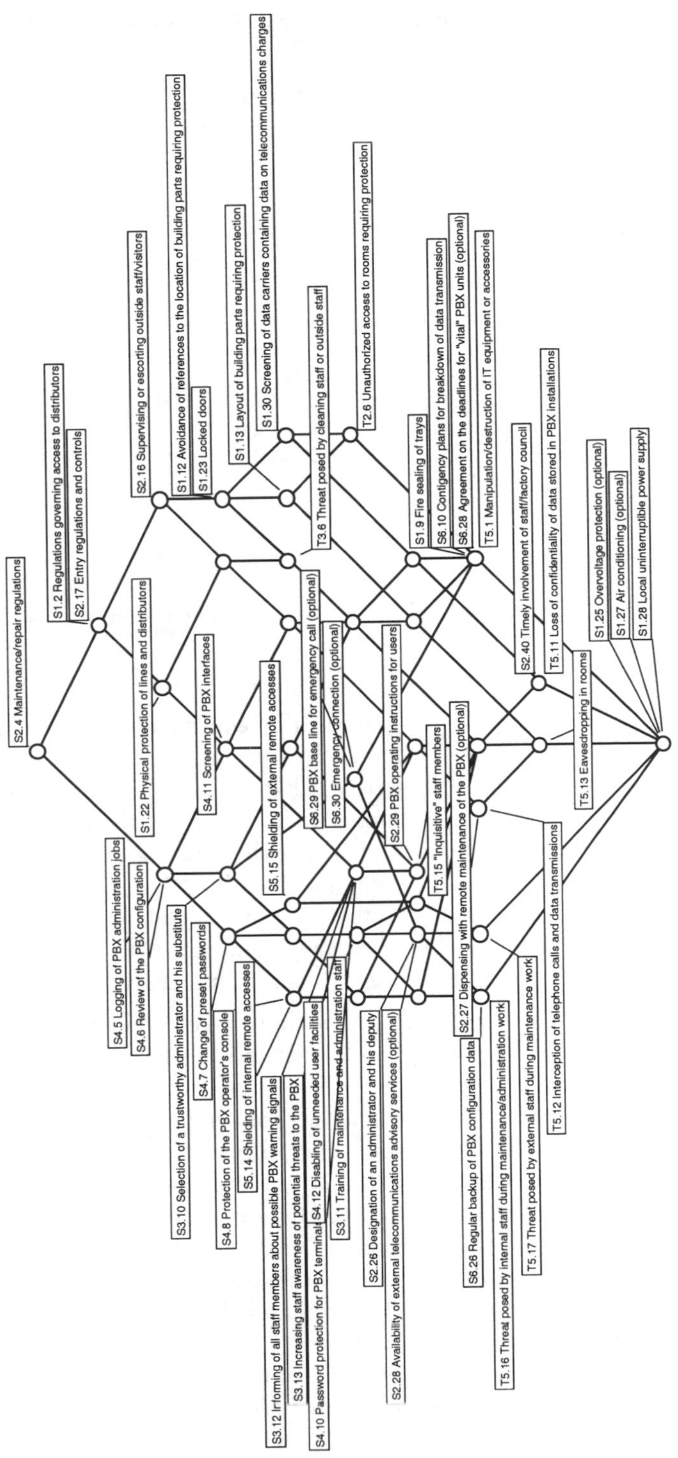

Fig. 3. The concept lattice presenting threats to telecommunication systems against which maintenance and repair is needed

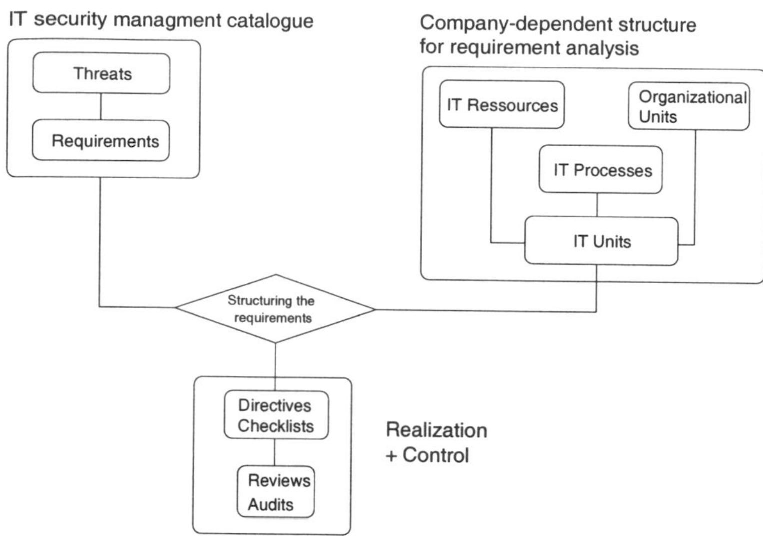

Fig. 4. The data model of the IT security management tool

We describe how TOSCANA supports IT security analysis by means of an example. Figure 5 shows a nested line diagram which is composed by the three conceptual scales 'Existence of directives', 'Key Control' and 'Faults'. When we first have a look at the large left ellipse of the diagram, then we see that there are $1+3+4+2=10$ requirements for which there are no directives formulated at the moment ('Maßnahme nicht vorhanden' = directives not existent). Two of them are key control, i. e., requirements which are considered as very important. Hence, for these two requirements, directives and checklists should be provided immediately, while the other requirements can be regarded later.

But also for key control requirements where directives are already present, one has to verify if they are appropriate. There are $1+1+2+9+2+3=18$ such requirements which can be found in the rightmost medium-sized ellipse which is determined by the attributes 'Maßnahme vorhanden' (= directives existent) and 'Key Control'. By drill-down into this ellipse, we obtain Figure 6. Here we can see in more detail how these requirements are distributed with regard to different types of faults. For instance, all requirements assigned to 'Human Resources' are related to 'Faults', 'Human failures' and 'Organizational Shortcomings'. Since we have zoomed into the rightmost ellipse of Figure 5 (Maßnahme vorhanden) we know that there are directives and checklists provided. By clicking on 'Maßnahme anzeigen' (= show directives), we can switch to the GUI based on ANACONDA where we obtain more information about these directives. The directives assigned to Human Resources include for instance regulations about security check procedures and immediate deleting of accounts when employees leave the company.

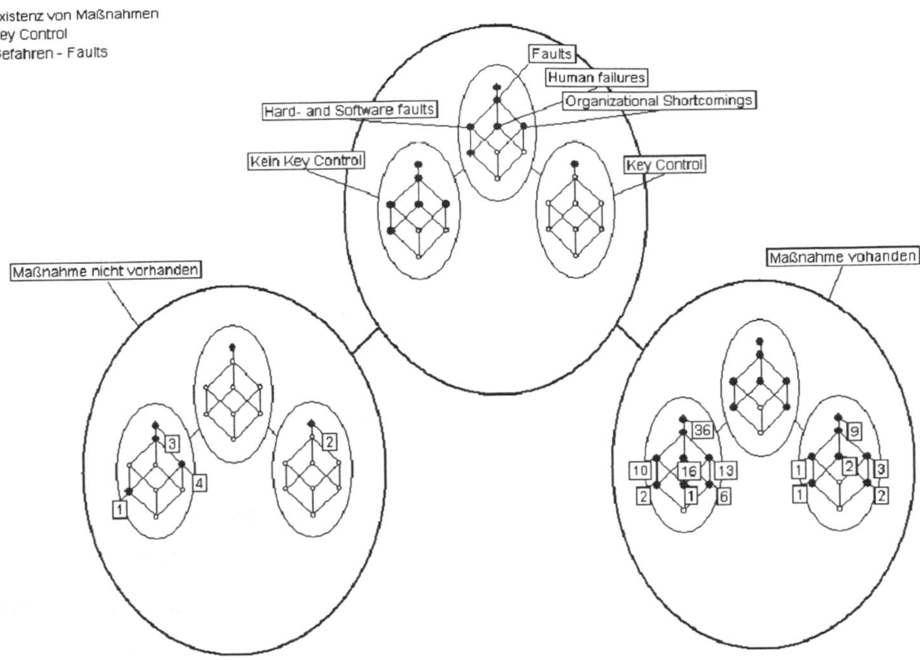

Fig. 5. Analysis of existing directives

Concluding this section, we discuss to what extent the system requirements provided by Brachman et al. (cf. Section 1) are fulfilled by the IT security management tool.

1. The entities of the data model (threats, requirements, IT resources, organizational units, etc.) reflect the way IT security experts see their organization. By differentiating these entities in conceptual scales, they can be activated in ad hoc queries. One remaining difficulty is that, in the present state, one entity type has to be chosen in advance as object type (in the formalization of Formal Concept Analysis). The extension of the theory in order to provide more flexibility in this aspect is in progress.
2. Categorical structures are described by conceptual scales which can be added to the system at any time. Even during the analysis process, new insights may give rise to further conceptual scales. In the case of the IT security tool, in order to create a new conceptual scale, it is sufficient to select the attributes describing these categories; the conceptual scale is then automatically derived from the present data by ANACONDA.

3.+ 4. The possibility of combining arbitrary conceptual scales provides an almost unlimited multitude of conceptual segmentations and patterns which offer each different views on the data.

5. At the moment, monitoring changes over time is not implemented in the IT security management system. However, one could extend the data model by

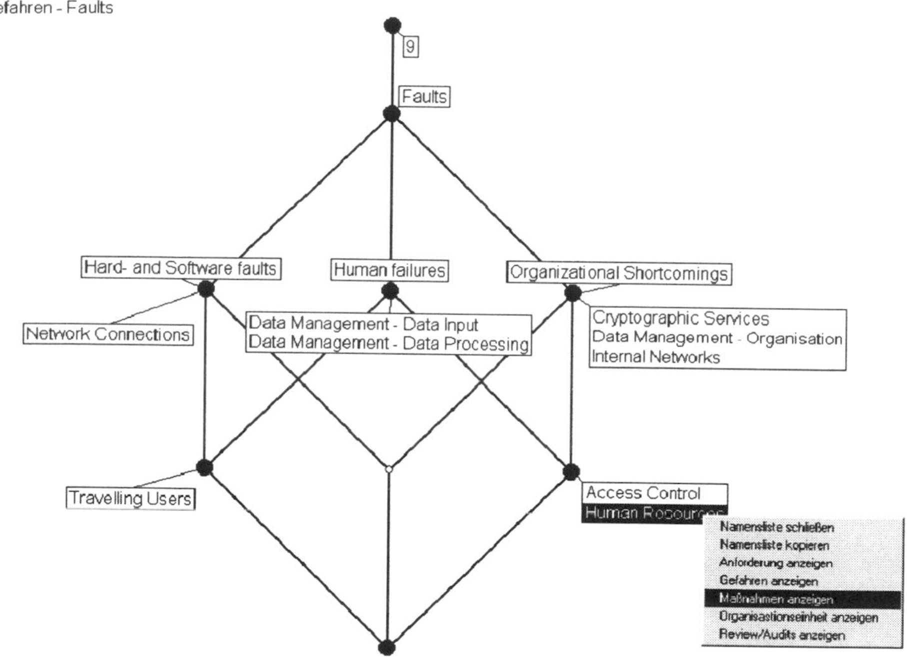

Fig. 6. Zooming into the rightmost concept of the nested line diagram in Figure 5

time stamps which indicate the moment of introducing new directives, and provide a conceptual scale covering this temporal aspect. This is implemented in other applications of Conceptual Information Systems, for instance in a system for monitoring an incineration plant ([9]).

6. The transparency of the analysis process is asserted by the fact that aggregation is only performed by set union. Hence all information about the individual objects is obtainable at all time.
   TOSCANA offers to the user a history drill- down. It lists the attributes to which the actual concept is restricted. A global history tracing the overall analysis process is not implemented at the moment.
7. Background knowledge of domain experts is represented in the structure of the conceptual scales in which the experts have explicitly coded formal aspects of their knowledge. The connection to implicit background knowledge is activated by the semantics of the attributes in the conceptual scales.
8. By visualizing the distribution of objects over related concepts, line diagrams are more appropriate than single numerical values (such as averages and standard deviations) to support the communication between experts and users.

Overall, Conceptual Information Systems offer conceptually shaped landscapes of structurally coded knowledge allowing diverse excursions, during which a learning process yields an increasingly better understanding of the domain (cf. [31]). The graphical representation of interesting parts of the landscape, in particular, supports intersubjective communication and argumentation.

5 Further Developments

Conceptual information systems have been developed up to now based on the management system TOSCANA. They have been implemented for many purposes in different research areas, but also on the commercial level. Their range covers a variety of tasks and applications for which the human-centered view is dominant. For instance, TOSCANA information systems have been established for *analyzing* data of children with diabetes [21], for *investigating* international cooperations [11], for *exploring* laws and regulations in civil engineering [13], for *retrieving* books in a library [12], [19], for *assisting* engineers in designing pipings [27], for *inquiring* flight movements at Frankfurt Airport [10], for *inspecting* the control system of an incineration plant [9], for *developing* qualitative theories in music esthetics [15], for *studying* semantics of speech-act verbs [8], for *examining* the medical nomenclature system SNOMED [20], for *controlling* the customer database of a mail-order company [16] etc.

Further research aims at developing conceptual information systems by extending the functionalities that are available by the management system TOSCANA. Conceptual information systems may be understood as *On-Line Analytical Processing* (OLAP) tools [24]. The conceptual scales can roughly be seen as dimensions of a multi-dimensional data cube. The zooming in one of the concepts of a scale corresponds to 'slicing' the data cube. 'Dicing' and 'Drill-Down' are also supported. Another direction of research is concerned with extending the *logic-based components*. Since Formal Concept Analysis and *Description Logics* are closely related and have similar purposes (cf., e. g., [5], [25]), first steps in integrating both theories have been made ([1], [23], [3], [17]). Furthermore, the extension of Formal Concept Analysis to *"Contextual Logic"* (see [30], [18]) allows to integrate developments in the field of *Conceptual Graphs*. For hybrid information processing, an extension of TOSCANA information systems is projected by incorporating *statistical and computational components* [26]. All this indicates a promising development of extending TOSCANA information systems toward a wider range of applications.

References

1. F. Baader: Computing a minimal representation of the subsumption lattice of all conjunctions of concepts defined in a terminology. In: *Proc. KRUSE'95*, 168–178.
2. K. Becker, M. Zickwolff: IT-Sicherheitsmanagement mit TOSCANA. Intl. Conf. of the Information Systems Audit and Control Association, Brussels, July 13, 1998
3. H. Berg: *Terminologische Begriffslogik*. Diplomarbeit, FB4, TU Darmstadt 1997.

4. R. J. Brachman, T. Anand: The process of knowledge discovery in databases. In: U.M. Fayyad, G. Piatetsky-Shapiro, P. Smyth, R. Uthurusamy (eds.), *Advances in Knowledge Discovery and Data Mining.* Cambridge, Mass.: AAAI/MIT Press, 1996.
5. R. J. Brachman, P. G. Selfridge, L. G. Terveen, B. Altman, A. Borgida, F. Halper, T. Kirk, A. Lazar, D. L. McGuinnes, L. A. Resnick: Integrated support for data archaeology. *International Journal of Intelligent and Cooperative Information Systems*, Vol.2, No. 2, 1993, 159–185.
6. Bundesamt für Sicherheit in der Informationstechnik: *IT-Grundschutzhandbuch 1996.* Bonn 1996.
7. B. Ganter, R. Wille: *Formal Concept Analysis: Mathematical Foundations.* Springer, Berlin-Heidelberg-New York 1999.
8. A. Grosskopf, G. Harras: Eine TOSCANA-Anwendung für Sprechaktverben des Deutschen. In: G. Stumme, R. Wille (eds.): *Begriffliche Wissensverarbeitung: Methoden und Anwendungen.* Springer, Berlin-Heidelberg-New York 2000, 273–295
9. E. Kalix: *Entwicklung von Regelkonzepten für thermische Abfallbehandlungsanlagen.* Diplomarbeit, FB13, TU Darmstadt, 1997.
10. U. Kaufmann: *Begriffliche Analyse über Flugereignisse – Implementierung eines Erkundungs- und Analysesystems mit TOSCANA.* Diplomarbeit, FB4, TU Darmstadt 1996.
11. B. Kohler-Koch, F. Vogt: Normen und regelgeleitete internationale Kooperationen. In: G. Stumme, R. Wille (eds.): *Begriffliche Wissensverarbeitung: Methoden und Anwendungen.* Springer, Berlin-Heidelberg-New York 2000, 325–340
12. W. Kollewe, C. Sander, R. Schmiede, R. Wille: TOSCANA als Instrument der der bibliothekarischen Sacherschließung. In: H. Havekost, H.J. Wätjen (eds.): *Aufbau und Erschließung begrifflicher Datenbanken.* (BIS)-Verlag, Oldenburg, 1995, 95-114.
13. W. Kollewe, M. Skorsky, F. Vogt, R. Wille: TOSCANA — ein Werkzeug zur begrifflichen Analyse und Erkundung von Daten. In: R. Wille, M. Zickwolff (eds.): *Begriffliche Wissensverarbeitung – Grundfragen und Aufgaben.* B.I.-Wissenschaftsverlag, Mannheim, 1994, 267-288.
14. R. Langsdorf, M. Skorsky, R. Wille, A. Wolf: An approach to automated drawing of concept lattices. In: K. Denecke and O. Lüders (eds.): *General Algebra and Applications in Discrete Mathematics.* Shaker, Aachen 1997, 125–136.
15. K. Mackensen, U. Wille: Qualitative text analysis supported by conceptual data systems. *Quality and Quantity: International journal of methodology* 2/33 (1999), 135–156
16. N. Mager: *Formale Begriffsanalyse und Cluster-Analyse – ein Vergleich anhand der Identifikation von Artikel- und Auftragsstrukturen.* Diplomarbeit, FB 1, TU Darmstadt 1998
17. S. Prediger: Logical scaling in formal concept analysis. In: D. Lukose, H. Delugach, M. Keeler, L. Searle, J. Sowa (eds.): *Conceptual Structures: Fulfilling Peirce's Dream.* Springer, Berlin-Heidelberg-New York 1997, 332–341.
18. S. Prediger: *Kontextuelle Urteilslogik mit Begriffsgraphen. Ein Beitrag zur Restrukturierung der mathematischen Logik.* Shaker Verlag 1998.
19. T. Rock, R. Wille: Ein TOSCANA-System zur Literatursuche. In: G. Stumme, R. Wille (eds.): *Begriffliche Wissensverarbeitung: Methoden und Anwendungen.* Springer, Berlin-Heidelberg 2000, 239–253
20. M. Roth-Hintz, M. Mieth, T. Wetter, S. Strahringer, B. Groh, R. Wille: *Investgating SNOMED by Formal Concept Analysis.* Preprint, FB4, TU Darmstadt 1997.

21. P. Scheich, M. Sorsky, F. Vogt, C. Wachter, R. Wille: Conceptual data systems. In: O. Opitz, B. Lausen, R. Klar (eds.): *Information and classification.* Springer, Berlin-Heidelberg 1993, 72–84.
22. H. Söll: *Begriffliche Analyse triadischer Daten: Das IT-Grundschutzhandbuch des Bundesamts für Sicherheit in der Informationstechnik.* Diplomarbeit, FB4, TU Darmstadt 1998.
23. G. Stumme: The conceptual classification of a terminology extended by conjunction and disjunction. In: N. Foo, R. Goebel (eds): *Topics in Artificial Intelligence.* Springer, Berlin-Heidelberg-New York 1996, 121–131.
24. G. Stumme: On-Line Analytical Processing with Conceptual Information Systems. *Proc. 5th Intl. Conf. on Foundations of Data Organization*, 12.–11. November 1998
25. G. Stumme, R. Wille, U. Wille: Conceptual knowledge discovery in databases using formal concept analysis. In: J. M. Żytkow, M. Quafofou (eds.): *Principles of Data Mining and Knowledge Discovery.* Proc. of the 2nd European Symposium on PKDD '98, LNAI 1510, Springer, Heidelberg 1998, 450–458
26. G. Stumme, K. E. Wolff: Computing in conceptual data systems with relational structures. In: G. Mineau, A. Fall (eds.): *Proceedings of the Second International Symposium on Knowledge Retrieval, Use, Storage for Efficiency.* Simon Fraser University, Vancouver 1997, 206–219.
27. N. Vogel: *Ein begriffliches Erkundungssystem für Rohrleitungen.* Diplomarbeit, FB4, TU Darmstadt 1995.
28. F. Vogt, R. Wille: TOSCANA — a graphical tool for analyzing and exploring data. In: R. Tamassia, I.G. Tollis (eds.): *Graph Drawing '94.* LNCS 894. Springer, Berlin-Heidelberg-New York 1995, 226-233.
29. R. Wille: Begriffsdenken: Von der griechischen Philosophie bis zur Künstlichen Intelligenz heute. *Dilthey–Kastanie*, Ludwig–Georgs–Gymnasium, Darmstadt 1995, 77–109
30. R. Wille: Conceptual graphs and formal concept analysis. In: D. Lukose, H. Delugach, M. Keeler, L. Searle, J. Sowa (eds.): *Conceptual Structures: Fulfilling Peirce's Dream.* Springer, Berlin-Heidelberg-New York 1997, 290–303.
31. R. Wille: Conceptual landscapes of knowledge: a pragmatic paradigm for knowledge processing. In: G. Mineau, A. Fall (eds.): *Proceedings of the Second International Symposium on Knowledge Retrieval, Use, Storage for Efficiency.* Simon Fraser University, Vancouver 1997, 2–13.

Translations of Ripple Down Rules into Logic Formalisms*

Rex B.H. Kwok

School of Computer Science and Engineering,
The University of New South Wales,
UNSW SYDNEY NSW 2052,
Australia 2052
rkwok@cse.unsw.edu.au

Abstract. The Ripple Down Rule (RDR) is a knowledge acquisition scheme which has been successfully used in large scale commercial applications. Most notable is the use of the scheme in building a knowledge base for interpreting pathology results. Unlike machine learning algorithms which construct theories for raw data, the commercial system using the RDR scheme requires some interaction with an expert to correct erroneous interpretations. However, the frequency of such interactions is very low. Furthermore, the simplicity of the interaction means that a knowledge engineer is not required when updating a knowledge base.
A number of RDR variants have been devised for different applications. While Scheffer has given operational semantics to one variant of RDR, translations of RDR into classical logics has not yet been presented in the literature. This paper will show how two variants of RDR, single classification RDR (SCRDR) and multiple classification RDR (MCRDR), have a propositional or first–order core tied with case specific defaults. Such a translation will be used to highlight properties of the RDR scheme which make it successful. Similarities and differences in the two variants will be discussed and RDR revision will also be analysed.

1 Introduction

The Ripple Down Rule (RDR) scheme is a simple and maintainable knowledge representation scheme which has proved successful in large and complex domains involving classification, configuration, and search[4,11,5]. Probably the most impressive application of RDR is in the interpretation of pathology reports. In commercial use, a rule base containing several thousand rules has been constructed by pathologists. When a case results in an inference which a pathologist disagrees with, the correct inference and distinguishing features of the case are collected from the pathologist. The rule base is automatically updated using this information. The pathologist's only task is to contruct rules to distinguish cases. Each case may contain the results of as many as two hundred tests (repeatedly recorded over a time period). From such a large amount of data, the current rule base interprets 95% of reports correctly[11,6]. Furthermore, this figure is still improving and the time required by an expert to update the rule base is only fifteen

* This is an extension of a paper presented at the Fourth Australian Knowledge Acquisition Workshop, 1999, Sydney Australia.

R. Dieng and O. Corby (Eds.): EKAW 2000, LNAI 1937, pp. 366–379, 2000.

minutes a day[6]. Given the success of the knowledge representation scheme and the update procedure, it is of interest to investigate the properties of RDR which lead to its success. For example, it will be shown how any error made during the construction of a rule base can always be corrected. Furthermore, the analysis will highlight the structural features which make rule base revision simple.

This paper will investigate two variants on the central RDR theme: single classification RDR (SCRDR) [3] and multiple classification RDR (MCRDR)[1]. Some analysis of the similarities and differences between the variants can be done empirically or by looking at how the schemes are specified, however, a more detailed analysis can be performed by translating the variants into logic formalisms. While, Scheffer[13] has already given operational semantics to SCRDR and translated it into decision lists, translations into classical logics have not been published in the literature. This paper will show how the RDR tree (SCRDR or MCRDR) corresponds to a propositional or first–order theory and how, because of the way cases are evaluated in RDR, defaults are also generated by a type of closed world assumption.

To facilitate a provably correct translation of the RDR scheme, algebraic specifications of SCRDR and MCRDR will be presented. This will be done in Section 2. These specifications will be used to define the translations. The translations and the results showing correctness will be presented in Section 3. One use for the translations is that they can be used to show some of the similarities and differences between SCRDR and MCRDR. Section 4 will look at this issue. The RDR scheme has been highly successful for knowledge acquisition because revising an RDR tree is simple. The revision is simple enough that a knowledge engineer is not required; the expert directly interfaces with a RDR system to update a knowledge base. How the revision methods appear across the translation and some of the properties of the revision will be presented in Section 5. A survey of related work will be presented in Section 6 to show how the RDR methodology compares with other approaches. Finally, a summary of the work and directions for future research will be presented in Section 7.

2 Algebraic Specifications of SCRDR and MCRDR

A SCRDR rule base is a finite binary tree with two distinct types of edges. These edges are typically called *true* and *false* edges. Underlying a rule base is a formal language $\mathcal{L}$ (either propositional or first–order) and a classical entailment operator, $\models$. The language is used to formulate the rules associated with each and every node in a tree. The form of each rule is: *if* α *then* β where α and β are elements of $\mathcal{L}$ such that α is called the *condition* and β is called the *conclusion*. An SCRDR rule base is defined as follows:

Definition 1. *A single classification RDR rule base RB is a pentuple* $(\mathcal{L}, N, F, T, R)$ *where:*

1. *$\mathcal{L}$ is either a propositional or first–order language.*
2. *N is a finite set called the set of* nodes.
3. *F and T, the* false edges *and* true edges *respectively, are partial irreflexive functions from N to N and there is a unique $n \in N$ (called the root node) such that*
   a. *For any other node $m \in N$, $F(m) \neq n$ and $T(m) \neq n$.*

b. *For any node $m \in N$, there exists a unique sequence of nodes $(n_1, n_2, ..., n_l)$ (called the path from n to m) such that:*
i. $n_1 = n$ *and* $n_l = m$.
ii. $n_i \neq n_j$ *if and only if* $i \neq j$.
iii. *For every* i, $1 \leq i < l$, *either* $F(n_i) = n_{i+1}$ *or* $T(n_i) = n_{i+1}$.

4. *R is a total function from N to $\mathcal{L} \times \mathcal{L}$.*

In this definition, the set N defines the set of nodes in the SCRDR tree. Each node is associated via the function R to a pair of formulae such that the first element is read as the condition and the second, the conclusion. To connect the nodes are two functions, F and T. The false edges are defined by F and the true edges are defined by T. To ensure that these functions structure the nodes into a binary tree, these relations are forced to satisfy a number of constraints. For instance, a root node is identified which is unique and does not have any edges leading to it. Furthermore, any node in the tree is reachable via a unique path from the root via a sequence of nodes. The other constraints ensure that a node only links to at most one other node via a false edge (similarly for a true edge).

A case, representing the results of pathology tests for example, can be represented as a subset of the language $\mathcal{L}$. A case will typically be denoted by the letter C. Cases in SCRDR are evaluated by passing a case through the rule base. Starting at the root of the tree, if the case entails the condition of the node, the case is said to *fire* the rule and the conclusion is temporarily accepted (overriding any other conclusion previously considered). The case is then passed on to the node (if it exists) connected via a true edge. When a rule does not fire, the case is passed to the node connected via the false edge. The process continues until a leaf node is reached. This evaluation algorithm defines a path through the rule tree for each case. The conclusion given by the algorithm is the conclusion of the last node along the path which fired. Following Scheffer[13], this evaluation procedure can be recursively defined.

Definition 2. *Let the case C be a subset of $\mathcal{L}$ and R be a SCRDR rule base. The evaluation function Eval(RB, C) takes a rule base and a case and returns an element of $\mathcal{L} \cup \{X\}$ (called the result). Let n_k be any node in RB and define the following function Ev from $N \times 2^{\mathcal{L}}$ to $\mathcal{L} \cup \{X\}$.*

$$Ev(n_k, C) = \begin{cases} b_k & \text{if } R(n_k) = (\alpha_k, \beta_k) \text{ and } C \models \alpha_k \text{ and if there exists} \\ & \text{a node } n_m \text{ such that } T(n_k) = n_t \text{ then } Ev(n_t, C) = X \\ Ev(n_t, C) & \text{if } R(n_k) = (\alpha_k, \beta_k) \text{ and } C \models \alpha_k \text{ and there exists} \\ & \text{a node } n_t \text{ such that } T(n_k) = n_t \text{ and } Ev(n_t, C) \neq X \\ Ev(n_f, C) & \text{if } R(n_k) = (\alpha_k, \beta_k) \text{ and } C \not\models \alpha_k \text{ and} \\ & \text{there exists a node } n_f \text{ such that } F(n_k) = n_f \\ X & \text{otherwise} \end{cases}$$

Let $Eval(RB, C) = Ev(n, C)$ where n is the root node of RB.

The recursive definition of Ev consists of four tests. The third and fourth tests handle nodes which do not fire. If a child does not exist down a false edge, Ev returns X to indicate that no conclusion has been reached[1]. On the other hand, when a false edge links to a child, Ev simply passes the case to that child node. The first and second tests handle the cases when a node fires. The conclusion at the node is adopted if a true edge does not link to a child. When such a child is present, evaluation is passed onto that child. Should it return X, indicating that no other conclusion has been reached, once again the conclusion at the node is accepted. Otherwise, the conclusion returned by the child node is accepted. To guarantee a conclusion, the root node normally has a condition which is always satisfied.

The MCRDR knowledge representation scheme is a generalisation of the SCRDR scheme. Instead of limiting a node to at most two children, any number of children are allowed. What is more, there is only one type of edge. With fewer constraints, the MCRDR structure is, in fact, more easily defined.

Definition 3. *A multiple classification RDR rule base RB is a quadruple* $(\mathcal{L}, N, E, R)$ *where:*

1. $\mathcal{L}$ *is either a propositional or first–order language.*
2. N *is a finite set called the set of nodes.*
3. E*, the set of edges, is an irreflexive binary relation on* $N \times N$ *such that there is a unique node* $n \in N$ *(called the root node) with the following properties:*
   a. *For any other node* $m \in N$, $(m, n) \notin E$.
   b. *For any node* $m \in N$*, there exists a unique sequence of nodes* $(n_1, n_2, ..., n_l)$ *(called the path from* n *to* m*) such that:*
      i. $n_1 = n$ *and* $n_l = m$.
      ii. $n_i \neq n_j$ *if and only if* $i \neq j$.
      iii. *For every* i, $1 \leq i < l$, $(n_i, n_{i+1}) \in E$.
4. R *is a total function from* N *to* $\mathcal{L} \times \mathcal{L}$.

The only difference in the syntactic descriptions of MCRDR and SCRDR rule bases is in the edges. In SCRDR, T and F shape the rule base into a binary tree. With MCRDR, E shapes the rule base as a tree with an arbitrary branching factor.

Cases in MCRDR are evaluated by passing a case to the root node of the rule base. Should a case result in a rule firing, the case is passed on to each child of the node containing that rule. Should a node not fire, the case terminates at that node and the case is not propagated. This procedure defines a set of paths through the MCRDR tree. The nodes of each path fire and the last node of each path only has children which do not fire. The result returned by this evaluation algorithm collects the conclusions from the last node of each such path. This is defined as follows:

Definition 4. *Let the case* C *be a subset of* $\mathcal{L}$ *and* RB *be a MCRDR rule base. The evaluation function Eval(RB, C) takes a rule base and a case and returns an element of* $2^{\mathcal{L}} \cup \{X\}$ *(called the result). Let* n_k *be any node in* RB *and define the following function* Ev *from* $N \times 2^{\mathcal{L}}$ *to* $2^{\mathcal{L}} \cup \{X\}$.

[1] This is necessarily not an element of $\mathcal{L}$.

$$Ev(n_k, C) = \begin{cases} b_k & \textit{if } R(n_k) = (\alpha_k, \beta_k) \textit{ and } C \models \alpha_k \textit{ and} \\ & \textit{for all nodes } n_m \textit{ if } (n_k, n_m) \in E \textit{ then} \\ & Ev(n_m, C) = X \\ \cup_{n_m \in Ch(n_k)} Ev(n_m, C) & \textit{if } R(n_k) = (\alpha_k, \beta_k) \textit{ and } C \models \alpha_k \textit{ and} \\ & Ch(n_k) = \{n_m | (n_k, n_m) \in E \textit{ and} \\ & Ev(n_m, C) \neq X\} \textit{ and } Ch(n_k) \neq \emptyset \\ X & \textit{otherwise} \end{cases}$$

Let $Eval(RB, C) = E(n, C)$ *where* n *is the root node of* RB.

This follows a similar pattern to SCRDR evaluation. The last 'catch–all' test handles nodes which do not fire. When this happens, X is returned to indicate that further evaluation is unnecessary. The first two tests handle the case when a node fires. In the first, the conclusion at the node is accepted if every child node does not fire. Otherwise, the case is passed to every child which does fire.

3 Translating SCRDR and MCRDR into a Formal Logic

Given the details of how cases are evaluated with SCRDR and MCRDR rule bases, it might be thought that a kind of prioritised default logic is necessary to formalise the reasoning process. However, this section will show that the SCRDR and MCRDR knowledge representation schemes have a propositional or first–order core (depending on the underlying language of the RDR) with a set of defaults arising from a type of closed world assumption when case information is scarce.

In evaluating cases with RDR, paths are traced out in rule trees. Along each path, as rules fire, conclusions are temporarily stored. Only the conclusion from the last node in the path which fired is ultimately accepted. This might indicate that rules at the bottom of a rule tree have greater priority. However, it turns out that the conditions under which a particular node gives an ultimate conclusion are definite and do not rely on the depth of the node. To understand why this is the case, consider a SCRDR rule base RB with root n and any other node n_k. Since there is only a single path from n to n_k, for a case to reach n_k, it must take the particular true and false edges along this path; either entailing or contradicting the conditions in the nodes along this path. This establishes a set of conditions for a case to reach n_k. Having reached n_k, the case must entail the condition at node n_k. For the conclusion at this node to be accepted, the case must trace out a path from n_k to a leaf node without satisfying any of the conditions in the nodes along this path. This path from n_k to the leaf node can be called the *exception branch* since the nodes along the path contain rules which can override the conclusion of n_k. The exception branch may be of 0 length if n_k is already a leaf node. Otherwise, since the condition of node n_k is satisfied, the exception branch contains the node on the true edge down from n_k and subsequently all the nodes down the false edges. This can be seen graphically in Figure 1. The bold edges are the ones traversed making the nodes from n_1 to n_k the path to n_k and the nodes from n_{k+1} to n_{k+m} the exception path.

A path from the root node to a leaf node of a SCRDR rule tree determines a set of relations between a case and the conditions along the path. For the path outlined above,

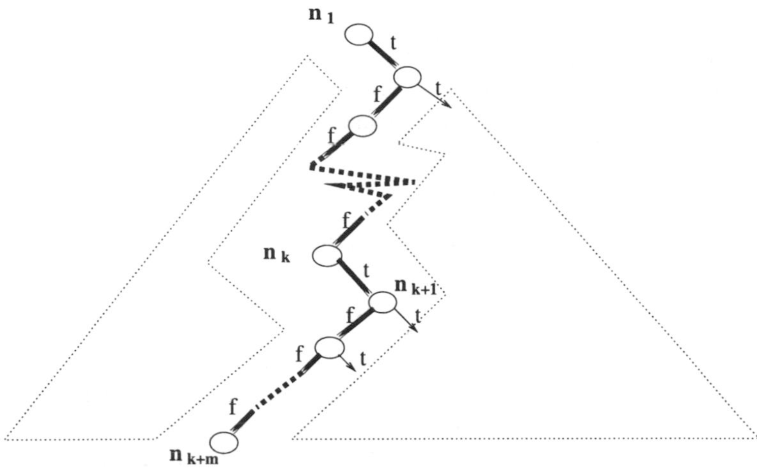

Fig. 1. The path a case must take for a node n_k to be the conclusion provider in SCRDR.

these relations are exactly the conditions under which a particular node provides the conclusion when evaluating a case. These conditions can be collected and converted into a formula which expresses this situation.

Definition 5. *Let RB be a SCRDR rule tree with root n_1. Suppose n_k is any node in RB with $R(n_k) = (\alpha_k, \beta_k)$. Let $(n_1, n_2, ..., n_k)$ be the path from n_1 to n_k. Let $(n_{k+1}, n_{k+2}, ..., n_{k+m})$, the exception branch from n_k, be a sequence of nodes such that $(n_k, n_{k+1}) \in T$ and for any l, $1 \leq l < m$, $(n_{k+l}, n_{k+l+1}) \in F$. The following set collects the conditions along the path from the root to n_k which must have been entailed by a case.*

$$NodeSat(n_k) = \{\alpha_i \,|\, (n_i, n_{i+1}) \in T \text{ and } R(n_i) = (\alpha_i, \beta_i) \text{ and } 1 \leq i < k\}$$

In a similar vein, the following set collects the conditions which were contradicted to reach node n_k.

$$NodeCont(n_k) = \{\alpha_i \,|\, (n_i, n_{i+1}) \in F \text{ and } R(n_i) = (\alpha_i, \beta_i) \text{ and } 1 \leq i < k\}$$

The conditions along the exception branch are collected by the following set:

$$Except(n_k) = \{\alpha_i \,|\, R(n_i) = (\alpha_i, \beta_i) \text{ and } k + 1 \leq i \leq k + m\}$$

Define the formula of node n_k, $Form(n_k)$, by:

$$Form(n_k) = \left(\bigwedge_{\alpha_i \in NodeSat(n_k)} \alpha_i \wedge \bigwedge_{\alpha_j \in NodeCont(n_k)} \neg\alpha_j \wedge \alpha_k \wedge \bigwedge_{\alpha_l \in Except(n_k)} \neg\alpha_l \right) \rightarrow \beta_k$$

The *formula* of a node n_k is a sentence expressing when the node provides the conclusion for an evaluation. In collecting the formulae of all the nodes in a SCRDR tree RB, it may be that we are ignoring some of the interactions between different nodes. However, this is not the case. The nodes in an SCRDR tree can be viewed in isolation so that collecting the formulae of nodes into a set, called the *theory* of RB, correctly represents the beliefs contained in RB.

Definition 6. *Let RB be a SCRDR tree. Define the* theory *of RB, $Th(RB)$ by:*

$$Th(RB) = \{Form(n_k) \mid n_k \in N\}.$$

This definition translates an SCRDR rule base into a set of clauses in propositional or first–order logic. However, to demonstrate that the translation is faithful, it is necessary to show that the use of an SCRDR rule base is preserved. The primary function of SCRDR is to classify cases. This is done according to the evaluation function in Definition 2. Case information is combined with the SCRDR rule base to determine a conclusion. The aim, then, is to show that the behaviour of the evaluation function is mimicked by logical entailment.

Having translated the content of a rule base, it is now necessary to see how cases are translated. The only issue that needs to be considered is that the information in a case may not contain enough information to directly entail or contradict the conditions in nodes. This is particularly the case in a diverse domain such as pathology test interpretation where a case may represent the results of a few tests and the rule base may contain references to hundreds of different tests. This is handled in RDR systems by taking the false edge as a default. When a case does not entail the condition of a rule, the case is transferred to the node down the false edge. This gives case evaluation some non–monotonic behaviour because adding information to a case can change the evaluation. The defaults carried by a case are exactly the negated conditions of rules that the case does not entail.

Definition 7. *Let RB be a SCRDR tree and C a case. The* defaults *of RB given case C are defined as follows:*

$$Def(RB, C) = \{\neg\alpha_i \mid n_i \in N \text{ and } R(n_i) = (\alpha_i, \beta_i) \text{ and } C \not\models \alpha_i\}$$

Several points are worth highlighting. Firstly, a default in $Def(RB, C)$ is the *negated* condition of a rule. A default is never the condition itself. Reflecting back on the formula of a node in Definition 5, the negations in the antecedent thus represent the notion of *negation as failure* in logic programming. This means that it is possible to translate SCRDR as a logic program without the need for defining a set of case relative defaults. However, it is more advantageous to translate RDR into classical logic because a number of RDR applications (including Beydoun and Hoffmann's work on the incremental acquisition of search knowledge[2]) assume that case information is complete. Under the above definition, this implies that the set of defaults is empty and that negations in $Form(n_k)$ should not be interpreted as negation as failure. A second point is that the translation is tractable in practice. Even though the default set is defined using a consistency test, additional constraints on the structure of case information and rule conditions allow the test to be performed simply. For instance, it is often the case that rule conditions and case information are sets of literals[6]. The consistency check in this case reduces to testing for the subset relation.

With these definitions, it is possible to show that the algebraic formulation of SCRDR has been faithfully translated into logic.

Theorem 1. *Let RB be a SCRDR rule base, C a case, and β_j any conclusion from a rule in RB.*

1. *If $Eval(RB, C) = \beta_j$ then $Th(RB) \cup C \cup Def(RB, C) \models \beta_j$.*
2. *Let $Th(RB)|_\beta = \{\phi \in Th(RB) \mid \phi$ is of the form $\psi \rightarrow \beta\}$.*
   If $C \cup Def(RB, C) \cup (Th(RB) \setminus Th(RB)|_{\beta_j}) \not\models \beta_j$ and $Th(RB) \cup C \cup Def(RB, C) \models \beta_j$ then $Eval(RB, C) = \beta_j$.

The condition in the second part of this result asserts that at least one formula from the theory of RB of the form $\phi \rightarrow \beta_j$ is needed to entail β_j. For instance, the case information and the defaults alone may logically entail a conclusion – with no input from the SCRDR theory. When this occurs, there is no guarantee that the evaluation process will give the same result. The reason for this restriction is that the entailment operator is much less restrained than the evaluation process in RDR systems. Using a stronger logic (such as prioritised default logic) will not alleviate this problem. However, there may be weaker assumptions which still allow the result to follow.

There are similarities and differences in the way cases are evaluated in SCRDR and MCRDR. For a node to contribute a conclusion, in both SCRDR and MCRDR, a case must reach the node. In SCRDR this happens through a sequence of false and true edges. In MCRDR, there are basically only true edges. After reaching a node, in SCRDR a case must not satisfy any of the conditions along the exception branch. The exception branch in SCRDR is exactly analogous to the children of a node in MCRDR. Thus for a node to contribute a conclusion in MCRDR, a case must entail all the conditions along the path from the root to the node. Furthermore, the case must not satisfy any of the conditions in the children of that node. The conditions under which a node contributes a conclusion in MCRDR are defined below.

Definition 8. *Let RB be a MCRDR rule tree with root n_1. Suppose n_k is any node in RB with $R(n_k) = (\alpha_k, \beta_k)$. Let $(n_1, n_2, ..., n_k)$ be the path from n_1 to n_k. The following set collects the conditions along the path from the root to n_k which must have been entailed by a case.*

$$NodeSat(n_k) = \{\alpha_i \mid R(n_i) = (\alpha_i, \beta_i) \text{ and } 1 \leq i < k\}$$

The conditions in the children of n_k are collected by the following set:

$$Except(n_k) = \{\alpha_i \mid R(n_i) = (\alpha_i, \beta_i) \text{ and } (n_k, n_i) \in E\}$$

Define the formula of node n_k to be the following sentence:

$$Form(n_k) = \left(\bigwedge_{\alpha_j \in NodeSat(n_k)} \alpha_j \wedge \alpha_k \wedge \bigwedge_{\alpha_l \in Except(n_k)} \neg \alpha_l \right) \rightarrow \beta_k$$

Following the procedure carried out with SCRDR, the formula from each node can be collected to form a theory.

Definition 9. *Let RB be a MCRDR tree. Define the* theory *of RB, $Th(RB)$ by:*

$$Th(RB) = \{Form(n_k) \mid n_k \in N\}.$$

Defaults are generated when evaluating a case in MCRDR in exactly the same way that defaults are generated for SCRDR. When a case is passed to a node, the default is that the case does not entail the condition.

Definition 10. *Let RB be a MCRDR tree and C a case. The* defaults *of RB given case C are defined as follows:*

$$Def(RB, C) = \{\neg\alpha_i \mid n_i \in N \text{ and } R(n_i) = (\alpha_i, \beta_i) \text{ and } C \not\models \alpha_i\}$$

Collecting these definitions together, it is possible to show that a faithful translation of the MCRDR scheme has been defined.

Theorem 2. *Let RB be a MCRDR rule base, C a case, and β_j any conclusion from a rule in RB.*

1. *If $\beta_j \in Eval(RB, C)$ then $Th(RB) \cup C \cup Def(RB, C) \models \beta_j$.*
2. *Let $Th(RB)|_\beta = \{\phi \in Th(RB) \mid \phi$ is of the form $\psi \rightarrow \beta\}$.*
   If $C \cup Def(RB, C) \cup (Th(RB) \setminus Th(RB)|_{\beta_j}) \not\models \beta_j$ and
   $Th(RB) \cup C \cup Def(RB, C) \models \beta_j$ then $\beta_j \in Eval(RB, C)$.

4 A Preliminary Comparison of SCRDR and MCRDR

From the translation presented in the previous section, several similarities and differences are highlighted between SCRDR and MCRDR. Similarities can be seen in the overall shape of theories extracted from trees and how defaults are generated. Differences show up in the relationship between nodes.

The formula generated for a node in SCRDR and MCRDR follow the same pattern. The template for generating the formula comes from the rule present in the node itself. This rule is altered by strengthening the antecedent of the rule; more conditions have to be satisfied before the rule contributes a conclusion. These extra conditions are garnered from the ancestors and children of the node. Defaults are used by both representation schemes in exactly the same way. When a case does not definitively entail or contradict a condition, the default assumption is that the case contradicts the condition.

The greatest formal difference between SCRDR and MCRDR is in the relationship between nodes in a tree. In SCRDR, distinct nodes give rise formulas which are orthogonal and mutually exclusive. More formally, the antecedent of the formula from one node always contradicts the antecedent of the formula from any other node. To understand why this is so, consider the paths to any two distinct nodes. These paths must diverge at some node. According to Definition 5, the condition of the rule at this node appears in positive form for one antecedent and in negative form for the other antecedent. The relationship between nodes in a MCRDR tree is more relaxed. With a MCRDR tree only nodes which are in an ancestor–descendent relationship have formulae which are necessarily orthogonal. The ancestor will have a formula with the negated conditions of its children. The descendent will necessarily have a formula with the condition of one of these children in positive form.

5 Revising SCRDR and MCRDR

One of the strengths of the RDR framework is that rule bases are so easily revised that an expert can update a rule base without consulting a knowledge engineer. The structure of the knowledge base is hidden from the expert and the expert merely answers a few simple questions posed by an RDR system. The algorithm which uses the answers of the expert to revise a knowledge base is motivated by studies which show that it is not possible to fully elucidate knowledge; only context dependent knowledge can be expressed which distinguishes cases[4]. With an RDR system, a knowledge base is revised when the rule base gives an evaluation which the expert does not agree with. The expert is then asked to isolate distinguishing features of the case. These features represent an exception to the rule in the RDR tree which generated the wrong conclusion. In SCRDR, a new node is added which extends the exception branch of the node which gave the wrong conclusion. The conclusion of the rule at this new node is the conclusion the expert believes the case implies and the condition contains the features isolated by the expert. This is formulated algebraically below.

Definition 11. *Let* $RB = (\mathcal{L}, N, F, T, R)$ *be a SCRDR rule base and* C *a case. Suppose that node* n_k *with the rule* (α_k, β_k) *provides the conclusion in evaluating* C*. Let* $(n_1, n_2, ..., n_k, n_{k+1}, ..., n_m)$ *be the path taken in* RB *when evaluating* C *where* $(n_1, ..., n_k)$ *is the path from the root of* RB *to* n_k *and* $(n_{k+1}, ..., n_m)$ *is the exception branch of* n_k[2]*. Suppose that an expert disagrees with conclusion* β_k*. Let* $RB' = (\mathcal{L}', N', F', T', R')$ *be the revision of* RB*. Then:*

1. $\mathcal{L} = \mathcal{L}'$[3].
2. $N' = N \cup \{n_x\}$ *where* n_x *is not an element of* N.
3. *If the exception branch equals* $()$*, then* $T' = T \cup (n_k, n_x)$ *and* $F' = F$*, otherwise,* $F' = F \cup (n_m, n_x)$ *and* $T' = T$.
4. R' *is a function from* N' *to* $\mathcal{L} \times \mathcal{L}$ *such that if* $n \in N$ *then* $R'(n) = R(n)$*. Otherwise* $n = n_x$ *and* $R'(n) = (\alpha_x, \beta_x)$ *where* β_x *is the desired conclusion for the case and* α_x *are the distinguishing features obtained from the expert*[4].

[2] Note that this is the empty sequence when n_k is a leaf node.

[3] In this treatment we do not consider the case when the expert introduces new terms into the language.

[4] In RDR these conditions come from the difference list between the case the has been incorrectly classified and the cornerstone case attached to the rule which gave the wrong conclusion. These details are not important for the treatment presented here. What matters is that some conditions are isolated by the expert.

Consider how a revision operation affects the theory of an SCRDR rule base as defined in Section 3. The formula of a node depends on the path to a node and the exception branch of the node. Suppose the newly added node is called n_x. Since n_x is added as a leaf node it can only affect nodes for which n_x lies at the end of its exception branch. Node n_x lies at the end of the exception branch of one and only one node; the node which gave the incorrect conclusion. Thus, revising a SCRDR tree causes very little change in the theory corresponding to the rule base. Suppose that an SCRDR tree has been updated according to Definition 11, then this difference is spelled out in the following result.

Theorem 3. $Th(RB') = Th(RB) \setminus \{Form(n_k)\} \cup$
$\{\left(\bigwedge_{\alpha \in NodeSat(n_k)} \alpha \wedge \bigwedge_{\alpha \in NodeCont(n_k)} \neg\alpha \wedge \alpha_k \wedge \bigwedge_{\alpha \in Except(n_k)} \neg\alpha \wedge \neg\alpha_x\right) \rightarrow \beta_k,$
$\left(\bigwedge_{\alpha \in NodeSat(n_k)} \alpha \wedge \bigwedge_{\alpha \in NodeCont(n_k)} \neg\alpha \wedge \alpha_k \wedge \bigwedge_{\alpha \in Except(n_k)} \neg\alpha \wedge \alpha_x\right) \rightarrow \beta_x\}$

This result shows that one rule has been split into two. The antecedent of the formula for n_k has been strengthened to include $\neg\alpha_x$ (thus excluding the error causing case). At the same time, a new formula is added which is exactly the same except that the antecedent contains α_x and the conclusion is β_x. This new formula activates for the new case. This shows that the context under which node n_k originally fired is carried to the new node. The difference is that a new discriminator α_x and $\neg\alpha_x$ has been introduced which leads to different conclusions.

The revision policy for RDR has two important properties. Firstly, the changes to the theory are highly local. While the theory may contain many formulae, the revision process only replaces one formula with two others. Secondly, the result shows that mistakes in the rule base can always be corrected. If the rule added to the RDR tree is (t, t) (where t represents the constant *true*), then the two formulae added to the theory during a revision become trivially true. The overall effect, then, is to contract the theory by the formula corresponding to the offending node.

The revision of a MCRDR tree results in much the same local changes as SCRDR revision. However, there is more freedom in placing a new node in MCRDR revision. Placing a rule at the end of an evaluation path has exactly the same effect as that outlined for SCRDR. One device which is commonly used when updating an MCRDR rule base is the *stopping rule*. When case evaluation gives an unwarranted conclusion, an exception node is added to the node giving that conclusion. This new node has the conclusion *true*. Thus the exception node serves only to strengthen the conditions under which its parent gives a conclusion. When a new node is placed at some location in the middle of the tree, it affects the formula of its parent (by creating a new exception) and introduces a new formula to the theory (the one corresponding to the new node).

6 Comparison with Other Work

While the suite of features characterising the RDR methodology is unique, it shares some of its ideas with a number of other approaches. The RDR knowledge representation scheme is closely tied with *extended logic programs* in logic programming [7,10,8] and decision lists in machine learning[12]. Also, the revision scheme used in RDR is related to the one used by Vere[14] for batch learning.

Current implementations of RDR trees are actually extended logic programs[7,10]. Recall that the general form of a formula extracted from an RDR tree is:

$$\bigwedge_{\alpha \in X} \alpha \wedge \bigwedge_{\beta \in Y} \neg\beta \rightarrow \gamma$$

where X and Y are sets of literals. The negation symbols in front of the formulae from Y can be read as *negation as failure*; it is sufficient if a case entails every formula in X and not entail any formula in Y to generate conclusion γ. The shape of such a formula matches those used for extended logic programs[7]. The general form of an extended logic program formula is:

$$\bigwedge_{l_i \in A} l_i \wedge \bigwedge_{l_j \in B} \mathbf{not}\ l_j \rightarrow l_k$$

where each l_n is a literal and **not** is negation as failure. Thus, RDR trees are extended logic programs.

Grosof's extension of extended logic programs to include prioritized labels has no parallel in SCRDR and MCRDR[5]. While a natural language specification of RDR trees may indicate that priorities are present; with rules lower in a branch having a higher priority since their conclusions can 'replace' conclusions higher in the tree. The translation presented here shows that negation as failure is strong enough to capture this behaviour. Finally, the strong relationships between rules in RDR (that only one rule in SCRDR and that only one rule along a branch in MCRDR can fire) are not stipulated in extended logic programs.

Another knowledge representation scheme which bears a close resemblance to the RDR tree is the decision list. As defined by Rivest[12], a decision list is a list of pairs:

$$(f_1, v_1), ..., (f_r, v_r)$$

where each f_i is a conjunct of literals (a proposition or its negation) and each v_i is a value in $\{0, 1\}$. Given an assignment $\mathbf{x}$ which gives each and every proposition a value of 0 or 1, the decision list returns v_j if j is the least index such that the boolean function f_j returns 1 for $\mathbf{x}$. Since conclusions earlier in the list take precedence over those occurring later, the decision list may be likened to a branch in an RDR tree with the pairs at the front of the decision list representing nodes close to a leaf and pairs at the end of the decision list representing nodes close to the root. However, as Rivest shows, the decision list actually represents a broad class boolean functions. There is no notion of negation as failure and the decision list only classifies complete truth assignments to propositions. Even so, the resemblance is close enough that Scheffer[13] has extended the definition of decision lists to encompass negation as failure and first–order sentences. This extension matches the expressibility of RDR trees.

[5] In a variant of RDR used for configuration[6], an inferencing mechanism is used which loops repeatedly over an RDR tree. Further study will be needed to whether this places some priorities over certain rules.

The revision of RDR trees is characterised by two features: locality and exception handling. As shown in Section 5, RDR revision changes a theory only very little. When an unwanted conclusion is produced, a trace of the inference procedure identifies the offending overly general node. To prevent the conclusion, the conditions under which the offending node fires is strengthened. To give the correct conclusion an exception is added to the offending node. Such exceptions can have their own exceptions. This revision procedure closely resembles Vere's[14] procedure for learning relational concepts. The aim of the system is learn a theory which distinguish whether an object belongs to a certain concept class or not. Input to the system consists of a set positive examples and a set of negative examples. This batch learning framework differs from the incremental framework in which RDR is set. However, what is crucial here is the way in which Vere's system learns. As a first step, Vere constructs an overly general theory which covers all positive examples. Since this theory may cover some negative examples, Vere turns the problem around and looks commonalities between all these covered negative examples. This represents the exceptions which the original theory must not satisfy. Repeating this process constructs a theory with nested exceptions:

$$\gamma_1 - (\kappa_{11} - (\kappa_{12} - (\kappa_{13} - ...)))$$

where γ_1 and each κ_{ij} is some first order formula and there is an implicit conjunction between each expression. This policy of repeatedly patching overly general rules coincides with the RDR revision policy.

Each knowledge representation scheme described in this section has algorithms for learning theories expressed in the scheme. This may devalue the worth of the RDR methodology because the most successful RDR applications[4,3,11] require an expert to construct the knowledge base. There are two answers to this charge. Firstly, several researchers have now proposed algorithms[9,5,13] for fully automated RDR learning. Secondly, in the pathology rule base, conclusions are actually strings in natural language. Determining when a case, with a certain desired natural language diagnosis, may conflict with the output of the RDR rule base is at present not feasible. Automatically repairing such a rule base would be even more difficult. As such, it may be argued that an expert is necessary for determining when conflicts occur and for phrasing correct diagnoses.

7 Summary and Discussion

This paper has presented a translation of two ripple-down rule schemes, SCRDR and MCRDR, into formal logic. This translation shows that both schemes contain a propositional or first–order core (depending on the language underlying a scheme) together with a set of case dependent defaults to reflect the policy that a case is thought by default to not satisfy conditions. The translation can also be used to give an interpretation to the revision policy of SCRDR and MCRDR. It gives a formal interpretation of the idea that an expert can only give context relative information to distinguish cases.

One area of RDR research generating interest is in the automated modification of rule bases. The translation of RDR rule bases into logic can be used to show the properties of algorithms which modify rule bases. For example, an algorithm which eliminate nodes to reduce the size of trees can be shown to preserve inference power by showing the logical equivalence of the original and revised trees.

References

1. P. Compton B. Kang and P. Preston. Multiple classification ripple down rules: Evaluation and possibilities. In *Proceedings of the 9th Banff Knowledge Acquisition for Knowledge Based Systems Workshop*, pages 17.1–7.20, 1995.
2. G. Beydoun and A. Hoffmann. Incremental acquisition of search knowledge. *International Journal of Human Computer Interactions*, 52:493–530, 2000.
3. P. Compton, G. Edwards, B. Kang, L. Lazarus, R. Malor, P. Preston, and A. Srinivasan. Ripple down rules: Turning knowledge acquisition into knowledge maintenance. *Artificial Intelligence in Medicine*, 4:463–475, 1992.
4. P. Compton and R. Jansen. A philosophical basis for knowledge acquisition. In *Proceedings of the 3rd European Knowledge Acquisition Workshop EKAW '89*, pages 75–89, 1989.
5. P. Compton, P. Preston, and B. Kang. The use of simulated experts in evaluating knowledge acquisition. In *Proceedings of the 9th AAAI-Sponsored Banff Knowledge Acquisition for Knowledge–Based Systems Workshop*, pages 12.1–12.18, 1995.
6. P. Compton, Z. Ramadan, P. Preston, T. Le-Gia, V. Chellen, and M. Mullholland. A trade–off between domain knowledge and problem–solving method power. In *Proceedings of the 11th Banff knowledge acquisition for knowledge–based systems workshop*, pages Banff, SRDG Publications, University of Calgary. SHARE 17, 1–19, 1998.
7. M. Gelfond and V. Lifschitz. Logic programs with classical negation. In *Proceedings of the Seventh International Conference on Logic Programming*, pages 579–597. MIT Press, 1990.
8. B. Grosof. Prioritized conflict handling for rules. ibm research report rc 20836(92273). available at htpp://www.research.ibm.com/people/g/grosof/. Technical report, IBM Research Division, 1997.
9. H. Mannila J. Kivinen and E. Ukkonen. Learning rules with local exceptions. In *Proceedings of the European Conference on Computational Learning Theory: EuroCOLT'93*, pages 35–46. Clarendon Press, Oxford, 1994.
10. R. Kowalski and F. Sadri. Logic prograns with exceptions. *New Generation Computing*, 9:387–400, 1991.
11. P. Preston and G. Edwards. A 1600 rule expert system without knowledge engineers. In *World Congress on Expert Systems, Lisbon, Portugal*, 1994.
12. R. Rivest. Learning decision lists. *Machine Learning*, 2(2):229–246, 1987.
13. Tobias Scheffer. Algebraic foundation and improved methods of induction of ripple down rules. In *Proceedings of the Pacific Knowledge Acquisition Workshop PKAW '96*, pages 279–292, 1996.
14. S. Vere. Multilevel counterfactuals for generalizations of relational concepts and productions. *Artificial Intelligence*, 14:139–164, 1980.

Generalising Ripple-Down Rules

Paul Compton[1] and Debbie Richards[2]

[1]School of Computer Science and Engineering, University of New South Wales
UNSW Sydney 2052, Australia.
compton@cse.unsw.edu.au

[2]Department of Computing, Division of Information and Communication Sciences,
Macquarie University, Sydney, Australia
richards@ics.mq.edu.au

Abstract. Ripple-Down Rules (RDR) has the goal of simple, incremental development of a knowledge-based system (KBS) while the KBS is already in use, so that over time an expert can evolve a sophisticated KBS as a minor extension of their normal duties. RDR has had considerable success in developing classification KBS. It has been extended to configuration, heuristic search and other tasks. This paper proposes a generalisation of RDR that may enable experts to evolve KBS for a range of tasks.

1 Introduction

RDR was developed to deal with the problem that experts never gave a comprehensive explanation for their decision making. Rather they justified that the conclusion was correct and the justification was created for and shaped by the context in which it was given [1]. The critical features of RDR as it has evolved are that:

- Knowledge is added to the system to deal with specific cases. These are cases for which the system has made an error.
- The system gradually evolves over time, whilst in use.
- The system rather than the knowledge engineer organises how knowledge is added.
- It validates any knowledge acquisition (KA) so that it provides an incremental addition to the system's knowledge and does not degrade previous knowledge.
- to add new knowledge, the expert only has to identify features in a case that distinguish it from other different cases retrieved by the system.

Together these features provide the central difference of RDR from other KA approaches. A guiding principle of human intellectual endeavour is seeking to make things understandable. Reasonably, most modern KA research is motivated by the same idea: that acquiring knowledge should be a process of organising, and making clear an area of expertise. Modern KA is perhaps even moving away from the goal of producing an artefact able to make expert-like decisions, to helping organisations structure and make clear its knowledge and expertise [2]. In this framework the expert and knowledge engineer are intimately involved in deciding how to organise

R. Dieng and O. Corby (Eds.): EKAW 2000, LNAI 1937, pp. 380-386, 2000.

and structure the knowledge and problem solving and KA tools and techniques are designed to assist the expert and knowledge engineer in this scientific activity.

RDR has the quite different goal of hiding the organisation of the knowledge from the expert (and knowledge engineer). RDR distinguishes between an expert as a rational practitioner who is able to justify his or her practical decisions in terms of the presence or absence of some observations, and an a expert as an authority or consultant in a domain able to develop and expound principles and theory. We see this scientific activity of developing models as very important and something for which RDR KBs may be a valuable resource [3,4,5], but in building the KBS we prefer to deal with the expert as rational practitioner. The expert identifies the features that distinguish between different conclusions, but they do not need to explain the logical connections between these features and the conclusion. This leads to a focus on KA based on cases and integrating this KA into the expert's routine processing of cases as a rational practitioner. In contrast KA as a scientific model building naturally focuses on a major initial period of model development.

RDR systems have been implemented for a range of application areas and tasks. The first industrial demonstration of this approach was the PEIRS system, which provided clinical interpretations for reports of pathology testing [6]. The approach has also been adapted to a of tasks: multiple classification [7], control [8] heuristic search [9], document management using multiple classification [10], configuration [11] and resource allocation [12]. The level of evaluation in these studies varies, but overall they clearly demonstrate very simple and highly efficient knowledge acquisition. RDR tools to build systems to provide interpretative comments for medical Chemical Pathology reports are now available commercially and at least 15 such KBs are in routine use. Results from this have not yet been published, but confirm that very large knowledge bases (>7000 rules) can be built and maintained very easily by pathologists with little computing experience or knowledge. A complete training course before pathologists start building and maintaining such systems takes less than one day (Pacific Knowledge Systems, personal communication).

These developments have all been particular extensions to the basic RDR strategy, but their success raises the question of whether a general strategy of incremental development is possible which could be applied to a wide range of problem types. We do not deny the utility of intensive knowledge modelling approaches, but consider consider that other possibilities need to be explored. This paper is an attempt at generalising the RDR approach

2 RDR Background

The key features of RDR that have resulted in successful commercial application are as follows:

- A task is identified which has the following characteristics:
    - there is an information system, which repetitively outputs data for cases being processed. (The origin of the case data is not important)
    - there is a need for expert interpretation of the case data

- it is normal or convenient for experts to monitor the output case data. (For example in pathology, it is common for pathologists or senior laboratory scientists to monitor reports. The rule addition (to correct errors) that this results in, takes 15 minutes or so per day, and does not interfere with the experts' normal duties.)

➢ Sufficient data modelling and software engineering is carried out to enable case data to be passed from the information system to the KBS and to be presented to experts in a suitable way for them to identify features and add rules.

➢ An RDR system is then put into routine use.
  - If during monitoring, a case is identified where the KBS output is incorrect in some way, the expert enters the correct conclusion for that part of the output and the case is flagged for rule updating.
  - The KBS is then updated. However, only a single component of the output, and so only a single rule conclusion is corrected at a time.
  - When rules are updated, the expert is shown a display of the case, perhaps also a previously stored case which perhaps may also highlight possibly important differences between the cases. It should be noted that this assistance is not critical as the expert has already identified features in the case in deciding it needs correction.
  - The expert selects sufficient features to construct a rule to eliminate previously stored cases. (The expert may also assign the conclusion to the stored case if appropriate. This can occur when a system is developed piecemeal and it has become appropriate to make a more complete response for a case.)
  - The system adds the rule to the KB, in such a way that the same case will always be processed by the same rule sequence.
  - The input case is added to a data base of such cases and linked to the new rule. These stored cases, which have prompted the addition of rules are called 'cornerstone cases'.
  - The case may be rerun and more components changed or added as required.

It is beyond the scope of this paper to fully describe the various RDR structures that fulfil the above. They include, binary trees, n-ary trees, multiple binary trees, and n-ary trees where there is repeat inference and some form of conflict resolution. However, the central features of all of them are that:

- When a correction is made a new rule is added; rules are not changed
- This rule is linked to the rule that gave the incorrect conclusion
- Only one conclusion is given by any rule path (a series of linked correction rules); i.e. the conclusion from the last rule satisfied in the path.
- As noted above, when a correction rule is added, it must exclude other cases appropriately satisfied by its parent rule and other rules in the system.
- Inference is organised so that the same cornerstone case will always be processed by the same sequence of rules despite any later additions to the KB.

3 Generalising RDR

The type of problems we are considering are broadly construction problems where the solution has a limited number of components and relationships between components. It does not cover more freeform activities such as artistic creation.

The central hypothesis we wish to propose is that for tasks of this nature, a solution to a problem can be assembled one component at a time with no need for backtracking and to change parts of the solution that have already been developed. In practice experts may start to assemble a solution and then revise it when they find problems. However, in theory an expert could propose a solution that did not need any such backtracking. After an expert has developed a solution, (perhaps with much backtracking) they could then propose this solution in a 'corrected' version without backtracking. They could describe how each component is added to the system and placed in an appropriate relation to the existing components and justify this only on the basis of the external data available and the components so far assembled. We do not see a problem that this is an artificial construction. RDR was originally motivated by the idea that any explanation by an expert is a construction created in a context to justify an hypothesis [1]. The point of RDR is to provide incremental maintenance to deal with the incompleteness of such constructions. The less expert the construction, the more maintenance is required, but as we have shown, convergence is still achieved without high levels of expertise [13]. This has also been theoretically validated [14].

With RDR the expert is only expected to deal with individual errors, but cumulative refinement over time allows the system to develop a very high level of expertise. We propose here that this approach can not only find the rules for individual decisions, but learn the appropriate order in which a solution should be assembled. The inference mechanism reasons without backtracking to assemble a solution, if this is incorrect the expert not only corrects the rules responsible for the individual components, but implicitly corrects the order in which the components are assembled – again with the constraint that the order in which solutions to previous problems were correctly assembled is not corrupted.

The reasons for attempting to develop such a solution are fairly straightforward. Firstly the backtracking and correction we observe in expert performance is not a virtue, but a limitation of the expert and certainly we would value more highly experts who do not make mistakes. RDR gradually learns how to achieve this despite having an imperfect human teacher. There seems then no reason to model human weakness by a revision step such as in propose and revise. Revision belongs to KA to improve the KB rather than inference. Finally, in the approach we are proposing, no search is used, only inference. The advantage of this is that is makes it easier to ensure that each case is processed in the same way by the same sequence of rules thus facilitating incremental maintenance.

3.1 Inference and Knowledge Acquisition

The following inference structure seems to support the requirements.
When a case is passed to the KBS:

1) inference starts with the first rule added to the knowledge base. The 'working tentative conclusion' referred to below is initially set as null. The current rule being processed is referred to as rule X.
2) process a set of sibling rules in order of age, starting with the eldest. The current rule being processed is referred to as rule X.

   if rule X fires
   then rule X's conclusion replaces the tentative conclusion.
      if rule X has any children
      then these are all evaluated in order of age (recursively repeating 2)
   if none of rule X's children fire
   then rule X's conclusion is acted on, making a permanent change to the case. The tentative conclusion is reset to the null conclusion. Control is passed to Rule X's next eldest sibling, or if it has no younger sibling, back to its parent.
3) inference is then repeated over the whole KB until no further changes are made to the case. There are variants on how this repeated inference may be carried out which are beyond the scope of this paper to consider,

Although this seems a fairly conventional inference structure it has significant differences from conventional inference. No conflict resolution strategy is required: rules are processed in a strict order and once the final conclusion on any refinement path is reached it is immediately added to the case and cannot be undone at a later stage of inference. The only way an addition to the case can be removed or changed is by an expert adding a refinement rule for the rule that gave the conclusion. A consequence of this policy is that a rule with the same (or an alternative) conclusion as a previous rule that has been acted on is not considered to fire and nor are its children evaluated. If they were, the requirement of only child rules being able to undo a conclusion and maintaining the same inference order may be broken.

Knowledge acquisition has the following steps:

1) The output of the system for a particular case is identified as not being correct and the case is rerun in knowledge acquisition mode.
2) In knowledge acquisition inference stops after each conclusion is added to the case.
3) If the expert disagrees with a particular conclusion, a refinement rule is added to correct (i.e. replace) that conclusion.
4) As usual in RDR the expert must select sufficient conditions for the rule to exclude any stored cases from firing the rule. The case that caused the addition of this rule is now also stored as a cornerstone case. It will be a cornerstone case for all rules that fire on this case in building the final output.
5) Inference continues step by step and further corrections are made until the correct solution is established.

As well as changing the priority of rule conclusions by refinement, the process above would correct the order in which rules were evaluated and acted on to reflect the 'ideal' order the expert implicitly proposes for different types of case. We see as one of the key attraction of this idea is that the expert is not being asked 'how' he or she might carry out problem solving. They provide an example of problem solving which has a specific order, but each decision in building this is based simply on the presence or absence of features in the case, features that were in the original data or have been added by a previous step in the proccss.

4. Conclusion

At this stage this a research proposal which needs demonstration However, we believe it is highly plausible. Incremental KA has been comprehensively evaluated for classification problems and works well. More importantly in one initial study it shows excellent convergence in the real construction problem of configuring ion chromatography methods [11]. This study and a preliminary development of RDR for resource allocation [12] depended on specific modifications to how RDR worked. The present paper is simply an attempt to generalise this. On the other hand there are limitations to more conventional approaches. For example, although propose and revise methods apply to a range of construction tasks, using case-based reasoning to find an appropriate starting point seems to provide significant improvement [15] We see that our proposal may well capture the advantages of the case-based approach, but in a more expert-focussed way, providing a generic solution to many KBS problems, and without the need for decisions on problem-solving methods.

More generally, we anticipate that gradual incremental development of KBS with development integrated into the normal workflow may be a valuable alternative to modelling-intensive approaches beyond the classification domains where the utility of the incremental approachhas already been demonstrated.

Acknowledgements. This research is supported by the Australian Research Council

References

1. Compton, P.J. and Jansen, R., A philosophical basis for knowledge acquisition, Knowledge Acquisition (1990) 2 :241-257.
2. Akkermans, H., Speel, P. and Ratcliffe, A., Problems, Opportunity and Feasability Analysis for Knowledge Management - An Industrial Case Study in B Gaines, R Kremer & M Musen, 12th Banff Knowledge Acquisition for Knowledge-Based Systems Workshop, (SRDG Publications, University of Calgary) (1999) 2-1.1-2-1.22.
3. Lee, M. and Compton, P., From heuristics to causality in J Lee, J Liebowitz & Y Chae, Proceedings of the third world congress on expert systems, 1996 (Seoul, Cognizant Communications, 1996), pp 946-953.
4. Richards, D. and Compton, P., Uncovering the conceptual models in ripple-down rules in D Lukose, H Delugach, M Keeler, L Searle & J Sowa, Conceptual Structures: Fulfilling Peirce's Dream, Proceedings of the Fifth International Conference on Conceptual Structures (ICCS'97) Lecture Notes in Artificial Intelligence, No 1257, (Berlin, Springer Verlag,) (1997) 198-212.
5. Suryanto, H. Compton, P. Discovery of class relations in exception structured knowledge bases, in International Conference on Conceptual Structures (ICCS-2000) in press

6. Edwards, G., Compton, P., Malor, R., Srinivasan, A. and Lazarus, L., PEIRS: a pathologist maintained expert system for the interpretation of chemical pathology reports, Pathology (1993) 25 :27-34
7. Kang, B., Compton, P. and Preston, P., Multiple Classification Ripple Down Rules : Evaluation and Possibilities in B Gaines & M Musen, Proceedings of the 9th AAAI-Sponsored Banff Knowledge Acquisition for Knowledge-Based Systems Workshop, (Banff, Canada, University of Calgary) (1995) 17.1-17.20.
8. Shiraz, G. and Sammut, C., Combining Knowledge Acquisition and Machine Learning to Control Dynamic Systems in 15th International Joint Conferences on Artificial Intelligence (IJCAI'97) (Nagoya, Japan, Morgan Kaufmann,), (1997) 908-913.
9. Beydoun, G. Hoffmann, A. Incremental Acquisition of Search Knowledge, International Journal of Human Computer Interaction, (2000) 52(3) 493-530.
10. Kang, B., Yoshida, K., Motoda, H. and Compton, P., A help desk system with intelligent interface, Applied Artificial Intelligence (1997) 11(7-8) 611-631
11. Compton, P., Ramadan, Z., Preston, P., Le-Gia, T., Chellen, V. and Mullholland, M., A trade-off between domain knowledge and problem-solving method power in B Gaines & M Musen, 11th Banff knowledge acquisition for knowledge-based systems workshop, (,SRDG Publications, University of Calgary,) (1998) SHARE 17,1-19.
12. Richards, D. and Compton, P., Revisiting Sisyphus I - an Incremental Approach to Resource Allocation Asking Ripple-Down Rules in B Gaines, R Kremer & M Musen, 12th Banff Knowledge Acquisition for Knowledge-Based Systems Workshop, (Banff, SRDG Publications, University of Calgary,) (1999) 7-7.1-7.20.
13. Compton, P., Preston, P. and Kang, B., The Use of Simulated Experts in Evaluating Knowledge Acquisition in B Gaines & M Musen, Proceedings of the 9th AAAI-Sponsored Banff Knowledge Acquisition for Knowledge-Based Systems Workshop, (SRDG Publications, University of Calgary), (1995) 12.1-12.18.
14. Beydoun, G. and Hoffmann, A. A Formal Framework of Ripple Down Rules, in Proceedings of the 5th Australian Knowledge Acquisition Workshop (AKAW99),Sydney (1999) 57-71
15. Zdrahal, Z. and Motta, E. Improving Conpetence by Intergrating Case-Based Reasoning and Heuristic Search in B Gaines & M Musen, 10th Banff Knowledge Acquisition for Knowledge-Based Systems Workshop (1996)

Monitoring Knowledge Acquisition Instead of *Evaluating* Knowledge Bases

Ghassan Beydoun and Achim Hoffmann

School of Computer Sciences and Engineering
University of New South Wales
Sydney, NSW 2052, Australia
ghassan@cse.unsw.edu.au

Abstract. Evaluating the success of a knowledge acquisition (KA) task is difficult and expensive. Most evaluation approaches rely on the expert themselves, either directly, or indirectly by relying on data previously prepared with the help of experts. In incremental KA, knowledge base (KB) errors are monitored and corrected by an expert. Thus, during its evolution a record of the knowledge based system (KBS) performance is usually easy to keep. We propose to integrate with the incremental KA process, an evaluation process based on a statistical analysis to estimate the effectiveness of the KBS, as the KBS is actually evolved. We tailor such an analysis for Ripple Down Rules (RDR), which is an effective incremental KA methodology where a record of the KBS performance can be easily derived and updated as new cases are processed by the system. An RDR KB is a collection of rules with hierarchical exceptions, which are entered and validated by the expert in the context of their use. This greatly facilitates the knowledge maintenance task which, characteristically in RDR, overlaps with the incremental KA process. The work in this paper aims to overlap evaluation with maintenance and development of the knowledge base. It also minimises the major expense in deploying the RDR KBS, that of keeping a domain expert on-line during maintenance and the initial period of deployment. The expert is not kept on-line longer than it is absolutely necessary. We use the structure and semantics of an evolving RDR KB, combined with proven machine learning statistical methods, to estimate the added value in every KB update, as the KB evolves. Using these values, the decision-makers in the organisation employing the KBS can apply a cost-benefit analysis of the continuation of the incremental KA process. They can then determine when this process, involving keeping an expert on-line, should be terminated.

1. Introduction

Development of KBs is normally divided into several *phases*. Commonly recognised phases are *requirement definition, analysis, design* and *implementation* [24]. In many domains the design stage may cause difficulties as a concrete model may not be available or modelling may be too expensive. Incremental construction of KBs omits the design stage and merges the implementation and maintenance stages. This is par-

R. Dieng and O. Corby (Eds.): EKAW 2000, LNAI 1937, pp. 387-402, 2000.

ticularly appealing, as experience has shown that the maintenance phase is critical for the continuous deployment of an expert system. Many systems have become obsolete when maintenance became too difficult [1, 7].

Incremental construction and refinement of KBs using RDR have proved successful in building many useful applications e.g. [8, 12, 26]. RDR is the result of work to simplify knowledge engineering. With RDR, knowledge maintenance is a simple process which can be done by a domain expert without a knowledge engineer. Developing RDR KBs relies on incremental refinement of acquired domain expert's knowledge. RDR is founded on the realisation that experts do not offer explanations of why they made a decision, rather they offer a justification based on the situation (context) [9]. RDR incorporates the idea introduced by Davis [13] in TEIRESIAS of knowledge acquisition within context of a shortcoming of the KB. In TEIRESIAS the task of localising the failure was left to the expert. In RDR this task is automated.

The current state of the art of RDR does not provide any formal testing methodology for the resultant knowledge base. Rather, testing normally involves some existing test data. The incremental knowledge acquisition process is continued until the KB gives an accuracy rate as close to 100% as possible over this test data. Clearly, the incremental development is interrupted to allow for evaluation, and this interruption may take place several times depending on the performance of the knowledge base on the test data. Allowing for these interruptions, this evaluation paradigm may be an effective method as long sufficient test data is available. However, using some data for testing presumes that the expected result over this data is known a priori, and hence this clearly mandates some prior expert involvement. If such test data is not possible, then the only way is to keep the expert on-line to ensure that the knowledge base is performing *sufficiently well*. This is an expensive brute force solution, as experts are highly trained professional who command a very high fee. It is important not to keep them longer than it is absolutely necessary.

Paper Contribution and Layout

In this paper, we propose a paradigm to evaluate and develop the knowledge base simultaneously. Towards this, we present an automatic evaluation process which runs parallel to the incremental knowledge acquisition process. This consists of applying a statistical evaluation step for every newly added rule, as this gets added to the knowledge base. Moreover, instead of requiring a separate test data, we apply our statistical evaluation to the actual cases which the expert oversees during the incremental development of the knowledge base. Combined with a consideration of the structure of the knowledge base (RDR tree), our statistical analysis allows the derivation of estimates of the incremental accuracy to the knowledge base, which new rules give. The trend of these estimates is then used to make the decision, of whether or not the knowledge acquisition process should be stopped.

This paper is organised as follows: In section 2, we overview the RDR methodology. In section 3, we briefly discuss related works, and we introduce our paradigm for evaluating knowledge bases as they are incrementally developed with RDR. In section 4, we extend a formal RDR framework which we presented in [4, 6]. We then employ this framework to describe the statistical details, which make evaluation possible concurrently with incremental development. This is illustrated with an example. In section 5, we discuss the utility of the approach from an organisational management perspective. In section 6, we conclude with a critical appraisal of the approach and highlight possible future efforts for this research.

2. RDR Basics

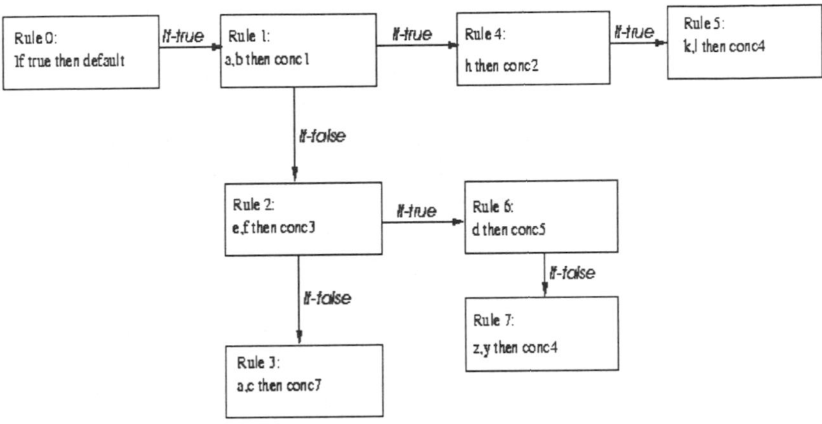

Figure 2.1. A single classification RDR tree. A case to be classified starts at the root default node and ripple down to a leaf node. The conclusion returned by the KB is the conclusion of the last satisfied rule to the leaf node.

An RDR KB is incrementally developed through direct interactions with a domain expert. It is a collection of simple rules organised in a binary tree structure. Every rule can have two branches to two other rules: A false and a true branch (an exception branch). An example is shown in figure 2.1. When a rule applies a true branch is taken, otherwise a false branch is taken. The root node of an RDR tree contains the default rule whose condition is always satisfied. The root node is of the form "*If true then default conclusion*". The default rule has only a true-branch. If a 'true-branch' leads to a terminal node *t*, and the condition of *t* is not fulfilled then the conclusion of the rule in the parent node of *t* is taken. In other words, if the conclusion of an exception rule ('true-branch' child rule) is satisfied, it overrides the conclusion of its parent rule. If a 'false-branch' leads to a terminal node *t*, and the condition of *t* is not fulfilled, then the conclusion of the last rule satisfied 'rippling down' to *t* is returned by the KB. Note, the classification starts at the root node, and the described conditional branching is repeated until a leaf node is reached. The KB is guaranteed to return a conclusion as at least the default rule is satisfied 'rippling down' to *t*. When the expert disagrees with the conclusion returned by the KB, the KB is said to fail and requires modification.

The key strength of the RDR knowledge acquisition framework is the fact that the KB can be easily modified. This strength has two reasons: Firstly, the cause of failure of the KB is automatically determined due to the tree like structure of the KB. A new rule is always added as a leaf node. It gets attached to the last visited rule before the KB failed (See above for conditions of failure). Secondly, the framework ensures newly added rules make the KB consistent with a new case, without becoming inconsistent with previously classified cases.

Every rule added to an RDR KB is a justification for a case classification given by the expert. RDR update policies are based on the idea that when a knowledge-based system makes an incorrect conclusion, a new rule *r* that is added to correct that conclusion should only be used in the same context in which the mistake was made. In RDR, this context is represented by the sequence of rules that were evaluated leading to a wrong conclusion which caused the addition of *r*. Rules are attached to such sequences of rules. Hence, rules are only in the context of their application. An added rule *r* satisfies the case for which the original sequence failed, and it excludes all cases covered by its predecessor rule. The strength of the approach is that rules are never corrected or changed because corrections are contained in rules added on to the end [9]. Corrections entered by the expert are always guaranteed to be valid, because of the way conditions of new rules are chosen (see above).

RDR KBs were successfully used in the medical expert system PEIRS [8]. This system was in routine use at St Vincents Hospital in Sydney until mid-90's. It was used to to provide clinical interpretations from pathology reports. The system went in routine use with about 200 rules and developed to 2000 rules during use. Its maintenace was undertaken by a resident pathologist without the use of a knowledge engineer. It resulted on average of only 2 to 3 rules per day [14]. The resultant average of 10 rules per hour is extremely economical. Most importantly, the time required to add a rule is independent of the size of the KB. More recently, RDRs were also successfully used to acquire complex control knowledge [27] and search heuristic knowledge [3]. As we briefly discussed in section 1, the current state of the art of RDR does not provide any formal testing methodology for the resultant knowledge base. In the next section, we briefly overview knowledge acquisition evaluation research. We then give a high level abstract description of the concurrent evaluation process, which we propose instead of the usually separate informal evaluation stage. We contrast our approach to the current approaches.

3. Integrating Evaluation with Incremental KA

Various knowledge acquisition evaluation techniques are discussed in the KA literature. Most are concerned with the performance of the system after it has been developed [17]. For example, Menzies discusses formalised success metrics in [21] to assess the benefits of an expert system *after* its deployment. These measures are domain dependents statistical assessment of an expert system which can only be applied in retrospect. Software engineering *goals checking techniques,* after the development of knowledge based management tools, have also been proposed in [23]. These target knowledge management goals in an organisation, and they are of little use in classification tasks where there is exactly one goal, that of classification, but this very goal is difficult to check.

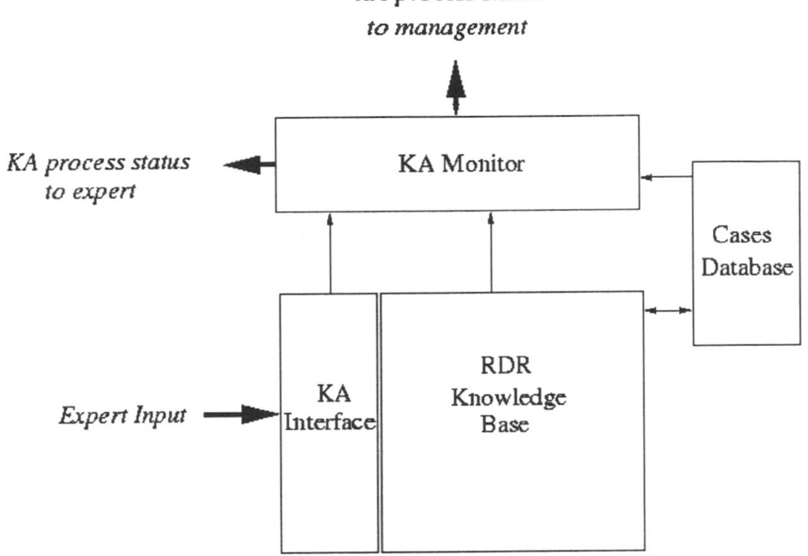

Figure 3.1. The knowledge acquisition process is supplemented with a statistical monitor which reports on the quality of the last interaction to the expert, and the progress of the whole KA process to the management overseeing the KA project in the organisation.

With respect to RDR classification tasks, a commonly used method for evaluating knowledge bases is evaluating their performance against machine learners performance on the same test data e.g. [11, 28]. This method is effective so long as sufficient data is available by the machine learner to induce the expert programs, and to then subsequently test them. Machine learners normally require a great deal of data, unlike manually constructed RDR which converge at a much faster rate. Therefore, in addition to the cases seen by the expert in the manually constructed RDR, extra cases are required to create the expert programs. These cases have to be correctly classified before hand, unless unsupervised machine learning (where the class of the cases can be unknown e.g. [2]) is used for evaluation, which to our knowledge has not yet been attempted anywhere.

Edwards and Compton etal e.g. [10, 15] supplemented RDR-based systems with mechanisms to let the user know of limitations of the knowledge base. Their concern addressed the need of the users of the system to know its limitations. Our concern in this paper is with making the job of the developers of the RDR-based system easier, by stultifying the need for a separate evaluation stage.

In the rest of this paper, we attempt to address a question similar to that addressed by Critical Success Metrics (CSM) [21]: If we lack an objective human expert capable of assessing a system, and if we lack a library of classified cases (desired behaviour), how can we assess an expert system? In addition, we have the extra criterion of conducting the assessment during the actual development of the knowledge base. We aim to provide a knowledge acquisition methodology which delivers ready to use knowledge bases, which do not require a separate testing phase distinct from the development phase. We achieve this extra criterion in using the RDR technology. In other words, we substitute the knowledge evaluation task after the KB is developed, by a *knowledge-monitoring* task during the incremental knowledge acquisition task. By this, the incremental KA process yields an effective knowledge base, which has already been successfully and positively evaluated during its development.

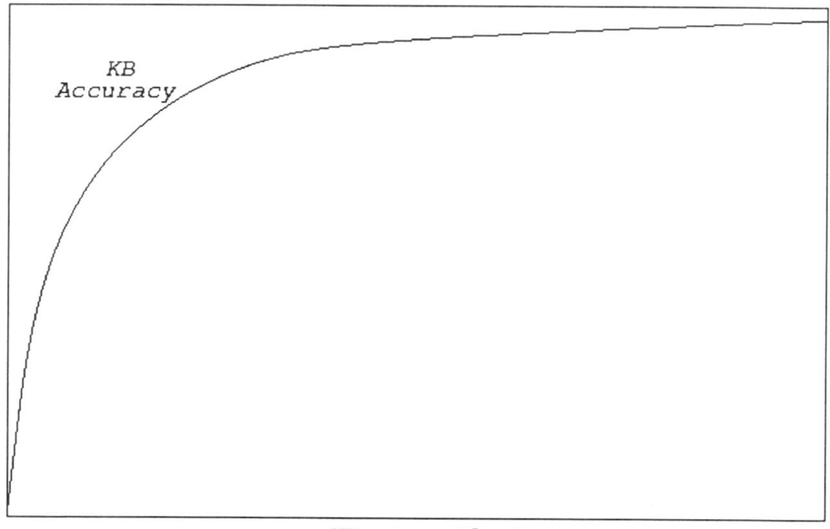

Figure 3.2. RDR convergence

In RDR, the expert enters rules validated for the context on hand. This context is represented by the case which the expert explains. This process ensures that the expert enters only valid rules, however the question remains: When is the knowledge base considered valid for the whole domain? As we discussed, the knowledge base could be evaluated against some available test data, but this test data itself requires that an expert classifies each test case. Instead, in what follows, we propose an ongoing testing procedure, which ensures delivery of an evaluated knowledge base without a separate evaluation stage. This is achieved by monitoring the actual knowledge acquisition, and evaluating the effectiveness of newly added rules by using statistical analysis and the structure of the actual knowledge base. We propose an incremental knowledge acquisition cycle as shown in figure 3.1, where the evaluation runs concurrently to the maintenance.

It has been empirically observed [9, 11, 18, 19], and formally argued [4, 5] that the convergence of an RDR knowledge base is inversely logarithmic to the number of added rules (see figure 3.2). That is, most knowledge is added in the early stage of the knowledge acquisition process. When the knowledge base convergence does not conform to the trend shown in figure 3.2, then most likely, RDR is not suitable for the domain on hand [5]. As the RDR tree becomes more accurate, the number of cases required to cause an addition of a rule increases. Hence, as the knowledge acquisition proceeds, the cost of each rule in terms of expert time increases. We propose to evaluate every single knowledge base update. If the newly added rules add little knowledge to the knowledge base than the expert's time may not be economically viable and the knowledge acquisition may be terminated. That is, the knowledge acquisition has reached its upper limit towards the right hand side of the horizontal axis in figure 3.2.

In the next section, we discuss how every new update is statistically evaluated. This constitutes the heart of the statistical process in the knowledge acquisition monitor (see figure 3.2).

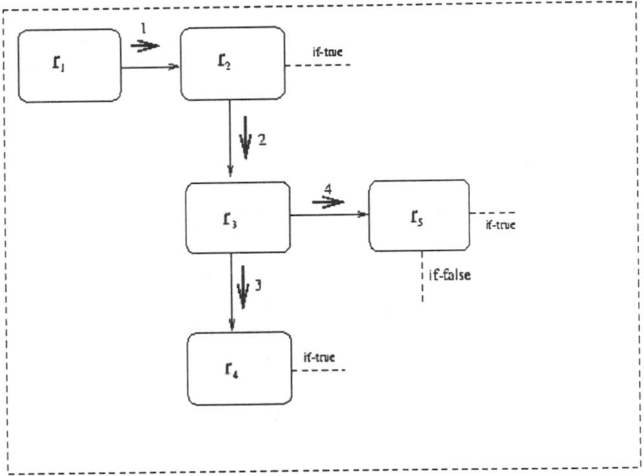

Figure 4.1: A typical representation of an RDR tree.

4. Statistical Monitoring of the KA Process

Empirical RDR research dwarfs formal and theoretical analysis of the methodology. Theoretical research on RDR KBs have been concerned with analysing the efficiency of their automatic induction e.g. [16, 20]. The work in this section extends the work done on formalising their manual construction, which has only been done in [4, 5]. A brief formal framework extracted from [4] is first presented, then this is used to describe the statistical process evaluating RDR. This is at the heart of the knowledge acquisition evaluator shown in figure 3.1.

4.1. RDR Formal Framework

The following three definitions follow [25]:

Definition 1: The context of a rule *r, context(r)* is the set of objects that reach *r* when they are in the process of being classified (see previous definition for how objects get classified in an RDR tree).

For example, in figure 4.1 $context(r_3)$ is the set of instances flowing down arrow 2.

Definition 2: The domain of a rule *r, dom(r)* is the set of objects that reach *r* and for which *r applies.*

Definition 3: The scope of a rule *r, scope(r)* is the set of objects that reach *r* and for which *r fires.*

Note, $scope(r) \subseteq dom(r) \subseteq context(r)$.

For example, in figure 4.1, $dom(r_3)$ is the set difference between the set of instances flowing down arrow 2 and the set of instances flowing down arrow 3.

Given $P(x): D \rightarrow [0,1]$ the distribution function over the domain of expertise *D,* we extend the above notions with the following:

Definition 4: The coverage of a rule *r, coverage(r)* is the probability that a case *x*, randomly drawn according to the distribution function *P(x),* is in *dom(r).* This is:

$$coverage(r) = \sum_{x \in dom(r)} P(x)$$

The *coverage* of a rule is a key measure of the impact of the rule on the rest of the knowledge base.

Definition 5: Predictivity measure *pred(r)* of a rule *r* is the ratio of all probabilities that objects in its domain are classified correctly. That is:

$$pred(r) = \frac{\sum_{x \in scope(r)} P(x)}{\sum_{x \in dom(r)} P(x)}$$

The *predictivity* measure is a useful measure of the quality of the rules entered by the expert. In combination with the coverage of a rule, it reflects the utility of a rule. That is, how often a rule fires correctly for given number of cases. Note that the probability distribution of cases is taken into consideration, because the actual performance of the knowledge base depends on instances with frequent occurrence, more than instances of rare occurrence. The *coverage* and the *predictivity* of a new rule *r* can be estimated based on a number of correctly classified cases. This is discussed in the next section.

Clearly, the most expensive resource in developing an RDR-based knowledge base is keeping the expert on-line during its use. Thence, it is desirable to free up this resource by terminating the knowledge acquisition process as soon as this is feasible. As we earlier discussed, as the knowledge base develops, more cases are required to cause a new rule addition. Further, as shown in figure 4.2, as the knowledge base develops, the coverage of a new rule decreases. Hence, the benefit of keeping the expert decreases dramatically as the knowledge base evolves. Later in section 5, we give guidelines for the decision to terminate the KA process based on a trade off between the cost of keeping the expert on-line and an error tolerance in the knowledge base performance. For example, a knowledge base with 99.9% accuracy would be assumed effective enough in most domains and the cost of keeping the expert would be hard to justify from an economic perspective. In the next section, we discuss how we can estimate the incremental accuracy, due to a new rule being added, based on the knowledge base performance on past seen cases.

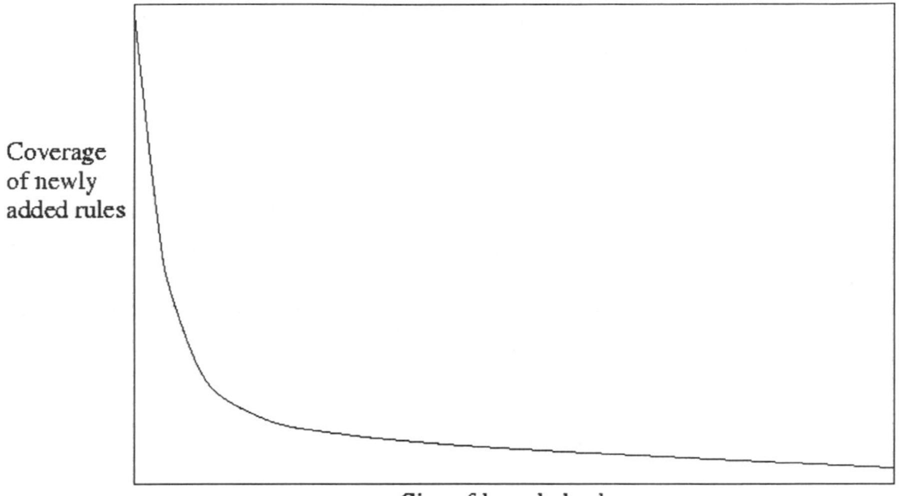

Figure 4.2. Domain of newly added rules as the knowledge base converges

4.2. Statistical Analysis of the Effectiveness of RDR

In what follows, we develop statistical estimate of the knowledge base error, which in turn can be used as a criterion to stop the knowledge acquisition process.

Theorem 1: Given an error tolerance ε for an RDR tree T, after classifying m cases correctly, the probability that the error of T is less than ε is given by:

$$P\,(Error\ of\ T < \varepsilon) > (1-\varepsilon)^m$$

Proof: The probability that the error of T is less than ε is greater than $(1-\varepsilon)$ for every correctly classified case. T performance is independent of the order of these m cases. Thus, theorem 1 follows. QED

Theorem 1 gives a confidence measure for a test that classifies m cases correctly. When a classification error by the knowledge base occurs, the expert modifies T by adding a new rule r.

From theorem 1, the following corollary immediately follows:

Corollary 1: Given an upper bound δ on the probability that a given error estimate ε of the knowledge base is exceeded after the knowledge base classifies m cases correctly, we have: $\varepsilon <= 1- \delta^{1/m}$

Following the correct classification of *n* cases, we use corollary 1 to calculate an upper bound on the error of the knowledge base E_k after the addition of a new rule *r*. Towards this, we make the following observation:

Observation 1: Following the addition of r, the error of the knowledge base E_k is given by: $E_k = Error\ (new\ rule\ r) + Error\ (KB\ without\ r\ )$

Given *n* correctly classified test cases, m_1 cases will be correctly classified by the new rule *r*, and m_2 cases by the rest of the knowledge base without *r*. That is, $m_2 = n - m_1$. The component of the knowledge base error due to a new rule *r,* depends on whether or not an arbitrary case *c* is actually classified by *r,* that is *coverage(r).* That is, the contribution of the new rule *r* to the error rate of the knowledge base is as follows: $coverage(r) * E_r$ (where E_r is the error rate in *r*)

Thus, observation 1 can be rewritten as follows:

Observation 2: Following the addition of r, the error of the knowledge base E_k is given by: $E_k = coverage(r) * E_r + (1 - coverage(r)) * Error\ (\ KB\ without\ r)$

To estimate *coverage(r),* we use the ratio *Q* of cases classified by r to all seen cases. That is, an estimate of *coverage(r)* is $Q = m_1/n$.

In expressing E_k in terms of the performance of the knowledge base on the seen correctly classified n cases, two questions must be considered: Firstly, How well do the correctly *n* seen cases reflect the real accuracy of the knowledge base. Secondly, how well does the ratio *Q* estimate *coverage(r).* These two questions are answered using statistical theory, normally applied in machine learning.

Statistical theory e.g. [22, 29] tells us that with N% confidence, the true probability that a case c belongs to the domain of r lies in the interval:

$$Q - Z_N\ \sigma < \text{coverage(r)} < Q + Z_N\ \sigma$$

An *N%* confidence interval for some parameter *p* is an interval that is expected with probability *N%* to contain *p* [22]. Our parameter of concern is *coverage(r),* estimated by $Q = m_1/n$. Z_N defines the width of the smallest interval about the mean that includes *N%* of the total probability mass under the bell-shaped Normal distribution. σ is the standard deviation over the sample of *n* cases. In our case, we use the standard deviation expression for binomial distribution, that is:

$$\sigma = \sqrt{\frac{Q(1-Q)}{n}}$$

The above interval gives the limits for two-sided *N%* confidence intervals. However, as we are interested in the upper bound of *coverage(r),* we prefer instead the single sided limit. The symmetry of the Normal Distribution Bell curve is used, and we assert with *M% (where M =N+1 (100 – N /200))* confidence that:

$$Q + Z_M \sqrt{\frac{Q(1-Q)}{n}} > coverage(r) \qquad (1)$$

Similarly, we develop an upper bound for *[1 – coverage(r)]* – the probability that a case belongs to the domain of a rule other than the new rule *r* – based on the lower bound of *coverage(r).* That is, the upper bound of *[1 – coverage(r)]* is given by:

$$1 - (Q - Z_M \sqrt{\frac{Q(1-Q)}{n}}) > [1 - coverage\,(r)] \qquad (2)$$

Thus, by observation 2 and substitution of expressions (1) and (2), an upper bound for error of the knowledge base E_k following the correct classification of n cases is given by:

$$E_k < [Q+Z_M \sqrt{\frac{Q(1-Q)}{n}}\,]\, E_r + [1 - (Q-Z_M \sqrt{\frac{Q(1-Q)}{n}}\,)] * Error(\text{ KB without } r)$$

Given *n* cases correctly classified, to estimate the knowledge base error E_k to a degree of certainty *M*, we use corollary *1*. This results in:

$$[Q+Z_M \sqrt{\frac{Q(1-Q)}{n}}\,]\,(1- M^{1/m}{}_1) + [1-(Q- Z_M \sqrt{\frac{Q(1-Q)}{n}}\,)]\,(1- M^{1/(n-m}{}_1{}^{)}) > E_k$$

In the statistical analysis of this section, we showed how to approximate the error of an RDR tree by considering a sequence of correctly classified cases. In doing this, we have estimated an upper bound on the *coverage* and the error of a new rule *r*. This error can be easily used to obtain the *predictivity(r)* using the following:

$$Predictivity\,(r) = 1 - error\,(r)$$

This *predictivity* can in turn be used to derive an expression for the upper bound on the probability that an arbitrary case *c* ∈ *scope (r):*

$$P(c \in scope\,(r)) = Predictivity\,(r) * coverage\,(r)$$

With respect to the knowledge acquisition process, all these statistical estimations can be calculated in its background, and the result can be reported as the knowledge acquisition proceeds.

As an example of how the statistical analysis discussed can be used, let's consider a sequence of *n* instances, which dictated the progress of the knowledge acquisition process:

$$I_1\, I_2\, I_3 \ldots \boldsymbol{I}_{M_1} \ldots \boldsymbol{I}_{M_2} \ldots \boldsymbol{I}_{M_3} \ldots \boldsymbol{I}_{M_4} \ldots \boldsymbol{I}_{M_5} \ldots\ldots \boldsymbol{I}_{M_s} \ldots I_n$$

Highlighted instances in the given sequence are misclassified instances which cause a knowledge base modification. In the above sequence, *s* modifications are shown. That is, the expert added *s* rules to the RDR tree, following observing and correcting its performance on that sequence. In our above analysis, cases correctly classified following each modification are used to measure the effectiveness of the knowledge base and the last modification undertaken by the expert. For example, the last part of the sequence $I_{M_s} \ldots I_n$ is used to evaluate both, the effectiveness of the last *s-th* update and the error in the knowledge base at that point. However, following every modification, adjacent sub-sequences of test cases can be merged to evaluate the effectiveness of the corresponding knowledge base modifications combined. This provides a more accurate estimate of the whole knowledge base error with an improved confidence level.

More concretely, say the last sub-sequence consists of 50 cases. Of these, 5 cases were correctly classified by the last added rule. That is, we have $n = 50, m = 5,$ hence $Q = 1/10$. Using these values, we have: $E_k < 0.0112$. That is, after classifying 50 cases correctly, we can be 90% certain that the KB error is less than 1.12%. Of this, 0.2% due to the new rule (its *coverage*). The higher the certainty, the wider the interval. For example, we can be 98% that the KB error is less than 9.2%.

The way these estimates are used in evaluating the progress of the KA process is discussed in the next section.

5. Discussion

The statistical analysis of the last section provides a way for estimating the coverage and predictivity of a new rule *r* to a given certainty level. The strength of this statistical analysis is that, it is based on the *correct performance* of the knowledge base on seen cases, *during* the actual knowledge acquisition process. These estimates can be made 'on the fly' as the knowledge acquisition proceeds. Thus, before an expert enters a new rule, an assessment of the last rule that s/he entered is made available with a given degree of confidence. The trend of these assessments is informative about three critical factors for evaluating the success of the KA process: The quality of the expertise, the progress of the knowledge acquisition process, and lastly whether or not the RDR methodology is effective for the domain.

The quality of the expertise is reflected in the predictivity estimate. The lower this predictivity is, then the lower the quality of expertise on hand is. On the other hand, if the predictivity is high, then to assess the effectiveness of the expertise the coverage of rules needs to be considered. Combined with high predictivity, the higher the rules coverage is, then the more effective the expertise is. This way of assessing expertise - in using the predictivity - applies only in the early stage of the knowledge acquisition process, because this is when we expect a proficient expert to be aiming to generalise the knowledge base over the whole domain. Later, when the knowledge acquisition process progresses, we expect the expert to be dealing mainly with exceptions. Thus, when the coverage of newly added rules is relatively high, this is an indication that the knowledge acquisition is still in its early stage. Lastly, when the coverage values are fairly constant, this is an indication that the convergence of the knowledge base towards acceptable accuracy is going at a linear pace. Whether or not, the KA process will yield an effective knowledge base will depend on the size of the domain and on the time resources which can be afforded towards this.

Table 4.1. Decision table used with KA monitor statistical output

KA parameters	**Early KA stage**	**Advanced KA stage**	**Comments**
High predictivity + Low coverage	Bad expertise/ and or domain is unsuitable for RDR	Good expertise/ Good domain	Low coverage is expected at later KA stages when we have logarithmic convergence
High predictivity + High Coverage	Good expertise and suitable domain for RDR	Good expertise/ possibly unsuitable domain	High coverage at a later stage may indicate slow linear convergence.
Low predictivity + High Coverage	Bad expertise and suitable domain for RDR	Bad expertise/ possibly unsuitable domain	As above
Low predictivity + Low Coverage	Bad expertise and unsuitable domain for RDR	Bad expertise/ possibly unsuitable domain	Linear convergence compounded with bad expertise

From a managerial perspective, the trend of the statistical assessment can lead to one of two actions: Replace the expert or terminate the KA project. Replacing the expert is required when the quality of expertise is low, as this may extend the time required to complete the knowledge base beyond the planned budget. This decision needs to be considered in the early stage of the knowledge acquisition process. The second decision to terminate the KA process, assumes that a proficient expert has been in place and one of two conditions prevails: First, the coverage of recently added rules have decreased to a level which does not justify the expert's time. This would indicate that the knowledge base has converged to an acceptable accuracy level. Secondly, the coverage of all rules has been steady. That is, expensive linear convergence is prevailing and the planned budget has been expanded. Summary of the discussion in this section is shown in table 4.1.

Our statistical analysis is not RDR specific. It can be used in any incremental KA environment. However, the decision table (table 4.1) assumes convergence behaviour as shown in figures 3.2 and 4.2.

5. Conclusion and Future Work

In this paper, we have outlined how, the incremental KA process with RDR can be evaluated without the need for a separate testing stage. This is achieved by a statistical estimation of key knowledge acquisition parameters: These were rules *coverage* and rules *predictivity*. Our monitoring process reduces the cost of keeping the expert more than it is absolutely necessary.

Combined with the RDR technology, our monitoring extension gives an off-the-shelf process for developing knowledge bases which combines three stages in one: Development, maintenance and evaluation.

Clearly, choosing the coverage threshold for newly added rules and the estimation confidence level to terminate the KA process depends on the actual domain, and how the knowledge base will be ultimately used. If the recommendation given by a knowledge base is a key determinant in a decision support system, then we want to be as sure as possible that it gives the right answer. On the other hand, if the knowledge base gives a number of solutions, and finally choosing a solution is undertaken by another source of knowledge (e.g. an evaluation function) - as in [3] - then choosing the confidence interval and the coverage threshold can be done less cautiously.

Future extension of this work will attempt to account for that error tolerance in the knowledge base in our current analysis.

References

1. Arinze, B., *A natural language front-end for knowledge acquisition.* SIGART Newsletter, 1989. 108 : p. 106-114.
2. Bégin, J. and Proulx, R., *Categorization in unsupervised neural networks: The Eidos model.* IEEE Transactions on Neural Networks, 1996. 7 (1): p. 147-154.
3. Beydoun, G. and Hoffmann, A. *Acquisition of Search Knowledge* . in *The 10th European Knowledge Acquisition Workshop (EKAW97)* . 1997. Spain: Springer.
4. Beydoun, G. and Hoffmann, A. *Simultaneous Modelling and Knowledge Acquisition using NRDR* . in *5th Pacific Rim Conference on Artificial Intelligence (PRICAI98)* . 1998. Singapore: Springer-Verlag.
5. Beydoun, G. and Hoffmann, A. *A Formal Framework of Ripple Down Rules* . in *The Fourth Australian Workshop on Knowledge Acquisition (AKAW1999)* . 1999. Sydney: University of New South Wales.
6. Beydoun, G. and Hoffmann, A. *A Holistic Approach for Knowledge Acquisition* . in *11th European Workshop on Knowledge Acquisition and Management (EKAW99)* . 1999. Germany: Springer.
7. Brown, B., *The taming of an expert: an anecdotal report.* SIGART Newsletter, 1989. 108 : p. 133-135.
8. Compton, P., Edwards, G., Kang, B., Lazarus, L., Malor, R., Preston, P., and Srinivasan, A., *Ripple down rules: Turning knowledge acquisition into knowledge maintenance.* Artificial Intelligence in Medicine, 1992. 4 : p. 463-475.
9. Compton, P. and Jansen., R., *A philosophical basis for knowledge acquisition.* Knowledge Acquisition, 1990. 2 : p. 241-257.
10. Compton, P. and Preston, P. *Knowledge based systems that have some idea of their limits* . in *10th Banff Knowledge Acquisition for Knowledge-Based Systems Workshop (KAW99)* . 1996. Canada: SRDG publications.

11. Compton, P., Preston, P., and Kang, B. *The Use of Simulated Experts in Evaluating Knowledge Acquisition* . in *9th AAAI-sponsored Banff Knowledge Acquisition for Knowledge Base System Workshop (KAW95)* . 1995. Canada: SRDG publications.
12. Compton, P., Ramadan, Z., Preston, P., Le-Gia, T., Chellen, V., Mulholland, M., Hibbert, D., Haddad, P., and Kang, B. *A trade-off between domain knowledge and problem-solving method* . in *11th Banff Knowledge Acquisition for Knowledge Base System Workshop (KAW98)* . 1998. Canada: SRDG Publications.
13. Davis, R., *Interactive Transfer of Expertise: Acquisition of New Inference Rules.* Artificial Intelligence, 1979. 12 : p. 121-157.
14. Edwards, G., *Reflective Expert Systems in Clinical Pathology (MD thesis)*, 1996, University of New South Wales.
15. Edwards, G., Kang, B.H., Preston, P., and Compton, P., *Prudent expert systems with credentials: managing the expertise of decision support systems.* International Journal of Bio-Medical Computing, 1995. 40 : p. 125-132.
16. Gaines, B.R. and Compton, P.J. *Induction of Ripple Down Rules* . in *Fifth Australian Conference on Artificial Intelligence (AI92)* . 1992. Hobart: World Scientific.
17. Grogono, P., Batarekh, A., Preece, A., Shingal, R., and Suen, C., *Expert system evaluation techniques: a selected bibliography.* Expert Systems, 1991. 8 (4): p. 227-239.
18. Kang, B., Compton, P., and Preston, P. *Multiple classification ripple down rules: Evaluation and possibilities.* in *9th AAAI-sponsored Banff Knowledge Acquisition for Knowledge Based Systems Workshop* . 1998. Canada.
19. Kang, B.H., Gambetta, W., and Compton, P., *Verification and validation with ripple-down rules.* International Journal of Human-Computer Studies, 1996. 44 : p. 257-269.
20. Kivinen, J., Mannila, H., and Ukkonen, E. *Learning Rules with Local Exceptions* . in *European Conference on Computational Theory* . 1993.
21. Menzies, T. *Evaluation Issues With Critical Success Metrics* . in *11th Banff Knowledge Acquisition for Knowledge Base System Workshop (KAW99)* . 1998. Canada: SRDG Publications.
22. Mitchell, T.M., *Machine Learning* . 1997, Singapore: McGraw-Hill.
23. Nick, M., Althoff, K.D., and Tautz, C. *Facilitating the Practical Evaluation of Organizational Memories Using the Goal-Question-Metric Technique* . in *12th Banff Knowledge Acquisition for Knowledge-Based Systems Workshop (KAW99)* . 1999. Canada: SRDG publications.
24. Parpola, P. *Seamless Development of Structured Knowledge Bases* . in *11th Banff Knowledge Acquisition for Knowledge Bases Systems (KAW98)* . 1998. Canada: SRDG.
25. Scheffer, T. *Algebraic foundations and improved methods of induction or ripple-down rules.* in *2nd Pacific Rim Knowledge Acquisition Workshop (PKAW96)* . 1996.

26. Shiraz, G. and Sammut, C. *Combining knowledge acquisition and machine learning to control dynamic systems* . in *15th International Joint Conference on Artificial Intelligence (IJCAI97)* . 1997. Japan: Morgan Kaufman.
27. Shiraz, G.M., *Building Controller for Dynamic Systems (PhD Thesis)* , in *School of Computer Science and Engineering* . 1998, New South Wales: Sydney. p. 260.
28. Wada, T., Horiuchi, T., Motoda, H., and Washio, T. *A New Look at Default Knowledge in Ripple Down Rules Method* . in *Pacific Rim Knowledge Acquisition Workshop (PKAW98)* . 1998. Singapore: National Univeristy of Singapore.
29. Walpole, R.E. and Myers, R.H., *Probability and Statistics for Engineers and Scientists* . 1989, New York: Macmillan Publishing Company.

Torture Tests: A Quantitative Analysis for the Robustness of Knowledge-Based Systems

Perry Groot[1], Frank Van Harmelen[1], and Annette Ten Teije[2]

[1] Division of Mathematics and Computer Science, Faculty of Sciences, Vrije Universiteit, De Boelelaan 1081A, 1081 HV Amsterdam, the Netherlands. {perry,frankh}@cs.vu.nl.

[2] Department of Computer Science, Universiteit Utrecht, PO Box 80.089, Padualaan 14, 3508 TB Utrecht, the Netherlands. annette@cs.uu.nl

Abstract. The overall aim of this paper is to provide a general setting for quantitative quality measures of Knowledge-Based System behavior which is widely applicable to many Knowledge-Based Systems. We propose a general approach that we call "degradation studies": an analysis of how system output degrades as a function of degrading system input, such as incomplete or incorrect inputs. Such degradation studies avoid a number of problems that have plagued earlier attempts at defining such quality measures because they do not require a comparison between different (and often incomparable) systems, and they are entirely independent of the internal workings of the particular Knowledge-Based System at hand.
To show the feasibility of our approach, we have applied it in a specific case-study. We have taken a large and realistic vegetation-classification system, and have analyzed its behavior under various varieties of missing input. This case-study shows that degradation studies can reveal interesting and surprising properties of the system under study.

1 Motivation

When asked about the essential differences between Knowledge-Based Systems (KBSs) and "conventional software", one often hears the claim that KBSs can deal with incomplete, incorrect and uncertain knowledge and data, whereas conventional software is typically very brittle in these respects (see e.g. [4] for a very early formulation of this claim). Although, nowadays researchers no longer view this distinction as either necessary or sufficient to define a KBS, it is believed that the ability of KBSs to deal with missing or invalid data is an essential dimension of KBS validation.

There has been both practical experience and theoretical analysis over many years to back up the mentioned claim. As an example of practical experience, we cite [7]: in a number of verification exercises, errors were found in the knowledge-base of KBSs which were nevertheless still functioning at acceptable levels. As an example of theoretical analysis, we point to our own work [12,13] where we proved that for a large class of diagnostic systems the computed set of diagnoses degrades gracefully and predictably when either the system input (observations) or the knowledge-base degrades in quality.

However, until now, the analysis of the robustness of KBSs in the face of incomplete, incorrect or uncertain knowledge and data has been limited to such practical experience

R. Dieng and O. Corby (Eds.): EKAW 2000, LNAI 1937, pp. 403–418, 2000.

and qualitative analysis. Little or no attempt has been made at a quantitative analysis of the proclaimed robustness of KBSs. A recent special issue of a journal was dedicated to methods for Evaluating Knowledge-Based Systems [6]. None of the papers in that special issue performed any quantitative analysis on the quality of Knowledge Based Systems. The editorial of this special issue lists only a hand-full of quantitative evaluation studies that have been performed over a decade or more of KBS research. In fact, one paper in that special issue [11] even seems to suggest that global qualitative evaluations are about as much as we can expect from KBS evaluation projects. Finally, one of the reviewers of this paper even remarked that "For a long time, the KA community has decried the lack of good evaluation metrics to measure the quality of the KA process and of the resulting knowledge bases." We consider this a serious defect in the study of KBSs, particularly since such robustness is often proclaimed as a unique characteristic of KBSs.

The central claim of this paper is that a quantitative analysis of the robustness of KBSs is both possible and useful.

To argue this claim, we present a case-study in which we perform such a quantitative analysis for a particular KBS. In section 2 we describe our approach to measuring robustness by degradation studies, and we give definitions for the basic notions involved in such degradation studies. In subsequent sections, we apply this approach in a case-study. Section 3 describes the KBS which we subjected to a degradation study and section 4 describes and analyzes the results that we obtained in this study. Section 6 summarizes the main points of the paper and looks at future steps to be taken.

2 Approach and Foundational Definitions

In this section we describe our approach to measuring robustness by degradation studies, and we give definitions for the basic notions involved in such degradation studies. Our aim is to define a very general set of notions that can be widely used in future degradation studies. We regard this section as a central contribution of this paper: the definitions in this section should form the basis of similar analyzes by other researchers and practitioners.

2.1 Robustness and Degradation

The IEEE Standard Glossary of Software Engineering Terminology [5] gives the following definition for robustness:

Informal Definition 1 (Robustness) *The degree to which a system or component can function correctly in the presence of invalid inputs or stressful environmental conditions.*

In other words, robustness of a KBS is concerned with the way in which the quality of the KBS output degrades as a function of a decrease in the quality of the KBS input. This definition immediately leads to the idea of degradation studies:

Informal Definition 2 (Degradation Study) *In a* degradation study *we gradually decrease the quality of the KBS input, and measure how the KBS output quality decreases as a result.*

2.2 Output Quality

Of course, we must be more precise about the rather vague notion of "quality" of the KBS input and output. Concerning the KBS output, we assume that this is always a *set* of answers. In fact, for many typical KBS tasks, this is a realistic assumption: a set of consistent classes in a classification task, a set of likely hypotheses in a diagnostic task, a set of potential designs in a configuration task, etc[i]. More explicitly stated:

Assumption 1 *For the KBSs that we consider we assume that their output can be interpreted as a discrete set of answers.*

Under this assumption, we will define two measures for KBS output quality. Let *correct (I)* be the set of all correct answers for a given input I, and *output (I)* be the set of actually computed answers for the input I.

Definition 1 (Recall) *The* recall(I) *of a KBS for a given input I is defined as:*

$$recall(I) = \frac{|correct(I) \cap output(I)|}{|correct(I)|}.$$

In other words: the recall is the fraction of correct answers that the system actually computes. It can of course happen that $correct(I) = \varnothing$ (when the system is presented with a case I for which no correct output exists, such as an inconsistent set of observations for a classification system, or an inconsistent set of requirements for a design system). In this case we define:

$$\text{if } correct(I) = \varnothing \text{ then } recall(I) = 1.$$

This reflects the intuition that the empty answer is always included in any set of answers.

Definition 2 (Precision) *The* precision(I) *of a KBS for a given input I is defined as:*

$$precision(I) = \frac{|correct(I) \cap output(I)|}{|output(I)|}.$$

In other words: the precision is the fraction of computed answers that are actually correct. In the case $output(I) = \varnothing$ (i.e. when the system returns no output), we define:

$$\text{if } output(I) = \varnothing \text{ then } precision(I) = \begin{cases} 1 & \text{if } correct(I) = \varnothing, \\ 0 & \text{otherwise.} \end{cases}$$

This reflects the intuition that the only correct answer in this case is the empty set.

We will simply write *recall* and *precision* when we mean the average of *recall*(I_j) and *precision*(I_j) over a given set of inputs $I_1, ..., I_n$.

It is a widely known fact in information retrieval that in general it is very hard to achieve both a high precision and a high recall. In general, a high recall must be paid for with a low precision. Consider for example a trivial system which always returns all

[i] Of course, even for KBSs which return a single answer, this assumption still holds since we can interpret such a single answer x simply as the singleton set $\{x\}$.

candidate answers. By inspecting the definitions above, it can be easily seen that such a system would have a recall of 1, but a precision close to 0.

There are two very attractive aspects to these definitions for the "quality of output". First of all, these definitions are well known from the literature on information retrieval (e.g. [10]), and have proven to be useful, informative and intuitive measures in many studies in that field and elsewhere (see for instance [3] for an application of these measures to deduction-based software component retrieval). Secondly, these measures are completely general, and make no commitment to either the task or the domain of the KBS that we wish to study. Consequently, the approach proposed in this paper can be directly applied to other KBSs, even when they are very different from the one that we happen to have chosen in our own case-study.

The above definitions are in fact gradual versions of the classical notions of soundness and completeness: recall corresponds to the degree of completeness of the system, and precision corresponds to the degree of soundness of the system. These measures provide a quantitative angle on our earlier work [14] which was strictly qualitative.

2.3 Input Quality

Unfortunately, the definition of input quality cannot in our view be defined in an equally generic manner. Our case-study is concerned with a classification task, and our input quality measures are directly based on this task-type, such as missing and incomplete observations. We expect that each task-type will come with its own measure for input quality.

Notice that we have already taken a step further than in [14]. In that paper we did not commit to any definition of quality on input or output, and only demanded that whatever the definition was, it should respect a partial ordering. In this paper on degradation testing, we commit to a specific definition of output quality, while leaving input quality open to be defined for each specific application.

2.4 Comparing Robustness

The only notion that is still left undefined is some ordering on robustness: when do we call a system more robust or less robust than another? Unlike output quality (where we have given a single widely applicable definition) and input quality (whose definition is deliberately left open to depend on the task-type), we have not been able to determine a good answer to this question. Instead, we offer a number of competing definitions:

Definition 3 (Monotonicity) *A robust system will show a monotonically decreasing output quality as a function of deteriorating input quality.*

The motivation for this property is that a system whose output quality oscillates as a function of input quality is much less predictable than a system with monotonically decreasing output quality. This demand corresponds precisely to the usual demand on anytime algorithms that their output quality monotonically increases with increasing run-time [2].

Definition 4 (Quality Value) *A system S_1 is more robust than a system S_2 for a set of inputs, if everywhere on that input set the output quality of S_1 is higher than the output quality of S_2.*

Definition 5 (Rate of Quality Change) *A system S_1 is more robust than a system S_2 for a set of inputs, if everywhere on that input set the output quality of S_1 decreases more slowly than the output quality of S_2.*

Definition 6 (Integral of Quality Value) *A system S_1 is more robust than a system S_2 for a set of inputs, if on that input set the integral of the output quality of S_1 is larger than the same integral for S_2.*

Formally speaking, definition 4 compares the output quality of two systems (and is concerned with which system produces the *best* output), while definition 5 compares the first derivative of the output quality of the systems (and is therefore concerned with which system produces the *most stable* output). Definition 6 compares the overall quality of the output quality over an entire interval even when neither system always dominates the other (as required in definition 4).

These definitions are illustrated in figure 1[ii]

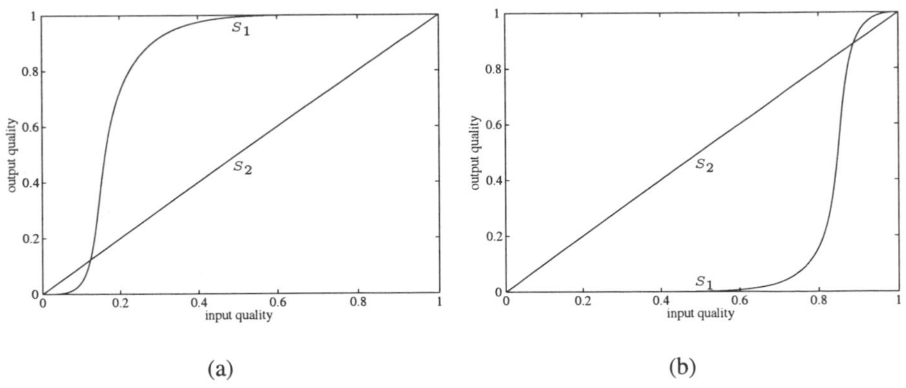

Fig. 1. Comparing robustness of systems.

In figure 1(a), system S_1 is more robust on for example the interval $[0.1, 0.3]$ according to definition 4, since on that interval its output quality is always higher than that of S_2. However, according to definition 5, S_2 is the more robust of the two, since its output quality decreases more gradually (reading the graph from right to left). Definition 6 allows to take a more overall perspective: it takes the size of the area under the output

[ii] In our figures, we plot input quality against output quality. When speaking about "robustness", we are interested in *decreasing* input quality, so the graphs must be read from right to left.

quality graph as measure of the overall quality. Under this definition, S_1 is more robust on the entire interval [0,1], since the value of $\int_0^1 output\ quality\ d(input\ quality)$ is larger for S_1 than for S_2. Note that the situation is rather different in figure 1(b). Although the output quality again increases from 0 to 1 over the same interval, the comparisons between S_1 and S_2 on various subintervals are very different.

At the current point in our research, we simply propose each of these definitions as reasonable, without claiming superiority of any definition in all cases. In fact, we believe that under different pragmatic circumstances, different definitions will be preferable: if steep drops in system performance are to be avoided, the second definition is preferable. If one is interested in upholding output quality as long as possible in the face of declining input, the other two definitions may be preferred.

3 Example Knowledge-Based System

An essential aspect of our proposed approach to measuring robustness through degradation experiments is that it is entirely independent of the particular problem-solving method employed by the KBS under study. All that is required is a description of the functional I/O-relation of the system[iii]. To emphasize this point, we will describe the particular KBS that we used in our case-study only in terms of its functionality, and refrain from describing the underlying problem-solving method.

For our case-study we have used a classification system for commonly occurring vegetation in Southern Germany. The plant-classification system was created with the D3 Shell-Kit which is a tool for the development of KBSs. We will not discuss this tool here but refer to a number of publications about D3 [8,9]. It is also possible to download a demo-version of the software from the URL `http://d3.informatik.uni-wuerzburg.de`.

The plant-classification system that we studied can have 40 different observables as input and has 93 different plant-names as output. The knowledge base consists of 7586 rules. Furthermore, with the system we received 150 test-cases. Each of these cases consisted of the set of observations for that case (color and shape of flowers, leafs, stem, etc.), together with the (supposedly correct) answer for these observations as given by a human expert. Around 97% could be answered correctly by the system.

The input observations can be entered in a graphical user interface, but the user is not restricted to the ordering in this interface. The observations can be entered in any order, thus the input can be seen as a *set*. This is not entirely true because some observations are dependent on other observations and will only appear when certain input-conditions are met. Because of these dependencies, the maximum number of observations that can be given for one case is 30.

The plant-classification system computes a score for every output class based on the given input. These scores result in an ordering on the output classes. All the classes with a sufficiently high score can be seen as a plausible candidate for the given input, but plants with a higher score are seen as more plausible candidates. All the scores are computed for a given input set and these scores are adjusted incrementally when new observations are added. The user does not actually see the numeric scores of the candidates, but only an

[iii] Sometimes referred to as "competence" in the Knowledge Engineering literature.

interpretation of the scores. For example, all plants with a score lower than -42 receive the status *ausgeschlossen* (i.e. excluded).

4 Results of the Degradation Study

In this section we present the robustness measures that we have obtained in empirical experiments with the plant-classification system. Before we discuss these results in some detail, we want to emphasize that this case-study only serves to illustrate our general approach to measure robustness through degradation testing. What's important in this section is the quantities we've decided to measure, and how we analyze them, not so much the specific results for the plant-classification system, since it only serves as a case-study to illustrate our proposal.

4.1 Which Input Quality Measure to Use?

According to the definitions from section 2 we must still decide on what to use as a measure on the input quality. In this case-study we choose the *completeness of the input* as the measure of input quality. In our classification system, completeness of the input can be directly translated as the *number of available observations*.

There are two reasons why this choice is reasonable and attractive: - **robustness:** in many practical classification settings, the input observations are not completely available. It then becomes an interesting question how robust the system functions under such incomplete input. - **Anytime behavior:** Even when all observations are present, there are practical settings where insufficient run-time is available to process all the observations: some output from the system is required before a given real-time deadline, and not all observations can be processed before this deadline. Those observations that could not be processed before the deadline can be regarded as "missing from the input".

As a result of this second reason, the degradation results that we present in this section can also be seen as *anytime performance profiles* for the plant-classification system. Performance profiles are a basic tool in the study of anytime algorithms [2]. They plot the output quality as a function of available run-time. Since available run-time can be interpreted as one aspect of "input quality", such performance profiles are simply a special case of our more general proposal: performance profiles only study output degradation as a function of decreased run-time, whereas our approach is applicable to any aspect of input quality that one chooses to model.

In the following we will present a number of graphs analyzing the robustness of the plant-classification system. Each of these graphs plot output-quality (measured by either recall or precision) against input-quality (measured by the number of observations that were available to the system). If one is interested in anytime behavior, these graphs can be read from left to right: "what happens when the system has time to process more and more of the inputs?". If one is interested in robustness, these graphs should be read from right to left: "what happens when the system is provided with fewer and fewer of the inputs?"

Before we discuss the results, a final remark must be made about the possible values of recall and precision in this case-study. Since for every case there is at most one correct answer (namely the name of the actual plant on which the observations were made), we have for any case I, $|correct(I)| = 1$ iff the case is in the knowledge base or $|correct(I)| = 0$ iff the case is not in the knowledge base. As a result, the only values that $recall(I)$ can assume are either 0 or 1. For the same reason, $precision(I)$ is either 0 or $\frac{1}{|output(I)|}$.

4.2 Using the Input Sequence from the Test-Cases

Now that we have established that the number of available observations will be the input-aspect that we will degrade in our studies, we have to decide in which order observations will be made available to the system. Our first choice is simply based on the order in which the observations appeared in the test-cases for the plant-classification system. Each such test-case consisted of a list of observables and their values for that case. Figure 2(a) shows how the precision of the answers from the system (as defined in definition 2) increases when longer initial-sequences of the test-cases were given to the system. The first surprise that this graph has in store for us is its monotonic growth:

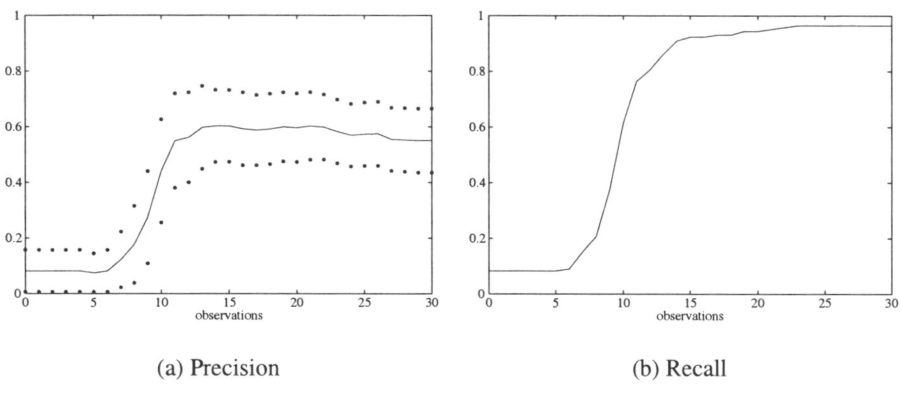

(a) Precision

(b) Recall

Fig. 2. Measures with test-case order.

Surprise 1 *Both average precision and average recall (see figure 2(b)) grow monotonically (or: almost monotonically in the case of precision) when adding more observations. This is somewhat* [iv] *surprising since this is not true for individual cases. The classification algorithm of the plant-classification system assigns both positive and negative scores. This means that the answer-set can both grow and shrink when adding more observations. In fact, only 58% of the test-cases has a monotonically growing answer-set. As mentioned above, such monotonic behavior is desirable from both a robustness and from an anytime perspective, so on a case-by-case basis, the plant-classification system does not score very well on this. Surprisingly, the average-case behavior of the system is apparently much better.*

[iv] This result is not completely surprising because it is well known that the average of several variables can indeed show a different distribution than the individual variables.

A second observation to make is that (as to be expected) initially the system is not able to make any sensible guess at likely solutions (this holds up to about 6 observations). For higher number of available observations, the graph is surprising for two reasons:

Surprise 2 *After about 12 observations, adding more observations does not increase the precision. This is surprising since most cases contain as much as 19-30 observations. Figure 2(a) suggests that 12 observations is sufficient to obtain the maximally achievable precision on average.*

Surprise 3 *The region in which additional observations actually contribute to an increase in precision is surprisingly small, namely between the 6 and 12 observations. Of the 19-30 observations per case, all the real work seems to be done by this small segment of observations!*

Figure 2(b) shows similar results for the other dimension of output quality, namely the recall from definition 1.

The dotted lines in figure 2(a) indicate the variance of the precision, and this variance is rather significant. It shows that the distribution of the actual precision-values that were obtained for the different cases are actually spread rather widely around the average[v].

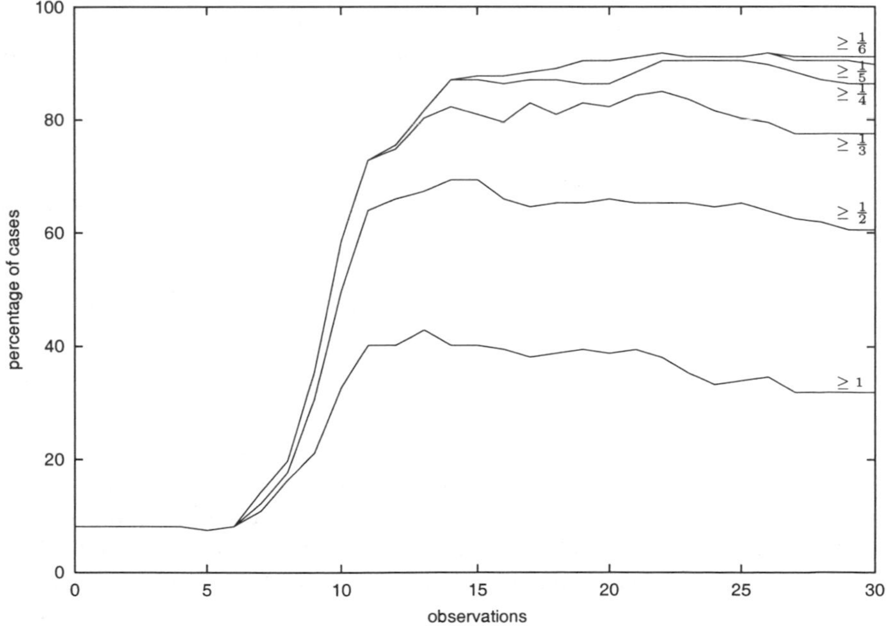

Fig. 3. Precision with multiple levels.

[v] No variance was plotted for the recall since, as explained above, in our application the recall is either 0 or 1. Because of this, the variance for recall is not a meaningful notion.

Figure 3 gives more insight in the distribution of the precision than the simple average from figure 2(a). Each line in this figure shows the percentage of cases that achieved a precision of at least a certain value after the given number of observations. The lowest line shows that after 12 observations, 40% of the cases have already reached the maximum precision (namely 1). Furthermore, and more surprisingly, this percentage then stops growing! This means that:

Surprise 4 *When aiming for the maximum precision of 1, there is no need to use any more than 12 observations (out of a maximum of 30!). If the maximum precision has not been reached after the first 12 observations, adding further observations will not help.*

This is actually a more precise version of surprise 2 above. There we claimed that extending beyond 12 observations was not useful *on average*. Here we see that for harder cases, a few more observations do actually help, although not more than 20 observations in total.

This is because at the other end of the scale (the top line in figure 3) , we see that the percentage of cases with a precision of at least 0.2 continues to increase during a longer interval. Apparently, harder cases (those that ultimately achieve a lower precision) benefit more from additional observations than easy cases (those that achieve precision 1). Nevertheless, even there we see that no increase is gained after about 20 observations:

Surprise 5 *Whatever the final precision that is ultimately obtained by the system, this level of precision is already obtained after at most 20 observations. It seems that asking for any more then 20 observations will not improve the output quality any further. This is surprising since many cases (in fact 98% of the test set) contain more than 20 observations.*

Looking at the initial segment of observations, we see another surprise: although we may expect that a low number of observations leads to a low average precision, it is surprising that the lines for the different precision-levels all *coincide* until the 6th observation:

Surprise 6 *No increase in precision can be gained from the first 6 observations.*

This means that in an anytime setting, interrupting the system before the 6th observation is completely useless, since no increase in precision will have been obtained yet.

Figure 3 is particularly interesting from an anytime perspective: it tells us for each partially processed input what the chance is that the system has already obtained a certain precision in its output: for instance, after having fed the system 10 observations, there is a 30% chance that it has already obtained the maximum precision of 1, a 45% chance that it has already obtained a precision of at least 0.5, and a 60% chance that it has already obtained a precision of at least 0.3.[vi] This information can be used by the user to determine if it is useful to continue feeding the system more input, or if a sufficiently high precision has already been obtained for the purposes of the user, so that processing (and acquiring potentially expensive observations) can be stopped. Our graph (when

[vi] Note that these chances are cumulative, which is why they add up to more than 100%.

interpreted as a performance profile) contains much more information than the usual performance profiles presented in the literature (e.g. [15]). These graphs typically give only a *single* expected value for the output quality at any point in time (compare our figure 2(a)), whereas we give a probability distribution of the expected output value, which is much more informative.

Note that the ideas behind figure 3 can in principle also be applied to the recall. We omitted this because in our case -study the recall is either 0 or 1, thus the resulting figure would be the same as figure 2(b).

4.3 Early Conclusions on Robustness

Since we are only studying a single system, we cannot apply the definitions from section 2.4, which only speak about one system being more or less robust than another. However, what is clear from the analysis until now is that the robustness of the plant-classification system is certainly not very uniform across the distribution of input quality. While degrading input quality (i.e. reading the previous graphs from right to left), the system at first appears extremely stable against missing observations: no quality loss occurs at all. This holds until we are left with somewhere between 12-15 observations (depending on the difficulty of the case). At that point, the robustness of the system is very low, and the input quality drops dramatically.

Is this desirable behavior or not? Would a more uniform behavior (e.g. a straight line connects bottom-left and top-right of figure 2(a)) be more attractive? In our view, this question cannot be answered in general, but depends on the pragmatics of the system in use. The "straight line" profile is on the one hand more attractive, because it avoids the dramatic drop in quality seen in the figures above (definition 5 from section 2.4); on the other hand, it would start loosing output quality straight away, while the profiles discussed above are all remarkably resistant to quality loss during early phases of input degradation (definition 4 from section 2.4).

4.4 Exploring Other Input Sequences

In all the profiles above, we have degraded the input by removing observations in the order in which they were listed in each test-case. Figure 4 shows what happens if the input is degraded by removing observations in a different order.

For reference, the dotted line shows the recall-profile from figure 2(b). The left-most line shows the theoretically optimal average-recall profile: at each step in each case, we computed which next observation would contribute maximally to an increase in recall. Of course, this cannot be done in practice, since which observation will contribute most in general depends on the observation-value that is obtained, so this computation can only be done theoretically for test-cases where all observations are already present. The value of the left-most line is therefore only to show what would be the theoretically fastest increase in recall by the system with the fewest possible observations. The right-most line in figure 4 does the same, but this time for the theoretically slowest average-recall profile. Every other possible recall profile must lie between these two lines (as is indeed the case with the earlier observed profile based on the test-case sequence). Finally, figure 4 shows a narrow bundle of recall profiles. Each of these profiles corresponds to a randomly generated order of the observations.

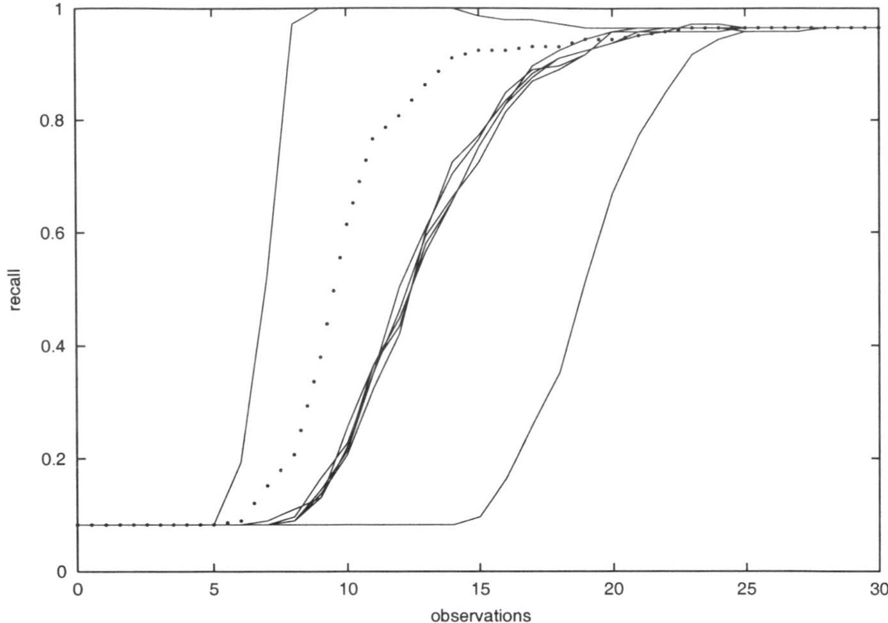

Fig. 4. Recall with various orderings.

The dotted line in this figure shows the profile based on the observation order obtained from the test-cases (as originally plotted in figure 2(b)). We can now see that this observation order actually scores rather well when compared with the random sequences:

Surprise 7 *The degradation sequence taken from the test-cases is surprisingly effective in obtaining a high recall after only a few observations. In fact, it is much closer to the theoretically optimal sequence than the randomly generated (information-free) sequences.*

Currently, we have no good explanation for this phenomenon. It is possible that the order of the input observables in the test-cases is influenced by the order in the graphical user-interface. We will look more closely at this ordering in section 4.6.

4.5 Further Conclusions on Robustness

The variation in the curves from figure 4 shows that the plant-classification is very sensitive to the specific order in which the observations are presented to the system. In other words: when the same set of observations are presented to the system in a different order, the behavior of the system may change dramatically.

This type of robustness is not covered by our robustness definitions in section 2.4. The definitions there are all concerned with comparing the behavior of different systems on the same degrading input. The phenomenon observed in figure 4 concerns the behavior of a single system on different ways of degrading the input. We leave it for further research how to include this type of robustness in our approach.

4.6 Which Sequence Does the System Actually Use?

The original plant-classification system has been designed in such a way that all observations can be entered at any time during the dialogue. The system does not enforce a particular order among the observations to be entered as input. Nevertheless, the user-interface of the system does suggest a particular input sequence, namely the order in which the observations occur on the input form. Although the user can enter observations anywhere from the input form, the top-to-bottom sequence of this form is suggestive.

The solid line in figure 5 shows the increase in recall for this user-interface sequence. The dotted lines show the theoretically fastest, the theoretically slowest gains in recall, and the gains from random observation orderings and the test-case ordering as well (all copied from figure 4). As can be observed in this figure, the user-interface sequence performs rather well when interpreted as an anytime performance profile (and certainly much better than a random ordering). This suggests that the user-interface has to some extent been designed with this behavior in mind. Although this behavior was not the reason for the plant-classification system, it would be interesting to see how a dedicated dialogue strategy can save time.

Actually, the real reason behind the ordering of the user-interface was the intended use of the system. This means that we have to place our results in this context. The ordering of the user-interface is based on the way people describe plants. First the system asks about the flower, which is the most specific part of the plant and asks about the leaves and stem afterwards. This specificity ordering may be the reason for the better curve in figure 5 when we compare it with a random ordering.

Furthermore, we like to note that the most optimal input order w.r.t. the recall or precision, may not be realizable in practice because it can decrease other factors like for example the user-friendliness of the user-interface. Some trade off will usually have to be made.

5 Future Work

Although the results above already yield interesting insights in the behavior of a realistic KBS, many other aspects could still be uncovered using further degradation studies. We discuss some of these extensions in this section:

The informal definition for robustness that we used as a starting point in section 2 has not been carried through entirely in the paper. Functioning correctly in the presence of invalid inputs has not been evaluated in the case study and should be included in future research.

[16] suggests a category of measures on output quality which is not yet covered by the recall and precision that we have used in the above, namely "specificity of a solution". This is intended to represent the degree of detail in the systems' answer. An example would be a system which can compute names of ever finer grained plant-families instead of only individual species (as above). This property was irrelevant in our case-study, since the plant-classification system only deals with a flat list of candidates, not with a hierarchically organized space of candidates. We have therefore ignored this potential third dimension of KBS output quality, but we expect that good measures can be devised for this just as well as for the other two dimensions which we did handle.

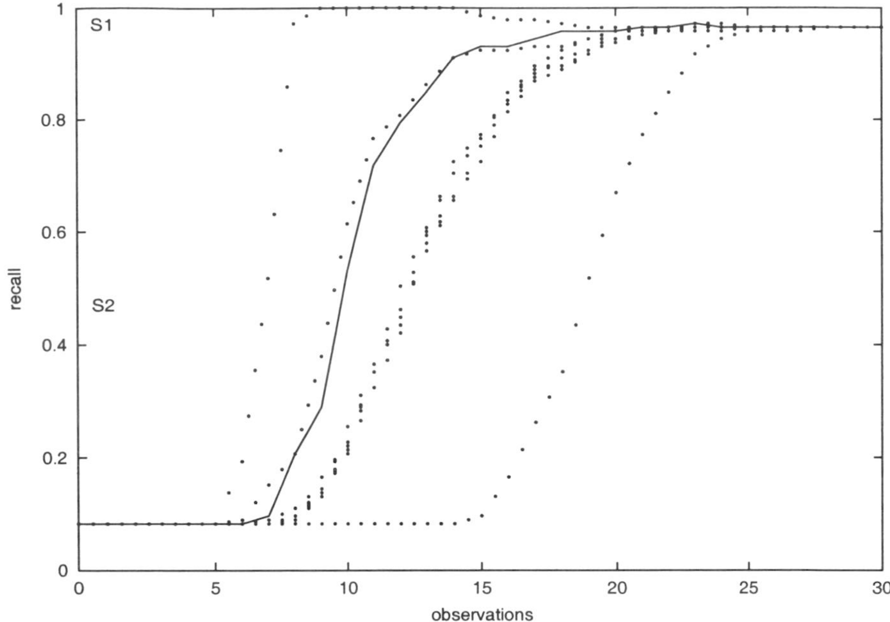

Fig. 5. Recall with user-interface ordering.

In this paper, we have studied the consequences of degrading the *input* quality of a KBS. It would be equally if not more interesting to study the effects of degradations of the knowledge-base itself. After all, the knowledge-base is most likely incomplete and often partially incorrect. We expect that the same approach as taken in this paper will apply to such a knowledge-base degradation study, and we intend to perform such a study in the near future.

The output quality measures we used (precision and recall) are geared towards systems with a discrete output (a set of answers). Some KBS applications return real-valued answers (e.g. ratings). We must study how these systems can also be subjected to degradation studies using acceptable measures. In fact, the plant-classification system not only returns a set of candidates, but indicates a numeric score for each candidate. Our current output-measures completely ignore this score. A further step would be to also include this score in the quality measures.

As mentioned in section 4.2, figure 3 can be interpreted as a prediction for the expected quality of the output after a given number of observations. In effect, figure 3 is the result of *learning the anytime performance profile* through the test-cases. As with any learning task, we can apply cross-validation to the set of test-cases [1]: use a subset of the test-cases to "learn" profiles as in figure 3, and use the remaining cases to check the accuracy of the predicted performance levels.

Our measures for output quality (recall and precision) can only be computed for cases where the correct answer is actually known. This is not as obvious as it may sound. In many applications (e.g. computing the best solution to a design problem) the correct (i.e. best) answer is not known to any human expert. In such cases, one must either resort to known approximations of the correct answer, or fundamentally different quality measures must be defined.

Our proposed definitions for output quality (precision and recall) focus on the correctness of the answers computed by a system. Of course, there are many more aspects to the "quality" of a KBS, such as the quality of its explanation, its computational efficiency, its interaction with its environment (be it users or other systems), etc. It is an open issue to us whether the same "degradation study" approach can be taken to quantifying any of these other aspects of the systems quality.

6 Conclusions

In this paper, we have argued for the need for *quantitative analysis* of the quality of KBSs. In particular, we have shown how *robust behavior* in the light of incomplete system-input is amenable to such quantitative analysis. Our quantitative analysis is based on the idea of *degradation tests*: analyze how the quality of the output degrades as a function of degrading input. We have proposed a set of *general definitions* which are general enough that they can be used in similar degradation experiments by others, even if the systems concerned are of a very different nature than the one in our case-study. The proposed approach of measuring robustness via degradation experiments is *entirely independent of the problem-solving method* used internally by the KBS under study. All that is required is a functional description of the I/O-relation of the KBS. We have shown the practicality of our approach by applying it to a particular *case-study*. This yielded a number of surprising insights into the behavior of the system under study.

The ultimate suggestion that follows from this work is that any KBS should upon delivery come accompanied with a set of degradation statistics such as discussed in this paper as a quantitative way of measuring interesting and important aspects of the systems quality. This would contribute to a more empirical and quantitative analysis of AI systems in general and of KBSs in particular, very much in the spirit of [1].

Acknowledgements. We like to thank Frank Puppe for the help he has given us. This paper was inspired by a discussion with him during the Banff'98 KAW workshop. He gave us access to the plant-classification software and explained in detail its working. He was also always available to answer any question by e-mail.

References

1. P. R. Cohen. *Empirical methods for artificial intelligence*. MIT Press, 1995.
2. T. Dean and M. Boddy. An analysis of time-dependent planning. In *Proceedings of the seventh National conference on artificial intelligence AAAI–88*, pages 49–54, Saint Paul, Minnesota, 1988.
3. B. Fischer and J. Schumann. NORA/HAMMR: Making deduction-based software component retrieval practical. In *Automated Software Engineering (ASE)'97*, pages 246–254. IEEE, 1997.
4. F. Hayes-Roth. Knowledge-based expert systems — the state of the art in the US. In J. Fox, editor, *Expert Systems: state of the art report*. Pergamon Infotech, Oxford, 1984.

5. IEEE. IEEE standard glossary of software engineering terminology, 1990. IEEE Standard 610.12-1990, ISBN 1-55937-067-X.
6. Tim Menzies and Frank van Harmelen. Evaluating Knowledge-Engineering Techniques. *International Journal of Human-Computer Studies*, 51(4):715–727, October 1999.
7. A. Preece, S. Talbot, and L. Vignollet. Evaluation of verification tools for knowledge-based systems. *Internationl Journal of Human-Computer Studies*, 47:629–658, 1997.
8. F. Puppe, U. gappa, K. Poeck, and S. Bamberger. *Wissensbasierte Diagnose- und Informationssysteme*. Springer-Verlag, Juli 1996.
9. F. Puppe, K. Poeck, U. Gappa, S. Bamberger, and K. Goos. Wiederverwendbare Bausteine für eine konfigurierbare Diagnostik-shell. *Künstliche Intelligenz*, 94(2):13–18, 1994.
10. G. Salton and M. J. McGill. *Introduction to Modern Information Retrieval*. McGraw-Hill, New York, 1983.
11. Nigel Shadbolt, Kieron O'Hara, and Louise Crow. The experimental evaluation of knowledge acquisition techniques and methods: history, problems and new directions. *International Journal of Human-Computer Studies*, 51(4):729–755, October 1999.
12. A. ten Teije and F. van Harmelen. Computing approximate diagnoses by using approximate entailment. In *Proceedings of the Fifth International Conference on Principles of Knowledge Representation and Reasoning (KR'96)*, pages 265–256, Boston, Massachusetts, November 1996.
13. A. ten Teije and F. van Harmelen. Exploiting domain knowledge for approximate diagnosis. In M. Pollack, editor, *Proceedings of the Fifteenth International Joint Conference on Artificial Intelligence (IJCAI'97)*, pages 454–459, Nagoya, Japan, August 1997.
14. F. van Harmelen and A. ten Teije. Characterising approximate problem-solving by partial pre- and postconditions. In *Proceedings of ECAI'98*, pages 78–82, Brighton, August 1998.
15. S. Zilberstein. Using anytime algorithms in intelligent systems. *Artificial Intelligence Magazine*, fall:73–83, 1996.
16. S. Zilberstein and S. J. Russell. Approximate Reasoning Using Anytime Algorithms. In S. Natarajan, editor, *Imprecise and Approximate Computation*. Kluwer Academic Publishers, 1995.

Certifying KBSs: Using CommonKADS to Provide Supporting Evidence for Fitness for Purpose of KBSs

Kieron O'Hara[1], Nigel Shadbolt[1], and Jeni Tennison[2]

[1]Dept. of Electronics and Computer Science, University of Southampton, Highfield, Southampton SO17 1BJ, UK
{kmo,nrs}@ecs.soton.ac.uk
[2]Epistemics Ltd, Strelley Hall, Nottingham, UK
Jeni.Tennison@epistemics.co.uk

Abstract. Certification is the process of showing that software meets its requirements and is fit for purpose. It occurs in sensitive contexts where it is essential for safety or other reasons that the software should never fail. Certifying KBSs can be seen as especially problematic, because KBSs' output, being heuristic rather than algorithmic, is less predictable than that of conventional software. By developing a detailed and extended case study, the authors show that KBS development governed by CommonKADS is, with very little adjustment, satisfactory for KBS certification.

Introduction

In this paper we will discuss problems with the certification of KBSs, and suggest that the use of CommonKADS [1] as a de facto standard is a reasonable solution to those problems. In any sensitive application, software needs to go through some sort of independent certification process to ensure that it is fit for purpose. Clearly, the certification process is closely related to verification and validation, and also to testing. However, the purpose of certification entails that there are important differences.

Certification is an issue for all safety-critical and mission-critical contexts, particularly for bespoke or little-used software in sensitive contexts such as military contexts [2], nuclear power [3], aviation [4] and sea transportation [5]. Software that has been used without problems by a wide user base can reasonably regarded as safe, but special-purpose software in, say, an aircraft needs to be certified before being brought into service.

The aim of certification is to establish the usability credentials of the application within its sponsoring organisation. The process is aimed at the users of the system, and in broad terms, is meant to give them the confidence to use the application. Certification therefore has two aspects to it: establishing that the requirements are met; and providing a reasoned case that the system is safe to use, which is more of a sociotechnical process that takes place within the particular organisational culture.

This safety case tries to establish that the developers followed a trustworthy development process, using by-products of V&V such as evidence from tests, reviews of the models and software, etc. This can be problematic for KBSs in particular; while

R. Dieng and O. Corby (Eds.): EKAW 2000, LNAI 1937, pp. 419-434, 2000.

there are a number of mature software engineering (SE) methodologies that have been used frequently in real-world contexts and whose properties are well-known, KBS development methodologies are relatively less mature.

We will show that KBS certification is possible, by sketching a case study using an amended version of CommonKADS. In the next section, we characterise certification, and discuss some difficult issues for certifying KBSs. In section 0, we discuss KBS development with CommonKADS in certification contexts, and section 0 gives a case study showing how certification evidence is produced. In section 0 we discuss related work, and in section 0 we will discuss some of the issues that this exercise has raised.

Certification: The Issues

2.1 The Certification Process

Certification itself is straightforward. The development process must produce, as well as the developed system, enough documentation to ensure that all of the requirements have been met and the development method followed rigorously. All the code must be checkable; it must be possible to find a rationale for any line of code. Such a rationale should be in the requirements, or in a design decision which must be properly documented. The requirements are checked against a *compliance matrix*, which measures the extent to which user requirements have been addressed.

Software requirements come from two sources. First there are requirements from any embedding systems, which would be monitored by the engineers of the wider system. More important are the requirements of the KBS itself, independent of the wider context. These are expressed in a *cardinal points specification.*

The compliance matrix expresses the compliance of the software with each of the cardinal points. For each point, the matrix shows the requirement's rationale, the method of showing compliance (e.g. tests, inspection, analysis etc.), and a statement of whether the system actually was compliant, partially compliant or non-compliant, together with any other documentation useful to the certification authorities (e.g. detailed test results, models, lists of evidence used etc.).

The safety case is less mechanical to produce. It draws upon the documentation produced by development and testing to establish that all procedures have been followed correctly and that the system is fit for purpose. This is an internal organisational issue, rather than a traditional KBS development issue; the level of detail here depends on how much rigour the sponsors require. Nevertheless, there are development implications; for a KBS to be certified, it has to have been developed using with a mature methodology that produces adequate documentation.

2.2 Relevant Issues

There are particular issues concerning certifying KBSs in particular. In this section we will review some of these issues, and suggest ways of circumventing problems.

- **Maturity**. Certification requires that a KBS be reliable. This can only be assured when it is developed using a methodology and software (e.g. KA tools) that have been used successfully over a long period and wide range of problems, user types and system types. The problem for KBS as opposed to conventional software is that there are fewer mature methodologies around, partly reflecting lack of effort in the KBS community in the evaluation of methodologies and software [6].

- **Documentation**. The methodology must produce sufficient documentation for certification. One way of ensuring this is to use model-based methodologies, whose models specify the KBS at various stages of development [7]. Most model-based methodologies include at least a design model, a conceptual model and a requirements specification, enabling certification authorities to compare the code with the design, the underlying knowledge/expertise and user requirements. However, such models, will have to be extensively annotated to explain modelling decisions. For example, a conceptual model would have to include explanations of particular sets of rules, perhaps pointing to the KA sessions where they were acquired.
- **Knowledge Intensiveness**. Conventional software can be tested straightforwardly, as the same input leads to the same output. However, because of the heuristic nature of knowledge and expertise, KBSs only have to produce *acceptable* output, whose range could be relatively wide. Hence, while certification should ensure that every line of code has been tested, this is less strong for KBSs than for conventional software.
- **Full Life Cycle**. Certification requires a methodology to be followed rigorously across the full development life cycle, from procurement, development planning, KA, design, implementation to testing. KBS development methodologies have generally focused on the theoretically interesting areas of KA, modelling, and design, as these are where KBS-specific problems tend to arise. This means that they tend not to be strong in many certification-relevant areas.
- **Software Engineering**. Certification procedures assume the standard phases of SE have been carried out, where all modelling prior to system design tends to be lumped together into 'requirements specification'. In a KBS project, however, modelling is central, and is the greater part of the effort spent. Hence certification procedures need to be flexible enough to accommodate the greater amount of knowledge modelling.
- **Integration**. An embedded KBS raises integration problems. KBS development needs to be integrated into the wider system development, and the KBS needs to be integrated into the wider system. This requires, for certification, a strong model of communication with the environment. An additional problem is that the wider context may impose limitations on choices of off-the-shelf hardware and software.
- **Traceability**. Certification requires links between items of importance to ensure traceability. For instance, each piece of code should have a traceable justification either in the user requirements, or a design rationale, or a KA session, and should be linked to relevant tests. All items in the code or models need to be extensively annotated with design rationales.

2.3 CommonKADS

Any KBS methodology needs to meet the above difficulties for certification. We have used CommonKADS in this paper, as it addresses them as follows.

- **Maturity**. CommonKADS has a wide user base, and has been used to develop knowledge-intensive systems in both academic and commercial contexts.
- **Documentation**. It produces six major models during development [1, pp.18-19].
- **Knowledge intensiveness**. It includes a number of formalisms to express non-deterministic, uncertain or heuristic knowledge, and can be used to suggest areas where rigorous testing/certification is required.
- **Full life cycle**. It covers most of the KBS development life cycle, though it is less specific about post-implementation phases [1, p.381].
- **Software engineering**. It can be mapped onto existing SE methodologies.
- **Integation**. The communication model models the interfaces rigorously [1, pp.215-240].
- **Traceability**. Each model can be decomposed and modules linked with their justifications, thereby allowing traceability support [1, pp.85-122]. The principle of structure-preserving design [1, p.273] means that there will be straightforward structural correspondences between the different models and the code.

CommonKADS in our judgement is a suitable methodology to address these key issues, though others might have done as well. Our aim is now to establish that CommonKADS can be adequate for KBS development in certification contexts.

CommonKADS and Certification

To test the hypothesis that CommonKADS could be used to develop certifiable KBSs, the authors, together with partners from Aerosystems International, developed a case study. The domain used was the hypothetical upgrading of an Airborne Early Warning (AEW) military helicopter which coordinates airborne defences for an aircraft carrier. The helicopter has a number of combat aircraft (CA) under its control. When a threat is detected, the helicopter sends a CA to intercept it.

The study involved two tasks, the development of a framework for the use of CommonKADS in this context, and development of the case study within the framework. The documentation produced was then evaluated. In this section we describe the development framework, moving onto the study in Section 0.

The framework involved understanding the processes in the development of an embedded KBS. Many of these were developing CommonKADS models, but the demands of certification entailed that further processes needed to be grafted onto the basic CommonKADS framework. The full set of processes, together with a rough set of connections (*not* to be understood as a life cycle model!) can be seen in Figure 1. Note that knowledge acquisition, as a key set of sub-processes that appears throughout KBS development, is placed as a separate set of processes. Note also that testing and refinement could be carried out as an integral part of modelling or KA by using principles of early operationalisation of parts of knowledge models and running them with scenario data, as advocated in the ACKnowledge project, for example [8].

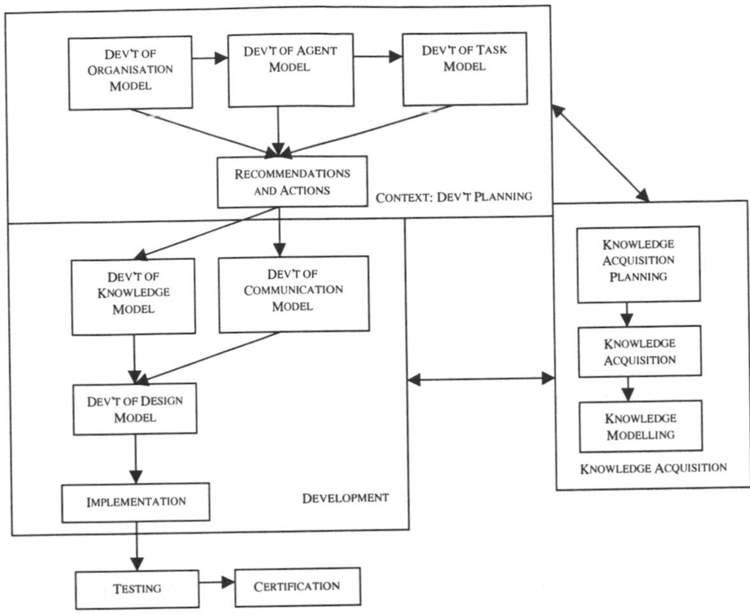

Fig. 1. KBS development processes in a certification context

Each process was further analysed in terms of (a) how it fitted into the development lifecycles of the KB, the KBS and the wider system, (b) the products it uses and creates, (c) the people and resources involved, and (d) quality measures. The relationships between KB development processes are well-known. However, the relationship between the development processes of the KBS and the wider system is more complex for the purposes of integration. Space does not permit a detailed account of this relationship here, though we hope to pursue this matter elsewhere.

The framework drew explicit links with conventional software development within sensitive contexts. The standard we used was the US Dept. of Defense's MIL-STD-498 [2], which is intended to provide contractors with a uniform set of requirements for software development and documentation, and is not meant to specify or discourage the use of any particular methodology, or life cycle.

MIL-STD-498 also provides a requirement for a set of documents to be used for certification. We therefore amended the framework to ensure that these documents would be produced; in general it was not difficult to integrate the MIL-STD-498 documents into the CommonKADS development processes.

The completed framework for development and certification of KBSs in effect adds extra instructions to the CommonKADS method as set out in [1]. These extras appear both as extra processes (e.g. implementation, testing), and as stronger prescriptions for the CommonKADS processes (e.g. adding suggestions as to how to break down the processes, which person should conduct different sub-processes, how many resources to expect to spend etc.). It was then used to develop substantial portions of a KBS, and the documentation produced was stored in order that a certification exercise could be held.

Case Study

4.1 Scoping

After a CommonKADS feasibility study [1, pp.28-35] on the 22 AEW tasks, the task selected for the KBS was the *assign mission*, where the AEW personnel selected a CA to intercept a target that had already been classified as a threat. The target's bearing would be the input, and the output would be one of the CA (chosen on the basis of its position, fuel status, whether or not it is armed, and current AEW tactics). The KBS was scoped to give advice to AEW personnel. This had the effect of making safety less of an issue, as the system would not be sending orders directly to the CA.

There are several types of outputs that it would be useful for the KBS to support.

- **Immediate Response**. Quick voice responses from the AEW personnel to the CA.
- **Decisions**. Back-up communications using encoded messages sent via the datalink system connecting the various operational units..
- **Explanation**. An account of the reasoning behind advice.
- **Gathered Data**. The system may gather previously unavailable data, and pass it on through the datalink to the central command (e.g. on the aircraft carrier).
- **Traces of Inferences**. Short term storage of inferences to facilitate reuse.

This scoping and feasibility was performed as part of CommonKADS organisation modelling, and hence used a full model of an aircraft carrier's organisation, tasks and agents. We will now set out some of the documentation created as part of KBS development, for the later models, implementation and testing. But note that the documentation resulting from organisational modelling would also be available for the certification authorities.

4.2 An Advice Module for a Military Helicopter

In this section we sketch some of the documents produced by this KBS development. We also show how some of this evidence would be used during certification. We focus on knowledge modelling, but this does not mean that a similar wealth of detail is not available in other processes too.

Knowledge Modelling. The task layer describes the assignment of CAs to missions, based on the *assignment* task; use of this well-known generic task helps increase the confidence as to the reliability of the method. The full task [1, pp.155-159] is:

```
TASK assignment;
/*Source: generic task from CommonKADS; Requirement_2;
KA session 20-Dec-1999*/
 GOAL:
 "Assign the subjects to the resources."
  ROLES:
  INPUT:
  subjects: "The subjects that need to get a resource";
  resources: "The resources that can be assigned";
```

```
    allocations: "Set of subject-resource allocations";
    OUTPUT:
    allocations: "Set of subject-resource allocations";
  END TASK assignment;
```

Note the documentation of sources in line 2, from the CommonKADS task, the user requirements, and a KA session. Annotated methods for realising the task were created, together with heuristics for choosing between them. All of this structure was justified via traceable links to KA sessions.

The inference and domain layers were also defined as usual. UML diagrams were supplemented by pseudocode which contained traceable links. The documentation of the entire model showed how the knowledge in the target system was specified, and where the justifications of that specification can be found. The knowledge model could be used to check against the design model and the code, and also as a source for the correct understanding of various test scenarios etc.

Software requirements specification. The content of the knowledge model was also expressed in the capability requirements section of a document conforming to the software requirements specification within MIL-STD-498 for the KBS as a whole. See [2] for the recommended structure. This adds nothing to the KBS development content, but it gives the information to the authorities in a form with which they will be comfortable.

Information sources used. The documentation also listed information sources used during modelling; in this case study, these included tactical manuals and reference books. Information about these included short summaries of content, full references, and pointers out to KA sessions where they were approved. Using this it can be established that only accepted and reliable sources were used.

Glossary. A glossary was also kept as a hypertext document, with links from terms in definitions to the definition of those terms.

Components used. The record of components used to develop the knowledge model is a very important document. Two types of reusable components were used in creating the knowledge model: the CommonKADS generic assignment task, and Ontolingua ontologies for basic concepts, simple geometry and simple time. In general, certification authorities should have a list of reliable and mature KBS development components, and that developers would have to make a case for the acceptability of any new ones used.

Scenarios. The format in Table 1 was used for listing scenarios, used for modelling, testing and V&V. The 'linkage' column shows how the scenario refers to other objects. It can then be judged how comprehensive the scenario coverage is. A scenario is likely to be at the end of a traceability trail, e.g. acting as the basis for a KA session. The source of the scenario acts as the ultimate guarantor.

Table 1. A scenario

Knowledge Scenario	**Information**	**Linkage**
Knowledge Scenario Identifier	*Knowledge Scenario 7* The closest CA has just completed an intercept and does not have enough fuel to complete the mission.	
Source	Written by Squadron Leader Ichabod Thrusthaven, 22nd Dec 1999.	May refer to KA sessions, and to SMEs
Agents Involved	• KBS (initiates communication) • track database • AEW Personnel • CA pilot	Refers to agents from the agent model
Context	The scenario represents typical maritime air defence with surface units preparing to mount an amphibious landing at a port NE of the display, on the SE coast of Ruritania. Threat is from NE and is expected to comprise a mixture of bomber and fighter sweep aircraft. The AEW helicopter is on the barrier. The CA has just completed an intercept. A track has just been identified as hostile, approaching from a direction nearest to the CA. *Other details, such as precise locations of entities involved and the amount of fuel and weapons for the CA would be specified here*	Refers to information objects from the knowledge model
Outcome	The KBS should not assign the mission to that CA, as it does not have enough fuel. Instead, it should select a further CA with enough fuel to complete the intercept.	Refers to information objects and agents
Quality and Performanc e	To fulfil requirement_10 — "Advice shall be provided in a timely manner, with messages being provided within 2 seconds of threat identification." — all reasoning to be carried out within 2 seconds.	

Elicitation material. Most of the material used to develop the knowledge model was elicited from SMEs. The elicitation records were stored as three tables, giving the plan (see Table 2), the session records, and a protocol of the session. Much of this material was justificatory, explaining design decisions by showing how they were demanded by SMEs' testimony. The session records indexed the protocols, ultimately giving access to actual transcriptions or audio or video recordings of the sessions if be required. The KA session plans would be laid out in the wider development plan based on expected knowledge requirements; if a plan were not followed, the authorities would need to know why, and there would have to be a justification if there was no attempt to cover the ground in subsequent sessions.

Table 2. A KA session plan

KA Session Plan	**Information Description**	**Linkage**
KA Session Plan Identifier	*Session Plan 8-Feb-2000* Identify the constraints governing what CA can intercept a threat, and the preferences governing which of those that can should be chosen.	
Date & Time	8th February 2000, 11:00-16:00	
Location	Military headquarters	
People	**Knowledge engineer:** Jeni Tennison **expert:** Nehemiah Bultitude	Refers to knowledge engineers and SMEs in the project plan
Techniques	20 Questions – a good technique for identifying the constraints and preferences of the situation that are important in performing a task, and the order in which they should be applied.	
Materials	Using context from Scenarios 1-15 to give the answers to the SME's questions	May refer to results of previous analysis or modelling

V&V results. The knowledge model was verified and validated by the knowledge engineer (ideally, but not in this case, together with SMEs). The justification for the content of the knowledge model is in terms of the processes that created it, the content of the model itself, and the validity of the tests that were applied to it.

Process validation. Validation of the process of developing the knowledge model should be carried out by performing the following checks:

- every detail within the model is the result of either information from validated models, items (e.g. KA sessions or reusable components) recorded in protocol records, or modelling decisions recorded through a design rationale
- all reusable components originate from a recognised, valid source and have been shown to be effective in a number of similar KBSs
- all KA and walkthrough protocols originate from a recorded KA session
- all KA sessions were planned as recorded in a KA session plan
- all SMEs are recognised experts in the domain
- all information sources are recognised and valid
- all modelling decisions comply with agreed criteria

Knowledge model validation. The knowledge model can validated in three ways: through direct validation by SMEs (carried out for all knowledge model structures), through testing against the knowledge scenarios, and by inspection. The following checks were made to ensure that it was correct and consistent, and had a complete specification of all components in knowledge schemas:

- all knowledge model transfer functions are given in the communication model
- all tasks in the communication model are detailed in the knowledge model

- all tasks in a control specification are given in the knowledge model task layer
- all inferences and roles are given in the knowledge model inference layer
- all domain constructs specified within a knowledge role, referenced by a relation or referenced by a rule type are detailed in the domain layer of the knowledge model
- all instances (or rules) defined in the KB are instances of a concept (or rule type) detailed in the knowledge model domain layer

V&V method validation. These checks ensured that the knowledge scenarios were correct, consistent and sufficiently covered the space of possible scenarios:

- all information items, tasks and inferences are involved in at least one scenario
- all agents in the knowledge scenarios are detailed in the agent model
- all substantively different situations are involved in knowledge scenarios

Other Processes. We have given a detailed account of the knowledge modelling documentation. For other processes, in the space available, we can suggest types of documentation that should be available for certification authorities.

Communication modelling. Communication modelling should provide:

- Communication scenarios, with different situations for communication between the KBS and other agents, characterised in terms of agents involved, content, the expected/intended outcome and quality and performance measures.
- An overall communication plan, made up of dialogue diagrams showing possible interactions between agents and the KBS, with pseudocode and explanatory text.
- Individual transactions, as in CommonKADS worksheet CM-1 [1, p.234].
- Information exchange specifications, as in worksheet CM-2 [1, p.235].
- Interface requirements specification, as in [2].
- V&V results, where the communication model is justified as above in terms of the validity of the development, the model content, and the validation tests.

Design modelling. Design modelling should provide:

- A system architecture, as in CommonKADS worksheet DM-1 [1, p.281].
- A target implementation platform, as in worksheet DM-2 [1, p.283].
- An architecture specification, as in worksheet DM-3 [1, p.290].
- An application design, as in worksheet DM-4 [1, p.292].
- A software design description, as in [2].
- V&V results.

Implementing and integration. Executable code, consisting of domain-specific instances of classes and rule types, is the main product of implementation. This equates to the static knowledge within the KB.

The integration of the KB with components of the wider system, such as the track database and datalink subsystem, is realised through the interface components of the KBS. The knowledge base is embedded within a conventional system that is given access to all aspects of its functioning. Message objects are used to structure the communication between the knowledge base and the outside world.

Testing. The V&V of the KB during and following implementation is the highest-profile testing that is involved in the development of the KB. Testing of the KBS occurs at several levels:

- knowledge base
- knowledge-based system (including conventional software components)
- wider system

The tests run on the KBS as a whole and on the wider system with the KBS integrated into it are determined within the wider system development process, and can be grouped under the following headings:

- **tests:** running the code with internal checks to examine the performance of the system
- **inspection:** examining the code to ensure that it originates from a proper source
- **demonstration:** running the code without internal checks to demonstrate the performance of the system
- **analysis:** formal analysis of the code to demonstrate consistency and completeness
- **similarity:** examining the code to show similarities between it and recognised software components

Accompanying these, there was also a software test plan, a software test description and a software test report for each test [cf. 2]. The fact that the requirements were met was established by completion of the compliance matrix.

Related and Future Work

The field of V&V and KBS evaluation has always been very sparsely populated [9], but certification is barely touched on all. The importance of this cannot be overemphasised; it will restrict the spread of KBS.

Safe-KBS [10] was an attempt to tie KBS development into a management structure reflecting concerns about safety. It put forward a life cycle with seven processes: development, V&V, safety management, quality management, certification, configuration management and project management. Formally, these were all at the same hierarchical level, so that no process took a leading role, and they all interacted with input/output relationships. However, the complexity of KBS development meant that unsurprisingly in Safe-KBS it became the most complex of the seven processes and had the highest number of relationships with the others. The work reported here shows that, as long as a comprehensive development methodology is used with care and precision, this would be sufficient to introduce a KBS into sensitive domains.

Alun Preece and colleagues at the Aberdeen have also worried about the problems of validating KBSs. For instance, the RECOVER project uses knowledge of system faults exposed by V&V techniques to repair and improve the KBS semi-automatically by adding a knowledge refinement capability to the verification tool COVER [11]. Issues include the use of completeness and consistency checking to help refinement, how testing techniques assist in creating and evaluating a KBS by means of example cases, and the background knowledge requirements of the refinement process. Preece has also investigated the use of formal methods within V&V [12].

The Safeware approach of Nancy Leveson and colleagues [13] applies software hazard analysis and hazard control procedures during software development, based on identified system hazards, to ensure that the software can avoid pitfalls as opposed to the traditional technique of verifying safety after development is complete. There is a range of techniques and tools available which can be used in an integrated and complementary way to spot a variety of problems. For example, one method, Software Deviation Analysis [14], can be used to provide assumptions about particular deviations in software inputs and hazardous outputs, and thereby to generate scenarios exploring those deviant outputs.

Both Safeware and RECOVER are more pessimistic than the approach we have described. We believe that there is enough material within (some) current KBS development methodologies to ensure certifiable software as long as procedures are followed correctly. Nevertheless, the use of such evaluation techniques alongside development has great potential, and may be helpful in addressing the knowledge management issue of how to develop a persuasive safety case.

One obvious angle for future work in this field is to perform more exercises of the type reported in Sections 0 and 0 above. Some exercises should take place using CommonKADS in different domains; others may focus on alternative methodologies, to establish whether or not they too can be employed in sensitive domains.

Another route would be to try to combine the sort of work described above with alternative objective KBS evaluation techniques, such as the use of critical success metrics [15]. Critical success metrics are numerical inferences from a KBS that express whether or not the system is a success. They have the advantage of being independent, domain-specific and reflective of the business concerns that prompted the commissioning of the KBS in the first place, and thereby can be keyed to specific concerns of certifying authorities.

Discussion

6.1 The Extent and Scope of Our Claim

During our analysis, a case study was developed in full, and the evidence collated. The evidence provided by the CommonKADS-guided development process met the requirements of military standards for software development and deployment, such as MIL-STD-498. To aid the comparison between CommonKADS and MIL-STD-498, some of the evidence was re-presented in forms required by MIL-STD-498. Military standards are as stringent as the requirements on any software that is to be inserted into highly safety-conscious or otherwise sensitive contexts. Hence our exercise has indicated that KBS development can meet rigorous safety and other standards.

It is worth emphasising the value of this result. We are not presenting Yet Another KBS Development Methodology. We are explicitly linking an *existing* development methodology with an *existing* certification practice, and showing that the two fit together well. Certification is not too much of a drag on KBS development, and KBS development can meet stringent certification requirements. This is an important, and happy, result.

Of course, this is only a single, though extensive, case study. We do not want to make claims that are too strong on the basis of it. We have certainly shown that it is possible to develop a KBS that meets certification requirements, and we have duly exhibited an existence proof. It may be that there are limits to such a development, and more work needs to be done to establish what such limits might be.

6.2 CommonKADS

In section 2.3 we laid out our detailed reasons for using CommonKADS in this case study; of these reasons, the relative maturity of CommonKADS was the most compelling. Clearly, there will be other development methodologies that would also meet many of the constraints. The work reported here says nothing about whether such methodologies would be suitable for certification purposes.

CommonKADS had to be amended to be used in a certification exercise; does this invalidate the results? The amendments to CommonKADS were straightforward adaptations to the new (certification) context in which it was to be applied. There were three types of amendment. The first type involved additions to the documentation produced; in this case study, these were documents required by MIL-STD-498 that either recast information already available from the development process, or that specified the development plans in detail. This is obviously a relatively small overhead to meet SE and organisational constraints. The second type involved additions to the information expressed in the documentation, in general being design rationales, or traceable links to and from models, KA sessions, information sources and code. This is to meet certification constraints. The third type involved the addition of phases beyond the development phases laid out in [1], in particular testing and certification phases. These phases are orthogonal to the CommonKADS structure, and are a clear requirement for certification. Recall also the suggestion that early operationalisation of models could help integrate testing and certification into KA and modelling phases [8].

Hence the amendments we made to CommonKADS were not ad hoc, but principled and justified. They were all additions; CommonKADS itself became the kernel of the augmented methodology. To our knowledge, no other knowledge engineering methodology covers all of the ground that certification requires. What amendments would be needed, and how principled they would be, would obviously depend on the methodology. On the other hand, SE methodologies do cover the ground, but would be inadequate because of their lack of detailed appreciation of the importance of KA and modelling for knowledge intensive applications, as noted in section 2.2. There is no SE notion of constructing models of knowledge using knowledge roles and components.

In carrying out the modelling there were no serious problems for certification. By following CommonKADS carefully and completely, and with the additions noted above, the models we produced were adequate for certification. This was even true for the embedded KBS that we were developing; the CommonKADS communication and design models proved adequate to model the wider system context. Without the additions we made, the models would not have been adequate; planning, traceability and rigorous testing in particular are essential, and vanilla-flavoured CommonKADS does not emphasise these. Hence we are confident that the additions to CommonKADS do not invalidate the claims we have made.

6.3 Methodological Issues

It is essential that KBS developers meet the basic methodological guidelines of SE.

- Plan everything;
- Perform the development activities;
  - Specify, design and implement;
  - Perform the V&V activities;
  - Perform safety and risk assessment;
- Transfer into service and maintain the KBS.

As everybody knows, it is rare for CommonKADS to be used completely and in full; the principle of structure-preserving design is not always adhered to, the early contextual models are not always fully specified, and knowledge models are not often amended as design amendments take place during debugging. This is no problem for development, but it is a serious one for certification; if the developers did not follow the methodology precisely, then the software could not be certified. It is possible to use CommonKADS rigorously; we did so in the case study. Of course, it may be more tedious to do this, but in sensitive contexts where certification is used, it is a justifiable overhead.

6.4 Certification and V&V

We should also emphasise once more the distinction between certification and V&V. V&V establishes that the system specified meets the user requirements, and that the system implemented is the one specified. This is obviously relevant to certification. However, much of certification is also concerned with demonstrating this to the system's users and stakeholders within an organisation. This clearly includes V&V issues, but also has a strong pragmatic element. Certification issues include: ensuring that a reliable methodology has been used and followed to the letter; ensuring that each line of code has been thoroughly tested; ensuring that each line of code is traceable back to a justification. So not only are a good set of test results essential for certification, but also *the fact that a full range of tests has been planned and carried out correctly*. Merely carrying out a V&V exercise would not be sufficient. The certification authorities would also need to know that the V&V methodology was reliable, and that any software used for V&V was itself certified.

This is why, for instance, there would be problems with the development of a KBS without using a specified methodology, or if a methodology was used with short cuts. It is also why model-based methodologies are useful, because the models act as predictors of behaviour, as guarantors of correct development, and as media for traceable links and logging of design decisions. On the other hand, a methodology such as Ripple-Down Rules (RDR), which does not produce models, may have problems with *certification*, however impressive its *V&V* results [16, 17].

6.5 Certification and KBSs

This may prompt the response that the certification proposed in this paper is the wrong sort for KBSs. After all, the procedures were developed for the certification of conventional software, and may be simply inappropriate for KBSs. To answer this question is beyond the scope of this paper, which is specifically aimed at establishing that CommonKADS provides documentation in sufficient quantity and of sufficient quality to satisfy a conventional certification authority. In the current managerial context, this is essential, because testing and traceability and following a recognised and reliable methodology are the standard bases for certification. One could certainly imagine specialised KBS V&V procedures being grafted onto the processes suggested here to improve KBS certification. However, it is unlikely that such procedures would *replace* any of the major certification requirements for conventional software, but would have to be *additional*. Therefore, in the current managerial climate, it is a *necessary* condition that any KBS methodology should meet something like the constraints we suggest in this paper for certification purposes.

We should also add that our result should help undermine a common view that KBS are necessarily more difficult to certify safe than conventional software. It is true that rather intensive, disciplined labour is required for producing certifiable KBSs, but the model suites that can be produced, and the clear articulation of model types, ensure that a KBS is very well-understood. Conventional software cannot always boast such clarity of specification; it also does not follow that such software can avoid non-determinism merely by avoiding heuristics.

6.6 Conclusion

Certification will become increasingly important as more KBSs are deployed in sensitive areas; certification of conventional software has been standard for some time. Despite the important differences between conventional and knowledge-based software, we have shown that it is possible to certify KBSs rigorously in the context of a mature and robust methodology with a wide user base. We have used CommonKADS, with orthogonal amendments, as an example of such a methodology – it may be that CommonKADS is the only example. It is essential that any such methodology be followed to the letter, and that the issues raised in section 2.2 are all addressed. Nevertheless, this is an important result for the spreading of KBS technology, and the management of knowledge in sensitive areas.

Acknowledgments. The research recorded here was performed by Epistemics Limited on behalf of Defence Evaluation and Research Agency, (DERA) Farnborough under Contract Number ASF/3582. The authors would like to thank their partners under this contract, Aerosystems International, for their work in evaluating the certification framework independently, and in forcing the clarification of ideas by repeatedly asking hard questions.

References

1. Schreiber, G., Akkermans, H., Anjewierden, A., de Hoog, R., Shadbolt, N., Van de Velde, W. & Wielinga, B. *Knowledge Engineering and Management: The CommonKADS Methodology*, M.I.T. Press, Cambridge, Mass (2000)
2. MIL-STD-498. US Dept. of Defense military standard, at http://www.pogner.demon.co.uk/mil_498/
3. IEC Pub 880. International Electrotechnical Commission, *Software for Computers in the Safety Systems of Nuclear Power Stations*, Geneva (1986)
4. DO-178-B/ED-12B. RTCA/Eurocae, *Software Considerations in Airborne Systems and Equipment Certification*
5. IEC 1508. International Electrotechnical Commission, *Draft International Standard 1508: Functional Safety: Safety-Related Systems*, Geneva (1995)
6. Shadbolt, N., O'Hara, K. & Crow, L. The experimental evaluation of knowledge acquisition techniques and methods: history, problems and new directions, in *International Journal of Human-Computer Studies*, 51 (1999), 729-755
7. Shadbolt, N. & O'Hara, K. Model-based expert systems and explanations of expertise, in P.J. Feltovich, K.M. Ford & R.R. Hoffman (eds.) *Expertise in Context*, AAAI Press/MIT Press, Menlo Park, CA (1997), 315-337
8. Terpstra, P., van Heijst, G., Nordbo, I, Ramparany, F., Reichgelt, H., Shadbolt, N. & Wielinga, B.. *KA Process Support in KEW*, ACKnowledge deliverable ACK-UVA-A2-DEL-002-A, University of Amsterdam (1992)
9. Preece, A. Building the right system right: evaluating V&V methods in knowledge engineering, in *Proceedings of the 11th Banff Knowledge Acquisition for Knowledge Based Systems Workshop*, Banff, Canada (1998)
10. Benini, M., Dondossola, G., Guida, G. & Lamperti, G. *Safe-KBS Life-Cycle Model Description Document*, SafeKBS/TR3.2-a (1997)
11. Preece, A. & Shinghal, R. Foundation and application of knowledge base verification, in *International Journal of Intelligent Systems*, 9 (1994), 683-702
12. Meseguer, P. & Preece, A. Assessing the role of formal specifications in verification and validation of knowledge-based systems, in *Proceedings of the 3rd IFIP International Conference on "Achieving Quality in Software" (AQuIS'96)*, Chapman and Hall (1996), 317-328
13. Leveson, N.G. *Safeware: System Safety and Computers*, Addison-Wesley (1995)
14. Reese, J.D. *Software Deviation Analysis*, Ph.D. thesis, University of California, Irvine (1996)
15. Menzies, T. Evaluation issues with critical success metrics, in *Proceedings of the 11th Banff Knowledge Acquisition for Knowledge Based Systems Workshop*, Banff, Canada (1998)
16. Compton, P., Preston, P., Edwards, G. & Kang, B. Knowledge based systems that have some idea of their limits, in *Proceedings of the 10th Banff Knowledge Acquisition for Knowledge Based Systems Workshop*, Banff, Canada (1996)
17. Beydoun, G. & Hoffman, A. Simultaneous modelling and knowledge acquisition using NRDR, in *Proceedings of the 5th Pacific Rim Conference on Artificial Intelligence (PRICAI 98)*, Springer-Verlag (1998), 83-95

Kinesys, a Participative Approach to the Design of Knowledge Systems

Aurelien Slodzian

Laboratoire d'informatique de Paris 6
aurelien.slodzian@lip6.fr

Abstract. Kinesys (Knowledge Integration for the Engineering of Systems) is a research and development project initiated at Tractebel Energy Engineering (TEE). Its goal is to provide a knowledge base to the design engineers that capitalizes their know-how in power plant design. Practically, we expect that the systematic elimination of redundancy in design activities will lead to an important reduction of delays in the context of calls for tender issued by potential clients. We also expect an improvement of the quality of the offers thanks to the validation of the designs; and a preservation of the know-how of the company.
The Kinesys project was developed by applying a knowledge-level methodology with a strong emphasis on the participation of users in the design of the knowledge system.

1 Introduction

1.1 Project Objectives

The Kinesys project originated as an attempt to optimize the design of power plants at the design department of Tractebel Energy Engineering (TEE). The engineers in charge of these installations have been looking for techniques to improve the reuse of technical and financial information about past installations. Hence, they met the knowledge-base experts of the company and asked them to produce an appropriate knowledge management system.

In this document, we will briefly present the COMMA methodology which was used for the development of this system (section 2) before illustrating its application to our particular case (section 3).

1.2 Characteristics of the Project

Before going any further, let us point out the issues and characteristics of the problem, which guided our choice of a methodology and, later, the way it was applied.

Great volume of correlated data The quantity of information directly involved in the design of a power plant is enormous (more than 300.000 items

R. Dieng and O. Corby (Eds.): EKAW 2000, LNAI 1937, pp. 435–448, 2000.

in the final layouts). And this information is only the *result* of decisions motivated by logical inferences or by the engineer's experience; it does not even reflect the amount of knowledge necessary to take these decisions, which is an order of magnitude greater. The financial aspects add yet another dimension to this complexity.

Context awareness The resulting software was intended to actively assist the design processes and not only to be a passive information retrieval tool. We will see further how this aspect greatly influenced its design.

Non algorithmical problems Not only the complexity of each engineer's task surpasses the abstraction capacities of computers, but these tasks furthermore combine into complex collaboration processes that are only partially formalized.

Personalization The design processes involve people with different competencies, different responsibilities and, for each project, different roles. The capacity of a teamwork software tool to adapt its interface to the goal of its user is of the greatest importance for its success. This capacity is a necessary condition for the information to be presented in a relevant way for the particular user, and hence for the *efficiency* of information restitution.

Hence, Kinesys is a *knowledge sharing* project. Firstly its information sharing aspects are already obvious (reuse of power plant configurations). Second, the explicit relationship between information and context (i.e. usage of information by people) gives to the modeled information the status of "knowledge" - although it apparently comes back to series of numerical data.

2 Methodology

2.1 Motivations for a Knowledge Based Approach

The fact that the goal of the Kinesys project was to produce an operational information system convinced us that the most adequate approach was to rely on a task-oriented knowledge-based methodology:

- A knowledge-base is a relevant way of organizing information with respect to its usage;
- A task-oriented analysis limits the risk of arbitrariness in problem decomposition because the resulting model derives from the observation of reality and not from the preliminary choice of a representation method (as it would be the case with purely object-oriented methods for example);
- The identification of players involved in each task helps focus the knowledge-acquisition phase (knowledge identification and transfer);
- The role of the software tool may then be specified on a task basis, taking into account the specific goal of each identified task;
- The ergonomics engineers apply the findings of this analysis when they design the interface.

2.2 A Participative Approach

We had at heart that the future users of the knowledge base should participate in the design of the system, from the design of knowledge-level model to the validation of the interface.

This was meant to increase our chance that the tools would fit the expressed needs. We furthermore think that it will improve the durability of the knowledge base. Indeed, more adequacy provides more effective usefulness and gives the users more incentive to make the necessary efforts for regularly updating the contents of the knowledge-base. It further derives from our choice that the necessary competence for knowledge-base maintenance will reside in the individuals of the user group itself.

Hence Kinesys was a experimentation of a participative approach to knowledge management where the knowledge-level model (described below) is at the same time the building-stone of the software application and the medium of the interactions of the users, the knowledge engineers, the ergonomics engineers and the programmers.

2.3 Elements of the Methodology

A knowledge oriented methodology In the context of the Kinesys project, we used a modeling methodology called COMMA [11], that derives from COMMET [12,14,4,10]. However, we will not compare the respective benefits of this or that methodology but rather present the lessons from the application of a knowledge-oriented methodology to a real-size case. For methodology comparison, the reader will usefully refer to [1].

COMMA is based on the notion of a *knowledge-level model*, which it shares with other methodologies like, for example, KADS [17] or Noos [9]:

- COMMA proposes to consider the observed system as an "agent" which uses rationally the knowledge at its disposal to reach its goals[1]. The metaphor of the rational agent was introduced first by A. Newell [10,6] and it reflects the knowledge aspect of the method.
- The second basis of COMMA is the notion of *model*, taken as a conceptual, abstract and formalized description of a system[2], like, for example, the mathematical models of physical phenomena.
- A *knowledge-level model* hence describes a system in terms of the knowledge it uses to reach the goal(s) it has.

In the case of COMMA, the knowledge-level model consists in the formalized description of the agents in terms of the tasks they execute, the knowledge they manipulate and the methods they apply to perform these tasks.

[1] Here, the term "agent" is to be taken in a general sense and has nothing to do with Internet agents or multi-agent systems.

[2] Here also, the term is to be taken in the broad sense of a physical system. It may be a mechanical system as well as a team of engineers.

COMMET already defined these three sorts of models that we can consider as three perspectives on the studied system:

- The *task model* describes the activities of the agents and the correlated knowledge flow;
- The *knowledge model* describes the used knowledge; more precisely, it describes the abstract structures that may be imposed to the pieces of knowledge manipulated during task execution. This knowledge decomposes into *case knowledge* (i.e. the parameters of the particular case treated by the agent) and *domain knowledge* which is reused across cases.
- The *method model* describes the methods that are used for performing the tasks (i.e. which operations, applied to which part of the knowledge allow to realize which task);
- The *cooperation model* (introduced by COMMA) describes the distribution of the tasks and the interactions among the agents.

To model is to impose a conceptual structure to data, hence to define a number of concepts that allow to organize raw information and put it to the service of selected goals. Of course, the concepts exist explicitly or implicitly in the mind of the design engineers independently of the modeling process, as proves the fact that they effectively design power plants. The role of the knowledge engineers is thus formalize those among the concepts that are useful for the development of the application and for its evolution.

The structure imposed to case knowledge is called the *case model* and the structure imposed to the whole domain knowledge is the *domain model.* Both models form the global *knowledge model.*

This is a very complex model. Knowledge engineers hence decompose it in order to simplify its design: functional model, classification model, description model, and so on, are as many points of view on the knowledge and its use. The reader will find in [13] a more complete description of COMMET models, together with a typology of tasks and knowledge models.

The *cooperation model*, introduced by COMMA, allows for the modeling of situations where several human agents cooperate with several artificial ones (e.g. software tools). Such a model is necessary in the context of Kinesys since the collaboration between design engineers is an intrinsic feature of their activity.

In section 3 we will show the development of these four models in the context of the Kinesys project.

Issues in knowledge-level modeling In the context of software production, the design of a knowledge-level model aims at identifying those processes and the related knowledge that will be implemented in electronic form, i.e. as software that processes data. The knowledge-level model is expected to improve the quality of the software, just like a more complete and precise mathematical model allows for better simulations of physical phenomena.

COMMET and similar methodologies tried to go a bit further: they were designed with the hope that the knowledge-level models of observed agents might be used as specifications for software systems that would perform the same tasks as the original agent. If this had been possible, then software might be designed in terms of *goals* (while programming languages focus on the *means*) and a new generation of programming tools would use concepts much closer to human mental models (and their production could hence be more easily verified).

But it was proved in the meantime [16][3] that each modeling methodology should be considered in the perspective of the indented use of the resulting models. This seems natural *a posteriori* since it is now generally admitted that it is not possible to dissociate knowledge from its use; and a model is nothing else than knowledge about the observed agent.

Hence, a number of expectations about knowledge-level modeling were illusory. Practice furthermore showed many times that the generality and the re-usability of models were much more limited than expected[3].

Knowing this, we took the precaution to define clearly the roles of the knowledge-level model in the Kinesys project:

1. Knowledge acquisition should be conducted within the bounds of a clear conceptual framework, which is part of the domain model;
2. We wanted that users could validate the model and, in particular, its functional part;
3. The model was intended to be used as a communication means between users and knowledge engineers on the one hand and between knowledge engineers and programmers on the other hand;
4. The model should be precise enough to serve as a guide, a functional model, for the implementation (although implementation did not need to derive directly from the knowledge-level model).

These aspects are developed and illustrated in the next section, were we address the application of this methodology to Kinesys. We will discuss this subject again in section 4 where we evaluate the methodology.

3 Application to Kinesys

3.1 The Problem

The engineers of the design department of TEE have established that the lack of tools allowing the systematic reuse of past projects imposed the repetition of similar tasks from a project to another and thus caused an important loss of time.

For example, they pointed out that time was wasted while elaborating commercial offers since the information collected from the electrical and mechanical equipment vendors was not capitalized. It thus happened frequently that several calls for tender were issued for identical equipment.

[3] The same problem arises in the context of ontologies, that may be considered as an attempt to model a part of the domain knowledge.

More precisely design engineers expressed the following wishes:

- when answering calls for tender, reuse the configurations calculated in the context of previous ones;
- access easily information about electrical systems and equipment (characteristics, diagrams, notes, operation procedures, investment and operating costs, etc.);
- avoid sending twice the same calls for tender to equipment vendors.

Finally they expected that a tool for capitalizing knowledge would dramatically reduce the risks of erosion of the company's know-how (which erosion is mainly due to human mobility).

3.2 Project Progress

The COMMA methodology defines the models to be built, and their application, but does not provide us with a procedure for designing these models. We do not anyway think that there exists a universal method that would be efficient or even relevant in all situations where a knowledge-level model is useful.

For Kinesys, we have chosen to design first a general model of the overall activities of the engineers. This required to identify their fundamental activities and the key concepts of the domain. This shallow model was then refined by decomposing each identified task into its sub-tasks and by investigating as much as necessary the nature and structure of the associated knowledge models.

This is a tricky matter since there are several ways to proceed to task decomposition, which produce different task models. If the knowledge engineer want to limit the amount of arbitrariness he necessarily introduces, then he should aim at discovering the implicit and informal model the "agents" have of their own work. And he will design with them a more formal model, more precise, while remaining synthetic. As a result of such a collaboration, the model will not only be more accurate, but also it will be shared with the users of the future system. This collaboration is of the greatest importance for ensuring the adequacy of the system to the users' needs and, later on, to measure this adequacy.

3.3 First Step: Building a Terminology

Let us now present the progress of the design of the model of the tasks involved in writing of commercial offers, a part of the jobs facing design engineers.

We first identified the key concepts of the domain. In theory, we could have achieved this by considering the task of writing a commercial offer as a whole and by asking design engineers to point out which knowledge they used and produced while performing this task. But such an approach would have required that design engineers be accustomed to knowledge-level modeling and had already analyzed their own activities and hence that they were also... knowledge engineers! This is obviously not the case.

We instead tried to construct simultaneously shallow models of the tasks and of the knowledge (including a terminology) so as to set up a framework that might be refined afterwards. We did so by asking the engineers to describe their everyday work, to explain the terms they used and the way they took their decisions. The resulting models were submitted to them and their criticism of our misunderstanding was at the source of very clarifying debates.

Figure 1 represents a subset of the network of concepts that surrounds the notion of a commercial offer. The main concepts that appear on the drawing are the following ones:

Installation The *industrial installation* is the object of the study. Its scope is defined by the project leader and may be either a new energy production unit or a part of an existing one which is to be upgraded.

System An installation may be decomposed into a number of functions or *systems*. Each such system is developed as a number of equipment connected by pipes. Conversely, each equipment relates to one and only one system (which is its functional localization).

Equipment Physical unit of the installation. The equipment provides the pieces of the puzzle that the design engineers assemble. In section 4 the reader will find some remarks on the relative arbitrariness of the notions of system and equipment. Equipment is connected between each other through *pipes*.

Commercial offer The document sent to the client for evaluation of the commercial and technical proposal of TEE.

With these notions we may propose a general definition of the plant design task: *describe a set of equipment and pipes such that their combined operation produces the result described in the call for tender issued by the client; and so that the investment and operation costs are minimal.*

The tasks associated to the design activities are gradually revealed: specify systems, find equipment configurations that achieve the required function, evaluate the cost of these configurations, document the result, and so on. We then reach the task analysis phase.

Of course, these are only informal definitions and we had to encode formally this terminology so as to construct an ontology of the domain [15].

3.4 Second Step: Task Analysis

Power plant design appears immediately as a complex activity. Indeed, as soon as a first draft of the installation is established, a team of design engineers is formed, each one of them being in charge of one aspect of the installation (in general of a system). Engineers will then mostly work on their own, yet interacting regularly with each other.

The first reason of the complexity of the task model lies in the apparent lack of well defined synchronism: engineers design, in several steps and with more and more precision, the various components of the installation; they sometimes backtrack and reconsider their choices; finally, they simultaneously evaluate the cost of the main equipment of the installation. There is no linear progress towards the goal of a completely specified installation. Nothing sequential in this.

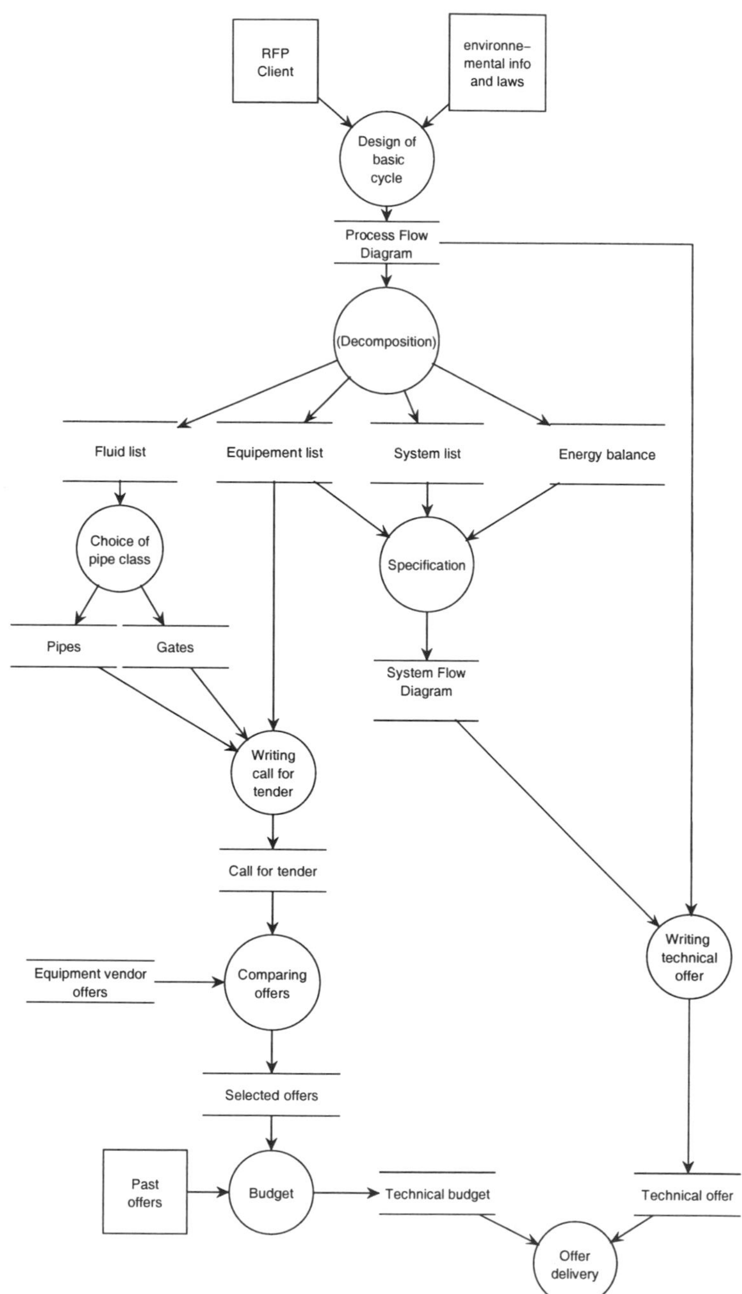

Fig. 1. Concepts underlying the writing of an offer

Nevertheless, this shallow analysis exhibits three main families of tasks:

- The fundamental design decisions are taken during *design tasks*;
- The *description tasks* consist in quantifying these decisions: specifying systems, equipment and pipes;
- During *evaluation tasks*, the cost of the systems is evaluated.

Figure 2 shows the main tasks executed during the preparation of a commercial offer. The model is represented as a diagram were circles represent tasks and where knowledge units are drawn as keywords between horizontal bars[4]. The arrows that link tasks and knowledge units indicate the knowledge flow (used knowledge vs. produced knowledge).

The detailed description of the individual tasks is out of the scope of this paper. The important point is that during the remainder of the modeling process, the structure of the knowledge units i.e. the knowledge model will derive from their use during the identified tasks.

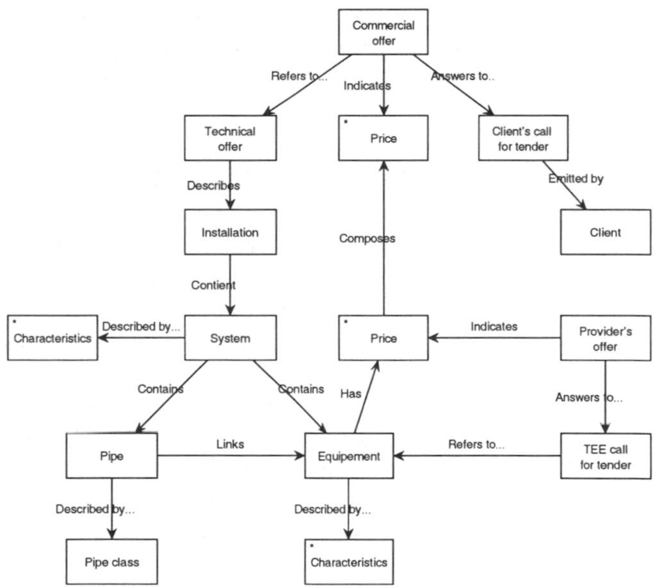

Fig. 2. Pre-Study phase of a power plant

3.5 Third Step: The Knowledge Model

The knowledge model was designed by constructing diagrams as the one presented in figure 1. The addition of each new element each new piece of knowledge

[4] Data Flow Diagram notation, as defined in [18]

was motivated by a precise need of information for a task. Then the relationships between the knowledge pieces were identified, but only those that correspond to an effective correlation in the mind of the design engineers.

The formalizable domain knowledge is essentially composed of reference tables about systems and all kinds of equipment and of past offers and installations. Domain knowledge consists mainly in the following items:

- The list of existing systems (and related information);
- The list of existing equipment (and related information);
- The possible relationships between systems and equipment;
- The list of pipe classes;
- The list of fluids and their properties (including the relationship with pipes).

On the other hand, case knowledge is for the moment restricted to the installations previously designed by the company.

We have not much formalized the know-how of the engineers but we are investigating the possibility to consider it as rules of good-practice in power plant design. Among those rules we already allow the engineers to edit a set of consistency constraints (relationships among specific equipment and systems).

3.6 Fourth Step: The Cooperation Model

The Kinesys project aims at providing an electronic support to human activities and this makes a difference with respect to classical software projects that generally aim at having the computer perform some tasks in place of some person. In classical cases, the nature of man/machine interactions is a *task delegation.*

In the context of Kinesys, the situation is made more complex by the great number of participants since several design engineers and several departments collaborate to the design of an installation.

To cope with this problem, we consider things as if people and machines were working in parallel on shared information, the computer trying to synchronize its activities with human activities. This is the framework of our cooperation model.

The way the various agents interact is regulated by what COMMA calls a *cooperation model.* Such a model defines which agent executes which task and how the agent's activities synchronize with each other. It also defines the knowledge flow among agents.

The cooperation model that has been chosen to describe the activities of the engineers is a standard cooperation model in COMMA called *Result Sharing.* According to this model, each agent (man or machine) brings its piece of information to a shared document which is, in Kinesys, the commercial offer. This model does not imply any *explicit* form of cooperation since the agents decide their behavior according to the state of the shared document. One might argue that engineers apply many other modes of cooperation during their daily interactions. This is true, but whatever the nature of these interactions is, they are out of reach of the software system and hence out of the scope of the model.

If we had aimed at an analysis of the quality of the internal communication of the design department, then a deeper analysis of cooperation modes would have been necessary. Here, once again, the scope of the model is clearly defined by its intended use.

A number of formal behavioral rules indicate to the system what kind of behaviour is expected. For example, there are consistency constraints to which the power plant design must obey. Howevere, those constraints are obviously not satisfied from the early beginning of the design. Hence, once rule is not to bother the users with error messages until a certain stage has not been reached in the design process. There are several such stages, and they are defined in terms of the degree of completion of equipment and system parameters.

The engineers may also fine tune the cooperation with the system by annotating the above mentionned consistency constraints. This way, and depending on the stage of the design process, the system will either automatically propagate constraints, or send alert messages,or simply do nothing.

The constraint mechanism in itself is not innovative. Its integration in the user control interface, as a way to tune the behaviour of the knowledge system, is however a new way to use such a mechanism.

3.7 A Word about Implementation

Without entering into the details of the implementation of Kinesys, we would like to mention its principles. Kinesys is designed as a set of interconnected Oracle[5] databases which the user accesses by means of an HTML browser. Between the SQL and the presentation layers one finds a module called HyperInfo [7, 8], which allows to prepare dynamic pages (interpreted on the server side) and which manages the user accounts. Both features were necessary to prepare our context and user sensitive interface.

Another set of software modules come into play that analyze the modifications of the data and send notifications about these modifications, about inconsistencies or incompleteness in the design. Indeed, the consistency constraints are expressed as mathematical equations (suited to the way of thinking of engineers) but they have to be turned into sets of triggers on the database tables and fields.

Figure 3 shows a screen-shot of the Kinesys interface. The upper part of the screen contains the Kinesys navigation bar that allows to browse through and inside the installations and to copy equipment and systems from one installation to the other. The reuse of the technological know-how is hence as simple as a cut and paste!

The tool also produces reports about part or the whole of the installation, and generates calls for tender to equipment vendors.

The left panel displays the list of installations, the list of systems in an installation or the list of equipment in a system. The latter two allow for a graphical presentation, as on figure.

[5] Oracle is a product of Oracle Corporation.

The right panel displays the characteristics of the item selected in the left panel (e.g.the specifications of an installation, a system or an equipment). Engineers may modify the data that appear there. As each entity (system or equipment) is characterized by hundreds of parameters, they are grouped in views or filters.

The access to the Kinesys server is controlled at user level. For each project, the role of each involved design engineer is recorded by the system and the access to various data is managed accordingly. This is an important element of personalization since views and filters are defined on a role basis. Hence, when an engineer accesses the data about a given system, he will not see the same list of parameters as one of his colleagues who plays a different role in the same project.

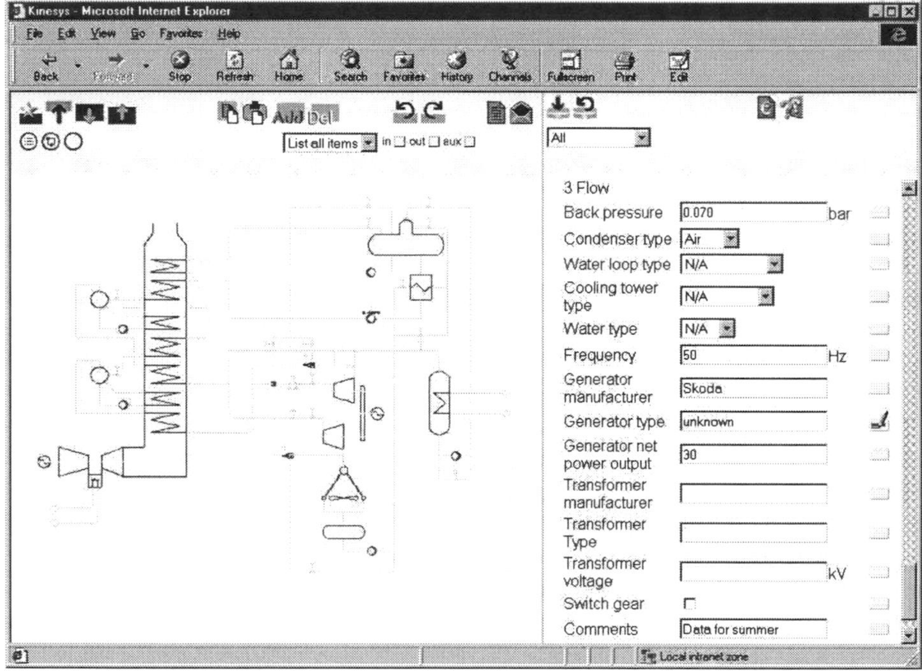

Fig. 3. A Kinesys screen-shot

4 Conclusion

4.1 Evaluation of the Methodology

We estimate the application of the described method saved time in the realization of a support system for the design of power plants. This saving is the result of our will to involve the users in the design of the system and to have them validate every step. Their participation guaranteed in a first stage the adequacy of the formal model to the mental model of the design engineers and, in a second stage, the adequacy of the tool to their needs.

We already have indications that the appropriation of the tool by the users is going on: their participation to the study makes Kinesys their tool. We hence expect to avoid the risk that the tool is rejected, as can be the case with those tools imposed from outside.

This validation and this appropriation were facilitated by the resorting to abstract models that the users could understand. This way, they participated not only to the design of the interface but also to the design of the knowledge base itself; and all this without being forced to integrate computer science concepts nor to constantly having to be concerned about filling the gap between their own model and its software representation. We furthermore think that they were motivated by the idea of reflecting about their own activity and discovering new aspects of it.

For example, the frontier between the notions of equipment and system appeared much fuzzier than they thought. The problem arose when considering large equipment, like heaters, which engineers consider as being decomposable into systems. This is in contradiction with the definition of equipment as the undecomposed units of a power plant. The specific problem of the heater was solved easily and this is rather an example of how the application of such a methodology benefited to design engineers, independently of the development of a knowledge base.

Another consequence of this collaborative modeling is that the interface is also built on concepts of the domain. We tried to reduce the gap between the mental model of the users and the model it gets back through the interface of the software tool.

Let us bear in mind, however, that the final evaluation of the tool will only be possible after a few months of usage, when we will be able to measure the involvement of the users in maintaining the knowledge base. This evaluation is to be initiated shortly.

4.2 Issues

We think without falling back to the utopia of a "modeling tool that compiles models into programs" that it is possible to link more closely the models and their implementation. In particular, it would be possible, using an adequate modeling formalism, to use models for commenting the code and/or determining data structures. It might also be possible to use task models to encapsulate code so as to allow for some form of goal-oriented programming.

However, our current perspective is to enrich our methodology by applying it to other applications so as to propose a *validated* set of good practices for the design of knowledge based systems projects are being set up in this direction.

References

1. N. Glaser. Contribution to knowledge acquisition and modeling in a multi-agent framework PhD Thesis. UHP Nancy I. 1996.
2. R. de Hoog, R. Martil, B. J. Wielinga, R. Taylor, C. Bright, W. van de Velde. The CommonKADS Model Set. ESPRIT Project P5248. KADS-II/M1/DM..1b/UvA/018/5.0, University of Amsterdam, Lloyd's Register, Touche Ross Management Consultants & Free University of Brussels, December 1993.
3. Marc Linsten Knowledge acquisition based on explicit methods of problem-solving. PhD thesis, University of Kaiserslautern, 1992.
4. A. Mc Intyre. KresT 2.5 user manual Knowledge Technologies nv. Brussels, 1993.
5. A. Newell. The knowledge level. Artificial Intelligence, 18:87-127, 1982.
6. A. Newell. Unified Theories of Cognition. Harvard University Press, Cambridge, MA, 1990.
7. D. Paten and M. Vassart. Hyperinfo: Building a dynamic intranet. Tractebel internal document.
8. D. Paten and M. Vassart. Hyperinfo easy access to corporate information. In Proceedings of the 9th European Oracle User Group, 1992.
9. E. Plaza and J.L. Arcos. Noos, an integrated framework for problem solving and learning. In Proceedings of the KEML '97 workshop on Knowledge Engineering Methods and languages, 1997.
10. A. Slodzian. Knowledge level reflection. Master's thesis, VUB, 1994.
11. A. Slodzian. A componential methodology for modeling multi-agent cooperation. PhD thesis, VUB/LIP6, 1998.
12. L. Steels. Components of expertise. AI Magazine, 11(2):29-49, 1990.
13. L. Steels. Knowledge systems (draft edition). Artificial Intelligence Laboratory, University of Brussels (VUB), 1991.
14. L. Steels. Reusability and configuration of applications by non-programmers. Technical report 92-4, VUB, 1992.
15. M. Uschold and M. Gruninger. Ontologies: principles, methods and applications. Knowledge Engineering Review. 11(2). 1996.
16. W. Van de Velde. Issues in knowledge level modeling. In J-M. David, J-M. Krivine and R. Simmons, editors, Second Generation Expert Systems, pages 211-231. Springer-Verlag: Heidelberg, Germany, Berlin, 1993.
17. B.J. Wielinga, W. Van de Velde, A. Th. Schreiber, and J.M. Akkermans. The KADS knowledge modeling approach. In R. Mizoguchi, H. Motoda, J. Boose, B. Gaines, and R. Quinlan, editors. Proceedings of the 2nd Japanese Knowledge Acquisition for Knowledge-based Systems Workshop, pages 23-42. Hitachi, Advanced Research Laboratory, Hatotama, Saitama, Japan, 1992.
18. R.J. Wieringa. Requirements Engineering: Frameworks for Understanding. Wiley, 1996. ISBN 0471958840.

An Organizational Semiotics Model For Multi-Agent Systems Design

Joaquim Filipe

Escola Superior de Tecnologia do Instituto Politécnico de Setúbal
Rua Vale de Chaves, Estefanilha, 2914-508 Setúbal, Portugal.
JFilipe@est.ips.pt

Abstract. This paper describes how the organizational semiotics field can provide a conceptual infrastructure for designing normative multi-agent information systems. Since 'information' is an ill-defined word we prefer to adopt the semiotics framework, which uses the 'sign' as the elementary concept. Information as a composition of signs is then analyzed at different levels, including syntax, semantics, pragmatics and the social level. Based on different properties of signs, found at different semiotic levels, we propose here a new agent model, designated by EDA (an acronym for its three component modules: Epistemic-Deontic-Axiological), to represent agent informational states and simultaneously define its conceptual communication framework. The norm-based and communication-based multi-agent social architecture defined in this paper is flexible enough to accommodate changes in social structure, including changes in role specification, role instantiation and even the dynamics of institutional relationships, including role removal or creation. Communication is supported by a technical infrastructure (JINI) that enables both direct message exchange and blackboard protocols. Agents are enabled with logical reasoning for a flexible implementation of conversations, which are conceptually described by finite state machines.

1 Introduction

Organizational Semiotics is a particular branch of Semiotics, the formal doctrine of signs [9], concerned with analyzing and modeling organizations as information systems. Core concepts such as *information* and *communication* are very complex and ill-defined concepts, which should be analyzed in terms of more elementary notions such as semiotic 'signs'. Business processes would then be seen as processes involving the creation, exchange and use of signs. Since organizational activity is an information process based on the notion of responsible co-operative agent, we propose a model that accommodates both the social dimension in organizational agents behavior and the relative autonomy that individual agents exhibit in real organizations.

The proposed model is an intentional model, based on three main components, trying to capture relevant agent mental attitudes. In section 5 we provide a comparative critical analysis of other intentional models that have been proposed in the Distributed Artificial Intelligence (DAI) literature for multi-agent systems

R. Dieng and O. Corby (Eds.): EKAW 2000, LNAI 1937, pp. 449–456, 2000.

modeling. However, previously to design and implement a model it is necessary to understand system requirements, using an adequate method for systems analysis. Many methods have been proposed to tackle this important problem [5] but, in spite of that, a high proportion of computer-based systems fail. Estimates vary between 40% and 50% of projects [13], which seems to indicate that the requirements specifications are often wrong. Organizational Semiotics [12] approaches the requirements specifications phase using a clear methodology for semantic analysis based on the concept of ontological dependency. The result is an overall specification of the organizational dependencies and activities.

Organizational Semiotics, however, is not sufficiently developed to provide an analytical model for designing each agent in the organizational social system. This paper extends the work that has been done in semantic analysis, which provides a way to clearly define overall system requirements, into the specification of individual agents at a pragmatic level, keeping a social and normative perspective.

2 Organizational Semiotics

In this paper we approach this problem using the Organizational Semiotics stance [12, 8] to provide adequate system requirements and a solid conceptual basis for simulation models. Semiotics, which was traditionally divided into three areas – syntax, semantics and pragmatics – has been extended by Stamper in order to incorporate three other levels, including a social world level. A detailed and formal account of these levels may be found in [12].

This approach is different from mainstream computer science because instead of adopting an objectivist stance – where it is assumed the existence of a single observable reality, external to the agent, which some modeling methods try to capture with the help of entity-relationship models and data-flow diagrams – it adopts a social subjectivist stance. This means that for all practical purposes nothing exists without a perceiving agent nor without an agent engaging in action [13]. Invariant behaviors available to an agent are called *affordances*. This philosophical stance ties every item of knowledge to an agent who is, in a sense, responsible for it.

The recent paradigm shift from centralized data processing architectures to heterogeneous distributed computing architectures, emerging especially since the 1990's, placed social concerns in the agenda of much research activity in Computing, particularly in the Distributed Artificial Intelligence field (DAI). In DAI, organizations are modeled as multi-agent systems composed by autonomous agents acting in order to achieve social goals, in a cooperative manner [15, 11]. Social goals can be seen as norms.

3 The EDA Model

Social psychology provides a well-known classification of norms, partitioning them into perceptual, evaluative, cognitive and behavioral norms. These four types of norms are associated with four distinct attitudes, respectively [13] :

- *Ontological* – to acknowledge the existence of something;
- *Axiological* – to be disposed in favor or against something in value terms;
- *Epistemic* – to adopt a degree of belief or disbelief;
- *Deontic* – to be disposed to act in some way.

Our agent model is based on these attitudes and the associated norms, which we characterize in more detail below:

- *Perceptual* norms, guided by evaluative norms, determine what signs the agent chooses to perceive. Then, when a sign is perceived, a pragmatic function will update the agent EDA model components accordingly.
- *Cognitive* norms define entity structures, semantic values and cause-effect relationships, including both beliefs about the present state and expectations for the future. Conditional beliefs are typically represented by rules, which being normative allow for the existence of exceptions.
- *Behavioral* norms define what an agent is expected to do. These norms prescribe ideal behaviors as abstract plans to bring about ideal states of affairs, thus determining what an agent ought to do. Deontic logic is a modal logic that studies the formal properties of normative behaviors and states.
- *Evaluative* norms are required for an agent to choose its actions based on both epistemic and deontic attitudes. If we consider a rational agent, then the choice should be such that the agent will maximize some utility function, implicitly defined as the integral of the agent's axiological attitudes.

Using this taxonomy of norms, and based on the assumption that an organizational agent behavior is determined by the evaluation of deontic norms given the agent epistemic state[1], we propose an intentional agent model, which is decomposed into three components: the epistemic, the deontic and the axiological.

Together, these components incorporate all the agent informational contents, according to the semiotics ladder [12], where it is shown that information is a complex concept, and requires different viewpoints to be completely analyzed.

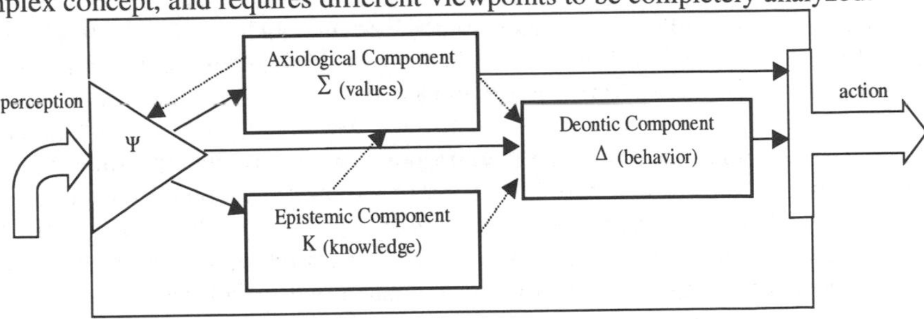

Figure 1: The EDA agent model.

Ψ is a pragmatic function that filters perceptions, according to the agent perceptual and axiological norms, and updates one or more model components.

Σ is an axiological function, that is used in two circumstances: to decide which signs to perceive and to decide which actions to execute.

[1] von Wright (1968) suggests that the study of deontic concepts and the study of the notions of agency and activity are intertwined.

K is a knowledge based component, where the agent stores his beliefs both explicitly and implicitly, in the form of potential deductions based on logical reasoning.

Δ is a set of available plans, either explicit or implicit, that the agent may choose to execute.

We provide here only a brief description of the knowledge representation chosen for each model component. A more detailed syntactic and semantic analysis of each component is provided in [3]. At the implementation level we have used a hybrid Artificial Intelligence paradigm, combining frames and rules.

3.1 Epistemic component

The semiotics methods proposed in [13] regarding requirements analysis and specification, state that the analysis process should start with a semantic analysis phase. The results of this phase can be displayed graphically as an ontology chart. However, since we are interested in trying to partially automate some of the organizational processes, we need a formal model.

A formal model of an organization must enable the representation for agents, affordances, and their ontological relationships. Furthermore, cognitive norms need to be included in the epistemic component of the agent informational model in order to provide an intensional form of knowledge representation.

Let $A = \{\alpha_1, \alpha_2, \ldots, \alpha_k\}$ be the set of agents and let $\Phi = \{\varphi_1, \varphi_2, \ldots, \varphi_m\}$ be the set of affordances, represented in the ontology chart; Let $P = \{\rho_1, \rho_2, \ldots, \rho_n\}$ be the set of relationships between them. An affordance may depend ontologically on one or two antecedents, which can be agent(s) or affordance(s). Formally, using the BNF notation: $\rho_i = \rho_i(\alpha_k \mid \alpha_j, \alpha_k \mid \varphi_k \mid \varphi_j, \varphi_k)$.

For the sake of simplicity we will adopt the sentential approach to formalize agents' knowledge. The sentential approach states that every agent knows every proposition that is stored in its knowledge base [7].

Following the recommendation of Liu [8] we use a semantic temporal database concept to keep track of affordances existence. In the implementation we use a knowledge-based tool for this purpose: affordances are represented by frame objects and ontological relationships are represented in frame slots. This kind of representation is particularly adequate for classification hierarchies where more general types subsume more specific ones and property inheritance is a useful inference mechanism. Other kinds of knowledge, not easily amenable to hierarchical class-subclass relationships, are represented using production rules and deductive inference.

Cognitive norms are represented as conditional beliefs, i.e. rules. We use a temporal qualifier to identify the time interval when the norm applies.

3.2 Deontic component

Norms, commitments and plans are represented in an unified way: as goals, according to the modal operator proposed in the EDA model description:

$G_i = O_{\alpha}^{\theta}(P, \tau, \sigma) = O$ ([α stit P] in-time-window $\Delta\Im$ with-utility [μ σ] commited-to θ)

where O is the standard deontic operator 'ought-to-be' and [α stit P] is an agency statement, with the semantics proposed by Belnap, saying that agent α sees-to-it-that proposition P becomes true. This means that α will perform a plan to bring about P in time window $\Delta\Im$, where $\Delta\Im$ is a time expression, specifying the time window during which proposition P is supposed to be satisfied. μ and σ are places to be filled in by the axiological component, with the utility of doing and of not-doing, respectively, the action [α stit P]. Although the exact values must be calculated by the axiological component, based on the current situation, the deontic component may fill in default values, eventually using common knowledge, i.e. norms, about the domain. The default value of μ indicates the expected value of [α stit P] for α, i.e. the expected benefit of α fulfilling its obligation; σ indicates the expected value of the sanction, i.e. the expected violation cost.

Planning becomes a goal-directed behavior simulation. We use the rule-based paradigm for representing a means-ends analysis process, which constitutes the base of our planning activity, and is based on a process of goal decomposition and sequencing. This is made using a backward chaining inference process, over rule sets where rule antecedents represent less general goals and consequents represent more general goals.

This basic concept is very similar to the *production rules* paradigm, used by most knowledge-based systems/expert systems. However, two changes had to be incorporate into the framework before it worked as desired:

- Firstly, it is necessary to avoid the automatic insertion of goals into the system's agenda. Goals can only be introduced into the agenda after being filtered by the axiological component, for value assignment and filtering;
- Secondly, time must be taken into account, both to trigger events that signal the start or finish of some affordance and to identify the existence of affordances during hypothetical reasoning, during the plan generation process.

According to the model dynamics defined in the previous section, the start and finish of affordances is registered in the semantic temporal database, by deontic norms and agents.

3.3 Axiological component

Agent preferences are represented as meta-norms, i.e. as rules in a meta-language outside the domain representation language. Objects in this meta-language define norm priority as a partial order relation between norms. This process has been represented as a knowledge-based system to be used exclusively by the axiological component of an EDA agent.

The axiological component of the EDA model provides preference relations both for the deontic component and for the epistemic component. In both cases, norms are represented as default rules. The problem is how to establish a preference amongst norms that would enable to solve dubious or conflicting situations.

A standard solution is to define a partial order between every pair of norms. For example, [2] provides an extension to Reiter's default logic – Prioritized Default Logic (PDL) – a meta-level approach to generate preferred extensions of default logic:

Reiter defines a default theory as a pair $\Delta = (W, D)$, where D is a set of default rules and W is a set of first-order logic well formed formulas. A prioritized default theory is a triple $\Delta = (W, D, \prec)$, where $\prec$ is a strict partial order over D, such that rule r_1 has priority over r_2 iff $(r1, r2) \in \prec$, or $r1 \prec r2$.

Given a set of formulae E, a default rule $a \to b \in D$ is active in E iff: $a \in E, \neg b \notin E, b \notin E$

Based on the notion of active default rule, Brewka presents the following definition:

E is an extension of Δ, generated by a total order□, containing $\prec$ iff $E = \bigcup E_i$ where $E_0 = Th(W)$ and for $i \geq 0$:

$$E_{i+1} = \begin{cases} E_i & \text{If there is no active default rule in } E_i \\ Th(E_i \bigcup \{c\}) & \text{where c is the consequent of the minimal □ active default rule in } E_i \end{cases}$$

This component permanently computes utilities associated to deontic norms and is able to suggest the best agent's next action whenever required to do so.

4 Organizational Normative Framework: Roles, Services and Policies

The organizational normative structure is essentially defined by the organizational roles and their relationships. Roles can then be instantiated by one or more agents. Conceptually, a role is a set of Services and Policies, and a Policy is a set of Obligations and Authorizations. At the implementation level, agents are represented by objects and services are defined by the object *interface*. Policies are sets of rules related to one or more EDA components, each of which includes at least one knowledge base (KB). When an agent is selected to perform a role, each of its EDA components downloads the adequate KB from an organizational role server.

Obligations are represented as goals, using the goal definition indicated in section 3.2. Authorizations are represented using the same syntax as goals but in a pattern format, and are interpreted as potential action enabling/blocking devices.

Conversations are modeled using a variant of the *conversation-for-action* scheme of Winograd and Flores, based on syntax-directed translation schemes (SDTS) [4], with the important differences that: (i) Each agent has its own finite-state machine – allowing for some autonomy, and (ii) SDTS allow for dynamic modification of the transition rules, thus enabling individual agents to learn and to incorporate exception-handling rules in their business models.

5 Related Work

Although inspired mainly in the semiotics stance, and the norms-attitudes relationships at different psycho-sociological levels, related to organizational modeling, the EDA agent model is related to several other models previously proposed, mainly in the DAI literature.

One of these is the BDI model (Belief, Desire, Intention) proposed by Rao and Georgeff [10]. This model is based on a theory of intentions, developed by Bratman [1]. The BDI perspective is more concerned with capturing the properties of human intentions, and their functions in human reasoning and decision making, whereas the EDA model is a norm-based representation of beliefs, goals and values, based on a semiotics view of information and oriented towards understanding and modeling social cooperation. BDI agents can easily abstract from any social environment because they are not specifically made for multi-agent systems modeling.

Singh also provides a social perspective to multi-agent systems. He adopts a notion of commitment that bears some similarity with our goals, in the sense that it relates a proposition to several agents, defining the concept of 'sphere of commitment' [11].

Jennings [6] proposes a social coordination mechanism based on commitments and conventions, supported by the notions of joint beliefs and joint intentions.

Yu and Mylopoulos [16] also recognized the importance of explicitly representing and dealing with goals, in terms of means-ends reasoning, and they have proposed the i* modeling framework, in which organizations and business process models are based on dependency relationships among agents.

6 Conclusions and future work

The EDA model described here is based on the organizational semiotics stance, where normative knowledge and norm-based coordination is emphasized. The main model components (Epistemic, Deontic and Axiological) reflect a social psychology classification of norms, therefore provide a principled norm-based structure for the agent internal architecture that is also oriented towards a norm-based social interaction in organizations.

The EDA architecture integrates also a number of important ideas gathered mainly from the DAI field and from deontic logic. Some of the most important ones were described in the previous section. We recognize the need for a semantics to underpin the proposed model but, at the present, we have focused mainly on conceptual issues.

Particularly important for organizational modeling is the notion of 'commitment'. Although we didn't formally define our notion of commitment, we do see commitments in terms of goals, emerging as a pragmatic result of social interaction. We believe that multi-agent commitments can be modeled as related sets of deontic-action statements, distributed across the intervening agents, based on the notion of unified goals as proposed in the deontic component of our model.

An axiological component seems to be a necessary part of any intelligent agent, both to establish preferred sets of agent beliefs and to prioritize conflicting goals. Since we adopt a unified normative perspective both towards epistemic issues and deontic issues, both being based on the notion of norm as a default or defeasible rule, the axiological component is conceptualized as a meta-level Prioritized Default Logic.

In a multi-agent environment the mutual update of agents' EDA models is essential as a result of perceptual events, such as message exchange. However, the specification of the EDA update using a pragmatic function is still the subject of current research, and will be reported in the near future. A related line of research that is being pursued at the moment involves the software simulation of EDA models, which raises some software engineering questions, related to the implementation of heterogeneous multi-agent systems implementation, where interaction aspects become a key issue, requiring a pragmatic interpretation of the exchanged messages.

References

[1] Bratman, M., 1987. *Intentions, Plans and Practical Reasoning*. Harvard University Press, USA.

[2] Brewka, G., 1994. Reasoning about Priorities in Default Logic. In *Proceedings of AAAI-94*, AAAI Press, Seattle, USA.

[3] Filipe, J. and K. Liu, 2000. The EDA Model: An Organizational Semiotics Perspective To Norm-Based Agent Design. Submitted to the Workshop on Norms and Institutions in Multi-Agent Systems, Barcelona, Spain.

[4] Fred, A. and J. Filipe (2000) "Syntax-Directed Translation Schemes for Multi -Agent Systems Conversation Modelling", ICEIS2000, Stafford, UK.

[5] Ghezzi, C., M. Jazayeri and D. Madrioli, 1991. *Fundamentals of Software Engineering*. Prentice-Hall, Englewood-Cliffs, NJ.

[6] Jennings, N., 1994. *Cooperation in Industrial Multi-Agent Systems*, World Scientific Publishing, Singapore.

[7] Konolidge, K., 1986. *A Deduction Model of Belief*. Morgan-Kaufman, Inc.

[8] Liu, K., 2000. Semiotics Information Systems Engineering. Cambridge University Press. Cambridge.

[9] Peirce, C. (1931-1935) Collected papers of Ch. S. Peirce, C. Hartshorne and P. Weiss (Eds). Cambridge, Mass.

[10] Rao, A. and M. Georgeff, 1991. Modeling Rational Agents within a BDI architecture. In *Proceedings of the 2nd International Conference on Principles of Knowledge Representation and Reasoning* (Nebel, Rich and Swartout, Eds.),439-449. Morgan Kaufman, San Mateo.

[11] Singh, M., 1996. Multiagent Systems as Spheres of Commitment. In Proceedings of the Int'l Conference on Multiagent Systems (ICMAS) - Workshop on Norms, Obligations and Conventions. Kyoto, Japan.

[12] Stamper, R., 1973. Information in Business and Administrative Systems. John Wiley & Sons.

[13] Stamper, R., K. Liu, M. Hafkamp and Y. Ades, 2000. Understanding the Roles of Signs and Norms in Organizations – a Semiotic Approach to Information Systems Design, Behavior and Information Technolog, 19(1), 15-27.

[14] von Wright, G., 1968. An Essay in Deontic Logic and the General Theory of Action. Acta Philosophica Fennica, 21. North-Holland.

[15] Wooldridge, M. and N. Jennings, 1995. Agent Theories, Architectures and Languages: A Survey. In Wooldridge and Jennings (Eds.) Intelligent Agents, Springer-Verlag, LNAI 890.

[16] Yu, E. and J. Mylopoulos, 1997. Modelling Organizational Issues for Enterprise Integration. In Proceedings of ICEIMT'97, 529-538.

Author Index